LEADERS
from the 1960s

LEADERS

from the 1960s

A Biographical Sourcebook of American Activism

EDITED BY

David DeLeon

Greenwood Press
Westport, Connecticut · London

Library of Congress Cataloging-in-Publication Data

Leaders from the 1960s : a biographical sourcebook of American
    activism / edited by David DeLeon.
        p.   cm.
    Includes bibliographical references (p.   ) and index.
    ISBN 0–313–27414–2 (alk. paper)
    1. Social reformers—United States—Biography.   2. Political
activists—United States—Biography.   3. Social change—United
States—Bio-bibliography.   4. Radicalism—United States—Bio-
bibliography.   I. DeLeon, David.
Z7164.S66L43   1994
[HN59]
016.30348'4'09730922—dc20   93–31603

British Library Cataloguing in Publication Data is available.

Library of Congress Catalog Card Number: 93–31603
ISBN: 0–313–27414–2

First published in 1994

Greenwood Press, 88 Post Road West, Westport, CT 06881
An imprint of Greenwood Publishing Group, Inc.

Printed in the United States of America

The paper used in this book complies with the
Permanent Paper Standard issued by the National
Information Standards Organization (Z39.48–1984).

10 9 8 7 6 5 4 3 2 1

CONTENTS

PREFACE

The radicals and liberals of the 1960s expressed beliefs and emotions that continued to attract or repel people decades later. There were "nostalgia" books on the mammoth Woodstock festival of 1969 and the protests of the 1960s. Politicians like Ronald Reagan and George Bush, by contrast, remembered the ferment of the era with overall unease. Newspaper obituaries in 1989 painted the virtues and the vices of Abbie Hoffman, Huey Newton, I. F. Stone, and Michael Harrington. Memoirs like Tom Hayden's *Reunion* (1988) received wide attention. Collections of readings have been published, such as *The Sixties Papers* (1984) and *The 60s without Apology* (1984). Skirmishes over the meaning of this period continued in politics, documentary films, the arts, and specialized university courses.

There has been no volume, however, which outlines what happened to many of the major activists of the 1960s through the 1970s and the 1980s, into the 1990s. Did their influence rise or fall? How did their goals, thoughts, and actions change? Had they continued to be radical, like Angela Davis, or liberal, like Ralph Nader? Had many become entrepreneurs like Jerry Rubin? Were the majority embittered, such as David Horowitz and Peter Collier? How many had become right-wing apologists like Eldridge Cleaver? This book provides information on a wide selection of nationally prominent activists of the 1960s.

The entries are grouped into broad categories for the general convenience of the reader, not because everyone fits into a neat box. Each section has a brief introduction that cites basic themes and provides some explanation why the individuals in that section were chosen. If an individual that is mentioned in the section introduction has an entry, there is an asterisk (*) after the name. For example, in Part One, "Racial Democracy," the section introduction mentions Louis Farrakhan (*). If an individual can be found in one of the other sections, that will be noted by including the section number by the sign, such as for Maulana Karenga (5*). Thus, there is an entry on Karenga in Part Five.

Some of the individuals in this volume were active before the 1960s (such as Herbert Marcuse), but became prominent in the 1960s; some became leaders or symbolic figures in the early 1970s (such as Leonard Peltier); but most are centered in the 1960s movements for democratic social change. Some were chosen because of a momentary notoriety, such as H. Rap Brown, while others have been widely known for many years, such as Tom Hayden. The entry on Brown is relatively brief; that on Hayden is longer. The longest entries are for individuals that the editor regards as having the greatest cultural, social, or political influence, such as Noam Chomsky. Readers will undoubtedly have some disagreements with these judgments. It should be noted, furthermore, that the selection process has several limitations. For example, the dominant culture has a greater willingness to publicize male leaders and English-speaking, Eurocentric people. Thus, this volume has a limited number of women, Chicanos, and indigenous Americans. While the editor made efforts to broaden the volume's selection, these inherent limitations remain. The section bibliographies direct the reader to other sources of information, such as the two volumes edited by Darlene Clark Hine, *Black Women in America* (Brooklyn: Carlson Publishing, 1992), and Jessie Carney Smith's *Notable Black American Women* (Detroit: Gale Research, 1992).

Each entry provides a biographical sketch of the individual's origins, development, and possible sources of activism. Most of each entry, however, focuses on the basic concepts or essence of the individual's work, writings, or persona, and the critical responses to these. Each entry provides some answers to questions such as these: What were the fundamental goals of this individual? What organizations or networks (if any) sustained the work of this activist financially, socially, and intellectually? What methods were used to achieve the individual's central goals? Did this person's goals, methods, and affiliations change fundamentally over the years? Why was this person of social importance? What were the major responses among other activists and within the general community to his or her work? What may be considered the overall strengths and weaknesses of that work? Although there are no footnotes for these comments, each entry does conclude with a list of some of the most important works by the individual (if he or she wrote significantly), and essays, articles, and book commentaries on the individual. Although the emphasis is on items that are readily available, there has been an effort to include a broad range of opinion.

An older reader, looking at the table of contents, may think that the selections are too obvious: "Everyone knows who they are." Many of these activists are known, however, for their work in the 1960s and not for their later fate. Many activists also have name recognition but little public understanding of what they thought or did. Younger readers, in addition, may not be familiar with "movement heavies" known to the previous generation since the educational system rarely transmits such information.

The editor attempted to cover a broad spectrum of national leaders, but there is no claim that this list is somehow complete. Some people originally scheduled for inclusion—such as Timothy Leary, Abbie Hoffman, Bert Corona, Rodolfo "Corky" Gonzales, Shulamith Firestone, and Stokely Carmichael (Kwame Toure)—have no individual entries in the present volume, though they are mentioned in the discussions of others' activities. Some subjects, such as gay and lesbian organizers, are covered less thoroughly than originally planned. However, the diversity of activists and movements in this book allows the editor to meet his fairly modest goals: to suggest that much can be learned, positively and negatively, from the activists of the 1960s, and to provide some introductions that might be useful for further study.

The reader also will find valuable these references:

The Alternative Press Index, 1967–present (Baltimore, Maryland).

Buhle, Mari Jo, Paul Buhle, and Dan Georgakas, eds. Encyclopedia of the American Left. New York: Garland Publishing, 1990.

Buhle, Mari Jo, Paul Buhle, and Harvey Kaye, eds. The American Radical. New York: Rutledge, Chapman and Hall, 1994.

The Left Index; A Quarterly Index to Periodicals of the Left, 1984–present (Santa Cruz, California).

Whitman, Alden, ed. American Reformers: An H. W. Wilson Biographical Dictionary. New York: H. W. Wilson, 1985.

INTRODUCTION

American conservatives had a golden age in the early 1950s. Most fundamental critics of U.S. foreign and domestic policies were dismissed as naive, ignorant, Communist, or pinko. Most Negroes still seemed to be docile, although there were reports of trouble caused by agitators. Only a few "bad girls" were uppity or went wrong. Homosexuals (the small number who lurked within wholesome American society) were isolated, silenced, and dismissed as fags or dykes. Non-WASPs were usually characterized in openly bigoted terms such as greasers, spics, or kikes. Schools rarely bothered students with irritating subjects such as civil rights, non-Christian religions, the value of languages other than English, respect for other cultures, or what a genuine democracy would mean socially, economically, and politically. The mass media were full of self-congratulations about the United States. This conservative world began to crumble in the 1950s.

Naive white racism was the first pillar of conservatism that was attacked. American blacks who had fought against Nazi racism were less willing to accept a legally sanctioned American apartheid which limited their education, jobs, housing, political rights, and entire futures. The introduction to Part One of this reference book, "Racial Democracy," describes the growing protests of the 1950s and the 1960s. Black demands invaded the white cultural ghetto. White men could no longer assume that they would dominate everything of importance in U.S. society. Native Americans, Puerto Ricans, and other races were stirred also by such massive rallies as the 1963 March on Washington that brought a quarter of a million people to the nation's capital. "Nonwhites" were increasingly unwilling to tolerate white society's definition of them as inferior.

Young people, from all races, would often be in the vanguard of the coming movements for social justice. Adult leftists and progressives, by the end of the

1950s, had been purged generally from the federal government and the labor unions. Presidents Truman and Eisenhower, for example, authorized about 6.5 million security checks on federal employees. Dissent had been chilled in many of the institutions of U.S. society. Although the election of John F. Kennedy in 1960 promised a New Frontier in which "the torch has been passed to a new generation of Americans," the margin of victory had been only a little more than 100,000 votes out of 68 million. The alternative in 1960, Richard Nixon, was quite as popular. Radicals such as Michael Harrington had suggested, at first, that beyond rhetoric, there wasn't much difference between Nixon and Kennedy.

Even if there was minimal substance to Kennedy, and he did little more than talk a good talk, the largely apolitical "silent generation" of the 1950s was beginning to be replaced or transformed by people who expected change. The 1960s experienced what one person called a "youthquake." The post–World War II baby boom generation rippled through American society, politics, and culture. In 1960 there were 16 million Americans between the ages of 18–24 (with 3 million in college); in 1970 there were 25 million (with 10 million in college). Although there had been relatively lonely critics of the United States in the 1950s, such as Dorothy Day, Norman Thomas, C. Wright Mills, James Baldwin, Allen Ginsberg, Lenny Bruce, Michael Harrington, Herbert Marcuse, and Norman Mailer—along with tiny groups and tiny publications (such as *Dissent* and *Monthly Review*)—there were few large and active white constituencies for change. Then the Civil Rights movement reverberated through American life. Some of the uglier realities of this society appeared in the press and on TV screens. Consciousness began to change among many people. Some white students joined the struggle, such as the one thousand who went into the South during Freedom Summer in 1964. Most of the older generation, however, and the vast majority of "responsible" leaders urged caution, when they did not condemn student activism and the Civil Rights movement. The most powerful changes of this era began in the streets and only later compelled some positive legal and legislative acknowledgments.

The new student activism could be seen at places such as Berkeley, California, where some University of California students formed SLATE in 1959, and where some students aided civil rights organizing, anti-ROTC activities, opposition to the House Un-American Activities Committee, and local student complaints. The latter came to include free speech, the right to due process when students complained about the university or when the university sought to punish them, student delegates on committees and on the board of trustees, student input for curriculum design, student evaluation of faculty, and less repressive campus living environments.

Most of the new activists of the late 1950s and early 1960s were liberals who wanted the system to be as democratic as they thought it claimed to be. Some were later radicalized by racial injustice and resistance to their demands, but relatively few turned to the Old Left (such as the Communist party and various Trotskyist sects), which most felt to be morally compromised by their slavish support for foreign dictatorships and by their own internal authoritarianism. As an alternative, the 1960s saw the emergence of a New Left represented by such organizations as the Students for a Democratic Society (formed in 1962), which advocated "participatory democracy" rather than the passive and often manipulated "representative democracy" of the dominant society.

The second major catalyst of the 1960s, other than race, was the war in Vietnam. This war was never legally declared by Congress, propped up an unpopular right-wing foreign government, and eventually exposed key U.S. leaders as mass murderers. When the 1964 victory of Lyndon Johnson, as a peace candidate, was followed by escalation of the war, a generation began to divide. Some of those who enlisted or were drafted discovered that the enemy was a landless peasant who hated the urban elites in Saigon who were protected by invading black and white soldiers. (About 10 percent of the males of the 1960s generation served in Vietnam.) Other young Americans found safe havens through legal deferments. For example, Dan Quayle, later a Republican vice president, had the right connections to get into the Indiana National Guard, even though, in theory, he was a "hawk" who supported the war. Similarly, Dick Cheney, a later secretary of defense, would candidly admit, "I had other priorities in the 60s than the military." Some young people, like William Jefferson Clinton, combined deferments and protests. According to one poll, 16 percent of the 60s generation actively protested. Another surprisingly large number, perhaps 125,000, took the radically disruptive solution of escape to Canada. Despite this level of resistance, most of the older generation, and much of the younger generation, was shocked by the "draft dodgers" and resisters. By 1970, one conservative youth group, the Young Americans for Freedom, had as many members as SDS at its height.

The war ultimately poisoned the Great Society hopes and programs of President Johnson. It diverted money and distracted public attention. Many of those who supported Johnson felt discouraged and betrayed. Some gave up, some supported the war, some turned to radical protest. In 1968, Johnson refused to run for re-election, and Senator Robert Kennedy, a hope for pragmatic idealism, was shot dead. At the end of the following race between Richard Nixon (Republican), Hubert Humphrey (Democrat), and George Wallace (independent), Nixon won with less than 50 percent of the popular vote. Although Nixon had packaged himself as the peace candidate, protests continued, especially after a 1970 military "incursion" into Cambodia that saw major demonstrations at 80 percent of U.S. colleges and universities (as 448 closed or went on strike). At Kent State, in Ohio, and Jackson State, in Mississippi, students were killed by the authorities. Many Americans were shocked, although polls indicated that a majority approved of the use of violence to suppress these protests. Major varieties of antiwar criticism are included in Part Two.

Growing frustration with peaceful political change in the 1960s encouraged some to drop out, whether turning to separatist black nationalism, the counterculture, and/or drugs to escape from the corrupt society around them. Rather than to continue to work with the existing legal and political structures, some people turned to cultural "solutions" to their problems. Such responses were tried by small numbers of people: only 5 percent of 1960s youth tried communal living; 42 percent tried marijuana (although Bill Clinton didn't inhale), and 15 percent tried LSD. Some of those who didn't experiment were attracted; others were horrified.

Out of all of this came a large number of counterculture publications, a looser attitude toward drugs, and more sexual experimentation. Although cultural radicals were quotable (such as Dr. Timothy Leary's call to "turn on, tune in, and drop out") and sometimes colorful (especially the showman Abbie Hoffman), the essential character of the surrounding society was not changed. Instead, it absorbed youth culture, repackaged it, and sold it for a profit. "Good vibes" or "the orgasm of immediate experience" (as Hoffman described it) could change individual people, but could it transform an entire society? Both the power and the limits of "radical culture" are considered in Part Five.

By the late 1960s there was a conservative backlash against such villains as unruly youth, crime, too aggressive minorities, and social welfare programs. The middle class had been burdened financially with much of the costs of the Great Society; the apparent defeat in Vietnam seemed a sign of weakness; many supported a return to "law and order." The intensity and breadth of support for critics also diminished with the winding-down of the war, the racial and political fragmentation of the Left (such as the splintering of SDS and SNCC's expulsion of all whites), the evanescent character of many of the institutions of the counterculture (like the Youth International Party, the "Yippies"), and the burning out or dropping out of some leaders and followers. Despite these changes, the struggles of the 1960s did not vanish in the 1970s and the 1980s, and some, such as the movements for women's rights, gay liberation, and ecology (all of which were quite small in the 1960s) became highly visible and influential. These are considered in Parts Three and Four of this book.

Conservatives were offended, bruised, fearful, and angry. They tended to characterize the 1960s activists as (1) immature, naive, ignorant, and self-indulgent youth; (2) noisily complaining racial minorities wanting special treatment; (3) violence-prone, disrespectful, unpatriotic radicals who were determined to destroy America; (4) immoral people who challenged the "natural order of life" (i.e., prosperous white males on top) and, thereby, God; (5) subversive intellectuals who were poisoning the minds of the impressionable; and (6) tax-and-spend liberal champions of "welfare queens," lazy workers, and slovenly riff-raff. Radicals had wanted to turn the world upside down.

Conservatives used various appeals and means to restore order. Whether in power or not, conservatives waged a cultural war to imply that they were more patriotic, more religious, and more American. The solutions to America's problems were primarily cultural: prayer in the schools, anti-abortion laws, respect for authority, and discipline ("just say no to drugs"/just say no to premarital sex). In power, conservatives sought to pack the Supreme Court and the federal judiciary with politically correct right-wing ideologues; appoint pro-business advocates to regulatory agencies such as the Environmental Protection Agency and the National Labor Relations Board; deny (if possible) any government funding for their critics through the National Endowment for the Arts and the National Endowment for the Humanities; belittle public education (preferring private schools); enact tougher sentencing laws; build more prisons; spend more money on the military; and reduce taxes, especially on the wealthiest, while expanding reliance on regressive taxes that most burdened the lower classes, such as the sales tax. Much of the American public acquiesced in or approved of these measures. In some cases, conservatives were able to use popular skepticism about the competence of government—which was derived partly from the failure of the Vietnam War, doubts about the effectiveness of centralized social engineering, and the pervasive corruption of the later Nixon presidential years (Watergate and more)—to advance their own agenda.

Most reformers and radicals had fundamentally dissimilar views of the 1960s and its aftermath, although there could be some overlapping of interpretations and attitudes. The most persistent general legacy of the 1960s was a pervasive questioning of American life. Critics compared the egalitarian principle of this society to its realities. To what degree did the actual complement the ideal? Racial minorities did not have the same opportunities as most whites. Women did not have the same opportunities as most men. The poor were often trapped by their dead-end environments and education. Most people had little power in their jobs and in the general society. Many people concluded that American democracy was, in practice, a fraud.

Some responded to this realization by withdrawing from the struggle to change the United States, and became escapist, cynical, and apolitical. Others, angry that their ideals had been blocked, or liberated from their former illusions, worked for improvements within the existing system. A relatively small few envisioned a fundamentally new society, and some of these people became socially and intellectually entrapped in cults. A wide range of people, during the 1960s, became aware of deep layers of injustice that few had previously recognized, such as the broad cultural dominance of white supremacy, basic assumptions of female inferiority, fears of homoeroticism, contempt for children and the aged, and devastating abuses of nature.

Beyond this questioning of authority, a second legacy of the 1960s was the common expectation (by most of the critics) of positive change. Average people began to fight back against racial injustice, sexual discrimination, and the arrogance of generals, politicians, and official experts. It was seldom the "leaders" of this society who formed the emerging movements. A Civil Rights movement began and then some politicians responded; a women's movement began and then some politicians responded; an ecology movement began and then some politicians responded. It was not the governing elites who began the gay movement or any of the other movements of the 1960s and early 1970s. Many of the implications of these movements were too disturbing for the powerful. The military, for example, was criticized in the 1960s and early 1970s because of the anti-democratic Uniform Code of Military Justice; soldiers were unable to form their own bargaining units; and the military was used to support anti-democratic regimes abroad. Some criticisms were later deflected, but much of the public was at least wary of the use of the military in foreign wars after the painful years of Vietnam. Even a successful later war, such as the 1990s reinstallation of the feudal despot of Kuwait and aid for the family dictatorships of the Arabian peninsula, created an enthusiasm that rapidly evaporated.

The 1960s put some issues permanently on the political and cultural map, whether conservatives wanted them there or not. Foreign policies were seldom bipartisan, but likely to be controversial. Many blacks declared that integration was not all that they wanted; they would define who they were, not whites. Sex discrimination laws emerged as a new area of legislation and litigation. Ecology laws and lawsuits proliferated. Many gay people came out of the closet. Radicals insisted that their versions of U.S. history were more accurate than that of white, upper-class, male, capitalist versions.

Most of the critics used liberal means to promote their goals: education, litigation, and legislation. By the 1990s, there were strong elements of technocratic elitism in most of the descendants of the 1960s and the 1970s. They had evolved (or devolved) into polite spokesmen and organizations to lobby for special interests. But each movement also had radical activists, such as Earth First! for ecology or ACT-UP and Queer Nation for gay liberation. By contrast, most of the sectarian parties had perished or withered into insignificance.

This era produced no unified vision and no central organization or confederation of organizations. It also raised more questions than it provided clear answers. Nonetheless, it was a defining period. Many Americans came of age intellectually and emotionally in the 1960s. They gained a sharper and more mature understanding of their own society and its place in the world. The failures and successes of this time can be instructive. By debating this past, we can gain a clearer knowledge of both our present and our future.

SELECTED BIBLIOGRAPHY

General Histories of the 1950s

Diggins, John. *The Proud Decades: America in War and Peace, 1941–1960*. New York: W. W. Norton, 1988.

Halberstam, David. *The Fifties*. New York: Random House, 1993.

Jamison, Andrew and Ron Eyerman. *Seeds of the Sixties*. Berkeley: University of California Press, 1994.

Jezer, Marty. *The Dark Ages: Life in the United States, 1945–1960*. Boston: South End Press, 1982.

O'Neal, William L. *American High: The Years of Confidence, 1945–1960*. New York: Free Press, 1987.

Pells, Richard H. *The Liberal Mind in a Conservative Age: American Intellectuals in the 1940s and 1950s*, 2d ed. Middletown, CT: Wesleyan University Press, 1989.

McCarthyism

Fried, Richard M. *Nightmare in Red: The McCarthy Era in Perspective*. New York: Oxford University Press, 1990.

Kutler, Stanley I. *The American Inquisition: Justice and Injustice in the Cold War*. New York: Hill and Wang, 1982.

Navasky, Victor. *Naming Names*. New York: Viking Press, 1986.

Early 1960s Politics

Bernstein, Irving. *Promises Kept: John F. Kennedy's New Frontier*. New York: Oxford University Press, 1991.

Burner, David. *John F. Kennedy and a New Generation*. Glenview, IL: Scott, Foresman, and Co., 1988.

Caro, Robert A. *The Years of Lyndon Johnson: The Path to Power*. New York: Vintage, 1988.

Conkin, Paul K. *Big Daddy from the Pedernales*. Boston: Twayne Publishers, 1986.

Goodwin, Richard. *Remembering America: A Voice from the Sixties*. Boston: Little, Brown, 1988.

Matusow, Allen J. *The Unraveling of America: A History of Liberalism in the 1960s*. New York: Harper and Row, 1984.

Reeves, Thomas C. *A Question of Character: John F. Kennedy in Image and Reality*. New York: Free Press, 1990.

Student Movement; New Left

Ali, Tariq. *Street Fighting Years: An Autobiography of the Sixties*. London: Collins, 1987.

Alpert, Jane. *Growing Up Underground*. New York: Morrow, 1981.

Aptheker, Bettina. *Academic Rebellion in the United States*. Secaucus, NJ: Citadel Press, 1977.

Breines, Wini. *Community and Organization in the New Left, 1962–1968: The Great Refusal*. New Brunswick, NJ: Rutgers University Press, 1989.

Buhle, Paul, ed. *History and the New Left: Madison, Wisconsin, 1950–1970*. Philadelphia: Temple University Press, 1990.

Castellucci, John. *The Big Dance: The Untold Story of Kathy Boudin and the Brink's Robbery Murders*. New York: Dodd, Mead, 1986. Reviewed: Annie Gottlieb, *New York Times Book Review* 91 (July 13, 1986): 26; Harvey Klehr, *Commentary* 52 (July 1986): 60–62.

Clecak, Peter. *America's Quest for the Ideal Self: Dissent and Fulfillment in the 60s and 70s*. New York: Oxford University Press, 1983.

———. *Radical Paradoxes: Dilemmas of the New Left, 1945–1970*. New York: Harper and Row, 1973.

Cowan, Paul. *The Making of an Un-American*. New York: Viking, 1967.

Daniels, Robert V. *The Year of the Heroic Guerilla: World Revolution and Counterrevolution in 1968*. New York: Basic Books, 1989.

Farber, David. *Chicago '68*. Chicago: University of Chicago Press, 1988.

Frankfurt, Ellen. *Kathy Boudin and the Dance of Death*. New York: Stein and Day, 1983.

Fraser, Ronald, et al. *1968: A Student Generation in Revolt*. New York: Pantheon Books, 1988.

Gitlin, Todd. *The Whole World Is Watching: Mass Media in the Making and Unmaking of the New Left*. Berkeley: University of California Press, 1980.

Goines, David Lance. *The Free Speech Movement; Coming of Age in the 1960s*. Berkeley, CA: Ten Speed Press, 1993.

Hayden, Tom. *Reunion: A Memoir*. New York: Random House, 1988.

Isserman, Maurice. *If I Had a Hammer: The Death of the Old Left and the Birth of the New Left*. New York: Basic Books, 1987.

Jacobs, Harold, ed. *Weatherman*. Berkeley: Ramparts Press, 1976.

Jacobs, Paul, and Saul Landau, eds. *The New Radicals: A Report with Documents*. New York: Random House, 1966.

Kaiser, Charles. *1968 in America: Music, Politics, Chaos, Counterculture and the Shaping of a Generation*. New York: Weidenfeld and Nicolson, 1988.

Katsiaficas, George. *The Imagination of the New Left: A Global Analysis of 1968*. Boston: South End Press, 1987.

Koning, Hans. *Nineteen Sixty-eight: A Personal Report*. New York: W. W. Norton, 1987.

Marin, Peter. "The Weathermen, Twenty Years On," *Harper's* 275 (Dec. 1987): 26–28.

Miller, James. *"Democracy is in the Streets": From Port Huron to the Siege of Chicago*. New York: Simon and Schuster, 1987.

Myers, R. David, ed. *Toward a History of the New Left: Essays from within the Movement*. Brooklyn, NY: Carlson Publishing, 1989.

Newfield, Jack. *A Prophetic Minority*. New York: New American Library, 1966.

Oglesby, Carl, ed. *The New Left*. New York: Grove Press, 1969.

Potter, Paul. *A Name for Ourselves*. Boston: Little, Brown, 1971.

Powers, Thomas. *Diana: The Making of a Terrorist*. Boston: Houghton Mifflin, 1971.

Rorabaugh, William J. *Berkeley at War*. New York: Oxford University Press, 1989.

Sale, Kirkpatrick, *SDS*. New York: Random House, 1973.

Stewart, Mary. "Bernardine Dohrn," in *The Biographical Dictionary of the American Left*, Bernard Johnpoll and Harvey Klehr, eds. (Westport, CT: Greenwood Press, 1986): 113–14.

Teodori, Massimo, ed. *The New Left: A Documentary History*. Indianapolis: Bobbs-Merrill, 1969.

Unger, Irwin. *The Movement: A History of the American New Left, 1959–1972*. New York: Dodd, Mead, 1974.

General Anthologies on the 1960s

Albert, Judith, and Stewart E. Albert, eds. *The Sixties Papers: Documents of a Rebellious Decade*. New York: Praeger, 1984.

Boskin, Joseph, and Robert Rosenstone, eds. *Seasons of Rebellion: Protest and Radicalism in Recent America*. Lanham, MD: University Press of America, 1980 (1972).

Churchill, Ward, and James Vander Wall, eds. *COINTELPRO Papers: Documents from the FBI's Secret Wars against Domestic Dissent in the U.S.* Boston: South End Press, 1990.

Cluster, Dick, ed. *They Should Have Served That Cup of Coffee: 7 Radicals Remember the 60s*. Boston: South End Press, 1979.

Haskins, James, and Kathleen Benson, eds. *The 60s Reader*. New York: Viking Kestrel, 1988.

Howard, Gerald, ed. *The Sixties*. New York: Paragon House, 1991.

Kessler, Lauren. *After All These Years; Sixties Ideals in a Different World*. New York: Thunder's Mouth Press, 1990.

Morrison, Joan, and Robert K. Morrison, eds. *From Camelot to Kent State: The Sixties Experience in the Words of Those Who Lived It*. New York: Times Books, 1987.

Oxford University Socialist Discussion Group, eds. *Out of Apathy: Voices of the New Left Thirty Years On*. London: Verso, 1989.

Sayres, Sohnya, et al., eds. *The 60s without Apology*. Minneapolis: University of Minnesota Press, 1984.

Schultz, Bud, and Ruth Schultz, eds. *It Did Happen Here: Recollections of Political Repression in America*. Berkeley: University of California Press, 1989.

Tischler, Barbara L., ed. *Sights on the Sixties*. New Brunswick, NJ: Rutgers University Press, 1992.

General Reflections on the 1960s

"After the Sixties: The Politics and Culture of Liberation," *Salmagundi* (theme issue) no. 81 (Dec. 1, 1988).

Berman, Paul. "Don't Follow the Leaders," *New Republic*, Aug. 10 and 17, 1987, pp. 28–35.

Berman, Ronald. *America in the Sixties: An Intellectual History*. New York: Free Press, 1968.

Blaser, Kent. "What Happened to New Left History?" *South Atlantic Quarterly* 85 (Summer 1985): 283–96; 86 (Summer 1987): 209–28.

Blum, John Morton. *Years of Discord, 1961–1974*. New York: W. W. Norton, 1991.

Breines, Wini. "The Sixties Again," *Theory and Society* 14 (1985): 511–23.

———. "Whose New Left?" *Journal of American History*, Sept. 1988, pp. 328–45.

Brinkley, Alan. "Dreams of the Sixties," *New York Review of Books*, Oct. 22, 1987, pp. 10–16.

Buhle, Paul. "Remembering the Sixties" (review article), *Oral History Review* 17 (Spring 1989): 137–42.

Buhle, Paul, and Robin D. G. Kelley. "The Oral History of the New Left in the United States: A Survey and Interpretation," *Journal of American History* 76 (Sept. 1989): 537–50.

Burns, Stewart. *Social Movements of the 1960s: Searching for Democracy*. Boston: Twayne Publishers, 1990.

Calvert, Gregory Navala. *Democracy from the Heart: Spiritual Values, Decentralism, and Democratic Idealism in the Movement of the 1960s*. Eugene, OR: Communitas Press, 1992.

Calvert, Gregory, and Carol Nieman. *A Disrupted History: The New Left and the New Capitalism*. New York: Random House, 1972.

Casale, Anthony, and Philip Lerman. *Where Have All the Flowers Gone? The Rise and Fall of the Woodstock Generation*. Kansas City, MO: Andrews and McMeel, 1989.

Chafe, William H. *Never Stop Running: Allard Lowenstein and the Struggle to Save American Liberalism*. New York: Basic Books, 1993.

Chalmers, David. *And the Crooked Places Made Straight: The Struggle for Social Change in the 1960s*. Baltimore: Johns Hopkins University Press, 1991.

Churchill, Ward, and James Vander Wall, eds. *The COINTELPRO Papers: Documents from the FBI's Secret Wars against Domestic Dissent*. Boston: South End Press, 1990.

Collier, Peter, and David Horowitz. *Destructive Generation: Second Thoughts about the Sixties*. New York: Summit Books, 1989.

———, eds. *Second Thoughts: Former Radicals Look Back at the Sixties*. Lanham, MD: University Press of America, 1989.

Conlin, Joseph. *The Troubles: A Jaundiced Glance Back at the Movement of the Sixties*. New York: Franklin Watts, 1982.

Davidson, Carl. *The New Radicals in the Multiversity and Other Writings on Student Syndicalism (1966–1967)*. Chicago: Charles H. Kerr, 1990.

Davidson, Sara. *Loose Change; Three Women of the Sixties*. Garden City, NY: Doubleday, 1977.

De Leon, David. *Everything Is Changing: Contemporary U.S. Movements in Historical Perspective*. New York: Praeger, 1988.

Dickstein, Morris. *Gates of Eden: American Culture in the Sixties*, new edition. New York: Penguin, 1989 (1977).

Echols, Alice. " 'We Gotta Get Out of This Place': Notes Toward a Remapping of the Sixties," *Socialist Review* 22 (April-June 1992): 9–33.

Eynon, Bret. "Look Who's Talking: Oral Memoirs and the History of the 1960s," *The Oral History Review* 17 (Spring/Fall 1991): 99–107.

Farber, David. *The Age of Great Dreams: America in the 1960s*. New York: Hill and Wang, 1994.

Flacks, Richard. *Making History: The Radical Tradition in American Life*. New York: Columbia University Press, 1988.

———. "Port Huron: Twenty-Five Years After," *Socialist Review* nos. 93–94 (May-August 1987): 140–47.

Garver, Paul, and George Abbott White. "What Was Old; What Was New? The New Left and American Exceptionalism" (review article), *Journal of American Studies* 22 (April 1988): 67–76.

Ghitelman, David. "Preparations for the Long March: The Seventies Revisited," *The Antioch Review* 49 (Winter 1991): 68–76.

Gitlin, Todd. *The Sixties: Years of Hope, Days of Rage*, rev. ed. New York: Bantam Books, 1993 (1987).

Gottlieb, Annie. *Do You Believe in Magic? Bringing the 60s Back Home.* New York: Fireside/Simon and Schuster, 1987.

Grele, Ronald. "A Second Reading of Experience: Memoirs of the 1960s," *Radical History Review* 44 (1989): 159–66.

Haskins, James, and Kathleen Benson, eds. *The 60s Reader.* New York: Viking Kestrel, 1988.

Henry, David. "Recalling the 1960s: The New Left and Social Movement Criticism" (review article), *The Quarterly Journal of Speech* 75 (Feb. 1989): 97–112.

Herf, Jeffrey. "The New Left and Its Fading Aura," *Partisan Review* 53:2 (1986): 242–52.

Issel, William. *Social Change in the United States, 1945–1983.* New York: Schocken Books, 1985.

Isserman, Maurice. "1968 and the American New Left," *Socialist Review* 18:4 (Nov./Dec. 1988): 94–104.

———. "The Not-So-Dark and Bloody Ground: New Works on the 1960s," *American Historical Review* 94 (Oct. 1989): 990–1009.

Isserman, Maurice, and Michael Kazin. "The Failure and Success of the New Radicalism," in *The Rise and Fall of the New Deal Order, 1930–1980*, Steven Fraser and Gary Gerstle, eds. (Princeton: Princeton University Press, 1989): 212–42.

Jackson, Rebecca. *The 1960s: An Annotated Bibliography of Social and Political Movements in the United States.* Westport, CT: Greenwood Press, 1992.

Jennings, M. Kent. "Residues of a Movement: The Aging of the American Protest Generation," *American Political Science Review* 81 (June 1987): 367–82.

Kann, Mark E. *The American Left: Failures and Fortunes.* New York: Praeger, 1982.

Knight, Douglas M. *Street of Dreams: The Nature and Legacy of the 1960s.* Durham, NC: Duke University Press, 1989.

Lerner, Michael. "The Legacy of the Sixties for the Politics of the Nineties," *Tikkun* 3 (Jan./Feb. 1988): 44–48, 87–91.

Levy, Peter B. "The New Left and Labor: The Early Years (1960–1963)," *Labor History* 31 (Summer 1990): 294–321.

———. *The New Left and Labor in the 1960s.* Urbana: University of Illinois Press, 1994.

"The New Left, Labor, and the Vietnam War," *Peace and Change* 15 (Jan. 1990): 46–69.

Magnet, Myron. *The Dream and the Nightmare; The Sixties Legacy to the Underclass.* New York: William Morrow, 1993.

Matusow, Allen. *The Unraveling of America: A History of Liberalism in the 1960s.* New York: Harper and Row, 1984.

Morgan, Edward P. *The 60s Experience: Hard Lessons about Modern America.* Philadelphia: Temple University Press, 1991.

O'Brien, James P. "The New Left," *Radical America*, May-June, 1968, pp. 1–25; Sept.-Oct. 1968, pp. 1–22; Nov.-Dec. 1968, pp. 28–43.

O'Neill, William L. *Coming Apart: An Informal History of America in the 1960s.* New York: Times Books, 1972.

Oglesby, Carl. *Who Killed JFK?* Berkeley: Odonian Press, 1992.

———. *The Yankee and Cowboy War: Conspiracies from Dallas to Watergate.* Mission, KS: Sheed, Andrews and McMeel, 1976.

Oglesby, Carl, and Richard Shaull, *Containment and Change.* New York: Macmillan, 1967.

Oppenheimer, Martin, Martin J. Murray, and Rhonda F. Levine, eds. *Radical Sociologists and the Movement: Experiences, Lessons, and Legacies*. Philadelphia: Temple University Press, 1991.

Port Huron Statement (1962). Chicago: Charles H. Kerr, 1990.

"Radical Historians and the Crisis in American History, 1959–1980" (round table), *Journal of American History* 76 (Sept. 1989): 393–488.

Rothman, Stanley, and S. Robert Lichter. *Roots of Radicalism: Jews, Christians and the New Left*. New York: Oxford University Press, 1982.

Smith, Michael Steven. *Notebook of a Sixties Lawyer*. Brooklyn, NY: Smyrna Press, 1992.

Snow, Richard. "The New Left Revisited: A Look at Recent Scholarship," *Journal of American Studies* 19 (Aug. 1985): 239–54.

Stein, Jane, and Michael Stein. *Sixties People*. New York: Knopf, 1990.

"Teaching the Sixties: A Symposium," *Radical History Review* 44 (Spring 1989): 93–107.

Tipton, Steven M. *Getting Saved from the Sixties: Moral Meaning in Conversion and Cultural Change*. Berkeley: University of California Press, 1982.

Unger, Irwin, and Debi Unger. *America in the 1960s*. St. James, NY: Brandywine Press, 1992 (original 1988 Scribner's title: *Turning Point: 1968*).

Viorst, Milton. *Fire in the Streets: America in the 1960s*. New York: Simon and Schuster, 1981.

Walter, Edward. *The Rise and Fall of Leftist Radicalism in America*. Westport, CT: Greenwood Press, 1992.

Weiner, Jon. "The New Left as History," *Radical History Review* 42 (Fall 1988): 173–87.

Whalen, Jack, and Richard Flacks. *Beyond the Barricades: The Sixties Generation Grows Up*. Philadelphia: Temple University Press, 1989.

Willis, Ellen. *Beginning to See the Light; Sex, Hope, and Rock and Roll*, 2d ed. with a new introduction. Hanover, NH: Wesleyan/University Press of New England, 1992 [1981].

Wohlforth, Tim. "The Sixties in America," *New Left Review* no. 178 (July-August 1989): 105–123.

Zinn, Howard. *The Twentieth Century; A People's History*. New York: Harper and Row, 1984 (a portion of Zinn's *A People's History of the United States* [1980]).

PART ONE

RACIAL DEMOCRACY

It is one of the ideals of American society that no one should be treated unequally because of the color of his or her skin. It is one of the realities of American society that white readers of these words, even those who believe that racism is declining or is a thing of the past, would be unlikely—if this were possible—to choose to be black, brown, or yellow. Most whites have some recognition that, if this were to happen, they would be treated differently, and probably unfairly.

Since Europe is the ancestral homeland of the majority of Americans, it is not surprising that European ways of life have been the standards of proper behavior and that people, ideally, should look European. Such customs were challenged sharply in the 1960s and the 1970s by various champions of the Other. Some of the native inhabitants of North America ("Indians") reasserted that they were not Europeans. They expressed their own cultural, religious, social, political, and economic values. Descendants of enslaved Africans, who had been stripped of even their ancestors' names, insisted upon speaking in their own voices. While these groups and others usually accepted major portions of the dominant culture, they demanded the right to define themselves, rather than to be defined by the majority.

This trend was lamented by nostalgic white supremacists and others who feared that these "grievance groups" would fragment the supposed unity of America. Defenders of these changes asserted that the emergence of a genuinely multiracial and multicultural America would give us a more realistic sense of our own past, present, and future, along with this nation's place in a largely nonwhite world. Some argued that blacks and other minorities were already at least bicultural, and that it would be good for more whites to become so.

African-Americans have been the largest minority in the United States, numbering thirty million people in 1990. They have remained also the most commonly feared by the white majority. Most black children continued to attend shabbily inferior schools that were virtually segregated. Teachers and employers often had expectations of inferior performance. The sight of several black teenagers on a street corner could arouse anxiety. A black customer in a store might be watched for shoplifting. Cab drivers could pass them by. A white person entering an elevator that was occupied only by a black man was likely to feel uncomfortable, if not threatened. Few whites lived next door to blacks, socialized with them, or went to church with them. White politicians regularly used white fears to win votes. Beneath the obligatory American optimism about progress there was considerable ignorance, suspicion, and anger. This sometimes burst into the open, such as with the shock, disgust, and violence that flamed up in 1992 following a jury's acquittal of Los Angeles police who had been videotaped while they were beating a black man, Rodney King, who was already lying on the ground.

Despite continued racial injustice in America, the Civil Rights movement that emerged in the 1950s and 1960s had positively shook the foundations of American society. Although it seemed to many at the time like a sudden convulsion, pressures had been building rapidly in the previous decades. By the end of World War II, "what to do with Negroes" was not "just a southern white question" that the rest of the country could ignore. While 90 percent of the black population had lived in the South in 1900, there had been immense migrations during World War I and World War II. There were growing black communities outside the South. The 1930s programs of the New Deal and the economic opportunities during the 1940s also encouraged change. During the 1940s, a half million black workers joined the CIO, hundreds of thousands of blacks served in the U.S. military, and the membership of the NAACP grew from 50,000 to 450,000. Black Americans increasingly challenged limits on their right to vote through such court cases as *Smith v. All-wright* (1944), which attacked the all-white primary election. Black America seemed poised for change.

White America, by contrast, was moving generally toward conservatism in the late 1940s and into the 1950s. The liberal agenda of President Harry Truman (including civil rights proposals) came to nothing, civil rights organizations were red-baited as Communist, and a man like John Rankin, a U.S. Representative from Mississippi, could stand on the floor of the House and rant "niggerniggerniggerniggernigger, and nobody would say anything" (*New York Times*, Nov. 21, 1991, D2).

Change came, not because of the spontaneous generosity of this society, but because many blacks and their white supporters demanded change. The Supreme Court, after a depressing parade of cases that upheld segregation for more than a half century, finally killed the principle of "separate but equal" in *Brown v. Board of Education* in 1954. The Montgomery Bus Boycott in

1955–1956 used the powerful weapon of economic boycott to challenge discrimination. The integration of the Little Rock High School in 1957 forced a weak and complacent President Eisenhower to send federal troops to prevent screaming white mobs from beating and perhaps killing nine black children who wanted to attend the white public school. The Reverend Martin Luther King, Jr., began the Southern Christian Leadership Conference in 1957. The first civil rights bill since Reconstruction was pried out of the Congress in 1957. Local actions grew; a mass movement was developing. Sit-ins began in 1960, the same year as the formation of the Student Nonviolent Coordinating Committee. The Civil Rights Act of 1964 and the Voting Rights Act of 1965 offered significant protections for basic political rights. Thousands of Americans, black and white, bore witness to their principles by assisting these struggles in the 1950s and 1960s.

Although the result may not have been the promised land, some of the malignant heritage of slavery was cut away. While the major institutions were seldom decisive, whether it was the "deliberate speed" of the courts, the vacillation of presidents, the frequent cynicism of the FBI and the Department of Justice, and the gridlocked special interests of the Congress, the mass movements pushed these institutions toward at least moderate change. This continued into the 1980s despite obstructions. For example, President Reagan never met the Congressional Black Caucus once during eight years in office; he filled the judiciary with politically correct conservatives who were acutely sensitive to the needs of business but not to individuals; he appointed ideologues to the Department of Justice and the U.S. Civil Rights Commission; he rarely found qualified black candidates for high office (unless they were black conservatives); he attempted to prevent extension of the civil rights laws; he supported the apartheid government in South Africa; he sought to give tax exemptions to segregated private schools; and he seldom spoke out, despite his reputation as a Great Communicator, for racial equality. He was followed by the administration, equally empty, of George Bush.

Racial progress has not come primarily because of the actions of politicians, who are usually followers after mass movements rather than the leaders of them, but because of the inspiration and work of genuine leaders like Mary Frances Berry (*), Shirley Chisholm (*), Fannie Lou Hamer (*), Martin Luther King, Jr. (*), and Robert Moses (*).

Since the 1960s, the goal of liberal integrationism has been dominant, but other perspectives have remained: the orthodox Islam of the later period of Malcolm X (*), the separatist Islam of Louis Farrakhan (*), the democratic socialism of Bayard Rustin (*) and Ron Dellums (6*), the communism of Angela Davis (6*), and various forms of cultural, political, and economic black nationalism found in the works of Amiri Baraka (*), Bobby Seale (*), and Maulana Karenga (5*). Such diversity should not surprise the reader any more than diversity in "the white community" (assuming that such an entity can be said to exist).

The protests of African Americans, the largest minority in U.S. society, have influenced movements by other minorities, although any group has its own distinctive history. For example, the modern protests of Indians (as the Europeans called them) and of Chicanos are not simply cultural side shows to the main events in U.S. history but illuminate both its strengths and weaknesses.

In the case of the native peoples, there were about two million in 1990 who claimed significant native ancestry. Most of them lived in cities. Less than one-half lived on the fifty-four million acres in more than two hundred reservations in twenty-six states. Various federal programs spent more than $3 billion a year for health, education, and maintenance, including the funding of the Bureau of Indian Affairs, an agency founded in 1824 that had 14,000 employees.

For many years, native peoples were "represented" in Washington, D.C., by whites who generally wanted them assimilated into European culture. The earliest reform groups, such as the Indian Rights Association (1882), saw no value in native cultures. White reformers such as Richard Henry Pratt, the head of the Carlisle Indian School, declared that it was necessary to "kill the Indian to save the man"—to re-create the Indian in the white man's image.

The first organizations created by native people, such as the Society of American Indians (1911), often shared assimilationist goals. While the SAI emphasized pride, it also sought a future of independent, Christian farmers. It was not until the New Deal programs of the 1930s, the military and defense jobs of World War II, and greater opportunities from increased urbanization that it was possible for national organizations to encompass large numbers of tribes. The National Congress of American Indians (NCAI) was established in 1944 and rapidly became the largest native opponent of harmful federal policies (such as the abrupt termination of previous commitments) and advocate of educational, economic, and political progress for native peoples.

As the 1960s began, younger Indians were dissatisfied with the slow pace of improvement and by some of the goals of the NCAI. Men such as Melvin Thom (1938–1984) and Clyde Warrior formed the National Indian Youth Council (NIYC) in 1961. They criticized the old leaders as "Uncle Tomahawks." The new association declared that "weapons employed by the dominant society have become subtler and more dangerous than guns—these, in the form of educational, religious, and social reform, have attacked the very centers of Indian life by attempting to replace native institutions with those of the white man." Warrior pointed to the militant protests of blacks and Chicanos. The NIYC began to sponsor such confrontations as "fish-ins" in Washington State over the violation of treaty rights for fishing. Warrior was also active in the election of Vine Deloria, Jr. (*), to the presidency of the NCAI in 1963.

The more activist leaders condemned the third world conditions on the reservations, the inefficiency and (they believed) corruption of much of the federal bureaucracy, and racist attitudes and practices by whites. They presented a very different version of American history than that found in many textbooks. For most of these leaders, Columbus was not a brave discoverer of a new world but the racist, mass-murdering invader of ancient lands. They pointed to the hundreds of broken treaties. They asked for recognition that native people had contributed much to America, including major portions of our modern diet. They insisted that their spiritual values and cultures were not just curiosities but deserved serious consideration.

One of the most militant groups founded in the 1960s was the American Indian Movement (1968), whose most prominent members included Vernon Bellecourt (*), Russell Means (*), and Dennis Banks (*). AIM members were active in the Mt. Rushmore protest (1971), the Trail of Broken Treaties march to Washington, D.C. (1972), the occupation of the BIA headquarters (1972), and the seventy-one-day armed occupation of Wounded Knee, South Dakota (1973), which had been the site of the last massacre of the Indian wars in 1890.

In the 1960s and the 1970s, native peoples sometimes benefited from the Great Society and New Federalism programs, along with civil rights cases and legislation. Although some critics were suppressed by possibly illegal means, such as Leonard Peltier (*), and the more radical groups declined in membership, there remained a wide range of groups dealing with specific approaches. These included Americans for Indian Opportunity (organized by LaDonna Harris in 1970) and the Native American Rights Fund (1970). Native people were increasingly able to defend themselves within this society and express their distinctive and diverse messages.

Just as the word "Indian" conceals an enormous range of different cultures, so does the word "Hispanic." The 1990 census recorded more than twenty-two million Hispanics, people with Spanish surnames. This category, however, was incredibly heterogeneous. It included, for example, people from all of the diverse and sometimes hostile cultures of Central and South America. My few specific cases in this section of the book primarily represent Chicanos (Chavez, Gonzales, Gutiérrez, and Tijerina). In 1990, there were approximately fourteen million people of Mexican ancestry within the United States.

Before the 1960s, most organizations, such as the League of United Latin American Citizens (1929) and the American GI Forum of the United States (1948) emphasized their patriotic concern for integrating their members into the mainstream of U.S. society. Such organizations had successes, for example, in challenging unequal treatment within the education system and the military.

The 1960s, however, saw more radical critics who felt that the United States had not provided equal treatment and that integration might not be a valuable overall goal. Reies López Tijerina (*) was active in attempting to regain ancestral lands in New Mexico. José Angel Gutiérrez (*) was a key founder of an electoral party, La Raza Unida (1969). Rodolfo "Corky" Gonzales organized the Crusade for Justice (1966), which was especially prominent for creating a series of national conferences, such as for Chicano youth. Cesar Chavez (*) and Dolores Huerta relied heavily upon the support of Mexican American farm workers to build the United Farm Workers of America (1966). All of these leaders declared, to varying degrees, pride in their distinct cultural heritage. Many organizations became more aggressive during this period, such as the Mexican American Political Association (1958), the Mexican American Community Service Agency (1964), the Movimiento Estudiantil Chicano de Aztlán (1966), and the Mexican American Legal Defense and Educational Fund (1967).

The later decline of some of these leaders and organizations can be attributed partly to the dismantling of programs related to the Great Society and the War on Poverty, integration of some of the militants into the Democratic party and other centrist institutions, growing skepticism about some of the more separatist ideals, and despair at the conservative trends of later decades. Nonetheless, political power had grown; multiculturalism was more widely respected; there had been economic progress for some; and there were major Spanish-speaking networks in publishing, radio, and television.

Many other ethnic protesters are not represented here. The relatively small number of Asians who organized during the 1960s came from a wide range of cultures. The reader can find some direction in the following sources: Philip S. Foner and Daniel Rosenberg, eds. *Racism, Dissent, and Asian Americans; A Documentary History* (Greenwood, 1993); Hyung-Chan Kim, ed., *Dictionary of Asian American History* (Greenwood, 1986); Hyung-Chan Kim, ed., *Asian American Studies; An Annotated Bibliography and Research Guide* (Greenwood, 1989); "Commemorative Issue: Salute to the 60s and 70s . . . ," *Amerasia Journal* 15:1 (1989); Jeffrey Paul Chan et al., eds., *Aiiieeeee! An Anthology of Asian American Writers* (new edition, Mentor, 1991); Jeffrey Paul Chan et al., eds., *The Big Aiiieeeee! An Anthology of Chinese American and Japanese American Literature* (Meridian, 1991), and William Wei's *The Asian American Movement* (Temple, 1993).

Puerto Ricans also saw a strong revival, after World War II, of concerns about how their language and history affected their present identity. In 1990, there were about 3.5 million Puerto Ricans on their home island and 2.75 million on the U.S. mainland. Although the island alone has a larger population than two dozen U.S. states, it has no senator and only one "resident commissioner" in the House of Representatives. That commissioner has a vote in committees, but not on final bills. There have always been political, economic, and cultural frustrations produced by situations like this. For some, it provokes stronger nationalism. Ruben Berrios, the head of the Puerto Rican Independence Party, has criticized U.S. domination, noting that "we are Latin Americans. We are a Nation. You don't swallow nations, because you get indigestion. Look at the Soviet Union" (*Washington Post*, Nov. 5, 1989, A26). Although a plebiscite on the island in November of 1993 showed little support for independence, the electorate was almost evenly split between statehood and an enhanced commonwealth status. Selected readings about modern Puerto Rican criticism can be found in the bibliographies presented below.

Will the demographic changes in the United States—with higher birth rates for "minorities" and accelerated rates of Asian and Latin immigration—stimulate cultural change? Or, as with previous eras of immigration and ethnic conflicts, will assimilation be the dominant theme? By one Census Bureau estimate, "minorities" will be almost 50 percent of the population by the year 2050 (*Washington Post*, Dec. 4, 1992, A10). While such long-term projections are extremely speculative, it is worth considering how this might affect the America of the future.

Would education be more multicultural in an America that was truly a "nation of nations" (as Walt Whitman already called it), as part of an increasingly interlinked global society? What perceptions should the public have of different regions, such as Asia and Latin America, and of non-Christian religions, such as Islam? Are other cultures only footnotes to the Euro-American national story of the United States? Should there be more emphasis on multilingualism? Would rising immigration in a weak economy mean increased social tensions? Will there be greater interethnic strife over jobs and political power? Is the basic theme of American civilization that of simple addition (the melting pot), Jesse Jackson's "rainbow," Mayor David Dinkins's "gorgeous mosaic," or that of fusion into something new?

SELECTED BIBLIOGRAPHY

Black Liberation

Civil Rights Movement

Blumberg, Rhoda Lois. *Civil Rights: The 1960s Freedom Struggle*, rev. ed. New York: Twayne Publishers, 1991.

Branch, Taylor. *Parting the Waters: America in the King Years, 1954–1963*. New York: Simon and Schuster, 1988.

Carson, Clayborne, David J. Garrow, Vincent Harding, and Darlene Clark Hine, eds. *Eyes on the Prize: A Reader and Guide*. New York: Penguin, 1991.

Carson, Clayborne, David J. Garrow, Gerald Gill, Vincent Harding, and Darlene Clark Hine, eds. *The Eyes on the Prize Civil Rights Reader: Documents, Speeches, and Firsthand Accounts from the Black Freedom Struggle, 1954–1990*. Boston: Blackside, Inc., 1991.

Dulaney, W. Marvin and Kathleen Underwood, eds. *Essays on the Civil Rights Movement*. College Station, TX: Texas A&M University Press, 1993.

Eagles, Charles, ed. *The Civil Rights Movement in America*. Jackson: University Press of Mississippi, 1986.

Fender, Stephen, and Michael Heale, eds. "Civil Rights and Student Protest," *Journal of American Studies* (special issue) 22 (April 1988).

Garrow, David. *Bearing the Cross: Martin Luther King, Jr. and the Southern Christian Leadership Conference, 1955–1968*. New York: Morrow, 1986.

————, ed. *We Shall Overcome: The Civil Rights Movement in the United States in the 1950s and 1960s.* 3 vols. Brooklyn, NY: Carlson, 1989.

Glen, John M. *Highlander, No Ordinary School, 1932–1962.* Lexington: University Press of Kentucky, 1988.

Goldfield, David R. *Black, White and Southern.* Baton Rouge: Louisiana State University Press, 1990.

Graham, Hugh Davis. *The Civil Rights Era: Origins and Development of National Policy, 1960–1972.* New York: Oxford University Press, 1990.

Hampton, Henry, Steve Fayer and Sarah Flynn, eds. *Voices of Freedom: An Oral History of the Civil Rights Movement from the 1950s through the 1980s.* New York: Bantam Books, 1990.

Klibaner, Irwin. *The Conscience of a Troubled South: The Southern Conference Educational Fund, 1946–1966.* Brooklyn, NY: Carlson Publishing, 1989.

————. "The Travail of Southern Radicals: The Southern Conference Educational Fund, 1946–1976," *Journal of Southern History* 49 (May 1983): 179–202.

Levy, Peter B., ed. *Documentary History of the Modern Civil Rights Movement.* Westport, CT: Greenwood Press, 1992.

Lowery, Charles D., and John F. Marszalek, eds. *Encyclopedia of African American Civil Rights from Emancipation to the Present.* Westport, CT: Greenwood Press, 1992.

Lyon, Danny. *Memories of the Southern Civil Rights Movement.* Chapel Hill: University of North Carolina Press, 1992.

McAdam, Doug. *Freedom Summer.* New York: Oxford University Press, 1988.

Meier, August, and Elliott Rudwick. *CORE.* Urbana: University of Illinois Press, 1975.

Mills, Nicolaus. *Like a Holy Crusade: Mississippi 1964–The Turning of the Civil Rights Movement in America.* Chicago: Ivan R. Dee, 1992.

Morris, Aldon. *The Origins of the Civil Rights Movement: Black Communities Organizing for Change.* New York: Free Press, 1984.

Murray, Paul T. *The Civil Rights Movement: References and Resources.* Boston: G. K. Hall, 1993.

O'Dell, Jack. "The FBI's Southern Strategies," in *It Did Happen Here: Recollections of Political Repression in America,* Bud and Ruth Schultz, eds. Berkeley: University of California Press, 1989: 279–88.

O'Reilly, Kenneth. *"Racial Matters": The FBI's Secret File on Black America, 1960–1972.* New York: Basic Books, 1990.

Powledge, Fred. *Free at Last? The Civil Rights Movement and the People Who Made It.* Boston: Little, Brown, 1991.

Raines, Howell. *My Soul Is Rested: The Story of the Civil Rights Movement of the Deep South.* New York: Putnam, 1977.

Rogers, Kim Lacy. *Righteous Lives: Narratives of the New Orleans Civil Rights Movement.* New York: New York University Press, 1993.

Rothschild, Mary Aickin. *A Case of Black and White: Northern Volunteers and the Southern Freedom Summers, 1964–1965.* Westport, CT: Greenwood Press, 1982.

Sitkoff, Harvard. *The Struggle for Black Equality, 1954–1992,* 2d ed. New York: Hill and Wang, 1992.

Stern, Mark. *Calculating Visions: Kennedy, Johnson, and Civil Rights.* New Brunswick, NJ: Rutgers University Press, 1992.

Weinberg, Jack. "Students and Civil Rights in the 1960s," *History of Education Quarterly* 30 (Summer 1990): 213–24.

Weisbrot, Robert. *Freedom Bound: A History of America's Civil Rights Movement*. New York: W. W. Norton, 1990.

West, Thomas R. and James W. Mooney, eds. *To Redeem a Nation: A History and Anthology of the Civil Rights Movement*. St. James, NY: Brandywine Press, 1993.

Williams, Juan. *Eyes on the Prize: America's Civil Rights Years, 1954–1965*. New York: Penguin Books, 1987.

Youth of the Rural Organizing and Cultural Center. *Minds Stayed on Freedom: The Civil Rights Struggles in the Rural South, an Oral History*. Boulder, CO: Westview Press, 1991.

Black Power

Barbour, Floyd B., ed. *The Black Power Revolt: A Collection of Essays*. Boston: Porter Sargent, 1968.

Bracey, John H., Jr., August Meier, and Elliott Rudwick, eds. *Black Nationalism in America*. Indianapolis: Bobbs-Merrill, 1970.

Carmichael, Stokely, and Charles V. Hamilton. *Black Power: The Politics of Liberation in America* new edition, with updated afterwords. New York: Random House, 1992 [1967].

Carson, Clayborne. *In Struggle: SNCC and the Black Awakening of the 1960s*. Cambridge, MA: Harvard University Press, 1981.

Cleage, Albert. *Black Christian Nationalism*. New York: Morrow, 1980 (1972).

Essien-Udom, Essien. *Black Nationalism: A Search for Identity in America*. Chicago: University of Chicago Press, 1962.

Haines, Herbert H. *Black Radicals and the Civil Rights Mainstream, 1945–1970*. Knoxville: University of Tennessee Press, 1988.

Jenkins, Betty L., and Susan Phillis, eds. *The Black Separatism Controversy: An Annotated Bibliography*. Westport, CT: Greenwood Press, 1976.

McCartney, John T. *Black Power Ideologies: An Essay in African-American Political Thought*. Philadelphia: Temple University Press, 1992.

Marsh, Clifton E. *From Black Muslims to Muslims: The Transition from Separatism to Islam, 1930–1980*. Metuchen, NJ: Scarecrow Press, 1984.

Van Deberg, William L. *New Day in Babylon: The Black Power Movement and American Culture, 1965–1975*. Chicago: University of Chicago Press, 1992.

Walters, Ronald W. *Pan Africanism in the African Diaspora: An Analysis of Modern Afrocentric Political Movements*. Detroit: Wayne State University Press, 1992.

Some Individual Examples

Abernathy, Ralph David. *And the Walls Came Tumbling Down: An Autobiography*. New York: HarperCollins, 1989.

Basil, Marilyn K. "Haki Madhubuti," in *Contemporary Authors*, vol. 24, New Revision Series. Detroit: Gale Research, 1988: 294–97.

———. "Sonia Sanchez," *Ibid.*, pp. 410–14.

Bechtel, Judith A., and Robert M. Coughlin. *Building the Beloved Community: Maurice McCrackin's Life for Peace and Civil Rights*. Philadelphia: Temple University Press, 1991.

Bray, Rosemary L. "A Black Panther's Long Journey" [on Elaine Brown, combined with a sketch "The Women of the Movement"], *New York Times Magazine*, January 31, 1993, pp. 21–23, 26, 68, 76.

Brown, Elaine. *A Taste of Power: A Black Woman's Story*. New York: Pantheon, 1993.

"Building Movements, Educating Citizens: Myles Horton and the Highlander Folk School" (commentaries), *Social Policy* 21 (Winter 1991): 2–79.

Cagin, Seth, and Philip Dray. *We Are Not Afraid: The Story of Goodman, Schwerner, and Chaney and the Civil Rights Campaign for Mississippi*. New York: Macmillan, 1988.

"Carmichael, Stokely," in *Contemporary Authors*, vol. 25, New Revision Series. Detroit: Gale Research, 1989: 64–66.

Carson, Clayborne. "Stokely Carmichael," in *Biographical Dictionary of the American Left*, Bernard K. Johnpoll and Harvey Klehr, eds. Westport, CT: Greenwood Press, 1986: 66–67.

Chafe, William H. *Never Stop Running: Allard Lowenstein and the Struggle to Save American Liberalism*. New York: Basic Books, 1993.

Chappell, David L. *Inside Agitators: White Southerners in the Civil Rights Movement*. Baltimore: Johns Hopkins Universty, 1994.

"Charles R. Garry, Fiery Lawyer for Radicals in 60s, Dies at 82," *New York Times*, August 18, 1991, p. 30.

Crawford, Vicki L., Jacqueline Anne Rouse, and Barbara Woods, eds. *Women in the Civil Rights Movement: Trailblazers and Torchbearers, 1941–1965*. Brooklyn, NY: Carlson Publishing, 1990.

Decker, Jeffrey Louis. *The Black Aesthetic Movement*. Detroit: Gale Research, 1991.

Dees, Morris, with Steve Fiffer. *A Season for Justice: The Life and Times of Civil Rights Lawyer Morris Dees*. New York: Scribner's, 1991.

Dorman, Michael. "Who Killed Medgar Evers?" *New York Times Magazine*, May 17, 1992, pp. 52–53+.

Drimmer, Melvin. "Roy Wilkins and the American Dream: A Review Essay," *Phylon* 45 (June 1984): 160–63.

Durr, Virginia. *Outside the Magic Circle: The Autobiography of Virginia Foster*. University: University of Alabama Press, 1985.

Edwards, Harry. *The Struggle That Must Be: An Autobiography*. New York: Macmillan, 1980.

Fleming, Cynthia Griggs. "Black Women Activists and the Student Nonviolent Coordinating Committee: The Case of Ruby Doris Smith Robinson," *Journal of Women's History* 4 (Winter 1993): 64–82.

Franklin, John Hope, and August Meier, eds. *Black Leaders of the Twentieth Century*. Urbana. University of Illinois Press, 1982.

Freccero, Carla. "June Jordan," in *African-American Writers*, Valerie Smith, Lea Baechler, and A. Walton Litz, eds. New York: Scribner's, 1991: 245–61.

Gates, Henry Louis. "Ishmael Reed," in *African-American Writers* (see Smith, Baechler, and Litz, eds.), pp. 361–77.

"Giovanni, Nikki," in *Contemporary Literary Criticism*, vol. 64. Detroit: Gale Research, 1991: 181–96.

Hamilton, Charles V. *Adam Clayton Powell, Jr.: The Political Biography of an American Dilemma*. New York: Macmillan, 1991.

Hauser, Thomas. *Muhammad Ali: His Life and Times*. New York: Simon and Schuster, 1991.

Hilliard, David, with Lewis Cole. *This Side of Glory: The Autobiography of David Hilliard and the Story of the Black Panthers*. New York: Little, Brown, 1993.

Hine, Darlene Clark, ed. *Black Women in American History*, 8 vols. Brooklyn: Carlson Publishing, 1990.

Horton, Myles, with Judith Kohl and Herbert Kohl. *The Long Haul: An Autobiography*. New York: Doubleday, 1990.

Horton, Myles, Brenda Bell, John Garenta, and John Marshall Peters. *We Make the Road by Walking: Conversations on Education and Social Change*. Philadelphia: Temple University Press, 1990.

Hurst, Catherine Daniels. "Haki R. Madhubuti," in *Afro-American Poets Since 1955*, Trudier Harris and Thadious Davis, eds., vol. 41 of *The Dictionary of Literary Biography*. Detroit: Gale Research, 1985: 222–32.

Innis, Roy, interviewed by Jeffrey Elliot, in *Black Voices in American Politics*, Jeffrey Elliot, ed. New York: Harcourt Brace Jovanovich, 1986: 241–63.

"John Lewis: Scarred Survivor Brings Home Lessons of '60s," *Washington Post*, March 6, 1990, A3.

"Jordan, June," in *Contemporary Authors*, vol. 25, New Revision Series. Detroit: Gale Research, 1989: 241–43.

Jordan, June. *Technical Difficulties: African-American Notes on the State of the Union*. New York: Pantheon Books, 1992.

"Joseph L. Rauh, Jr., a Life of Activism," *Washington Post*, Sept. 3, 1992, A1, A9.

Joyce, Joyce Ann. "Richard Wright," in *African American Writers* (see Smith, Baechler, and Litz, eds.), pp. 505–23.

King, Mary. *Freedom Song: A Personal History of the 1960s Civil Rights Movement*. New York: William Morrow, 1987.

Lewis, John. "Where did the Civil Rights Movement Go Wrong?" (interviewed by Vicki Quade), *Human Rights* 15 (Fall 1988): 18–22+.

Lipsitz, George. *A Life in the Struggle: Ivory Perry and the Culture of Opposition*. Philadelphia: Temple University Press, 1988.

"The Long, Long Journey of James Meredith: From Civil Rights Symbol to Jesse Helms's Aide," *Washington Post*, Nov. 3, 1989, C1, C2, C3.

McFadden, Grace Jordan. "Septima P. Clark and the Struggle for Human Rights," in *Women in the Civil Rights Movement: Trailblazers and Torchbearers, 1941–1965*, Vicki L. Crawford, Jacqueline Anne Rouse, and Barbara Woods, eds. Brooklyn, NY: Carlson Publishing, 1990: 85–97.

"McKissick, Floyd," in *Current Biography Yearbook 1991*. New York: H. W. Wilson, 1991: 650–51.

McKissick, Floyd. "Making Black Capitalism Work" (interview), in *Black Voices in American Politics*, Jeffrey M. Elliot, ed. New York: Harcourt Brace Jovanovich, 1986: 281–95.

McLaurin, Melton A. *Separate Pasts: Growing Up White in the Segregated South*. Athens: University of Georgia Press, 1987.

"Memorial Honors the Victims of Racial Violence," *New York Times*, Nov. 4, 1989, p. 7.

Moody, Anne. *Coming of Age in Mississippi*. New York: Dial Press, 1968.

Mueller, Carol. "Ella Baker and the Origins of 'Participatory Democracy'," in *Women in the Civil Rights Movement: Trailblazers* (see Crawford, Rouse, and Woods, eds.), pp. 51–70.

Nelson, Emmanuel. "Critical Deviance: Homophobia and the Reception of James Baldwin's Fiction," *Journal of American Culture* 14 (Fall 1991): 91–96.

Newton, Huey. Obits: *Current Biography* 50 (Oct. 1989): 59; *New York Times Biographical Service* 20 (Aug. 1989): 806–7.

"Old Hands, Young Blood: Student Activists of the 60s Meet Campus Organizers of the 80s," *Southern Exposure* 16 (Summer 1988): 47–58 (Casey Hayden, Howard Zinn, Charles McDew, Joyce Ladner, Clayborne Carson, and others).

Payne, Charles. "Ella Baker and Models of Social Change: Tribute," *Signs* 14 (Summer 1989): 885–99.

Porter, Horace A. *Stealing the Fire: The Art and Protest of James Baldwin*. Middletown, CT: Wesleyan University Press, 1989.

"The Radical Departure of Bobby Rush," *Washington Post*, May 3, 1993, C1, C8, C9.

Robinson, Jo Ann Gibson. *The Montgomery Bus Boycott and the Women Who Started It: The Memoir of Jo Ann Gibson Robinson*, David Garrow, ed. Knoxville: University of Tennessee Press, 1987.

Salem, Dorothy C., ed. *African American Women: A Biographical Dictionary*. New York: Garland Publishing, 1993.

Sellers, Cleveland, and Robert L. Terrell. *The River of No Return: Autobiography of a Black Militant and the Life and Death of SNCC*. Jackson: University Press of Mississippi, 1990 (1973).

Shakur, Assata. *Assata: An Autobiography*. Westport, CT: Lawrence Hill, 1987.

Sinsheimer, Joe. "Never Turn Back: An Interview with Sam Block," *Southern Exposure* 15 (Summer 1987): 37–50.

"Slain Panther Leader Fred Hampton Honored by City of Chicago," *Jet* 79 (December 10, 1990): 9.

Smith, Jessie Carney, ed. *Notable Black American Women*. Detroit: Gale Research, 1992.

Smith, Valerie, Lea Baechler, and A. Walton Litz, eds. *African-American Writers*. New York: Scribner's, 1991.

Stalvey, Lois Mark. *The Education of a WASP*. Madison: University of Wisconsin Press, 1989.

Toner, R. "[Andrew] Young as Candidate," *New York Times Biographical Service* 21 (May 1990): 492–93.

Weiss, Nancy J. *Whitney M. Young, Jr., and the Struggle for Civil Rights*. Princeton, NJ: Princeton University Press, 1989.

Wilkins, Roger. *A Man's Life*. Woodbridge, CT: Ox Bow Press, 1991 (1982).

Wilkins, Roy, with Tom Mathews. *Standing Fast: The Autobiography of Roy Wilkins*. New York: Viking, 1987.

Zehner, Harry. "How Roy Innis Ravaged CORE," *Saturday Review* 6 (April 28, 1979): 21–24.

Overall Black Impact

Button, James. *Blacks and Social Change: Impact of the Civil Rights Movement in Southern Communities*. Princeton, NJ: Princeton University Press, 1987.

Collier, Peter, and David Horowitz, eds. *Second Thoughts about Race in America*. Lanham, MD: University Press of America, 1991.

Elliot, Jeffrey, ed. *Black Voices in American Politics*. New York: Harcourt Brace Jovanovich, 1986.

Fairclough, Adam. "Historians and the Civil Rights Movement" (review article), *Journal of American Studies* 24 (December 1990): 387–98.

Fendrich, James Max. *Ideal Citizens: The Legacy of the Civil Rights Movement*. Albany, NY: SUNY Press, 1993.

Haddad, Yvonne Y., ed. *Muslims of America*. New York: Oxford University Press, 1991.

Harding, Vincent. *Hope and History: Why We Must Share the Story of the Movement*. Maryknoll, NY: Orbis Books, 1990.

Harris, Fred R., and Roger W. Wilkins, eds. *Quiet Riots: Race and Poverty in the U.S.; The Kerner Report Twenty Years Later*. New York: Pantheon Books, 1988.

Lawson, Steven F. "Freedom Then, Freedom Now: The Historiography of the Civil Rights Movement," *American Historical Review* 96 (April 1991): 456–71.

———. *In Pursuit of Power: Southern Blacks and Electoral Politics, 1965–1982*. New York: Columbia University Press, 1985.

———. *Running for Freedom: Civil Rights and Black Politics in America Since 1941*. Philadelphia: Temple University Press, 1990.

Marable, Manning. *Black American Politics: From the Washington Marches to Jesse Jackson*, rev. ed. New York: Routledge, Chapman and Hall, 1991.

———. *Race, Reform, and Rebellion: The Second Reconstruction in Black America, 1945–1990*, 2d rev. ed. Jackson: University Press of Mississippi, 1991.

Marwell, Gerald, Michael T. Arken, and N. J. Demerath. "The Persistence of Political Attitudes among 1960s Civil Rights Activists," *Public Opinion Quarterly* 51 (Fall 1987): 359–75.

Reed, Adolph, Jr., ed. *Race, Politics, and Culture: Critical Essays on the Radicalism of the 1960s*. Westport, CT: Greenwood Press, 1986.

Robinson, Armstead L., and Patricia Sullivan, eds. *New Directions in Civil Rights Studies*. Charlottesville: University Press of Virginia, 1991.

Walton, Hanes, Jr. *When the Marching Stopped: The Politics of Civil Rights Regulatory Agencies*. Albany: State University of New York Press, 1988.

Chicano

Acosta-Belen, Edna, and Barbara R. Sjostrom, eds. *The Hispanic Experience in the United States: Contemporary Issues and Perspectives*. New York: Praeger, 1988.

Acuña, Rodolfo. *Occupied America: A History of Chicanos*, 3d ed. New York: Harper and Row, 1988.

Caballero, Cesar, and Susan A. Delgado. *Chicano Organization Directory*. New York: Neal-Schuman, 1985.

Calderón, Héctor, and José David Saldívar. *Criticism in the Borderlands: Studies in Chicano Literature, Culture and Ideology*. Durham, NC: Duke University Press, 1991.

Camarillo, Albert, ed. *Latinos in the United States: A Historical Bibliography*. Santa Barbara, CA: ABC-Clio Press, 1986.

Catalano, Julie, ed. *Mexican Americans*. New York: Chelsea House, 1989.

Corona, Bert. "Bert Corona: Labor Radical" (interviewed by Diane Campbell), *Socialist Review* 19 (January-March 1989): 41ff.

De la Garza, Rodolfo O., et al., eds. *The Mexican American Experience: An Interdisciplinary Anthology*. Austin: University of Texas Press, 1985.

DuBois, Ellen Carol, and Vicki L. Ruiz, eds. *Unequal Sisters: A Multi-Cultural Reader in U.S. Women's History*. New York: Routledge, 1990.

Eysturoy, Annie O., and José Antonio Gurpequi. "Chicano Literature: Introduction and Bibliography," *American Studies International* 28 (April 1990): 48–82.

Foley, Douglas, et al. *From Peones to Politicos: Class and Ethnicity in a South Texas Town, 1900–1987*, rev. ed. Austin: University of Texas Press, 1988.

Gann, L. H., and Peter J. Duignan. *The Hispanics in the United States: A History*. Boulder, CO: Westview Press, 1986.

García, Eugene E., Francisco A. Lomelí, and Isidro D. Ortiz, eds. *Chicano Studies: A Multidisciplinary Approach*. New York: Teachers College, Columbia University, 1984.

García, F. Chris. *Latinos and Politics; A Selected Research Bibliography*. Austin: University of Texas Press, 1991.

García, Ignacio M. *United We Win: The Rise and Fall of La Raza Unida Party*. Tucson: MASRC; the University of Arizona, 1989.

García, John A., Theresa Córdova, and Juan R. García. *The Chicano Struggle: Analysis of Past and Present Efforts*. Binghamton, NY: Bilingual Press, 1984.

Garcia, Mario T. *Memories of Chicano History: The Life and Narrative of Bert Corona*, foreword by David Montgomery. Berkeley: University of California Press, 1994.

Garcia, Mario T. *Mexican Americans: Leadership, Ideology, and Identity, 1930–1960*. New Haven: Yale University Press, 1989.

Gómez-Quiñones, Juan. *Chicano Politics: Reality and Promise, 1940–1990*. Albuquerque: University of New Mexico Press, 1990.

"Gonzales, Rodolfo," in *Chicano Literature: A Reference Guide*, Julio Martínez and Francisco A. Lomelí, eds. (Westport, CT: Greenwood Press, 1985): 221–28.

Gonzales, Sylvia Alicia. *Hispanic American Voluntary Organizations*. Westport, CT: Greenwood Press, 1985.

Gutíerrez, David G. "Sin Fronteras? Chicanos, Mexican Americans, and the Emergence of the Contemporary Mexican Immigration Debate, 1968–1978," *Journal of American Ethnic History* 10 (Summer 1991): 5–37.

Hammerback, John, Richard J. Jensen, and José Angel Gutíerrez. *A War of Words: Chicano Protest in the 1960s and 1970s*. Westport, CT: Greenwood Press, 1985.

Huerta, Dolores. "Reflections on the UFW Experience," *The Center Magazine* 18 (July/August 1985): 2–8.

Jankowski, Martin Sanchez. *City Bound: Urban Life and Political Attitudes among Chicano Youth*. Albuquerque: University of New Mexico Press, 1986.

Jenkins, J. Craig. *The Politics of Insurgency: The Farm Worker Movement and the Politics of the 1960s*. New York: Columbia University Press, 1985.

Kanellos, Nicolás, ed. *Biographical Dictionary of Hispanic Literature in the United States: The Literature of Puerto Ricans, Cuban Americans, and Other Hispanic Writers*. Westport, CT: Greenwood Press, 1989.

Limón, José E. "The Daemonizing Epic: Rodolfo 'Corky' Gonzales and the Poetics of Chicano Rebellion," in *Mexican Ballads, Chicano Poems*. Berkeley: University of California Press, 1992: 115–29.

Lomelí, Francisco A., and Carl R. Shirley. *Chicano Writers*. Detroit: Gale Research, 1989.

Marín, Christine. *A Spokesman of the Mexican American Movement: Rodolfo 'Corky'*

Gonzales and the Fight for Chicano Liberation. San Francisco: R and E Research Associates, 1977.

Marin, Marquerite V. *Social Protest in an Urban Barrio: A Study of the Chicano Movement, 1966–1974*. Lanham, MD: University Press of America, 1991.

Marquez, Benjamin. *Power and Politics in a Chicano Barrio: A Study of Mobilization Efforts and Community Power in El Paso*. Lanham, MD: University Press of America, 1985.

Martínez, Eliud. "*I Am Joquin* as Poem and Film: Two Modes of Chicano Expression," *Journal of Popular Culture* 13 (Spring 1980): 505–15.

Meier, Matt S. *Mexican American Biographies: A Historical Dictionary, 1836–1987*. Westport, CT: Greenwood Press, 1988.

Meier, Matt S. and Feliciano Ribera. *Mexican Americans/American Mexicans: From Conquistadores to Chicanos* (rev. ed. of *The Chicanos*). New York: Hill and Wang, 1994.

Montejano, David. *Anglos and Mexicans in the Making of Texas, 1836–1986*. Austin: University of Texas Press, 1987.

Rocard, Marcienne. *The Children of the Sun: Mexican-Americans in the Literature of the United States*. Tucson: University of Arizona Press, 1990.

Rosaldo, R., R. G. Seligmann, Jr., and R. A. Calvert, eds. *Chicano: The Evolution of a People*, 2d ed. Melbourne, FL: Krieger, 1982.

Rose, Margaret. "From the Fields to the Picket Lines: Huelga Women and the Boycott, 1965–1975," *Labor History* 31 (Summer 1990): 271–93.

Rosenbaum, Robert J. *Mexicano Resistance in the Southwest: "The Sacred Right of Self-Preservation."* Austin: University of Texas Press, 1981.

Samora, Julian. *A History of the Mexican-American People*, rev. ed. Notre Dame, IN: Notre Dame University Press, 1992.

San Miguel, Guadalupe, Jr. *Let Them All Take Heed: Mexican Americans and the Campaign for Educational Equality, 1929–1981*. Austin: University of Texas Press, 1987.

Shirley, Carl R. *Understanding Chicano Literature*. Columbia: University of South Carolina Press, 1988.

Shorris, Earl. *Latinos*. New York: W. W. Norton, 1992.

Skerry, Peter. *The Mexican Americans; The Ambivalent Minority*. New York: Free Press, 1992.

Stone, Les. "Luis Valdez," in *Contemporary Authors*, vol. 32, New Revision Series. Detroit: Gale Research, 1991: 442–44.

Indian

Bataille, Gretchen M., ed. *Native American Women; A Biographical Dictionary*. New York: Garland Publishing, 1992.

Cadwalader, Sandra L., and Vine Deloria, Jr., eds. *The Aggressions of Civilization: Federal Indian Policy since the 1880s*. Philadelphia: Temple University Press, 1984.

Calloway, Colin, ed. *New Directions in American Indian History*. Norman: University of Oklahoma Press, 1988.

Churchill, Ward, and James Vander Wall. *Agents of Repression: The FBI's Secret Wars against the American Indian Movement and the Black Panther Party*. Boston: South End Press, 1988.

Clifton, James A. *Being and Becoming Indian: Biographical Studies of North American Frontiers*. Chicago: Dorsey Press, 1989.

Cloutier, Candace. "N. Scott Momaday," in *Contemporary Authors*, vol. 14, New Revision Series. Detroit: Gale Research, 1985: 335–40.

Cornell, Stephen. *The Return of the Native: American Indian Political Resurgence*. New York: Oxford University Press, 1988.

Davis, Mary B., ed. *Native America in the Twentieth Century: An Encyclopedia*. New York: Garland, 1994.

Deloria, Vine, Jr. *American Indian Policy in the Twentieth Century*. Norman: University of Oklahoma Press, 1985.

Deloria, Vine, Jr., and Clifford M. Lytle, Jr. *The Nations Within: The Past and Future of American Indian Sovereignty*. New York: Pantheon Books, 1984.

Edmunds, R. David, ed. *American Indian Leaders: Studies in Diversity*. Lincoln: University of Nebraska Press, 1986.

Green, Rayna. *Native American Women: A Contextual Bibliography*. Bloomington: Indiana University Press, 1983.

Jaimes, M. Annette, ed. *The State of Native America: Genocide: Colonization, and Resistance*. Boston: South End Press, 1991.

Josephy, Alvin M., Jr., ed. *Red Power: The American Indians Fight for Freedom*. Lincoln: University of Nebraska Press, 1985.

La Potin, Armand S., ed. *Native American Voluntary Organizations*. Westport, CT: Greenwood Press, 1987.

Moses, L. G., and Raymond Wilson, eds. *Indian Lives: Essays on Nineteenth- and Twentieth-Century Native American Leaders*. Albuquerque: University of New Mexico Press, 1986.

Nabokov, Peter, ed. *Native American Testimony: A Chronicle of Indian- White Relations from Prophecy to the Present, 1492–1992*. New York: Viking, 1991.

Olson, James S., and Raymond Wilson, eds. *Native Americans in the Twentieth Century*. Urbana: University of Illinois Press, 1986.

Prucha, Francis Paul. *The Great Father: The United States Government and American Indians*. Lincoln: University of Nebraska Press, 1984.

Roscoe, Will, ed. *Living the Spirit: A Gay American Indian Anthology*. New York: St. Martin's Press, 1988.

Stannard, David E. *American Holocaust; Columbus and the Conquest of the New World*. New York: Oxford University Press, 1992.

Stuart, Paul. *Nations within a Nation: Historical Statistics of American Indians*. Westport, CT: Greenwood Press, 1987.

Swann, Brian, and Arnold Krupat, eds. *I Tell You Now; Autobiographical Essays by Native American Writers*. Lincoln: University of Nebraska Press, 1987.

Tickner, J. Ann. *Self-Reliance vs. Power Politics: American and Indian Experiences in Building Nation States*. New York: Columbia University Press, 1986.

Williams, Robert A., Jr. *The American Indian in Western Legal Thought; The Discourses of Conquest*. New York: Oxford University Press, 1990.

Puerto Rican

Abramson, Michael. *Young Lords Party*. New York: McGraw-Hill, 1971.

Acosta-Belen, Edna, ed. *Puerto Rican Woman*, 2d ed. New York: Praeger, 1986.

Carr, Raymond, *Puerto Rico: A Colonial Experiment*. New York: Random House, 1984.

Carrion, Arturo Morales. *Puerto Rico: A Political and Cultural History*. New York: Norton, 1984.

Fernandez, Ronald. *Los Macheteros: The Violent Struggle for Puerto Rican Independence*. New York: Prentice Hall, 1988.

———. *The Disenchanted Island: Puerto Rico and the United States in the Twentieth Century*, foreword by William M. Kunstler and Ronald L. Kuby. New York: Praeger, 1992.

Fitzpatrick, Joseph P. *Puerto Rican Americans: The Meaning of Migration to the Mainland*, 2d ed. New York: Prentice Hall, 1987.

Fowlie-Flores, Fay, comp. *Index to Puerto Rican Collective Biography*. Westport, CT: Greenwood Press, 1987.

Lemann, Nicholas. "The Other Underclass," *Atlantic Monthly* 268 (Dec. 1991): 96–102+.

López, Alfredo. *Doña Lucha's Island: Modern Colonialism in Puerto Rico*. Boston: South End Press, 1987.

Meléndez, Edgardo. *Puerto Rico's Statehood Movement*. Westport, CT: Greenwood Press, 1988.

"Puerto Rico: A Colonial Dilemma," *Radical America* (double issue) 23:1 (Jan.-Feb. 1989).

Rodriguez, Clara. *Puerto Rican; Born in the USA*. Wincester, MA: Unwin Hyman, 1989.

———. "Puerto Rican Studies," *American Quarterly* 42 (Sept. 1990): 437–55.

Sanchez, Maria, and Antonio Stevens-Arroyo. *Toward a Renaissance of Puerto Rican Studies*. Boulder, CO: Westview Press, 1987.

Wagenheim, Olga Jimenez de. *Puerto Rico's Revolt for Independence: El Grito de Lares*. Boulder, CO; Westview Press, 1985.

Zavala, Iris M., and Rafael Rodriguez, eds. *The Intellectual Roots of Independence: An Anthology of Puerto Rican Political Essays*. New York: Monthly Review Press, 1980.

DENNIS BANKS (1930–)

American Indian Movement founder, Indian activist

Dennis Banks was one of the founders and leaders of the American Indian Movement (AIM), an organization established in Minneapolis, Minnesota, in 1968 to help improve Indian conditions and to protect Indians against civil rights violations by the police. Banks participated in major demonstrations throughout the 1960s and 1970s, drawing attention to the horrid conditions that urban and reservation Indians faced. In the 1990s, he and Russell Means, another well-known Indian activist, continued to be recognized as significant voices of Indian protest against discriminatory practices against their people.

Born on April 12, 1930, on the Leech Lake Reservation in northern Minnesota, Banks, a full-blood Chippewa, was taken from his home at age five and sent to Pipestone Indian School, 400 miles away. He later attended schools in North and South Dakota and at Leech Lake. In 1953 Banks joined the U.S. Air Force and served in Japan and Korea. After his discharge he became a jobless drifter. He received prison sentences in the mid-1960s for burglary and check forgery. While working as a recruiter for Honeywell Corporation, he and two other Chippewas, George Mitchell and Clyde Bellecourt, founded AIM in 1968. For the next several years AIM's militant activities made national headlines, and Banks would often be in the center of the controversies.

In November 1969 Banks was among the Indians who temporarily occupied Alcatraz Island in San Francisco Bay. It was then abandoned federal property and they had hoped to create an Indian cultural center on the island. Banks became executive director of AIM in 1971 and helped make the organization a national movement. He played a major role in convincing white authorities in Gordon, Nebraska, to apply equal justice in the murder case of Raymond Yellow Thunder by white men and to hear Indian grievances on other matters.

Banks was involved in the planning of the Trail of Broken Treaties, a protest rally of Indian tribes who traveled to Washington, D.C., in November 1972 to cite treaty violations and to present twenty demands to rectify matters. When promised federal housing proved inadequate, the Indians took over the Bureau of Indian Affairs building, renaming it the Native American Embassy. During the occupation, Banks was in charge of security and internal operations. After five days of negotiations, the Indians agreed to vacate the building. The government promised to study Indian grievances and paid for transportation of Indians back to their homes. The violence associated with this incident probably hurt the Indian movement more than it helped it.

In February 1973 Banks and other AIM members intervened in the stabbing death of Wesley Bad Heart Bull in Custer County, South Dakota. They

Dennis Banks *(right)* with Russell Means. Copyright *Washington Post*; Reprinted by permission of D.C. Public Library.

were outraged that the white man who stabbed an Indian was charged with second-degree manslaughter instead of murder. Negotiations broke down, and violence resulted, causing injuries to several policemen and Indians. Banks would later be arrested and found guilty of riot and assault with a deadly weapon in 1975 for his involvement at Custer. Facing a maximum sentence of fifteen years, Banks fled and, for the next ten years, evaded South Dakota authorities (discussed below).

After the Custer incident in 1973, Banks and other AIM members occupied Wounded Knee, the site of the last major battle between the Sioux and the U.S. Army in December 1890. Beginning on February 28, 1973, the occupation lasted until May 9, 1973. The Indians were protesting against the oppressive tribal government at Pine Ridge, demanding the removal of Dick Wilson, the tribal chairman, and asking for a U.S. Senate investigation of treaty violations and of the BIA.

The FBI and federal marshals did not launch a major attack against the Indian protesters, although sporadic fighting ensued, and two Indians were killed in the seventy-one-day encounter. The government consented to conduct investigations of the tribal government at Pine Ridge and of the status of the 1868 Treaty of Fort Laramie. Again, the violence at Wounded Knee II tended to draw attention from Indian grievances.

Banks and Means stood trial for their participation at Wounded Knee on

February 12, 1974, in St. Paul, Minnesota. Among the lawyers defending them were William Kunstler (6*) and Mark Lane. The eight-month trial ended on September 16 when federal judge Fred Nichol dismissed all charges against Banks and Means because of government misconduct in the case that included illegal wire taps, lying under oath, and altered documents.

Banks later clashed with William Janklow, assistant attorney general of South Dakota, when he charged Janklow with sexual misconduct with an Indian girl. Janklow would become attorney general and then governor of South Dakota. As attorney general, he prosecuted the case against Banks for his involvement at Custer in 1973. Found guilty in 1975, and facing a maximum sentence of fifteen years, Banks failed to appear for sentencing because he believed he would be killed in prison.

For the next ten years, Banks found sanctuary in California and in New York. Governor Jerry Brown refused to extradite Banks to South Dakota. Movie actors Marlon Brando and Jane Fonda (5*) supported the governor's decision. In California Banks taught at Deganawidah-Quetzalcoatl University at Davis, a two-year college stressing minority studies. In 1978 Banks organized the Longest Walk, a protest march to Washington, D.C., to lobby against anti-Indian legislation and other issues. He, of course, remained in California.

George Deukmejian, a Republican, won the governorship in 1983. He declared that he would not protect Banks from extradition. Banks then fled to a new sanctuary at the Onondaga Reservation near Syracuse, New York. While the governor of New York, Mario Cuomo, was not as supportive as Governor Brown, Cuomo did block the use of state police to arrest Banks while he resided among the Iroquois at Onondaga.

Banks kept busy on the reservation by jogging, coaching a cross-country team, doing chores, and organizing drives for the needy. In 1984 he decided that his reservation life was too confining. He returned to South Dakota and was sentenced, in October of 1984, to three years in prison. He was not jailed for that long, however, being paroled on December 9, 1985.

Banks secured employment in 1985 as an alcoholism counselor at the Pine Ridge Reservation. He became involved in economic development projects on the reservation that included a computer assembly business. In addition, he hosted a radio program which entertained as well as informed its listeners. In December of 1990 he participated in events commemorating the Battle of Wounded Knee centenary.

Dennis Banks continued to be a leading advocate of Indian rights. In the 1990s he turned to acting, playing minor roles in such films as *Thunderheart* and *The Last of the Mohicans*.

Bibliography

"Banks, Dennis," in *Current Biography* 53 (June 1992): 6–11.

Davis, Ann Leslie. "The Ride Back," *Mother Jones* 16 (Jan./Feb. 1991): 79–80.

Dewing, Rolland. *Wounded Knee: The Meaning and Significance of the Second Incident.* New York: Irvington Publishers, 1985.

Jensen, Richard E., R. Eli Paul, and John Carter. *Eyewitness at Wounded Knee.* Lincoln: University of Nebraska Press, 1991.

Lazarus, Edward. *Black Hills/White Justice: The Sioux Nation Versus the United States, 1775 to the Present.* New York: Harper/Collins, 1992.

Matthiessen, Constance. "The Hounding of Dennis Banks," *The Nation* 238 (March 24, 1984): 343–46.

Matthiessen, Peter. *In the Spirit of Crazy Horse*; new afterword. New York: Viking, 1991 (1983). Reviewed: *Atlantic* 251 (March 1983): 112; *New Republic* 188 (March 7, 1983): 31+; *New York Review of Books* 30 (April 14, 1983): 21+; *New York Times Book Review*, March 6, 1983, p. 1+.

———. *Indian Country.* New York: Viking, 1984.

United States. Congress. Senate. Select Committee on Indian Affairs. *Proposed Wounded Knee Park and Memorial . . .* (congressional hearings). Washington, DC: U.S. Government Printing Office, 1991.

United States. Congress. Senate. Committee on Interior and Insular Affairs. Subcommittee on Insular Affairs. *Occupation of Wounded Knee. . . .* Washington, DC: U.S. Government Printing Office, 1976.

United States. Congress. Senate. Committee on the Judiciary. Subcommittee to Investigate the Administration of the Internal Security Act and Other Internal Security Laws. *Revolutionary Activities within the United States: The American Indian Movement. . . .* Washington, DC: U.S. Government Printing Office, 1976.

Vizenor, Gerald. "Dennis of Wounded Knee," *American Indian Quarterly* 7 (Spring 1983): 51–65.

Raymond Wilson

IMAMU AMIRI BARAKA
[LEROI JONES] (1934–   )

Black cultural revolutionary

The man who was then known as LeRoi Jones published his first book of poetry, *Preface to a Twenty Volume Suicide Note,* in 1961. In the years that followed, he wrote numerous plays, poems, and short stories, along with commentaries on literature, music, and society. Most of this writing focused on white racism and black liberation. During these decades, Jones moved from Greenwich Village to Harlem, and then to Newark. His political outlook changed from liberalism to black nationalism, then to Marxism-Leninism, and, later, to socialism. Along the way, he joined the Kawaida branch of the Islamic faith and changed his name to Imamu Amiri Baraka. Throughout these changes, he remained a radical spokesman for the black community.

LeRoi Jones was born in Newark, New Jersey, the son of middle-class par-

Imamu Amiri Baraka
[LeRoi Jones] speaking
at Howard University
1973. Copyright
Washington Post;
Reprinted by permission
of D.C. Public Library.

ents. He demonstrated unusual oratorical skills as a child when he memorized
and recited lengthy speeches for family gatherings. He became a gifted student who graduated two years early from high school. Although he received
a two-year scholarship in 1951 from Rutgers University, he apparently felt an
outsider there and transferred to Howard University in Washington, D.C.,
after one year. He arrived at Howard as an enthusiastic young student, but
soon came to despise most of the school, except for a few classes with Sterling
Brown in jazz criticism. By 1954 he had concluded that Howard trained blacks
for token positions in a white-dominated society, creating only the illusion of
significant progress.

Jones was shocked particularly by blatant discrimination among the Howard
students. Lighter-skinned blacks refused to associate with darker-skinned

blacks. The students who had come from urban areas like Philadelphia or New York ridiculed those who had come from rural areas in the South. African-American students detested blacks from the Caribbean or Africa. Furthermore, all Howard students apparently believed that they were superior to blacks from other historically black colleges and universities. Jones interpreted these biases as the products of a prejudiced white society. The overall effect of a Howard education, Jones believed, was to make black students adhere to a white aesthetic: to value white ideals, white standards of beauty, and, ultimately, "whiteness."

Jones left Howard University in 1954. Several biographers claim that Jones graduated with a Bachelor of Arts degree, but he later asserted that he had "flunked out of school" because of poor academic performance. He was uncertain of his future, and he joined the U.S. Air Force as an immediate way of fulfilling the military requirements of that time. After completing both basic and advanced training, Jones was assigned to be a member of a bomber crew at an air base in Puerto Rico. There, the tranquil routine of military life allowed him to immerse himself in the world of literature. He read widely, both in the European classics and the best-seller list, but he came to believe that he was a black outsider in a predominantly white world. Again, as had happened at Rutgers and Howard, Jones came to a sense that there was something about the white way of doing things, of expressing one's self, of being artistic, that limited his ability to reflect himself and his experience in his art.

During his last year in the air force in 1957, Jones became fascinated with the goal of living as a writer in New York City. He spent several of his furloughs in Greenwich Village, where old friends and acquaintances introduced him to the periphery of the Beat culture movement. Jones was intrigued by the irreverence of the Beats, their decidedly unconventional ideas, and their free lifestyles. When he was prematurely discharged from the military because of a rumor of communist sympathies, he quickly found his way to the Village, where he would pursue his artistic and intellectual dreams.

His New York debut was less than triumphant. After he found an apartment, he worked as a stock employee in a record shop. When mail orders came in, Jones would retrieve the albums from the stacks and fill the orders. Jones soon earned extra income and notability, however, by drawing upon the knowledge of jazz that he had developed under the guidance of Professor Brown. He began to review jazz albums for *Downbeat* magazine, and he occasionally penned the liner notes for new jazz releases.

Simultaneously, Jones made inroads into the artistic community by editing or co-editing a series of small, Beat-oriented literary magazines. Together with Hettie Cohen, a white co-worker whom he married in 1958, Jones founded the magazine *Yungen*. He soon had a creative hand in the literary projects *Floating Bear*, *Fuck You!*, and *Zazen*. As an editor, Jones worked closely with authors such as Diane DiPrima, Allen Ginsberg (5*), and Jack Kerouac. He was regarded as a significant, although minor figure in the Beat movement.

The couple was nonetheless far from economic solvency. The magazines were sold usually for contributions rather than an established cover price. The small revenue from each issue was used to pay for the next issue. During this period, Jones was also gathering material for his first book of poetry, the 1961 *Preface to a Twenty Volume Suicide Note*. Between 1958 and 1961–1962, the couple was supported almost entirely by Hettie Cohen's income.

While Jones was a starving artist, he had a discernible and growing role in the Village. His white friends included many rising artists and writers, and his black peers included many of the established or emerging jazz musicians. He both organized and attended parties and intellectual gatherings where he established social contacts.

His politics between 1958 and 1961 were a combination of liberalism, anti-authoritarianism, and nascent black consciousness. His experiences at Rutgers and Howard soured him on the benefits of integration. Nonetheless, he maintained a dichotomy between art and politics. He never attempted, during his early career, to explore the potential differences between being a writer and being a "black writer." At first, his rejection of "white" artistic values was satisfied by his activities within the Beat culture.

Jones's 1961 visit to Cuba shifted his political outlook. Although he had been a member of the Fair Play for Cuba Committee since 1958, his travel produced a deeper appreciation of the positive aspects of the Cuban Revolution. Jones witnessed black- and brown-skinned peoples who won their liberation from oppression by force and now enjoyed the dignity that independence had brought.

It was during this trip that Jones met and talked with Robert Williams. Williams had made international news in the 1950s when, as director of the Monroe, North Carolina NAACP, he formed a gun club for Monroe's black residents to oppose Klan terror. After one shoot-out, Williams's group disarmed several members of the local Klan. Williams would later author the book *Negroes with Guns*.

The militance of Williams, the spirit of the Cuban Revolution, and the examples of African revolutions against European colonization all stimulated Jones to question the nonviolent integrationist struggles in the United States. When he returned, he criticized the pretentiousness of Greenwich Village intellectuals who imagined that they were superior to "in the streets" politics. Jones's relationship with his white colleagues grew more strained. He now condemned white liberals and rapidly earned a reputation as an extremist who hated whites and particularly Jews. Ironically, it was during 1961 to 1964 that Jones received his broadest critical acclaim from white Americans.

His first effort to increase his political awareness and commitment came in 1961 when he formed the Organization of Young Men. This group was comprised of blacks from the Village such as Archie Shepp, Harold Cruse, and A. B. Spellman. While Jones was the nominal leader, he was unsuccessful in articulating a clear direction for the group. There was no formal political agenda, only a shared impatience with nonviolent protests, and a preference for an unspecified but more vigorous form of black politics. Activities beyond these general discussions were rare or nonexistent. While Jones had no clear alternatives, he now derided liberal activism by both blacks and whites. When Malcolm X (*) referred to the March on Washington in 1963 as the "Farce of Washington," Jones fully agreed that it was merely "showmanship" that masked the cruel realities of racist inequality in America.

As Jones embraced a militant form of black politics, he concluded that he had to live and work among black people for his own artistic and cultural development. In 1964, the same year that his play *Dutchman* won an Obie Award, Jones founded the Black Arts Repertory Theatre/School in Harlem. Although he remained married to Hettie Cohen, and still lived in the Village, he now split his time between the Harlem school and the remnants of his integrated world in the Village.

Jones, like many other black Americans, watched the schism within the civil rights movement between the activists who adhered to integration and non-violence and those who espoused radical political and cultural separatism. By 1964, the black nationalism that was articulated by leaders such as Malcolm X and Stokely Carmichael found favor with many black Americans. These people had grown weary and skeptical of the nonviolent tactics of Dr. Martin Luther King (*). Even members of the first generation of blacks who could enter previously segregated schools and jobs often perceived themselves limited by covert forms of white prejudice. There seemed to be a glass ceiling preventing them from achieving all that their ability and character deserved.

Jones remembered such discrimination at Rutgers in 1951. His later experience at Howard University convinced him that integration was not a solution but a method of instilling self-hatred in black Americans. Black nationalists were attracted to the ideal of blacks controlling their own financial, political, educational, and cultural organizations. A vision of "black power" was emerging.

This new black nationalism differed from its antecedents in two important ways. First, unlike the Garveyite philosophy of the 1920s, the black nationalists of the 1960s sought to develop autonomous black enclaves in Newark, Watts, or Harlem, as opposed to repatriating black Americans to Africa. Second, whereas Marcus Garvey had called for the removal of blacks from the American economic and political system, Carmichael, Malcolm X, and LeRoi Jones (among others) fought to carve out their own colored niche within the capitalist system.

When Malcolm X was murdered in February of 1965, Jones took the loss personally. The contradiction of being a black nationalist leader with a white wife proved too much to bear, and he separated from Hettie Cohen. By March of 1965, Jones moved to Harlem to fully commit himself to the Black Arts Repertory Theatre/School.

The Black Arts School was to function as a cultural liaison between the black community in Harlem and the nationwide struggle for "black liberation." Throughout the spring and summer of 1965 the school's members performed plays, poetry readings, dance recitals, and concerts that sought to affirm "blackness" and the African heritage of black Americans. Jones and the other BART/S members also tried to use impromptu gatherings to initiate street theatre or poetry readings. It was the art, drama, and literature of what Larry Neal referred to as the "Black Aesthetic." This asserted that black artists and writers, to be useful to the black community, had to be both technically proficient and socially and politically relevant. The Black Arts School attempted to establish new criteria by which Afro-Americans could judge the worth of a poem, painting, or piece of music.

The Black Arts School was an eclectic gathering of individuals at various levels of talent and commitment to the cause. Jones was their leader only in the sense that he had achieved a greater notoriety than the other participants. The press also centered on him because of the anti-Semitism, homophobia, and anti-white animus contained in many of his works. Jones, in both his poetry and his politics, fostered a highly confrontational style that caused many whites and blacks to dismiss his work as pure invective.

The school was able to survive financially because the rents were low and because, in the collective spirit of the times, artists who got money from their work contributed to the expenses. In 1965, for example, Jones and the playwrights Nat White and Charles Patterson had a total of four plays running in Off-Broadway theatres. Jones charged $20 per ticket downtown so that he could repeat the same performance for free in Harlem. The school, in addition, received about $40,000 in federal money when the Johnson administration tried to end the "disturbances" in northern ghettos by funding local social programs. While Jones later conceded that some of this money was used illegally by BART/S members to cover their personal expenses, most of it was spent hiring residents of Harlem as school employees.

The school had a short life. Jones displayed little enthusiasm for the burdens of leadership. He failed to instill either discipline or purpose into the BART/S membership, and did not provide any clear political or social agenda for the group. Internal quarrels became so pervasive that some members carried weapons. The final crisis came when Jones refused to allow Sargent Shriver to enter the school's facilities. Shriver was a major figure in the Johnson administration. He had arrived unannounced to investigate charges that federal assistance was being misused by anti-white extremists. Shriver, with a group of reporters, was refused admission. Shortly thereafter, Jones's OEO assistance was cut off and the school was quickly reduced to penury. In the midst of this decaying situation, Jones moved back to Newark, where he continued to organize black nationalist artistic and political groups. A subsequent police raid on the Harlem building turned up a "cache of weapons" and ammunition. This effectively killed this project.

In early 1967, Jones founded the Spirit House. This artistic enclave in Newark was a maturer version of the Black Arts School. Newark became a center for black nationalist activities when Jones attracted artistic contributions from such prominent blacks as Sonia Sanchez, Yusef Imam, and Ed Bullins.

After Jones established himself in Newark (and married his second wife), he traveled west to accept a teaching position at San Francisco State College. SFSC was undergoing a wave of protests prompted by the Black Student Union's agitating for minority cultural and academic programs. Jones soon participated as both advisor and activist. He encouraged black students to use confrontational methods, such as threatening to beat up white student council members.

It was during the 1967 protests that Jones met Maulana Karenga (5*). Karenga was a cultural black nationalist and founder of the Kawaida faith. Jones was impressed by Karenga's organization, which had an almost military discipline and strictly enforced its values. Jones used some of his time on the West Coast to absorb Karenga's leadership concepts.

At the core of Karenga's success was the Kawaida faith. This is an ersatz religion which borrows elements of Islam and mixes them with selected African religious and cultural practices to create a non-Western ideology for African-Americans. The faith was based upon adherence to the Nguzo Saba, or seven principles. Its followers were forbidden to smoke tobacco, use drugs, eat pork, or consume alcohol. The Kawaida faith has also been extremely patriarchal. Women are required to accept subordinate roles as wives and mothers.

When Jones became a Kawaida member in late 1967, he discarded his "slave name" for a traditional African or Islamic one. LeRoi Jones became Imamu Amiri Baraka, which one biographer has interpreted as meaning Spiritual Leader—Blessed Prince (Hudson, p. 34). After his return to Newark, Baraka sought to implement the central concepts of Kawaida.

His first goal was to create pragmatic outlets for the energies of Newark's black nationalists. By 1968, he decided that he would seek to unite all black political organizations in Newark under one umbrella group, which would determine goals and policies for the membership. Baraka hoped to use this power to help blacks to control the city government. Black nationalists would use the ballot to create their own enclave.

Baraka's political orientation had changed. He had moved from hollow rhetoric to real politics. When he had issued his 1965 call for Harlem to secede from the United States and to nationalize all of the white-owned businesses in the newly independent region, he had no plans to achieve this goal—beyond a tacit invitation to begin looting. By 1968, Baraka's goals had been clarified by Karenga. First, he sought to elect many blacks to the city government. Second, he wished to elect a black mayor. These officials, along with black activists who did not hold office, would promote black economic and cultural development. The Committee for a Unified Newark completed this campaign by electing Newark's first black mayor in 1970. This event may have been Jones's biggest political success. His subsequent political endeavors, particularly his efforts to create a nationwide black political party, met with less approval.

Baraka realized the limitations of organizing under the banner of black nationalism by 1974. His adoption of a Marxist-Leninist political philosophy expressed his desire to elevate economics and class to a level equal to that of race. Baraka was convinced that capitalism played a large part in the underdevelopment of black Americans and that nationalism contained serious shortcomings as a liberation program because it failed to adequately address economic issues.

Baraka's political and literary influence peaked between 1964 and 1970. During the following years, he was unable to capture the prominence that he had once enjoyed. Nonetheless, Baraka held visiting professorships at prestigious universities such as Yale and Rutgers, which underscored his continued status as a major literary figure. As the 1990s opened, he was a full professor at the State University of New York at Stony Brook and had just been denied a similar rank at Rutgers. His appointment had been blocked, he asserted, by "Klansmen," "Europhilic elitists and white supremacists" within the English Department.

LeRoi Jones/Amiri Baraka represented a transition that many black Americans made during the 1960s, a transition from integration and nonviolence to militancy and separatism. The transformations from LeRoi Jones to Amiri Baraka, from Greenwich Village to Harlem, and from the Beat movement to the Black Arts movement, were all portions of Baraka's personal life that symbolized the larger quest of black America to define itself in terms of a Black Aesthetic. Blacks increasingly did not want to be judged by the dominant white standards of beauty, value, and intelligence. Although Baraka was not the seminal influence of the black nationalist movement of the 1960s, he embodied many of the promises and the problems of that movement.

Bibliography

Baraka, Imamu Amiri. *The Autobiography of LeRoi Jones/Amiri Baraka*. New York: Freundlich Books, 1984.
———. *The LeRoi Jones/Amiri Baraka Reader*, William J. Harris, ed. New York: Thunder's Mouth Press, 1991.
Brown, Lloyd. *Amiri Baraka*. Boston: Twayne Publishers, 1980.
Cook, Mercer, and Stephen E. Henderson. *The Militant Black Writer in Africa and the United States*. Madison: University of Wisconsin Press, 1969.
Cruse, Harold. *The Crisis of the Negro Intellectual*. New York: Quill, 1967.
Fox, Robert Elliot. *Conscientious Sorcerers: The Black Postmodernist Fiction of LeRoi Jones/Amiri Baraka, Ishmael Reed, and Samuel R. Delany*. New York: Greenwood Press, 1987.
Harris, William J. *The Poetry and Politics of Amiri Baraka: The Jazz Aesthetic*. Columbia: University of Missouri Press, 1985.

Hudson, Theodore R. *From LeRoi Jones to Amiri Baraka*. Durham, NC: Duke University Press, 1973.

Jones, Hettie. *How I Became Hettie Jones*. New York: E. P. Dutton, 1990.

Karenga, Maulana. *Introduction to Black Studies*. Los Angeles: Kawaida Publications, 1984.

Neal, Larry. *Visions of a Liberated Future: Black Arts Movement Writings*. New York: Thunder's Mouth Press, 1989.

Alan Spears

VERNON BELLECOURT [WABUN-ININI] (1931–   )

American Indian Movement Leader; international activist

Vernon Bellecourt and his younger brother Clyde were part of the inner circle of urban Indians that led the American Indian Movement (AIM) to a leadership position in New Left politics during the late 1960s and early 1970s. The Bellecourt brothers, along with Dennis Banks (*) and Russell Means (*), were the most visible spokesmen for AIM, an urban organization that modeled itself after the militant black power movements of that era. Their political philosophy was based on conflict and confrontation to preserve the heritage of the native American, to protest racial discrimination, to protect Indian rights, and to rectify past wrongs.

Bellecourt's troubled early years no doubt nourished his militancy. He and Clyde were part of a family of twelve children raised in a home with no running water or electricity on the White Earth reservation in northern Minnesota. Their main support came from a small veteran's pension allotted to their father who was wounded and disabled by mustard gas in France in World War I. Clyde was sent to reform school at age ten and was soon labeled incorrigible. The rest of the family moved to Minneapolis, where Vernon studied at St. Benedict's parochial school. Although considered a disciplined student, he dropped out of school in the eighth grade and drifted into the Minneapolis ghetto. At age nineteen Vernon was sentenced to the St. Cloud Reformatory for robbing a tavern in St. Paul. There he studied barbering and ingratiated himself with prison authorities with his excellent haircutting. His Mr. Vernon beauty salons propelled him into a middle-class lifestyle. In the mid-1960s he sold his salons and moved near Aspen, Colorado, where he styled hair and skiied.

Back in Minneapolis Clyde became the AIM director for Minneapolis shortly after it was founded by Chippewas Dennis Banks and John Mitchell in July 1968. Funded mainly by grants from the Office of Economic Opportunity and the American Lutheran Church, AIM enjoyed such success in the Twin Cities that it soon expanded into a national organization.

Vernon Bellecourt [WaBun-Inini]. *Source*: ICC File

Vernon Bellecourt rejected his white middle-class orientation and founded the AIM chapter at Denver in 1971. Despite his limited education Bellecourt was very articulate and had more leadership experience and maturity than most of the other AIM leaders. Consequently, he often served as the spokesman for the organization. He was also a fund-raising leader, where he enjoyed success in obtaining grants from the federal government and from various religious denominations, especially the American Lutherans. Paradoxically, AIM identified the Christian church and the federal government as two of the worst enemies of the American Indian. Bellecourt was appointed to the post of national director of AIM by the movement's central council in the spring of 1972.

AIM strategy focused on demonstration, confrontation, and occupation. Vernon Bellecourt played a key role in these activities during the organization's period of peak activity from the fall of 1972 to the summer of 1973. He helped lead the Trail of Broken Treaties caravan to Washington, D.C., at election time 1972. When AIM occupied the Bureau of Indian Affairs building in Washington, Bellecourt served as a key negotiator and mediator.

After the successful confrontation in Washington, AIM converged on South Dakota. AIM was anxious to disprove the constant criticism that it was an urban organization that did not represent grassroots reservation Indians. They sought to depose Pine Ridge tribal council president Richard Wilson, an outspoken AIM critic, and replace him with Russell Means, a member of the

Oglala Sioux tribe. A Pine Ridge civil rights group opposed to Wilson invited AIM to the reservation to assist them.

When an impeachment attempt against Wilson failed, AIM decided to stage a dramatic confrontation by occupying historic Wounded Knee. During the much publicized seventy-one-day occupation Bellecourt chose to remain on the outside and serve as a spokesman and fund-raiser. During the occupation Bellecourt addressed the United Nations, pleading for protection of Indian rights. In April 1973 *Penthouse* magazine interviewed him. He was pictured in full traditional Indian dress and described as "the most militant Indian since Geronimo." Referring to the damage at Wounded Knee, Bellecourt said, "If to destroy a small amount of your possessions is the only way to make you listen, then maybe it is time we made you listen." He was arrested and indicted several times for his militant activities during this period but never was convicted on any charges. When he was arrested in Chicago on federal charges of inciting a riot in South Dakota, he requested and received the assistance of the Reverend Jesse Jackson (6*). Later, Bellecourt became one of the founders of Jackson's Rainbow Coalition.

After Wounded Knee AIM was decimated by numerous arrests and bitter internal strife. Many native Americans who were originally attracted by the vitality of AIM became alienated by its violence and its lack of integrity. Don Allery, historian for the Red Lake tribe in Minnesota, said he was involved with AIM during its formative years but became disenchanted when it didn't follow through on complaints about such things as job discrimination. "The route they took, I guess it served a purpose," Allery said. But he said he thinks AIM failed "on anything that required a consistent on-going followup." Tim Giago, editor of the *Lakota Times* (then a weekly Indian newspaper in South Dakota) said, "The violence of their tactics created a backlash against people on the reservations." AIM funding from government and church sources virtually stopped after Wounded Knee.

In an apparent attempt to adjust to the criticism, Vernon Bellecourt returned to Minneapolis and took a less militant stance, trying to turn AIM into an "educational organization" and urging his followers to increase their appreciation for Indian culture. He also became more international in outlook and philosophy and assumed a leadership position in the International Indian Treaty Council. It is a nongovernmental organization in the United Nations Economic and Social Council. As a representative of AIM Bellecourt attended numerous international meetings promoting the cause of indigenous people and nonaligned nations. But he was still eager to have an opportunity to lead his people at the grassroots level on the reservation.

In 1978 Bellecourt returned to the White Earth reservation and won election to the tribal council, serving as secretary-treasurer for four years. He holds the distinction of being the only nationally known AIM leader to hold elected office on a reservation. Gerald Vizenor, a well-known Chippewa author, commented:

The radical figures were not elected to speak for tribal reservation people, nor were they appointed to represent the interests and political views of elected tribal officials. In response to this criticism, several tribal radicals returned to reservations. Vernon Bellecourt . . . was elected representative. Bellecourt was an ambitious reservation politician, no less out-spoken than he had been in urban tribal politics, and he served his constituents with distinction.

Bellecourt ran for tribal council chairman twice, but was defeated both times by his longtime political rival, Darrell (Chip) Wadena, who attacked Bellecourt's self-styled world diplomacy and lack of interest in local issues. "Why are we dealing with those countries?" Wadena asked. "We have a number of causes here that could be helped, such as alcoholism, unemployment and abuse. You're not going to find him around those kind of problems," said Wadena, who labeled his opponent a sensationalist.

Since his defeat at White Earth, Bellecourt's main focus has been the International Treaty Council. This association has led him to visit Libya at least seven times and Nicaragua three times, and to attend assorted other international gatherings concerned with racism and racial discrimination. In the process he has met with foes of the U.S. government like Colonel Muammar Qaddafi of Libya, PLO Chairman Yassir Arafat, and Nicaraguan President Daniel Ortega.

Bellecourt's most controversial relationship has been with Libya. In January 1989 Bellecourt and 150 others gathered in Tripoli for the Libyan-sponsored First International Conference for the Liberation of the Indian Peoples of the Americas. Representatives from North, Central, and South America as well as native people of the Pacific islands attended. Bellecourt introduced Muammar Qaddafi and joined him in a prayer for world peace. Critics such as Tim Giago suggested that Bellecourt's motives were more materialistic than altruistic.

In September 1989 Bellecourt was arrested and jailed for refusing to testify to a grand jury investigating activities of alleged Libyan foreign agents. A federal probe had led to the arrest of eight men charged with illegally diverting money intended for Libyan students in the United States to activities that supported Libya's government. The FBI reported that most of the men were members of the People's Committee for Libyan Students, a group the Libyan government created in 1981. Some of the committee's activities included bringing minority group leaders such as Bellecourt to Libya for tours and, in some cases, for rallies opposing U.S. policies. Bellecourt had been held in a New York City jail for two months for his refusal to cooperate when a federal judge signed an order to release him from prison unconditionally.

This victory did not spell an end to Bellecourt's battles with the federal government, though. While attending the Central American Congress of Indian Nations at Panama City, Panama, in March 1989, he took several rolls of pictures. On March 22, 1989, Bellecourt took two rolls of film to a photo development store in Minneapolis. After he left, FBI agents entered the store and without a search warrant examined the negatives and were allowed to buy a set of prints.

Bellecourt sued in federal court, contending the FBI was predisposed against him and had violated his constitutional rights. The court ruled that Bellecourt had no expectation of privacy because he took the photos to a store that briefly displayed customers' photos during processing. The U.S. Eighth Circuit Court of Appeals upheld the ruling, much to Bellecourt's dismay. He claims that some of his associates have been approached by FBI agents who suggest he is using Libyan funds to train Indian youths in the United States in terrorism. "They're (the FBI) terrorists.... They say it was some clandestine, undercover meeting where we were plotting something. It wasn't like that.... There's no big conspiracy," Bellecourt said. Although not all Indian leaders are enamored of Vernon Bellecourt and his tactics, they all condemn the actions of the FBI. The case may be appealed to the United States Supreme Court.

In response to his critics Bellecourt admits it would be safer to distance himself from Qaddafi and other political extremists. He maintains, however, that the U.S. public is not getting accurate information about foreign policies, such as Qaddafi's revolution and the slaughter of thousands of Indians in Guatemala and Brazil. He asserts that as a descendant of the Crane clan of the Chippewa tribe, he will follow his roots as a messenger and continue to speak out.

Although much of his energy has been diverted to the international scene, Bellecourt remains active on domestic issues as well. "We continue the struggle against the continued erosion of God given inherent and treaty rights of land, natural resources, hunting, fishing, gathering, spiritual, cultural, and political rights which are under constant attack," he states in an information sheet. In September 1990 he led AIM protesters to the Pigeon River bridge on the Canadian border to support the Mohawks in their land dispute with Canada. In April and June Bellecourt represented AIM in support of Chippewa spearfishing rights in northern Wisconsin.

Bellecourt has not gained personal wealth from his highly visible activities. He rents a small house in south Minneapolis, drives a 1979 Mercury, and rents out his mobile home at the White Earth reservation. He survives on his wife's income and honoraria from speaking engagements.

Karen Northcott, president of the Twin Cities chapter of the National Lawyers Guild, describes Bellecourt's current role:

> Vernon Bellecourt has been for many years a political activist concerned about human rights here and abroad. He is frequently an outspoken critic of the U.S. government policies concerning Indian nations in the United States, Central and South America as well as a staunch opponent of U.S. complicity in apartheid in South Africa and U.S. backed wars in Angola, Mozambique, and Palestine.

As the 1990s began, Vernon Bellecourt remained as radical and controversial as he had been two decades earlier.

Bibliography

Burnette, Robert, and John Koster. *The Road to Wounded Knee*. New York: Bantam Books, 1974.

Dewing, Rolland. *Wounded Knee: The Meaning and Significance of the Second Incident*. New York: Irvington Publishers, 1985.

———, ed. *The FBI Files on the American Indian Movement and Wounded Knee* (twenty-six reels of microfilm), guide by Martin Schipper. Frederick, MD: University Publications of America, 1988.

Lawrence, Bill. "Interview: Vernon Bellecourt," *Penthouse*, February 1983, pp. 34–38.

McDonald, Marci. "Following the OKA Example," *Maclean's* 103 (Oct. 8, 1990): 34.

Matthiessen, Peter. *In the Spirit of Crazy Horse*, with a new afterword. New York: Viking Press, 1991.

Treaty Council News (official bulletin of the International Indian Treaty Council, 710 Clayton Street, #1, San Francisco, California 94117).

Vizenor, Gerald. *The People Named the Chippewa*. Minneapolis: University of Minnesota Press, 1984.

Rolland Dewing

MARY FRANCES BERRY (1938–)

Civil rights/anti-war activist; co-founder, Free South Africa Movement; commissioner, U.S. Commission on Civil Rights

"Today I am in Vietnam and we are *not* winning the war." With this declaration and observation, Mary Frances Berry opened each hard-hitting report she filed in the summer of 1967 as an accredited journalist with the University of Michigan's *Michigan Daily*. An anti-war and civil rights activist, recent Ph.D. graduate of the University of Michigan, and assistant professor at Central Michigan University, Berry had formulated an anti-war position and taken a public stance as a result of her analysis of U.S. history and policy. Persuaded that the general populace was receiving limited information and disinformation, Berry established a statewide reputation as an anti-war activist-professor with her news accounts and interviews with marine ground troops regarding the United States' involvement, escalation, and the impact of the war on the citizenry.

Primary focus on anti–Vietnam War activities, however, gave way to that which had been a constant in Berry's life and a persistent problem in the United States, systemic racism, when Martin Luther King, Jr. (*), was assassinated in April 1968. In Berry's analysis this tragedy directed attention to violence in the nation, racist discrimination, racial antipathies, ineffective national policies, and the limited progress of civil rights groups in the accomplishment of national goals related to desegregation or integration, establishment of equal

Mary Frances Berry. *Source*: Library of Congress

rights, and recognition of human equality. In response to both the tragedy of King's assassination and its immediate aftermath, Berry felt compelled to re-prioritize. Although completing studies at the University of Michigan's Law School and teaching in not only Michigan but also Maryland during the last years of the 1960s and the early 1970s, Berry became even more outspoken in her protest of legal and extralegal manifestations of racism. Leadership of campus demonstrations in conjunction with the Black Action Movement (BAM), supervision of the University of Maryland's establishment of an Afro-American Studies Program, and provision of a "safe house" for members of the Black Panther party and other radical African-American activists marked not only her identification by movement activists as a trusted comrade, strategist, analyst, and organizer, but also the beginning of her rise to prominence as a civil rights/black liberation activist.

Since the latter 1960s and early 1970s Mary Frances Berry has engaged in protests against war and against discrimination on the basis of race, gender, and disability. She has, as well, widely championed human rights. From her campus activism of the 1960s to her 1984 arrest while protesting apartheid at the South African embassy in Washington, D.C., however, Berry's particular prominence and reputation have come to be primarily associated with advocacy of social justice.

Mary Frances Berry was born in Nashville, Tennessee, on February 17, 1938, to Frances Southall Berry and George Ford Berry. Periods of her childhood—like that of her brothers George Jr. and Troy Merritt—were marred by severe poverty and rampant racism. A strong and resourceful child, Berry survived inhuman treatment in an orphanage for a time and daily defied attempts to devalue her. These constituted her first acts of resistance. Berry was a pupil in the public schools of Nashville and the surrounding rural area. Challenged particularly by Minerva Hawkins, Berry was graduated with honors from Pearl High School. After graduation, she attended Fisk University of Nashville and Howard University in Washington, D.C. Having earned the Bachelor of Arts degree from Howard in 1961, Berry continued her studies as a graduate student of history and law. From Howard she obtained the Master of Arts degree in 1962, and from the University of Michigan at Ann Arbor she earned both the Ph.D. in history (with a concentration in U.S. constitutional history) and the Juris Doctor degree by 1966 and 1970, respectively. Throughout her college and graduate school years she worked in hospitals and laboratories to finance her education and support herself.

Mary Frances Berry's early academic career included appointments to the faculties of Central Michigan University in Mount Pleasant, Michigan; Eastern Michigan University of Ypsilanti, the University of Michigan at Ann Arbor; and the University of Maryland. Her exceptional ability and scholarly productivity, however, were recognized by administrators and regents of not only the University of Maryland but also the University of Colorado; Professor Berry was appointed to positions of increasing administrative responsibility at both universities. Between 1970 and 1976 she served at the University of Maryland as director of the Afro-American Studies Program, chairperson of the Division of Behavioral and Social Sciences, as well as provost of that division. In 1976 she was appointed chancellor and professor of history and law at the University of Colorado in Boulder; she held the latter position until 1980.

In 1980 she joined the faculty of her alma mater, Howard University, where she taught for six years. She accepted the Howard appointment after having been assistant secretary for education under President Jimmy Carter from 1977 to 1980. Carter also appointed her a commissioner of the U.S. Commission on Civil Rights in 1980. Considerable notoriety attended her years as a commissioner during the Reagan administration when the president sought in 1983 to oust Berry because of her civil rights stance. She currently holds the Geraldine Segal Professorship of Social Thought and a professorship of history at the University of Pennsylvania. Berry's record of scholarship—including numerous scholarly articles and books such as *Black Resistance/White Law, Stability, Security, and Continuity*, and *Why ERA Failed*—has resulted in professional acclaim and honors. In 1990 Professor Berry began serving her term as the first African-American female president of the Organization of American Historians and served with distinction through mid-1991.

Mary Frances Berry's longevity as a respected political activist and advocate for justice has its roots in the consistency of her analysis and praxis since the late 1960s. She may be distinguished from other activists, however, not only because as a professional historian her analysis of conditions of oppression grows out of prodigious historical research, but also because that research directly informs and heavily influences her ideological stance. Having labored under the triple burden of racism, poverty, and sexism during her youth and young adult years, Berry was prompted by her background, her continued exposure to discrimination, her observations, and her studies to research the history, nature, and scope of systemic racism in the United States. The initial result was her 1971 monograph, *Black Resistance/White Law*, in which she made the argument that "whether its policy was action or inaction, the national government has used the Constitution in such a way as to make law the instrument for maintaining a racist status quo" (p. x). In a second study of African-American citizenship, military necessity, and civil rights policy during the Civil War era, Berry demonstrated that one significant basis for enactment of civil rights measures during Reconstruction was military necessity. She further argued that the study suggested two propositions. First, "the best atmosphere in which to enact legal changes in black status is a crisis in which black reactions are perceived by whites, especially governmental officials, as having a significant bearing on the outcome." Second, "the attainment of blacks to the legal status of citizens . . . had to be won through sacrifice on the part of blacks and concessions on the part of whites to meet their own needs and fears" (*Military Necessity and Civil Rights Policy*, Kennikat Press, 1977; p. x).

Continuing to establish and articulate a firm, scholarly foundation for activism and dissent against the racist status quo, Mary Frances Berry (with John W. Blassingame) stressed in a 1982 survey of the African American experience, *Long Memory*, that there were minimally eight lessons to be learned from African-Americans' history:

1. "Politics . . . could provide access to patronage and elected officials but not economic rewards for the group."

2. "Nonviolent protest could gain the passage of laws and some enforcement."

3. "Violent protest needed to be organized in such a way that repression was expected and counter measures planned."

4. "Economic problems . . . were rooted in racism and were not of a different order."

5. "To nurture the struggle [for racial justice in the United States] and the will to survive, black institutions—family, church, schools—needed to be maintained."

6. "[I]nternational problems [have created and] create international opportunities for finding supporters in the struggle."

7. There remained a "persistence of oppressive conditions and [a] decreased probability that equality would come without an ever-increasing emphasis on struggle."

8. African Americans historically have evidenced "the strength to survive despite the odds."

Mary Frances Berry's publications also revealed sources for her own persistence in struggle. The avoidance of discouragement in the face of temporary setbacks found its origin in both her knowledge of African-American history and her analysis of changes over time in the United States. In *Why ERA Failed,* she demonstrated that since the era of the Bill of Rights, "the more substantive the change" sought, the more probable that it would require considerable time—decades rather than years" to alter fundamental law in the United States (p. 3).

Mary Frances Berry's ability to shed light on situations with historical scholarship and to reinforce the validity of demands by reference to specific grievances or abuses over time has repeatedly distinguished Berry among activists. Always she has functioned in the dual role of scholar-activist. When queried, Roger Wilkins, the Robinson Professor of History at George Mason University, an activist himself and a former aide to Lyndon Johnson, described qualities of mind and character he had observed: "Mary Frances Berry is one of the ablest and most effective activists I have ever encountered. She has a brilliant mind, high idealism, staying power, and a wonderful sense of humor" (Roger Wilkins to author, November 26, 1991). Particularly telling in regard to the dual role, however, has been Berry's use of history for advocacy in connection with civil rights litigation. For example, on behalf of Brenda Patterson in *Patterson v. McLean Credit Union* during the October 1987 term of the United States Supreme Court, Berry, with other historians, demonstrated and argued the intent of nineteenth-century legislators to prohibit public and private acts of racial discrimination through the Civil Rights Act of 1866. (See Brief of *Amicus Curiae* of Eric Foner, John Hope Franklin, Mary Frances Berry, et al., in *Brenda Patterson v. McLean Credit Union,* Supreme Court of the United States, October Term 1989.)

The scholar-activist role, in her estimation, has necessitated Mary Frances Berry's participation in the indispensable tasks of community organizing and mass protest. Marches on Washington, marches on the White House, marches to the capitol for the purpose of demonstrating displeasure about racial, gender, and economic discrimination in the United States have commanded much of Berry's time and attention. Equally compelling concerns about unjust foreign policy and its impact upon persons of African descent have placed Mary Frances Berry in massive demonstrations. Sylvia Hill, professor of criminal justice at the University of the District of Columbia and member of the Steering Committee of the Free South Africa Movement, has been involved in African liberation support actions in the United States since the 1970s. She has recalled: "One of my fondest memories of the Free South Africa Movement's year-long campaign of arrests at the South African Embassy [was] seeing Mary Frances alight from her car, open the trunk and drag out the placards for the day's protest activities" (Sylvia Hill to author, December 18, 1991). Having observed and worked with Berry, Jesse Jackson (6*) has recalled: "I have seen her work tirelessly and with immeasurable integrity and wisdom for the liberation of South Africa, for civil rights in this country, and for a fair and equal education for all children" (Jesse Jackson to author, January 21, 1992).

Mary Frances Berry, as was the case with numerous African-Americans emerging as activists during the 1960s, came first to positions of local leadership. Consistent with her personal orientation toward solutions and results, when there were needs that local communities or student groups were determined to meet, Berry was able to offer galvanizing ideas for action and mobilized people to achieve identified goals. What was accomplished in Ann Arbor, Michigan; Mt. Pleasant, Michigan; and College Park, Maryland, through a group-centered, history-infused leadership style to compel the acknowledgment of not only the presence and voices of African-Americans, but also the significance of students as unrelenting advocates of equity in allocation of resources for improvement of academic and social-economic conditions of African-Americans created a particular legitimacy and reputation. While Berry did not seek and did not become the object of national media attention in the 1960s, her emergence from among students and local Michiganders as a leader was unmistakable.

Credence given Mary Frances Berry's ideas by other activists and the African-American community's increasing recognition of her since the early 1970s provide evidence of Berry's growing acceptance as an effective spokesperson and political activist. Primarily associated with civil rights and African liberation networks, Berry's political activism has found expression in her work with established organizations such as the NAACP and TransAfrica, particularly engaged in advocacy with Althea Simmons (until her death), Wade Henderson, and Randall Robinson. As a result of the quality and extensiveness of Mary Frances Berry's advocacy of racial justice, she has been given awards and honors by a number of traditional African-American organizations, including the National Association for the Advancement of Colored People (NAACP) and the Southern Christian Leadership Conference (SCLC). Additionally, however, Mary Frances Berry has also played important roles in the creation of new organized expressions of protest and empowerment, such as the Rainbow Coalition and the Free South Africa movement. "It was she, along with Walter Fauntroy and Randall Robinson, who went to jail to call the nation's attention to the need to end apartheid in South Africa," Jackson has reminded us, but he also has been quick to note that Mary Frances Berry "helped to chart the course of two historic presidential campaigns, and . . . continues to share her very profound insights to help us build a Rainbow Coalition for change" (Jackson to author, January 21, 1992).

Sylvia Hill, a co-founder of the Free South Africa movement, has identified—with others—Berry's "intellect," "social consciousness," "energy," and "sense of humor" as qualities that have established Mary Frances Berry as such a valued colleague among activists in civil rights and African liberation struggles. Hill, however, has also significantly observed and explained sources of the respect given Berry:

> Never one to be afraid of work, she's the kind of leader who will not only show up at a demonstration rally to speak, but she's willing to distribute posters and leaflets. . . .
> Mary Frances [Berry's] political acumen is unique and grounded in the needs of our people. . . . Her context for action is an understanding of history and the contradictions of this society that can be challenged. . . . In any political meeting you can usually bank on her coming up with a good action idea! (Hill to author, December 18, 1991)

The content of Mary Frances Berry's ideology is both constant and in process because her ideology reflects the integration of ongoing research and her praxis with fundamental beliefs of a moral nature. On one occasion Berry explained her commitment to political activism: "When it comes to the cause of justice, I take no prisoners and I don't believe in compromising" (Brian Lanker, I Dream A World, p. 84). "Justice" is a fundamental constant of Berry's ideology. Its meaning for her is discoverable by careful attention to praxis and pronouncements. For Berry, justice is a moral and political principle of fair, but not identical treatment. Its indispensable corollary is the principle of equality. Thus, in a just society, human beings have an equal entitlement to justice by virtue of their birth. For Berry, the struggle must continue "until the day when opportunity is [not only] truly free of the discriminatory results, which have advantaged white males," but also free of "the persistence of sex and race and handicap discrimination in our society." The goal is for all to have "an equal opportunity."

To achieve justice, however, there must be remedies to address discrimination. Justice as fairness, therefore, requires recognition of violations of rights and effective, far-reaching responses. For example, in 1983 Berry argued that to ignore the centuries-long privileging of white males in the discourse of affirmative action by referring to them "as 'innocent victims' when they are, in fact, beneficiaries who have been unjustly enriched by . . . employers' past discrimination," was to fail to recognize "that had no original discrimination occurred, women and minorities would have been in the workforce, and there would have been no need for the court to order their hiring" (Berry, "Turning Back the Clock on Women and Minority Rights," *Negro History Bulletin* 46, no. 3 [July-August-September 1983]: 83). That justice as fairness requires recognition of the impropriety of identical treatment in the face of discrimination is further illustrated in Berry's discussion of reparations in "Reparations for Freedmen, 1890–1919: Fraudulent Practices or Justice Deferred?" (*Journal of Negro History* 57 [July 1972]: 219–30). Finally, as the fundamental principle of equal entitlement to justice has found expression in Mary Frances Berry's praxis, it has become clear that its extension to human beings regardless of nationality is an important element of Berry's understanding.

Mary Frances Berry's critics have labeled her an "extremist" for her "radical vision of civil rights, of America, and of the world." (See Ben Wattenberg, Editorial, *Washington Post*, September 16, 1983.) Critics of her radicalism have included conservatives of different races and party affiliations. Berry, who is an independent, has taken on her opponents forcefully, the most powerful having been former President Ronald Reagan. After the Reagan administration announced its duty in regard to civil rights "[to be] responsible for seeing that the civil rights of all individuals are protected," Reagan notified Berry and two other members of the U.S. Commission on Civil Rights that he was terminating their service effective October 1983. The attempt to fire Berry, Blandina Ramirez, and Murray Saltzman and replace them with persons more sympathetic to Reagan's conservative views was confronted in court by Berry and Ramirez, who brought a federal suit against Reagan and used the opportunity to clarify the purpose of the Commission. Berry asserted that the Commission served as "the conscience of the nation on civil rights" and that Reagan and members of his administration "have taken it over so that they could use the wreckage . . . to do studies that will prove that Blacks are to blame for our social and economic problems, that government has no role to play. . . . The[ir] point is to get Blacks to accept the idea of not asking the government to do anything to overcome the legacy of discrimination and, indeed, to forget about this legacy altogether" (Reynolds, p. 12). When the Reagan-Bush era ended with the November 1992 election, President Clinton appointed Berry to be the first female head of the commission in 1993.

Confronting with equal force and vigor the Reagan-backed opponents of sanctions for South Africa and apologists for "constructive engagement" with South Africa's apartheid regime, Mary Frances Berry withstood a storm of criticism regarding her position on black South Africans' liberation. Her response to her critics further defined her ideology. Not only did she emphasize the pivotal importance of economic sanctions as a catalyst for ending apartheid, but also underscored the essential relationship between racist policies at home and abroad. Yet, in the final analysis, she linked justice with morality. After nearly twenty hours in police custody following her arrest for the 1984 sit-in at the South African Embassy, Berry declared: "There comes a time when you have to bear witness" against the "immorality" (*Washington Post*, November 23, 1983, p. B–1).

Any careful observer of Mary Frances Berry's activism is struck by its moral foundation. Because the goals of a just society as well as a just world and the objective to bring about justice as an equal entitlement for all persons have a moral "ought" at their base, those with whom she has most often been a colleague in struggle consider her a "trusted friend." Roger Wilkins perhaps best summarized the impact of Berry's integration of morality and ideology on those with whom she advocates justice: "I have done civil rights with her. I have done politics with her, and South Africa. And if I had to go to war, she'd be one of the first people I'd want to be in my foxhole" (Wilkins to author, November 26, 1991).

Mary Frances Berry's activism and scholarship continued unabated into the 1990s. She accompanied Jesse Jackson to South Africa on the occasion of Nelson Mandela's release and later returned with Gay McDougall of the Lawyers' Committee on Civil Rights to assist the African National Congress in its efforts to frame acceptable constitutional principles for black South Africans' empowerment and protection. She completed *The Politics of Parenthood* (1993) in which she explores historically issues of justice in relation to child care and the impact of race, economics, and gender on access to child care. In the opinion of Jesse Jackson, "Mary Frances Berry's contributions to the human family reverberate in every sphere." Her outspoken critique of racial and economic injustice as well as opposition to opponents of affirmative action (such as Clarence Thomas) continues to provoke wide-ranging criticism from conservatives. As any political activist, she expects it. "We are engaged in a struggle," Berry maintains, "for the minds and hearts of Americans on major domestic and foreign policy issues in our society" (Berry in "Turning Back the Clock," p. 82). In regard to anti-war, civil rights, and other social justice issues, since the late 1960s it has been this struggle to influence citizens and affect "major domestic and foreign policy" in the United States that has been Berry's focus. While she has not proposed solutions characteristic of the radical left, her opposition to a racist status quo and her ideological position on equality have been and may be appropriately viewed as radical in the context of the United States.

Bibliography

Berry, Mary Frances. *Black Resistance/White Law: A History of Constitutional Racism in America.* New York: Appleton-Century-Crofts, 1971; Prentice Hall, 1974.
———. "Civil Rights under Seige," *Peace and Freedom* 45 (Sept./Oct. 1985): 18–19.
———. "The Constraints and Opportunities for Black Women in the 1980s," *The Creative Woman* 5 (Fall 1981): 18–21.

―――. "The Federal Role in Increasing Equality of Educational Opportunity—Responses," *Harvard Educational Review* 62 (Nov. 1982): 462–66.

―――. "How Hard It Is to Change," *New York Times Magazine*, Sept. 13, 1987, pp. 93–94+.

―――. "Increasing Women's Influence in Government and Politics: The Inclusion of Women of Color," *Proteus* 3 (Fall 1986): 1–5.

―――. *Military Necessity and Civil Rights Policy.* Port Washington, NY: Kennikat Press, 1977.

―――. *The Politics of Parenthood; Child Care, Women's Rights, and the Myth of the Good Mother.* New York: Viking Press, 1993.

―――. "Reparations for Freedmen, 1890–1919: Fraudulent Practices or Justice Deferred?" *Journal of Negro History* 57 (July 1972): 219–30.

―――. "Repression of Blacks in the South, 1890–1945: Enforcing the System of Segregation," in *The Age of Segregation: Race Relations in the South, 1890–1945,* Derrick A. Bell and Robert Haws, eds. (Jackson: University Press of Mississippi, 1978).

―――. *Stability, Security, and Continuity: Mr. Justice Burton and Decision Making in the Supreme Court, 1945–1958.* New York: Greenwood Press, 1978.

―――. "Taming the Civil Rights Commission," *The Nation* 240 (Feb. 2, 1985): 106–8.

―――. *Why ERA Failed: Politics, Women's Rights and the Amending Process of the Constitution.* Bloomington: Indiana University Press, 1986.

Berry, Mary Frances, and John Blassingame. *Long Memory: The Black Experience in America.* New York: Oxford University Press, 1982.

"Mary Frances Berry" in Brian Lanker, *I Dream a World: Portraits of Black Women Who Changed America.* New York: Steward, Tabori and Chang, 1989.

"Mary Frances Berry" in *Notable Black American Women,* Jessie Carney Smith, ed. Detroit: Gale Research, 1992.

"Mary Frances Berry" in *Who's Who among Black Americans, 1990/91.* Detroit: Gale Research, 1991.

Poinsett, Alex. "Colorado University's Chancellor," *Ebony* 30 (Jan. 1977): 58–60, 65–66.

Reynolds, Barbara. "The Woman the President Couldn't Fire," *Essence* 15 (Oct. 1984): 12, 158.

Smith, Carol Hobson. "Black Female Achievers in Academe," *Journal of Negro Education* 51 (Summer 1982): 323–27.

Genna Rae McNeil

JULIAN BOND (1940–   )

Civil rights and anti-war activist

"The greatest problem in the United States," Julian Bond stated in an interview in 1962, "is the country's inability to really provide the democracy they preach." Compelling the nation to live up to its ideals has been the motivating force behind Julian Bond for his entire adult life. From his early involvement

Julian Bond. Copyright
Washington Post; Reprinted by
permission of D.C. Public Library.

in the sit-in movement, through his struggle to be seated in the Georgia House
of Representatives, to his later advocacy of mass participation in the political
arena, Bond has stood as one of the most consistent advocates of democracy,
both in the United States and abroad.

Julian Bond was born in Nashville, Tennessee, in 1940. He was the descendant of a distinguished black family that valued education and Christian
morality. His grandfather, James Bond, the son of a slave, studied at Berea
and Oberlin colleges and received a Bachelor of Divinity from the latter. His
father, Horace Mann Bond, a contemporary of W.E.B. DuBois, received his
Ph.D. from the University of Chicago and became one of the most prominent
black educators in the country, serving as president of Lincoln University in
Pennsylvania through much of Julian's youth. Julian attended a private Quaker
school in Bucks County, Pennsylvania, where he excelled in sports and co-
edited the high school newspaper. He grew up in relative comfort. In 1957,

Julian moved with his family to Atlanta when his father accepted a post as Dean of the School of Education at Atlanta University. Shortly afterwards, Julian enrolled at Morehouse College, which was part of the Atlanta University complex.

Julian's involvement in the civil rights movement began in February 1960. Three days after four North Carolina A.T. & T. students sat down at a Woolworth's lunch counter for whites only, Bond's classmate, Lonnie King (no relation to Martin Luther King, Jr.) showed Bond a headline story on the sit-ins that appeared in the Atlanta *World*. Let us "make it happen here," King prodded Bond. Though not politically active prior to the Greensboro sit-ins, Julian responded favorably to King's invitation. Together they organized an Atlanta University student movement which protested against segregated facilities. Subsequently, Bond helped organize COAHR, the Committee on Appeal for Human Rights, a city-wide civil rights group which staged nonviolent campaigns against Jim Crow and conducted a series of voter registration drives. One protest led to the arrest of fellow Atlantan Martin Luther King Jr.—this event compelled Robert and John F. Kennedy to directly contact the King family and a southern judge. Many political scientists argue that this gesture produced John F. Kennedy's slim margin of victory over Richard Nixon in the November election. Hence, Bond, who prodded King to join COAHR's protests, was indirectly responsible for electing Kennedy president.

Representing the Atlanta student movement, Bond attended the founding meeting of the Student Nonviolent Coordinating Committee, or SNCC, in Raleigh, North Carolina, in April 1960. Following the meeting, Bond returned to Atlanta, where he helped build one of SNCC's most dynamic affiliates. By mid-1961, Bond had dropped his studies, married, and become a full-time civil rights worker. In order to better publicize the goals and objectives of the Atlanta movement, Bond launched an alternative newspaper, the Atlanta *Inquirer*. Unknowingly, in doing so, he was carving out a niche for himself within the Civil Rights movement as an expert on generating publicity. Bond's work caught the attention of SNCC's executive secretary, James Forman (*), who offered him the post of director of public relations for SNCC. Bond accepted, despite the terrible pay (about $40 a week) and the fact that his wife was about to have a baby.

As SNCC's liaison to the mass media, Bond came to symbolize the cutting edge of the Civil Rights movement. He was young, articulate, well groomed, determined, and defiant. In other words, he fit the mold given to SNCC by historian and activist Howard Zinn: he was one of the "new abolitionists." Although Bond never completed his formal education at Morehouse College and did not attend church or profess to any deep religious convictions, it would be inaccurate to see Bond's activism as a rejection of the values of his parents or as evidence of a generational rebellion. He did not break from his family's historical reverence for education and religion. Rather, he built on his grandparent's and parent's accomplishment by becoming an educator of the masses and a national spokesman for a nonviolent revolution within the Christian tradition.

In an organization that valued action and physical bravado, Bond was the odd man out. He spent much of his time in SNCC's Atlanta office drafting press releases and attending to the organization's logistical concerns. Whereas many of SNCC's best known members earned their fame by risking their lives on the front lines and spending time in jail, Bond was jailed only once and more often than not stayed out of harm's way. Yet, throughout the first half of the decade, Bond was one of the most prominent and well-liked members of SNCC. He steered clear of factional disputes and was respected by his peers for unselfishly playing his assigned role. Without his press releases and savvy editorial direction of SNCC's newspaper, the *Student Voice*, which gained the attention of the national media and sympathizers across the country, SNCC's various field activities, from the Southwest Georgia project to Mississippi Summer, would have been less effective.

In 1965, Bond ran for the Georgia House of Representatives from a predominantly black district of Atlanta. In part, his campaign reflected SNCC's turn from nonviolent direct action to black power. Although SNCC leader Stokely Carmichael would not popularize the term "black power" for another year, already SNCC saw black political empowerment as one of the keys to attaining equality. Building on years of voter registration work, Bond translated SNCC's new tendency into a reality, winning 82 percent of the vote in the November election, thus becoming one of the first blacks in the South to be elected to office as an outgrowth of the civil rights movement.

Shortly after Bond was elected, but before he was sworn in as a representative, SNCC publicly declared its opposition to the war in Vietnam. In a strongly worded statement, SNCC called the war immoral and hypocritical and announced its support for draft resistance. Bond openly endorsed SNCC's declaration and allied himself with the budding anti-war movement. Local politicians and both the local and national media immediately attacked Bond for taking an anti-war stance. The Atlanta *Constitution* proclaimed that Bond backed "draft card burners." Prominent Georgians questioned Bond's patriotism, with Georgia Lieutenant Governor Peter Zack stating that SNCC's stance, which Bond supported, suited the Kremlin. The FBI announced that it would investigate SNCC to see if it had broken federal laws. And members of the Georgia House of Representatives declared that they would move to have Bond stripped of his seat in the state legislature.

Indeed, when the Georgia House convened on Monday, January 10, 1966, Bond was requested to step aside while the rest of the legislature was sworn in to office. The Georgia Assembly established a committee to consider a petition to expel Bond and in short order did so. A special election was held in Bond's Atlanta district and he was once again elected. But the Georgia House still refused to seat him. Hence, Bond filed a suit, which called for the courts to declare the actions of the House unconstitutional, on the grounds that the state of Georgia had violated his First Amendment rights. In a land-mark decision, the U.S. Supreme Court unanimously ruled in Bond's favor. The decision not only allowed Bond to take his seat in the Georgia House of Representatives, but it expanded the First Amendment rights of all elected officials and candidates for public office.

In the same period, Bond left SNCC, which had moved away from its commitment to nonviolence and toward black nationalism. Bond stated that he left SNCC for practical reasons: since he no longer had the time to work for SNCC, he could not justify continuing to draw a paycheck from it. But SNCC's more militant style, under the leadership of Stokely Carmichael and subsequently H. Rap Brown (*), led to the departure of several of SNCC's founders, including John Lewis and James Forman, and influenced Bond's decision to leave the organization, as well. His views on the Vietnam War and the political empowerment of blacks still paralleled those of SNCC, but the organization's militant rhetoric did not mesh with Bond's more deliberate style and willingness to continue to prod the system, from within, to live up to its ideals.

In 1968, Bond once again gained national headlines, becoming the first black man in U.S. history to be nominated for the vice presidency. Bond's nomination grew out of his continued involvement in politics and the anti-war movement. Bond was part of the "new politics" of the latter part of the 1960s and early 1970s which challenged the traditional rules and leaders of the two major political parties. Bond was one of the organizers of the New Politics Conference in 1967, an unsuccessful attempt to establish a left-wing political organization out of the anti-war, civil rights, and student movements. In 1968 he joined the Loyal Georgia Democrats, a group of dissidents within the Democratic party that sought to challenge the so-called Regular Demo-crats of the state, which were led by white supremacist Lester Maddox. Bond also supported Eugene McCarthy's attempt to win the Democratic party's presidential nomination.

Initially, few political pundits gave the Loyal Georgia Democrats a chance of unseating the Regular Democrats at the party's national convention in Chi-cago. But with the help of several McCarthy staff members and Joe Rauh, who had served as the Mississippi Freedom Democratic party's counsel in 1964, and through Bond's astute and charismatic leadership at the convention, the dissidents won a startling victory. The credentials committee agreed to split the Georgia vote in two, with half of the votes going to the Regular Democrats and the other half going to the Loyal Democrats. Many of the Regular Democrats left the convention rather than share their seats with the insurgents.

With McCarthy's run for the presidency derailed, much of the press focused on Bond as the symbol of the new politics. He became an overnight spokes-person for the insurgents, voicing their criticism of the war and demand for major racial and economic change. One sign of Bond's status came when

Allard Lowenstein, the prime mover behind the McCarthy campaign, placed Bond's name into nomination for the vice presidency. Though he turned down the nomination, on the grounds that he was too young to accept, he left the convention with a substantial national following.

Following the 1968 Democratic convention, Bond remained active in electoral politics and was a prominent anti-war and civil rights spokesperson. In 1974, he was elected to the Georgia State Senate, a post he retained until 1986, when he decided to run for a seat in the United States Congress. The seat he sought, the Fifth Congressional District of Georgia, was one whose lines he was largely responsible for drawing, pushing for the creation of a predominantly black district as a state senator, and after the legislative body rebuffed his efforts, as a litigant in the courts. Ironically, his main opponent was his former SNCC colleague, John Lewis. The battle between the two veteran activists was a hard one, and reporters tended to emphasize the differences between the two. The press presented Bond as the articulate intellectual who emphasized the need for black solidarity and pride. It portrayed Lewis as the soft-spoken footsoldier who had maintained his commitment to building a black and white coalition. But beneath the alleged differences between Bond and Lewis was their common history. Both had been leaders of SNCC; both had vocally opposed the Vietnam War and fought for the political empowerment of blacks. And both had maintained their commitment to making America a more democratic society long after the movement had waned. Put another way, both had made it possible for blacks in Atlanta to elect a black man as their congressperson, in the first place. Lewis won the election.

For the past twenty years Bond has served on tens of boards of various civil and human rights organizations, including the Atlanta chapter of the NAACP, the Southern Poverty Law Center, the Highlander Center, various voter education projects, and the Atlanta Black-Jewish Coalition, and has been a prominent guest lecturer on college campuses. In speeches to today's students Bond argues that ordinary people can make a difference. SNCC's history shows that students can change society. Students, like himself, Bond reminds his audience, staged the sit-ins and freedom rides, challenged white supremacy in Mississippi, and led the protests against the war in Vietnam. As a result, Jim Crow laws were toppled, southern blacks gained the right to vote, and the Vietnam War was brought to an end. Bond urges youth to follow the examples of their predecessors, to build a mass movement dedicated to addressing the problems that still plague America, foremost among them the continued economic oppression of millions of black Americans. The failure to do so, Bond warns, will be the perpetuation of inequality and "half" citizenship for America's nonwhite population.

Bond continues to be politically active and financially secure. He has worked as a narrator of documentary shows and films (including the highly acclaimed series on the Civil Rights movement, "Eyes on the Prize"); he has written a syndicated column; he has been a speaker; he has taught at several schools. In the 1990s, he held positions at American University, Williams College, and the University of Virginia. Based upon his history of activism, there was little doubt that as long as America continued to fall short of its ideals, Bond would remain an ardent proponent for democracy and equality.

Bibliography

"Atlanta's Coke Controversy," *Newsweek* 109 (April 27, 1987): 36.

Bond, Julian. *Black Candidates: Southern Campaign Experiences*. Atlanta: Southern Regional Council, 1969.

———. "Color Blinders," *The Nation* 251 (Aug. 13–20, 1990): 152–53.

———. Intr. to *Eyes on the Prize: America's Civil Rights Years, 1954–1965*, by Juan Williams. New York: Viking, 1987.

———. Intr. to *If They Come in the Morning: Voices of Resistance*, by Angela Y. Davis. New York: Third Press, 1971.

———. Intr. to *Memories of the Southern Civil Rights Movement*, by Danny Lyon. Chapel Hill: University of North Carolina Press, 1992.

———. Intr. to *Urban Minority Administrators: Politics, Policy and Style*, Albert K. Karnig and Paula D. McClain, eds. Westport, CT: Greenwood Press, 1988.

———. "The NAACP Judged Thomas by His Character, not by the Color of His Skin," *The Black Scholar* 22 (Winter 1991/Spring 1992): 148–49.

———. "A Perspective on the Present Status of Diversity in the United States," *William Mitchell Law Review* 17 (Spring 1991): 419–38.

———. "Putting the Spin on the N.A.A.C.P.," *New York Times*, Feb. 27, 1993, p. 19.

———. "Remembering Dr. King." *TV Guide* 38 (Jan. 13–19, 1990): 26–27.

———. *A Time to Speak, A Time to Act: The Moment in Politics*. New York: Simon and Schuster, 1972.

———. "We Have Reached Only Half of 'Dream'," *Atlanta Journal Constitution*, April 4, 1993, G1:5.

———. "Where We've Been, Where We're Going: A Vision of Racial Justice in the 1990s," *Harvard Civil Rights–Civil Liberties Law Review* 25 (Summer 1990): 273–85.

Bond, Julian, and Adolph Reed. "Equality: Why We Can't Wait," *The Nation* 253 (Dec. 9, 1991): 733–37.

"Memories of an Era Form Basis of Lessons," *New York Times Biographical Service* 17 (Dec. 1988): 1326–27.

Neary, Julian. *Julian Bond: Black Rebel*. New York: William Morrow, 1971.

Newman, Debra. "Julian Bond," in *The Encyclopedia of World Biography: 20th Century Supplement* (Palatine, IL: Heraty and Associates, 1987): pp. 80–82.

Raines, Howell. *My Soul Is Rested: Movement Days in the Deep South Remembered*. New York: Penguin, 1977.

Robinson, Armstead L., and Patricia Sullivan, eds. *New Directions in Civil Rights Studies*. Charlottesville: University Press of Virginia, 1991.

Urban, Wayne J. *Black Scholar: Horace Mann Bond, 1904–1972*. Athens: University of Georgia Press, 1992.

Peter B. Levy

H. RAP BROWN [JAMIL ABDULLAH AL-AMIN] (1943–   )

SNCC leader, Muslim convert

For many Americans, H. Rap Brown embodied black power in the 1960s. His threat to "burn America down" if it didn't reform represented the defiance and determination of part of the younger generation of black students in the late 1960s, between the assassinations of Malcolm X (*) in 1965 and Martin Luther King, Jr., (*) in 1968. H. Rap Brown appears to have taken his leadership cue from Malcolm X, whose funeral he attended after riding almost twenty hours from Jackson, Mississippi, to New York City.

Hubert Brown was born in Baton Rouge, Louisiana, of a father who was a World War II veteran and hardworking employee of the Esso Oil Company and a mother who frequently held two jobs, both as a maid and as a teacher at an orphanage. His mother even attended night school to improve her employment opportunity and enable her two sons and a daughter to complete school. Hubert's own school education was supplemented with extracurricular activities such as the Boy Scouts, trips to athletic contests, and occasional hunting trips with his father.

Hubert found that a black child's life in the African-American community was difficult to negotiate. "I knew dudes who were old men by the time they were seven. . . . [If] you acted like a child, you didn't survive." He remembered his boyhood friends as exceptionally bright since they had to survive "either by fighting, running, or tomming." He soon encountered many people in "negro America" who had learned to live "by the wine bottle, reefer, or Jesus." By the time he was old enough to attend high school, he was dismissive of much of official culture. For him, there was "no sense in reading Shakespeare. . . . It was obvious that [he] was a racist." He later was moved by his mother from the all-black McKinley High School to the integrated Southern High School, where he was suspended on several occasions for challenging the authorities. He then became more recalcitrant and adamant about identifying with other downtrodden African-American students. His effort to become more streetwise led to a great facility in playing the "dozens." This is a crude game in which a man tries to humiliate his opponent with shrewd verbal jousting. His brother Ed nicknamed him "Rap" because of his skill in besting others in this game.

During his high school days, Brown worked as a waiter in a nightclub, construction employee, and cleaner of the hulls of ocean cargo ships. At the same time, Brown became interested in the political and economic problems

H. Rap Brown [Jamil Abdullah Al-Amin]. *Source:* Library of Congress

of blacks. He participated in a campaign to register more black voters, led by a local organization known as Phalanx. When he graduated from high school, where he had been at least a fine athlete, Brown attended Southern University on a work scholarship and played quarterback on the football team from 1960 to 1962. In college, he joined other students in a sit-in demonstration to protest the poor facilities and segregated conditions at the Greyhound Bus Terminal in Baton Rouge.

Brown followed his brother to Howard University in Washington, D.C., in 1963. His racial consciousness was stimulated by interaction with the Howard University student intelligentsia and by his reading of such men as W.E.B. DuBois, Frederick Douglass, Marcus Garvey, and Richard Wright. Brown's involvement in civil rights activities increased during the summers of 1963 and 1964. He participated in the March on Washington in 1963 and attended the Democratic National Convention in Atlantic City in 1964. At the latter, the Mississippi Freedom Democratic party (MFDP) made a powerful challenge to an officially elected all-white delegation from Mississippi. Brown was disgusted by the way that the MFDP was treated by conventional politicians, whether conservative or liberal.

Because of his activities, Brown's recognition began to grow. In 1965, he became the chairman of a little known political organization called the Non–Violent Action Group (NAG). As the head of this group, Brown attended, along with other civil rights representatives, a meeting in the White House with President Lyndon Johnson. The purpose was to discuss the apparent laxity of the federal government in preventing an attack on black citizens on Edmond Pettis Bridge in Selma, Alabama. Brown, who felt that all of the other blacks quickly entered their "tomming" routines, spoke directly to the president in ways that newspaper reporters described as disrespectful. His behavior was a sign, however, of the brashness and impatience of many younger black students. Brown admired the blunt speech that came out of the members of the Student Nonviolent Coordinating Committee (SNCC), formed in 1960. He joined this group himself in 1966.

In 1966, Brown began to devote all of his time to working for SNCC. At first, he organized voters in Greene County, Alabama. Brown knew the South well. He understood that a Negro on a lonely road at night without a gun was in a dangerous position. According to many SNCC workers, Brown carried a gun which he claimed he stole from a sporting goods store. His first arrest came in 1966 in Alabama for carrying a gun. Although he was annoyed at the lassitude SNCC workers showed in coming to his rescue, Brown nonetheless redoubled his organizing efforts in Alabama, leading to greater recognition for him and eventually his election as the chairperson of SNCC in 1967. Brown's tenure as leader was brief, but stormy. He stated upon his election that "it was obvious when I became Chairman that I was in for trouble." His prophecy proved to be correct. In 1967, he went to Cambridge, Maryland, to speak in the black community. There had been a local resurgence of racist activities by the Ku Klux Klan and a States Rights party. Brown's exhortations for blacks not to tolerate attacks or racial slights were later offered as evidence by authorities that he provoked a riot in which white stores were looted and burned. During the night of the rioting in Cambridge, Brown was caught in police crossfire and suffered gunshot wounds. While he managed to escape, he was charged with arson, despite the lack of evidence showing direct involvement. The following year, the National Advisory Commission on Civil Disorder concluded that police "overreaction" and civil officials in Cambridge had been responsible for the rioting.

Cambridge was the beginning of Brown's major legal woes and subsequent arrests that made it impossible for him to function in SNCC other than as a symbol. Brown thought there was an agreement with the FBI, in the aftermath of the Cambridge conflagration, that he would surrender in New York City. This was foiled with his arrest at the Washington, D.C., airport. He was released on bail, but faced additional criminal charges stemming from an appearance in Dayton, Ohio, where rioting also had occurred. His legal problems mounted further when Brown flew roundtrip from New York to New Orleans to visit his family in Louisiana and handed his registered rifle to a stewardess aboard the plane. Brown's indictment in Maryland during the trip and his arrest by officers of the Alcohol and Tobacco Division of the Justice Department for carrying a gun across state lines while under indictment led to his being held on a $25,000 bond. He was eventually returned to New Orleans. Brown was soon trapped in the labyrinth of the legal system, with many resulting arrests and subsequent run-ins with local law officials and the FBI. He would soon lament that he had been arrested in almost every state in the nation. He was on a forty-day hunger strike in his cell in Parrish, Louisiana, when he heard the news in 1968 that Martin Luther King had been murdered.

Soon after his release from the Louisiana jail, Brown married in May of 1968 to Lynne Doswell, a schoolteacher in New York City. Despite his new relative freedom and stability, it became increasingly difficult for Brown to guide SNCC because of his legal problems. In 1968, SNCC turned to "collective leadership," thereby superseding Brown as chairman. Nonetheless, by the summer of that year, Brown stated publicly that he was in control of SNCC, and he sought to change the organization's name to Student National Coordinating Committee. In March 1970, two of Brown's close SNCC allies and workers, Ralph Featherstone and William H. ("Che") Payne, were killed in a car bomb explosion in Bel Air, Maryland. They had been leaving the courthouse where Brown was to be tried for charges arising out of the Cambridge civil disturbances. There were rumors that Brown had been the intended victim. Amidst the fear that this may have been an assassination plot against him, Brown went underground. He was reportedly seen in various countries, with Canada and areas of Africa being mentioned.

In 1971, he was wounded by a New York policeman near a Manhattan bar which he was accused of attempting to rob. His subsequent trial and conviction led to incarceration from 1971 to 1976. While in jail, he was moved nearly twice a year through the New York State prison system, spending time at Greenhaven, Sing Sing, and Attica, among other jails. He converted to Islam while in prison, taking the name Jamil Abdullah Al-Amin. He was paroled in 1976 and went to live in Atlanta, Georgia. There, he began to serve as the Imam to a small group of Muslims in the city's West End, near the Atlanta University complex. He and fellow Muslims patrolled their neighborhood to prevent crime and drug abuse in the community in which he now lived with his wife and two sons. He worked toward the goal of building a mosque that would open by the 1996 Olympics in Atlanta. The mosque would serve as a place of worship for his own followers and those Muslims coming to the city for the athletic events. He hoped that Islam would provide balance in the lives of his people, commenting that "the Prophet didn't pray all day and he didn't play all day" (*New York Times*, May 3, 1993, B7). His influence grew beyond Atlanta to such cities as New York, Chicago, and Detroit.

In his new identity as Jamil Abdullah Al-Amin, the old H. Rap Brown continued to be concerned about blacks establishing their own identity, rather than adopting the cultural roles of Europeans. In an August 1991 interview, he insisted that "as long as Blacks remain committed to the Greco-Roman,

Judeo-Christian concept of civilization and ethics, they are not prepared to deal with the reality of this system or anything else. . . . History bears witness to the fact that any people who have waged a successful struggle have done so based on the application of Islam." His old militance had taken a new form.

Bibliography

Barboza, Steven. *American Jihad: Islam After Malcolm X.* New York: Doubleday, 1994.

"Black Muslims Enter Islamic Mainstream," *New York Times*, May 3, 1993, A1, B7.

Brown, H. Rap. *Die, Nigger, Die.* New York: Dial Press, 1969.

———. Interviewed August 15, 1991, Atlanta, Georgia.

———. (writing as Jamil Al-Amin). *Revolution by the Book (The Rap is Live).* Beltsville, MD: Writers' Inc., International, 1993. Reviewed: *The American Muslim Journal*, Sept. 3, 1993, 23:1.

Carson, Clayborne. *In Struggle: SNCC and the Black Awakening of the 1960s.* Cambridge: Harvard University Press, 1981.

"H. Rap Brown, now Jamil Al-Amin, is still speaking out against oppression, but in a less radical way than in the 60s," *Detroit News*, Feb. 5, 1993, B3:1.

Vertical files, Schomburg Library, New York.

Vertical files, Woodruff Library, Atlanta University Center, Atlanta, Georgia.

Maceo Dailey, Jr.

CESAR CHAVEZ (1927–1993)

Organizer of farm workers, civil rights leader

In 1962, Cesar Chavez moved from San Jose to Delano, California, to begin organizing a union among farm workers. Because earlier unions among agricultural workers had failed, most labor leaders considered the task impossible. Without co-workers, personal wealth, political power, or formal education past the seventh grade, Chavez appeared to be no match for the wealth and power of the growers. However, Chavez was undaunted. He slowly and carefully organized workers through a campaign which stressed one-on-one communication with potential members and speeches to farm-worker audiences. In 1965 his newly founded union joined with Filipino workers in a prolonged strike which vaulted Chavez and his organization into national prominence.

By 1970 powerful opponents set out to destroy the growing union. It then represented most of the agricultural workers in the grape fields and was ready to begin organizing lettuce growers. The Teamsters Union mounted an organizing drive in direct opposition to Chavez while prominent politicians in California and in Congress attempted to legislate roadblocks to the farm work-

Cesar Chavez. *Source*: Library of Congress

ers' success. Meanwhile, Chavez's union faced internal dissension which surfaced in the 1970s and continued into the 1980s.

Although Chavez's persistent campaign did produce many remarkable successes, including the nation's first collective-bargaining legislation for farm workers, setbacks have been frequent and his union never fully organized the farm workers. Yet the influence of the labor movement he founded cannot be measured solely by union victories; it also served as a powerful impetus for civil rights in the United States. Because of his campaign for justice during three decades Chavez became not only one of the best-known and admired dissenters of the 1960s but also an enduring folk hero.

Chavez was born in 1927 in Yuma, Arizona, and fondly remembered his early years spent on a family farm near town. When the land was lost during the depression of the 1930s, his family joined the migrant workers who crisscrossed the nation looking for work. The loss of his family's land and his humiliating experiences as a migrant instilled in him an intense desire to improve the lives of farm workers. Chavez's father, other members of the family, and then he himself joined farm worker unions which soon collapsed.

Cesar quickly learned, even as a young man, how difficult it would be to create an agricultural union.

In the 1940s Cesar Chavez moved to San Jose where he married, worked in a variety of jobs, and met two men who significantly influenced his ideas and career. Father Donald McDonnell, a Catholic priest, tutored him in the ideas of *Rerum Novarum*, Pope Leo XIII's encyclical pledging the church's support for workers and social justice. Fred Ross, an activist whose Community Service Organization (CSO) worked to pressure American institutions into granting rights which were denied to the underprivileged, convinced Chavez to become active in the CSO and became Chavez's mentor in grassroots organizing. Chavez became an effective CSO organizer, eventually rising to general director of the organization. As years went by, however, he became increasingly frustrated over the CSO's unwillingness to organize farm workers.

In 1962 Chavez resigned from the CSO and moved to Delano to begin creating an agricultural union. He chose Delano because of its large population of workers who had year-round jobs in the area. They might be easier to organize than migrant workers. He hoped to find a formula for success in Delano that could be applied to other farm workers. His quest would be easier, he believed, because his brother Richard lived in Delano and would offer him the support of his family.

Once in Delano, Chavez embarked on an intense campaign to recruit members. He worked in the fields during the day and then drove to farm workers' camps and homes virtually every night, speaking to individuals and groups at house meetings and in other settings on hundreds of nights in eighty-seven communities within a 100-mile radius of Delano. He had workers fill out cards detailing the improvements they felt needed to be made in their lives. His conversations and the information he received in the surveys helped Chavez to understand the problems and needs of the workers. The meetings helped him to identify potential leaders who might join the seasoned organizers whom he had attracted from the CSO.

In 1962 the farm workers held their organizing convention in Fresno, California, taking the name the National Farm Workers Association (NFWA) and selecting Chavez as their president. The NFWA created a dues schedule and adopted a flag with an Aztec eagle on a red backdrop as its symbol. Aided by Protestant ministers, some Catholic priests, and outside volunteers who had worked in the civil rights movement in the South, Chavez planned to organize the union slowly and carefully over several years. By 1965, with the membership at more than 2,000, Chavez had a cautious strategy of avoiding strikes until the union was more fully organized. History then intervened to change his plans.

On September 8, 1965, the Agricultural Workers Organizing Committee (AWOC), a Filipino farm workers union, announced a strike against grape growers in the Delano area. AWOC called upon Chavez and his union to join them. The two unions merged into the United Farm Workers Organizing

Committee (UFWOC) and joined the AFL-CIO. As the strike persisted, Chavez and his organization attracted national attention through tactics which they have continued to use for decades. The boycott was probably the most famous. It was first used to target selected growers but later expanded to all grape growers. Union organizers ultimately canvassed all major markets in an attempt to eliminate the sale of grapes. In 1970, following a bitter five-year strike, Chavez scored a startling victory when the majority of growers signed contracts with his union.

After the success in grapes, the farm workers shifted their efforts to lettuce workers. Many growers refused to bargain with Chavez. Instead, they signed agreements with the Teamsters Union. Following a difficult and distracting battle for several years, the two unions reached a settlement: Chavez's union was granted jurisdiction among field workers, the Teamsters among workers in the packing sheds and among truckers. In 1973 many of the contracts of Chavez's union, now named the United Farm Workers (UFW), were up for renewal. The Teamsters violated their earlier agreements by openly challenging the UFW. They often used physical brutality and other forms of intimidation of UFW supporters. The Teamsters signed highly favorable agreements with many growers previously contracted to the UFW. The union's membership dropped from its high of 55,000 to 6,000 by 1975.

Established political forces both helped and hindered Chavez. The Nixon administration first unsuccessfully attempted to pass laws outlawing the union's most successful tactics, and then backed legislation in California, Arizona, and Oregon to outlaw boycotts. As in the interunion conflicts, Chavez's struggle to overcome these new challenges diverted energy from his efforts to build an effective union. Prospects brightened in 1975 with the passage of the California Agricultural Labor Relations Act. This established the Agricultural Labor Relations Board (ALRB) to supervise elections and disputes. The UFW, given new life by the ALRB, began to win elections to represent workers.

By 1980 Chavez's union could count significant achievements from its nearly twenty-year struggle. Workers had acquired pension plans, health-care benefits, access to credit union, and other precedent-setting services and concessions from growers. The UFW had won the right to bargain while accumulating a fair measure of political influence in California, Arizona, and Texas. As in the past, however, success arrived in the midst of formidable challenges and dangers, this time from both inside and outside the UFW. In 1977 Chavez moved the union's headquarters from Delano to La Paz, a former tuberculosis sanitarium in the Tehachapi Mountains south of Bakersfield, California. Complaining that this move separated leaders from workers, and also troubled with what they perceived as Chavez's consistent inability to delegate authority and inordinate fear of communist infiltration in the union, many members—including major leaders like Gil Padilla—left the union in the late 1970s and early 1980s. Moreover, in 1982 newly elected California governor

George Deukmejian appointed ALRB board members who were openly hostile to Chavez. Without the board's support, the UFW again declined in power and numbers.

To revive his lagging movement, Chavez reinstituted a boycott to accompany his ongoing campaign of persuasive speaking and writing. While continuing to take national and regional speaking tours, he intensified his use of written persuasion by using the sophisticated computer equipment at La Paz to send millions of pieces of mail to those sympathetic to his cause. A major theme of his later speeches, written messages, and boycott was the indiscriminate use of pesticides by growers and the effects of those pesticides on workers.

Throughout Chavez's career his beliefs and actions remained consistent. Keys to understanding the man and his motives are found in his experiences as a migrant, as an organizer for the CSO, and in his personal faith or theology.

Chavez carried with him many vivid memories of the low wages, poor working conditions, and social injustices suffered by workers. Rather than leading to a sense of hopelessness or anger, these experiences left him with a strong desire to improve the lives of workers so that they could avoid the poverty and injustices that he had faced in his early life. Intimately familiar with the day-to-day problems of farm workers, he spoke to his audiences as one of them as well as their leader.

As an organizer for the CSO, Chavez acquired practical skills that he could later use in building his union. He discovered the power of face-to-face organizing. He learned how to organize groups, to form coalitions among existing groups, to work with local leaders to recruit members, and to persuade members to carry the financial load rather than seeking outside funds from contributors who might want control over the organization. He also came to understand that an organizer must establish trust through personal relationships. With these skills and insights he would translate his personal desires into successful action to improve the squalid working and living conditions that he had once experienced and that many farm workers continued to experience. Chavez led not as an outsider imposing the form and structure of a traditional union on farm workers but as a fellow worker building a unique organization to meet the particular needs of its members.

Throughout his years as a farm worker, with the CSO, and as a labor leader, Chavez based his actions on his personal theology. A devout Roman Catholic, he believed that the church must care for the poor and that Christ's model of nonviolence was admirable. Accordingly, he called upon the Catholic church to join with the workers, to carry out its sacred duty to improve the lives of poor people, and to demonstrate its love for people by helping achieve social justice through social change. Although initially not siding with Chavez's movement, church leaders gradually shifted their support to him. This support was particularly important because most farm worker–union members were Catholics.

Much of the history of the UFW has been built around traditional Catholic religious practices. The union used pilgrimages, fasting, retreats, public prayers, and public masses as an integral part of its practices. The Virgin of Guadalupe became an especially powerful symbol. Also, many advisors in the union were either Catholic priests or Protestant ministers.

Chavez's spiritual faith was also reflected in his lifelong commitment to nonviolence. His study of the works of Gandhi and St. Paul, and his training in the CSO, revealed to him the practical power and moral correctness of nonviolent tactics. One of his toughest challenges was to remain nonviolent in strikes, a setting which invited violence.

Chavez's religious beliefs and personal experiences led him to a millennial interpretation of history. During the turbulent 1960s he concluded that the poor were on the march in a revolution to change the nation. Viewing the UFW as a unique union because it represented the poor and downtrodden who were part of a revolutionary movement to change social conditions, he considered his union to be a family bound together in a common struggle for justice. Because he was convinced that God's plan included a millennial future, and thus that history was on the side of the farm workers, Chavez believed that he would inevitably reach his goals.

Although Chavez saw his ends as divinely sanctioned, success rested upon earthly means. To him, the elimination of injustice required that the public receive a righteous message of facts, arguments, and explanations. If he presented his case clearly and with ample facts and thoughtful arguments, listeners and readers would eventually recognize its truthfulness and respond to his persuasive appeals. With public address his central tool of reform, he reached out widely to his audience through public letters, manifestos, marches, and fasts, as well as through addresses before congressional committees, interviews on television and in magazines, and speeches. Further expanding his audience, Chavez emerged as a leading spokesperson for civil rights. His union, comprised mainly of racial minorities, has often been described as a civil rights movement.

The shy and gentle Chavez at first disliked public speaking, but he quickly realized its importance in recruiting followers, raising money, and communicating his case for reform. Working hard and systematically to improve his abilities as an orator, he developed impressive skills in using evidence, organizing ideas, and creating arguments, all appropriate rhetorical qualities for a persuader who believed that God would ineluctably guide the public to the proper decision once that public was aware of the facts and logic of a righteous cause. Chavez's own humble lifestyle and consistent dedication to his ideals projected an appealing personal image which added impact to his persuasive message. His understanding of the speaking styles of Mexican-Americans, most notably their use of anecdotes, *dichos* or aphorisms, and gracious formality, contributed to his rhetorical prowess.

As Chavez's influence increased, opposition to him intensified. In the 1960s the John Birch Society and others labeled him a communist who exploited the poor to achieve his own evil ends. Some antagonists claimed that he had never been a farm worker and was becoming wealthy from his union work. Meanwhile, an alternative union was formed and claimed to represent the true sentiments and interests of farm workers. (It was later proven to be financed by growers.) Among the many politicians who backed the growers were President Richard Nixon and Governor Ronald Reagan, both of whom publicly ate grapes during the boycott. In the years of the Vietnam War the Nixon administration bought vast supplies of grapes for U.S. troops. Less dramatic but no less threatening were the persistent attempts to pass federal and state legislation to outlaw tactics used by the UFW.

In 1993, Chavez's salary was about $5,000 a year. He had dedicated his life and resources to his cause, saying that love meant sacrifice. While he was in Arizona testifying at a trial—and following a seven-day fast—he died in his sleep. His health had been undermined by his years of service. He was survived by his wife, eight children, and his union.

His California funeral brought out at least 25,000 people, from the average to the famous. Speakers celebrated his life: that in a world of quitters, he had endured; that he had used economic boycotts, strikes, fasts, and civil disobedience to achieve his goals; that he achieved more dignity and a better life for some agricultural workers. Speakers were also fearful about what would happen to the UFW, which had shrunk to somewhere between 10,000 and 20,000 members. Child labor was still common; workers were still surrounded by dangerous pesticides and herbicides; real wages had declined in the 1980s; and most employers were quite willing to use illegal immigrants and, if necessary, violence, to intimidate their field labor. Chavez had understood the power of his enemies: "Everything is interwoven with agriculture. When you take on the growers, you're also taking on the large insurance companies who also happen to be owners of land, and you're taking on the large banks, and the railroads, and the pesticide and fertilizer companies. Talk about a power base against you" (*Washington Post*, May 1, 1993, A23). His idealism highlighted the widespread hypocrisy of American life. There is much that can be learned about both the shame and the promise of this society from an understanding of the life of Cesar Chavez.

Bibliography

"After Chavez, Farm Workers Struggle," *New York Times*, July 19, 1993, A12.

Bardacke, Frank. "César's Ghost; Decline and Fall of the U.F.W.," *The Nation* 257 (July 26/August 2, 1993): 130–35.

Corwin, Miles. "The Grapes of Wrath Revisited," *Los Angeles Times*, September 29, 1991, A1.

Daniel, Cletus E. "Cesar Chavez and the Unionization of California Farm Workers," in *Labor Leaders in America* Melvyn Dubofsky and Warren R. Van Tine, eds. Urbana: University of Illinois Press, 1987: 350–82.

Garcia, Richard A. "Dolores Huerta: Woman, Organizer, Symbol." *California History* 72(Spring 1993): 56–71.

Hammerback, John C., and Richard J. Jensen. "'A Revolution of Heart and Mind': Cesar Chavez's Rhetorical Crusade," *Journal of the West* 27 (April 1988): 69–74.

Huerta, Dolores. "Reflections on the UFW Experience," *The Center Magazine* 18 (July/August 1985): 2–8.

Levy, Jacques E. *Cesar Chavez: Autobiography of La Causa*. New York: W. W. Norton, 1975.

Martínez, Elizabeth. "Walking with Cesar," *Z Magazine* 6 (June 1993): 21–25.

Meier, Matt S. "Cesar Chavez," in *Mexican American Biographies: A Historical Dictionary, 1836–1987*, Matt S. Meier, ed. Westport, CT: Greenwood Press, 1988: 55–57.

Obits: *New York Times*, April 24, 1993, A1, A29, April 30, 1993, A13; *Washington Post*, April 24, 1993, B6, April 30, 1993, A1, A21, May 1, 1993, A23.

Ross, Fred. *Conquering Goliath: Cesar Chavez at the Beginning*. Detroit: Wayne State University Press, 1992.

Zimmerman, Joy Ann. "An Organizer's Organizer," *The Progressive* 52 (December 1988): 12–13.

John C. Hammerback
Richard J. Jensen

SHIRLEY CHISHOLM (1924–   )

African-American congresswoman, 1969–1982, and 1972 presidential candidate

Shirley Chisholm is probably most well known as the first African-American woman to serve as a member of the United States House of Representatives and also the first black person to actively seek the presidential nomination of a major U.S. party. During the 1960s Chisholm was in the vanguard of those African Americans who wanted to solidify the civil rights victories wrought by the Supreme Court's desegregation decision of 1954 and the success of various protests. Her career benefitted from the momentum of the Montgomery, Alabama, bus boycott of 1956–1957, lunch-counter sit-in demonstrations, freedom rides on interstate buses, and other forms of legislative and civil disobedience.

Chisholm knew that committed black elected officials on the local, state, and federal level were needed to prod the government to respond to the needs of the poor and disenfranchised. She emphasized employment, education, housing, political representation, and criminal justice. Chisholm was an eloquent voice for not only African Americans but also for Hispanics and other minorities. She was equally interested in women's employment and repro-

Shirley Chisholm. Copyright *Washington Post*: Reprinted by permission of D.C. Public Library.

ductive rights. Chisholm often told her audiences that she suffered more discrimination because of her sex than because of her race.

Born to a poor family on November 30, 1924, in Brooklyn, New York, Shirley Anita St. Hill, was the eldest of four daughters. Because her parents, Charles and Ruby, were struggling to establish themselves in the city, they sent their three eldest girls to Barbados, an island where 90 percent of the population is of African origin. Their maternal grandmother gave them love, pride, and rigorous discipline. She was responsible for the girls' secular and religious education for several years. Shirley attributes her success largely to this early training. She did not suffer from the racial constraints that exist for black children in the United States.

When Shirley was ten years old, she returned to Brooklyn where she attended public schools. By the time of her high school graduation Shirley's excellent grades won her tuition scholarships to several prestigious colleges. She needed to live at home, however, because her family lacked the money for her room and board. She decided to pursue her degree in early childhood education at nearby Brooklyn College. Shirley was active in several organizations at Brooklyn College. These groups included the Harriet Tubman Society for Negro History, the debating society, and a black women's professional sorority, Delta Sigma Theta. She was commended regularly for her oratorical skill. She graduated with honors in 1946 and twelve years later earned a Master of Arts from Columbia University. In the time between these two degrees, she worked as a nursery school teacher, childcare center director, and an educational consultant in the division of day care of the New York City Bureau of Child Welfare. She also served on the boards of several community-based organizations.

Married at twenty-five to Conrad Chisholm, an insurance investigator who frequently traveled, Shirley often found herself with time on her hands. Like her father, who had been a follower of back-to-Africa leader Marcus Garvey, Shirley was a keen observer of the political scene. She decided to spend her free time learning more about local political organizations. Her years of debating at college as well as her work among blacks and Hispanics made her want to help the poor to benefit from social and government programs. She especially wanted to assist the poor with employment, education, and housing. Bedford-Stuyvesant had slowly become a predominantly black and Hispanic neighborhood, but the Democratic party representatives were all white and largely insensitive to the new majority.

Chisholm began her involvement in political work with African-American members of the Bedford-Stuyvesant Political League. This had been founded to ensure that blacks and Hispanics would be fairly represented at all levels of government. She left that organization soon and began to work with local Democratic clubs. As a door-to-door precinct worker and fund-raiser, Chisholm found that women traditionally sponsored most events to raise money for the local party organization, but men usually held all the leadership positions and determined the rewards black supporters received through the party hierarchy. Chisholm became interested not only in more power for minorities but also in elevating the status of females within the Democratic ranks. After campaigning for black male candidates in several elections, Chisholm ran for the New York State Assembly herself.

As a virtual unknown with little money, she had to be creative and industrious to put her name before the public. She spoke to various church and civic groups including Hispanic ones where she impressed them with her fluent Spanish. She spoke out on issues even when the sidewalk was her only podium. Since her college days she had been an orator who could rivet the attention of her audience and regularly outwit her verbal opponents. Hard work did not deter her. Whether she was researching materials relating to her district or the state, stuffing envelopes, or telephoning voters, she diligently pursued her goals and usually succeeded. In 1964 she was elected to represent Brooklyn in the state legislature. She was the second black woman to become a member of that body.

Chisholm finally had an opportunity to translate her many ideas for the improvement of the community into real programs that would meet pressing social and economic needs. During the four years that she was in the New York State Assembly, she introduced fifty bills, eight of which were passed into law. One of these made domestic workers eligible for unemployment insurance; another provided state scholarships to black and Puerto Rican students whose parents could not afford to give them a college education. In addition to the scholarship, students could receive counseling and tutoring to help them hone their skills. Chisholm also supported other educational programs, aid for day-care centers, abortion reform, tenure retention for teachers during maternity leave, and the curtailment of use of weapons by police officers.

Because of her diligent work for her constituents, she received their overwhelming support. Even though her district lines were repeatedly redrawn, causing her to campaign for her assembly seat three different times during her four-year tenure, she won easily each time.

In 1967 the district lines were redrawn again creating the Twelfth U.S. Congressional District with a vacant seat slated for the 1968 election. Chisholm decided that she wanted to run for the seat. Her opponent was the noted civil rights leader James Farmer (*), who had served as the director of the Congress of Racial Equality (CORE), an organization that had been in the vanguard of the civil rights movement. Possibly because Chisholm was a well-known resident of Bedford-Stuyvesant, while Farmer lived in Manhattan, she won a landslide victory. She remained in the U.S. House of Representatives from the ninety-first through the ninety-seventh Congresses (1969–1982).

As the first black female ever to serve in the House of Representatives, Chisholm generally had a trail of reporters at her heels. She used this to her advantage. Always considering herself a political maverick, Chisholm focused as much attention as she could on social programs which benefitted the poor, minorities, and women. The Democratic party position did not always coincide with her views.

Chisholm immediately protested that the military budget was indefensible because social programs were suffering. She stated during one congressional session that she would not vote to spend any money for the military while Americans were hungry, ill-housed, and poorly educated. She actively opposed U.S. involvement in the Vietnam War. She also began to support legislation allowing abortions for women who chose to have them. Abortions were not only illegal then, they were socially unacceptable. Although she was personally opposed to abortion because of her religious beliefs, Chisholm was appalled by the casualties from illegal abortions. She decided that each woman should have a right to choose. The sexual revolution caused by a change in national values and the ease in obtaining inexpensive birth-control pills gave rise to the sentiment, especially among young people that reproductive choices should belong to women.

Chisholm was also in the vanguard of those protesting the limited job opportunities for women, such as being secretaries, teachers, and librarians. African-American women were too often shunted into stereotypical maid and nanny roles from which they needed liberation both by legislation and self-effort. Chisholm's anti-war and women's liberation views made her a popular figure among college students, who besieged her with invitations to speak at college campuses.

Chisholm served on several House committees: Agriculture, Veterans' Affairs, Rules, and Education and Labor. During her first term, when she was assigned to the Forestry Subcommittee of the Agriculture Committee, Chisholm protested, saying that there were no forests in Bedford-Stuyvesant. During one of her first congressional meetings, she insisted on being placed on committees that could deal with the "critical problems of racism, deprivation, and urban decay," not one that was totally unrelated to her constituency or her personal abilities. Although new members generally do not have their pick of appointments, Chisholm's public and private protests got her on the Veterans' Affairs committee.

In 1972 Chisholm made the stunning announcement that she would run for the presidency. She spoke out about the inequities in the judicial system in the United States, police brutality, prison reform, gun control, the right to dissent, drug abuse, and numerous other topics. She appeared on the television show "Face the Nation" with three other Democratic presidential candidates: George McGovern, Henry Jackson, and Edmund Muskie. Although McGovern won the nomination at the Democratic National Convention, Chisholm captured 10 percent of the votes. As a result of her campaign, she was voted one of the ten most admired women in the world.

After her unsuccessful presidential campaign, Chisholm continued to serve in the House for another decade. As a member of the Black Caucus she watched the number of African-American representatives grow, including additional black congresswomen. Chisholm remained a strong supporter of social reforms urging less money for defense and more for domestic programs. The 1978 *Congressional Record* documents that she supported educational aid and training opportunities for poor students, cost-of-living pay increases for federal employees, a full-employment program for the nation, an end to discrimination against women through the passage of the Equal Rights Amendment, the protection of abortion rights, the establishment of a voting representative in

Congress for Washington, D.C., a cessation of U.S. involvement in South Africa, and quality health care for black Americans.

She announced her retirement from Congress in 1982, when she was bitter over the reduction of social programs under the Reagan administration. She taught various political courses at Mount Holyoke College and Spelman College in Atlanta. In 1984 after the Democratic National Convention, she spearheaded the formation of the National Political Congress of Black Women, which by 1988 boasted 8,500 members and chapters in thirty-six states. The group was organized to endorse and raise funds for candidates.

Still in popular demand as a public speaker, Chisholm continued to campaign for her beliefs like a candidate for election. She deplored the abdication of social justice programs under Republican administrations and continued to support the rights of African Americans, other minorities, the poor, and women to full and complete participation in the American society. In 1993, President Clinton appointed her ambassador to Jamaica, a tribute to her past successes and continuing abilities.

Bibliography

Chisholm, Shirley. *The Good Fight*. New York: Harper and Row, 1973.

———. "Racism and Anti-Feminism," *The Black Scholar* 14 (Sept./Oct. 1983): 2–7.

———. *Unbought and Unbossed*. Boston: Houghton Mifflin, 1970.

Duckworth, Alan. "Shirley Chisholm," in *Notable Black American Women*, Jessie Carney Smith, ed. Detroit: Gale Research, 1992: 185–89.

Duffy, Susan. "Shirley Chisholm," in *American Orators of the Twentieth Century*, Bernard K. Duffy and Halford R. Ryan, eds. Westport, CT: Greenwood Press, 1987: 63–68.

———, compiler. *Shirley Chisholm: A Bibliography of Writings by and about Her*. Metuchen, NJ: Scarecrow Press, 1988.

Haskins, James. *Fighting Shirley Chisholm*. New York: Dial Press, 1975.

LeVeness, Frank P., and Jane P. Sweeney, eds. *Women Leaders in Contemporary U.S. Politics*. Boulder, CO: L. Rienner, 1987.

Debra Newman Ham

ELDRIDGE CLEAVER (1935–)

Leading figure in the Black Panther party

Eldridge Cleaver, author of the widely read collection of prison writings, *Soul on Ice* (1968), and minister of information for the Black Panther party for Self-Defense (1967–1971), was one of the most visible and controversial figures in the black liberation movement. Wounded in an April 1968 shoot-out with police that left another Panther, Bobby Hutton, dead, he ran as the Peace and

Freedom party candidate for president of the United States; engaged California Governor Ronald Reagan in a running free-speech debate; and finally fled the country when it appeared that he would be returned to prison for parole violation. From exile in Algiers, his voice turned increasingly nihilistic, contributing little to the revolution of which he dreamed and much to the fratricide that plagued the Panthers during the early 1970s.

Cleaver came to Los Angeles from rural Arkansas as a child and would spend more than a third of his first thirty years in state prisons. This odyssey began in a California Youth Authority institution where he also experienced the first of many conversions by joining the Roman Catholic church. Caught with what he called "a shopping bag full of love" (marijuana) at the age of eighteen, he entered San Quentin Prison in 1954, about a month after the United States Supreme Court's historic school desegregation decision, *Brown v. Board of Education.* A conviction for rape would follow, and he would spend nine of the next twelve years in San Quentin and Folsom. He joined the Nation of Islam in 1960, becoming assistant minister of the San Quentin Mosque, and remained an active Muslim when transferred to Folsom in 1963. While consigned to solitary confinement for being an agitator, he demonstrated wide-ranging and eclectic reading interests. He remained in the Nation of Islam until Muhammad put out Malcolm X (*).

Paroled in December 1966, Cleaver began writing for *Ramparts*, the muckraking, anti-war magazine published in San Francisco, and preparing his prison writings for publication. He also began speaking at college campuses, including Fisk University, where he met Kathleen Neal. The two soon married. Back in the Bay Area, Black Panther party founders Huey Newton and Bobby Seale (*) heard Cleaver on the radio one evening and rushed down to the station. "Huey related to Eldridge as a Malcolm X, coming out of prison," Seale recalled, adding that they were especially impressed with Cleaver's writing abilities. Newton wanted to start a newspaper and thought Cleaver was the man to do it. Cleaver remained noncommittal, though he was equally impressed, particularly after he witnessed an armed Panther bodyguard escorting Malcolm's widow, Betty Shabazz, during her trip to San Francisco and Oakland. He joined Newton and Seale a few months later, simply by announcing that he was a Panther, and in April 1967 *The Black Panther* newspaper began publication. Both Eldridge, as minister of information, and Kathleen Cleaver, as communications secretary, were on the paper's editorial staff.

Until this time the Panthers concentrated on recruiting a revolutionary cadre of disaffected young blacks, many of whom had criminal records, from the Oakland ghettos. Armed with shotguns and handguns, they policed the police, following cop cars around on their own community patrols and reading law books to officers making routine traffic stops or arrests. Their ideology, such as it was, came from the "Off the Pig!" slogan and Frantz Fanon's *Wretched of the Earth,* and their range of operation was strictly limited to the Bay Area. This changed in October 1967, when Oakland police stopped a car

WANTED
BY THE
FBI

INTERSTATE FLIGHT - ASSAULT WITH INTENT TO COMMIT MURDER
LEROY ELDRIDGE CLEAVER

FBI No. 214,830 B

Photograph taken 1966   Photographs taken 1968

Aliases: Eldridge Cleaver, Leroy Eldridge Cleaver, Jr.

DESCRIPTION

Age:	33, born August 31, 1935, Little Rock, Arkansas		
Height:	6' 2"	**Eyes:**	Brown
Weight:	185 to 195 pounds	**Complexion:**	Medium
Build:	Medium	**Race:**	Negro
Hair:	Black	**Nationality:**	American
Occupations:	Author, clerk, laborer, magazine editor, reporter, writer		
Scars and Marks:	Numerous pock scars on back		
Remarks:	Sometimes wears small gold earring in pierced left ear lobe		

Fingerprint Classification: 24 L 13 U OOM 19
I   2 U OOI

CRIMINAL RECORD

Cleaver has been convicted of assault with intent to commit murder, assault with a deadly weapon and possession of narcotics.

CAUTION

CLEAVER ALLEGEDLY HAS ENGAGED POLICE OFFICERS IN GUN BATTLE IN THE PAST. CONSIDER ARMED AND EXTREMELY DANGEROUS.

A Federal warrant was issued on December 10, 1968, at San Francisco, California, charging Cleaver with unlawful interstate flight to avoid confinement after conviction for assault with intent to commit murder (Title 18, U. S. Code, Section 1073).

IF YOU HAVE ANY INFORMATION CONCERNING THIS PERSON, PLEASE NOTIFY ME OR CONTACT YOUR LOCAL FBI OFFICE. TELEPHONE NUMBERS AND ADDRESSES OF ALL FBI OFFICES LISTED ON BACK.

DIRECTOR
FEDERAL BUREAU OF INVESTIGATION
UNITED STATES DEPARTMENT OF JUSTICE
WASHINGTON, D. C. 20535
TELEPHONE, NATIONAL 8-7117

Wanted Flyer 447
December 13, 1968

Eldridge Cleaver on F.B.I. Wanted Flyer. *Source*: Library of Congress carrying Huey Newton. Officer John Frey died and Newton was wounded in the shoot-out that followed. Involuntary manslaughter charges led to the "Free Huey" campaign that brought the chapter recruits in dozens of cities in the Midwest and Northeast. Cleaver brought white radicals into the Free Huey campaign and staged the famous pose Newton assumed for a photograph that first appeared in the Panther newspaper and then was widely reproduced as a poster. In black leather, Newton sat in a wicker chair holding a shotgun against a background of African shields and a pelt.

Prominence for Cleaver himself came with publication of *Soul on Ice* and the handful of passages where he described the rape of white women as an insurrectionary act. He traced this view to his prison cell, where he kept a white pin-up on the wall, and the 1955 Money, Mississippi, lynching of Emmett Till, a young boy from Chicago who had gone South to visit relatives and died because he wolf-whistled at a white woman. When Cleaver saw a picture of the woman, he said he "felt that little tension in the center of my chest I experience when a woman appeals to me." A breakdown followed, and he came out of prison intent on carrying out as many insurrectionary acts (rapes) as possible. This put him back in prison where he eventually concluded that he was suffering from "a revolutionary sickness" and began writing to expunge from his soul the guilt of his crimes. Ultimately, the message of *Soul on Ice* was that rage was self-destructive. "The price of hating other human beings is loving oneself less," Cleaver wrote. "From my prison cell, I have watched America coming awake. It is not fully awake yet, but there is soul in the air and everywhere I see beauty."

The Cleaver who joined the Black Panther party respected the goals and gains of the Civil Rights movement and counseled Newton and Seale to reach out to the white Left. This bore fruit with the Free Huey campaign and the Peace and Freedom party, culminating in Cleaver's nomination as that party's candidate for president and Kathleen Cleaver's nomination for a seat in the California State Assembly. But it ended in disaster when the Panthers tried to form a coalition with Stokely Carmichael and the Student Nonviolent Coordinating Committee (SNCC).

Cleaver admired SNCC, particularly its own coalition building during the Freedom Summer of 1964 in Mississippi. About the racist Neshoba County murder of three young civil rights workers, two of whom were white, Cleaver wrote: "I wonder if James Chaney said, as Andrew Goodman and Michael Schwerner stood helplessly watching, as the grizzly dogs crushed his bones with savage blows of chains—did poor James say, after Rufus Scott—'You took the best, so why not take the rest?' Or did he turn to his white brothers, seeing their plight, and say, after Baldwin, 'That's your problem, baby!' I say, after Mailer, 'There's a shit-storm coming.' " By 1968, however, SNCC had changed. The quiet Bob Moses (*) had given way to the shrill Carmichael, and the group was entirely black. When Cleaver and Seale visited SNCC's Washington, D.C., office, they found what Seale called "black racist" ideas.

"We couldn't operate in a black racist thing," Seale said, yet for a brief time Carmichael joined the Panthers before falling out amid mutual name calling and acrimony.

Largely at Cleaver's insistence, the Panthers continued to call for a "united-front struggle," a coalition of black and white people "against their common oppressor." This "integrated" revolution moved away from black nationalism to identify capitalism rather than racism as the principal problem facing the people. The Panthers increasingly relied on a Marxist-Leninist and Maoist rhetoric, and in Cleaver's case this was done in an increasingly profane way. He spent much of the time making his run for the presidency and talking about the governor of California, proving himself adept at getting college students to chant "Fuck Ronald Reagan" and making purposefully absurd campaign promises. When asked what he would do first upon being elected and moving into the White House, he said, "I'll burn the mother fucker down."

Having lost his bid for the presidency and convinced that he would also lose a parole revocation hearing, Cleaver fled to Cuba. He surfaced in North Korea to praise the ideas of Korean communists; in Moscow to pose with his wanted-by-the-FBI poster; and in Hanoi to urge black GIs to desert and otherwise sabotage the American war effort in Vietnam. In *The Black Panther*, he called for the formation of a North American Liberation Front patterned after the Vietcong and Castro's guerrillas in Cuba. Armed struggle at home would work, he wrote, because "the United States has more mountains than all of these other areas." A concrete house facing the Mediterranean coast in Algiers became home and the operational base of the Black Panther party's International Section.

In exile, Cleaver's voice took on the tone of a crazed revolutionary. America became "Babylon" and Kathleen called Eldridge "Papa Rage." He built a revolutionary theory that included anti-Semitism and calls for terrorism. The powerful voice of *Soul on Ice* that dreamed of conciliation between the races and a day when America would rid itself of racism and other institutional diseases, now called for "hit lists" of "targets that I actually want to aim at and pull the trigger." These lists, ranging from Richard Nixon to Oakland Police Chief Charles Gain, would place the Panthers, Cleaver said, "in a position to implement head-up murder. We can guarantee the total destruction of Babylon—with a form of struggle that pigs will call madness." To overthrow the government, he added, the initial target would not be Washington, D.C., but Long Island—because "Long Island controls New York, New York controls the country and the country controls the world." This could all be accomplished because black people have "the ultimate political consequence in their power," the "power to unleash . . . RACE WAR."

Ultimately, "the Lumpen" would have no choice but to do so. Nor would there be any guiding force, Cleaver claimed, since "a determined revolutionary doesn't require an authorization from a Central Committee before offing a pig. As a matter of fact, when the need arises a true revolutionary will off the Central Committee."

While the exiled Cleaver championed "the angels of destruction" and the "great educational value" of murder ("it teaches people to kill the enemy and hate the enemy"), Huey Newton increasingly emphasized the Black Panther party's community service programs. The party was splitting into two factions, and in 1971 Cleaver found himself accused of placing the Panthers in a "twilight zone" with his advocacy of a black-white alliance; endangering Panther survival with his suicidal advocacy of terrorism; and even undermining Panther support in the black community with his compulsive swearing. There were other charges in *The Black Panther* that Cleaver abused his wife and murdered another Panther in Algiers. Cleaver responded by criticizing the "bureaucratic" Newton's refusal to emphasize "military struggle." Newton and Cleaver expelled each other's faction in March 1971. The Black Panther party would continue, but its heyday, and Cleaver's as well, had come and gone.

Another and perhaps last conversion brought Cleaver back to the United States in 1976 to vote for Jimmy Carter and face weapons charges in an Oakland courthouse. The autobiographical *Soul on Fire* (1978) emphasized the importance of constitutional liberties, the inhumanity of government acting in the name of the proletariat, and the centrality of religious values. Simply put, he said he "stopped being a communist or socialist and developed an understanding and respect for free enterprise and the democratic political system." Searching for a church, he joined the Mormons. Searching for a way to make a living, he turned to the conservative lecture circuit, the selling of ceramic pots and other objects, and eventually a recycling business. He sought, and failed to get, conservative Republican backing for a run at the United States Senate. He even turned up at the Republican National Convention in 1984 to sing the praises of Ronald Reagan. The father of two and divorced from Kathleen, who went on to Yale Law School, he later lived alone in a modest Berkeley apartment. His only trouble with the police involved a cocaine-possession charge.

Though troubled by his radical 1960s image, Cleaver remains proud of his work with the Panthers. "I think the Black Panther Party played a very positive role at a decisive moment toward the liberation of Black people in America." Further progress, in his new worldview, depended on the benevolence of capitalism and the willingness of black Americans to enter the capitalist class.

Cleaver spoke well for himself in *Soul on Ice*. But the ideology he developed as a Black Panther, no matter how exciting to hear in the long-gone days of rage, was as shallow as it looked on the printed page. "The ideology of the Black Panther Party is the historical experience of black people in their struggle against the System of racist oppression in Babylon," he wrote in the days before the police and the Panthers' own feuding broke the party down, "interpreted through the prism of Marxist-Leninist analysis by our minister of defense, Huey P. Newton." The emptiness of this should not obscure the existence of an admirable Panther vision that stressed the involvement of people in their own lives and in the solutions to their own problems. Here, where the Panther legacy is worth something, the articulate Cleaver contributed few ideas and nothing of an ideology.

"There is soul in the air and everywhere I see beauty," he wrote in *Soul on Ice*. By the early 1990s, Cleaver felt the bitterness of irrelevance. For years, there had only been death in the air. In March of 1994, he suffered a brain hemorrhage following an arrest on drug charges. Cleaver, who had once classified himself as "an extremist by nature," symbolized the hopelessness of empty rhetorical militance.

Bibliography

"Cleaver Confronts His Past," *Washington Post*, March 16, 1994, C3.

Cleaver, Eldridge. *Eldridge Cleaver: Post-Prison Writings and Speeches*, Robert Scheer, ed. New York: Viking, 1969.

———. Interview with Bill Kauffman and Lyn Scarlett, in *Reason* 17 (Feb. 1986): 22–28.

———. *Soul on Fire*. Waco, TX: Word Books, 1978.

———. *Soul on Ice*, Ishmael Reed, intr. New York: Dell/Laurel, 1992 [1968].

"Cleaver, Eldridge," in *Contemporary Literary Criticism*, vol. 30. Detroit: Gale Research, 1984: 53–69.

Jensen, Richard J., and John C. Hammerback. "From Muslim to Mormon: Eldridge Cleaver's Rhetorical Crusade," *Communication Quarterly* 34 (Winter 1986): 24–40.

O'Reilly, Kenneth. *"Racial Matters": The FBI's Secret File on Black America, 1960–1972*. New York: Free Press, 1989.

Parks, Gordon. "Eldridge Cleaver in Algiers: A Visit with Papa Rage," *Life*, Feb. 6, 1970, pp. 20–23.

Reese, Michael. "A Bizarre Race in California," *Newsweek* 107 (March 10, 1986): 46.

Rout, Kathleen. *Eldridge Cleaver*. Boston: Twayne Publishers, 1991.

Schanche, Don A. "Panthers against the Wall," *Atlantic*, May 1970, pp. 55–61.

"Whatever Happened to . . . Eldridge Cleaver," *Ebony* 43 (March 1988): 66–68.

Kenneth O'Reilly

VINE DELORIA, JR. (1933–   )

Executive director, National Congress of American Indians (1964–1967), author, organization activist

While Vine Deloria, Jr., did not attract national attention until his best-selling book, *Custer Died for Your Sins* (1969), and his appearance on "The Dick Cavett Show" with pictures of brutality against Indian fishermen of the Tacoma, Washington, area, his range of 1960s activities is chronicled in Stan Steiner's book, *The New Indians* (1968).

Vine Deloria, Jr., Executive Director, National Congress of Indians. *Source*: Library of Congress

Deloria represented a subtle kind of Indian activism which was present in the 1960s but little publicized. His great-grandfather was a Sioux medicine man and his grandfather one of the first Sioux chiefs to adopt the Christian way and become a native missionary to his own people. His father, Vine, Sr., was the most prominent Christian Indian of the past sixty years, eventually becoming the Episcopal archdeacon of South Dakota. It might have been predictable that Vine Deloria, Jr., would become an activist in the same vein as the black churchmen who led the civil rights movement of the 1960s. Instead, the young man broke away. He struggled through college, served a hitch in the U.S. Marine Corps, and generally rebelled against the conventions and institutions of his early youth. For example, he worked his way through the Augustana Lutheran Seminary in Rock Island, Illinois, although he had no intention of becoming a minister or using his degree. He was simply interested in theology.

Vine Deloria, Jr.'s rise in national Indian politics was just short of spectacular. In 1963 he took a position with the United Scholarship Service in Denver, Colorado, where he developed a program to enroll Indian high school–aged students in eastern independent schools. This program was later picked up by the poverty programs and retitled "A Better Chance." In 1964, while attending a convention of the National Congress of American Indians (NCAI) in Sheridan, Wyoming, he ran for and was elected to the directorship of that organization, the largest national political organization of American Indian tribes. His election represented a distinct break with Indian tradition. Previous directors had been of the same age group as the incumbent tribal chairmen. With Deloria's election the NCAI jumped down a generation to choose a much younger man to lead the tribes in their political battles. His election is generally attributed to Clyde Warrior, leader of the National Indian Youth Council who was a skilled organizational politician.

When the older tribal leaders discovered that the younger Indians had in effect engineered a major political coup in Deloria's election, they withheld funds from the NCAI, hoping to force Deloria's resignation and the appointment of an older Indian leader more in tune with their views. Deloria's response was simply to announce that he was filing bankruptcy for the organization, a very unexpected move that brought the reluctant tribal leaders into line and gave Deloria tremendous influence with both Indian youth and longtime organizational dissidents. By the spring of 1966 Deloria had established himself sufficiently so that he was able to hold a low-key protest against Stewart Udall when Udall met in Santa Fe, New Mexico, to organize the Bureau of Indian Affairs program so that it could seek legislation which would have mortgaged Indian trust lands. The Indian tactics used at this protest were the reverse of existing black models of highly publicized protests. Deloria negotiated a set of considerable concessions from the Interior Department based on the threat to hold a public protest. Interior, not wishing to become part of the civil rights headlines, conceded the Indian points.

In the fall of 1966 Commissioner Robert Bennett toured Indian country ostensibly to get Indian opinion on legislative reforms. In fact, a piece of legislation had already been written and John Belindo, Deloria's capable assistant in Washington, D.C., had secured a copy of the proposed legislation. Belindo and Deloria alternately attended each of Bennett's meetings and handed out copies of the proposed legislation. By May 1967 the proposal was so controversial that it was introduced in Congress "By Request," a certain sign that its sponsors did not want the legislation attached to their political careers. During the spring of 1967 Deloria put together a coalition of tribes to protest the construction of Stampede Dam on the California-Nevada border. The tribes pledged to oppose all Interior legislation unless Indian water rights were protected. When the Bureau of Indian Affairs was able to wear down this coalition by administrative pressures against each member tribe, Deloria saw the need for Indian attorneys and decided to resign his directorship and attend law school, one of the first Indians of that day to do so.

In the fall of 1967, Belindo, now director of the NCAI, and Deloria led a protest against the ABC television program on General Custer. They developed the technique of having tribes file fairness petitions against ABC affiliates, and the program aired for only eleven episodes and then disappeared.

During the spring of 1968, the Indian Civil Rights Act was attached to the Black Housing Bill by Senator Sam Ervin of North Carolina. The tactic was designed to have the housing bill committed to the House Interior Committee because it had an Indian provision. Deloria and Belindo arranged that the bill would go directly to the House Judiciary Committee thereby ensuring the passage of the Indian Civil Rights Act and the amendment of PL 280 which gave states jurisdiction over Indian reservations.

During the fall of 1968, Deloria was elected to the Executive Council of the Protestant Episcopal Church. Prior to his first meeting as a member, in fact as the first American Indian ever to serve on a Protestant church's governing board, Deloria sent out a form letter to native clergy across the United States demanding "More Real Involvement" in church affairs. Accordingly, a resolution was passed at his first meeting authorizing a complete overhaul of the church Indian mission work. Deloria resigned from the church board in late August 1969 after having begun a movement within the Protestant churches which saw about six major denominations establish "Indian Desks" to place the church mission work in the hands of American Indians.

In early 1969, Deloria organized a meeting of the urban Indian centers in the United States which produced the first national urban Indian organization—American Indians United. He worked sporadically with urban Indians during that year and began to work with Menominee Indians who were seeking to repeal the Menominee termination act which had transformed their federal reservation into Wisconsin's smallest and poorest counties. In July *Playboy* magazine published a chapter on anthropologists from Deloria's forthcoming book, *Custer Died for Your Sins*. Indians all over the country began to rally and protest against the way in which government, scholars, and churches were treating them. By fall this tide of protest produced the occupation of Alcatraz Island in San Francisco Bay. Deloria had become one of the best-known Indian activists, and when *Time* magazine did an article on Indian activism, it was astonished to learn that he was younger than most of the "new" Indian personalities in the protest movement.

Deloria worked with small tribes on small projects during the early 1970s, assisting the Tonto Apaches and Nooksacks to obtain federal recognition and helping with the fishing rights struggle in the Pacific Northwest. He helped to organize anti-terminationist Colville Indians to oppose pending legislation and to eventually gain control of their tribal council from pro-termination advocates. He worked with the Six Nations peoples in New York State to get legislation to return sacred wampum belts which the State Museum of New York had illegally taken decades before. And he attended several protest meetings in Canada where the Trudeau government was proposing terminal legislation for Canadian Indians.

As the Indian movement gathered steam, Deloria remained in the background and gave advice and provided information for many of the public protests of the period. Answering activist complaints that he was not personally at Wounded Knee, Deloria replied that he could be in court either as an expert witness and attorney or as a defendant and he felt he would be more valuable as an attorney. He was the only Indian attorney to participate in the Wounded Knee trials and was both an expert witness and defense attorney in four of the trials. It was his testimony in the Means-Banks trial in St. Paul, Minnesota, that got the 1868 treaty introduced as evidence of motive for the Indian defendants.

In 1978 Deloria became a professor of political science at the University of Arizona and quickly developed an American Indian Graduate Program with an M.A. degree. He felt that his job was to help train the coming generation of Indian scholars and attorneys. Graduates of this program now serve in tribal programs, teach in community colleges, and are studying for their Ph.D. degrees in various social science fields. Between 1969 and 1985 Deloria published eleven books and approximately 100 articles on a wide range of subjects but most notably Indian political issues. He has been connected with most of the major movements in Indian politics in the past two decades but has adopted a style of action that seeks to minimize public presence because "it eventually makes me ineffective to be too well known." But it is a rare issue that does not have his footprints somewhere in the background.

Deloria's activist tactics can be analyzed under a certain set of rubrics. The first technique is wherever possible to turn a major institution in upon itself so that it is unable to confront Indian opposition effectively. This tactic is probably best illustrated in his Episcopal church resolution but can be seen in his involvement with the issue of reburial of Indian human remains now in the possession of American museums. Here he has been moderately successful in getting cultural anthropologists to support Indians against the archaeologists. When working on the recognition of the Tigua Indians of El Paso, Texas, he was able to pit the state of Texas against the Bureau of Indian Affairs and later with the Tonto Apaches got the Bureau to oppose the Bureau of the Budget.

His most prominent rhetorical technique is to represent radical ideas in conservative language hopefully thereby lulling the opposition to sleep. He is currently advocating a return to a commission form of negotiating with tribes, a modest step which would restore much of the old treaty-making status to the tribes. In early confrontations with the Interior Department he demanded self-determination instead of termination, thereby sounding like a states' rights advocate but in effect helping to establish the procedures for transferring large amounts of federal money directly to tribal governments. His ideas on ecology and land conservation sound like a stuffy Republican of the 1920s but in fact seek to return large areas of North America to a buffalo pasture.

Deloria is extremely wary of American society and consequently refuses to be drawn into issues and controversies that are ideologically attractive but politically impossible to win. He refused, for example, to support the Poor People's March in 1968 because he felt its goals were too broadly stated. But during that period of time he was engaged in smaller problems of federal recognition of tribes, on the theory that if more tribes were recognized than were terminated, Indians would be ahead. He was successful in every venture during this period. Deloria will, however, gladly take a beating from his own Indian constituency if he feels the issue has future importance. He supported the occupation of the Bureau of Indian Affairs, much to the disgust of elected tribal leaders, and participated in the Wounded Knee trials when other Indian attorneys refused on the grounds it would hurt their careers. He has been a stalwart friend and supporter of eastern Indian communities even though their efforts to gain federal rights have been consistently attacked by western Indians.

Much of Deloria's activist work is spent sowing seeds of discontent which he hopes will eventually produce protests and movements. Thus when he advocated support of tribal sovereignty in *Custer Died for Your Sins*, many people accused him of introducing outmoded European ideas into federal Indian law. Within the decade, however, tribal sovereignty had become the catchphrase for much of what tribes wanted to do. He consistently supports traditional religions and the traditional customs even though he lives in an urban area and hardly ever goes to traditional events. He is presently advocating the spiritual dimension of land use planning, an exotic idea that even he is not certain about but which he believes has potential for changing tribal priorities for the future.

Although Deloria serves on a large number of boards, an examination of his organizational affiliations will show that he prefers to align himself with regional groups or with groups devoted to a single issue. He serves as vice chairman of the proposed National Indian Museum, but only as a vehicle to enable him to raise the issue of repatriation. Serving on minor organizational boards was a deliberate tactic because it provided him with a recognizable constituency but did not commit him to national policy shifts as a member of a national board. He was therefore free to criticize national activities on behalf of vaguely defined constituencies.

Vine Deloria, Jr., appeared to be a product of the 1960s and early 1970s but didn't really fit into a comfortable category in either decade. He has such an enigmatic image that he can appear to be both nationally prominent and nationally obscure at the same time. It is only when his perceived interests and ideals are approached that he has taken any action at all. But then he is usually well organized and has some definite goal in mind and is able to raise support to deal with the problem. For example, he helped to hamper and postpone the production of *Hanta Yo*, a dreadful book about the Sioux Indians. When the book did reach television, it was entitled "Mystic Warrior" and was a ratings disaster. By the early 1990s, his persona was that of a regional tribal elder. That is to say, a familiar face. But it was still difficult to tell what was behind that face.

Note

Deloria's 1994 address was at the Department of Ethnic Studies, University of Colorado at Boulder.

Bibliography

Deloria, Vine, Jr. *American Indian Policy in the Twentieth Century*. Norman: University of Oklahoma Press, 1985.

————. *Behind the Trail of Broken Treaties; An Indian Declaration of Independence*. Austin: University of Texas Press, 1985 (1974). Reviewed: *American Indian Quarterly* 10 (Fall 1986): 347–48.

————. "Commentary: Research, Redskins, and Reality," *American Indian Quarterly* 15 (Fall 1991): 457–68.

————. *Custer Died for Your Sins: An Indian Manifesto*. New York: Macmillan, 1969.

————. "Felix S. Cohen's Handbook of Federal Indian Law," *University of Colorado Law Review* 54 (Fall 1982): 121–42.

————. *God Is Red*. New York: Grossett and Dunlap, 1973.

————. "The Invented Indian" (book review), *The American Indian Quarterly* 16 (Summer 1992): 397–410.

————. "It's Time to Be Interested in Indians Again," *The Progressive* 54 (April 1990): 24–27.

————. "Laws Founded in Justice and Humanity: Reflections on the Content and Character of Federal Indian Law," *Arizona Law Review* 31 (1989): 203–23.

————."Minorities and the Social Contract," *Georgia Law Review* 20 (Summer 1986): 917–33.

————. *We Talk, You Listen*. New York: Macmillan, 1970.

Deloria, Vine, Jr., and Sandra L. Cadwalader. *The Aggressions of Civilization: Federal Indian Policy since the 1880s*. Philadelphia: Temple University Press, 1984.

Deloria, Vine, Jr., and Clifford M. Lytle, Jr. *American Indians, American Justice*. Austin: University of Texas, 1983. Reviewed: *American Indian Quarterly* 8 (Fall 1984): 349–50; *American Bar Foundation Journal* 1984 (Summer 1984): 659–71; *Christian Century* 101 (March 7, 1984): 256–57; *Human Rights* 11 (Winter 1984): 37; *Pacific Historical Review* 54 (Feb. 1985): 88–89.

————. *The Nations Within: The Past and Future of American Indian Sovereignty*. New York: Pantheon Books, 1984. Reviewed: *American Indian Quarterly* 11 (Spring 1987): 146–47; *American Political Science Review* 80 (March 1986): 319–20; *Natural History* 94 (Jan. 1985): 76+; *Social Science Journal* 24:3 (1987): 341–42.

Deloria, Vine, Jr., and John G. Neihardt. *A Sender of Words: Essays in Memory of John G. Neihardt*. Salt Lake City: Howe Brothers, 1984.

Johansen, Bruce E. "Dead Indians Out, Live Indians In," *The Progressive* 53 (Dec. 1989): 15–16.

Josephy, Alvin M. *America in 1492: The World of the Indian Peoples before the Arrival of Columbus*. New York: Alfred A. Knopf, 1992.

Lyons, Oren, Vine Deloria, Jr., et al. *Exiled in the Land of the Free: Democracy, Indian Nations, and the U.S. Constitution*. Santa Fe, NM: Clear Light Publishers, 1992.

"Vine (Victor) Deloria, Jr.," in *Contemporary Authors*, vol. 2, New Revision Series. Detroit: Gale Research, 1987: 130–32.

Warrior, Robert Allen. "Vine Deloria, Jr.," *The Progressive* 54 (April 1990): 24–27.

Clifford M. Lytle, Jr.

JAMES FARMER (1920–   )

National director of the Congress of Racial Equality (CORE), 1961–1965; civil rights leader

James Farmer became national director of the Congress of Racial Equality in 1961, after having served as program director of the NAACP since 1959. As head of CORE, Farmer was a prominent spokesman for the civil rights movement. In addition, he acted as tactician and activist and in that capacity instigated the successful Freedom Ride 1961. As an original founder of CORE in 1942, Farmer had experimented with nonviolent, direct-action tactics. When black college students began their lunch counter sit-ins in Greensboro, North Carolina, in 1960, they called upon organizers from CORE to train them in the nonviolent technique. Thus, Farmer must be considered a preeminent figure in the mid-century civil rights movement.

James Leonard Farmer, Jr., was born in Texas on January 12, 1920. He was the first son and second of three children of the former Pearl Houston, a teacher, and Dr. J. Leonard Farmer, the offspring of impoverished former slaves. The elder Farmer, having worked his way through Boston University to a doctorate in theology, became an Old Testament scholar and minister of the Gospel, as well as the first African-American Ph.D. in the state. He qualified as a member of W.E.B. DuBois's "Talented Tenth." Of black, white, and American Indian ancestry, James grew up on the black college campuses where his father taught. While the senior Farmer's position conferred special status in the black community upon his son and gave him partial protection from virulent southern racism, James learned that it did not shield his father, nor ultimately the family, from the indignities of prejudice and segregation in the South.

His autobiography, *Lay Bare the Heart*, describes Farmer's experiences as a PK (preacher's kid) following his father as he moved from one southern black college to another. In 1933, the family returned to Wiley College, in Marshall, Texas, where Farmer had been born and from which he graduated in 1938. Ultimately they arrived at Howard University in Washington. Displaying his gifts early, Farmer entered and won an oratorical contest that earned him a four-year scholarship to college. In 1936 he joined and was elected vice-chair of the National Council of Methodist Youth. This experience awakened his interest in pacifism. Farmer then served as national chair of the Youth Committee Against War and subsequently declined military service in World War II. Although he applied for conscientious objector status, the draft board chose instead to grant him a ministerial deferment. Even though Farmer

James Farmer. *Source*: Library of Congress

was not an ordained minister, the government did not want to add to the ranks of "radical" conscientious objectors. Farmer eased his conscience for taking the easy way out by insisting that the board place on file his personal statement explaining his opposition to war as mass murder and his refusal to fight for democracy in the racially segregated U.S. military.

Upon entry into Howard University, Farmer was introduced to the philosophy of Mohandas Gandhi. Like A. Philip Randolph before him, Farmer realized the applicability of nonviolent direct action as a weapon against racial discrimination. Although he earned a Bachelor of Divinity from Howard in 1941, Farmer refused ordination. Instead, at age twenty-one, he moved to Chicago and became race relations secretary of the pacifist Quaker organization, Fellowship of Reconciliation (FOR). Through FOR, Farmer met other like-minded pacifists and democratic socialists who were also opposed to racial segregation. The interracial group lived in the Hyde Park–Kenwood section near the University of Chicago and staged its first successful sit-in demonstration at the neighborhood Jack Spratt Coffee House, which had refused service to African Americans.

After the success of this strategy in opening the local restaurant and the White City Roller Rink to black patrons, Farmer began to formulate the theoretical underpinnings for a nonviolent, direct-action mass movement against segregation. He drafted a memorandum, "Provisional Plans for Brotherhood Mobilization," for the head of FOR, Rev. A. J. Muste, in which he recommended the organization extend its use of nonviolence to protest against racism. The FOR National Council considered the proposal and voted not to "sponsor" but rather to authorize Farmer, on FOR time, to start a pilot organization in one city—Chicago—along the lines he had suggested. The Chicago FOR group began, in April 1942, what ultimately became the Congress of Racial Equality as an interracial group employing nonviolent direct action. During the 1940s CORE established local chapters in northern, eastern, and western states; developed an unsalaried national staff; and formed an advisory committee. Farmer left the FOR in 1945 because of disagreements with Muste, while remaining active as a volunteer in CORE. He married, although the union lasted only briefly, and, in 1946, found employment with the Upholsterer's International Union of the American Federation of Labor coordinating its southern organizing drive. In 1950 Farmer became youth secretary for the democratic-socialist League for Industrial Democracy in New York City. He then returned to labor, in 1955, when he found work with Jerry Wurf's District Council 37 of the State, County, and Municipal Employees Union, a position which provided him with the opportunity to visit fifteen African countries.

In 1959, Roy Wilkins invited Farmer to join the staff of the National Association for the Advancement of Colored People as program director. In that capacity, Farmer wrote a memo interpreting the motivation, philosophy, and goals of the student sit-ins, but because of the NAACP's emphasis on legal action, they found it difficult to understand "any tactic which involved violation even of the local law." The old-line, hierarchical NAACP shied away from activism for fear of antagonizing its contributors. This stand brought it into conflict with the newer, democratic, protest-driven southern groups. The former wanted to pursue equality through the courts, while the latter thought that street demonstrations were more effective. Differences developed between Farmer and Wilkins, in part because of the restraints imposed on Wilkins by his position as head of the bureaucratic organization. In his autobiography, Farmer revealed how organizational rifts became personal and petty as the civil rights groups competed for publicity and funds.

Meanwhile, Farmer and a few colleagues like James Robinson, Bernice Fisher, James Peck, George Houser, and Lula Peterson, who became Farmer's second wife, had kept CORE going as a voluntary group devoted to nonviolently fighting racial discrimination. Lacking full-time leadership, the organization made only slow progress toward its goal. The Montgomery bus boycott of 1955 and the emergence of Martin Luther King, Jr. (*), revived CORE's fortunes by popularizing the techniques the members had been using and experimenting with on a smaller scale through the years. Then, in February 1960, four black college freshmen sat down at a segregated dime-store lunch counter (Woolworth's) in Greensboro, North Carolina. They refused to move until they were served. A white businessman, Ralph Johns, had read CORE's pamphlet, *Erasing the Color Line*, which documented the organization's sit-ins of the 1940s. Johns had tried for several years to convince students to sit in. He finally "struck pay dirt" with the four students in 1960 and called in CORE organizers to train them. Thus there was an intellectual connection between CORE's previous nonviolent demonstrations and the students. Early in 1961, overcoming their objections to his interracial marriage, the faithful decided to offer Farmer the job as the first national director of CORE. They hoped he would be able to provide the leadership to move the group to the forefront of the Civil Rights movement. Farmer accepted the job, leaving the NAACP.

Fulfilling his sponsors' hopes, Farmer helped to make much of the history of the mid-century Civil Rights movement. Prior to 1961 the organization had only a few salaried staff members. Farmer changed the structure, adding new departments and staff both at headquarters and in the field. By 1964 there were 124 affiliated CORE groups, and the income of the national went from $60,000 in 1959 to $900,000 in 1964. Reaching back into the past, Farmer embellished FOR and CORE's 1947 Journey of Reconciliation idea. This had tested enforcement in the upper South of the Irene Morgan decision barring discrimination in interstate travel. Farmer developed the Journey into Freedom Ride 1961, wherein integrated groups of nonviolent activists rode interstate buses into the Deep South to verify whether buses, terminals, restaurants, and rest rooms were complying with Supreme Court orders to desegregate their facilities. According to Farmer, "Whites will sit and eat in 'Colored Sections' and Negroes will sit and eat in the 'White Sections.' They will refuse to accept segregation in any form: if need be they will accept threats, violence and jail sentences." Participants were selected from volunteers who had been active in nonviolent demonstrations. They were specially trained to cope with the brutality they expected to encounter. Replacements were also chosen to take the places of any participants who might be arrested.

The Freedom Riders, with Farmer among them, were subjected to attacks by unruly mobs of segregationists. At that point, members of the Student Nonviolent Coordinating Committee (SNCC), which had been formed by the student activists, came to the aid of the beleaguered Freedom Riders with fresh recruits. News coverage of the protesters' travail did not stave off white rage as the Freedom Riders finished their journey from Montgomery, Alabama, to Jackson, Mississippi. The Freedom Rides not only played an important role in desegregating interstate transportation facilities, but they also catapulted CORE into the front ranks of the civil rights movement.

In one of the most moving chapters in his autobiography, Farmer revealed his reluctance to join the Freedom Ride to Jackson after he had missed the Alabama portion of the Ride because of his father's funeral. He confessed that only after a young girl shamed him into it, did he board the bus at the last moment. Farmer was proud of the fact that, although afraid, he participated in the Freedom Ride while Martin Luther King avoided some of the more perilous situations, even when confronted by student activists.

The publicity accorded the Freedom Rides made Farmer one of the "Big Six" civil rights leaders. He took his place beside A. Philip Randolph, head of the Negro American Labor Council; Martin Luther King, Jr., and his Southern Christian Leadership Conference; Roy Wilkins, Whitney Young of the National Urban League; and John Lewis of the SNCC. In addition to the Freedom Rides, CORE held classes in nonviolent resistance and organized sit-ins and picketing which desegregated variety store lunch counters in the South in 1960. In the North they picketed Woolworth's, asking people to assist the southern movement by boycotting the dime-store chain. Farmer also masterminded the Freedom Highways project of 1962, which opened Howard Johnson and Holiday Inn facilities along the southeastern coast to African Americans. The demonstration on opening day of the New York World's Fair in 1964 called attention to local employment, housing, and school discrimination.

CORE joined with the Southern Regional Council, the SNCC, and the SCLC to register black voters. The 1964 Mississippi Summer Project was a joint effort of CORE, SNCC, SCLC, and the NAACP, which, as the Council of Federated Organizations (COFO), worked in voter registration, community centers, and freedom schools. Two CORE members, black James Chaney and white Michael Schwerner, along with COFO summer recruit Andrew Goodman, became the first fatalities of the Mississippi Freedom Summer of 1964. The discovery of their bodies buried beneath an earthen dam near the town of Philadelphia brought CORE further notoriety.

During the 1950s, CORE groups with a primarily black membership had been established in southern and border states. The interracial character of the northern chapters also changed during the 1950s and 1960s, as more blacks than whites joined the organization. While initially the northern CORE groups directed their activities against discrimination in public accommodations, later the emphasis shifted to employment, education, and housing. As these goals proved to be more threatening to many whites, however, they had limited success.

At the height of the movement, in the early sixties, the civil rights groups began to bicker among themselves as they contested for funds and prestige. In his books, Farmer revealed much of the dissension that occurred within the Council of United Civil Rights Leadership, to which all the organizations belonged. Yet he indicated that in many ways the leaders continued to work together. Farmer alerted King that he was under electronic surveillance by the FBI; Wilkins sent a check for a thousand dollars to the hard-pressed CORE. Most important, Thurgood Marshall supplied $300,000 from the NAACP Legal Defense and Education Fund which provided bail bond money for CORE activists jailed in Jackson, Mississippi.

As the Civil Rights movement was beset by discord, CORE's nonviolent tactics and interracial philosophy faced growing opposition. Younger activists came to see the goal of equal rights and opportunities as a "kind of cruel joke" and began to demand "compensatory and remedial" treatment to improve the quality of life in the ghettos. The rise of the black nationalist ideology divided the organization's staff, officers, and membership. Many of CORE's black leaders and workers believed not only that the civil rights drive was being stymied by white violence in the South, but also that white leadership undermined black self-esteem and that white inactivity at the federal level had the effect of co-opting the movement.

Under pressure, although the staff remained interracial, Farmer made certain CORE's top leadership was in the hands of African Americans. The primary goal became organization of the masses. Realizing the potential power of the ghetto, CORE workers decided to drop their traditional policy of political neutrality "and organize the Negro community, house by house, block by block, into political units." They then planned to form the small units into larger alliances. Instead of expending all their energies making demands on the "power structure" from outside, CORE intended to act as a catalyst so African Americans could create their own centers of political power with leadership coming from the ghetto. While Farmer respected Randolph and Bayard Rustin's broad alliance of black and white poor, organized labor, church groups, and white liberals, he thought that the black poor had to first organize themselves so they could enter into the coalition with power and on a basis of equality. African Americans should be free to integrate if they desired, he argued, but by 1965 the emphasis had shifted to black pride.

Thus CORE went from a middle-class, predominantly white, group of pacifists to a predominantly black action group, but the price was internal disruption. CORE's interracial policy was the greatest point of contention, but the philosophical basis of the entire Civil Rights movement, nonviolence as well as interracialism, was being challenged by the Black Power movement, and black consciousness clashed with white participation.

Farmer himself was not immune from the strife, barely surviving several attempts to replace him as head of CORE. In 1961, James Robinson, a white CORE officer, tried unsuccessfully to remove Farmer and put Rev. Fred Shuttlesworth in his place. In 1964, a group led by A. J. Muste, his old mentor, tried to replace Farmer with Bayard Rustin (*) as CORE's leader. Realizing that because of his white wife he would not survive another coup attempt by Black Power forces in CORE, Farmer resigned in 1965. Farmer planned to head an adult literacy drive, reasoning that although the civil rights movement had opened the doors of opportunity, millions of people might not be able to walk through because of their inadequate education. His literacy plan was thwarted when Adam Clayton Powell, Jr., head of the Labor and Education Committee of the House of Representatives, capitulated to a request from President Lyndon Johnson and recommended against funding Farmer's project at the last moment. Johnson returned this favor by having a libel suit against Powell dismissed.

Disappointed, Farmer began to teach civil rights courses at Lincoln University in Pennsylvania and at New York University. In 1968 he ran for a congressional seat from Brooklyn on the Liberal ticket, but lost to Democrat Shirley Chisholm (*). Farmer later became an assistant secretary in the U.S. Department of Health, Education, and Welfare in the Nixon administration. Farmer argued that civil rights proponents needed an ally in the Nixon White House. He resigned after two years because the administration sought his endorsement of G. Harold Carswell, a segregationist, to the Supreme Court. In 1975 Farmer returned to the labor movement, becoming executive director of the Coalition of American Public Employees. Having secured the position through the intercession of Jerry Wurf, Farmer found himself without regular employment after Wurf's death in 1981. Farmer also began losing his sight, eventually becoming totally blind. In 1987 he suffered a minor heart attack.

While he was still involved in his first brief marriage, Farmer met Lula Peterson, a Phi Beta Kappa in economics from the University of Chicago, at a CORE meeting. They subsequently married, in 1949, and had two daughters, Tami Lynn and Abbey Lee. Lula Farmer remained active in CORE work through the years. She died of Hodgkin's disease in 1977, leaving Farmer distraught. After his departure from the Public Employees Coalition, Farmer moved to Fredericksburg, Virginia, where, as a distinguished visiting professor, he taught classes on the history of the Civil Rights movement at Mary Washington, a state-run, liberal arts college. His students' papers had to be read to him and he graded them orally.

Farmer was still on the lecture circuit in 1993 and working on a book about current issues in the African-American community, a project he envisioned taking two or three more years to complete. Progress was slow because Farmer had to dictate the work. He was involved in a Thirtieth Anniversary Commemoration of the Freedom Rides held in Jackson, Mississippi, July 18–21, 1991. The theme, "A Look Back—A Leap Forward," reflected Farmer's desire to make the occasion an opportunity to deal with current problems as well as a reunion for the Freedom Riders.

Farmer's philosophy evolved through the years from a simple concern with the elimination of racial discrimination and the opening of "opportunity," a "colorblind" approach to American society, to "color-consciousness" and the belief that American blacks should identify with their African heritage. He had tried to mediate between middle-class blacks and their demands for equal opportunity and middle-class whites who would have had to forgo some of their privileges in order for black demands to be met. It was movement work that caused Farmer to become concerned with his identity as an African American. In his book *Freedom—When?*, Farmer traced the way in which his ideology, and that of CORE, altered as a result of experience to an emphasis on race and nationalism and the acquisition of a mass base. Farmer admitted his philosophical debt to Malcolm X (*). African Americans had to rid themselves of their self-hate and accept their blackness. No one else could give them their freedom; they had to "achieve freedom for themselves." For CORE, that meant the organization no longer existed to "serve Negroes," but rather it became "a Negro organization." Yet, for all his emphasis on individual self-respect and racial awareness, Farmer never personally advocated black chauvinism.

In the beginning CORE, like the early abolitionists, operated under the belief that "truth alone" would convert segregationists. From their encounters with reality, CORE members learned that what men believed ultimately mattered less than the way, as a result of external pressure, they could be made to behave. Although a pacifist, Farmer agreed with Gandhi that it was preferable to resist evil with force than to fail to resist out of fear.

As the Civil Rights movement expanded beyond its original middle-class base to encompass the masses in the streets, the potential for violence increased. Nevertheless, Farmer argued that demonstrations were effective in gaining their objectives, in encouraging mass action, and engendering self-confidence in the participants. Farmer's original theory in *Freedom—When?* lay in his observation that street demonstrations really acted as a safeguard against violence. He pointed out there were no riots in Harlem in the summer of 1963 when there were hundreds of mass demonstrations, but Harlem erupted in a major riot in 1964 when there were few street demonstrations. Likewise, during the civil rights demonstrations in Birmingham, Alabama, in 1963, that city also experienced a decline in crime. Perhaps, he concluded, the impulse to riot could be channeled into orderly demonstrations.

His more black-conscious philosophy was not appreciated by President Lyndon Johnson, however. Farmer and Johnson had had a good working relationship, and Farmer had enjoyed an open door to the president. But after passage of the Civil Rights Act, in the summer of 1964, Johnson asked the Big Six civil rights leaders to stop street demonstrations because he thought they would have a detrimental effect on Johnson's campaign for the presidency. Roy Wilkins called a meeting in which he and Bayard Rustin asked for a Moratorium on Demonstrations. They did not specifically say they were acting at the behest of the White House, but they implied that the request came from Johnson. Farmer refused to sign the Moratorium as did John Lewis, while Wilkins, Young, King, and Randolph agreed to the Moratorium because of their desire to defeat Barry Goldwater for president. In part, Farmer resisted because he thought it would be a disaster if they said they were going to call off demonstrations and the demonstrations continued because the leaders did not have the power to stop them.

After he voted against the Moratorium, however, Farmer could no longer reach the president by telephone. Johnson became even more enraged and less accessible after a CORE resolution, which Farmer opposed, calling for withdrawal of American troops from Vietnam. Personally against the war, Farmer did not favor CORE's becoming involved in the anti-war movement because he thought it would draw attention away from the race problems, and it might open the door to Communist infiltration. As Johnson became more deeply involved in Vietnam, in 1965, his priorities changed and his commitment to civil rights lessened. Farmer's refusal to accept the Moratorium and the war probably contributed to Johnson's refusal to support Farmer's literacy project.

Following his resignation, in March 1965, Farmer endorsed Floyd B. McKissick over the more integrationist George Wiley as his successor to the post of national director of CORE. Meeting in convention in July, under the leadership of McKissick, CORE officially endorsed black separatism and discarded its former commitment to nonviolence. At its 1967 convention, National CORE omitted "multiracial" from its constitution. At the 1968 convention, Roy Innis ousted McKissick and changed the CORE constitution to exclude persons not of African descent, a course previously taken by SNCC. These actions cost CORE its liberal white support, however, and the organization neared collapse. Farmer noted that before Black Power there had been disagreement over tactics, but after Black Power there was disagreement on goals and objectives which led to the disintegration of the movement.

There is no question that a major part of CORE's success in the early 1960s came as a result of Farmer's charismatic leadership. Yet according to August Meier and Elliott Rudwick in their book on CORE, Farmer was a poor administrator and had difficulty making decisions. Certainly there were contradictions in Farmer's behavior. Did he accept the position in the Nixon administration because, as head of CORE, he had become used to the spotlight and did not want to give it up? Like Randolph, Farmer was both a democratic socialist and a committed anti-communist. In 1944, he fought successfully for a provision in CORE's constitution excluding communists. Does antipathy to communism explain his relationship with FBI executive Cartha (Deke) DeLoach, who warned Farmer of a planned coup to replace him as head of CORE with someone more amenable to the communists?

In his autobiography, Farmer candidly admitted his personal shortcomings. He berated himself for what he called the "greatest tactical oversight" of his life, failing at the time of the Freedom Rides, in 1961, to "move for a merger between CORE and SNCC," a step that "would have unified the action wing of the movement." Farmer also acknowledged being somewhat jealous of King's success with the bus boycott in Montgomery; Farmer had been preaching nonviolent civil disobedience for many years without recognition.

Yet one cannot gainsay Farmer's stewardship and creativity, his effectiveness as a fund-raiser and communicator, his friendly charm and approachability. Farmer was notable as well for his willingness to participate in local demonstrations and identify with the hardships and sacrifices of his followers. In contrast to King, who preferred to be bailed out quickly, Farmer stayed in jail with the other demonstrators. He was the only member of the Big Six, for example, to pass up the opportunity to make a speech at the March on Washington in 1963, choosing instead to remain incarcerated in Plaquemine, Louisiana. He was also loyal. Unlike the other civil rights leaders, Farmer developed a personal relationship with Malcolm X and was the only one of the group to attend the slain Muslim's funeral. Perhaps most important, by refusing to give in to his handicap and continuing to be a productive citizen, Farmer provided an exemplary role model.

Farmer's place in the history of the mid-century Civil Rights movement is assured. From his experiments with nonviolent civil disobedience and the founding of CORE in 1942, to his resignation from that organization in 1965, Farmer played a major role in the fight for civil rights. He continued his work by imparting knowledge of the movement to the young.

Bibliography

Bell, Inge Powell. *CORE and the Strategy of Nonviolence.* New York: Random House, 1968.

"Civil Rights Activist James Farmer Feted at 73rd Birthday Jubilee," *Jet* 83 (April 17, 1993): 16–17.

Collison, Michele N-K. "One of the 'Big Four,' A Civil-Rights Leader Keeps History Alive," *Chronicle of Higher Education* 35 (Feb. 22, 1989): A3.

Farmer, James. *Freedom—When?* New York: Random House, 1965.

———, interviewed by Harri Baker (Oct. 1969) and Paige Mulhollan (July 20, 1971); Oral History Collection, Lyndon Baines Johnson Library, Austin, Texas.

———, interviewed by Paula Pfeffer, via telephone, May 30, 1991.

———. *Lay Bare the Heart: An Autobiography of the Civil Rights Movement.* New York: Arbor House, 1985. Reviewed: *The Crisis* 92 (June/July 1985): 18+; *Dissent* 33 (Winter 1986): 116–19; *The Humanist* 46 (Jan./Feb. 1986): 44; *Journal of Southern History* 52 (May 1986): 326–27; *Labor History* 28 (Winter 1987): 112–14; *The Nation* 240 (May 4, 1985): 535–37; *New Leader* 68 (March 25, 1985): 14–15; *New Republic* 192 (April 1, 1985): 33–34+; *New York Times Book Review* 90 (March 24, 1985): 20–21.

———. "Where Does the Civil Rights Movement Stand Today?" *The Humanist* 45 (Nov./Dec. 1985): 5–10.

Forman, James. *The Making of Black Revolutionaries*, 2d ed. Washington, DC: Open Hand Publishing, 1985.

Meier, August, and Elliott Rudwick. *CORE: A Study in the Civil Rights Movement, 1942–1968.* New York: Oxford University Press, 1973.

Newman, Debra. "Farmer, James," in *The Encyclopedia of World Biography: Twentieth Century Supplement.* Palatine, IL: Heraty and Associates, 1987: 459–60.

Papers of the Congress of Racial Equality, 1941–1967. State Historical Society of Wisconsin, Madison, Wisconsin.

Papers of the Congress of Racial Equality: Addendum, 1944–1968. Martin Luther King, Jr. Center of Nonviolent Social Change, Inc., Atlanta, Georgia.

Peck, James. *Freedom Ride*. New York: Simon and Schuster, 1962.

Paula F. Pfeffer

LOUIS ABDUL FARRAKHAN (1933–   )

Minister of the Nation of Islam

At the beginning of the 1990s Minister Louis Farrakhan had emerged as one of the most controversial black leaders and one of the strongest proponents of black nationalism. From Los Angeles to Boston and from the rural counties of the Mississippi Delta to the black metropolis of Detroit, Minister Farrakhan has been able to draw large audiences, often numbering from 5,000 to over 40,000 people. On television and radio, his audiences are even larger. He has the forensic ability to deliver silver-tongued oratory or he can lash out with angry denunciations and veiled death threats. Surrounded by Fruit of Islam security guards with closely cropped hair and dressed in suits and bow ties, Minister Farrakhan remains an enigma to the American public. Who is he? What does he want and what is his message?

Born Louis Eugene Wolcott in 1933 in the Bronx, New York, he was raised in Boston by his West Indian mother. Deeply religious, Louis faithfully attended the Episcopalian church in his neighborhood and became an altar boy. With the rigorous discipline provided by his mother and his church, he did well academically and graduated with honors from the prestigious Boston English High School, where he also participated on the track team and played the violin in the school orchestra. In 1951, he attended the Winston-Salem Teachers College in North Carolina for two years before he dropped out to pursue a career in music. Able to play the violin and piano as well as sing, Wolcott performed in the Boston nightclub circuit as a singer of calypso and country songs. In 1955 at the age of twenty-two, Louis Wolcott was recruited by Malcolm X (*) to the Nation of Islam. Following the custom of the Nation, he dropped his surname and took an X, which meant "undetermined," ex-slave, ex-Christian, ex-smoker, ex-drinker, ex-mainstream American. However, not until he had met the Honorable Elijah Muhammad, the supreme leader of the Nation of Islam, on a visit to the Chicago headquarters did Louis X convert completely and dedicate his life to building the Nation. After Louis had proved himself for several years, Elijah Muhammad gave Louis his Muslim name of "Abdul Farrakhan." As a rising star within the Nation, Minister

Louis Abdul Farrakhan.
Source: Library of Congress

Farrakhan also wrote the only song, "A White Man's Heaven is A Black Man's Hell," and dramatic play, "Orgena" or "A Negro" spelled backwards, allowed by Muhammad.

If anyone in the Muslim movement closely resembles Malcolm X in career and style, it is Louis Abdul Farrakhan. Although he is shorter than Malcolm, he is also as fair-skinned as Malcolm was. Both of them also had mothers who came from the Caribbean. Moreover, Minister Farrakhan's career path has been almost exactly the same as Malcolm's. After a nine-month apprenticeship with Malcolm at Temple No. 7 in Harlem, Minister Louis X was appointed the head minister of the Boston Mosque, which Malcolm founded. Later, after Malcolm X had split with the Nation, Farrakhan was awarded Malcolm's Temple No. 7, the most important pastorate in the Nation after the Chicago headquarters. He was also appointed National Spokesman or National Representative after Malcolm's demise and began to introduce the Hon. Elijah Muhammad at Savior Day rallies, a task which once belonged to Malcolm. Like his predecessor, Farrakhan is a dynamic and charismatic leader and a powerful speaker with the ability to appeal to the masses of black people. Both men also started newspapers for the Nation. Malcolm founded *Muhammad Speaks* (now called the *Muslim Journal*) in the basement of his home. In 1979 Louis Farrakhan began printing editions of *The Final Call*, a name which he resurrected from early copies of a newspaper that Elijah Muhammad had put out in Chicago in 1934. The "final call" was a call to black people to return to Allah as incarnated in Master Farad Muhammad, or Master Fard, and witnessed by his Apostle Elijah Muhammad. For Farrakhan, the final call has an eschatological dimension; it is the last call, the last chance for black people to achieve their liberation (Mamiya, 1982; 1983).

The major difference between them is that while Malcolm X was evolving, changing his views from the proto-Islamic black nationalism of the Nation to that of Sunni orthodoxy, Louis Farrakhan has remained more or less consistently the same. In fact, after Malcolm left the Nation, it was Minister Louis X who led the public attack in a series of scathing articles in *Muhammad Speaks* in 1965, denouncing Malcolm's new position and calling him an "international hobo." Some passages read like a veiled death warrant although Louis eventually leaves vengeance to Allah (Goldman, 1979:248):

Only those who wish to be led to hell, or to their doom, will follow Malcolm. The die is set, and Malcolm shall not escape, especially after such evil, foolish talk about his benefactor.... Such a man as Malcolm is worthy of death, and would have met with death if it had not been for Muhammad's confidence in Allah for victory over his enemies.

Fifteen years later in a speech in Harlem on May 18, 1980, Farrakhan still described Malcolm X's defection from the Nation and his turning his back on Elijah Muhammad as a negative example:

Yes, I even stand on Malcolm X. If Malcolm had not made the turn that he did, I would not have a guide to keep me from making the same mistake. He was an example for me instead of me being an example for him. He knew one day that I would be the National Representative. Because he died I have a chance to live.

The assassination of Malcolm X on Sunday, February 21, 1965, however, has remained problematic for the Nation of Islam. Some black people, including some in the generation who were born after the 1960s, have blamed the Nation of Islam for Malcolm's death. While the final responsibility for Malcolm's death still remains unclear, Minister Farrakhan has claimed that as far as he knew, no one in the Nation's hierarchy of leadership, neither Elijah Muhammad, the other ministers, nor himself, ever gave any orders, directly or indirectly, to kill Malcolm. However, he said, "we may have created a climate that contributed to his death." Malcolm's martyrdom has continued to haunt the Nation.

The death of the Honorable Elijah Muhammad in February 1975 also contributed to major internal problems for the Nation of Islam and led to the largest schism that the movement has experienced in its history. The leadership hierarchy of the Nation chose one of Elijah's sons, Wallace Deen Muhammad, as Supreme Minister, replacing his father as the head of the organization. In April 1975 Wallace, who later took the Muslim name Warith Deen Muhammad, declared that whites were no longer considered "devils" and could become members; there were neither black Muslims nor white Muslims, "all were children of God" (*Nashville Tennessean*, April 19, 1975). He began to make radical changes within the organization, disbanding the Fruit of Islam, getting rid of racist and separatist teachings, and reinterpreting other doctrines for consistency with orthodox Sunni Islam. Imam Warith Muhammad also changed the name of the organization. In 1976 Muhammad renamed it the "Community of Al-Islam in the West," and in 1980 he changed the name to the "American Muslim Mission." In 1985 he disbanded the central organization and allowed independent masjids. Many members left immediately after the radical reforms by Warith Muhammad, and a number of schismatic groups were formed by some disaffected leaders like Silas Muhammad in Atlanta, John Muhammad in Detroit, and Caliph in Baltimore. Minister Louis Farrakhan, however, did not make a schismatic break until 1978, when he succeeded in resurrecting the old Nation of Islam, retaining the black nationalist and separatist beliefs and doctrines which were central to the teachings of Elijah Muhammad. From 1975 until 1978, Farrakhan traveled extensively to Muslim countries and found a need to recover the focus upon race and black nationalism that the Nation had emphasized. In the early years of the resurrected Lost-Found Nation of Islam, he was introduced as the spiritual reincarnation of the Honorable Elijah Muhammad at Savior Day celebrations in February 1981 and 1982. Farrakhan's own position on the death of Elijah Muhammad is somewhat elusive. Sometimes he claims that Elijah did not die in a Chicago hospital but is still alive, and at other times he is proclaimed as the spiritual reincarnation of Elijah Muhammad. In 1982 it was estimated that Farrakhan's charismatic presence had attracted a hard-core membership of about 20,000 followers, which has probably tripled in size in 1993.

The message and the program of Louis Farrakhan's "second resurrection" of the Nation of Islam are basically the same as those under Elijah Muhammad. Black nationalism exhibits itself in the following ways. First, Farrakhan has kept the Black Muslim creed (Shahadah), which views Master Fard as Allah incarnate (God is Black), and his Apostle, the Honorable Elijah Muhammad who personally knew and saw Allah. Second, he has left intact the central myth of Yakub, the black mad scientist who rebelled against Allah by creating the white race as a weak hybrid race, as well as other doctrines like the Black

Man as the Original Man, the Battle of Armageddon, and whites as Devils. Farrakhan has also elaborated on a belief of Elijah Muhammad that Unidentified Flying Objects are satellite ships sent from a gigantic mothership, which is shaped like a wheel, and eventually this wheel will rescue righteous black people from the coming apocalypse that will engulf the earth and wicked people. In September 1985 Farrakhan claimed to have a vision of the mothership and its satellites (*Washington Post*, March 1, 1990: p. A16ff.). These myths and doctrines function as a theodicy for the Black Muslims, as an explanation of and rationalization for the pain and suffering inflicted upon black people in America.

Third, Farrakhan's program includes the same ten demands for the liberation of all black people found in every issue of the earlier *Muhammad Speaks* newspaper. But he has placed strong emphasis upon the demand for a separate territory or land for black people. The reason for this emphasis is that at a time when black nationalism has waned in the 1980s and assimilation has continued apace with a large increase in the black college student population since the 1960s, the demand for a separate land underlies in the strongest way possible the continued alienation of the members of the Nation from American society and their rejection of the American way of life. When asked about the realism of demanding a separate territory, Farrakhan replied, "Anything is possible. Blacks are owed this land as reparation for centuries of slave labor. Besides, whoever thought that the Vietnamese would win against the United States? Yet they defeated the mightiest power in this world. Anything is possible in this world. Insh'allah" (Mamiya, Interview, 1980; Mamiya, 1982).

Prior to the 1984 presidential campaign of the Reverend Jesse Jackson (6*), Minister Louis Farrakhan was largely unknown to the American public and the media. Part of his strategy for avoiding the media was again due to Malcolm X's negative example of being a favorite media personality. The Jackson campaign, however, led to a change in that strategy by focusing media attention on Farrakhan and the Nation. In the fall of 1983 Minister Farrakhan transformed one of the cardinal rules of the Nation of Islam by registering to vote and by providing the Fruit of Islam security guards for the Jackson campaign. Under Elijah Muhammad Black Muslims were enjoined not to participate in electoral politics since they did not regard themselves as "Americans" and owed no allegiance to this country. Elijah and some of his sons even spent time in prison for refusing the draft. However, with Farrakhan's decision that members of the Nation could now participate in politics, there were deep hopes in the black community that the earlier split between the heroic black leaders, Martin Luther King, Jr., (*) and Malcolm X, could be reconciled by the joining of forces by Jackson and Farrakhan; the uniting of the civil rights movements with the black nationalist contingent. In February 1984, Jackson used the words "Hymie" and "Hymietown" in his conversation with a black reporter, Milton Coleman, of the *Washington Post*. Coleman's publication of the incident and Jackson's attempt to defend himself stirred a storm of protest by Jewish groups and the media. Minister Farrakhan entered the fray by threatening to "make an example" of Coleman for betraying a heroic black leader and leaving the punishment in the "hands of Allah."

After leaving the Jackson campaign because of the controversy he stirred, Farrakhan continued to exacerbate the tensions between African Americans and Jews by making a series of allegedly anti-Semitic remarks in his public speeches. For example, he is accused by the B'nai B'rith of viewing Judaism as a "gutter religion"; calling Hitler a "great man" but "wickedly great"; and criticizing a "Jewish-controlled media." His criticisms of Israel and Zionism in the Middle East conflict were also viewed as anti-Semitic by mainline Jewish groups. Farrakhan has defended himself by protesting that his comments and speeches were taken out of context and distorted by the media. He has also claimed that his remarks were directed against the mistreatment of Palestinians by Zionists in Israel rather than against Judaism as a religion (*The Final Call*, June 1984; Walter Goodman, *The New York Times*, March 29, 1990: p. C22). "Louis Farrakhan is not an enemy of America, not an enemy of Jews, not an enemy of white people," he said in a *Washington Post* interview. "To say that Louis Farrakhan is antisemitic is an unfair characterization of me" (Nathan McCall, *Washington Post*, March 2, 1990).

The reactions to the Farrakhan controversy in the national black community have been diverse. Some mainstream black leaders like Mayor David Dinkins of New York City, Mayor Tom Bradley of Los Angeles, and author Paul Robeson, Jr., have been highly critical of Farrakhan's alleged anti-Semitism. Other leaders like the Reverend Calvin Butts of the Abysinnian Baptist Church in Harlem have recognized Minister Farrakhan's growing constituency and influence. However, Butts has also disagreed with some of Farrakhan's public statements as "divisive" and "irresponsible" (DeWayne Wickham, Gannett News Service, *Poughkeepsie Journal*, December 1990). But the majority of black leaders and clergy, while disagreeing with some of Farrakhan's views, have also resisted the efforts of Jewish groups to pressure them to publicly denounce and repudiate him. As Les Payne, national editor of *New York Newsday*, said on Gil Noble's show "Like It Is":

> Forced repudiation is not repudiation at all, it's a kind of moral extortion. The demands for black leaders to repudiate someone is not only dangerous, but also racist because it assumes that black leaders have collective responsibilities for Minister Farrakhan's public utterances.

It is clear that after a decade of attempting to rebuild and re-establish the base of the Nation of Islam, Minister Farrakhan is fully in charge of deciding the new directions for the Nation of Islam. In recent years, he has repurchased the building of the former Temple No. 2, the Nation's headquarters in Chicago, from Warith Muhammad and renamed it Mosque Maryam. He has also encouraged his followers to re-establish the economic base of the Nation through small businesses like distributing Power Pac cosmetics. Black Muslims also took part in anti-drug crusades across the country, and in Washington, D.C., they patrolled the Mayfair Mansions. Besides allowing his followers to vote in American elections, Farrakhan has made it possible for some of them to run for office in Washington, D.C. In 1990 Abdul Alim Muhammad ran for a seat in the House of Representatives, and George X Cure campaigned for the D.C. delegate seat, while Shawn X Brakeen was a candidate for the school board (McCall, *Washington Post*, May 5, 1990: p. B1). Although they were unsuccessful, Minister Farrakhan has hinted that members of the Nation may enter other elections since there was a need for moral leadership among black people (McCall, *Washington Post*, May 9, 1990: p. D1). By allowing political participation in American politics, he has cleared the path of the separatist barriers that Master Fard and Elijah Muhammad had erected, which had earlier blocked Malcolm X's deep desires to actively participate in the upheavals of the civil rights movement (James Cone, 1991).

Besides political participation, another innovation that Farrakhan has supported is the move toward Muslim unity among the varying sects of African-American Muslims. At the second General Meeting of the Continental Council of Masajid of North America in the fall of 1990, he surprised everyone by reciting the "Shahadah," the basic Muslim creed that affirms belief in Allah, the One Lord and Creator, and belief in the Prophet Muhammad. But in his address to the Continental Council, Minister Farrakhan also encouraged other Muslims to re-evaluate the work and contributions of the Honorable Elijah Muhammad and his teacher Master Fard Muhammad. These two leaders had paved the way for the widespread acceptance of Islamic teachings in black communities. In a rare show of Muslim unity, both Imam Warith Deen Muhammad and Imam Sarraj Wahaj, leaders of the largest groups of orthodox African-American Muslims, accepted Minister Farrakhan into their fold on the basis of his profession of faith. "I have made the decision to accept Minister Louis Farrakhan," said Warith Muhammad, "upon what he has said today. . . . I think we can accept him and let him have his role and let us respect him in his role. That's my decision today" (*The Final Call*, October 31, 1990: pp. 2, 6). This move toward creating "Ummah" (community) among the different Muslim groups in the United States and the respect shown to Farrakhan have left him in a favorable position. While there has been some speculation that his profession of the Shahadah was merely pragmatic, especially to open the Nation of Islam to more contributions from oil-rich Arab nations besides those from Colonel Qaddafi and Libya, only time and Farrakhan's future actions will allow fair judgment.

Originating in 1930 as an obscure group, the Nation of Islam, or the Black Muslim movement in its various forms, is the longest lasting and most enduring of the black militant and separatist movements in the United States (Mamiya and Lincoln, 1988). For about forty years, Minister Louis Farrakhan has been closely associated with the Nation, rising through the leadership ranks and emerging as its supreme charismatic leader in the 1980s and 1990s. Through leaders like Elijah Muhammad, Malcolm X, and Farrakhan, one of the most significant accomplishments of the Nation of Islam was to help change the self-perception and ethnic definition of more than thirty million black Americans from a stance of self-hatred, identity confusion, and inferiority to one of self-affirmation, ethnic pride, and dignity. Spearheaded by the efforts of the Nation, the Black Consciousness movement of the late 1960s and early 1970s helped to change the symbolic language of an entire country from "Negro" to "Black." The terms "Negro" and "Colored" are now used only to refer to past historical periods.

Another important accomplishment involves the reclamation of the broken lives of several million poor black people who either were in prison or trapped by drugs, alcohol, and crime. With the growth of the sector of the black poor to more than one-third of the black population and with the dismantling of the civil rights gains and programs of the 1960s during the Reagan-Bush era, Minister Farrakhan's messages of black unity, self- knowledge, independence, and critique of American society have struck a responsive chord among the black masses. Rap groups and rappers like Public Enemy and Prince Akeem have helped popularize the appeal of the Nation, with songs such as "It Takes a Million to Hold Us Back" and "Coming Down Like Babylon" (*Final Call*, June 17, 1991: p. 6). Membership in the Nation of Islam has reached beyond 60,000, with a much larger number who have been influenced by the minister's preaching and teaching.

In the meantime, Minister Louis Abdul Farrakhan has shown himself to be remarkably adept at both stirring and surviving a broad range of controversies throughout his career in the Nation of Islam.

Bibliography

Cone, James. *Martin and Malcolm and America: A Dream or a Nightmare?* Maryknoll, NY: Orbis Books, 1991.

Essien-Udom, E. *Black Nationalism: A Search for Identity in America.* Chicago: University of Chicago Press, 1962.

Farrakhan, Louis. *Back Where We Belong: Selected Speeches by Minister Louis Farrakhan,* Joseph D. Eure and Richard M. Jerome, eds. Philadelphia: PC International Press, 1989.

———. Interview by Nathan McCall, *Washington Post,* March 1, 1990, A16ff.

Final Call, 1979–June 1991.

Goldman, Peter. *The Death and Life of Malcolm X.* Urbana: University of Illinois Press, 1979.

Haddad, Yvonne Y., and Adair T. Lummis. *Islamic Values in the United States: A Comparative Study.* New York: Oxford University Press, 1987.

Lincoln, C. Eric. *The Black Muslims in America,* 3d ed. Grand Rapids, MI: Erdmann, 1993.

———. "The Black Muslims and Black Acceptance," in *The Black Experience in Religion,* C. Eric Lincoln, ed. Garden City, NY: Doubleday, 1974.

Lomax, Louis F. *When the Word Is Given*. New York: Signet Books, 1963.

Maesen, William A. "Watchtower Influences on Black Muslim Eschatology: An Exploratory Story," *Journal for the Scientific Study of Religion* 9 (Winter 1970): 321–35.

Mamiya, Lawrence H. "From Black Muslim to Bilalian: The Evolution of a Movement," *Journal for the Scientific Study of Religion* 21:2 (1982): 138–51.

———. "Minister Louis Farrakhan and the Final Call: Schism in the Muslim Movement," in *The Muslim Community in North America*, Earle Waugh, Baha Abu-Laban, and Regula Qureshi, eds. Edmonton: University of Alberta Press, 1983: 234–51.

Mamiya, Lawrence H., and C. Eric Lincoln. "Black Militant and Separatist Movements," *Encyclopedia of the American Religious Experience*, Charles H. Lippy and Peter W. Williams, eds. New York: Scribner's, 1988: II; 755–71.

Marsh, Clifton E. *From Black Muslims to Muslims: The Transition from Separatism to Islam, 1930–1980*. Metuchen, NJ: Scarecrow Press, 1984.

Muhammad, Elijah. *Message to the Black Man in America*. Chicago: Muhammad Mosque of Islam No. 2, 1965.

———. *The Supreme Wisdom: Solution to the So-Called Negroes' Problem*. Chicago: Muhammad Mosque of Islam No. 2, 1957.

Muslim Journal (previously *Muhammad Speaks*, *The Bilalian News*, and *The American Muslim Journal*), 1964–June 1991.

Waugh, Earle, Baha Abu-Laban, and Regula B. Qureshi, eds. *The Muslim Community in North America*. Edmonton: University of Alberta Press, 1983.

X, Malcolm and Alex Haley. *The Autobiography of Malcolm X*. New York: Grove Press, 1964.

Lawrence H. Mamiya

JAMES FORMAN (1928–   )

Leading figure in the Student Nonviolent Coordinating Committee, revolutionary black leader

James Forman achieved national recognition in the early 1960s as a central leader of the Student Nonviolent Coordinating Committee (SNCC), the most radical of the civil rights organizations. By the mid-1960s, Forman was one of a handful of the best known and respected revolutionary black organizers and theorists in the United States.

Forman was born in Chicago and served in the U.S. Air Force during the Korean War. In the late 1950s he continued his education, receiving a B.A. from Roosevelt University and pursuing graduate work at Boston University. Working for the Chicago *Defender*, he traveled to the South to report on the growing civil rights movement. But he could not remain an observer. By 1961, he was elected executive secretary of SNCC. He held this position until 1966.

James Forman. *Source*: Library of Congress

The high point of Forman's political life was his time with SNCC, an organization which constituted the left wing of the Civil Rights movement. SNCC initiated or participated in important activities of the movement in its most active phase (1960–1965). In 1961, SNCC members took up the Freedom Rides in Montgomery, Alabama, when they appeared to have been stopped by racist violence. SNCC worked to register black voters throughout the South. In November 1963, SNCC organized a "Freedom Vote" in Mississippi, where blacks throughout the state, denied a role in the regular election, participated in a mock election. In 1964, SNCC initiated the Mississippi Freedom Summer, comprehensive activities to register voters and attack segregation. The summer culminated in the formation of the Mississippi Freedom Democratic party (MFDP), which challenged the legitimacy of the segregated regular Democratic party. The MFDP was denied all but a token role at the national Democratic party convention in Atlantic City.

But SNCC came to an impasse after Freedom Summer. The organization turned inward as it confronted the new post–civil rights phase of the struggle. Although Forman continued to be associated with SNCC, he stepped down from the position of executive secretary, in part due to ill health.

In February 1968, Forman was drafted into the leadership of the Black Panther party as minister of foreign affairs, but in July 1968, he resigned. After attending a Black Economic Development Conference (BEDC) in Detroit, in April 1969, Forman became the leader of the permanent BEDC organization which arose from that meeting. BEDC, essentially an amalgamation of Forman's SNCC supporters with members of the Detroit-based League of Revolutionary Black Workers (LRBW), demanded reparations from white churches for their role in the historical degradation of blacks. Simultaneously, Forman joined the LRBW leadership, where he was a foremost advocate of the creation of a Black Workers Congress (BWC). Although the BWC's founding convention in 1971 drew more than 400 delegates from across the country, the organization soon disintegrated. In the mid-1970s Forman returned to graduate school, receiving a Ph.D. from the Union for Experimental Colleges and Universities in 1982.

Like Black Panther leaders Huey Newton and Bobby Seale (*), Forman attempted to develop a political theory which synthesized black nationalism with Marxian class analysis. The most important of Forman's writings is *The Making of Black Revolutionaries* (1972), a comprehensive personal and political autobiography. Speeches and writings from the late 1960s are collected in *The Political Thought of James Forman* (1970). Forman's doctoral thesis, a theoretical work written mainly in the late 1970s is published as *Self-Determination and The African-American People* (1981).

Forman's political trajectory through the 1960s closely parallels that of the left wing of the black movement. In 1961, when he began working for SNCC, Forman adopted, with some reticence, the philosophy of nonviolence. His distinctive contribution to SNCC in the early 1960s was the level of organizational sophistication he imparted to a group that generally mistrusted organized leadership. When SNCC nearly split between direct action and voting rights factions, Forman welded them together by pointing out that the hostile reaction of white racists to any efforts to promote black rights rendered this distinction secondary. By the mid-1960s Forman accepted the turn to armed self-defense and black nationalism, which culminated in the Black Panther party's ideas and activities.

Between about 1965 and 1967, SNCC was at the center of the transformation of the black movement. Fresh on the heels of significant victories in national politics (the passage of the 1964 Civil Rights Act and the 1965 Voting Rights Act), the black movement was forced to face the more daunting task of challenging racism embedded in the economic, political, and social institutions of the whole society, not just the South. This led SNCC to turn inward in an examination of its basic principles. Confronted with racist violence,

SNCC abandoned the philosophy of nonviolence, in practice, by 1965, in favor of armed self-defense. By then most SNCC field workers were carrying guns.

A more serious problem was the role of whites in the black movement. A logical extension of the ideal of black self-determination in the black community was black control of their own organizations. This was a delicate subject in SNCC because hundreds of northern white students had participated in Freedom Summer, and eighty-five had been put on the paid staff afterward. This created tensions, as blacks felt whites were playing too great a role. The most extreme critics argued that organizations for the advancement of black self-determination should be exclusively black. Eventually Stokely Carmichael took up this position, as he became an internationally known advocate of Black Power. Grudgingly, Forman accepted this idea as well.

Forman's overall worldview in the late 1960s is perhaps best understood in contrast to Carmichael's. Carmichael argued that African-Americans constituted a colonized people. This condition necessitated that they close ranks in black separatist organizations for the promotion of a positive self-identity and for self-determination. Black Power signified a struggle for full participation for blacks in decisions that affected their own lives. This outlook explicitly rejected class analysis. As Carmichael said at a Black Panther rally in 1968, neither communism nor socialism was suited to blacks because neither addressed the problem of racism. Blacks must develop "an African ideology which speaks to our blackness—nothing else." There was no place in this outlook for white allies or for "white" doctrines such as Marxism.

Forman accepted part of this outlook. He argued that the first priority was developing a *black* organization, although he was clearer than Carmichael in advocating an explicitly revolutionary group. But Forman rejected Carmichael's separatism as "pure skin analysis." There had to be some reckoning between black nationalism and class analysis. For one thing, a class analysis of the independent black African states showed that many were controlled by "bourgeois nationalists" who continued to exploit the African masses. Applied to SNCC, Forman's class analysis criticized the role of middle-class black liberals. SNCC failed to identify sufficiently with poor and working-class blacks.

Forman believed that self-determination in the black community could not succeed without fundamental changes in the political and economic system of the United States. The ultimate victory against racism would come only with socialist society. Such a society would replace the profit system with production for human needs. It could be created only by a revolutionary party of which blacks would form the vanguard. Because Forman viewed the process of revolutionary change as directed by a revolutionary elite, he never confronted the problem of changing the consciousness of the majority of white workers. Instead, he thought only of white radicals who would play a supportive role for the black vanguard.

It was much easier for Forman to put his politics into practice in 1960–

1965 than it was afterward. In the early years of SNCC the issues and the tactics were practically ready-made: segregation and disenfranchisement were already being fought by sit-ins, street demonstrations, and campaigns to register voters. Forman's organizational skills made SNCC's efforts more effective, but he did not invent the tactics or devise SNCC's program of activities. After 1965, it was more difficult for Forman to link his political outlook to concrete activities or specific organizational objectives. Like many black leaders in the late 1960s, Forman was increasingly ideological and abstract.

Forman's later work, *Self-Determination*, attempts to set forth a theoretical justification for African-American political autonomy in the Black Belt of southern states. Blacks constitute an oppressed nation in their "historic homeland," a region roughly coterminous with the states of North Carolina, South Carolina, Georgia, Alabama, and Mississippi, and including parts of other states. In much of this region, blacks once formed the majority of the population. Forman calls for autonomy within the United States, not an independent African-American state, which was long a stated demand of the Communist party. Forman argues that black organizations should immediately initiate negotiations with the U.S. government for autonomy in the Black Belt. This immediacy appears to be the main advantage of the autonomy demand; Forman does not counterpose it to continued progress toward an independent African-American state nor to a struggle for socialism.

The main problem with Forman's thesis is that he did not counter the argument that African-Americans constituted a small and shrinking part of the southern population (18 percent in 1980, down from 25 percent in 1930). This was due to massive out-migration, mostly to northern and western cities. Since the 1970s the majority of American blacks have lived outside the South. This population shift weakened the argument that blacks comprise an oppressed nation (as opposed to an oppressed racial or national minority) in the Black Belt, since "concrete territorial boundaries" are crucial to Forman's definition of a nation. *Self-Determination* may reflect a post-1960s pessimism in Forman, as he speaks of the creation of no new organizations, nor of popular struggle, relying instead on negotiations by existing black organizations for autonomy.

Forman lists a host of black nationalist thinkers and writers as the main sources of his thought. In the late 1950s he digested works of Gandhi on nonviolence. Forman agreed with the position of Kwame Nkrumah, president of Ghana, who argued for nonviolence if possible, but action of all kinds against racism. Forman justified the rural orientation of SNCC in the early 1960s in terms of Che Guevara's works. Forman met Guinea's president Sékou Touré on a trip to Africa in 1964. Touré convinced Forman that American black organizers should see exploitation, not just racial oppression, as the central problem to be addressed. Forman credits, above all, the work of Frantz Fanon for its influence on his thought in the 1960s. Fanon was a psychiatrist who participated in the Algerian national liberation struggle in the 1950s, and authored *Black Men, White Masks* (1952) and *The Wretched of the Earth* (1963).

Forman embraced Fanon's left-wing nationalism, with its critique of bourgeois nationalism in the independent African states, its advocacy of an armed struggle against imperialism, and its identification of the "lumpenproletariat," or black urban underclass, as the central force for revolutionary change. Although Forman explicitly embraced Marxism in the late 1960s, he does not identify specific writers from the socialist tradition for their influence on him.

Forman, a leading figure in SNCC, played a key role in destroying segregation in the South. It is unlikely that the victories so often attributed to Martin Luther King, Jr. (*), could have been achieved in the 1960s without the heroic intervention of SNCC workers at the local level. The registration of almost three million new black voters in the South between 1962 and 1968 laid a foundation for the rise of black electoral politics. SNCC was also the first organization of national importance to promote a radical black nationalism in the 1960s.

During the early 1960s, SNCC developed a distinctive style of organizing. SNCC's grassroots radicalism led it to be suspicious of leaders who were not accountable to members. Central to its critique of other civil rights organizations was SNCC's advocacy of "group-centered leadership" instead of "leader centered" organizations. This radicalism led SNCC to become a model for black militancy and for the New Left, which emulated SNCC's idea of a movement which strove to develop everyone as a leader.

Much of the criticism of Forman has been based upon political differences. The national Democratic party saw SNCC as a nuisance, at best, and, at worst, a dangerous and destabilizing threat. Civil rights leaders such as Roy Wilkins of the NAACP and Whitney Young of the Urban League openly attacked SNCC's direct-action philosophy.

Within SNCC, Forman was the foremost leader of those who emphasized organizational discipline and administration. People who were more individualistic criticized him as dictatorial. After 1965, Forman also clashed with separatists who rejected any alliances with whites. Although Forman shared much of the Black Panther leadership's political outlook, he was never fully integrated into its leadership, and relatively spurious personal differences appear to have led to his resignation.

In their book on the League of Revolutionary Black Workers (LRBW), *Detroit: I Do Mind Dying*, Dan Georgakas and Marvin Surkin criticize Forman's role in the disintegration of the LRBW. They argue that Forman intensified factionalism within the LRBW, and contend that his thought was an unsystematic series of demands coupled with organizational suggestions. They attack Forman for shifting the LRBW's focus from organizing over shop floor issues to a vague ideological struggle. Thus, in the Black Workers Congress, Forman never formulated concrete local activities as the focus of ongoing work. On the other hand, they contend that "more than anyone else associated with the League, James Forman had been an open advocate of the women's liberation movement."

The theoretical task set by Forman by the late 1960s was the fusion of Marxism with black nationalism. There are inherent problems in this project. First of all, Forman and other black nationalists had trouble identifying *which* Marxism they were drawing on. In *Rediscovery of Black Nationalism*, Theodore Draper speaks of "do-it-yourself Marxism" which fails to distinguish Marx from Lenin, or Trotsky from Stalin and Mao. As a result, there are basic confusions. For instance, Fanon spoke of the lumpenproletariat as the central force for revolutionary change in a colonized situation; Lenin insisted on the leading role of the industrial working class, even in a country such as turn-of-the-century Russia, with its overwhelmingly peasant population. Although Forman considered himself a revolutionary, he defined revolution in a variety of ways. Sometimes it referred to "any struggle for dignity." While Forman termed the nonviolent students of SNCC to be revolutionary almost from the very start, he ultimately argued that only armed struggle could bring about revolutionary change. The term lost the precision it had, at least in the classical Marxist tradition. To the extent that he defined it, Forman's socialism was of an elitist variety. Change was directed from above, by a black revolutionary vanguard, in the interests of the masses. Forman may have defined revolution in this way because Maoism was the most popular form of Marxism in the Third World during the 1960s.

Bibliography

Cagin, Seth. "Children of Radicals," *Rolling Stone*, Sept. 26, 1985, pp. 91–92+.

Carson, Clayborne. *In Struggle: SNCC and the Black Awakening of the 1960s*. Cambridge: Harvard University Press, 1981.

Draper, Theodore. *The Rediscovery of Black Nationalism*. New York: Viking Press, 1975.

Forman, James. *The Making of Black Revolutionaries*, 2d ed. Seattle: Open Hand Publishing, 1985.

———. *The Political Thought of James Forman*. Detroit: Black Star Publishing, 1970.

———. *Sammy Younge, Jr.: The First Black College Student to Die in the Black Liberation Movement*. Seattle: Open Hand Publishing, 1986.

———. *Self-Determination and the African-American People*. Seattle: Open Hand Publishing, 1981.

Georgakas, Dan and Marvin Surkin. *Detroit: I Do Mind Dying*. New York: St. Martin's Press, 1975.

Haskins, James. *Profiles in Black Power*. Garden City, NY: Doubleday, 1972.

Jefferson, Alphine W. "Forman, James," in *The Encyclopedia of World Biography: 20th Century Supplement*. Palatine, IL: Heraty and Associates, 1987: 492–93.

Kunstler, William Moses. *Deep in My Heart*. New York: Morrow, 1966.

"Paying for the Sins of the Past," *Newsweek* 112 (May 22, 1989): 44.

Glenn Perusek

JOSÉ ANGEL GUTIÉRREZ (1944–   )

Founder of La Raza Unida; Chicano leader

The multitalented José Angel Gutiérrez served as a foremost spokesperson, organizer, and theorist for the Chicano or Mexican-American protest movement. He was the driving force behind the creation of two significant cultural and political organizations in the movement, the Mexican-American Youth Organization and La Raza Unida (The United Race); and drawing upon his graduate studies in political science, he used his speeches and writings to lay out influential plans for Chicano political action. Early in his career he gained national attention and illustrated the successful application of his own theories for obtaining power when he created a movement which overthrew the Anglo power structure in Crystal City, Texas. He soon became the head of the city's school board and then county judge. After the Chicano Movement lost its force, Gutiérrez moved to a career as a college professor in Oregon and subsequently returned to Texas to become a lawyer. He continued to speak frequently for improvements in the lives of Mexican-Americans in the Southwest.

The son of a medical doctor, José Angel Gutiérrez was born in Crystal City, Texas, in 1944, into a family free of the poverty which plagued many Mexican-American families in his community. Although he was president of the student body and a star debater in high school, shortly after graduation he served notice that his future would be spent combatting rather than joining the established order. In 1963 he first attracted national attention by helping elect five Mexican-Americans to the Crystal City city council and consequently instilling in Mexican-Americans a new awareness of their potential political power in the community. As a student at St. Mary's University in San Antonio in 1967, he continued to demonstrate the power of organizing when he and four other young Chicanos founded the Mexican-American Youth Organization (MAYO), an activist group which sought social change and trained young Chicanos for leadership positions in the community. Upon receiving an M.A. in political science in 1969 he returned to Crystal City and began organizing Mexican-Americans to pursue various causes. In that year he also served as an advisor to protesting Chicano students who staged a walkout at the local high school.

In 1970 Gutiérrez helped organize a Chicano political party, La Raza Unida, to gain power in Crystal City. The party immediately elected several members to the city council and enough members to control the school board—who chose Gutiérrez as the first Mexican-American president of the board. After expanding into other parts of Texas and then into other states, La Raza Unida became a national political party and elected Gutiérrez as its chairman. He

José Angel Gutiérrez.
Source: Legal Center of
José Angel Gutiérrez

left that position in 1979 to spearhead efforts to link La Raza Unida with various groups in other nations. From 1974 to 1980, even as he labored to further the Chicano Movement and while he was completing his Ph.D. in political science from the University of Texas, he served as county judge in Zavala County, Texas, and hence as chief administrative officer, chief fiscal officer, and chief election officer. Upon resigning as judge, he moved to Oregon where he first directed the International Studies Department at Colegio Cesar Chavez in Mt. Angel. He then taught political science at Western Oregon State College as well as headed its effort to recruit minority students. In 1986 he returned to Texas to begin law school in Houston. By the 1990s, he worked in Dallas as a lawyer and executive director of the Greater Texas Legal Foundation, a nonprofit organization which sought justice for poor people.

His original goals and methods in the 1960s raised basic questions about Mexican-Americans within U.S. society. He was convinced that Mexican-Americans should unite to challenge the Anglo power structure in the Southwest, that the Republican and Democratic parties had not been and would not be responsive to the needs of Mexican-Americans, and that the traditional Mexican-American organizations failed to develop young leaders or engage in direct-action projects and community organization. He created activist political organizations such as MAYO and La Raza Unida. MAYO was founded as a vehicle for young Chicanos to create meaningful change. Well educated and unafraid of confrontations with Anglos, MAYO's young leaders sought control of the educational systems in Chicano communities and the creation of Chicano businesses and cooperatives which would break the economic domination of Anglos. La Raza Unida exemplified a common phenomenon of the period: young, educated Chicanos returning home to organize their communities in order to change conditions. Gutiérrez had a definite program to allow Mexican-Americans to end their dependence on Anglos and improve their lives. Once members of La Raza Unida gained control of the school board, for example, they instituted a program of bilingual education from kindergarten to the third grade and bicultural education (Chicano studies) in secondary education. They also eliminated the use of I.Q. and English proficiency tests, adopted textbooks which told of the contributions of Chicanos to American society, and provided free breakfasts and lunches for all students. Thus for once Mexican-Americans were making major decisions on subjects which affected their lives, inspired by Gutiérrez who had shown them how to use the political system.

Gutiérrez relied heavily on effective organizing and skillful public address as means to his ends. His organizing reflected a pattern born of a series of his insights: members of the community should first raise complaints and concerns; the organizer should mobilize the people, highlight their issues, and build on the people's frustration; and ultimately the organizer must propose and work for a solution.

Gutiérrez also developed a set of practical principles for the organizer-persuader. Concerning time and space, for example, he learned that commitments could be gained from men by talking to them in bars in a particular manner; that most people willingly listened and discussed issues early in the evening; and that listeners were most responsive in common settings, such as when men were sitting in cars waiting for women to finish shopping or women were in the laundromat or under the hairdryer in the beauty shop. Moreover, he discovered that to engender unity he should speak at churches, bars, and other places people voluntarily went rather than at special events called for the purpose of a speech.

Gutiérrez's early experiences as a high school debater and later experiences as an organizer taught him additional principles of persuasion. He learned to adapt to his audience's needs and expectations. He discovered differences between speaking in English and Spanish, in rural versus urban settings, and at college campuses versus other settings. He understood the need to show proper deference to cultural differences and to symbols important to particular audiences. His own speeches reflected several primary purposes: to create a sense of unity among Mexican-Americans, to change their perceptions of themselves and of Anglos, and to stimulate confrontations with the power structure. He attempted to achieve unity by employing positive terms around which Mexican-Americans could unite. Those terms include "Chicano" to identify the community; "Aztlan" to define a Chicano homeland; "La Raza" and "La Raza Unida" to signify a sense of unity against a common foe; and "Brown" to refer to skin color. He also frequently talked of the Catholic church because of its significance to Mexican-Americans. At the same time he built solidarity by applying negative terms such as these to the Anglo: devil, Gringo, bigot, un-American, racist, animalistic, foreigner, thief, exploiter, and barbarian.

His goal was to restructure the reality of Mexican-Americans to instill a sense of pride in them and in their communities. Anglos had portrayed Chicanos as lacking any history of dissent or worthwhile culture and as being decidedly inferior to Anglos. Historians, social scientists, the media, popular culture, and even the government had created this false image of Chicanos, and many Chicanos had accepted it. To transform the community first required removing these negative images.

One means Gutiérrez used to elevate Chicanos' self-esteem was to make Anglos responsible for the problems of Mexican-Americans. For example, he argued that policies and practices of Anglos caused Mexican-Americans to suffer from poor health care, unfair treatment by police and the legal system, disproportionately high percentages of those sent to fight and die in foreign wars, and inadequate formal education which resulted in unemployment and underemployment. Once aware of the extent of and consequences of this devastating treatment by Anglos, Chicanos would be more willing to fight for change. Although Gutiérrez saw organizations like La Raza Unida as essential to providing social, economic, and political means in the necessary confrontations with the Anglos, he warned that violence may at times be necessary in the struggle.

Gutiérrez's writings complemented his oratory. He expressed his theories on Chicano organizing, the need for dissent, and Chicano politics in works like *La Raza and Revolution* and *El Politico: The Mexican American Elected Officials in Texas*. In *A Gringo Manual on How to Handle Mexicans*, written in English and Spanish, he discussed clever tricks used by Anglos to keep Chicanos in an inferior position. Employing many means of persuasion, he wrote a poem, "22 Miles," which created a haunting image of the first twenty-two years in the life of a Mexican-American.

While Gutiérrez's quest to improve the lives of Mexican-Americans never changed, he did alter his tactics to conform to the nature of organizations he led and to changes in society. As a young college student and as an organizer in his hometown, he angrily confronted the Anglo power structure and formed MAYO and La Raza Unida—composed of young, educated Chicanos who rejected established organizations—alternatives to traditional political groups. Similar to many African-Americans, American Indians, and white college students of the period, young Chicanos rejected many of the values, beliefs, and institutions of society. And like the other activist groups, Chicano organizations lost prominence, popularity, and power in the mid-1970s because of a variety of reasons, including the loss of the Vietnam War as a focal point of dissent, a lack of central organization and unified methods, harassment by government agencies, the emotional and physical burn-out of many activists, and the rise of a wide range of other issues including ecology, energy concerns, gay rights, and women's rights.

A strength of the movement, its youth and spontaneity, also may have been a weakness. Because its leaders were often inexperienced, much of the protest lacked direction and was driven by anger rather than visions for change. Moreover, there were conflicting political ideologies, strategies, and personalities.

After the demise of the Chicano Movement, Gutiérrez joined with many other militants in returning to college and redirecting his activism into local movements within the established system. As a university professor and later as a lawyer, he has worked for change through more mainstream channels. At the end of the 1970s, for example, he spoke out about the importance of the census to minorities, saying that the undercounting of minorities lost them political representation and social benefits. Broadening his emphasis of population numbers, he pointed out that nonwhites would soon be a majority and would one day witness a White House painted brown.

By 1980, political life for Mexican-Americans had clearly improved in the Southwest. To Gutiérrez, however, the triumph of seeing the Democratic and Republican parties both court Mexican-American voters was diluted because these parties had co-opted issues of the Chicano Movement as well as some of its leaders. Gutiérrez himself reflected this pattern in 1984 when he ran as an independent for the Oregon legislature. His campaign literature highlighted his experience as a college professor, member of a local school board, and six years as a county judge, but omitted the location of the school board and any mention of his affiliation with La Raza Unida. His platform stressed increasing jobs, reducing property taxes, educating youth, outlawing nuclear waste, paying attention to senior citizens, respecting law and stopping crime, reducing school dropout rates, and encouraging proficiency in languages other than English.

As a lawyer in the 1990s Gutiérrez continued to work for the concerns of Hispanics in the Southwest. Although he had softened his confrontational style, he still advocated many of the same positions he favored when a member of La Raza Unida. As executive director of the Greater Texas Legal Foundation, he orchestrates an effort to overcome institutional barriers which limited Hispanic representation in American society by promoting such issues as redistricting of voting districts and helping farm workers recover lost wages. His broad goal is to help people improve their lives and to upgrade the quality of justice for poor people throughout the country.

Gutiérrez, in the 1990s, spoke and wrote on a broad range of issues. Changing world conditions had convinced him that the traditional concept of nation was outmoded. The United States' strong ties to Mexico and Central and South America, he argued, required opening the border between Mexico and the United States, teaching immigrants how the system can work for them, and granting resident aliens the right to vote. He also advocated providing working mothers with free health care before and after their children are born, cutting school dropout rates to increase students' ability to contribute to the new technological-informational age, reducing the influence of extraterritorial lobbies like those of the Japanese and Israelis, and making structural changes in governmental institutions in order to reduce tensions between Hispanics and African-Americans.

The Chicano Movement brought many significant changes to the United States. It left Mexican-Americans with a more positive self-image, increased pride in culture, reinforced rights to exercise their language and traditions, a greater sense of community, higher national visibility of their community, and new Chicano Studies programs in colleges. The movement headed by Gutiérrez and others also brought forth a new class of Hispanic political leaders and created a climate of activism and opportunity which subsequently allowed mainstream Hispanic political figures like San Antonio Mayor Henry Cisneros and Denver Mayor Federico Pena to reach once-unobtainable offices. When Mexican-Americans in the Southwest learned the necessity of acquiring the skills for organizing, they began to mobilize, speak up, assume leadership positions, and then change the world. Perhaps the most symbolic testimony to the impact of Gutiérrez was in Crystal City, where Hispanics still maintained a majority on the school board and in the offices of city and county governments.

Bibliography

"Former Flamethrower Gutiérrez Still Scorching Dems," *Houston Chronicle*, April 4, 1993, D2:2.

García, Ignacio M. *Until We Win: The Rise and Fall of La Raza Unida Party*. Tucson: MASRC, the University of Arizona, 1989.

Gutiérrez, José Angel. "A Youth Manifesto," in *Manifesto Addressed to the President of the United States from the Youth of America*, ed. Alan Rizler. London: Collier Books, 1970.

———. "Mexicanos Need to Control Their Own Destinies," in *La Raza Unida Party in Texas*. New York: Pathfinder Press, 1971.

———. *La Raza and Revolution: The Empirical Conditions of Revolution in Four South Texas Counties*. San Francisco: R & E Research Associates, 1972.

———. *El Politico: The Mexican American Elected Officials in Texas*. El Paso: Mictla Publications, 1972.

————. " 'Societal Pie' Sliced Wider for Hispanics," *The Progressive* 54 (Nov. 1990): 25–26.

Hammerback, John C., Richard J. Jensen, and José Angel Gutiérrez. *A War of Words: Chicano Protest in the 1960s and 1970s.* Westport, CT: Greenwood Press, 1985.

Jensen, Richard J. "An Interview with José Angel Gutiérrez," *Western Journal of Speech Communication* 44:3 (Summer 1980): 213–19.

Jensen, Richard J., and John C. Hammerback. "Radical Nationalism among Chicanos: The Rhetoric of José Angel Gutiérrez," *Western Journal of Speech Communication* 44:3 (Summer 1980): 191–202.

Meier, Matt S. "José Angel Gutiérrez," in *Mexican American Biographies: A Dictionary, 1836–1987* (Westport, CT: Greenwood Press, 1988): 98–99.

"Where to From Here?" (a symposium by the Left, including Gutiérrez), *The Progressive* 54 (Nov. 1990): 4, 17–32+.

Richard J. Jensen
John C. Hammerback

FANNIE LOU HAMER (1917–1977)

Black community organizer

Fannie Lou Hamer changed her life and the lives of countless other black and white Americans by the simple act of raising her hand at a meeting. The time was late August 1962. The place was a small church in Ruleville, Mississippi. She publicly declared that she was willing to challenge white power by insisting upon her right to vote. When she later attempted to register, Mrs. Hamer was fired from her job. Her life began to change. She became a voter registration leader and was severely beaten in a Mississippi jail. She went on to gain wide notoriety by challenging the president and vice president of the United States, the Democratic party, and the U.S. House of Representatives.

Fannie Lou Hamer was the twentieth of twenty children of Jim and Ella Townsend. She was born in Montgomery County, Mississippi, on October 6, 1917. Her parents, who were sharecroppers, had moved to Sunflower County two years later. Although they lived within the constraints of a harsh economic system, they imbued Fannie Lou with the sense that she could resist, not simply react. They had a pride in themselves that led her to question authority based solely on a person's being white. She also learned a deep religious faith that encouraged physical endurance and spiritual strength. Despite all that happened to her at the hands of whites, Fannie Lou Hamer refused to hate them. "Ain't no such thing as I can hate anybody and hope to see God's face," she would say.

Fannie Lou had a sixth-grade education. She attended school for six years during those few months that black children in Mississippi were not working

Fannie Lou Hamer. *Source*: Library of Congress

in the cotton fields. She was nonetheless a voracious reader. She sometimes jumped off a truck to pick up a scrap of paper to read, or picked up whatever book or magazine she found in her boss's house when she was cleaning or sitting with someone who was ill.

When Fannie Lou was little, her father managed to scrape together the money to rent land and buy machinery and farm animals. But a jealous white neighbor poisoned the stock; the family was hard hit by the loss. After each cotton crop was harvested, her mother would take several of her children and get landowners' permission to pick the hard-to-get wisps of cotton left in the fields. Through this "scrappin' cotton," she earned money to help the family exist through the winter. Fannie Lou's father died in 1939; her mother, infirm and virtually blind, lived with her youngest child until she died in 1961.

Fannie Lou Townsend married Perry Hamer in 1944. He was a strapping young farm worker who had come to the Delta from the hill country around Kilmichael, Mississippi. The Hamers took in two girls whose parents could not raise them themselves. When the older daughter, Dorothy, died in 1967, the Hamers adopted her two small daughters, Lenora and Jacqueline, and raised them as well.

Known as a leader around the W. D. Marlowe plantation outside Ruleville where she worked as a timekeeper, Mrs. Hamer had long questioned the inequalities she saw around her. Then, in the summer of 1962, young people from the Student Nonviolent Coordinating Committee came to Sunflower County. They had begun voter registration drives in several parts of Mississippi and were trying to win the confidence of the people in Ruleville. At one community meeting, James Forman (*) and the Reverend James Bevel spoke about how black people could start taking control of their lives. They could register to vote and elect officials who cared more about them than did the existing sheriffs and mayors. Mrs. Hamer was convinced. She put up her hand when they asked who would go with them to try to register.

She and seventeen others were soon on a bus heading for the courthouse in Indianola. They were frightened about how they would be treated at the registrar's office. They also worried about what would happen when they got home that night. In the midst of the fear came a woman's voice, singing every spiritual she knew; it was Fannie Lou Hamer. Singing became integral to her mission, as in years to come she would use music to calm people's fears, or to get them to start talking to one another, or to send them out to work rededicated. She would sing with people on the Boardwalk outside the Democratic National Convention, in demonstrations with Dr. Martin Luther King, Jr. (*), and on the same platform with Malcolm X (*) or Harry Belafonte or Judy Collins. Her public speaking compared in cadence and content, although hardly in polish, with the better educated Dr. King, but her singing gave her an added motivational power as her voice soared over those in her audience.

No one registered that day in August 1962. The registrar asked Mrs. Hamer to interpret a section of the Mississippi Constitution. It dealt with "facto laws." Hamer said later, "I knowed as much about a facto law as a horse knows about Christmas day." When Mrs. Hamer got home that night, she was fired from her job and told to leave the plantation. A few nights later, while she was staying with friends in Ruleville, nightriders fired shots into that home; she was out of the house at the time. Tensions ran so high that she briefly left Sunflower County, but when she came back she said she didn't care what happened to her, she was in civil rights to stay. She started speaking throughout the country to raise money for the voter registration work.

In 1963, she attended training workshops sponsored by the Southern Christian Leadership Conference. Returning by bus from one such workshop in Charleston, South Carolina, she and several other civil rights workers were arrested at the bus station in Winona, Mississippi, and charged with disorderly conduct. Several of the members of the group had tried to use the lunch counter and washroom. Such facilities were supposed to be integrated, following court decisions, but many places in the South, including Winona, had not complied. Several of the jailed group were beaten by law officers. The leader of the group, Annell Ponder, an SCLC worker, was struck repeatedly because she refused to call the law officers "sir." Several officers directed two black inmates to use a blackjack on Mrs. Hamer, who suffered pain for the rest of her life as a result of that beating. After several days, the group was released on bail. They then learned that while they had been in jail, NAACP leader Medgar Evers had been shot and killed in front of his Jackson home.

The Justice Department brought civil and criminal charges against the law officers. When the trial was held in the federal court in Oxford in December of 1963, the U.S. attorney, H. M. Ray, made an emotional plea for conviction, but the men were all acquitted. The all-white jury took the word of the white law officers, not the black plaintiffs and the U.S. government.

At this point, SNCC called for outside help to register voters. SNCC reasoned that only when white America's college students were involved in the drive (as they had been in small numbers during the fall of 1963) would the brutality stir the country. Others argued vehemently against the move, saying it would undermine development of local leadership. Mrs. Hamer, a SNCC staff member, was involved in that planning. She argued that local black registration workers needed all the help they could get. She also helped orient the Freedom Summer volunteers in Oxford, Ohio, and worked with them in Ruleville, which became a center of movement activity.

SNCC and the Freedom Summer volunteers signed up potential voters and helped organize a new political party to challenge white domination. Everything that the Mississippi Freedom Democratic party did had the same aim: to involve local people and to show them the role that they could have in governing themselves. MFDP might not win an election or a lawsuit or a challenge, but it always pressed its case so that these voters, with so little experience in democracy, would see what was possible. Mrs. Hamer was a strong advocate of education through participation. She ran for office and filed lawsuits, confronting the local hierarchy.

In August 1964 the Freedom Democrats challenged the all-white delegation to the Democratic National Convention in Atlantic City. The regular party had not only denied blacks any participation, but had demonstrated its disloyalty to national Democratic tickets by backing Republican candidates. The most eloquent testimony on what the civil rights efforts had cost came from Fannie Lou Hamer before the credentials committee. "All of this is on account we want to register, to become first-class citizens, and if the Freedom Democratic Party is not seated now, I question America, is this America, the land of the free and the home of the brave where we have to sleep with our telephones off the hook because our lives be threatened daily because we want to live as decent human beings in America?"

Lyndon Johnson, who wanted nothing to upset his nomination for a full term as president, sent vice presidential hopeful Hubert Humphrey to negotiate this impasse. He got nowhere. The national leaders proposed a compromise under which the MFDP would get two seats and the promise of change in the future. "We didn't come all this way for no two seats!" Mrs. Hamer roared, and MFDP rejected the compromise. The convention passed recommendations for change, however, and over the next several conventions, these became the basis for opening the party to greater participation by blacks, other minorities, and women.

Thwarted in this arena, MFDP turned next to Congress. At the opening of the 1965 session, Mrs. Hamer, Annie Devine of Canton, and Victoria Gray of Hattiesburg challenged the seating of Mississippi's well-entrenched House delegation. Again they charged that these politicians had not been legally elected because so many blacks were disenfranchised in Mississippi. The matter was referred to a committee, although the five congressmen were seated in the meantime. One by-product of the challenge was the deployment of an army of attorneys into Mississippi to take depositions that outlined in chilling detail the repression of black citizens of Mississippi. The challenge dragged on through the summer. Mrs. Gray was jailed in Washington at one point and Mrs. Devine was arrested in Jackson because of protests. The House ultimately rejected their demand in September 1965, but history had been made. Mrs. Hamer, Mrs. Devine, and Mrs. Gray were seated as guests on the floor of the House to hear the final debate. They were the first black people from Mississippi seated there since Reconstruction and the first black women ever. Not until Mike Espy was elected from the Delta in 1986 was a black Mississippian officially seated in the House.

Mrs. Hamer had been active on the legal front as well. In 1965, she filed suit against the Sunflower County voter registrar on grounds that, despite federal court orders, he was still making it difficult for blacks to register. The Supreme Court ruled that she was right. It ordered new elections in the spring of 1967 in two small Delta towns, Moorhead and Sunflower. Blacks ran slates of candidates in both towns, Mrs. Hamer traveled the country to raise funds, and all the black candidates lost. Mrs. Hamer tried to run for the state Senate in 1967 but was denied a place on the ballot under new state laws that made independent candidacies more difficult. She joined an MFDP lawsuit challenging these laws because they had not been cleared through the Justice Department as required by the Voting Rights Act of 1965. The Supreme Court also decided this suit in favor of the MFDP. Mrs. Hamer ran for office the last time in 1971, losing a campaign for the state Senate. Black candidates charged that election officials cheated them at several polling places in Sunflower County.

The 1968 Democratic National Convention in Chicago finally seated an integrated challenge delegation from Mississippi instead of the virtually all-white delegation. Mrs. Hamer was a member of this Loyalist Democratic party delegation, which consisted of a coalition including MFDP. She did not, however, play as major a role in the delegation as she had at Atlantic City although she did speak from the platform in favor of the challenging black delegations from Alabama. She also backed the Georgia challenge led by Julian Bond (*). She showed that she was willing to compromise with liberal Mississippians even when she did not feel they were as firm in their challenge of the existing system as was the MFDP, but she stood firm in her adherence to MFDP's basic opposition to the way her state was run, politically and economically. Despite her adamant opposition to the 1964 compromise, she could be flexible when that would bring the greatest gains, whether she was fighting over the leadership of a county Head Start program or working with a white lawyer who had previously had civil rights demonstrators arrested but now could provide some service to her.

Fannie Lou Hamer also wanted to provide the fundamentals of life for people. Her first brush with Mississippi's notorious internal spy agency, the Sovereignty Commission, came in early 1964 when she was distributing clothing to people who would try to register to vote. This was a suspicious act in the eyes of local white politicians. Later she organized Freedom Farm cooperative to provide vegetables for area families and to give them some economic, and therefore political, independence from whites. With the help of the National Council of Negro Women (NCNW), she ran a Pig Bank that provided meat for people's tables. NCNW also set up a day-care center, named after her, in Ruleville.

With NCNW, she also organized one of the first conferences in 1967 that brought poor women together with county officials to discuss what the residents needed from anti-poverty programs. She was involved in a long struggle between a grassroots organization that was running its own Head Start program and the more cautious county Head Start program. The grassroots program had more militant objectives, and more parents seeking fundamental change who were involved, but ultimately it lost. The federal government, stepping back from its war on poverty, consolidated the programs. The battle cost Mrs. Hamer some local allies who thought that she had sold out, but she had seen what was going to happen and tried to salvage as much as possible.

By the time of the 1972 convention, Mrs. Hamer was in ill health. She went as a delegate, however, and delivered a seconding speech for the vice presidential candidacy of Frances "Sissy" Farenthold of Texas. Mrs. Hamer believed in the need to advance women in politics; she had been one of the founders in July 1971 of the National Women's Political Caucus. With Congresswoman Shirley Chisholm (*), she urged the NWPC women not to forget the special concerns of their black sisters. She had also gotten some of the caucus founders, such as Betty Friedan (3*) and Liz Carpenter, to come to Mississippi to campaign with her in her race for state Senate in the fall of 1971.

Fannie Lou Hamer, in her last years, continued working to bring better housing to Sunflower County and to advance black politicians. But she suffered from years of medical neglect and from overwork. She had hypertension and she developed breast cancer a year before she died. When she no longer had the money or the strength to help people, many of her visitors stopped coming and she was often frustrated and lonely. She worried about how black professionals had gotten complacent and didn't care about those who were still oppressed. She was concerned about legal rulings that forced voters to re-register despite all they had gone through to register in the first place. But, as she told a caller not long before she died, she was joyful that one of her little girls had gotten a Christmas gift from a little white friend, something unheard of fifteen years earlier.

She died on March 14, 1977, in Mound Bayou, Mississippi. She was buried in a field on the outskirts of Ruleville, only a few blocks from the small church where she had put up her hand fifteen years earlier. Her grave marker reads: "I am sick and tired of being sick and tired."

The Mississippi Delta in the 1990s had changed, but there were still huge inequalities of opportunity, education, and income. But because Fannie Lou Hamer and her allies in SNCC and the Mississippi Freedom Democratic party had worked there, there was also more hope. Black children were not automatically denied political and economic hope simply because of the color of their skins. There were more genuine possibilities in life. She had demonstrated that productive resistance was possible, and through her speaking, her singing, and her example, inspired others. One of her favorite songs had been "This Little Light of Mine." Her light had shone brightly within the dark places of Mississippi and in the night of American racism.

Bibliography

Bramlett-Solomon, Sharon. "Civil Rights Vanguard in the Deep South: Newspaper Portrayal of Fannie Lou Hamer, 1964–1977," *Journalism Quarterly* 68 (Autumn 1991): 515–21.

DeMuth, Jerry. "Tired of Being Sick and Tired," *The Nation* 198 (June 1, 1964): 548–51.

Grant, Jacqueline. "Fannie Lou Hamer," in *Notable Black American Women*, Jessie Carney Smith, ed. Detroit: Gale Research, 1992: 441–44.

Hall, Carla. "The 'Little Light' of Civil Rights," *Washington Post*, April 28, 1993, C1, C4.

Hamer, Fannie Lou. Foreword to *Stranger at the Gates: A Summer in Mississippi*, by Tracy Sugarman. New York: Hill and Wang, 1966.

————. Interview, in oral history collection of the Moorland-Spingarn Research Center, Howard University, Washington, D.C.

————. Interview by Anne Romaine, in "The Mississippi Freedom Democratic Party through August 1964," M.A. thesis, Corcoran Department of History, University of Virginia, Charlottesville, Va., June 1970.

————. "It's in Your Hands," in *Black Women in White America*, Gerda Lerner, ed. New York: Vintage Books, 1973.

————. Papers: Fannie Lou Hamer papers, Amistad Research Center, Tulane University, New Orleans, Louisiana; Collection on Legal Change, Coleman Library, Tougaloo College, Jackson, Mississippi; Lyndon Baines Johnson Library files, Austin, Texas; Measure for Measure files, Wisconsin State Historical Society, Madison, Wisconsin; Mississippi Freedom Democratic Party papers, Wisconsin State Historical Society, Madison, Wisconsin; Mississippi State Archives; National Council of Negro Women files, National Archives for Black Women's History, Washington, D.C.; Student Non-Violent Coordinating Committee papers, 1959–1972, NYT microfilm; Sanford, N.C., Voter Education Project files, in the Southern Regional Council papers, 1944–1968, microform from NYT Microfilming Corp. of America (New York City).

————. "To Praise Our Bridges," *Mississippi Writers: Reflections on Childhood and Youth*, vol. 2: nonfiction, Dorothy Abbott, ed. Jackson: University Press of Mississippi, 1986.

Locke, Mamie E. "Is This America? Fannie Lou Hamer and the Mississippi Freedom Democratic Party," in *Women in the Civil Rights Movement*, Vicki L. Crawford et al., eds. Brooklyn: Carlson Publishing, 1990: 27–37.

Mills, Kay. *This Little Light of Mine: The Life of Fannie Lou Hamer*. New York: New American Library/Dutton, 1993.

"Never Turn Back: The Life of Fannie Lou Hamer," 1983 16mm film; 60 mins; Rediscovery Productions.

O'Dell, Jack H. "Life in Mississippi: An Interview with Fannie Lou Hamer," *Freedomways* 5 (Second Quarter 1965): 231–42.

Reagon, Bernice Johnson. "Women as Culture Carriers in the Civil Rights Movement: Fannie Lou Hamer," in *Women in the Civil Rights Movement* (cited above); 203–17.

Kay Mills

MARTIN LUTHER KING, JR. (1929–1968)

Baptist pastor; founding president of the Southern Christian Leadership Conference; winner of the Nobel Peace Prize

When the Montgomery bus boycott of 1955 and 1956 plucked Martin Luther King, Jr., from obscurity, he became one of the most powerful spokesmen for social justice in mid-twentieth-century America. His life and work embodied many traditions of reform. He was rooted, from his earliest years, in the faith and style of the southern black church. He later was influenced by the social gospel of Walter Rauschenbusch, the Boston school of theological personalism, the tempered political radicalism of Reinhold Niebuhr, and Mahatma Gandhi's tactics of nonviolent social protest. Drawing on these ideals, Dr. King challenged the nation to live up to its liberal political values.

King was born on January 15, 1929, in Atlanta, Georgia, the son and grandson of pastors of the city's Ebenezer Baptist Church. He was educated in local public and private schools for black youth and skipped several grades to enter Atlanta's Morehouse College at fifteen. There, he matured under the influence of President Benjamin Mays. Young King was ordained at Ebenezer and graduated from Morehouse in 1948. At nineteen, he entered Crozer Theological Seminary at Chester, Pennsylvania. King was drawn to the liberal evangelical

Martin Luther King, Jr. *Source*: Yanker Collection, Library of Congress

theory of Crozer's faculty. He served as president of the student body in his senior year and graduated with highest honors in 1951. Entering Boston University for graduate study in theology later that year, he absorbed the school's insistence on the sacred worth of human personality as the immanent manifestation of the transcendent Person. On June 18, 1953, King married Coretta Scott, a student at the Boston Conservatory of Music.

In September 1954, the Kings moved to Montgomery, Alabama, where he became the pastor of Dexter Avenue Baptist Church. When Mrs. Rosa Parks was arrested for refusing to give up her seat on a Montgomery bus to a white man on December 1, 1955, the city's black leaders organized the Montgomery Improvement Association (MIA) and chose King to lead a massive bus boycott. As negotiations failed, the black community prepared for a lengthy protest, and the city retaliated with a "get tough" policy. On January 30, King's home was bombed, and with eighty-eight others, he was indicted for conspiracy to organize an illegal boycott on February 21, 1956. King was found guilty of conspiracy on March 21, but a federal court later held that laws requiring segregation in public transportation were unconstitutional. The U.S. Supreme Court confirmed the lower court's decision on November 13. Six weeks later, King and others ended the boycott by boarding a desegregated bus. Within two days, King's home was fired upon, and in the next month, four other homes, four black churches, and a business were also attacked.

After the organization of the Southern Christian Leadership Conference (SCLC) at Atlanta's Ebenezer Baptist Church on January 10, 1957, King became its first president. SCLC joined other civil rights organizations in a Prayer Pilgrimage to Washington four months later. There, King stressed the importance of school desegregation and the franchise for black Southerners. In September 1958, while autographing copies of *Stride Toward Freedom*, his account of the Montgomery bus boycott, King was stabbed by a woman who was later found insane. On trips to Africa in March 1957, and to India in February 1959, Martin Luther King affirmed the solidarity of the American Civil Rights movement with the Third World's struggle against imperialism and deepened his own commitment to Gandhian nonviolent resistance to oppression.

In January 1960, King became co-pastor of Atlanta's Ebenezer Baptist Church. He supported the sit-in movement that began in February and convened a meeting of student activists at Raleigh, North Carolina, in April. This led to the formation of the Student Nonviolent Coordinating Committee (SNCC). When King was given a four-month prison sentence for violating probation on a charge of driving without a Georgia driver's license, Democratic presidential candidate John F. Kennedy intervened to win his release on bail. Kennedy's action may have substantially increased black support for his candidacy in the closely contested race with Richard M. Nixon. But when Freedom Riders sponsored by the Congress of Racial Equality (CORE) were greeted by violent white mobs in Birmingham and Montgomery, King rejected Attorney General Robert Kennedy's call for a cooling-off period. He went to Albany, Georgia, in December 1961, to give leadership to the civil rights movement in the southwest Georgia city. The demonstrations continued through the summer of 1962, but King and the movement won no concessions from the city's white leadership. By the end of the year, Albany was considered a clear defeat for Martin Luther King.

In 1963, King launched demonstrations at segregated lunch counters and a boycott of businesses in Birmingham, Alabama. After his arrest on Good Friday, April 12, he wrote his "Letter from Birmingham Jail" to local white clergymen. It summarized their lack of leadership in race relations, the grievances of the black community, and his nonviolent protest for social change. King was found guilty of criminal contempt. The Birmingham campaign reached a climax when children began demonstrating in large numbers, and

Commissioner of Public Safety Eugene "Bull" Connor ended a period of restraint. On May 2, 900 children were arrested. As demonstrators prepared to march the next day, they were attacked by police dogs and policemen wielding clubs and fire hoses. As the media reported the story, public opinion shifted in King's favor, and the Kennedy administration sought to intervene. When police attacks provoked several thousand blacks to riot, Birmingham's black and white leaders reached a settlement. While bombings led to another riot, the agreement survived, although narrowly interpreted by the city's white leadership. Birmingham was a turning point, however, as President Kennedy called for new civil rights legislation on public accommodations, desegregation, and employment.

His position of leadership in the movement restored, King joined other civil rights leaders in addressing 250,000 followers at the March on Washington in August 1963. His "I Have a Dream" oration repeated biblical and democratic themes underlying many of his earlier sermons and speeches. When a bomb exploded in a black church in Birmingham on September 15, 1963, killing four young black girls, Martin Luther King demanded federal intervention to prevent a "racial holocaust." In March 1964, his attention turned to St. Augustine, Florida, where demonstrators were attacked by white mobs. Five months later, public facilities in St. Augustine were desegregated by federal court order. During the summer, King toured Mississippi to encourage black people there to support the Mississippi Freedom Democratic party (MFDP). He supported the MFDP'S challenge to the all-white regular Mississippi delegation at the Democratic National Convention.

Shortly after the announcement that Martin Luther King, Jr., was to receive the Nobel Peace Prize, FBI Director J. Edgar Hoover attacked him as "the most notorious liar in the country." King had suggested that the FBI was ineffective in protecting the civil rights of black people in the South. While King avoided public confrontation with Hoover, the federal agency had been taping his telephone and hotel room conversations for two years. After he received the Nobel Prize, on December 10, 1964, King and his wife received a tape recording purporting to reveal his infidelity to her. An accompanying letter strongly suggested that Dr. King should commit suicide to avoid public humiliation. They rightly suspected that the tape and the letter had come from the FBI.

In January 1965, King's attention turned to Alabama, where civil rights leaders sought a march on Montgomery to protest the brutality in Selma. On March 7, a mounted posse of white volunteers and state troopers led by Colonel Al Lingo and Sheriff James Clark stopped a column of 500 demonstrators led by SCLC's Hosea Williams and SNCC's John Lewis at Selma's Edmund Pettus Bridge. Then they charged the line of marchers with cattle prods, clubs, and tear gas. Despite a federal court injunction and pressure from the Johnson administration, King led a similar march two days later. When confronted by troopers, he knelt with his marchers in prayer and then turned the line back toward Selma, a gesture widely criticized by black militants. President Johnson addressed a joint session of Congress on March 15, denouncing the violence in Selma, calling for passage of a voting rights bill, and concluding that "We Shall Overcome." A federal court authorized the march two days later, and on March 25, 1965, Martin Luther King led 25,000 demonstrators into Montgomery and up Dexter Avenue to the state capitol. Six months later, he met other civil rights leaders at the White House where President Johnson signed the Voting Rights Act into law.

In 1966, when he attacked discrimination in Chicago, King met the indifference of Mayor Richard Daley's regime and hostile white mobs. The campaign was interrupted when James Meredith was shot on a march from Memphis to Jackson, Mississippi. When King joined SNCC's Stokely Carmichael and CORE's Floyd McKissick to complete the march with a closing rally at Jackson, divisions surfaced within the movement. The NAACP's Roy Wilkins and the Urban League's Whitney Young refused to subscribe to its "massive public indictment" of American society. King signed the statement, but he balked at Stokely Carmichael's invocation of "black power." Returning to Chicago, King led demonstrations at city hall and met with Mayor Daley. After a three-day riot in the city's West Side ghetto, his marches into Chicago's white neighborhoods to protest housing discrimination attracted hostile counterdemonstrators. Two days before a march into Cicero, King reached an agreement with the city's establishment to halt the demonstrations. The agreement was only a pledge by the white leadership to curb discrimination. King was increasingly aware of the tenacity of problems in the urban ghetto and outspoken about the need for radical change.

After the Montgomery march, Martin Luther King grew more critical of the U.S. role in the Vietnam War and called for greater attention to the plight of the urban poor. The war not only offended his nonviolence, but it also diverted important resources from domestic needs. Yet his criticism of American foreign policy alienated King from the Johnson administration and other civil rights leaders. King continued to argue that nonviolent methods could produce genuine social change, but he was less optimistic about white America. By late 1966, the civil rights coalition for which he spoke had been undermined by internal dissension, and King pursued a new agenda which attacked both the Vietnam War and poverty and racial discrimination in the urban North.

When the U.S. Supreme Court upheld a contempt of court conviction stemming from the 1963 Birmingham demonstrations in 1967, Martin Luther King spent his prison sentence planning for an interracial coalition of poor people to press for new anti-poverty legislation. His plans, completed in February 1968, called on poor white, black, Indian, and Hispanic-Americans to march on Washington. They would urge federal legislation to guarantee jobs and a viable income to the poor and to end discrimination in education and housing. The campaign faced strong opposition from the Johnson administration and won little support from other civil rights groups. In March, King took time away from planning the Poor People's Campaign to go to Memphis to lead a mass march in support of the city's striking sanitation workers. The demonstration was marred when some protesters began smashing windows and looting stores, but King returned to Memphis to lead a second march a month later. At 6:00 P.M. on April 4, while he was standing on the balcony of his motel, Martin Luther King was shot in the head and died almost instantly. Two months later, James Earle Ray was arrested in London, and in March 1969, after being charged with King's murder, Ray pleaded guilty.

Critical reflection upon the life and thought of Martin Luther King, Jr., suggests that he was a more complex figure than the public knew in his own lifetime or than his early biographers recognized. Current scholarship emphasizes the importance of his nurture in a black family, a black church, and black schools. Precisely what the "blackness" of King's roots and background means for understanding his later career is much less certain because all of the biographers' attention has been given to his later public career. King's years of study at Crozer Theological Seminary and at Boston University were undoubtedly important for his remarkable capacity to communicate with northern white audiences, but even those years are given relatively slight attention in the biographies. It is as if he were a tree without roots. Once the roots are more fully examined, we may begin to appreciate the tree itself in new ways.

Similarly, the whole of King's intellectual and religious development needs careful re-examination. We know too little about the religious background which he once dismissed as "fundamentalist" in order to evaluate its influence upon his development. We know too little about his youthful experience at Morehouse College, where Benjamin Mays, Walter Chivers, George D. Kelsey, Lucius Tobin, and Samuel Williams introduced him to a world of ideas and served as important role models of the black male as the Christian intellectual social critic. Once these influences have been explored, we will be prepared to appreciate his confrontations with Marx and Nietzsche, his appropriations of Crozer's evangelical liberalism and Boston's theological personalism, and the meaning of his extensive appropriation of other people's scholarship without proper citations.

Finally, the exploration of King's background and early life are likely to reshape our understanding of his public career, but evaluation of that career is also tied inextricably to changing attitudes toward the movement with which he was so closely identified. The end of the first reconstruction was followed by a half century of negative historiography. Martin Luther King has been officially enshrined as a national hero and the central achievements of the second reconstruction are rarely directly challenged, but there are signs that we are entering a similar period of negative retrospection. Critics on the left decry the civil rights movement's failure to accomplish more radical social change, while those on the right breathe deeply and polish King's rough edges into a more acceptable and harmless national icon. Perhaps only his own message can save King from such an entombment.

Bibliography

Albert, Peter J., and Ronald Hoffman, eds. *We Shall Overcome: Martin Luther King, Jr., and the Black Freedom Struggle*. New York: Pantheon Books, 1990.

Bennett, Lerone, Jr. *What Manner of Man: A Biography of Martin Luther King, Jr.* Chicago: Johnson Publishing Co., 1968.

Branch, Taylor. *Parting the Waters: America in the King Years, 1954–1963*. New York: Simon and Schuster, 1988.

Fairclough, Adam. *To Redeem the Soul of America: The Southern Christian Leadership Conference and Martin Luther King, Jr.* Athens: University of Georgia Press, 1987.

Garrow, David J. *Bearing the Cross: Martin Luther King, Jr., and the Southern Christian Leadership Conference, A Personal Portrait*. New York: William Morrow, 1986.

———. *The FBI and Martin Luther King, Jr.: From 'Solo' to Memphis*. New York: W. W. Norton, 1981.

King, Coretta Scott. *My Life with Martin Luther King, Jr.* New York: Holt, Rinehart and Winston, 1969.

King, Martin Luther, Jr. *I Have a Dream: Writings and Speeches That Changed the World*, James M. Washington, ed; Coretta Scott King, intr. San Francisco: Harper/Collins, 1992.

———. *Papers of Martin Luther King*, Clayborne Carson, Ralph E. Luker, et al., eds. Berkeley: University of California Press, 1992–   .

———. *Stride Toward Freedom: The Montgomery Story*. New York: Harper, 1958.

———. *Where Do We Go From Here? Chaos or Community?* New York: Harper and Row, 1967.

King, Martin Luther, Sr. *Daddy King: An Autobiography*. New York: William Morrow, 1980.

Lewis, David L. *King: A Critical Biography*. New York: Praeger, 1970.

Oates, Stephen B. *Let the Trumpet Sound: The Life of Martin Luther King, Jr.* New York: Harper and Row, 1982.

Ralph, James R., Jr. *Northern Protest; Martin Luther King, Jr., Chicago, and the Civil Rights Movement*. Cambridge, MA: Harvard University Press, 1993.

Reddick, Lawrence D. *Crusader without Violence: A Biography of Martin Luther King, Jr.* New York: Harper and Brothers, 1959.

"A Round Table: Martin Luther King, Jr.," *Journal of American History* 74 (Sept. 1987): 436–81.

Smith, Kenneth, and Ira G. Zepp, Jr. *Search for the Beloved Community: The Thinking of Martin Luther King, Jr.* Valley Forge, PA: Judson Press, 1974.

Ralph E. Luker

RUSSELL MEANS (1939–   )

American Indian Movement leader, Indian activist

Among the leading Indian activists of the late 1960s and 1970s was Russell Means, an Oglala Sioux and one of the leaders of the American Indian Movement. He was involved in several well-known demonstrations throughout the United States that focused on the mistreatment of Native Americans and numerous treaty violations by the federal government. And in 1992, the year of the Columbus quincentenary, which celebrated the 500th anniversary of Columbus coming to the New World, Means was still active in Indian protest movements. He was one of the Indian leaders who organized a successful demonstration that stopped a Columbus Day Parade in Denver, Colorado.

Born on November 10, 1939, on the Pine Ridge Indian Reservation in South Dakota, Russell Means was the eldest of four boys born to Harold (Hank) Means, a mixed-blood, and Theodora (Feather) Means, a full-blood Sioux. During World War II, his father, a welder and auto mechanic, moved his family to California and secured employment at the Mare Island Navy Yard near San Francisco, California.

Means attended public schools in Vallejo, California. He earned good grades, became a Catholic, and participated actively in the Boy Scouts. When he entered San Leandro High School, he was a promising athlete, but after he faced severe discrimination, his grades and involvement in sports suffered. As a result, he became a juvenile delinquent and experimented with drugs. Means moved to Los Angeles and kicked the drug habit, but became an alcoholic. He continued to drift from place to place and job to job. In San Francisco he worked briefly as a ballroom dance instructor. He also worked as a laborer, farmhand, rodeo hand, and janitor. In 1964 he participated with other Indians in an unsuccessful attempt to take over Alcatraz Island. Hoping to earn a college degree, Means attended several colleges, including the University of California at Los Angeles, Arizona State University, and Cleveland State College. He never graduated.

In the late 1960s Means worked briefly for the tribal council at Rosebud Reservation, South Dakota. He later moved to Cleveland, Ohio, and became director of the Cleveland American Indian Center, a government-funded operation. He showed promise as a skillful demonstrator. In 1969 Means met Dennis Banks (*), a founder of the American Indian Movement (AIM), an Indian protest group started in Minneapolis, Minnesota, in 1968. Impressed with its confrontational tactics, Means founded the second AIM chapter in Cleveland. On Thanksgiving Day, 1970, Means and other Indians attracted national attention by taking over the *Mayflower II* in Plymouth, Massachu-

Russell Means at the Bureau of Indian Affairs, 1972. Copyright *Washington Post*; Reprinted by permission of D.C. Public Library.

setts. In June 1971, he participated in an AIM demonstration at Mount Rushmore, which focused on Lakota claims to the Black Hills.

Over the next several years, Means and Banks became well-known AIM activists throughout the nation. In September 1971 Means and about sixty Indians were unsuccessful in their attempt to take over the Bureau of Indian Affairs (BIA) in Washington, D.C. Means also filed suit against the Cleveland Indians baseball team, declaring that its mascot, Chief Wahoo, was a symbol of racism against Indian people.

In February 1972 Means was involved in AIM's condemnation of race-biased justice when several white men were leniently treated after murdering Raymond Yellow Thunder in Gordon, Nebraska. Several hundred Indians protested that too many times, Indian deaths resulted in minor punishments for whites. Means and AIM forced the authorities to handle the case properly. In addition, Gordon officials formed a board to hear Indian complaints. AIM's involvement enhanced both its reputation and that of Means among reservation Indians.

By mid-1972 Means had resigned his position at the Cleveland Indian Center and returned to South Dakota. He helped plan the Trail of Broken Treaties, a major demonstration, involving Indian tribes throughout the nation, that sent caravans to Washington, D.C., to protest the numerous broken promises to Indian people made by the federal government. They planned to meet in the nation's capital during the final week of the presidential race in November. On November 2, the Indians arrived.

AIM wanted the nation to understand how native peoples had been mistreated and treaties violated. These goals were not accomplished. Instead, promised housing by government officials proved inadequate, and Means and others led a protest at the BIA headquarters. A confrontation ensued, resulting in AIM's occupying the building and renaming it the Native American Embassy. The occupation was apparently a spontaneous action. The Nixon administration immediately engaged in negotiations in which Means played a prominent role. The result was that the government agreed to look into Indian grievances (the Indians had presented twenty demands), promised limited amnesty, and allocated $66,500 to transport Indians home. Indian acts of destruction and vandalism could be prosecuted. The occupation of the BIA may have harmed the Indian movement because the acts of violence received more attention than the discussion of the Indians' twenty demands.

Means returned to Pine Ridge, where he locked horns with tribal chairman Dick Wilson. Wilson, a staunch opponent of AIM, secured a tribal council resolution that prohibited AIM from holding meetings on the reservation. Violence broke out on the reservation, pitting AIM members against Wilson's group, called the "goon squad" by Wilson's opponents.

In February 1973 Means and other AIM members protested the second degree manslaughter charge against a white who had stabbed to death Wesley Bad Heart Bull in Custer, South Dakota. They demanded a murder charge. Discussions went nowhere, and a riot ensued in which several policemen and Indians were injured. Means, Banks, and other Indians were arrested. Means would eventually serve a brief jail term for this action.

Political conditions at Pine Ridge also deteriorated in February. Means played an active role in the attempted impeachment charges against Chairman Wilson, who was accused of violating the tribal constitution and misusing tribal funds. According to Wilson's accusers, impeachment charges were dismissed because they did not have time to prepare their case and Wilson controlled the trial proceedings. Means and approximately 200 followers, many of them armed, then occupied Wounded Knee, the site of a December 1890 Army massacre of the Sioux. On February 27, 1973, the occupiers declared that they were the new traditional tribal government. They demanded the removal of Wilson as tribal chairman, and requested a U.S. Senate investigation of treaty violations and of the BIA.

Mass media coverage of the event discouraged the FBI agents and federal marshals from launching a major assault against the Indians. Despite this, fire fights did occur, and two people were killed during the seventy-one-day siege. During the occupation, Means and other AIM leaders were permitted to go to Washington, D.C., in April to negotiate a settlement. Means had agreed to be taken to Rapid City, South Dakota, for arraignment. He was released under a $25,000 bond. The talks broke down, and Means was later held until the occupation ended. The government finally agreed in May to investigate the tribal government at Pine Ridge and the status of the 1868 Fort Laramie Treaty with the Sioux. Again, many observers believe Wounded Knee II hurt the Indian movement more than it helped it because not enough attention was paid to the Indians' grievances.

Means faced ten felony charges for his involvement at Wounded Knee. If found guilty, he could have received a maximum sentence of eighty-five years in prison and $96,000 in fines. Before standing trial, Means challenged Wilson for the office of tribal chairman. Means accused Wilson of not representing Indians and won the primary, defeating Wilson by over 150 votes. During the election, however, Wilson retained his chairmanship by beating Means, 1,709 to 1,530. Means appealed the results, citing threats, bribery, and ballot frauds by Wilson. Although irregularities certainly existed, Wilson retained his position.

The trial of Means for his involvement at Wounded Knee began on February 12, 1974, in St. Paul, Minnesota. Means and other AIM members had top defense lawyers, including William Kunstler (6*) and Mark Lane. The trial ended in September when federal judge Fred Nichol dismissed all charges against Means because of government misconduct in the case, which included lying under oath, illegal wire taps, and altered documents.

After the trial Means continued his activism, sustaining several injuries that included a stabbing and two bullet wounds. For example, in 1975 at Standing Rock Reservation, North Dakota, he was shot in the stomach by a BIA policeman during a bar altercation. By the end of the 1970s, Means had been exonerated of most of the charges against him but did serve some jail time and one year at the South Dakota State Penitentiary for armed rioting at Sioux Falls in 1974. He also participated in the "Longest Walk," a demonstration march to Washington, D.C., to protest anti-Indian legislation and other matters.

In the 1980s Means became an advocate for environmental protection in South Dakota. He helped establish Camp Yellow Thunder (named after Raymond Yellow Thunder, who had been murdered in Gordon, Nebraska, in 1972) in the Black Hills. The camp was built as a spiritual and educational center and in condemnation of the 1980 U.S. Supreme Court monetary settlement dealing with the illegal seizure of the Black Hills. Mean again tried to become tribal chairman at Pine Ridge in 1983. Because of his legal status as a convicted felon, he was declared ineligible.

For the remainder of the 1980s and into the 1990s, Means continued his efforts on behalf of Indian people. He spoke out against the mistreatment of native peoples in Latin America. He opposed the expansion of government facilities like Fort Riley, Kansas, and the holding of the annual Little Bighorn celebration in Hardin, Montana. Means also demonstrated for many years against Columbus Day activities, and in October of 1992, he and his supporters were able to cancel the Columbus Day parade in Denver, Colorado. To him, this was a symbolic victory since Colorado had been the first state to have a legal holiday for Columbus, enacting a law in 1907. He hoped that this would become a new model where the crimes (rather than the achievements) of Columbus would be remembered.

Russell Means remained a significant voice for Indian America. His impressive figure and speaking abilities served him well. He became, to many, a symbol for native Americans, whether as an activist or, more novel, a major actor in the movie *The Last of the Mohicans* in 1992. The last of Russell Means has not yet been heard.

Bibliography

Carrier, Jim. "Russell Means: Last of the Militants," *Denver Post*, Oct. 4, 1992, A1:2.

Churchill, Ward. "Goons, G-Men, and AIM: At Last the Story Will Be Told," *The Progressive* 54 (April 1990): 28–29.

Churchill, Ward, and Jim Vander Wall. *Agents of Repression: The FBI's Secret Wars against the Black Panther Party and the American Indian Movement*. Boston: South End Press, 1988.

D'Emilio, John. "Russell Means," in *Political Profiles: The Nixon-Ford Years*, Eleanora W. Schoenbaum, ed. New York: Facts on File, 1979: 431–32.

"Indian Group Still Plans a Super Bowl Protest," *New York Times*, Jan. 4, 1992, p. 29.

Josephy, Alvin M., Jr. *Now That the Buffalo's Gone*. New York: Alfred A. Knopf, 1982.

Lynch, Karen. "Custer Loses Again" [Custer Battlefield renamed], *The Progressive* 55 (Sept. 1991): 11.

Mason, W. Dale. " 'You Can Only Kick So Long . . . ': American Indian Movement Leadership in Nebraska, 1972–1979," *Journal of the West* 23 (July 1984): 21–31.

O'Neil, Floyd, June K. Lyman, and Susan McKay, eds. *Wounded Knee 1973*. Lincoln: University of Nebraska Press, 1991.

"Russell Means," *Current Biography 1978*. New York: H. W. Wilson, 1978: 294–97.

Weyler, Rex. *Blood of the Land: The Government and Corporate War against the American Indian Movement*. New York: Vintage, 1984 (1982).

Raymond Wilson

ROBERT PARRIS MOSES (1935–   )

Activist in the Student Nonviolent Coordinating Committee

Robert Parris Moses was born in 1935 into the tradition of the black church. His grandfather had been a charismatic Southern Baptist preacher and fundraiser for the National Baptist Convention. The Great Depression, though, aborted his father's career. Forced to take a janitorial job in Harlem, the elder Moses inculcated in his sons a drive to succeed.

Bob Moses was a precocious youth with a taste for philosophy. He was educated at excellent schools: Stuyvesant High School, Hamilton College in upstate New York, and Harvard University, where he earned an M.A. in philosophy in 1958. Many classmates regarded Moses as bright, but he displayed no early interest in questions of race and civil rights.

While teaching at Horace Mann High School in New York, Moses in 1960 took his first trip to the South. He visited his uncle, who taught at Hampton Institute. Moses experienced a "release" from prejudice by participating in a civil rights demonstration there. In Newport News, Virginia, he met Wyatt Tee Walker, an associate of Martin Luther King, Jr. (*). Moses decided to work in New York for Bayard Rustin (*), who was running the Committee to Defend Martin Luther King.

During the summer of 1960, Rustin persuaded Moses to go to Atlanta to work for the Southern Christian Leadership Conference on a voter registration project. There he became acquainted with the fledgling Student Nonviolent Coordinating Committee which shared the SCLC office. He soon became a tireless figure on the picket lines. His intensity and quiet intellectuality, however, led some SCLC members and students to believe that Moses was a communist.

To escape this uncomfortable situation, Moses volunteered to go on a SNCC drive through the Deep South recruiting for an upcoming conference. Ella Baker, the outgoing SCLC coordinator, had befriended Moses. She sent him in the direction of Amzie Moore, a local NAACP leader in Mississippi. Moore changed Moses' thinking and thereby the direction of SNCC. Moore was convinced that blacks could best improve their position through the ballot box. Moore eventually shifted the emphasis away from direct-action campaigns like sit-ins or freedom rides to voter registration. Moses now believed that political power addressed the economic concerns of blacks that direct action could not.

Moses returned to New York to fulfill his teaching contract but returned

Robert Parris Moses.
Source: Library of Congress

full-time to Mississippi and Moore in the summer of 1961. In SNCC, meanwhile, debate raged over whether direct action or voter registration was the better policy. Moses refused to use his growing prestige to sway the debate one way or another. This was typical of Moses, whose reticence and introspection were to become legendary. He merely asked that SNCC consider a registration project developed with Amzie Moore. Moore, however, realized the freedom rides had stirred up Mississippi to the point of violence. Because of Moore's discomfort, Moses agreed to start a voter registration school in a slightly less reactionary part of the state.

Moses moved to McComb, Mississippi, where he worked to set up a voter registration school. His aim was not simply to register voters. This was a virtually impossible task at that moment. Instead, he wanted to destroy the Mississippi mindset that kept blacks in a stupefying deference. Moses believed that once the state of mind of the Mississippi Negro was changed, newly empowered blacks would more readily seek their constitutional rights. Moses possibly also expected that the federal government would offer some assistance.

Moses' activities soon attracted other rights workers. Some were interested only in voter registration. Others recognized the possibilities that Moses' campaign offered for challenge and confrontation. Once Mississippi's whites got over their shock at Moses' activities, they cracked down hard. People suffered physical attacks and economic intimidation. Moses was severely beaten on the way to the McComb courthouse, yet he persevered. His status of martyr energized the local black community. Once again, the whites responded, this time with the fatal shooting of a local black who had been helping Moses. Moses and his workers were arrested and the registration movement collapsed. After his release from jail he spent the winter and spring planning for the next summer.

In the summer of 1962, the recently revived Council of Federated Organizations (COFO) intervened to resolve the bickering among the various rights groups. Moses was named program director and given funds from the Voter Education Project (VEP). This had been organized to funnel philanthropic funds for his work. The summer of 1962, though, was frustrating, as Moses admitted, "We are powerless to register people in significant numbers anywhere in the state." Moses blamed the federal government for not exerting pressure on Mississippi whites to enforce the federal laws.

For a while in the spring of 1963, it seemed that the federal government would get involved in the Delta town of Greenwood. The local government had cut off federal surplus food distributions through the winter. SNCC had attempted to provide "food for those who want to be free." After the shooting of a local black, whites attacked a voter registration rally headed for the courthouse. This attracted the media and thereby the federal government. The Justice Department wanted to file suit against the town, but the Kennedys chose, under pressure in Birmingham and elsewhere, to compromise with the whites rather than face the moral challenge hurled at them by SNCC.

In the summer and fall of 1963 Moses and SNCC shifted tactics. They organized a Freedom Vote to parallel the white elections. This effort would be less directly confrontational while raising the awareness of local blacks about political power. It would also involve some white students from the North. This participation brought greater media attention. Moses and SNCC soon hit upon the idea of a full-scale program bringing whites to Mississippi to work for voter registration.

While the upcoming Freedom Summer of 1964 offered tantalizing publicity opportunities, it also divided SNCC. SNCC had always worked toward raising the consciousness and self-esteem of local black Mississippians. This influx of educated white Northerners would cause resentment and threaten the progress SNCC had made in transforming the mentality of the black community. Moses pushed for it with uncharacteristic assertiveness, putting his prestige in the movement on the line. Moses stepped in after the killing of a witness to the murder of a local black who had worked with Moses. Declaring that "we can't even protect our own people," Moses won the rights workers to Freedom Summer.

Freedom Summer began grimly with the murder of three participants traveling in Mississippi. Despite this, the registration work continued. Although not a success if measured by black registration, it gained great publicity and, more important, the creation of a separate party challenge to the Mississippi Democrats in the 1964 presidential convention. The publicity brought summer-long exposure of the treatment of blacks in the Deep South. The convention challenge, though, marked the beginning of a shift of the civil rights movement from cooperation to confrontation with the federal government and with whites in general.

Moses fought at the 1964 Atlantic City Democratic Convention to have the all-white delegation from Mississippi replaced by one representing the Mississippi Freedom Democratic party. The latter had been chosen in a separate primary that had been open to all Democrats, black and white. Although the Freedom Democrats gained publicity at the convention, the political establishment found their pleas to be extreme. Moses and others were shocked by a manipulative politics that seemed to be devoid of any moral foundation. They left the convention.

For Moses, this was the end of his effective role in the movement. The years of work with little reward had caught up with him. He was thoroughly disgusted with the federal government and with politics. Radicalized, he floated around the movement for a while, spoke against the Vietnam War, cut off contact with whites, and fled the country in 1966 to avoid the draft. During the next several years Moses and his second wife, Janet, worked as schoolteachers in an obscure village in Tanzania. His absence from the United States added to his almost mythological stature.

The couple and their children returned to the United States after the Carter amnesty program in 1977 and settled in Cambridge, Massachusetts. Moses subsequently was awarded a five-year grant from the MacArthur Foundation of Chicago. Moses used the funds to organize the Algebra Project in the Boston public schools, intended to teach mathematics to inner-city youth. His methods had echoes of his work in Mississippi. He emphasized the centrality of families to the work of organizing, the empowerment of grassroots people and their recruitment for leadership, and organizing in the context in which one lives and works, focusing on issues found in that context. "The computer revolution that we are going through now," he told a group of newspaper editors in 1991 in Atlanta,

is a new math and literacy requirement [that] is going to affect who is and who is not a citizen. . . . There are things that must be done if we are not going to have a generation of people who function as serfs in our inner cities, just as the people that we worked with in the '60s on the plantations in Mississippi were serfs in society then. . . . The voting efforts that took place in the '60s and centered around the question of empowerment, and particularly empowering black people so they could participate in the political arrangements, now has a new dimension.

By 1992, the Algebra Project had been copied in ten states across the United States. Children were being trained in the analytic skills that would allow them to succeed in the modern world.

One of these projects was especially meaningful to Bob Moses. In the early 1990s he began to work, once again, in Mississippi. The state had changed, but there was still residential segregation, public schools were black (as a rule) and private schools were white, and poor children were still at a severe disadvantage. Without the proper education, they would have no future. They would be thrown away like the earlier sharecroppers. "Empowerment" and "democracy" continued to be vital goals of Bob Moses, but the means to achieve these goals had changed.

Bibliography

Branch, Taylor. *Parting the Waters: America in the King Years, 1954–1963*. New York: Simon and Schuster, 1988.

Burner, David. *And Gently He Shall Lead Them: Robert Parris Moses and Civil Rights in Mississippi*. New York: New York University Press, 1994.

Cagin, Seth, and Philip Dray. *We Are Not Afraid: The Story of Goodman, Schwerner, and Chaney and the Civil Rights Campaign for Mississippi*. New York: Macmillan Publishing, 1988.

Carson, Clayborne. *In Struggle: SNCC and the Black Awakening of the 1960s*. Cambridge: Harvard University Press, 1981.

———. "Moses, Robert Parris," in *Biographical Dictionary of the American Left*, Bernard K. Johnpoll and Harvey Klehr, eds. Westport, CT: Greenwood Press, 1986: 280–81.

Carson, Clayborne, David J. Garrow, Gerald Gill, Vincent Harding, and Darlene Clark Hine, eds. *The Eyes on the Prize Civil Rights Reader: Documents, Speeches, and Firsthand Accounts from the Black Freedom Struggle, 1954–1990*. Boston: Blackside, Inc., 1991; 170–76 and *passim*.

Jetter, Alexis. "Mississippi Learning" [an article on Bob Moses], *New York Times Magazine*, Feb. 21, 1993, pp. 28–32, 35, 50–51, 64, 72.

Lichtenstein, Nelson, ed. *Political Profiles: The Johnson Years*. New York: Facts on File, 1976: 437–38.

———. *Political Profiles: The Kennedy Years*. New York: Facts on File, 1976: 374–75.

McAdam, Doug. *Freedom Summer*. New York: Oxford University Press, 1988.

Moses, Robert Parris. "Commentary," in *We Shall Overcome: Martin Luther King, Jr., and the Black Freedom Struggle*, Peter J. Albert and Ronald Hoffman, eds. New York: Pantheon Books, 1990: 69–76.

———. "Letter from a Mississippi Jail Cell," in *Documentary History of the Modern Civil Rights Movement*, Peter B. Levy, ed. Westport, CT: Greenwood Press, 1992: 94–95.

———. "Mississippi: 1961–1962," in *The First Harvest; The Institute for Policy Studies,*

1963–1983, John S. Friedman, ed. New York: Grove Press, 1983: 185–200. (First published in *Liberation* 14 [Jan. 1970]: 6–17.)

Moses, Robert Parris, Mieko Kamii, Susan McAllister Swap, and Jeffrey Howard. "The Algebra Project: Organizing in the Spirit of Ella," *Harvard Educational Review* 59 (Nov. 1989): 423–43.

Raines, Howell, ed. *My Soul Is Rested: The Story of the Civil Rights Movement in the Deep South*. New York: G. P. Putnam's Sons, 1977.

                                                                    Eric Burner

LEONARD PELTIER (1944–   )

American Indian Movement activist, political prisoner

Bitter cold persuaded the demonstrators who had gathered outside the federal courthouse in Kansas City, Kansas, on December 3, 1990, to cancel their dancing and the smoking of the pipe. Instead, they prayed on the steps of the courthouse. Inside, an attorney filed a motion requesting the release from federal prison of Leonard Peltier, convicted in 1977 of murdering two FBI agents at the Pine Ridge reservation in South Dakota. The U.S. Supreme Court had decided not to review the case three years earlier. In 1990, the federal judge denied the new motion. Peltier remained in his cell at Leavenworth Federal Penitentiary, serving two consecutive life sentences.

Leonard Peltier, an Ojibwa-Sioux political leader affiliated with the American Indian Movement (AIM), has been remembered not so much for his political philosophy or his enduring spiritual vision born of the human rights struggles of the 1960s as for his trial and sentence. This has seemed to many people, including leaders of foreign governments, a spectacular miscarriage of justice and an abuse of power orchestrated by the Federal Bureau of Investigation hardly restrained by the revelations of misdeeds during the Watergate scandal.

Born on September 12, 1944, in Grand Forks, North Dakota, Peltier was raised by his paternal grandparents at Turtle Mountain after his parents separated. He attended the Wahpeton (Sioux) Indian School beginning in 1953. In 1958, at age fourteen, he participated in his first Sun Dance at the Turtle Mountain Reservation. He then went out to Oakland California to live with his mother's relations and seek work. Except for family, he had little contact with an Indian community at home or a larger, urban Indian community. By 1965, at age twenty, he owned part of an auto body repair shop in Seattle.

Peltier's first encounter with ethnic militancy came five years later. Inspired by the takeover of the abandoned federal penitentiary at Alcatraz in San Francisco Bay, where Indians claimed rights to abandoned "surplus" federal property, numbers of Washington Indians occupied Fort Lawton outside Seattle. Arrested with fourteen other militants, Peltier refused to leave the army stockade until all his companions had been freed. After his initiation into direct action at Fort Lawton, Peltier traveled to Arizona, where he heard from Navajo workers about AIM. He went to that organization's Denver office where he met Vernon Bellecourt (*). He accompanied Bellecourt to an AIM meeting at Leech Lake, Minnesota. That meeting fired his resolve. He foreswore alcohol and dedicated himself to the cause of Indian rights.

Peltier participated in scattered demonstrations throughout the West, traveled to Hollywood to raise money, and eventually joined Herb Poweless of the Milwaukee AIM chapter and concentrated most of his efforts in alcohol rehabilitation. He joined the Trail of Broken Treaties in 1972 that led from the West Coast to Washington, D.C. AIM hoped to coordinate its arrival in the capital with election day.

The Trail of Broken Treaties, far from reminding the nation of the hour's urgent need regarding native people, became a justification for suppression of AIM by the federal government. The occupation and "trashing" of the Bureau of Indian Affairs by AIM demonstrators was a precipitating event for federal intervention. Under the justification of "national security," the favorite rationale of the Nixon administration, the FBI accelerated a COINTELPRO (Counterintelligence Program) against AIM and its leadership. By the winter of 1972–1973 this program included manufactured evidence, spurious charges against persons, physical assaults, and, according to some AIM partisans, a number of assassinations of AIM leaders and open warfare on the Pine Ridge Reservation, South Dakota, between 1973 and 1976.

In the late morning of June 26, 1975, Peltier was resting in his house on the Pine Ridge Reservation when rifle fire from outside the house killed two FBI agents. It was later claimed that the agents were coming to issue an arrest warrant on a person they believed to be in the house. Actually, they may have been hoping to precipitate a confrontation with AIM supporters residing at the community of Oglala. Although large numbers of FBI agents, Bureau of Indian Affairs (BIA) police, state troopers, sheriff's deputies, and vigilantes surrounded the property within an hour of the first shots, the numerous Indians involved in the shoot-out escaped the cordon.

The death of the agents inspired one of the biggest manhunts in FBI history, including those that followed the political assassinations of the 1960s. Four men eventually were indicted for the killings. One was later released because the evidence was weak. Two were acquitted in July of 1976 when a jury concluded that they had fired at the agents in self-defense. The fourth man, Leonard Peltier, was indicted on the same charges as his companions, but he was not tried until the following year. After the fire fight, Peltier fled to western Alberta. He was arrested in 1976 and returned to the United States, despite severe doubts by Canadian magistrates in British Columbia. Peltier was then tried in the federal court of Judge Paul Benson in Fargo, North

Dakota, where he was convicted of aiding and abetting the deaths of the FBI agents. At the trial there was considerable evidence of Peltier's innocence, and this evidence has increased over the years. Some people have claimed that there was an FBI frame-up which included the manufacture of some trial information while other data potentially helpful to the defense was suppressed.

Despite numerous pleas for both a change of jurisdiction and the granting of a new trial, Peltier remained in jail into the early 1990s. By 1993, there existed a large and diverse international movement that regarded Peltier as a political prisoner and sought to have him freed. The Human Rights Commission of Spain, for example, honored him for "defending the historical and cultural rights of his people against the genocide of his race." The London-based organization Amnesty International listed him as perhaps the foremost political prisoner in the United States.

Following his conviction, Peltier spent three years in solitary confinement in Marion Federal Penitentiary, in Illinois. This institution was notorious for using shock therapy and behavior modification on inmates. A hundred years before, leaders of the Ghost Dance religion among the Sioux were imprisoned at Fort Marion following the slaughter of Big Foot's band of Minneconjous at Wounded Knee on the Pine Ridge Reservation. In time, the Sioux ghost dancers were sent out of the country for two years with Buffalo Bill's Wild West Show. Peltier would enjoy no such release. He survived an assassination attempt when transferred from Marion to a minimum security prison at Lompoc, California. Although he attempted to escape from Lompoc, charges against him following his recapture were dropped. Many of his supporters suggested that the government did not wish to prosecute him for fear that its questionable tactics would be challenged in open court.

By early 1993, it remained unclear whether a recent news story to appear on CBS's immensely popular "Sixty Minutes" or "Incident at Oglala," a documentary produced and narrated by Robert Redford, a popular actor turned filmmaker, would have much effect on winning Leonard Peltier a new trial. He never claimed to hold special status with AIM; but because of his arrest and conviction Peltier had become an international figure.

During November and December of 1993, various groups conducted a campaign to generate one million petitions, ten thousand phone and fax messages, and one thousand resolutions, proclamations and declarations. These were sent to President Clinton as part of a campaign urging him to commute the sentence of Leonard Peltier. The campaign noted that the Oglala shooting had grown out of extreme tensions during 1973–1975, and that the FBI conceded later that they could not directly prove that Peltier had killed the two FBI agents. Given the long history of general European abuses of the native peoples, and of specific FBI and court injustices toward minorities, the petition argued against the continued imprisonment of Peltier, who had already been in jail seventeen years. The organizers wanted clemency as an act of reconciliation during the 1993 UN Year of Indigenous People. They noted that this plea had been endorsed by many groups, such as Amnesty International and the National Association of Christians and Jews, along with many prominent people, including Bishop Desmond Tutu of South Africa and the Archbishop of Canterbury. Would Leonard Peltier remain a symbol of injustice or an acknowledgement of past wrongs and the hope of healing?

Bibliography

Churchill, Ward, and James Vander Wall. *Agents of Repression: The FBI's Secret War against the Black Panther Party and the American Indian Movement*. Boston: South End Press, 1988.

Clifton, James A., ed. *The Invented Indian: Cultural Fictions and Government Policies*. New Brunswick, NJ: Transaction Publishers, 1990.

Dewing, Rolland, ed. *The FBI Files on the American Indian Movement and Wounded Knee* (twenty-six reels of microfilm), guide by Martin Schipper. Frederick, MD: University Publications of America, 1988.

Hentoff, Nicholas. "The Peltier Case," *The Nation* 240 (June 22, 1985): 756.

"Incident at Oglala" (1992 film). Reviewed: *New Republic* 206 (June 8, 1992): 32; *New York Times*, May 4, 1992, C11; *New York Times*, May 8, 1992, C15; *New York Times*, May 10, 1992, H22; *The New Yorker* 68 (June 1, 1992): 59–60; *People Weekly* 37 (May 4, 1992): 36–39.

"Indian Protester Renews Appeal of Conviction in Slaying of Agents," *New York Times*, Dec. 10, 1992, A21.

Matthiessen, Peter. *In the Spirit of Crazy Horse*, with a new foreword. New York: Viking, 1991 (1983).

  Reviews of the 1983 edition: *The Atlantic* 251 (March 1983): 112+; *Christian Century* 100 (Aug. 3–10, 1983): 721–22; *Commonweal* 110 (May 20, 1983): 305–7; *New Republic* 188 (March 7, 1983): 31–34; *New York Review of Books* 30 (April 14, 1983): 21–24+; *New York Times Book Review* 88 (March 6, 1983): 1+; *Newsweek* 101 (March 28, 1983): 701; *Time* 121 (March 28, 1983): 70.

———. "The Trials of Leonard Peltier," *Esquire* 117 (Jan. 1992): 55–57.

———. "Who Really Killed the FBI Men; New Light on Peltier's Case," *The Nation* 252 (May 13, 1991): 613+.

Messerschmidt, Jim. *The Trial of Leonard Peltier*, with a new afterword. Boston: South End Press, 1989 (1983).

Peltier, Leonard. "War against the American Nation," in *It Did Happen Here: Recollections of Political Repression in America*, Bud Schultz and Ruth Schultz, eds. Berkeley: University of California Press, 1989: 212–29.

Russell, Dick. "Another Page in the Peltier Drama," *In These Times*, Aug. 7–20, 1991, pp. 7, 10.

Weyler, Rex. *Blood of the Land: The Government and Corporate War against the American Indian Movement*. New York: Vintage, 1982.

L. G. MOSES

BAYARD RUSTIN (1912–1987)

Radical pacifist and integrationist

The March on Washington in 1963 has taken its place among the momentous events that have shaped and changed the course of American history. Many people have heard excerpts from the powerful "I Have a Dream" speech that Martin Luther King (*) delivered at the march. By comparison, few people know of the life of the central organizer of that march, Bayard Rustin. Despite his decades of vital work as a radical pacifist, integrationist, and advocate of coalition politics, Rustin remained generally in the background. Nevertheless, he remained active until his death in 1987, espousing a consistently democratic vision of America's future.

Rustin's social and educational background made him different from most blacks from the beginning. While most black children born in the early years of the twentieth century grew up in a southern, conservative, rural, and poverty-stricken social system, Bayard was the product of a northern, urban, liberal, and working-class upbringing. His exposure to radical urban politics at an early age had a profound influence on his intellectual growth.

Bayard Rustin, the son of West Indian immigrants, was born in West Chester, Pennsylvania, in 1912. As a young man, he participated in radical experiments in school integration through his grandparents' association with a Pennsylvania Quaker group. He was an honor student at West Chester High School, where he also excelled in football, track and field, and tennis. In fact, he experienced his first serious encounter with racial prejudice as a member of the West Chester High School football team when he was refused service in a restaurant with his white teammates. Later he attended Cheyney State College in Pennsylvania and Wilberforce College in Ohio where he developed an interest in pacifist philosophy.

When he was financially unable to remain in college, Rustin traveled to Harlem, which was a hotbed of communist and socialist activity in the 1930s and 40s. There at the age of twenty-six, he joined the Young Communist League (YCL) as an organizer. In addition, he continued his formal education by enrolling at the City College of New York and supported himself by entertaining as a singer in local cafes and nightclubs.

The early 1940s were eventful years for Rustin. His pacifist convictions led him to resign from the YCL because of its support of Russia's military activities in World War II. He joined A. Philip Randolph as an organizer in 1941 for a proposed march on Washington. He criticized Randolph severely for calling off the march although its threat resulted in President Franklin Roosevelt's issuing an executive order that banned discrimination in defense industries

Bayard Rustin. *Source*: Library of Congress

and the creation of the Fair Employment Practices Commission. During the same year he joined the Fellowship of Reconciliation, a pacifist organization that began in England during World War I and later became active in the United States. Rustin refused to serve in the armed forces after he was drafted and received a jail sentence of twenty-eight months in the federal penitentiary at Lewisburg, Pennsylvania.

After the war, Rustin worked closely with the Congress of Racial Equality, which was formed in 1942, and the Fellowship of Reconciliation. These organizations were dedicated to improving race relations in the United States and, at the same time, adopting nonviolent protest as a tactic in fighting racial discrimination. Their first target was to use nonviolent means to protest segregated carriers in interstate travel.

In 1946, the Supreme Court held unconstitutional, in *Morgan v. Commonwealth of Virginia*, state laws requiring the racial segregation of passengers in interstate bus and train service. During the spring of 1947, members of the

Congress of Racial Equality and the Fellowship of Reconciliation wanted to test the efficacy of the Court's decision by organizing a Journey of Reconciliation through the South. Bayard Rustin volunteered to accompany the interracial group on train and bus rides into the South.

The riders experienced only minor problems between Washington, D.C., and the North Carolina border. At that point, their journey prompted minor confrontations with white passengers, bus drivers, and local police. Although the group encountered some potentially serious incidents as they went farther South, they had expected more aggressive hostility. It is likely that southern whites perceived them as little more than a nuisance since the group was small and had received little publicity in the South. Several protesters, nonetheless, were arrested for violating state segregation laws. Rustin, for example, was sentenced to thirty days on a North Carolina chain gang for violating a Jim Crow law in Chapel Hill.

Rustin concluded at the end of this protest that many people in the South, black and white, bus drivers, and police, were ignorant of the Irene Morgan case and its constitutional significance. Local policemen and bus drivers either did not know that their actions violated the Constitution or were interested more in enforcing local and state regulations against interracial mixing on motor carriers.

The protesters met southern blacks who pleaded with them to observe the law. To Rustin, their open hostility to the Journey of Reconciliation indicated that some blacks in the South had a vested interest in keeping the status quo. This should not have surprised Rustin and his friends. Even southern blacks were not immune from suspicion of strangers. This was true especially of northern strangers who came South and demanded that blacks support their agendas in fighting racial discrimination and then returned to the safety and security of their homes in the North. The riders were more prepared for verbal threats and hostility from whites, which should have forewarned Rustin that even nonviolent protest in the Deep South would be subjected to violence. Southern whites who were adamantly opposed to liberalization of state segregation laws were unlikely to be swayed by the moral strength of peaceful protest.

While nonviolent protest in the South might not shield its advocates from racial violence, black leaders in both the North and South were correct essentially in believing that aggressive militant tactics might be counterproductive. Therefore, some type of nonviolent mass protest or legal challenge to segregation in the South, like the strategy that led to the *Brown* decision, seemed to Rustin to be the most pragmatic strategy.

This theory was tested in Montgomery, Alabama, in 1955. The Women's Political Council (WPC) of Montgomery had planned to challenge the segregated bus system in the city. The WPC sought to find a black woman who had been arrested for violating the city's segregated seating codes on public buses and use her as a symbol for a boycott. The chance for a test case seemed possible when a policeman arrested a young black girl for violating the seating code. To the chagrin of the WPC, the girl was pregnant and unmarried. Fearing a moral backlash if this person were used to challenge the code, the Council waited for another candidate. This later turned out to be Rosa Parks, a married woman of impeccable moral integrity.

For Rustin, the significant point was that the WPC and later the Montgomery Improvement Association and the Montgomery ministers headed by the Reverend Martin Luther King agreed that their protest should be a peaceful bus boycott. Rustin, Ella Baker, and others formed In Friendship, a New York interracial group which raised several thousand dollars for nonviolent protests in Montgomery.

Rustin traveled to Montgomery in April of 1956 to file a report on the boycott for *Liberation* magazine. He had displayed more than a reporter's fascination for the protest in Montgomery and talked to A. Philip Randolph and other colleagues about offering his assistance. Some of his associates were concerned about his safety as well as adverse reaction to the boycott should he become intimately involved in its activities. Their fears resulted primarily from rumors about both his past and his private life. Rustin had a police record that contained a morals conviction resulting from an incident in the backseat of a car with male passengers in Pasadena, California, in 1951. His friends feared that if information about this issue became public, the opposition might use it to undercut the boycott. Black leaders in Montgomery, therefore, at least in private, worried about Rustin's participation and suggested that he return to New York.

Rustin had a further problem, which he had also faced when riding through the South to protest racial segregation in interstate bus and train service in 1947: he was not a native Southerner. His presence in Montgomery raised the fear and suspicion of both blacks and whites. Insofar as blacks were concerned, however, his closeness to A. Philip Randolph, a man widely respected among blacks in the North and South, helped to ameliorate their uneasiness.

Rustin impressed the leaders of the boycott enough so that he became an advisor to the boycott. He also contributed the wisdom of bringing some of the loose-knit groups in the South under one central structure, leading to the formation of the Southern Christian Leadership Conference (SCLC) in 1957. Ironically, his background prevented him from attaining a high office in SCLC just as it precipitated his departure from Montgomery when the press began to focus on his morals conviction and a stint in the Young Communist League.

When only partial successes resulted from nonviolent demonstrations in the South, the leaders of the major civil rights organizations were asked to consider initiating a march on Washington, D.C. By January of 1963, Rustin circulated a memo on the proposed march. Many civil rights leaders gradually realized its potential benefits. Roy Wilkins, Whitney Young, Walter Reuther, Martin Luther King, and Adam Clayton Powell approved of what had been primarily Rustin's idea. As the proposal gained momentum, controversy surrounded Rustin's participation. Should he be the principal organizer? Adam Clayton Powell, then a congressman, resented Rustin's influence in the civil rights movement and openly expressed disgust about Rustin's sexual proclivities. Gay males were not well thought of in the black community, and Powell disdained any black man who appeared effeminate. Powell's opposition aside, a compromise was made. A. Philip Randolph agreed to be the principal organizer of the march with Rustin as his deputy. The final event, nonetheless, bore the organizing imprint of Rustin.

To move several hundred thousand peaceful demonstrators in and out of Washington, D.C., was a complicated task. Accommodations, food, and transportation had to be provided. Bathroom facilities, first aid stations, and medical supplies must be furnished. Staging and parking areas for thousands of buses needed to be found. Local and federal demonstration permits required completion and approval. The program and speaking agenda must be arranged. Perhaps most important, the activities of various civil rights, religious, labor, and other groups had to be coordinated with near military precision. The unenviable task of bringing all of these components and logistical problems together and making them work was delegated to Bayard Rustin, pacifist, labor leader, political activist, Social Democrat, and second in command to A. Philip Randolph.

Some believed that it would be impossible to assemble so large a crowd without major confusion. The Kennedy administration had a civil rights bill pending in Congress. The leaders of the march were warned that the march could provoke a backlash in the Congress. Some congressmen exacerbated fears by predicting mass rioting, looting, and violence. Their forebodings seemed plausible to local and national law enforcement agencies. As a result, the Washington, D.C., National Guard and other military units were put on alert.

Ausust 28, 1963 was not marked, however, by chaos. There were no major disruptions as 250,000 people of all races, colors, and religions assembled at the Lincoln Memorial. The dire predictions of the doomsayers melted away in rituals of festivity and solemness of purpose. Marchers were transported to and from the demonstration efficiently, and minor problems were minimized by the security personnel. The Metropolitan Police Department and the U.S. Park Police remained in the background and allowed the organizers to solve minor problems that occurred.

The only significant problem materialized when John Lewis, one of the principal speakers, appeared likely to deliver a fiery and provocative call for blacks to march through the South as General Sherman did during the Civil War. Patrick O'Boyle, the Catholic archbishop of the Washington, D.C., archdiocese, threatened to withdraw if Lewis made his comments as planned. March organizers, including Rustin and Randolph, persuaded Lewis to modify his inflammatory language. This prevented a confrontation.

The success of the march represented, in many respects, a personal triumph and vindication for both Rustin and Randolph. They attributed its success to sound planning and organizing, rightness of purpose, and adherence to the moral strength of nonviolent protest. In their view, the mass demonstration represented a victory for the philosophy of peaceful protest and interracial cooperation to which they both had dedicated their lives. It was conceded generally that Rustin, more than any other individual, had been critical to the success of the march. Nonetheless, he was not invited to the White House after the demonstration to meet with President Kennedy as were several other march leaders. Bayard Rustin remained a social and political pariah no matter what he accomplished.

While moderate black civil rights leaders like Whitney Young and Roy Wilkins perceived Rustin as an embarrassment to the movement, they were willing to use his advice, knowledge of labor, organizational and intellectual skills, and contacts with white liberals. They did not, however, want to be identified closely with him. Young once suggested sarcastically that Rustin should not be considered a major civil rights leader because he did not head a major organization. Some civil rights leaders, nevertheless, wanted Rustin to remain in the background and go about his business in a quiet but effective manner.

Militant black leaders were more critical of Bayard Rustin than moderates. They saw no need to use his considerable skills in the struggle for black equality. They believed that he aligned himself too closely with white liberals and often defended their right to be major players in the struggle, failing to understand the need for blacks to control their own destiny. In addition, both militants and moderates disliked Rustin's propensity for publicly criticizing black leaders and supporting white liberals. When Daniel Patrick Moynihan, for example, published his critical report on the black family suggesting that its structure and composition were destructive, most blacks and some whites criticized his conclusions severely. Rustin, however, defended Moynihan, saying that he had always supported blacks in their struggle for equality and that he should not be blasted as a racist. He believed, instead, that blacks should scrutinize the report closely to determine if Moynihan's conclusions were valid and, if so, to get about solving the problem.

The schism between Rustin and black militants continued to grow after the March on Washington. Their views of the world and their political philosophies were too incompatible for reconciliation. There were those, nonetheless, who hoped that blacks could forget their philosophical differences to present a united front in the fight for equality. The events at the Democratic National Convention in Atlantic City, New Jersey, in 1964, destroyed any hope of accommodation.

The controversy in Atlantic City originated in the poverty-stricken and predominantly black rural areas of Mississippi, where one of the goals of the Mississippi Summer Project of 1964, led by Robert Moses of the Student Nonviolent Coordinating Committee, included registering poor blacks to vote. Moses and other leaders in SNCC and CORE had been unable to participate in the white-controlled Democratic party in Mississippi. As a result, they organized the Mississippi Freedom Democratic party (MFDP) in accordance with rules established by the National Democratic Committee, including a pledge to support the national Democratic ticket. The latter was something the regular Democratic party in Mississippi refused to do. MFDP challenged the seating of the regular Mississippi Democratic party delegates at the convention. President Johnson, fearing a white backlash in the South and a walkout of southern delegates on the convention floor if MFDP delegates were seated, requested that black and white civil rights leaders stress the need for MFDP to compromise. Johnson sought the assistance of such men as Martin Luther King, Walter Reuther, Bayard Rustin, and Joseph Rauh, attorney for MFDP.

Rustin believed it vital to accede to Johnson's wishes strictly on pragmatic grounds. If Johnson were elected, it would be easy to deal with him and liberals like Hubert Humphrey and Walter Mondale. All of these men had supported civil rights legislation. A compromise proposed that two delegates from MFDP would be seated with the right to vote. Any regular delegate who refused to support the nominee would not be seated. Most significant for those who hammered out the compromise was the promise not to accept delegates in the future from states which discriminated against blacks. This gave blacks latitude and leverage that they did not have before.

MFDP rejected the compromise and accused those who participated in its formulation of selling out poor blacks in the South and rejecting the moral rightness of their challenge. The compromise split SNCC from moderate civil rights organizations and provided credibility to black militants who contended that the white establishment could not be trusted. On the other hand, the landslide election of Lyndon Johnson and his subsequent support of Great Society legislation suggested, at least to Bayard Rustin, the accomplishments of coalition politics. Depending on one's perspective, the compromise was a shrewd victory or a denigrating defeat.

The events in Atlantic City unquestionably reeked of backroom political intrigue. Rustin and the others, in their haste to appease Lyndon Johnson, gave a perfunctory consideration to the broader political realities of the time. It appeared unlikely that Johnson, a former vice president in an administration considered anathema by the white South, would carry the region in the election. On the other hand, his opponent, Barry Goldwater, held such extremist views on issues unrelated to civil rights that his election by a national electorate usually centrist in its attitudes seemed improbable. It seemed reasonable to assume, therefore, that even if MFDP had been seated, the outcome of the election would have been unaffected. As it turned out, Johnson did not win Alabama, Georgia, Mississippi, Louisiana, or South Carolina. Rustin and the others succeeded only in further alienating and radicalizing SNCC.

After 1964, Bayard Rustin found himself on the opposite side of almost every position that radical blacks articulated. The white press often seized this as an opportunity to present the radicals as irrational hate-mongering revolutionaries, while Rustin came across as a rational civil rights leader who understood how to achieve black equality the right way. It appeared that as the black power movement grew, Rustin became an acceptable alternative, at least philosophically. The differences between black radicals and Rustin were played out in the fullest view of the public arena.

One issue on which radical blacks and Rustin disagreed passionately was the idea to establish black studies programs in colleges and emphasize Afro-American history as early as elementary school. This idea found acceptance among a broad spectrum of blacks. Bayard Rustin, nonetheless, remained unconvinced and perceived the establishment of such programs as separatist and an endeavor to isolate blacks culturally and politically from whites. He believed that it was impossible to separate the black experience historically from the American experience and that black studies would remove blacks from the context of American history. To Rustin, courses in black history and culture should be integrated into regular course work. He was convinced, for example, that there should be no separate Italian-American history, no separate Jewish-American history, no separate ethnic history of any kind, only American history that portrayed the contributions of all Americans.

Rustin accused colleges of placating radical blacks by accepting proposals for black studies programs. He suggested, instead, that colleges develop remedial programs to improve the scholastic levels of black students so that they could succeed in college and private life. He believed that math and English should be stressed among black students because these tools were required to succeed in a white-dominated society. He saw little value in instructing blacks in "soul" classes that were "meaningless" in the real world.

Rustin condemned as little more than criminals the black students who armed themselves, marched into a building at Cornell University in April 1969, and held the building in protest against university policies. He viewed such behavior as outlandish and implied that if administration officials could not control their campuses then the police ought to be called. A college campus was no place for armed students. He ridiculed college administrators who succumbed to student blackmail.

While it may be difficult to argue with Rustin's logic regarding the invasion of a college campus by armed students, his views on black studies programs reflected his integrationist stance rather than an objective appraisal of what the programs entailed and how such curricula might benefit black students. First, he surmised that, instead of black studies, most black students needed remedial education in math and English. In reality, most of the students who were demanding that universities create black studies programs were well-educated blacks from moderate or middle-class families. Contrary to his belief, they did not need remedial training. Most black students, in addition, attended predominantly black colleges that usually offered some black-related courses that were not taught at white colleges. The black students' challenge, therefore, represented an attempt to make universities responsive to the needs of its black students in an environment where most of the resources went to white students. Second, theoretically, if the white-dominated society had integrated the achievements of blacks into college curricula, the issue of black studies might have been moot. Rustin's misplaced criticism should have been directed at the system and not the black students.

Rustin and radical blacks also disagreed on the related issue of affirmative action as a solution to years of discrimination against blacks. Affirmative action required employers to establish goals and timetables for increasing the percentage of blacks among their employees. First, blacks had to be qualified for the position but not necessarily the best qualified. Second, there had to be a job vacancy. In other words, a white employee could not be fired in order to give a job to a black applicant. The critics of affirmative action, nonetheless, ridiculed the concept as reverse discrimination and an effort to employ unqualified blacks at the expense of other qualified workers.

Bayard Rustin, in a way, bought into this creative mythology by criticizing so-called racial quotas. In fairness to Rustin, he did not oppose the idea of affirmative action but quickly condemned the concept of racial quotas. Quotas differed from affirmative action in that employees with few or no black workers were required to hire blacks in numbers to reflect the percentage of blacks in the general population. Rustin and others who opposed quotas argued that if enough qualified blacks were unavailable then the employer or university recruiter was required to lower standards to meet the necessary quota.

Rustin viewed quotas as a cheap way of handling the crisis in black underemployment. He felt that funds should be available to train blacks to obtain the necessary skills to do well in whatever jobs they chose. Hiring unqualified blacks in a competitive job market might provoke an anti-black response from other ethnic groups and whites who lost job opportunities for which they were qualified. Perhaps more significantly, he questioned the inherent fairness of a policy that seemed to provide special consideration for Afro-Americans.

In reality, affirmative action was more complex than simple job quotas and reverse discrimination. This was something that its critics never understood. The hope of redressing the discrimination to which most blacks had been subjected resisted a solution acceptable to all sides. As a concept, affirmative action represented a moderate and short-lived solution to the serious problem of black unemployment and underemployment resulting from institutional racism. After all, many militant blacks preached that the problem of recompensing blacks for past discrimination should be addressed only through a reparations program of some kind. When compared with radical solutions like this, affirmative action appeared less threatening.

It was impractical to expect that the federal government would allocate massive funds to train blacks to compete for jobs with whites, as Rustin advocated. In the 1970s, Congress did pass the Comprehensive Employment and Training Act (CETA) that provided funds to train the unemployed for low-wage public service jobs. Later training slots were reduced, along with wages, until the act had little impact or significance for unemployed blacks. While Rustin supported the CETA program, it fell short of the enormous aid that he wanted Congress to allocate to train blacks for the job market.

Bayard Rustin not only opposed the idea of racial quotas but also the concept of black capitalism. The belief that black capitalism could provide some relief for the economic woes of blacks had been suggested in the past. Marcus Garvey's Universal Negro Improvement Association engaged in capitalistic ventures in the 1920s. The Black Muslims' slogan of self-help in the 1960s consisted, in reality, of an attempt to develop black businesses in the black community. Rustin viewed these attempts and others like them as endeavors in separatist economics and ideology. He doubted that a separate capitalist economy within the national economy would prove workable. If the American capitalist economy with enormous industrial capacity had been unable to solve the problems of black unemployment and economic stagnation, how did the proponents of black capitalism believe that a black capitalism with limited resources could do so?

Rustin failed to listen carefully to the advocates of black capitalism. They never considered it a panacea for black economic ills. Rather, they perceived it as black control of the economics of black neighborhoods. One of its basic tenets was that blacks were disadvantaged economically because they spent most of their money outside their communities but very little was returned to them. Advocates of black capitalism argued that establishing and supporting black businesses would help to prevent the loss of black resources within black communities. Bayard Rustin never viewed the issue in that light. He perceived it, instead, as an alien and separatist ideology. He believed the only hope for blacks was a strengthened coalition of trade unions, minorities, and liberals. He remained convinced that blacks could prosper only in a fully integrated society.

Bayard Rustin continued his social activism until his death in 1987 at the age of seventy-five. During the last ten years of his life he often embroiled himself in controversial issues such as U.S. policies toward Israel, Southeast Asia, and the Caribbean. He likened the plight of the Jews with that of American blacks. He supported consistently the cause of Jews in Israel and accused those who were critical of Israeli policies, including many blacks, of acquiesing in the politics of terrorism. His views on Israel elicited sharp criticism from some blacks who objected to Israeli intransigence in the Middle East. These blacks were most alarmed, however, over Israel's continuing support of the white racist regime in South Africa. Such critics could not offer unconditional support of Jews in Israel.

In his later years, Rustin gave more attention to international issues than he had during the 1960s and the early 1970s. In 1980, he traveled to Southeast Asia to appraise the condition of the Vietnamese boat people and the ravages of the Khmer Rouge insurgents in Cambodia. This was done to focus attention on their problems. He visited Haiti in the same year to draw attention to the plight of blacks in that beleaguered country. He also went to Sweden to participate in an international effort to force the Soviet Union to release the imprisoned dissident Anatoly Scharanski.

Until his death, Bayard Rustin continued to criticize his friends, colleagues, and fellow blacks when he believed they were wrong. During the economic crisis in the black community in the 1970s, which resulted from a steady rise in the black unemployment rate, Rustin criticized those blacks who argued for the deportation of illegal aliens who they believed took jobs from poor blacks. He accused the advocates of this position of making illegal aliens, most of whom were Mexicans, Asians, and poor blacks from Latin America and Haiti, scapegoats for failed economic policies. He rejected as absurd the contention that illegal aliens exacerbated the economic condition of blacks. The wages that they received, mainly from menial jobs in farming, service, and industry, would not have provided unemployed blacks with a decent living.

This analysis may have been accurate, but Rustin overlooked the influence of rising numbers of both illegal and naturalized aliens on the psyche of Afro-Americans. By the 1980s, there was a growing nativist ideology among blacks that resulted, in part, from the influx of aliens into black communities. There was a growing hostility, for example, between blacks and Koreans who often moved into black communities, opened small businesses and, in order to make a profit, charged prices for their goods that poor blacks could not easily afford. This led to frequent and sometimes violent confrontations. The issue of illegal aliens to blacks was considerably more complex than the question of jobs.

Despite Bayard Rustin's many controversial views, he was admired for his integrity and loyalty to his beliefs. Unlike some civil rights activists and radicals of the 1960s, his major positions remained consistent. He believed adamantly in an integrated society and the effectiveness of coalition politics. He severely criticized the positions of blacks when he believed their solutions advocated separatism. He supported labor and sought to include it as part of coalition politics while he was director of the A. Philip Randolph Institute. He identified with the new gay liberation movement. He championed the cause of Israel. He supported rights for illegal aliens. His voice was often raised in dissent, and he made his opinions known through a syndicated column that appeared in several black newspapers. When he died at the age of seventy-five in 1987, the nation lost one of its most humane activists.

Bibliography

Byron, Peg. "No More Back Seat: Civil Rights Activist Bayard Rustin Refused to Move Gay Pride to the Back of the Bus," *Southern Exposure* 16 (Fall 1988): 45–46.

Chinn, H. "Bayard Rustin: Six Decades of Fighting," *Gay Community News* 13 (June 29, 1986): 8.

Garrow, David. "Rustin, Bayard," in *The Biographical Dictionary of the American Left*,

Bernard K. Johnpoll and Harvey Klehr, eds. Westport, CT: Greenwood Press, 1986: 337–39.

Gates, Henry Louis. "Blacklash?" *The New Yorker* 69 (May 17, 1993): 42–4.

Morehead, Caroline. *Troublesome People: The Warriors of Pacifism*. Washington, DC: Adler and Adler, 1987: 253–59.

Obits: *Current Biography* 48 (Oct. 1987): 58; *Dissent* 35 (Winter 1988): 114–15; *Jet* 72 (Sept. 7, 1987): 54; *National Review* 39 (Sept. 25, 1987): 20; *New Leader* 70 (Sept. 7, 1987): 2, *New Republic* 197 (Sept. 28, 1987): 10–11; *New York Times Biographical Service* 18 (Aug. 1987): 857–58; *Newsweek* 110 (Sept. 7, 1987): 75; *Time* 30 (Sept. 7, 1987): 64.

Rustin, Bayard. "A. Philip Randolph," *Yale Review* 76 (Spring 1987): 418–27.

————. *The Bayard Rustin Papers* (22 reels of microfilm), John H. Bracey, Jr. and August Meier, eds. Bethesda, MD: University Publications of America, 1990.

————. "Black Power and Coalition Politics," *Commentary*, Sept. 1966, pp. 35–40.

————. "Civil Rights: 20 Years Later," *Newsweek*, Aug. 29, 1983, p. 11.

————. *Down the Line: The Collected Writings of Bayard Rustin*, intr. by C. Vann Woodward. Chicago: Quadrangle Books, 1971.

————. "The Failure of Black Separatism," *Harper's Magazine*, Jan. 1970, pp. 1–9.

————. "From Protest to Politics: The Future of the Civil Rights Movement," *Commentary*, Feb. 1964, pp. 1–8.

————. "How Has the United States Met Its Major Challenge since 1945?" *Commentary*, Nov. 1985, pp. 89–92.

————. "An Interview with Bayard Rustin," *New Perspectives* 17 (Winter 1985): 27–31.

————. Interviewed by Patricia Cooper, *The Crisis* 92 (March 1988): 24–29+.

————. "The King to Come: The Holiday and the Future Racial Agenda," *The New Republic* 196 (March 9, 1987): 19–21.

————. "Mobilizing a Progressive Majority," *The New Leader*, Jan. 25, 1971, pp. 7–10.

————. Review of *The Myth of Black Progress* by Alphonso Pinkney, in *The Atlantic* 254 (Oct. 1984): 121–23.

————. *Strategies for Freedom: The Changing Pattern of Black Protest*. New York: Columbia University Press, 1976.

Wiloch, Thomas. "Rustin, Bayard," in *Contemporary Authors*, vol. 25, New Revision Series. Detroit: Gale Research, 1989: 395–96.

Donald Roe

BOBBY SEALE (1936–   )

A founder of the Black Panther party

Bobby Seale was one of the boldest founders and champions of the Black Panther party during the 1960s and early 1970s. In the 1990s, Seale was a relatively low-profile private citizen who still represented, in many ways, the life of an African-American man.

Bobby Seale with Huey Newton. *Source*: Library of Congress

Bobby George Seale was born on October 22, 1936, in Dallas, Texas. Like most African people raised in the United States, Seale encountered and endured pain both outside and inside his family. Seale described his early years this way:

I grew up just like any other brother. We didn't always have money. During the war we had a little money, but after my father built the house he went to San Antonio, and we were back in poverty again. It was still wartime and there was some money around, but I remember that whenever my mother and father rented a house, they would rent half out to some other people. (*Seize the Time*, pp. 6–7)

Seale first began to oppose injustice when his family was living in Cordonices Village, a Berkeley, California, government housing project. Seale and his family, along with the other people living in Cordonices, were poor, and their living spaces were extremely crowded and "always dirty."

Seale's opposition to social inequality grew by the time he was sixteen. He was aware that the people who were indigenous to the country now called "the United States of America"—the native Americans—had become outcasts on their own land. He was emotionally and intellectually prepared to develop a radical critique of American society.

After completing high school, Seale spent some time in the U.S. Air Force. His military service concluded with his being court-martialed and given a "bad conduct" discharge. Seale had considered his treatment belittling and military personnel found his attitude unacceptable. This negative experience further sharpened his awareness of, his disdain for, and his resistance of European American authority.

Seale began attending Merritt Junior College in Oakland, California, during 1960. In 1962, upon returning to classes after having dropped out for one semester, Seale met Huey P. Newton. Many people around campus viewed Huey as a genius. Newton had a reputation on campus as well as in the East and West Oakland communities as a bright and aggressive man. In a short time, Bobby had the utmost respect for Newton, who influenced him profoundly. Newton coaxed, catalyzed, and offered a framework for Bobby's emotions, hopes, and ideas. As Seale remembered:

I met Huey . . . during the [time of the] Cuban blockade when there were numerous street rallies going on. . . . Huey was holding down a crowd of about 250 people . . . 'shooting everybody down'—that means rapping off information and throwing [a whole lot of] facts. . . . [Huey and the audience] got me caught up. They made me feel that I had to help out, be a part and do something. (*Seize the Time*, pp. 13, 14)

While Huey Newton may have been the flame which originally lit Bobby's mind, Minister Malcolm X (*) was even more of a prophetic fire. For Seale, both the life and the death of Malcolm became central to his emerging activism. When Seale heard that Malcolm had been murdered, his response was: "Fuck it, they killed him—I'll make a god damn Malcolm out of me" (*A Lonely Rage*, p. 175).

Seale was disappointed, however, with cultural nationalists who were long on theory and extremely short on programs to help people. Bobby Seale and Huey Newton began to think about creating an organization which would serve and empower poor African people in their everyday lives. They drew broad inspiration from Frantz Fanon's *The Wretched of the Earth*, Malcolm X's autobiography, Mao Tse-tung's *Little Red Book*, Robert Williams's *Negroes with Guns*, and some of the writings of Karl Marx and V. I. Lenin.

The Black Panther Party for Self-Defense evolved out of a Merritt College creation of Bobby and Huey called "The Soul Students Advisory Council." Sometime between late September and mid-October of 1966, the Black Panther Party for Self-Defense took shape. They adopted their name and their symbol, the Black Panther, from a freedom rights group based in the South, "the Black Panther Party of Lowndes County, Alabama," which started in 1965, and which called itself initially "the Lowndes County Christian Movement."

Newton was the minister of defense of the new organization; Seale was the chairman; and "Lil'" Bobby Hutton was the organization's first member and minister of finance. Hutton was a young man whom Seale had taught during the summer of 1966 as part of the summer youth work program at the Oakland Neighborhood Anti-Poverty Center. The group wrote a "Platform and Program" that contained ten points. The points were written in direct and simple terms since, as Seale put it, "a bunch of esoteric bullshit and a long essay" would not attract the people that they were speaking to.

Although the party never developed an elaborate ideology, each of the ten points did express basic elements about "What We Want" and "What We Believe." Consider the following:

1. We want freedom. We want power to determine the destiny of our Black Community.

   We believe that black people will not be free until we are able to determine our destiny.

2. We want full employment for our people.

   We believe that the federal government is responsible and obligated to give every man employment or a guaranteed income.

The third point of the Panthers' program expressed the necessity for Euro-American society to end its robbery of African-Americans and to provide reparations for its past sins of slavery and exploitation. Point four urged public housing fit for human habitation. The fifth point promoted education that would expose the decadence of the United States, teach African-American people their whole and true history, and encourage African-Americans to contribute to building a better society. Point six stated that all African-American men should be exempt from military conscription. The seventh point denounced police brutality. Point eight advocated the release of all African-

Americans held captive in any American jail. The ninth point demanded fair trials, in accordance with the Fourteenth Amendment to the U.S. Constitution, with juries composed of defendants' peers, meaning persons "from a similar economic, social, religious, geographical, environmental, historical, and racial background." Finally, point ten essentially reiterated all of the prior points. If African-Americans could not get "justice and peace" within the United States, they should exercise their right of revolution.

To fulfill these principles, Seale and the Black Panthers organized activities which served and empowered the African-American community. For example, from late 1966 through late 1967, with law books, sometimes with cameras, and always with guns, Seale and the Panthers followed and observed police—patrolled police—to make sure that the police did not abuse black people. In one instance, on May 21, 1967, Seale, Newton, and other Panthers served as armed escorts for Betty Shabazz, the widow of Malcolm X. Their work also began to be publicized through their own newspaper, *The Black Panther; Black Community News Service*, which began in May of 1967. As the Black Panther Party for Self-Defense expanded its activities, it dropped from its name "for Self-Defense" in 1967.

By 1969, Seale and the Black Panthers were engaged in many community service activities. They served free breakfasts to children; they provided communities with senior citizen escort services; they operated health clinics, "liberation schools," dental services, ambulance services, and free legal aid; they distributed free clothing and shoes; they worked to register voters; they sought to establish a commissary program for prisoners. And they continued to debate their goals.

At its zenith, the Black Panther party consisted of approximately 10,000 members, with forty or more Panther branches across the country. In 1972, Newton and the Panthers updated some aspects of their Ten-Point Platform and Program. The revisions generally made the document more class-and gender-inclusive, using the phrases "our black and oppressed communities," "all Black and oppressed people," and "Black people and other people of color." The tenth point was revised also to include a greater consciousness of the government's evolving ability to oppress people via advanced technology; "We want land, bread, housing, education, clothing, justice, peace and people's community control of modern technology." The party began to fade from national and international prominence by the mid-1970s. The party suffered partly because of ideological disputes, personality conflicts, and organizational disorder. Additionally, some part of the Panthers' decline was related to criticisms from other African-Americans. Most of the responsibility for the organization's collapse should rest, however, with the U.S. government.

From the moment that the Panthers became a visible, public reality, its members suffered from constant surveillance and harassment. White police made frequent, contrived, and annoying arrests, citing Panthers for alleged weapons violations and/or minor traffic violations. Attempts were made by various police agencies to halt publication and distribution of the Panther newspaper. The California State legislation attempted to restrict the constitutional right to bear arms. In October of 1967, shots were fired when a white patrolman stopped a car in Oakland that contained Huey Newton and another Panther. The patrolman was killed and Newton was injured badly. Though a second patrolman who arrived on the scene said that Newton had no weapon, Newton was still arrested for voluntary manslaughter. This began a series of costly and emotionally draining legal assaults.

In February of 1968, Seale and his first wife were arrested in their home without a warrant. Charges of conspiracy to murder were dropped ultimately. Later, in August of 1968, Seale, convicted of "disturbing the peace," began serving almost six months in a maximum security section of the Alameda County Courthouse. In addition, as a result of his participation in a demonstration of 10,000 persons at the 1968 Democratic convention in Chicago, Seale, along with seven white protesters, was put on trial for conspiracy. The trial, which lasted from September of 1969 through February of 1970, accused the men of forming a conspiracy to incite a riot at the Democratic convention. During the trial, Seale's protests resulted in him being gagged in the courtroom, shackled, and even hit in the testicles. Eventually the judge ruled that Seale had mistried, charged Seale with sixteen counts of contempt of court, and announced that Seale would be tried again the following year.

In 1969, Seale and Ericka Huggins were charged with murder and kidnapping. After a trial from late 1970 through May 1971, the case was dismissed. Seale and Huggins were "free." In between and during many of the aforementioned trials, Seale was kept in jail. He missed at least two years of his first child's development.

Many other Panthers were tried falsely. Some were killed with premeditation, such as the famous case of Fred Hampton in Chicago, considered as an official murder even by such establishment figures as Roy Wilkins and Ramsey Clark. Some Panthers remained in foreign exile even in the 1990s, such as Assata Shakur. Others continued to be in prison. The weight of these attacks, along with internal divisions in the party (including many government agents), shattered and finally crushed the Black Panther party.

In 1973, with the help of Newton, a few remaining Panthers, Ron Dellums (6*), and a variety of other supporters, Seale ran as an independent candidate for mayor of Oakland. The Panther party's leading spokesperson, Elaine Brown, ran for city council. Seale's campaign pivoted on a "14-Point Program to Rebuild Oakland." Seale spoke of "community control of the police department and all [other] city agencies and functions—to transform them so that they . . . serve the people." His programs, in many ways, resembled extensions of the community service and empowerment activities of the Panthers.

Seale ran for mayor with the major intention of educating the community. When the campaign was over, he had almost won, much to his own surprise. First he succeeded in defeating all of the other candidates in the primary election. Then, however, he was defeated by the incumbent Republican mayor in a head-to-head runoff. Nonetheless, his political effort had contributed to grassroots organizing, akin to the efforts of the Mississippi Freedom Democratic party of the 1960s.

Seale's ideas and actions in his later life were less dramatic than during his Panther years, although they were not fundamentally inconsistent. Seale argued that he remained committed to the quest for the creation of a just society. When the twentieth anniversary of the party's founding was celebrated in 1986, Seale spoke at the Harriet Tubman School in Harlem:

> The character of future movements will be about first class citizenship here [in the United States] and around the world. . . . Revolution is not a need for violence as portrayed by the corporate monopoly racist structure. Revolution is about the need to return political and economic power back into the hands of the people. [When] in the process of people doing that they get attacked by the corporate monopoly structure, they [the people] have every right to defend themselves. (*The National Alliance*, Oct. 31, 1986, pp. 13, 15)

Seale continued to have at least his share of ideological, economic, and legal criticisms in his later years. In 1988, some people questioned Seale for his publication of *Barbeque'n with Bobby*, a cookbook. They presumed that this proved his conversion to capitalism. Seale offered this explanation:

> I'm still a political revolutionary. . . . The fire never went out of me, but perceptions and realizations change. [To implement my goal of creating a foundation which assists in educating young African Americans and which gives two or three million dollars a year to grassroots programs working to eradicate illiteracy and hunger in the United States and apartheid in South Africa,] I need to get a cash flow. (*Richmond Time-Dispatch*, Aug. 25, 1988, E3)

Seale has never lived a luxurious life, and his business ventures were frequently clouded by failure if not actual charges of misconduct. His commercial inadequacies did not offer proof of criminality, however.

As the 1990s opened, Seale occasionally lectured and was connected to Temple University in Philadelphia. He worked with the Department of African American Studies and was a part-time assistant to the dean of the College of Arts and Sciences. He still hoped to "seize the time" to transcend a society where too many people are not free to develop all of their capacities. These people often have been dismissed as "black bums." Seale has had the vision to see what they could become in a more humane society.

Bibliography

Benjamin, Playthell. "The '60s Radicals: Where Are They Now?" *Emerge*, April 1991, pp. 20–27.

Freed, Donald. *Agony in New Haven: The Trial of Bobby Seale, Ericka Huggins, and the Black Panther Party*. New York: Simon and Schuster, 1973.

Heath, G. Louis, ed. *The Black Panther Leaders Speak: Huey P. Newton, Bobby Seale, Eldridge Cleaver, and Companions Speak Out.* Metuchen, NJ: Scarecrow Press, 1976.

———. *Off the Pigs! The History and Literature of the Black Panther Party.* Metuchen, NJ: Scarecrow Press, 1976.

Moore, Gilbert. *A Special Rage.* New York: Harper and Row, 1971.

Newton, Huey P. *To Die for the People: The Writings of Huey P. Newton.* New York: Vintage Books, 1972.

Pinkney, Alphonso. *Red, Black, and Green: Black Nationalism in the United States.* New York: Cambridge University Press, 1976.

Seale, Bobby. *A Lonely Rage: The Autobiography of Bobby Seale.* New York: Bantam Books, 1978.

———. *Seize the Time: The Story of the Black Panther Party and Huey P. Newton,* with a new introduction. Baltimore: Black Classic Press, 1991 (1968).

Shakur, Assata. *Assata: An Autobiography.* Westport, CT: Lawrence Hill, 1987.

The "Trial" of Bobby Seale (with special contributions by Julian Bond and others). New York: Priam Books, distributed by Grove Press, 1970.

Wilkins, Roy, and Ramsey Clark. *Search and Destroy.* New York: Harper and Row, 1973.

Rev. Cecil Gray

REIES LÓPEZ TIJERINA (1926–   )

Founder of the Alianza, minority leader

During the turbulent period of activism of the 1960s, Reies López Tijerina emerged as one of the most charismatic leaders of Mexican-American protest. His own campaign centered in New Mexico. For nearly a decade, he skillfully and incessantly built and led an organization of Hispanic-Americans who demanded a return of Spanish and Mexican land grants. Attracting national attention in 1967 by leading a violent raid on the Tierra Amarilla County courthouse in northern New Mexico, he became a revolutionary folk hero who was celebrated in books, articles, and songs. He soon shared the speaker's platform with national leaders of various radical groups. His prominence ended abruptly in 1969 when he began a prison sentence for parole violation. After his release from prison, he moderated his tactics and message and never regained his earlier popularity or power. As the 1990s began, he lived in relative obscurity with a small group of followers on a land grant he claimed in northern New Mexico.

Born on September 21, 1926, near Falls City, Texas, Reies Tijerina was one of ten children of Herlinda and Antonio Tijerina, sharecroppers and migrant workers. Growing up in the deprived world of migrant workers, young Reies

Reies López Tijerina seeks to arrest Warren Burger. *Source*: Library of Congress

suffered poverty and discrimination. His formal education was acquired in some twenty different rural schools. His mother was his primary teacher, reading him religious and other stories. She also encouraged him to take seriously his early mystical experiences. The first took place at age four when he dreamed that Christ took him by the hand and led him to a beautiful country. Others occurred throughout his life and provided inspirations and guidelines for his actions. After his mother's death when he was six years old, he worked in the fields with his father and older brothers and sisters. He quickly showed natural gifts as a speaker and persuader, earning him the title "abogado sin libros," or lawyer without books.

His mother's early training gave Tijerina a strong religious foundation. During his mid-teens he received a Bible from a traveling Baptist minister. He carefully read and incorporated its teachings into his life. At the age of nineteen, he abandoned his Catholic upbringing to enter an Assembly of God Bible college in Ysleta, Texas. After studying for three years, he began preaching in Victoria, Texas. Soon known as a fiery and effective preacher, he lost his ministerial credentials because he opposed tithing and believed that the church should help the poor rather than asking them for money. This was a portent of his later emphasis on social rather than religious issues. He demonstrated his commitment to his principles when, on at least three occasions, he gave all of his possessions to the poor. He spent most of the next decade preaching as an itinerant minister throughout the Southwest, seeing firsthand the misery and poverty of Mexican-Americans in the region. As a traveling preacher he developed a powerful speaking style which could convert the most skeptical of listeners and would later bring him success as a firebrand leader of Mexican-Americans.

During the 1950s he focused increasingly on social justice. In 1955 he founded a utopian religious community at Valle de la Paz (Valley of Peace), midway between Tucson and Phoenix. Although initially successful, the experiment collapsed because of harassment by local Anglos. Meanwhile, Tijerina had visited New Mexico and become interested in the issue of land grants. He had a powerful dream which included images of tall pines, frozen horses, and three angels. This convinced him that his mission in life was to help New Mexicans regain the land which had been given to them originally by Spanish and Mexican land grants. He subsequently traveled to Mexico several times and once to Spain to study the history and laws of land grants.

In the late 1950s Tijerina drifted into northern New Mexico. This was an economically impoverished region dominated by Spanish-speaking residents of towns and villages long isolated from most outside influences. Many of the local people traced their lineage to the Spanish and Mexicans who had settled in the area beginning in 1598. They often called themselves Hispanos. They were distrustful of outsiders, whom they blamed for their loss of several million acres of their community and privately owned land. Much of this lost land was claimed by the federal government for parks and recreation areas.

By 1960 Tijerina settled in Albuquerque and began a seven-year campaign to persuade New Mexicans that they should work to regain their lost lands and take pride in their culture. He traveled from house to house, speaking to men in the fields and to women in their homes. He addressed formal and informal gatherings at land-grant meetings, in churches, and wherever else he found an audience. He supplemented his personal contact with a daily radio show, "The Voice of Justice"; a newspaper column in Spanish in the Albuquerque *News Chieftan*; and for a short time, a weekly television program.

In February of 1963 he founded the Alianza Federal de Mercedes, an organization dedicated to restoring land grants to their rightful heirs. His efforts quickly bore fruit. Alianza membership multiplied with Tijerina claiming 30,000 members, although most authoritative estimates put the figure at 10,000 to 15,000. In 1966 he rejoined the Catholic church and married a young heir to a land grant. He admitted that both actions gave him more credibility among the Catholic Hispanos who formed most of his audiences in northern New Mexico.

From 1960 until 1966 he worked through established legal and political systems to create change. When these efforts failed to regain any land, he adopted more militant—and sometimes illegal—tactics. After he led a sixty-mile march from Albuquerque to Santa Fe to present demands to the governor of New Mexico yet recaptured no land, he presided over an occupation of the Echo Amphitheatre in a national forest in order to create the Republic de San Joaquin de Rio Chama. He hoped that this challenge to the jurisdiction of the Forest Service would illustrate the need for self-determination by Hispanos and force the courts to consider the issue of land grants. While the occupation led to his arrest, it also dramatically increased his following, particularly among young Chicanos.

By 1967, after more violence against Anglo-owned and government property, Rio Arriba County district attorney Alphonso Sanchez initiated action to suppress Tijerina and his followers. In response, Tijerina reconstituted the Alianza into the Alianza Federal de Pueblo Libres (Federal Alliance of Free Towns). He led an attempted citizen's arrest on the district attorney at the Rio Arriba County Courthouse in Chama. Although Sanchez could not be found, Tijerina's band seized and shot up the courthouse in perhaps the most daring, dramatic, and publicized single action in the Chicano Movement. Motivated by fears that the raid signaled a full-scale revolution, and that pro-Castro communists hidden in the hills might be joining Tijerina, a massive manhunt by police, national guard unit, and tanks tracked down "El Tiger" and his small group. Although Tijerina was later arrested, tried, and found guilty of charges surrounding the earlier events at the Echo Amphitheatre, he was acquitted of charges stemming from the courthouse raid. Adding to his reputation as an orator, in the latter trial he successfully argued his own case.

Tijerina's career paralleled the fortunes of many protesters and their causes. In 1968 he reached his greatest prominence and power. He led Chicanos at the Poor People's March on Washington, D.C., unsuccessfully ran for governor of New Mexico on a People's Constitutional party ticket, and called upon the president of Mexico to bring the land grant issue before the United Nations. The next year his increasingly daring antics included other well-publicized confrontations with the Forest Service and unsuccessful attempts at citizen's arrests on Supreme Court Justice Warren Burger, New Mexico's Governor David Cargo, and the director of the Los Alamos National Laboratory. During the latter part of the 1960s he became a celebrity to the New Left and to the nation's most militant protesters, sharing the platform with many radical speakers. In 1969 his quixotic quest ended when he began a three-year federal prison term for parole violation.

Tijerina was paroled on July 27, 1971, under terms that he hold no office in the Alianza, whatever its name, for five years. He nevertheless dominated the organization, although his tactics moderated. In 1976, again the formal leader of the Alianza, he revived his efforts to win the president of Mexico's support for taking the land grant issue to the United Nations. No longer the firebrand of his pre-prison years, he tempered his style of leadership and held a series of conferences devoted to brotherhood awareness.

With the Alianza split into a variety of factions in the 1990s, Tijerina's remaining support comes largely from the older heirs to land grants. The primary source of his publicity has been his puzzling depictions of Jews as responsible for problems plaguing all Mexican-Americans.

Yet even after considering himself as more a spiritual than a political leader, he has continued to strive to reclaim lands in the San Joaquin land grant in northern New Mexico. In 1979 he and his followers blocked a logging road in the area to assert their control over the half-million acres in the land grant. Although the blockade was broken, Tijerina and several families have occupied a version of the community of San Joaquin. He has served there as Alacalde (mayor) and as judge.

Tijerina relied on skilled rhetoric and appeals to history throughout his career. His message reflected his personal research in Mexico and Spain. In a typical presentation he would outline the basis for Mexican-American ownership of land, citing the results of his research on the *Laws of the Indies*— the laws by which the Spanish ruled the New World. Those documents, he argued, contained laws which were inalienable and consequently still applied. Individuals in northern New Mexico, therefore, could create free city-states like those outlined in the *Laws of the Indies* or like the city-state of San Joaquin, where he resided in 1990.

In the *Laws of the Indies* Tijerina also discovered his explanation for much of past, present, and future history. The *Laws* justified the marriage of Spanish and Indians in the New World, creating what Tijerina called the "New Breed." Only 450 years old, the New Breed would serve as a link between the United States and Latin America, bring together minorities and whites in the United States, and use its moral values to satisfy the world's hunger for moral order. Eventually this new race would lead older and dying races to a millennium characterized by peace and happiness.

Tijerina's message concentrated not only on the abstract and glorious future but also on the concrete and dismal present. He argued that Anglos had robbed Mexican-Americans of their lands through legal and illegal means ever since the United States wrested control of the region from Mexico. His research also convinced him that the land was stolen in violation of the Treaty of Guadalupe Hidalgo, which ended that war and required protection of the rights of property of land grant heirs.

Because the terrible treatment of Hispanos had stimulated not a single organization or institution to help the people, Tijerina concluded, Hispanos must publicize their own claims and promote their own interests. He claimed that the police and Forest Service had attempted to murder him, and that established institutions such as the educational system and news media had distorted Chicano history and created a false image of him as a violent troublemaker. Consequently, he proposed to alter the structure of education in northern New Mexico so that young people would be taught their history and accomplishment.

Tijerina's discourse reflected the conservative values and beliefs of his audience of the Hispanos of northern New Mexico. To these listeners, who were more traditional than radical, he stressed family, justice, religion, manliness, and unity. He advocated using the law courts to achieve their goals. He rested his arguments on the conservative sources of historical events and laws. It is also true, however, that he employed illegal means to gain national attention, expanded his themes to broader civil rights issues, and became politically linked to the New Left.

Tijerina's willingness to speak and write incessantly in an apparently hopeless cause, and his efforts to develop his arguments by conducting research in foreign countries all grew out of his view of himself as an agent of God. Through his visions he received God's plan for the future, where he was chosen to spread a message of facts and ideas that would inevitably persuade listeners, who in turn would change the world. Thus he was convinced that success would be certain if he only kept speaking and writing, for as a shepherd selected by God he could overcome whatever obstacles he encountered as he led a new breed of people toward a millennium of unity and brotherhood. Even while in prison Tijerina continued his campaign, writing his "Letter from the Santa Fe Jail" to maintain his hold on followers and further explain his ideas.

Consistencies as well as changes marked Tijerina's thirty-year crusade. Throughout his career he sought to improve the lives of Hispanos and all Mexican-Americans, developed his arguments with the facts discovered through his study of history and religion, believed he had the moral high ground, and centered on the immediate goals of regaining land and raising ethnic pride. Yet while he began his campaign as a fiery challenger of the entrenched Anglo power structure, in 1993 he was more subdued and contemplative and rarely spoke in public despite receiving numerous offers.

Tijerina's later views reflected changes which are difficult to understand. He believed that the problems of land grants required a resolution of international problems and that a nuclear holocaust was imminent. Laced throughout these themes was his scapegoating of Jews, whom he saw as an international conspiracy and blamed for many problems including the Hispanos' loss of land.

Notwithstanding the impotence of his later years, Tijerina left indelible marks in New Mexico. His powerful words and actions built the Alianza into the first movement for civil rights in New Mexico which gained national attention. Moreover, he helped Hispanos to break through their hopelessness and confront the established order. His long campaign bolstered the self-image of Hispanos, contributing to his followers' pride in their language and culture, sense of community, and ties to their origins in Spain and Mexico. To the young in particular, he became a symbol of courage and heroic activism after the courthouse raid and other attempted takeovers of federal properties.

Tijerina's influence reached far beyond New Mexico. By 1968 he was one of the widely recognized national leaders of Mexican-Americans, its spokesperson with the most explosive appeal, and a sought-after speaker by black, red, and brown power groups. Although he worked occasionally with the nation's best-known militant leaders in the last years of the 1960s, he never formally linked his organization to those of other protest movements.

The changes Tijerina brought to New Mexico did not result in the return of land to its original heirs. Perhaps too much power in Alianza rested with Tijerina. When he was in jail, the organization lost its effectiveness. Yet even changes in organizational structure could not have resolved a larger problem: it was unlikely that the lost acres would ever be recovered. It would have been more realistic to seek increased use rather than ownership of lands controlled by the federal government. But Tijerina was driven by dazzling visions. His proposals grew out of an unshakable belief that divine will would insure his success regardless of temporal obstacles.

Bibliography

Blawis, Patricia Bell. *Tijerina and the Land Grants*. New York: International Publishers, 1971.

Gardner, Richard. *Grito! Reies Tijerina and the New Mexico Land Grant War of 1967*. New York: Harper and Row, 1971.

Hammerback, John C., and Richard J. Jensen. "The Rhetorical Worlds of Cesar Chavez and Reies Tijerina," *Western Journal of Speech Communication* 44:3 (1980): 166–76.

Hammerback, John C., Jensen, Richard J., and José Angel Gutiérrez. *A War of Words: Chicano Protest in the 1960s and 1970s*. Westport, CT: Greenwood Press, 1985.

Jenkinson, Michael. *Tijerina*. Albuquerque, NM: Paisano Press, 1968.

Meier, Matt S. " 'King Tiger': Reies López Tijerina," *Journal of the West* 26 (April 1988): 60–68.

———. "Reies López Tijerina," in *Mexican American Biographies: A Historical Dictionary, 1836–1987*, Matt S. Meier, ed. Westport, CT: Greenwood Press, 1988: 219–21.

Nabokov, Peter. *Tijerina and the Courthouse Raid*. Berkeley: Ramparts Press, 1970.

Tijerina, Reies López. "The Land Grant Question," a speech at the University of Colorado, November 20, 1967, in Robert Tice, "The Rhetoric of La Raza," unpublished manuscript, Chicano Studies Collection, Hayden Library, Arizona State University, Tempe.

———. "Letter from the Santa Fe Jail" (August 15–17, 1969), in *We Are Chicanos: An Anthology of Mexican American Literature*, Philip D. Ortega, ed. New York: Simon and Schuster, 1973: 88–98.

———. *Mi lucha por la Tierra*. Mexico: Fondo De Cultural Cultura Económica, 1978.

John C. Hammerback
Richard J. Jensen

MALCOLM X [EL-HAJJ MALIK EL-SHABAZZ] [MALCOLM LITTLE] (1925–1965)

Muslim spiritual and racial teacher

Malcolm X, in cold black rage, stared into the eyes of white Americans. They were devils who had a long history of violence toward people of color. They were hypocrites who did not live up to their own ideals of Christianity and democracy. Blacks would not benefit from integrating with such depraved beings. It was better to create a separate black society. Malcolm's comments, best remembered in his autobiography published in 1965, angered some, jolted others, and pleased those who heard their own frustration and bitterness.

Malcolm was born in Omaha, Nebraska, on May 19, 1925—"born in a segregated hospital of a segregated mother and a segregated father." He was the seventh child of Earl Little, an itinerant construction worker and Baptist minister, and the fourth child of Louise Little. Malcolm's early years were poisoned by both poverty and racism. His family was not like that of Martin Luther King, Jr. (*), who was nurtured in a stable middle-class home in Atlanta and educated by a prominent and respected minister. Malcolm's father had neither the community credentials of the Reverend Martin Luther King, Sr., nor his moderate views. Earl Little was a champion of Marcus Garvey, and life in Omaha was apparently none too quiet for trouble-making blacks.

Shortly after Malcolm was born, the Littles moved first to Milwaukee and then to various locations in and around Lansing, Michigan. Even if Malcolm's memories of those years were not always accurate, it is clear that white America, for him, was not so much a land of opportunity as a maze of racial and class contradictions. His last home with his mother and father was a four-room shack with tar shingles, bare floors in all the rooms, and uncovered light bulbs for illumination.

Racism was found even within the family. Malcolm believed that his father, who was mahogany black, treated him the best because "he was subconsciously so afflicted with the white man's brainwashing of Negroes that he inclined to favor the [lightest-skinned], and I was his lightest child." Louise Little, however, was a Grenadian who was pale enough to pass for white and may have been harder on Malcolm because she did not want him to be spoiled.

Malcolm's childhood had no happy memories of vacations, play, and cheerful surroundings. Life became even worse when Earl Little was killed under mysterious circumstances in 1931. Malcolm was then six years old. His family sank further into poverty. Meals might consist of stale surplus bread and dan-

Malcolm X [El-Hajj Malik El-Shabazz].
Source: Library of Congress

delion greens, and the children's clothes were shabby. Malcolm began to steal. When he was thirteen, his mother had an eighth and illegitimate child. She drifted into insanity and was committed to a mental hospital in Kalamazoo, Michigan, where she remained for twenty-six years. The family was now scattered to state agencies, boarding homes, and relatives.

Malcolm, despite this discouraging history, was successful in school and was elected class president one year, although he recalled feeling "unique in my class, like a pink poodle." He also remembered that his school books said virtually nothing about his own people and that when he informed his favorite English teacher that he hoped to become a lawyer the man responded "you've got to be realistic about being a nigger. . . . Why don't you plan on carpentry?" Malcolm's formal education stopped after the eighth grade.

He moved to the Roxbury section of Boston in 1940 to live with his half-sister Ella. At this point, he had no positive black identity. He straightened ("conked") his hair with a burning lye compound. He got a blonde girlfriend.

He held various jobs regarded as suitable for his education and race, such as hotel bus boy, soda jerk, and waiter in a dining car. He also began his street education, learning how to play numbers, steer johns to prostitutes, smoke marijuana, and wear zoot suits. He absorbed the capitalist ethic that the whole world is a hustle and became "a predatory animal." All of this occurred not in the so-called backward and prejudiced South, but in the North. As Malcolm later noted, "I know nothing about the South. I am a creation of the northern white man and his hypocritical attitude toward the Negro."

He went to Harlem in 1942, at the age of seventeen, and continued his education, which soon included robbery. After spending most of his teenage years in the ghettos of Boston and New York, where he learned about drugs, prostitution, gambling, and theft, he was arrested for robbery in 1946. Not yet twenty-one, he was sentenced to eight to ten years in the prison at Charlestown, Massachusetts. He had "sunk to the very bottom of the American white man's society."

At this point, what could be the source of his redemption? Prison systems did not have a good record at rehabilitating people. Civil rights groups like the NAACP and the Urban League had little interest in convicts. The Left, both black and white, was being shattered and repressed in the late 1940s and the 1950s. By chance, Malcolm became aware of the teachings of a small subcult of Islam led by Elijah Muhammad. Four of Malcolm's siblings had already joined when his brother Reginald put him into contact with the group. Elijah Muhammad had served more than three years in prison in the 1940s for draft refusal and had begun to recruit in jail what he called "Negroes in the mud." Muhammad told Malcolm that white society had created Malcolm. White society had given him a negative identity as an ignorant and inferior member of U.S. society, destined to failure or to minimal income from menial jobs, and reconciled by a European-defined Christianity. Elijah said that Malcolm could re-create himself as a strong black man through the discipline of Muslim values.

Malcolm had a conversion experience where he was reborn, just as others have their lives transformed by Holiness churches or some secular ideology such as Marxism. But Malcolm's new faith was neither privatistic (a Muslim version of "I've got Jesus and that's all that matters") nor universalistic, such as the communism of W.E.B. DuBois and Paul Robeson. He now saw himself as strictly a race man who was obligated to contribute to the race by spreading "the natural religion of the black man, Islam." He had felt lost and alone. Now he had a sense of belonging, meaning, and hope.

Some of Elijah's teachings were Orthodox Islam, such as the focus on one God (in Arabic, the word for God is Allah), not some cluttered Christian trinity. Allah can never be actually depicted, unlike Christian artwork of God, usually as a fair-skinned male. The word of Allah is expressed in the Koran, including the requirement of five daily prayers (in the direction of Mecca), the obligation of charity, the duty of fasting during the month of Ramadan, and the expectation (if possible) of making a pilgrimage (a *hajj*) to Mecca. "Islam," in Arabic, means submission to Allah. Some of Elijah's teachings, however, were purely sectarian, such as the cult's founding role by W. D. Fard of Detroit, the status of Elijah Muhammad as the Messenger of Allah (whereas orthodox Muslims consider Muhammad of Arabia, who died in A.D. 632, as the last prophet of Allah), an elaborate mythology of the origin of the races (with whites as an inferior, bleached race created by an evil man from the original black race), and the limitation of membership in the Nation of Islam solely to blacks (whereas orthodox Islam is not racially exclusive). Elijah preached that a divine day of judgment was coming when the white devils would be destroyed. Blacks should stop being the "mental slaves, beggars, and servants of white America" and build their own temples, schools, businesses, and (ideally) state. For believers, righteous living meant no alcohol, no tobacco, no drugs, no gambling, no loud speech, no gluttony, no idleness, no flamboyant clothing, no movies, no dancing, and no extramarital sex.

Malcolm was an uncritical convert. His new religion provided him with an emotional and intellectual emancipation. He wanted to preach his new gospel but quickly realized the flaws in his education: "I didn't know a verb from a house." He started over by copying words and meanings from a dictionary, methodically progressing from A through Z. When he completed this task he said that, for the first time, he could pick up a book and understand what it was saying. He then read widely in history (which he complained had been whitened), philosophy, literature, law, and religion. He enrolled in prison correspondence courses in English and Latin. While his self-education left gaps, his later knowledge was not limited, then, to comic books, but included Herodotus, Socrates, Milton, Kant, Spinoza, Nietzsche, and Schopenhauer. As he later remarked: "I didn't know what I was doing, but just by instinct I liked books with intellectual vitamins."

When Malcolm was paroled in 1952, at the age of twenty-seven, he traveled to Chicago to meet Elijah Muhammad and be accepted into the movement. He was given the name Malcolm X, with the "X" symbolizing the African history and family that had been destroyed during slavery. The name "Little" represented the white oppressors. Malcolm's second life, a kind of reincarnation, was as Minister Malcolm. He traveled from city to city "fishing on corners" to convert his people. By 1953, he lived with Elijah Muhammad, who developed him as chief minister and spokesman of the Nation. In 1954 he was made the minister of Harlem's Temple No. 7.

Malcolm swept others into the Nation by his enthusiasm, wit, and personality. His speeches did not scream and rant, but spoke in carefully modulated tones, as he expressed considerable humor and vivid images. He appealed to his urban lower-class audiences by noting that he did not come out of the seminary or the university, unlike Dr. King, but out of the penitentiary. He was a "field Negro," not a middle-class "house Negro." He tried to speak to people in ways that they could understand. Although he was a Muslim, part of his success came from his thorough understanding of the metaphors of the Bible, which he reinterpreted to black Americans to prove the doctrines of Elijah Muhammad. Malcolm argued, for example, that the Bible justified the separation of the races, since "nowhere in the scriptures did God ever integrate his enslaved people with their slave masters. God always separates his oppressed people from their oppressor and then destroys the oppressor." Malcolm concluded that blacks should escape the wicked white race just as the Hebrews had the oppressive Egyptians.

The general public, black and white, began to be aware of what was commonly called the Black Muslims. In 1957, after a police beating of Hinton Johnson, a New York City member of the Nation, Malcolm summoned more than two thousand people to surround the local precinct station. He successfully demanded to see Johnson and got him medical attention. (Johnson later won a police brutality suit against the city.) Malcolm began to develop ties with other black activists, such as Representative Adam Clayton Powell. In 1959, Malcolm traveled to Egypt, Saudi Arabia, the Sudan, Nigeria, and Ghana as an emissary of Elijah Muhammad. Also in 1959, the public spotlight was put on him and the group by a critical but serious CBS documentary, "The Hate That Hate Produced." In 1961 he met and had a long conversation with Fidel Castro. At that point, the Nation had perhaps forty temples and missions, more than two dozen radio stations, businesses, schools, and tens of thousands of members, most of them between the ages of eighteen and thirty-five.

Despite this success, Malcolm began to have doubts, which he did not express publicly, about some of the church's religious principles. He also wanted it to be more socially and economically active. The Nation talked a strong moral talk, but it did little. Although Malcolm was critical of the civil rights movement, he understood that millions of people were being moved by activities for immediate political, economic, and social gains while the Nation was preoccupied with the apparently utopian goal of total separation in the future.

The Chicago organization became increasingly fearful that Malcolm was too influential as an individual, rather than as a spokesman for the organization. By 1963, Malcolm was one of the most requested people on the college lecture circuit. Strains between Malcolm and Elijah Muhammad intensified when Malcolm investigated rumors that Elijah had committed adultery with several of his secretaries and had fathered numerous illegitimate children. Elijah then shifted the focus to Malcolm in 1963 when he "silenced" Malcolm for ninety days. Malcolm was supposedly punished for endangering the public image of the Nation by his comment that the assassination of President Kennedy was an example of "the chickens coming home to roost"—that the United States had a history of violence at home and abroad.

Malcolm sensed that he was being set up for excommunication. Although Malcolm had once believed in Elijah "the way that Christians do in Jesus," he now felt that he was bleeding inside his own head. During the next year he established the Muslim Mosque, made a pilgrimage to Mecca, traveled in Africa (meeting several African leaders), and created the secular Organization of Afro-American Unity. By the spring of 1964 there had been major changes in his views. Islam remained a spiritual center—and secular intellectuals, then and later, seldom appreciated this—but it was now a universal, orthodox Sunni Islam that did not talk about "superior" and "inferior" races. Malcolm no longer saw any reason to isolate himself from millions of people in the Muslim world because they were not "black." After this self-described spiritual rebirth he took the name El-Hajj Malik El-Shabazz, as a Muslim who had made the holy journey to Mecca and was a master in the original tribe of the black people.

Black nationalism, also redefined, remained vital. He accepted white allies, but said that blacks must first organize themselves. There should be a strong sense of their own historical identity, which did not begin with slavery's chains. Blacks could not understand where they were until they understood where they had come from. "History," he said, "is a people's memory, and without memory man is demoted to the lower animals."

Black nationalism, he felt, should continue to be expressed in black political and economic control of black communities. Politicians should speak for the race. There should be black businesses "so that we can provide jobs for our own people instead of having to picket and boycott and beg someone else for a job." Socially, "we feel that it is time to get together among our own kind and eliminate the evils that are destroying the moral fiber of our society, like drug addiction, drunkenness, adultery that leads to the abundance of bastard children and welfare programs." His black nationalism, though, was not in the conservative tradition of Booker T. Washington which was centered on vocational training, economic self-help, hard work, black unity, and staying out of social and economic reforms in the broader white society. The white establishment loved most of this. By contrast, Malcolm was in the radical tradition of black nationalism that was Pan-Africanist (seeking to link black Americans with others of African origin), anti-capitalist ("show me a capitalist, I'll show you a bloodsucker"), and anti-imperialist ("you don't know where you stand in America until you know where America stands in the world"). His tentative solutions ranged from local voter registration drives to petitions for the United Nations, as a symbolic forum for the nonwhite majority of the world, to investigate human rights abuses within the United States.

Who were his audience while he was still alive? Liberal integrationists still found him too tainted by nationalism and radicalism. Christians were wary of his Muslim faith. Socialists and communists thought that he didn't understand the central importance of class. Some black nationalists felt that he wasn't saying enough about race. And some members of the Nation of Islam now ridiculed him as a traitor who deserved to die. Louis X (later Louis Farrakhan [*]) ominously proclaimed in a December 1964 issue of *Muhammad Speaks* that "the die is set, and Malcolm shall not escape. . . . Such a man as Malcolm is worthy of death." There were disturbing rumors that Elijah Muhammad had decided that "it's time to close his eyes" and various temples had received tapes from Chicago that Malcolm was about to be "blasted off the face of the earth." Malcolm was convinced that Elijah's Muslims were preparing to kill him: "anyone who chooses not to believe what I am saying doesn't know the Muslims in the Nation of Islam."

One week before Malcolm's death, the Nation of Islam got a court order to evict Malcolm, his four small daughters, and his pregnant wife from their home. Malcolm claimed that the house was theirs. After this notice, there was an unusual fire one evening. Then, on the afternoon of February 21, 1965, as he began to speak to a small gathering at the Audubon Ballroom in Harlem, he was struck by shotgun blasts and numerous bullets fired by several black attackers. He died quickly. He was three months short of his fortieth birthday.

Three Muslims were convicted, although their exact guilt, the possibility of other accomplices and assassins, and the role of the FBI and local police organizations in protecting (or not protecting) Malcolm continued to be disputed. Louis Farrakhan and other members of the old Nation of Islam later sought to deflect attention from their own activities, which at least contributed to a murderous climate. Malcolm's widow, Betty Shabazz, remembered the comments of Louis X and remained angry at the Nation's abandonment of her and her children after the murder of her husband. Even when Malcolm's autobiography was published in 1965, he remained a nonperson among the Nation's faithful although, by the 1990s, some were willing to allow the impression that Malcolm was about to be reconciled with the Nation at the time of his death (for the truth, see his *Final Speeches* [1992]). Some of the followers of Louis Farrakhan implied that they were somehow the legitimate descendants of Malcolm.

Malcolm X was a complicated man who was reduced frequently, by both his critics and his friends, to a cartoon. Many dismissed him as a black racist, a poisonous hate-monger, or preacher of violence. *Newsweek* labeled him "Satan in the Ghetto" and *The Nation* announced that he was "the most articulate member of the Negro lunatic fringe." Most black newspapers and magazines were no more complimentary. By contrast, "black power" advocates of the 1960s, nationalists, other Muslims, rap musicians, and even conservatives (such as Clarence Thomas, Thomas Sowell, and the *Wall Street Journal*) later scavenged through his speeches and literary remains to find proof of their own ideological or racial beliefs. In truth, Malcolm left no lasting organizations, no coherent program, and no specific strategy or set of strategies. Even his final racial views naively urged a black unity that little understood the powerful defining (and dividing) roles of class, gender, and geography. W.E.B. DuBois, by comparison, had a more sophisticated understanding of race, both in the United States and abroad.

Such criticisms, even if fundamentally valid, do not explain why three million copies of his autobiography had sold by the early 1990s. Nor does it tell us why millions of people were interested in Spike Lee's $33 million epic movie, or why millions displayed the symbol "X" or the face of Malcolm. Perhaps the central reason is that racism (tangled up with class) remained throughout American life and few public figures aggressively challenged it. A young Malcolm growing up in the 1990s was as likely to be born into poverty: one-half of all African-American children were in poverty as the 1990s began (and more than 30 percent of all African-Americans). A young Malcolm in the 1990s was as likely to live in crumbling urban surroundings and attend an inferior school. Why bother with education if there were few jobs? Why resist drugs if there was little hope or future? Why not have children early as a sign of some virility and success? A young Malcolm might have ended up in jail. The United States, with more than one million inmates in 1993, had the largest percentage of its population in prison of any country in the world and almost 50 percent of those prisoners were African-Americans. How could such a person develop a sense of self-worth? It was not surprising that a 1980s update of a 1947 study of young African-American children found that most had absorbed the larger culture's views: 65 percent of them, given a choice between white dolls or black dolls, preferred white dolls: "Black is dirty"; "I want to be white"; "I'm tired of being black" (*Time*, May 17, 1993, p. 48). The U.N. Human Development report for 1993 noted that while the United States, overall, ranked number 6 out of 173 nations in terms of quality of life (which included education, health, and real purchasing power), if African-Americans were considered a separate nation they would rank number 31—and the remaining whites would be number 1 in the world (*Washington Post*, May 18, 1993, A7). Even successful African-Americans have been shocked by episodes such as the Rodney King trials. Was the second trial a success? Had racism diminished? As Malcolm had said earlier: "You don't stick a knife in a man's back nine inches, and then pull it out six inches and say you're making progress."

This is what Malcolm X offered.

First, and most shallowly, he was a vivid image. Some people interpreted this as pride, others militance or male strength. His head was not bowed; he stood up to the white man with blunt talk of "no sellout" and "by any means necessary." This image, of course, can be commercialized, trivialized, or used only (as Stanley Crouch said) like "a voodoo doll—something to shake at white people and say, 'I'm not happy here. I'm not satisfied yet.'"

Second, and more significant, the image could be used as a role model. Malcolm overcame poverty, drugs, and jail. He grew, cleaned up his life, and ended with tantalizing glimpses of a unifying vision. He became somebody.

Third, he didn't do this by himself; he was aided by his family, the Nation of Islam (at first), and his friends. Religious, social, political, and economic institutions can help to create decent and productive people, just as institutions can keep them caged and baffled. In the case of Islam, Americans could learn to differentiate between such narrow sectarians as Louis Farrakhan and the orthodox Sunni Islam of Wallace Muhammad, son of Elijah Muhammad. Wallace and Betty Shabazz became part of the Muslim world of one billion people, concentrated in 57 countries where more than one-half of the population are Muslim.

Fourth, Malcolm's life illustrated the importance of values, certainly in the case of Islam, but also the role of history and culture in establishing one's identity. Europeans have largely ignored the ancient and complex history of Africa; this is a history that is as old as that of mankind. Even African-Americans have been brainwashed to see Africa as totally negative. Few look to African cultures or seek to form Africa support groups to influence U.S. political and economic ties. They have consciously or subconsciously absorbed European definitions of history, art, religion, literature, and society. Malcolm argued that by hating Africa they ended up hating themselves. African-Americans needed to decide who they were, not merely accept the definitions of the dominant white society. African-Americans needed to understand their own history, both in Africa and in North America. A naive Eurocentrism should be confronted by Afrocentrism.

Fifth, what was the goal of all of this? It was no longer a genetic determinism (like that of the "ice people" and the "sun people" of Dr. Leonard Jeffries) or xenophobic nationalism. But it was also not simple integrationism, which usually meant that blacks are supposed to become more like whites, not that whites are supposed to change. Malcolm was an African-American Muslim. He did not wish to become a copy of a white Christian. This perspective would be called, later, multiculturalism. It was a smashing attack on the reductionist melting pot.

Sixth, the last days of both Malcolm and Dr. King displayed a greater consciousness that the coming battlefields would necessarily include economics. Neither black nationalism nor liberal integration had done much for those at the bottom. Economic injustice would prove to be a far more difficult opponent than overt segregation.

The life of Malcolm X could be portrayed in three major acts, each reflected by his name. Malcolm Little was a stepchild of white America. Malcolm X was redeemed by the teachings of Elijah Muhammad, but remained confined in a ghetto world. El-Hajj Malik El-Shabazz escaped into an international world where he became Muslim, African-American, and radical.

Bibliography

Breitman, George, Herman Porter, and Baxter Smith. *The Assassination of Malcolm X*, 3d ed. New York: Pathfinder Press, 1991.

Carson, Clayborne. *Malcolm X: The FBI File*, David Gallen, ed. New York: Carroll and Graf, 1991. See the critique of this volume by David Garrow, *Journal of American History*, Dec. 1992, p. 1250.

Clarke, John Hendrik, ed. *Malcolm X: The Man and His Times*. Trenton, NJ: Africa World Press, 1990 (1969).

Cone, James. *Martin and Malcolm and America: A Dream or a Nightmare?* Maryknoll, NY: Orbis, 1991.

Davis, Lenwood G., and Marsha L. Moore, eds. *Malcolm X: A Selected Bibliography.* Westport, CT: Greenwood Press, 1984.

Dyson, Michael Eric. "Who Speaks for Malcolm X? The Writings of Just about Everybody," *New York Times Book Review,* Nov. 29, 1992, pp. 3, 29, 31, 33.

Frady, Marshall. "The Children of Malcolm," *The New Yorker,* Oct. 12, 1992, pp. 64–72, 74–81.

Gallen, David, et al. *Malcolm X: As They Knew Him.* New York: Carroll and Graf, 1992.

Garrow, David. "Does Anyone Care Who Killed Malcolm X?" *New York Times,* Feb. 21, 1993, E17.

Goldman, Peter. *The Death and Life of Malcolm X,* 2d ed. Urbana: University of Illinois Press, 1979.

———. "Malcolm X: Witness for the Prosecution," in *Black Leaders of the Twentieth Century.* Urbana: University of Illinois Press, 1982: 304–30.

Haddad, Yvonne Yazbeck, ed. *The Muslims of America.* New York: Oxford University Press, 1991.

Horne, Gerald, " 'Myth' and the Making of 'Malcolm X'," *American Historical Review* 98 (April 1993): 440–50.

Johnson, Timothy V. *Malcolm X: A Complete Annotated Bibliography.* New York: Garland Publishing, 1986.

Lee, Spike, with Ralph Wiley. *By Any Means Necessary: The Trials and Tribulations of Making 'Malcolm X'.* New York: Hyperion, 1992.

"Malcolm X: Make It Plain." Washington, DC: Blackside, Inc. for the Public Broadcasting System, 1994 (film: 150 minutes).

Marable, Manning. "On Malcolm X: His Message and Meaning" (pamphlet). Westfield, NJ: Open Magazine Pamphlet Series, 1992.

Perry, Bruce. *Malcolm: The Life of a Man Who Changed Black America.* Barrytown, NY: Station Hill Press, 1991.

Strickland, William and the Malcolm X Documentary Production Team. Malcolm X: Make It Plain, with oral histories by Cheryll Y. Greene. New York: Viking Press, 1994.

White, John. "Malcolm X," in *Black Leadership in America: From Booker T. Washington to Jesse Jackson,* John Clark, ed. 2d ed. New York: Longman, 1990, pp. 145–71.

Wood, Joe, ed. *Malcolm X: In Our Own Image.* New York: St. Martin's Press, 1992.

X, Malcolm. *The Autobiography of Malcolm X,* with the assistance of Alex Haley. New York: Grove Press, 1965.

———. *Malcolm X: The Last Speeches,* Bruce Perry, ed. New York: Pathfinder Press, 1989.

———. *Malcolm X: Speeches at Harvard.* New York: Paragon House, 1991 (1968).

———. *Malcolm X Speaks,* George Breitman, ed. New York: Grove Weidenfeld, 1990.

David DeLeon

PART TWO

PEACE AND FREEDOM

The old law, 'an eye for an eye,' leaves everyone blind.
—*Rev. Martin Luther King, Jr.*

Americans generally consider themselves peace-loving, although they are avid consumers of television programs, movies, newspapers, and magazines that describe, in thrilling detail, brutal attacks on people, and are strewn with bruised, torn, and bloody bodies. This is not some contemporary quirk. If the history books of this society eliminated all references to preparations for wars, actual wars, and the aftermath of wars, how much would be left? In fact, this society began with wars against the native peoples, was established in a war against the mother country, was expanded by further wars against Indians and Mexicans, was preserved in a civil war, and has expanded its worldwide influence by additional wars. By the latter decades of the 1900s, the United States was the largest seller of military weapons on the entire planet.

During the 1960s, contradictions between the ideal and the real in American society produced explosions of consciousness and protest within the United States. At first, there were only a few individuals and tiny groups that challenged the reigning mythology, usually in the name of such troublemakers as Micah, Isaiah, and Jesus. These defenders of the absolute sanctity of human life were commonly members of historic peace churches such as the Quakers and pacifist organizations such as the Fellowship of Reconciliation (1915), the American Friends Service Committee (1917), the War Resisters League (1923), the Women's International League for Peace and Freedom (1919), and the Committee for Nonviolent Action (1957). While some organizations emphasized counseling for conscientious objectors to military service, such as the

Central Committee for Conscientious Objectors (1948) and the National Interreligious Board for Conscientious Objectors (1940), others had links to emerging social reform movements. The Fellowship of Reconciliation, for example, influenced Bayard Rustin (1*), James Farmer (1*), and other activists in the Congress of Racial Equality (1943). Pacifists had also created a small publishing network that included *Liberation* (1956–1977) and *WIN* (Workshop in Nonviolence, 1966–1983). Some radical pacifists, such as David McReynolds (*), David Dellinger, and A. J. Muste, criticized the violence of both capitalism and communism, espousing a "third camp" where nonviolent direct action might be used to challenge such major forms of oppression as militarism and racism.

While pacifists have been a persistent and sometimes influential core within the anti-militarist movements in the United States, they seldom have been numerous. At the beginning of the 1960s, there were many more people who were not pacifists, but were opposed to nuclear weapons. They urged the cessation of nuclear testing and progress toward disarmament. The Committee for Nonviolent Action, the National Committee for a Sane Nuclear Policy (SANE; 1957), and the Student Peace Union (1959) held vigils, circulated petitions, organized demonstrations, and engaged in nonviolent direct action. Although such groups were dismissed frequently as idealistic and even unpatriotic, they reflected widespread fears about nuclear fallout and nuclear war. One of the most effective advertisements for SANE was one in 1962 that portrayed a concerned Dr. Benjamin Spock (*), the famous pediatrician, which implied a doubtful future: "Dr. Spock is worried." The 1963 Test Ban Treaty, while apparently a success for this movement, saw a temporary decline in membership and support for organizations which no longer seemed so necessary.

When the U.S. government began to pour money and troops into South Vietnam in 1965 (after years of less dramatic support of the Saigon government), the pacifist, anti-nuclear, and anti-military organizations began to grow. Although many Americans were first aware only of campus protesters, the range of dissenters became extraordinarily broad. There were students like Mark Rudd (*) and Mario Savio (*), pacifists such as Dr. Martin Luther King, Jr. (1*), Dorothy Day (6*) and the Berrigans (*), and nonpacifists like the Reverend William Sloane Coffin, Jr. (*). Coffin, for example, helped to coalesce some opponents of the war into Clergy and Laity Concerned About Vietnam (1965). The anti-war movement eventually included an amazing spectrum of opinion, from those opposed as part of a larger radical perspective, such as the SDS leader Tom Hayden (6*) and the libertarian socialist Dr. Staughton Lynd (*), to "average Americans" who may have condemned the war because it was not (in their opinion) being fought vigorously enough. Most dissenters worked within the law; others broke it, burning draft cards, refusing military induction, and fleeing the country. Two mammoth coalitions eventually emerged: the National Peace Action Coalition, which was dominated by the Socialist Workers party, but focused on the single issue of peaceful protest against the war, and the multi-issue National Mobilization to End the War in Vietnam, which included some direct resistance that virtually invited arrest. The governing elites of this society finally concluded that the war was too costly, neither defeating the enemy in Vietnam nor the protesters at home. The Vietnam Peace Accords were signed in January of 1973.

It was often forgotten after the war—and little understood during it—that many GIs dissented from within the military. This caused considerable alarm among their superiors. These protests had ranged from refusal to serve in Vietnam (such as the cases of the Fort Hood Three in 1966 and that of Captain Howard Levy, a doctor, in 1967), demonstrations by black soldiers ("no Vietnamese ever called me nigger"), participation in public demonstrations while in uniform, mass resistance to go into combat in Vietnam (combined with growing drug use), desertions, and hundreds of attacks on officers. The war transformed many of those in it, such as Ron Kovic (*), who began as a naive believer in the clichés of the cold war and became a paralyzed vet who worked to build the Vietnam Veterans Against the War (1967).

During the war there were dozens of coffeehouses near U.S. military bases, draft counseling centers, and more than three hundred GI publications (beginning in 1967) with such names as *Aerospaced, All Hands Abandon Ship, As You Were, Eyes Left! FTA* [Fuck the Army], *Fat Albert's Death Ship Times, Green Machine, The Hunley Hemorrhoid, The Last Harass, Left Face, Now Hear This, Star-Spangled Bummer, Up Against the Bulkhead, Veterans Stars and Stripes for Peace,* and *Winter Soldier.* The slogan for *POW* may have summarized the general attitude of these papers: "Every G.I. is a prisoner of war." Perhaps there was no major national newspaper because local papers had more direct interest, publishing letters and articles complaining about "the brass," "Pentagoons," and career "war pigs." Such complaints were made not solely by drafted college students but by discontented or embittered enlistees who may have discovered that the military life was not what they expected.

The anti-war movement within the military deserves greater recognition because it raised fundamental questions that illuminated aspects of American society and its place in the world. Some GIs were asking whether they retained rights as U.S. citizens to meet (as in anti-war coffeehouses), to read and distribute uncensored literature (such as independent GI papers), and to speak out at demonstrations beyond the gates of their military bases. In almost all cases, the military establishment loudly answered that GIs did not or should not have such rights. A base commander laments in one GI cartoon that "there's got to be an effective way to prevent ungrateful Americans from taking advantage of free speech." Does this mean that military regulations can violate the essence of the Constitution? Is the Uniform Code of Military Justice primarily a system of justice within our democratic values, or is it mainly a system of undemocratic discipline necessary to meet the unique needs of military service?

At various times during the war in Vietnam, GIs protested health and safety conditions; nebulously defined rules; arbitrary restrictions on freedom of speech, press, and assembly; the absence of trial by peers; and limited rights of appeal (perhaps through civilian review boards). Robert Sherrill cataloged many of these criticisms in his book *Military Justice Is to Justice as Military Music Is to Music* (1970). Reformers like David Cortright offered broad remedies for these problems under a general call for "the civilianization of military law."

Specifically, Cortright and some others boldly proposed the formation of GI unions similar to those found in various European countries. If the United States is such a democratic society, why is it that U.S. soldiers have so few legal protections and rights? In December of 1967, Andy Stapp formed the American Serviceman's Union (ASU). This was one of the reasons that he was expelled from the army in 1968 for "subversion and disloyalty." Although the ASU and its newspaper *The Bond* never reached more than a few thousand people, the idea of unionizing the military ranks was considered in the 1970s by the American Federation of Government Employees (AFGE), the Teamsters, the National Maritime Union, and the Association of Civilian Technicians.

Major organizations eventually backed off because of varying combinations of their own timidity, limited public support, and sharp official condemnation. Upholders of the established order believed that democracy *should* stop at the barracks door. It was asserted that being a soldier was a patriotic calling, not a job; it had unique requirements of sacrifice and discipline. Soldiers, it was argued, must obey orders, cannot "punch out" of the barracks, cannot bargain for binding contracts, and should not be able to strike. European unions were not comparable because temporary conscripts were their primary membership, and these temporary soldiers expected rights similar to those of civilians.

Supporters of military unionization presented many alternatives to this conventional wisdom. The radical ASU urged the election of officers from below, collective bargaining, minimum wages, democratic control of court-martial boards, and the abolition or reduction of many petty regulations. Moderate organizations such as the AFGE talked more ponderously about the possibilities for institutionalized consultation and, if there were disputes, binding arbitration rather than strikes. It was claimed that unions would allow channels of communication and allow orderly hearings of grievances, thereby making military service more humane and attractive. On the question of discipline, some advocates of unionization pointed to possible comparisons with the International Association of Fire Fighters (founded in 1918 and encompassing more than 90 percent of professional firemen in the United States) and the Fraternal Order of Police (founded in 1915 and having more than 200,000 active and associated members). Police unions, for example, fulfilled needs to express complaints; bargain for wages, benefits, and working conditions; re-solve disputes; and lobby for the profession. This was all done without dis-rupting command structures. These groups were not, of course, unions, but professional associations, varieties of which existed in the U.S. military. Still, they provided some models for military unionization, especially if such union-ization emphasized career soldiers, along with the examples of European mil-itary unions.

After 1973 there was an official crackdown on "poor discipline" and dissent within the military. Since the new military had become all-volunteer, the for-merly draftable middle classes were no longer very concerned about military reform, and military authorities usually disposed of internal dissenters through rapid dismissals. David Cortright has noted that resistance continued in the military, but it was less organizationally coherent. Peace societies also contin-ued, but tended to focus their attention on specific weapons systems or specific U.S. aid programs, such as in Nicaragua and El Salvador.

During the 1980s a substantial portion of the American public supported vast new military spending because of their belief, after Vietnam, that the United States had become weak. From 1981 through 1987, the U.S. govern-ment put more than $2 trillion into the military. The Pentagon, in this peace-time, maintained its rank as the largest bureaucracy in the world; there were hundreds of military installations within the United States; there were hun-dreds of military installations outside the United States (in several dozen coun-tries); more than a half-million U.S. troops were abroad; and there were U.S. ships and submarines in all of the major seas of the globe. This was the biggest military establishment in the world. It was occasionally used to keep the (usu-ally dark-skinned) natives in their places in such instances as the invasion of Grenada, navy shelling of Lebanon, bombing in Libya, covert aid to Nicara-guan rebels, overt and covert aid to wealthy elites in El Salvador, and the invasion of Panama. This military buildup served various purposes beyond protecting U.S. business interests in foreign countries. It also stabilized the U.S. economy through massive spending, provided huge federal subsidies to high-tech research (such as Reagan's "star wars" projects), and tied many Americans economically to the military welfare state. Although the military empires of communism had rotted away by the 1990s, the U.S. military empire was trimmed but not dismantled.

The use of this military machine had some political limits, however, partly because of public skepticism after Vietnam. When the U.S. military restored the emir of Kuwait, a despot who didn't even bother with the pretense of a sham parliament, the United States carefully explained that it was not fighting for democracy but to defeat the aggressive leader of Iraq and to protect U.S. oil supplies. Although some people asked disturbing questions about previous U.S. support for Iraq—and noted that almost all of Iraq's weapons had been purchased in the West—the public was willing to support a brief and colorful war that was entertaining on television so long as it was not painfully costly in U.S. money or U.S. lives. Thus, the American government supplied most of the weapons and more than a half-million mercenary troops, but other nations paid the bills. Iraq, a nation the size of California with a population of eighteen million, was first magnified into a major threat and then swatted down.

Although President Bush announced that the victory over Iraq proved that the United States had gotten over "the Vietnam syndrome" (which was defined as the fear of using American military power) there remained broad doubts about long-term foreign involvements. The 1992 election also demonstrated that Vietnam had not been forgotten entirely, whether it was unease about Dan Quayle's use of his class privileges to find a comfortable refuge in the National Guard during the war or Bill Clinton's manipulation of the draft regulations. While the candidates were willing to impugn the character of their opponents, none were willing, however, to draw any major lessons about why the United States had become involved in the Vietnam War, how it had been fought, and whether the later peace (which included a long boycott of the unified Vietnam and dramatic posturing about theoretical U.S. prisoners of war) was actually reasonable. Such a discussion could affect every taxpayer, since a majority of the money sent to the federal government goes to pay for past wars or preparations for future wars. This situation has continued for so long that the consciences and imaginations of most Americans seem to have been numbed.

Some of this apathy may be attributed also to the apparent absence of any threat of major war or nuclear disaster. Cora Weiss, a longtime leader of SANE, commented in 1990 that "when the situation is outrageous, you can count on people to get out there and demand change. If the situation is not outrageous, they do their laundry" (*Washington Post*, June 3, 1990, A3). Even so, it is troubling that many people casually accept the military's absorption of so many resources while there are enormous needs for affordable housing, health care, and education, along with decent, well-paying civilian jobs. The priorities of American society, in the 1990s, continued to be challenged by the groups mentioned earlier, along with others such as Pax Christi (1973), the National Mobilization for Survival (1977), SANE/Freeze (1987), Physicians for Social Responsibility (1961), and Citizen Soldier (1976). The federal government made a tiny but symbolic step in 1984 when it chartered the U.S. Institute of Peace as a counterpart to military academies (though scarcely as well funded!). There are alternatives to the existing military budgets and programs, but values and institutions that are a basic part of this society will not be easily changed.

SELECTED BIBLIOGRAPHY

Cold War

Diamond, Sigmund. *Compromised Campus: The Collaboration of Universities with the Intelligence Community, 1948–1955*. New York: Oxford University Press, 1992.
LaFeber, Walter. *America, Russia and the Cold War,* 5th ed. New York: John Wiley and Sons, 1988.
May, Lary, ed. *Recasting America: Culture and Politics in the Age of the Cold War*. Chicago: University of Chicago Press, 1989.
Whitfield, Stephen J. *The Culture of the Cold War*. Baltimore: Johns Hopkins University Press, 1991.

Vietnam War; Mass Resistance

Baritz, Loren. *Backfire: A History of How American Culture Led Us into Vietnam and Made Us Fight the Way We Did*. New York: Morrow, 1985.
Baskir, Lawrence M., and William A. Strauss. *Chance and Circumstance: The Draft, the War, and the Vietnam Generation*. New York: Vintage, 1978.
DeBenedetti, Charles, and Charles Chatfield. *An American Ordeal: The Antiwar Movement and the Vietnam War*. Syracuse, NY: Syracuse University Press, 1990.
Farber, David. *Chicago '68*. Chicago: University of Chicago Press, 1988.
Ferber, Michael, and Staughton Lynd. *The Resistance*. Boston: Beacon Press, 1971.
Foster, Catherine. *Women for All Seasons: The Story of the Women's International League for Peace and Freedom*. Athens: University of Georgia Press, 1989.
Franklin, H. Bruce. *M.I.A., or, Mythmaking in America*. Brooklyn, NY: Lawrence Hill Books, 1992.
Gioglio, Gerald R. *Days of Decision: An Oral History of Conscientious Objectors in the Military during the Vietnam War*. Trenton, NJ: Broken Rifle Press, 1989.
Gottlieb, Sherry Gershon. *Hell No, We Won't Go: Evading the Draft during Vietnam*. New York: Viking Press, 1991.
Hall, Mitchell K. *Because of Their Faith: CALCAV and Religious Opposition to the Vietnam War*. New York: Columbia University Press, 1990.
Halstead, Fred. *Out Now! A Participant's Account of the American Movement against the Vietnam War*. New York: Anchor Foundation, Pathfinder Press, 1978.
Herring, George C. *America's Longest War; The United States and Vietnam, 1950–1975,* 2d ed. Philadelphia: Temple University Press, 1986.
———. "America and Vietnam: The Debate Continues" (review article), *American Historical Review* 92 (April 1987): 350–62.
Karnow, Stanley. *Vietnam; A History,* rev. and updated. New York: Viking, 1991.
Katz, Milton S. *Ban the Bomb: A History of SANE, the Committee for a Sane Nuclear Policy*. New York: Praeger, 1986.
Kohn, Stephan M. *Jailed for Peace: The History of American Draft Law Violator, 1958–1985*. New York: Praeger, 1986.
Levy, Peter B. *The New Left and Labor in the 1960s*. Urbana: University of Illinois Press, 1994.
McMahon, Robert J., ed. *Major Problems in the History of the Vietnam War; Documents and Essays*. Lexington, MA: D. C. Heath, 1990.

Olson, James S. *The Vietnam War: Handbook of Literature and Research.* Westport, CT: Greenwood Press, 1993.

Powers, Thomas. *Vietnam: The War at Home: The Antiwar Movement, 1964–1968.* Boston: G. K. Hall, 1984 (1973).

Rowe, John Carlos and Rick Berg, eds. *The Vietnam War and American Culture.* New York: Columbia University Press, 1992.

Schell, Jonathan. *The Time of Illusion.* New York: Random House, 1975.

Shafer, D. Michael, ed. *The Legacy: The Vietnam War in the American Imagination.* Boston: Beacon Press, 1990.

Sherrill, Robert. *Military Justice Is to JUSTICE as Military Music Is to MUSIC.* New York: Harper and Row, 1970.

Sheehan, Neil. *A Bright Shining Lie: John Paul Vann and America in Vietnam.* New York: Random House, 1988.

Small, Melvin. *Johnson, Nixon and the Doves.* New Brunswick, NJ: Rutgers University Press, 1988.

Small, Melvin, and William D. Hoover, eds. *Give Peace a Chance; Exploring the Vietnam Antiwar Movement.* Syracuse, NY: Syracuse University Press, 1992.

Terry, Wallace. *Bloods: An Oral History of the Vietnam War by Black Veterans.* New York: Random House, 1984.

Tollefson, James W. *The Strength Not to Fight: An Oral History of Conscientious Objectors of the Vietnam War.* Boston: Little, Brown, 1993.

Vietnam Generation (journal), University of Minnesota, Minneapolis, 1989– .

Wittner, Lawrence S. *Rebels against War: The American Peace Movement, 1933–1983,* rev. ed. Philadelphia: Temple University Press, 1984.

Wyatt, David. *Out of the Sixties: Storytelling and the Vietnam Generation.* New York: Columbia University Press, 1993.

Zaroulis, Nancy, and Gerald Sullivan. *Who Spoke Up? American Protest against the War in Vietnam, 1963–1975.* Garden City, NY: Doubleday, 1984.

Major Campus Protests

Bates, Tom. *Rads* (on the 1970 bombing of the Army Math Research Center at the University of Wisconsin, Madison). New York: HarperCollins, 1992.

Bills, Scott L., ed. *Kent State/May Fourth: Echoes across a Decade.* Kent, Ohio: Kent State University Press, 1988.

Caute, David. *Year of the Barricades: A Journey Through 1968.* New York: Harper and Row, 1988.

Heineman, Kenneth. *Campus Wars: The Peace Movement at American State Universities in the Vietnam Era.* New York: New York University Press, 1993.

Lipset, Seymour Martin. *Rebellion in the University: A History of Student Activism in America.* Woodstock, NY: Beekman Publishers, 1972.

McGill, William. *The Year of the Monkey: Revolution on Campus, 1968–69.* New York: McGraw-Hill, 1982.

Report on the President's Commission on Campus Unrest; Including the Killings at Jackson State College. Salem, NH: Ayer Company, 1970.

Spofford, Tim. *Lynch Street: The May 1970 Slayings at Jackson State College.* Kent, OH: Kent State University Press, 1988.

Peace Movements; Peace Activists

Adams, Judith Porter, ed. *Peacework: Oral Histories of Women Peace Activists*. Boston: Twayne Publishers, 1990.

Albertson, Dean. "Dellinger, David," in *The Encylopedia of World Biography: 20th Century Supplement*. Palatine, IL: Jack Heraty and Associates, 1987: 367–68.

Alonso, Harriet Hyman. *Peace as a Women's Issue: A History of the U.S. Movement for World Peace and Women's Rights*. Syracuse, NY: Syracuse University Press, 1992.

"America's Peace Movement, 1900–1986" (symposium), *The Wilson Quarterly* 11:1 (1987): 94–147.

Annual Review of Peace Activism. Boston: Winston Foundation for World Peace, 1989.

Barnet, Richard. *The Rocket's Red Glare: When America Goes to War—The Presidents and the People*. New York: Simon and Schuster, 1990.

Blanchard, Bob, and Susan Watrous. "Daniel Ellsberg," *The Progressive* 53 (Sept. 1989): 17–21.

Chatfield, Charles, and Robert Kleidman. *The American Peace Movement: Ideals and Activism*. New York: Twayne Publishers, 1992.

Chatfield, Charles, and Peter van den Dungen, eds. *Peace Movements and Political Cultures*. Knoxville: University of Tennessee Press, 1988.

Cluster, Dick, ed. *They Should Have Served That Cup of Coffee*. Boston: South End Press, 1979.

Cooney, Robert, Helen Michalowski, and Marty Jezer. *The Power of the People: Active Nonviolence in the United States,* updated and enlarged. Philadelphia: New Society, 1987.

Cornell, Tom. "U.S. Pacifism Attacked and Defended," *Cross Currents* 41 (Summer 1991): 234–42.

Cortright, David. "GI Resistance during the Vietnam War," in *Give Peace a Chance*, Melvin Small and William D. Hoover, eds. Syracuse, NY: Syracuse University Press, 1992: 116–28.

———. *Peace Works: The Citizen's Role in Ending the Cold War*. Boulder, CO: Westview Press, 1993.

Cortright, David, and Max Watts. *Left Face: Soldier Unions and Resistance Movements in Modern Armies*. Westport, CT: Greenwood Press, 1991.

Cummings, Richard. *The Pied Piper: Allard K. Lowenstein and the Liberal Dream*. New York: Grove Press, 1985.

DeBeneditti, Charles, ed. *Peace Heroes in Twentieth-Century America*. Bloomington: Indiana University Press, 1986.

Dellinger, David. *From Yale to Jail: The Life Story of a Moral Dissenter*. New York: Pantheon, 1993.

———. *More Power Than We Know: The People's Movement toward Democracy*. Garden City, NY: Anchor Press, 1975.

———. *Vietnam Revisited: From Covert Action to Invasion to Reconstruction*. Boston: South End Press, 1986.

Dellinger, David, and Michael Albert. *Beyond Survival: New Directions for the Disarmament Movement*. Boston: South End Press, 1983.

D'Emilio, John. "Sam Brown," in *Political Profiles: The Nixon-Ford Years,* Eleanora W. Schoenebaum, ed. New York: Facts on File, 1979: 81–82.

Deming, Barbara, and Jane Meyerding. *We Are All Part of One Another: A Barbara Deming Reader*. Philadelphia: New Society, 1984.

Garson, Barbara. "GI Coffee House Movement," in *The Encyclopedia of the American Left*. Mari Jo Buhle, Paul Buhle, and Dan Georgakas, eds. New York: Garland Publishing, 1990: 269–70.

Georgakas, Dan. "Halstead, Fred," in *The Encyclopedia of the American Left* (see above), p. 288.

Harris, David. *Dreams Die Hard*. New York: St. Martin's Press/Marek, 1982.

Howlett, Charles F. *The American Peace Movement: References and Resources*. Boston: G. K. Hall, 1991.

Howlett, Charles F., and Glen Zeitzer. *The American Peace Movement: History and Historiography*. Washington, DC: American Historical Association, 1985.

Irwin, Robert A. *Building a Peace System: A Book for Activists, Scholars, and Concerned Citizens*. Monroe, ME: Common Courage Press, 1993.

Josephson, Harold, et al., eds. *Biographical Dictionary of Modern Peace Leaders*. Westport, CT: Greenwood Press, 1985.

Landau, Saul. "From the Labor League to the Cuban Revolution," in *History and the New Left; Madison, Wisconsin, 1950–1970,* Paul Buhle, ed. Philadelphia: Temple University Press, 1990: 107–12.

Lynn, Conrad. *There Is a Fountain; The Autobiography of Conrad Lynn*, with an introduction by William Kunstler. Brooklyn; Lawrence Hill, 1993 (1979).

Roberts, Nancy L., ed. *American Peace Writers, Editors, and Periodicals: A Dictionary*. Westport, CT: Greenwood Press, 1991.

Robinson, Jo Ann C. *Abraham Went Out: A Biography of A. J. Muste*. Philadelphia: Temple University Press, 1981.

———. *A. J. Muste: Prophet in the Wilderness of the Modern World*. Bloomington: Indiana University Press, 1986.

Rudenstine, David. "The Pentagon Papers Case: Recovering Its Meaning Twenty Years Later," *Cardozo Law Review* 12 (June 1991): 1869–913.

Scheer, Robert. *Thinking Tuna Fish, Talking Death: Essays on the Pornography of Power*. New York: Noonday/Farrar, Straus and Giroux, 1988.

Schultz, Bud, and Ruth Schultz, eds. *It Did Happen Here: Recollections of Political Repression in America*. Berkeley: University of California Press, 1989.

Schultz, John. *The Chicago Conspiracy Trial,* with a new introduction by Carl Oglesby. New York: Da Capo Press, 1993 (1972).

Segrest, Mab. "Barbara Deming: 1917–1984," *Southern Exposure* 13 (March/June 1985): 72–75.

"60s Radical, Linked to a Killing, Surrenders After Hiding 23 years," *New York Times,* Sept. 16, 1993, A1; "In 23 Years 'Alice' Never Escaped Katherine," *New York Times,* Sept. 17, 1993, A1, A22; "Woman Ends 23 Years as a Fugitive," *Washington Post,* Sept. 16, 1993, A1; "The Return of the Fugitive," *Time,* Sept. 27, 1993, pp. 60-61 (all on Katherine Ann Power).

Swerdlow, Amy. *Women Strike for Peace: Traditional Motherhood and Radical Politics in the 1960s*. Chicago: University of Chicago Press, 1993.

"War Protester Abandons Life in Underground, a Fugitive Surrenders to Face a 1969 Charge" [Jeffrey David Powell], *New York Times,* Jan. 7, 1994, A14.

Wells, Tom. *The Battle Within: America's Battle over Vietnam*. Berkeley: University of California Press, 1994.

Williams, Tom. "Dellinger, David," in *The Biographical Dictionary of the American Left,* Bernard Johnpoll and Harvey Klehr, eds. Detroit: Gale Research, 1986: 107–8.

Williams, William Appleman. *A William Appleman Williams Reader,* Henry W. Berger, ed. Chicago: Ivan R. Dee, Publisher, 1992.

PHILIP BERRIGAN (1923–   )

Co-founder of Jonah House Resistance Community;
peace activist

Philip Berrigan responded to the call of Old Testament prophets Micah and Isaiah by beating swords into plowshares. He has opposed all war since the early 1960s by repeatedly trespassing on government, corporate, and church property with his graphic message of resistance. Berrigan is one of a small number of radical Christians whose life is devoted entirely to his cause. Unshakably convinced that the elimination of nuclear arms and war is required by the Gospel command to love God and neighbor, Berrigan is uneasy with the religious establishment, the modern warfare state, and the military-industrial complex. Since his release from prison for draft board raids during the Vietnam War, Berrigan and his family have lived in a small community of Christian war resisters. At Jonah House adult activists and their children work, pray, and oppose nuclear arms.

Philip Berrigan's spiritual odyssey toward peace was rooted in a strict traditional Catholic upbringing later combined with a wide range of secular and religious influences. The youngest of six sons, Philip was raised in a working-class household where traditional religion was strictly enforced. Frida Berrigan, his mother, was a long-suffering housewife who placidly endured and modified her husband's volatile moods. His father, a self-proclaimed socialist and admirer of Gene Debs in his younger days, was a staunch American Federation of Labor unionist when his sons reached adulthood. Thomas Berrigan was stubbornly loyal to the church that he had abandoned as a young man and returned to after marriage. He devoted himself to trade unionism throughout his adult life. By the 1940s he became interested in racial relations and was one of the founders of the Syracuse, New York, branch of the Catholic Interracial Council.

World War II interrupted Philip Berrigan's higher education, but he served in Europe with distinction. Like his American contemporaries, Berrigan welcomed the atomic devastation of Japan, which was then commonly credited with saving the lives of U.S. soldiers. Of his five brothers, two were already studying for the priesthood when Philip completed his education at Holy Cross College in 1950. Much to the surprise of his friends, the gregarious young man announced that he would enter a seminary of the Josephite Fathers to begin training for the priesthood.

Daniel Berrigan (1921–) had been the first of Philip's brothers to seek and gain acceptance into seminary. When he was eighteen years old, he chose the Jesuit order, a religious community noted for its rigorous intellectual and spir-

Philip Berrigan. Copyright *Washington Post*; Reprinted by permission of D.C. Public Library.

itual program. Daniel was a zealous seminarian who wrote poetry, excelled in foreign languages, and showed concern for social issues. He was an advanced student when his older brother Jerome, a veteran, and later Philip became members of the Josephites. This was a religious community exclusively devoted to serving the spiritual needs of African-Americans. When Daniel began reading European theologians who advocated spiritual and social renewal, he shared these ideas with Philip, who remained in the Josephites after Jerome had left to marry. A year in France and Germany at the conclusion of his seminary education introduced Daniel to some legendary French worker-priests who profoundly influenced his thought. Daniel understood that when the church ignored social injustice the victims of oppression sought aid in labor activities or in politics. Daniel proposed to retain church members by mobilizing spiritually active Catholics for social change. Philip caught Daniel's enthusiasm. The two young men preached that a mature faith was expressed by prayer, study, and working for justice. These ideas anticipated and eventually coincided with the liberal ethos of the Kennedy era and the spirit of Catholicism embodied in the Second Vatican Council (1962–1965).

The brothers established a variety of volunteer programs. These included an experimental community, International House, that sought to include Daniel's students at LeMoyne College. The views of the Berrigans, already supporters of labor and civil rights, scandalized those Catholics who privatized religious belief. The Berrigans' sense of priesthood and the role of the laity was expansive: the spiritual realm could not be artificially separated from social responsibilities. Their message also alarmed their superiors who wanted a respectably noncontroversial image. During the early sixties, religious censors clamped down on the Berrigans' publications. Daniel occasionally countered by signing a pseudonym to his printed work. The Berrigans, eager to join the Freedom Rides, which in 1961 attempted to desegregate interstate bus travel throughout the Deep South, were deterred by superiors. Philip Berrigan was arrested for the first time in 1965 in Selma, Alabama. As they became more involved in the peace movement during the Vietnam War, clashes with superiors escalated. Peace was a prickly cause for church leaders. Catholic immigrant families had sacrificed for their country in two world wars to earn respect. Cold war Catholicism, furthermore, shared the anti-communist impulse of mainstream America. The peace movement, in this context, seemed unpatriotic. The Berrigans were not alone, however, in their peacemaking. Even from within the church a variety of thinkers and activists had challenged cold war militarism. More than any other person, Dorothy Day (6*) made it possible for American Catholics to advocate peace. Day, a journalist and radical who joined the church as an adult, advocated nonviolent social revolution. A self-styled Christian anarchist, she founded what became an international network of houses of hospitality where the poor were provided food and shelter. Day attracted intellectuals to her movement with the *Catholic Worker*, a lively paper that endorsed voluntary poverty, personal responsibility for others, direct aid for the poor, pacifism, and social revolution. The two priests also formed a friendship with Thomas Merton, a Trappist monk who was an established spiritual author. Merton lent his clerical credentials to the fledgling American Catholic peace movement. Thus, the Berrigans could build on a legacy of American Catholic social concern.

Other persons and forces nurtured the Berrigans' growing radicalism and their awareness of the inadequacy of words without deeds. The presidency of John F. Kennedy, despite its limited success in legislating reform, advocated social change and a partial ban on nuclear testing. Kennedy made reform acceptable to a larger public. Pope John XXIII, who convened the Second Vatican Council, seemed to encourage a pacifist option for Catholics. The early nonviolent civil rights campaign of Martin Luther King, Jr. (1*), suggested how much could be accomplished through mass protest and imprisonment. King's reliance on the nonviolence of Gandhi introduced the Berrigans to a theory of civil disobedience that resonated with Christian renewal. Later, when they turned to war resistance, the Berrigans were impressed by the existentialism of Albert Camus, Jacques Ellul's critique of Western technology, and Andre Trocme's personal witness and his teachings on Jesus. But the core of their spiritual insight has come from the Bible. Scripture study has deepened the roots of their social commitment as they have probed the inherent radicalism of the Judeo-Christian tradition.

They began their peace advocacy with liberal practices such as organizing, petitioning, speaking, writing, and demonstrating with others. They gradually felt dissatisfied. Peaceful protest failed to stop or even mitigate the Vietnam War. As thousands of young Americans and Asians died in Indochina, and war resisters languished in prison, the Berrigans demanded greater self-sacrifice for peace.

Impatient with talk as a substitute for anti-war action, Philip Berrigan founded the Baltimore Interfaith Peace Mission in 1966. They immediately began to plan nonviolent direct-action protests against the war. By October 1967, Philip Berrigan had turned from protest to resistance. With three others, he seized government Selective Service records and damaged them. He then convinced his brother Daniel to join a second raiding group, the Catonsville Nine, although Elizabeth McAlister (1939–), then a young religious sister and art historian who was drawn to the radical peace movement, reluctantly decided to wait. Daniel Berrigan's poetry readings, lectures, essays, and stature among intellectuals inspired young radicals. The 1968 raid became a catalyst for further raids on draft boards and war industries. At least 53 actions of this kind took place between 1967 and 1973. Still, resistance to government and war industry involved a radical minority within the broader peace movement.

The moral stature of the Berrigans was enhanced by their going to prison. Their sacrifice of personal freedom for the anti-war cause attracted some favorable publicity and new recruits to the peace movement. Probably close to one million copies of mass market paperbacks by or about the Berrigans were in the hands of readers by the early seventies. Readers clarified their opposition to war as they read the outpouring of letters, interviews, poetry, essays, and journals penned by the brothers, even while incarcerated. The new direction signaled by these first draft board raids appealed particularly to anti-war people who despaired of liberal politics by 1968. John Kennedy, the Reverend King and Senator Robert Kennedy had been killed and the major parties nominated cold warriors for the presidency. The Berrigans offered one alternative to the violence of the highly politicized Weather Underground, buffoonery of the Yippies, and exhaustion.

The draft board raids created a new tendency within the Vietnam era anti-war movement. This continued during the nineties with the plowshares movement against nuclear weaponry. While adhering to the principle of non-violence toward persons, these raids illustrate the frustration of radical peace advocates with the compromises and slowness of political process. The refusal of resisters like the Berrigans to endorse candidates for political office or party platforms emphasizes their refusal to work within the political system, it reinforces the primacy of conscience over civil obligation.

In key respects their anti-war actions resembled classic civil disobedience: the law was openly broken and the dissenters submitted to arrest and punishment. The radical impulse behind civil disobedience emerged clearly in their thoughts and deeds. Accompanying the raids was a scathing critique of American materialism and its reliance on military domination to preserve economic hegemony. This message was quite different from the optimistic tones of their reform-minded efforts of the early sixties. Since the beginning of the seventies, the Berrigans have spoken of themselves sometimes as Christian anarchists.

These raids, rich in religious ritual, relied on symbols of the Judeo-Christian tradition to convey the belief behind the activism. The actual destruction of war material at government or corporate locations underscores the radical vision of these resisters.

Despite this obvious radical outlook, the resistance movement of the Berrigans has maintained a tension with certain liberal values. Courtroom defense has been premised on two key features of modern liberalism: education of the public and an appeal to the ideals of the Bill of Rights for protection. With great zeal, the Berrigans, McAlister, and their co-defendants, while focusing on their motivation, have sought to arouse the courtroom and the informed public with thoughtful testimony about their spirituality interspersed with data to defend their arguments for peace. Their elaborate defense has been conducted by celebrity lawyers with the assistance of prominent character witnesses. If the draft board and disarmament raids suggested a profound alienation from civil authority, behavior in the courts suggested an expectation of protection under the law.

In 1970 the Berrigans decided to delay their impending imprisonment after the Catonsville trial by going underground. Daniel Berrigan resurfaced several

times before his apprehension by the FBI. The Berrigan underground eloquently expressed a loss of faith in the legal system; and at the same time it
heightened the visibility of two major peace leaders. The courts had confirmed
that these dissenters, conscientiously opposed to war, were ordinary felons.
More disappointing was the refusal of the federal court system to find the
legal means to end an unpopular, immoral, and debatably unconstitutional war.
The Berrigans ultimately questioned the moral authority of the courts to conduct a fair trial and impose a fitting punishment in cases of anti-war resistance.

While the imprisonment of the Berrigans hobbled effective and inspiring
anti-war leaders, their writings and work with inmates attempted to sustain
their supporters and created a new constituency for resistance. Prisoners like
Mitch Snyder, later a Community for Creative Nonviolence member and tireless advocate of the homeless, found new meaning in life from the example
of the jailed priests.

The experience of life in a federal prison might have broken the spirit of
some war resisters. Although the prison experience was depressing to Philip
and physically harmful to Daniel, it provided further evidence for the Berrigans' increasingly radical critique of society. The incarceration of unrepentant
war resisters suggested that the United States operated a lesser gulag of its
own. The social backgrounds of the nonpolitical prisoners indicted middle-
class materialism and the persistent poverty and lack of opportunity endemic
in society even after a decade of impassioned reform.

As we know from declassified Central Intelligence Agency and Federal Bureau of Investigation documents as well as presidential papers, the anti-war
movement and its imprisoned leaders terrified federal officials, including presidents Lyndon Johnson and Richard Nixon and FBI director J. Edgar Hoover.
No evidence of communist control was uncovered by thorough federal investigation. Still, officials were burdened by the persistence of demonstrators,
growing anti-war sentiment in the general public, and the longevity of the
expensive war. Anxious to break the troublesome anti-war movement, Hoover
startled the nation with charges that the Berrigans, McAlister, and others had
plotted to kidnap presidential advisor Henry Kissinger and to destroy heating
tunnels in Washington, D.C.

The resulting 1972 trial in Harrisburg, Pennsylvania, further debilitated a
declining anti-war movement. Using an unsavory paid informant and confis-
cated correspondence of Philip Berrigan and Elizabeth McAlister, which
among other things disclosed their secret physical relationship, government
prosecutors failed to prove the major charges. The media's effort to sensa-
tionalize the love of a nun and priest did not help public approval of the anti-
war resistance. Internal dissension within the politically and culturally divided
anti-war coalition, the prospect of a peace candidate on the national ballot,
Nixon's Vietnamization program, and the public's negative view of the anti-
war movement generally, were reasons why the Harrisburg spectacle was not
the worst disaster to befall the anti-war movement. It was already in decline.

The Berrigans responded to these depressing events by turning to self-evaluation. The result was the creation of a genuine community of war resisters. Sketched out by Elizabeth McAlister and discussed among friends, the plan was one creative and practical response to criticism directed at the antiwar movement, especially to the draft board raiders. Philip Berrigan and his wife Elizabeth McAlister have been the core members of the community since that time.

Jonah House, the resistance community founded in 1973, has sought to resist war and nuclear weaponry nonviolently. The community has organized activities at the Pentagon, the White House, churches, and weapons industries. Uncompromising in its radical view that the law of God supersedes civil law, Jonah House's activism is rooted in prayer and scriptural study. Scripture provides community values. The Berrigans and McAlister have closely studied the Psalms, Revelation, the Beatitudes, among other aspects of Judeo-Christian scripture and spirituality. The community publishes a newsletter, *Year One,* which is but one outlet for the writing of community members. Various radical Christian publications, such as the *Other Side* and *Sojourners,* offer exposure to a larger readership, although Philip Berrigan, Elizabeth McAlister, and community members such as Ched Myers have shared their thoughts on spirituality and activism in their books. Writing and lecturing acquaint the public with a message of radical evangelical Christianity and provide royalties that sustain the community.

Jonah House affirms a modest lifestyle. Located in an racially mixed inner-city neighborhood, the community lives in an old brick row house. Property is held in common. By engaging in manual labor such as house painting the community supplements its small income from royalties without the automatic withholding of federal taxes which support the military establishment. Jonah House's preference for plain living is clearly reminiscent of the economic precariousness of the Berrigans' youth and the spirit of voluntary poverty which the Berrigans and McAlister experienced in their religious communities. By refusing the seduction of bourgeois comforts, the community is reinforcing its anti-militarism and offering an ecologically responsible choice of lifestyle.

Within the community, decisions are made collectively. Tension between the individual conscience of a strong personality and deference to community required of resisters complicates shared life. Residing within individualism are potentially destructive behaviors such as emotional withdrawal and unilateral activity. At Jonah House the common vision has been occasionally challenged by one or more community members. Normally such conflicts are countered by community discussion and prayer, sometimes by parting from the group.

From experience, Jonah House chooses to remain small and intimate; no more than eight or nine adults are permanent community members at any time. Smallness permits the community to preserve its values and to support its members. The community forms an extended family for the children of imprisoned resisters. Each of McAlister and Berrigan's three children has faced temporary separation from a parent at an early age, but the presence of familiar adults has eased the adjustment of the children. On occasion the children have joined in protests. The eldest child of Berrigan and McAlister, Frida Berrigan was first arrested at age nine, when she was part of a group of four hundred at the U.S. Capitol responding to the 1983 State of the Union Address.

Jonah House is linked to a network of resistance groups that share similar visions of justice and nonviolent social change. This has helped to sustain radical peace activists over the long run through shared spirituality and community support networks. While the Berrigans advocated celibacy for peace activists in the late sixties, since then Philip Berrigan and Elizabeth McAlister have built a new movement that has redefined marriage and family in ways that enable families to resist nuclear arms responsibly.

In short, Jonah House is an intentional community centered on radical Christian values and resistance to war. Adult members who share basic values live in an arrangement that provides an alternative to the deficiencies of the small, private, and often fragmented nuclear family of the late twentieth century.

Since the end of the Vietnam War, community-based resistance of the Berrigans and McAlister has focused primarily on the nuclear arms race, the issue which had initially propelled them into the peace movement early in the sixties. After more than two decades of resistance to war and nuclear weaponry, they promote an insight originally made by Dorothy Day in 1945: nuclear weaponry is the anti-Christ of the modern age. McAlister and the Berrigans have explained how nuclear arms actually heighten public fears. The nuclear idol promises a false sense of security while denying the power of Christian love.

The Berrigans and McAlister have claimed that reliance on doomsday weaponry has enslaved citizens of the nuclear nations without assuring survival; they believe these weapons raise the potential for nuclear holocaust. Wealthy Western nations, they have asserted, have relied on the threat of their nuclear arsenal to maintain an imbalance of wealth and to protect access to resources needed for a high standard of living. Jonah House's commitment to voluntary poverty underscores the way in which nuclear arms may be used to equate national security with access to international resources. Many of their actions allow for varying levels of commitment—vigiling, leafleting, civil disobedience, disarmament—to promote the cooperation of individuals who may not be willing to break laws and serve time in jail.

During the 1970s and 1980s, the meaning of nonviolent resistance was further explored by the Berrigans and McAlister. Unconvinced that the Paris Peace Accords of 1973 could deliver peace to Southeast Asia, the Berrigans protested against American assistance to South Vietnam until the regime fell in 1975. Jonah House demonstrated at the embassies of the nuclear powers that year, and Daniel Berrigan turned his attention to other troubled areas of the world: the Middle East, Ireland, and Central America. His criticism of the Israeli government's reliance on military solutions to the complex problems of the Middle East resulted in an acrimonious assault on his position, including baseless charges of anti-Semitism. A few years later the Berrigans signed an appeal to the revolutionary government of Vietnam to protect human rights, an action that endangered their relationship to some on the Left.

Since the seventies the Berrigans and McAlister also have defended the rights of the unborn. Their "seamless garment" ethic of inclusive nonviolence has positioned the Berrigans and McAlister in a vulnerable place, for antinuclear activists have not normally embraced the inclusive position and prolifers generally abhor pacifism and resistance, which they find wanting in patriotism. Elizabeth McAlister has included in the seamless garment ethic opposition to war, nuclear weapons, abortion, capital punishment, the availability of guns, and hunting licenses. Positioning herself between the pro-life and pro-choice mainstream, McAlister has warned that both sides need to discuss meaningful alternatives to their hardened positions. In 1991, Daniel Berrigan, expressing his belief that there exists an "interlocking directorate" of death in our society, was arrested at a Planned Parenthood office in Rochester, New York, where he had attempted to block access to the facility, one day after the group protested U.S. involvement in the Gulf War.

While Jonah House and Daniel Berrigan share a common spirituality, a commitment to nonviolent resistance, and mutual support, the consensus is not absolute. On such issues as relationship to the church, personal priorities relating to causes other than war, nuclear arms, and justification of violence, variant positions coexist as each person struggles to define authentic faith.

The Berrigans and McAlister have challenged the church establishment to live up to the law of love, and they have proposed an alternative vision of the church. Their spirituality is rooted deeply in their Catholicism. However because Philip Berrigan and Elizabeth McAlister were married without official church agreement, both he and McAlister have been excommunicated from the Catholic church. Daniel Berrigan, however, has remained within the church. A Jesuit for fifty years and a priest for forty, his community life has been centered with a small group of Jesuits who live modestly in New York City. An enthusiastic supporter of Jonah House, today Daniel is considered by some Jesuits an exemplar of Christian social concern and of the original intent of Ignatius Loyola, founder of their order.

Poet, theologian, and philosopher, Daniel Berrigan has taught at several universities on limited-term appointments that allow him freedom to pursue nonviolent resistance. He has also been visible in movements other than the anti-nuclear cause that has been Jonah House's focus since the 1970s. First as a volunteer orderly at St. Rose's Home, a hospital for the cancerous poor, and more recently as a volunteer working with AIDS patients, Daniel has integrated several contemporary concerns. His arrest and conviction for criminal trespass at a Planned Parenthood clinic resulted from a desire to support nonviolence consistently.

The permissibility of revolutionary violence is another area where distinctions prevail. In his statements about Central American affairs, Daniel has doubted the efficacy of revolutionary violence while Philip has justified revolutionary violence as a last resort.

Allowing for these variations, the Berrigans and McAlister have launched a vital movement to resist nuclear weapons and war. Rooted in a common spirituality, community-based resistance has proved its faithfulness to its goal of promoting nonviolence and nuclear disarmament. By the 1980s, with the development of the plowshares movement, the Berrigans, McAlister, and members of the resistance network have regularly destroyed government or corporate property in a series of nonviolent demonstrations aimed at weapons manufacturers and the military. The Plowshares Eight of 1980, which included Daniel and Philip Berrigan, damaged a Mark 12A nuclear missile nosecone at a General Electric plant in Pennsylvania. Shortly after the first plowshares action in Europe took place, Elizabeth McAlister, a member of the Griffiss Plowshares, participated in damaging a bomber at Strategic Air Command base in central New York on Thanksgiving 1983. These and other plowshares actions, conducted by mature activists after much discussion, prayer, and preparation, have been accompanied by a resurgence in public anti-nuclear activism throughout the Western world during an era of conservatism. Philip Berrigan was arrested and served six months in prison for joining the Nuclear Navy Plowshares in 1988, a group charged with trespass when they boarded the USS *Iowa* and damaged the battleship's cruise missiles. The plowshares actions have had an international appeal, with interventions in Germany, Sweden, and Britain. The frequency of the plowshares actions and other anti-nuclear civil disobedience indicated a deep public concern; during the decade of the eighties it resulted in 37,000 arrests in the United States and Canada.

As Elizabeth McAlister has explained, the disarmament activities of the plowshares movement do not amount to simple civil disobedience. Civil disobedience is predicated on a high level of trust in the legal system and its ability to reform itself. The Berrigans and McAlister are disabused of such complete trust in legal process from experience and from their belief in a higher law.

Borrowing sociologist Robert Bellah's concept of civil religion to explain a mainstream religious political consensus promoted by the state, Elizabeth McAlister has argued in court that the religious beliefs of certain individuals are not currently protected. Civil religion protects the mainstream at the expense of radicals, whom it marginalizes. What constitutes acceptable religious belief and practice is narrowed by civil religion. One example of McAlister's point is the requirement that citizens pay taxes that support war and weapons, a violation of the basic beliefs of radical Christians who have faith in the way of love called for in the New Testament. The taxation requirement, which developed gradually, infringes on the right of a religious minority to live its beliefs.

The ideals of the Bill of Rights, according to McAlister and the Berrigans, have been tainted by such powerful institutions as multinational corporations. Industry, academia, and labor promote and protect their own interests, claiming that these represent the general good. Plowshares actions, then, express a spiritual struggle between institutional power and radical Christian belief. The overhaul of the legal system is not of primary concern to the present generation of Christian war resisters.

When in the late sixties and early seventies, the Vietnam anti-war movement turned to resistance and violence, informed popular opinion saw the draft board raid movement as an escalation of the anti-war movement in response to the escalation of the war. Nonviolent disarmament of today seems rooted more in hope than in frustration. McAlister has frequently mentioned how her resistance relates to her children's future. While rooted in the draft board raids of the sixties, the plowshares actions have responded to both the strengths and weaknesses of the previous movement. Community and networking offer needed spiritual, emotional, and financial support. Adherence to Christianity and nonviolence grounds activists in shared values, thus enhancing unity and defending against impulsive individual behavior. Emphasis on faithfulness over success enables activists to continue their resistance without agonizing over their effectiveness and the size of their following.

Bibliography

Berrigan, Daniel. *Daniel Berrigan: Poetry, Drama, Prose,* Michael True, ed. Maryknoll, NY: Orbis Books, 1988.

————. "No Longer the Enemy of My Enemies," *U.S. Catholic* 57 (May 1992): 25–27.

————. *To Dwell in Peace; An Autobiography.* San Francisco: Harper and Row, 1987. Reviewed: *America* 158 (May 28, 1988): 564–65; *Commonweal* 115 (Feb. 12, 1988): 93–94; *New York Times Book Review* 93 (Feb. 21, 1988): 31.

Berrigan, Philip, and Elizabeth McAlister. *The Time's Discipline: The Eight Beatitudes and Nuclear Resistance.* Baltimore, MD: Fortkamp Publishing, 1989.

Deedy, John G. *Apologies, Good Friends . . . An Interim Biography of Daniel Berrigan, S.J.* Chicago: Fides/Claretian, 1981.

Fisher, James Terrence. *The Catholic Counterculture in America, 1933–1962.* Chapel Hill: University of North Carolina Press, 1989.

Klejment, Anne. *The Berrigans: A Bibliography of Published Works by Daniel, Philip, and Elizabeth McAlister Berrigan.* New York: Garland, 1979.

Laffin, Arthur J., and Anne Montgomery, eds. *Swords into Ploughshares: Nonviolent Direct Action for Disarmament.* San Francisco: Perennial, 1987.

Lippy, Charles H., ed. *Twentieth-Century Shapers of American Popular Religion.* Westport, CT: Greenwood Press, 1989: 30–37.

McNeal, Patricia. *Harder Than War: Catholic Peacemaking in Twentieth-Century America.* New Brunswick, NJ: Rutgers University Press, 1992.

Meconis, Charles. *With Clumsy Grace: The American Catholic Left, 1961–1975.* New York: Seabury, 1979.

Merton, Thomas. *The Hidden Ground of Love,* William Shannon, ed. New York: Farrar, Straus, Giroux, 1985. Includes letters to the Berrigans, Thomas Cornell, Dorothy Day, and James Forest.

Occhiogrosso, Peter. *Once a Catholic.* Boston: Houghton Mifflin, 1987.

Phelps, Teresa Godwin. "Voices from Within: Community and Law in Three Prison Narratives," *Journal of American Culture* 15 (Spring 1992): 69–73.

Wilcox, Fred A. *Uncommon Martyrs: The Berrigans, the Catholic Left, and the Plowshares Movement.* Reading, MA: Addison-Wesley, 1991.

Anne Klejment

REV. WILLIAM SLOANE COFFIN, JR. (1924–)

Civil rights, peace, and social justice activist; executive secretary of Clergy and Laity Concerned About Vietnam; president of SANE/FREEZE: Campaign for Global Security

The weekend of October 21, 1967, in Washington, D.C., saw some of the great efforts of the peace movement. On Friday afternoon, draft resisters stood on the steps of the Justice Department. College students from across the country deposited their draft cards and the cards of others back on campus in a bag that was to be presented to the attorney general. The leader of this demonstration was an ex-army paratrooper and former CIA man Rev. William Sloane Coffin.

The scene at the Justice Department was recorded by Norman Mailer in *The Armies of the Night.* Mailer, in his account of that weekend, described Coffin as having

> one of those faces you expected to see on the cover of *Time* or *Fortune* as the candidate for Young Executive of the Year. Coffin had that same flinty eye, single-minded purpose, courage to bear responsibility, absorption in the details in the program under consideration, and absolute lack of humor.

Although Mailer's description of Coffin as the ideal of what a chaplain to future leaders should be is arguable, this civil rights, peace, and social justice activist became a key figure of the 1960s and one who continued his commitment.

Coffin was born in New York City in 1924. He and an older brother and younger sister had private schools, tutors, governesses, servants, chauffeurs, penthouse apartments, country homes, and summers in France. The family wealth was depleted, however, by the early years of the depression. In 1933, when he was nine, his protected world collapsed. His father died of a heart

Rev. William Sloane Coffin, Jr. Copyright *Washington Post*; Reprinted by permission of D.C. Public Library.

attack, and his mother decided to start anew in Carmel, California, where the children attended public school for the first time. Both having wealth and losing it were learning experiences for him. On the one hand, he always felt equal to the moneyed class. On the other hand, attending public school with Mexican-American children taught important lessons in American democracy. His family moved five years later to Paris so he could study music with Nadia Boulanger. After a year at Yale Music School, he began a four-year stint in the army. Like most young men of his generation, he was eager to get involved in the war, especially in the European theater.

His involvement in World War II, particularly with the repatriation of Russians who for various reasons had fought for the Germans, had a profound effect upon him. He felt guilty for his part in sending 2,000 officers back to Russia. He later found out that they were imprisoned or killed; this fact haunted him. He wrote that this "showed me that in matters of life and death the responsibility of those who take orders is as great as those that give them." This burden of guilt also influenced his decision in 1950 to spend three years in the CIA opposing Stalin's regime.

After the war, he attended Yale University and studied philosophers and theologians. "Why do human beings behave the way they do, which is to say with unbelievable cruelty to each other or by falling on a grenade there's no time to throw back, very heroically, very generously?" When he heard theologian Reinhold Niebuhr speak "of the need for church people to protest injustice in the name of God," he made a decision to enter the seminary. "The religious questions were the interesting ones for me when I went to college, so I read religious people and all the good atheists who were also interested in religious questions."

In 1958, at age thirty-four, married to Eva Rubinstein, the pianist's daughter, and the father of a newborn daughter, he returned to his alma mater as its chaplain. It was during his eighteen years at Yale that he gained recognition for his civil rights and anti-war activities. Soon after Coffin arrived at the university, Rev. Martin Luther King, Jr. (1*), was invited to speak. Coffin was stirred by his passionate eloquence and impressed by the power of direct action. It was by spending time in Africa in 1960, however, that he began to understand the urgency of the civil rights crusade. He joined the struggle after reading about the violence inflicted on civil rights activists in Anniston, Alabama, in 1961. "I doubt that I'd ever been angrier and certainly never more ashamed of the United States than I was looking at the pictures of the beatings," he later wrote. He went to Montgomery, Alabama to witness for his religious and political faith. There he was arrested as one of seven freedom riders and spent three nights in jail for challenging racial segregation at bus stations.

When violence broke out in the streets of Birmingham in 1963, Coffin went south again. "It was there that I drew my inspiration, it was there I saw most clearly the goal and the means." But it was not until he walked into black leader Ralph Abernathy's house and saw the frightened look in the eyes of Abernathy's son, who said "White man, are you going to hurt me?" that he understood "the qualitative difference between the intellectual ascent to feeling all men are created equal to feeling the monstrosity of inequality." It was a value-forming experience. Upon returning to Yale he stated that the eradication of both de facto and de jure segregation was the "number one challenge to American democracy."

Like most peace and social justice activists, Coffin voted for President Lyndon Johnson to defeat Senator Barry Goldwater in the 1964 election. He thought that "Johnson would be remembered for the lives he saved in Vietnam, not for those he lost." He was "stunned" two months later when the president announced his plans to use more force in Vietnam. Coffin didn't know how to react. The New Left troubled him, for "although staunch in its opposition to totalitarianism and violence on the right, it tended to be agnostic when it came to the violence and totalitarianism of Communists." He was never tempted to become anti-American. He agreed with United Nations Secretary General U Thant that the American people were great, but more important, they could even be good. But now he felt they were also callous. Although the political Left were correct in condemning the immorality of the war, they seemed incapable of persuading the center, without whose opposition there could never be an effective anti-war movement.

In 1965 Coffin trained his moral indignation on the war in Vietnam. In the fall of that year an ad hoc group called Clergy Concerned About Vietnam had been organized in New York under the leadership of the Reverend Richard Neuhaus, Rabbi Abraham Joshua Heschel, and Father Daniel Berrigan. The following month the group sponsored a study forum on Vietnam for five thousand area clergymen. Coffin was one of the main speakers. At the urging of Rev. Richard Neuhaus, Coffin and several prominent leaders, met in the apartment of John Bennet, the president of the National Council of Churches. On January 11 they formed a National Emergency Committee of Clergy Concerned About Vietnam. By the end of the month, the Committee had a prestigious board, predominantly Protestant but with significant Jewish leadership from Rabbi Heschel and a Catholic presence in Daniel Berrigan. Coffin was named executive secretary.

According to historian Charles DeBenedetti, the committee emphasized political realism, with an occasional moral critique of the war. It recommended persuasion and traditional political action, hoping to accumulate "that massiveness and momentum which enabled the clergy to help turn the tide in the civil rights struggle." Its leaders, including Coffin, opposed immediate withdrawal from Vietnam, denied any pacifist proclivities, and promised that they were organizing only on an emergency basis. Rabbi Heschel explained, "We came into being specifically to provide a religious comment on the war that would not be allied to the traditional peace movement and that did not stem from a body . . . committed to its own continuation beyond the cessation of the crisis." By April, though, interest from lay people and the further escalation of the war led the committee to change its name to Clergy and Laity Concerned About Vietnam (CALCAV). The group now prepared for a long struggle. This became a key organization; the anti-war movement had enlisted people with direct access to the American center.

By the time of the CALCAV mobilization in Washington in January 1967, Coffin, like many clergy, began to wonder if words were enough. He met with others to discuss what to do. Some people decided to challenge section 12 of the Selective Service Act, which declared that anyone "who knowingly counsels, aids or abets another to refuse or evade registration of service in the armed forces shall be liable for imprisonment." As pastors, they would not counsel young men to break the law, only to obey their consciences. If that led them to refuse induction, so be it. Coffin argued, as others had before him, that we are only obligated to obey good laws. Acts of civil disobedience dramatized what was wrong with bad laws. Examples ranged from the early Quakers to Henry David Thoreau, Eugene Debs, the abolitionists, the suffragettes and Martin Luther King, Jr. These people were all nonviolent and willingly accepted their punishment; none could be accused of trying to destroy the legal system.

The passivity of Congress pushed him toward civil disobedience. "If Johnson could be forced to arrest not a handful of young people but hundreds of older ones, if we could pack the jails, Congress might act, if not for the sake of our dying soldiers then for the sake of the domestic tranquility it so feared to disrupt." When letters to the Yale alumni magazine criticized Coffin for his "treasonable suggestions," he answered these accusations through the same magazine. He argued that there was a difference between just and unjust wars. He opposed this war for many reasons including U.S. intervention in another country's civil war and the fact that the Saigon governments from Diem to Ky did not represent the hopes and desires of the Vietnamese people. In addition, Coffin was upset that the war was being waged with great brutality and that the war cut funds that might be applied to anti-poverty efforts at home and abroad. Finally, he felt that the war could be ended through negotiations if we stopped bombing North Vietnam. Coffin had decided to participate in civil disobedience only after he had tried other means for years. Despite everything, the war continued to grow. For Coffin, civil disobedience was viewed "as a kind of radical obedience to conscience, to God . . . which would add to the best traditions of this country which won for us the respect of allies we no longer have in this venture."

During the summer of 1967 Coffin and Neuhaus prepared a statement on civil disobedience which was approved by the national board of CALCAV and later signed by hundreds of clergy nationwide. In it they promised to "counsel, aid and abet" those who refused induction. More specifically, they urged all churches and synagogues to declare themselves "sanctuaries for conscience." The idea was to allow draft resisters awaiting arrest to do so in places of worship. This would dramatize conflicts between the demands of law and the demands of conscience. In the fall, on the day before the March on the Pentagon to protest the war, Coffin and Mitchell Goodman organized a demonstration at the Justice Department in Washington to turn in draft cards. When they reached the Justice Department, Coffin spoke out:

> This week once again high government officials described protesters against the war as "naive," "wild-eyed idealists." But in our view it is not wild-eyed idealism but clear-eyed revulsion that brings us here. For as one of our number put it: "If what the United States is doing in Vietnam is right, what is there left to be called wrong?"

After stating his admiration for draft resisters, he said:

We cannot shield them. We can only expose ourselves as they have done. The law of the land is clear. Section 12 of the National Selective Service Act declares that anyone "who knowingly counsels, aids or abets another to refuse or evade registration or service in the armed forces . . . shall be liable to imprisonment for not more than five years or a fine of ten thousand dollars or both."

We hereby counsel these young men to continue in their refusal to serve in the armed forces as long as the war in Vietnam continues, and we pledge ourselves to aid and abet them in all the ways we can. This means that if they are now arrested for failing to comply with a law that violates their consciences, we too must be arrested, for in the sight of the law we are now as guilty as they.

Coffin was now an extremely controversial public figure. The president of his university, Kingman Brewster, disagreed with the chaplain's call for draft resistance. His mail was filled with obscenities, his family was subjected to hate calls, and his kids were told, "Tell your Daddy we're going to kill him." Coffin, along with Dr. Benjamin Spock (*), Mitchell Goodman, Marcus Raskin, and Michael Ferber were indicted on January 5, 1968, for conspiracy to counsel, aid, and abet draft resistance. Although he wanted to plead guilty and go to jail as a moral statement against the war, the others persuaded him to fight the conspiracy charge. The trial was held in May. Although the accused wanted to confront the constitutionality of the war and the legality of its conduct, the judge would not allow it. All of the defendants except Raskin were found guilty of conspiracy, not counseling. The sentence was two years in jail and a $5,000 fine. According to Coffin, "the trial of the Boston Five was dismal, dreary, and above all demeaning to all concerned." At Yale's commencement, however, when Coffin stepped up to give the opening prayer, the entire senior class rose to clap and cheer. Most surprising was that President Brewster stated his unqualified support. The Yale Corporation gave him administrative tenure (indefinite extension), and former Supreme Court Justice and U.N. ambassador Arthur Goldberg took his appeal. In July 1969 he was acquitted and all charges dropped.

It was during that year that Coffin had serious doubts about the efficacy of anti-war demonstrations. In the fall, CALCAV sponsored an emotional anti-war service at the National Cathedral in Washington, D.C., where Coffin delivered an ecumenical prayer. Although this service and the Mobilization March that followed the next day were impressive, Coffin was increasingly concerned over the violent streak in the radical Left. He hated to hear anyone justify violence. "That violence was inevitable in a sinful world was obvious," he wrote. "It might even be that physical violence could occasionally be a necessary evil. But I was convinced it should never be resorted to with a good conscience, only with a bad one."

In 1972 he was invited to Hanoi, North Vietnam, with Dave Dellinger, Cora Weiss, and Richard Falk to inspect the widespread destruction of non-military targets by U.S. bombing and to accept the release of three American

POWs. When he was asked by a reporter at the airport, "Aren't you really hoping North Vietnam will win?" he gave his standard reply: "I am rooting for neither side, I am simply against our massive military intervention in the civil affairs of another country." The sight of the victims of American bombing, in and out of the hospitals, especially the children, hurt him deeply. This trip further convinced him that in North Vietnam "our destruction had long ago exceeded the limits of decency, but had never reached any level of effectiveness." He appealed for amnesty within the U.S. for those convicted of antiwar protests.

After the war Coffin continued the commitment to social activism he began in the 1960s. In 1975 he left Yale and two years later became senior minister of the famed Riverside Church in New York City. Many people said that he transformed Riverside, built in the 1930s by John D. Rockefeller, Jr., into a more joyful, hopeful place dedicated to improving a world wracked by inequality and warfare. Coffin devoted himself and the church to helping the poor, the homeless, those afflicted with AIDS, and the refugees fleeing the political violence in Central America. He also started a full-time disarmament program that worked towards a freeze in nuclear weapons. Although some critics believe that he was less a minister than an advocate of social and political concerns, Coffin infused in Riverside a Christian philosophy that made words and deeds inseparable.

Ten years after he accepted the position at Riverside, he left to become president of SANE/FREEZE: Campaign for Global Security, the largest peace and justice organization in the United States. (This was later renamed Peace Action.) In that capacity, he was widely acknowledged as a leading proponent of a new political thinking that recognized the fundamental connection between peace, the environment, and social justice. The world was living "in the shadow of Doomsday in which poverty is not addressed and nuclear arsenals are bulging." He traveled throughout the nation lending his moral vision of a world where we spend less on the military and more on the poor and homeless. He did not really step down from the pulpit. He broadened his congregation for "a full-time peace and social justice ministry." "God presents us with choices we have to make ourselves," he often said. "I believe God calls each of us to be a co-creator, to help make the crooked straight and the rough places plane, to exalt the valleys and not to be deterred by high mountains."

Not everyone agreed with Coffin's "social gospel" liberal Christianity or even his moral vision. He was one of the favorite targets of the conservative *National Review,* and evangelical Christians found his positions on many international and domestic social issues appalling. "He's quite a liberal, he gives great comfort to the communists and socialists, to our enemies," stated Rev. Carl McIntire, president of the International Council of Christian Churches and a longtime opponent of Coffin. "During the Vietnam years, he contributed to the spirit of surrender that finally gripped our country." On the other hand, Coffin has been a hero to many, especially those who came to maturity in the

1960s. He continued his witness for the controversial social and moral issues of the day. He even became the obvious model for a "Doonesbury" cartoon character Scott Sloan, the self-described "fighting young priest who can speak to the young."

Coffin had a "lover's quarrel" with America for several decades. He worked to fulfill the dream of justice for all. He said that his anger helped him to preserve his sanity and kept him from tolerating the intolerable. He was part of a prophetic minority. The President of Yale, A. Bartlett Giamatti, once praised Coffin for keeping Yale socially and morally sensitive. Giamatti gratefully said to him, "You gave us energy." Coffin's durable optimism, steady commitment to justice, and sustained moral engagement not only energized Yale, but continued to energize and illuminate our world.

Bibliography

Coffin, William Sloane, Jr. *The Courage to Love*. New York: Harper and Row, 1982.
———. "The Gulf: Self-Righteousness (and Oil)," *Christianity and Crisis* 50 (Nov. 12, 1990): 342–43.
———. "The Gulf: Wrong Before, During, and After," *Christianity and Crisis* 51 (March 4, 1991): 57–58.
———. Interview, with Milton S. Katz, Overland Park, KS, Dec. 9, 1990.
———. *Living the Truth in a World of Illusions*. New York: Harper and Row, 1985.
———. *Once to Every Man: A Memoir*. New York: Atheneum, 1977.
———. *A Passion for the Possible: A Message to U.S. Churches*. Louisville, Ky: Westminster/John Knox, 1993.
———. "Peace Movement Hasn't Run Out of Work," *New York Times*, March 24, 1990, A24:5.
DeBenedetti, Charles. *An American Ordeal: The Antiwar Movement of the Vietnam Era*. Syracuse, NY: Syracuse University Press, 1990.
Flaherty, Francis. "An Interview with William Sloane Coffin," *America* 138 (April 1, 1978): 263–65.
Hall, Mitchell Kent. *Because of Their Faith: CALCAV and Religious Opposition to the Vietnam War*. New York: Columbia University Press, 1990.
Harris, Michael P. "Rev. William Sloane Coffin: Theology in Action from Montgomery to Harlem," *Perspectives* [U.S. Commission on Civil Rights] 15 (Summer 1983): 22–25.
Katz, Milton S. *Ban the Bomb: A History of SANE, the Committee for a Sane Nuclear Policy, 1957–1985*. Westport, CT: Greenwood Press, 1986.
Mailer, Norman. *The Armies of the Night*. New York: New American Library, 1968.
Marriott, Michel. "Dr. Coffin Says Goodbye to Riverside," *New York Times Biographical Service* 18 (Dec. 1987): 1349–50.
Marx, Paul. "Skeptics but Never Cynics: Coffin and Brewster at Yale," *The Christian Century* 92 (July 9–16, 1975): 656–58.
Shapiro, Fred C. "God and That Man at Yale," *New York Times Magazine*, March 3, 1968, pp. 30, 31, 52–62, 73, 74.
Solo, Pam. *From Protest to Policy: Beyond the Freeze to Common Security*. Cambridge, MA: Ballinger, 1988.

Steinfels, Peter. "Reshaping Pacifism to Fight Anguish in Reshaped World," *New York Times,* Dec. 21, 1992, A1, A13.

Ungeheuer, Frederick. "America's Last Peacenik" (interview), *Time* 133 (June 5, 1989): 76–77.

Milton S. Katz

RON KOVIC (1946–   )

Vietnam veteran, leader of Vietnam Veterans against the War, anti-war activist, author, and film writer

A human life may be viewed as a story which the person writes by living it and other people read as they try to make sense of what he does. Just as stories in the literal sense do not exist on the printed page but only in the minds of readers and there are different stories for different people in the same text, so there is no authoritative or true version of a person's life; there are only the many versions which readers create as they view it from different angles. This applies to the person's own version, the story which he reads as he reflects on his own life. It is one more version, more insightful in some ways than others, but often less so in other ways.

Some people seek to shape the story which will be read in their life by reducing what they have done and what has happened to them to words in the form of a memoir, autobiography, or autobiographical novel. They commit the act of literature in their struggle to come to terms with their life. In doing so they may deepen their understanding of their persona, but they also enrich it and add to its ambiguities.

Ron Kovic sought insight into his life and the understanding of others by writing *Born on the Fourth of July* (1976). It was ostensibly a memoir of Kovic's experiences in the portion of his life which began with his youth in Massapequa, New York, and culminated in an epiphany at the Republican National Convention in 1972. The narrative, however, is no mere chronology of events. Kovic shapes it by literary devices which bring coherence and meaning to the turmoil of experience. The book is brief. It singles out vivid scenes and charges them with meaning through reverberations of past events and intimations of ones to come. The narrative moves back and forth in time through an artful use of flashbacks. It shifts between voices: the first person to force readers to realize that a real human being is speaking to them and wrench from them compassion and outrage; the third person to distance readers and present the protagonist's story as representative of his generation, to persuade them to accept his generalizations about himself and his society.

Kovic begins his narrative with the moment he suffers a cataclysmic wound

Ron Kovic at the 1976 Democratic Convention. *Source*: Library of Congress

in combat in Vietnam. He closes the circle by returning at the end to the events which immediately preceded the wound. When readers finish the book, they find themselves where they were when they started, staring at the calamity for which the author has been seeking meaning. But now they ask themselves Kovic's own questions about it. Whether or not they accept his answers, they recognize the validity of the questions.

As Kovic reconstructs his life, it displays the classic form of tragedy. Experiences of childhood instill values and illusions in a favored and naive youth which are to lead him to disaster. On the basis of these values, he chooses a course of action. He becomes a "winner" by serving in the U.S. Marine Corps in Vietnam. His illusions, then his hopes, and finally his values disintegrate under the blows he suffers. First, his illusions die when he kills innocent villagers and possibly one of his own comrades in the insanity of battle. Then, his hopes perish when he suffers the wound which left him paralyzed from the chest down and sexually impotent. Finally his values collapse when as an alienated veteran in a callous and hypocritical society he slides into degradation, drunkenness and rowdiness, the paid intimacy of prostitutes, and estrangement from family, community, and religion. The last chapter of the story recounts his rebirth and regeneration which come through finding a cause (ending the Vietnam War) and fellowship in a new community (other veterans in the same cause).

The last portion of the narrative describes the activism which makes Kovic stand out from other victims of the war. He becomes active in a group, Vietnam Veterans Against the War. He participates in demonstrations which include a march on Washington at which veterans trash their medals on the Capitol steps.

The climax is the scene at the Republican Convention at which President Nixon is nominated for his second term. Kovic manages to work his way past guards onto the convention floor. He is interviewed by Roger Mudd and protests the war on national television. With two other handicapped veterans he interrupts Nixon's speech with shouted protests. He reports his feelings at that moment. "We had done it. It had been the biggest moment of our lives, we had shouted down the president of the United States and disrupted his acceptance speech. What more was there to do but to go home?"

It remained, however, to write his story, to spell out its significance. Then came Oliver Stone's film a decade later in 1986, for which Stone and Kovic wrote the screenplay. With the film Kovic's life was once more distilled and transmuted by art. It became a text in a new medium with new conventions for a new audience, written in collaboration with a co-creator with a new sensibility.

In movies, which are designed to entertain whether or not they illuminate, there is even less reason than in a novel or memoir to expect the story that is communicated to be faithful to the chaotic details of the story that was lived. It is impossible to determine and perhaps it is meaningless to ask whether the movie is faithful to Kovic's actual life, though he reports the eerie feeling on the set and looking at the film that he was watching his past unfold. What is more important than the literal accuracy of either the book or the movie is the validity of the message which they convey and their impact on their audiences. The meaning of Kovic's tragedy will be determined by how the various narratives, such as of the book, the movie, Kovic's reminiscences and the observations of those who know him, are read.

The eventual success of the anti-war movement in the 1970s won a degree of acceptance for Kovic. He was invited to speak to the 1976 Democratic National Convention. At the same time he expanded his circle of friends and comrades and worked to overcome his private demons. He lived in Redondo Beach, California, and enjoyed something of celebrity status because of the film and his association in people's minds with the actor who played him, Tom Cruise.

Kovic makes appearances on college campuses and other public forums to share his experiences and help empower people to overcome adversity, a subject on which he speaks with authority. He is thinking about writing another book, a follow-up to *Born on the Fourth of July*. He has thought of running for Congress or for president, not in the expectation of winning but as a way of communicating his message.

Ron Kovic's political message is a simple one. The Vietnam War was an exercise in genocide carried out by the many for the profit of the few. The government lied to its young men and exploited their patriotism to promote economic, political, and ideological causes in which they had no real stake. It cast them aside as broken tools when they had served their purpose. Those who were maimed were consigned to the inhumane regime of underfunded VA hospitals. Ambulatory veterans were exploited to fan the fires of hyperventilating patriotism. If the psychological and physical cripples refused to play the game, the public averted its gaze in embarrassment or turned upon them with venom.

Kovic believes that the same pattern is visible in most, if not all, of the other wars into which our leaders have taken us. He spoke out against the invasion of Panama and the Gulf War. In opposition to the latter, he made an appearance at the September 1990 Berkeley Teach-In, which was videotaped and circulated among peace groups. He stands ready for further efforts if the forum presents itself. In March 1990 he wrote, "When a system goes astray, it is the right and obligation of citizens to oppose it and change it—for themselves and for generations to come." The only remedy when the general public is fooled is to go into the streets, as the Chinese did in Tiananmen Square and the Czechs in Wencelas Square. Despite the failure of the peace movement to grow during the Panama and Iraq incursions, Kovic remained convinced that social activism in the 1990s would be more relevant than ever before.

As the 1990s began, he was a man in his forties. He was groping for the right medium for his message. He had successfully communicated in several formats, such as print, film, demonstrations, and lectures. He had become the winner that he set out to be as an eighteen-year-old naive patriot, although not in the way that he had dreamed.

Bibliography

Bryan, C.D.B. "Barely Suppressed Screams: Getting a Bead on Vietnam War Literature," *Harper's Magazine* 268 (June 1984): 67–72.

Harris, David. "Ask a Marine," *Rolling Stone*, June 11, 1992, pp. 77–81.

Keerdoja, Eileen. "Kovic: Some of the Wounds Have Healed," *Newsweek* 101 (May 9, 1983): 13–14.

Kovic, Ron. *Born on the Fourth of July*. New York: McGraw Hill, 1976.

———. *Born on the Fourth of July*, screenplay with Oliver Stone, 1986. Reviewed: Christopher Appy, "Vietnam According to Oliver Stone," *Commonweal* 117 (March 23, 1990): 187–89; Vincent Canby, "How an All-American Boy Went to War and Lost His Faith," *New York Times*, Dec. 20, 1989, C15, C16; J. Jones, "Kovic Buoyed by Audience Response," *Guardian* (New York) 42 (Jan. 17, 1990): 20; Stanley Kaufman, *New Republic* 202 (Jan. 29, 1990): 26–27.

———. "To Hell and Back" (interview), *American Film* 15 (Jan. 1990): 28–31, 56.

Ringnalda, Donald. "Fighting and Writing: America's Vietnam War Literature," *Journal of American Studies*, April 1988, pp. 25–42.

"Ron Kovic," *Current Biography* 51 (Aug. 1990): 33–37.

John Kultgen

STAUGHTON LYND (1929–   )

Historian, attorney, political activist, author

Staughton Lynd's widest notoriety was gained when, in 1965, he flew to North Vietnam with Tom Hayden (6*). This violated a federal ban on travel to restricted countries. Lynd's passport was revoked shortly after his return, and he was denied tenure at Yale University, where he was a professor of history. Lynd and Hayden wrote an account of their trip, *The Other Side*. These events propelled Lynd into a prominent position in the early anti–Vietnam War movement. Lynd's radical political activism, however stretched back to the 1940s, and continued into the 1990s. He remained consistent in his political outlook, even when involved in such diverse activities as the organized socialist left, a utopian community, the civil rights movement, the anti–Vietnam War movement, community organizing, rank-and-file labor organizing, and anti-imperialist activity.

Partly under the influence of his parents, Robert S. and Helen M. Lynd, who wrote the classic sociological study *Middletown* (1929), Staughton Lynd became a socialist at the age of fourteen. For a very short time in 1949 he was a member of the Socialist Workers party and then the Independent Socialist League. He quickly became disillusioned with what he calls their ponderous style of organizing which relied more on book learning than contact with ordinary workers and their struggles. He attended Harvard and was drafted into the army, agreeing to serve as a noncombatant. But amidst Senator Joseph McCarthy's investigations of the army he was discharged for his radical past. With his wife Alice, a consistent collaborator in his political activities, Lynd lived for a time in a communal group, the Macedonia Cooperative Community. He received a Ph.D. in history from Columbia University and took a teaching job at Spelman College in Atlanta (1961–1964) to be close to the Civil Rights movement. Among his students was Alice Walker, the well-known black author. The Student Nonviolent Coordinating Committee asked him to direct the Mississippi Freedom Schools, part of the Mississippi Freedom Summer in 1964. He then moved to Yale (1964–1967), but was focused now on the incipient anti–Vietnam War movement. He spent much of his time speaking, in the United States and abroad, against the American government's foreign policy. This high profile led to a confrontation with Yale University, which

Staughton Lynd. Photo courtesy of
Alice Lynd.

could not accept his radical public image. He was eventually denied tenure.
In 1967 Lynd moved with his wife and three children to Chicago to do community organizing. In Chicago the history departments of four different universities offered him teaching positions, which the administrations of each
school then rescinded. Lynd was too controversial to get a regular teaching
position, even though historians respected his scholarship. For the next eight
years the Lynds pieced together a living from a variety of sources. Alice wrote
We Won't Go, a book on war resisters, and did draft counseling; Staughton
worked at several community-organizing jobs.

Two projects led the Lynds to the law and a new focus on labor organizing.
During 1970–1972 Staughton Lynd worked on a project for the Institute for
Policy Studies. He investigated the impact of new occupational health and
safety legislation. At about the same time, the Lynds interviewed working
people for *Rank and File,* a model of oral history. They frequently met workers

with legitimate grievances against their companies but who received little or no assistance from their unions. The Lynds saw that they could earn a livelihood and engage in labor organizing through practicing law. After Staughton attended the University of Chicago Law School (1973–1976), the Lynds moved to Youngstown, Ohio. Staughton and Alice Lynd, as the 1990s began, were attorneys for the Legal Services Corporation.

Staughton Lynd participated in the important labor struggles against steel mill closures in Youngstown from the late 1970s to 1980, and wrote of this experience in *The Fight against Shutdowns*. Even after the last steel mill closed, however, Lynd continued to find numerous outlets for his organizing energies. He was a founding member of the Workers Solidarity Club of Youngstown. This is a small group comprised mainly of rank-and-file workers who act as an unofficial labor union. Their activities include education for workers and the support of strikes. He is an attorney for Solidarity USA, a group of retired steelworkers who since 1986 have been fighting to restore medical insurance benefits cut off by firms declaring bankruptcy. He also represents a group of disabled workers, Workers Against Toxic Chemical Hazards (WATCH), from the Lordstown, Ohio, plant of General Motors.

In addition, starting in 1985 Staughton and Alice Lynd used their summer vacations to visit Nicaragua, where they studied the experiment in combining religious and Marxian approaches to organizing. In the early 1990s they were at work on an oral history of the struggle of the Palestinian people.

Much of Lynd's thought expresses three ideas: radical democratic socialism, personal pacifism, and a commitment to local organizing. In the 1940s, after reading Trotskyist and other anti-Stalinist literature, such as Trotsky's *Literature and Revolution* and *The History of the Russian Revolution,* Edmund Wilson's *To the Finland Station,* and Bertram Wolfe's *Three Who Made a Revolution,* Lynd developed what he terms a libertarian socialist critique of the now-collapsed Soviet Union. He emphasized workers' democratic control of economic and political life. Institutions such as workers' councils, which existed during the early years of the Russian revolution, could provide a framework for the thorough development of economic and political democracy.

Lynd has connected this view, developed in the appraisal of the Soviet experiment in socialism, with American radical traditions. Lynd argued, in *The Intellectual Origins of American Radicalism,* that there is an Anglo-American radical tradition which shares much with non-Stalinist Marxism. In America this tradition stretches from Thomas Paine and William Lloyd Garrison to Edward Bellamy, Eugene Debs, and the 1960s radicals of Students for a Democratic Society (SDS).

Broadly speaking, this tradition expressed several key ideas. First, there is a right to revolution. An oppressed people has the right to throw off the government that oppresses them. Short of that, disobeying unjust laws is morally justifiable. Second, freedom consists of the nondelegable power of self-direction. As a result, representative bodies are necessarily suspect. A superior model is the New England town meeting where everyone can speak. Third, society should promote the satisfaction of human needs, not property rights. Finally, people owe their ultimate allegiance not to their nation, but to humanity as a whole.

Lynd thus speaks of a highly decentralized system in which the greatest power would be at the local level. Ideally, Lynd envisions a society in which the whole citizenry of a community would meet at least once per year to pass laws and elect public officials. Officials would be subject to continual review by the citizens, and may be subject to immediate recall. Representative bodies above the local level might be elected but, as Bellamy suggested in *Equality,* they might have functions similar to those of congressional committees. They would play an advisory or information-gathering role; at most they would coordinate decisions between localities. In developed industrial societies, workers' councils, based on factories or working-class communities, could play the role of town meetings.

By identifying a broad Anglo-American radical tradition and connecting it to versions of twentieth-century "participatory democracy" (thinkers and movements as diverse as Robert LaFollette, Rosa Luxemburg, G.D.H. Cole, the Industrial Workers of the World, French syndicalism, English guild socialism, and workers' councils in Russia), Lynd effectively synthesizes the essential aims of the libertarian socialist left. Necessary corollaries of Lynd's libertarian socialism are active opposition to racism, support for feminism, and support for anti-imperialist struggles.

An especially important element of Lynd's libertarian socialism is his critique of the bureaucratization of unions. Lynd argues that the divide between rank-and-file workers and their salaried full-time union officials is fundamental within the labor movement. Full-time bureaucrats have interests that are different from rank and file workers. While many historians portray the CIO unions as models of class struggle in their first decade, Lynd argues that they developed tendencies toward bureaucratization from the very start. In particular, unions which signed contracts containing clauses that banned strikes during their term handicapped rank-and-file attempts to improve their conditions. The dues check-off, which changed the collection of union dues from a regular interaction between union members and their representatives into a bank transaction, further cemented the division between bureaucracy and shop floor unionists.

Within the labor movement, advocates of CIO-style organizations—with a large paid staff of international representatives, serving local unions but paid by and accountable to the top leadership—argue that this is the most effective way to safeguard and advance workers' economic interests. What the rank and file gives up in accountability they reap in wages. Lynd's experience in Youngstown suggested that centralized national unions have lost much of their effectiveness in fighting against increasingly mobile firms. The activities of foreign workers such as Polish Solidarity and Russian miners suggests to Lynd that there are alternative models of unionism. It may be possible to coordinate workers' struggles without falling into the trap of bureaucratization. On a much smaller scale, the Youngstown Workers Solidarity Club is an attempt to create a rank-and-file alternative to traditional unionism. One strand of Lynd's current research is the examination of the potentialities of such an alternative model of unionism.

Lynd combines his libertarian socialism with what he calls "personal pacifism." Although he concedes that some popular movements, such as the 1979 Nicaraguan revolution against the U.S.-backed dictator Somoza, require the use of armed force, he is committed to nonviolence. Personal pacifism signifies that Lynd would not attempt to impose his own viewpoint on others. In addition, he would work side by side, accompanying those driven to armed means, in a worthwhile struggle. He has sought to infuse such struggles with nonviolence, to the greatest extent possible. Lynd sees great respect for human life in many national liberation struggles. For instance, after the overthrow of Somoza, the Sandinistas did not kill captured national guardsmen. Similarly, he argues, most Palestinians want Moslems, Christians, and Jews to live together in a democratic and secular Palestine.

For Lynd, the experiences of the radical student movement of the early 1960s constitute an important expression of the American radical tradition. Lynd argues that the concept of "participatory democracy" is of enduring value because it describes so well the democratic process in an ideal society. Lynd considers his activities since the early 1960s as an experiment, testing the validity of the idea of participatory democracy among industrial workers. Another aspect of this experimental outlook is to shun dogmatism and divisions on the left. Even when activists use widely different vocabularies, Lynd believes that it is better to proceed experimentally, to see if common values can be implemented in practice, rather than to focus on hammering out a unified theoretical or programmatic viewpoint. Lynd says, "It is better for people to associate with one another in an experimental spirit on the basis of shared values than to insist that everyone believe the same theory or the same creed. I think pushing fully formed ideas on other people has a tendency to divide. Taking experimental action on the basis of shared values tends to bring people together."

During the late 1960s and early 1970s two important shifts occurred in Lynd's organizing focus, one toward local organizing and the other toward labor. During the early anti-war movement, from approximately 1965 to 1968, Lynd was an internationally known critic of the Vietnam War. When he became disillusioned with the rhetoric and style of the late-1960s anti-war movement Lynd shifted back to local organizing. As Lynd points out, this was a shift that many groups and organizers were unable to make. For example, after the national publicity that followed the SNCC protest at the 1964 Democratic party convention in Atlantic City, most of its organizers found it difficult to return to day-to-day work in the rural south.

Second, Lynd shifted in the early 1970s from civil rights and the anti-war movement to political activity among workers. He concluded that as the student movement of the late 1960s engaged in increasingly radical activities on college campuses, it became isolated from ordinary Americans. The social power of students to effect change was reaching its absolute limit; only industrial workers could be the agent of more profound change. Only industrial workers had the power, because of their crucial role in the production process. They could challenge capitalism in a fundamental way.

How could this challenge be organized? Marxists usually asserted the need to create a working class *party* that was national and indeed international in scale, which could educate workers, lead them in economic actions, and represent their ultimate interests in the class struggle. Lynd dissented from this orthodoxy. Lynd rejects the revolutionary left which wants to build such parties as "ponderous," "shrill," and "sectarian." A reformist version of such parties would be no more attractive. A reformist party would unite workers in an organization dominated by professional politicians and full-time union officials. Ordinary workers would not control such a party. Thus, Lynd decisively rejects the organization of a party on the national level as the central strategic aim for the left. His practical activity, particularly since his move to Youngstown in 1976, has been building a local alternative to the union bureaucracy. He is interested in the economic and political organization of industrial workers at the local level.

This is not to say that Lynd considers local organizing to be sufficient. He agrees that today's local organizing and single-issue work, such as environmental protest, women's rights, and international solidarity, are important but fail to capture the sense, so prevalent in the 1960s, of a broad movement attempting to transform society. Thus when Lynd thinks of something larger than local organizing, he does not envision a politically and organizationally unified party, but rather of a diverse movement working on several fronts simultaneously.

Staughton Lynd is a remarkable figure because of his consistently radical outlook and his strong commitment to activism. During his active political life, Lynd withstood two major shifts to the Right in American national politics. First, he weathered the McCarthy era, when many left-wing intellectuals abandoned socialist principles during a time of witchhunts. Second, he did not quit the radical movement in the early 1970s when student protest waned. Many of his radical contemporaries deserted the left when activism receded. The conservative cast of American politics, into the 1990s, and the apparent renunciation of the "socialist" project in Eastern Europe, did not discourage Lynd. For him, "nothing that has happened in the world of late has given me reason to be anything but a socialist." Lynd's radical democratic thought was never founded upon belief in Communism. He had always been convinced that the Russian installed regimes of Eastern Europe, for example, had nothing to do with participatory workers' control, which was the defining feature of his own political objectives. At the same time, Lynd has a broader perspective on the historical development of radical ideas. While others became disillusioned by McCarthyism or the end of the student movement, Lynd identified with long traditions of radicalism. He always found productive means for organizing, even in the most difficult circumstances.

Lynd remained an activist. Of those 1960s radicals who remained on the Left, many assumed academic positions, leaving activism behind. In contrast, Lynd persisted in day-to-day organizing. For instance, he and his wife picketed daily against the Gulf War in 1991, despite the danger that they would be thoroughly ostracized from the community in which they had lived for over thirteen years. Lynd suggested a parallel between his own work and the organizing strategy of priests and nuns he has met in revolutionary Nicaragua. The latter practice a "preferential option for the poor" by working and living side by side with impoverished peasants and workers.

Elements of Lynd's politics have been criticized by his contemporaries. Many SDS organizers, such as Tom Hayden and Rennie Davis, were moving from local organizing to nationally oriented activity by the late 1960s, just as Lynd was moving in the opposite direction. They clashed over, for instance, the value of focusing major attention on the 1968 Democratic National Convention. Kim Moody criticized Lynd's emphasis on local labor organizing because the globalization of capitalism rendered it insufficient.

Perhaps the most profound criticism of Lynd's political outlook may be that there is little to connect his day-to-day activity with his long-range objectives. His decisive rejection of a socialist political party illustrates the failure of the American Left to solve its organizational problems. Lynd downplays the importance of the Left's seeking a common political outlook, opting for an experimental and thoroughly anti-sectarian approach. But if Lynd's socialism, defined as workers' democratic power, is ever to be realized, then some unified political organization beyond the local level will be necessary. A vague movement, an amalgamation of leftists with vastly differing ideas and activities, no matter how large, will not be equal to the task of revolutionary political change. A party-like organization would have the ability to educate workers in consistent socialist politics. Such an organization could evaluate its experience through democratic debate and then make decisions about common action. Only such an organization could coordinate the efforts of radicalized workers throughout the country. Such an organization would have to find some balance between sectarian hairsplitting and abandoning its principles. Lynd shunned the organized Left because it too often failed to make its ideas relevant to ordinary workers and their struggles. Yet, the problem of organizing a principled socialist group remains. Lynd has been aware of this problem. In "Prospects for the New Left," published in 1973, he argued that mass organizations could make democratic decisions about common action without suffocating independent initiatives of local groupings. In the 1990s, he still actively pursued ideas about how to amalgamate local organizers and single-issue groups into a broader movement.

Bibliography

Gitlin, Todd. *The Sixties: Years of Hope: Days of Rage*. New York: Bantam Books, 1987.

Hayden, Tom. *Reunion: A Memoir*. New York: Random House, 1985.

Hazlett, Joseph M. "Staughton Lynd," in *The Biographical Dictionary of Neo-Marxism*, Robert A. Gorman, ed. Westport, CT: Greenwood Press, 1985: 270–72.

Keerdoja, Eileen. "A '60s Activist Fights a New Fight," *Newsweek* 101 (Jan. 17, 1983): 10.

Lynd, Staughton. "Communal Rights," *Texas Law Review* 62 (1984): 1417–41.

———. *The Fight against Shutdowns: Youngstown's Steel Mill Closings*. San Pedro, CA: Singlejack Books, 1983. Reviewed: *Journal of Economic Issues* 8 (Sept. 1984): 950–53; *Labor History* 26 (Fall 1985): 605–7.

———. "The Genesis of the Idea of a Community Right to Industrial Property in Youngstown and Pittsburg, 1977–1987," *Journal of American History* 74 (Dec. 1987): 926–58.

———. *The Intellectual Origins of American Radicalism*. New York: Pantheon Books, 1968.

———. "Intellectuals, the University and the Movement," *Journal of American History* 76 (Sept. 1989): 479–86.

———. Interview, in *Visions of History*, Henry Abelove, Betsy Blackmar, Peter Dimock, and Jonathan Schneer, eds. New York: Pantheon Books, 1983: 149–65.

———. "The New Left," *Annals of the American Academy of Political and Social Science* 382 (March 1969): 64–72.

———. "Prospects for the New Left," in *Strategy and Program: Two Essays Toward a New American Socialism*. Boston: Beacon Press, 1973: 1–49.

———. "Resisting Plant Shutdowns," *Labor History* 30 (Spring 1989): 294–300.

———. Review of Guenter Lewy's *Peace and Revolution*, in *Commonweal* 116 (Feb. 10, 1989): 85–86.

———. "Toward a Not-for-profit Economy: Public Development Authorities for Acquisition and Use of Industrial Property," *Harvard Civil Rights–Civil Liberties Law Review* 22 (Winter 1987): 13–41.

———. "Trade Unions in the USA," *New Left Review* no. 184 (Nov.- Dec. 1990): 76–87.

———. "Youngstown: Rebuilding the Labor Movement from Below," in *Fire in the Hearth: The Radical Politics of Place in America*, vol. 4 of *The Year Left*, Mike Davis et al., eds. London: Verso, 1990: 177–94.

Lynd, Staughton, and Alice Lynd. "Labor in the Era of Multinationalism: The Crisis in Bargained-for Benefits," *West Virginia Law Review* 93 (Summer 1991): 907–44.

———. eds. *Rank and File: Personal Histories of Working-Class Organizers*. Princeton: Princeton University Press, 1981.

Moody, Kim. "A Reply to Staughton Lynd," *New Left Review* no. 184 (Nov.-Dec. 1990): 87–95.

Sale, Kirkpatrick. *SDS*. New York: Random House, 1973.

Glenn Perusek

DAVID McREYNOLDS (1929–   )

Peace activist, democratic socialist, writer

David McReynolds emerged as an important leader of the peace movement during the war in Vietnam. He wrote one of the first demands for unconditional and immediate withdrawal of American forces from Indochina. McReynolds was a key figure in building large coalitions to oppose the war. As a pacifist who rejected all wars, he worked diligently to keep large demonstrations from becoming violent. Twice during the war and again in the 1980s he traveled to Vietnam, where he stated his opposition to all wars, even though, with time, he became sympathetic to Ho Chi Minh. His many articles of political analysis were among the best written from a pacifist perspective. One of his objectives was to keep alive the philosophy of active nonviolence which had been developed by A. J. Muste. Since 1960 McReynolds has been associated with the War Resisters League and is the chief author of that organization's various position papers.

David McReynolds is from a conventional American family. His father, a veteran of World War II, worked for McGraw Hill Publications. His mother, though trained as a nurse, was a housewife after marriage. His brother is a journalist and his sister a teacher and homemaker. The family was Protestant, and as a youth David attended a Baptist church where he became active in the temperance movement. He later worked with the Prohibition party which, he recalls, linked alcoholism to exploitation of the poor. When a high school teacher introduced him to Lincoln Steffens's *Autobiography* and John Steinbeck's *Grapes of Wrath,* he began to develop a critical view of American society. Other writings which influenced his thinking were the first three books of the New Testament and Otto Rank's *Beyond Psychology* (1941). He later read widely in the scriptures of Hinduism and Buddhism, the anti-war poetry of Kenneth Patchen, and the writings of Eugene V. Debs, the Marxists and psychiatrists. He was as influenced by some individuals as by books. Alvin Ailey introduced him to the marvel of modern dance. Bayard Rustin (1*) confirmed his faith in nonviolence and became a vital inspiration in David's life. McReynolds also admired the life of Gandhi, but it was A. J. Muste, who "morally and intellectually did more to put my head where it is now than any other single person."

In 1969 McReynolds published "Notes for a More Coherent Article" in *WIN Magazine* in which he publicly discussed his homosexuality. He had never hidden his sexual orientation, but this was the first time he wrote about it. Being a homosexual added to his insight about the treatment of minorities. Because he neither glorified the gay lifestyle nor attempted to conceal it as

David McReynolds. Photo
courtesy of David McReynolds.

something shameful, he has been criticized by puritans in the peace movement
as well as by some gay activists.

Ironically, David, who started his political career as a prohibitionist, became
an alcoholic in the 1960s. In 1974, when he became aware of his severe
problems, he joined Alcoholics Anonymous. He has avoided alcohol ever since.
His private life includes a love of animals, especially cats, the cultivation of
bromeliads (a variety of house plants), photography, a wide range of music,
especially New Orleans blues and jazz, and cooking.

Democratic socialism, which promotes a society where the means of production are publicly owned and operated, and where civil liberties are protected and electoral politics practiced, is of special importance to David
McReynolds. He joined the Socialist party in 1951 while a student at UCLA.
He held several important leadership positions before he resigned to protest
its support for the Vietnam War. When the Party was reorganized in 1973,

he once again became an active member. In 1958 he was a write-in candidate for Congress. A decade later he again ran for Congress on a Peace and Freedom ticket headed by Eldridge Cleaver (1*). McReynolds viewed the electoral process as a way to build an awareness of socialist ideas. He is convinced that local campaigns are most effective for this purpose since it is conceivable that a socialist might be elected to Congress while there is no possibility of electing a socialist president.

Nevertheless, in 1980 McReynolds was the presidential candidate for the Socialist party. This campaign added to his national reputation and visibility as an American radical. He thought it would be useful to show people a "real live socialist and that this would help us more than an abstract discussion." He also welcomed the opportunity to "advance the cause of unilateral nuclear disarmament at a very dark point in U.S. foreign policy."

David's fundamental goal is revolutionary change through nonviolence. While he is a pacifist, he realizes that most people will only consider pacifism seriously as a tactic. He also defines himself as "essentially religious," though he rejects the concept of a personal God. His religion is an amalgam of the teachings of Jesus, Gandhi, Eastern sacred writings, and Marx. He would like to see pacifists "involved in a movement that would be nonviolent since violence is an obstacle to deep change, but where the emphasis is not on the nonviolent but on social change." He envisions a future society with a nonviolent defense force, full employment, health care for all, the dismantling of the American empire, and very different penal institutions.

Since the 1950s, David McReynolds has worked for various peace movement organizations. After a brief stint as part-time field secretary for the Fellowship of Reconciliation on the West Coast, he moved to New York in 1956 to became the editorial secretary for *Liberation,* a journal of the radical pacifist movement. Since 1960 he has been on the national staff of the War Resisters League (WRL). In the mid-sixties he began working with the War Resisters International (WRI), where he served ten years on its council. Much of his time there was spent opposing any pro-Soviet influence from the East European sections. He later became chair of the WRI, but lost his bid for re-election. In 1991 the War Resisters League created a part-time position for David to free him for more writing, travel, and speaking.

From the beginning of his work with the peace movement, McReynolds emphasized direct action and demonstrations, including civil disobedience. He was indicted and tried as a draft resister during the Korean War, but the case was dismissed on a technicality. During Vietnam he publicly burned his draft card. His participation in New York demonstrations against civil defense drills led to a twenty-five-day stint in jail, which he wrote about in *The Village Voice.* He was one of 14,000 arrested in Washington during the May Day demonstrations of 1971. He was one of seven WRL members who demonstrated for peace in Moscow's Red Square, while several others were doing the same thing on the White House lawn. His numerous articles and speeches helped to publicize these actions.

If anything, David became more radical over the years. He was strongly influenced by his trip to North Vietnam, where he found himself sympathizing with Ho Chi Minh and his movement. Seeing the Vietnamese defending themselves from attacks by the strongest nation in the world forced him to reevaluate his dedication to nonviolence. Nevertheless, he concluded that nonviolence was still the stronger and preferable force.

Those who are dedicated to change through nonviolence admire David McReynolds and appreciate his contribution. Evidence of this appreciation can be found in the special issue of the *Nonviolent Activist* for January and February of 1991. Although McReynolds is seen commonly as a man of principle, some radicals who are not committed to nonviolence view him as impractical and naive. He can be somewhat abrupt and impatient with those who disagree with him. Despite such personal traits, he is one of the most effective spokesmen and activists for nonviolence in the United States.

In a society that favors either comfortable cynicism about the possibility for genuine reforms or naive optimism, David McReynolds persisted in his work for several decades. As the 1990s began, there were, as always, reasons for both despair and hope. On the negative side, the peace movement was in decline. The general public seemed to conclude that the collapse of the Soviet Union and the apparent end of the Cold War made peace issues less important. Military spending was declining, the Selective Service program was ending (that is, no more required registration and, potentially, forced military labor), and many foreign issues appeared to be more bafflingly complex. As a result, some peace groups died, such as the U.S. Peace Council, the Mobilization for Survival, and the Pledge of Resistance. Others shrank, including Women Strike for Peace and the War Resisters League.

McReynold's argued that there continued to be an urgent need for a peace movement. Too much of the federal budget was spent on the military, even after reductions, and death continued to be a big business. The culture of the U.S. and many other societies were pervaded with images of violence. There were "little wars" across the planet. Nuclear weapons continued to spread. There needed to be some plan for conversion of military plants and military personnel to serve human needs. There needed to be a clearinghouse for peace projects and events that went beyond the modest "Key List" that the WRL published each month. Existing movement groups should do more than tend their own sectarian gardens. Instead, the peace movement might have a conference to regather and re-energize its supporters, while reaching out to other movements for democratic social change among environmentalists, feminists, organized workers, and people of color. McReynolds, as a co-chair of the Socialist Party, was convinced that peace can be achieved only through social justice.

The decline of the arms race of the Cold War had been a positive development, but McReynolds believed that it opened new opportunities for progress. It was time to move on. As he summarized his views in an article entitled "The Changing Scene" (p. 7):

It is as if we have awakened from a nightmare and are so glad to find that we are not really falling from a cliff, that we briefly forget we lost our job, the rent isn't paid, we have an infected wisdom tooth, we are going bald, our oldest child may be taking hard drugs, there are termites in the basement, and if the car doesn't get fixed it will stop suddenly and strand us without transportation. That is, the situation is desperate but it isn't as terminal as it seemed in the dream, and we relax for a minute.

OK—that minute is up.

Bibliography

"Anti-War Movement Suffers Peace Deficit," *Washington Post,* June 3, 1990, A3.

Fitrakis, Bob. "McReynolds, David," in *The Biographical Dictionary of the American Left,* Bernard K. Johnpoll and Harvey Klehr, eds. Westport, CT: Greenwood Press, 1986: 273.

McReynolds, David. "The Changing Scene," *The Nonviolent Activist,* Sept.-Oct. 1993, pp. 6–8.

———. "A New Look at the Cold War," *New Politics* 3 (Summer 1991): 178-82.

———. "Socialism," in *War Resisters League Organizer's Manual,* 2d ed., Ed Hedemann, ed. New York: War Resisters League, 1986: 16–22.

———. *We Have Been Invaded by the 21st Century,* introduction by Paul Goodman. New York: Praeger, 1970.

———. "The Words and the Will to Talk about Change," *The Progressive* 55 (March 1991): 28–30.

The Nonviolent Activist, Jan.-Feb. 1991. (The issue is devoted to McReynold's thirty years with the War Resisters League. It includes excerpts from his FBI and CIA files.)

Larry Gara

MARK RUDD (1947–   )

Students for a Democratic Society leader

In 1968 Columbia University exploded over the Vietnam War. The most visible student protester was Mark Rudd, head of the local chapter of Students for a Democratic Society (SDS). Kicked out of college, Rudd in 1969 helped organize the SDS Weatherman underground. They were pledged to and plotted revolution.

Rudd, son of a Defense Department employee and military reserve officer,

Mark Rudd on F.B.I. Wanted Poster. Copyright *Washington Post*; Reprinted by permission of D.C. Public Library.

grew up in suburban, middle-class Maplewood, New Jersey. After entering Columbia University, he became involved in campus politics. In early 1968 his "action faction" took over the local SDS chapter. His group believed that radical social change could be accomplished only by militant confrontation.

In an open letter to Grayson Kirk, Columbia's president, Rudd wrote, "If we win, we will take control of your world, your corporation, your university and attempt to mold a world in which we and other people can live as human beings. Your power is directly threatened, since we will have to destroy that power before we take over."

SDS decided to protest Columbia University's military contracts. In March 1968 a demonstration inside Low Library, the main administration building, led the university to impose discipline upon six demonstrators, including Rudd.

On April 23 SDS rallied students against the administration in front of the library. Student opinion, however, was divided. Someone in the crowd shouted that the students should immediately go and block construction of a new university gymnasium. The crowd surged to the gym site with Rudd following. He did not know where the gym was located.

For years the university had suffered from inadequate physical education facilities. Finally, the university had persuaded the city, over objections from Harlem's black residents, to allow a gym to be built in a public park between the university and Harlem.

Rudd quickly used this issue to build support among white students, black students, and nearby black residents. Building a biracial political movement was always of interest to Rudd.

The protesters took over as many buildings on campus as possible. Radical graduate students seized the math building; blacks, Hamilton Hall; and the main SDS group, three buildings, including Low Library.

Rudd and his friends occupied President Grayson Kirk's office, where they sat in his comfortable chair, read his mail, smoked his cigars, and drank his liquor. Although campus police had sealed off building entrances, students came and went by climbing through windows. SDS found documents that proved that the university's complicity in military research went even deeper than had been charged.

Amid so much turmoil many students left campus. Others stayed to hand food through the windows into the occupied buildings. Still others, opposed to the sit-in, tried to block access. Classes were cancelled, and for practical purposes the school year was over.

One week later, on April 30, the administration called the New York police, who cleared the buildings ruthlessly. The police officers loathed these arrogant, rich college kids. Many students were taken to hospitals with cuts and bruises. On this occasion, Rudd escaped arrest.

Angered by this repression and frustrated by failure, Rudd and his "action faction" looked for a larger field for revolutionary activity. Almost giddy from the publicity that made them heroes to other radicals, they moved to take over the national SDS organization.

In June 1969 Rudd's group, increasingly led by Bernardine Dohrn, William Ayers, and others, issued a manifesto, based on a Bob Dylan song, entitled "You Don't Need a Weatherman to Know Which Way the Wind Blows." This document, accepted by a portion of SDS, advocated going underground to commit acts of sabotage and violence to stop the war and cause a revolution.

Those who accepted the document became known as the Weathermen, or, after women's liberation, as the Weatherpeople. In October 1969 Rudd participated in the Days of Rage street violence in Chicago, but his life underground remains obscure.

In 1977, after seven years as a fugitive, including much time on the FBI's ten most wanted list, Rudd voluntarily surrendered to authorities and pleaded guilty to minor charges in a plea bargain.

In the 1980s Rudd, totally disinterested in politics, became a teacher in Albuquerque, New Mexico. Reflecting upon his revolutionary past in 1988, he said, "We were completely out of touch with reality. I now believe the Vietnam War drove us crazy."

Bibliography

Avorn, Jerry L. *Up Against the Ivy Wall: A History of the Columbia Crisis.* New York: Atheneum, 1968.

Cox Commission. *Crisis at Columbia.* New York: Vintage Books, 1968.

Harrison, Thomas L. "Mark Rudd," in *Political Profiles: The Johnson Years,* Nelson Lichtenstein, Eleanora W. Schoenebaum, and Michael L. Levine, eds. New York: Facts on File, 1976: 531–32.

Jacobs, Harold, ed. *Weatherman.* Berkeley: Ramparts Press, 1970.

Powers, Thomas. *Diana: The Making of a Terrorist.* Boston: Houghton Mifflin, 1971.

Rader, Dotson. *I Ain't Marchin' Anymore!* New York: David McKay, 1969.

Rudd, Mark. "Sixties' Lesson: Guilt-Motivated Militancy Can Be Dangerous," *The Guardian* (New York), Jan. 18, 1989, p. 19; Abbie Hoffman, "Hoffman to Rudd: Don't Apologize," *The Guardian* (New York), Feb. 22, 1989, p. 19.

Sale, Kirkpatrick. *SDS.* New York: Random House, 1973.

Spender, Stephen. *The Year of the Young Rebels.* New York: Random House, 1969.

W. J. Rorabaugh

MARIO SAVIO (1942–   )

Berkeley Free Speech Movement student leader

In 1964 the University of California at Berkeley suddenly banned political activity on campus. This action angered student civil rights activists, who organized the Free Speech Movement (FSM). Mario Savio, a brilliant orator played a key role. After much agony the FSM won. It was one of the student movement's greatest victories.

Savio, the son of devout, working-class Italians, had been born and raised in New York. He nearly became a priest, took the social gospel seriously, and in 1963 worked on a church-sponsored project in rural Mexico. In the fall he transferred to Cal and became a philosophy major.

Increasingly restless, he told a friend, "I'm tired of reading history. Now I want to make it." He joined the civil rights struggle and in the summer of 1964 went to Mississippi, where he was attacked. He returned to school "very angry."

That fall Savio and other activists challenged the university's new rules that

Mario Savio speaking at Berkeley, 1966. *Source*: Library of Congress

prohibited students from collecting funds or gathering supporters' names from card tables that had traditionally been placed at the edge of campus.

Savio emphasized a philosophical position. He said that the university had no right to regulate the content of speech and that only the courts, operating within the First Amendment, could impose restrictions. He envisioned the university as a free market for ideas.

Savio was also skeptical about American society. In a biting essay called "The End of History," he wrote that at the end of World War II the older generation had established a society designed to be perpetual. To Savio, whose Catholic values were now tempered by Marx, this society was too unjust to deserve preservation. He resented being told that nothing could change.

There were noon rallies nearly every day in front of Sproul Hall, the main administration building. Savio spoke to thousands of students. Meanwhile, other activists systematically defied the campus rules by setting up political card tables.

On October 1, university police arrested Jack Weinberg and placed him in a patrol car. Several hundred students surrounded the car and sat down. For thirty-two hours Weinberg and the car were held captive, while students, including Savio, climbed on top to debate. Weinberg remained at the site for more than a day.

By the end of November support for the FSM was growing. About one-third of the students, some 8,000, supported both the FSM's goals and its militant tactics. With broad support, the FSM leaders planned a sit-in inside Sproul Hall.

On December 2, Savio told a rally, "There is a time when the operation of the machine becomes so odious, makes you so sick at heart, that you can't take part; you can't even passively take part, and you've got to put your bodies upon the gears and upon the wheels, upon the levers, upon all the apparatus and you've got to make it stop. And you've got to indicate to the people who run it, to the people that own it, that unless you're free, the machines will be prevented from working at all."

Joan Baez (5*) sang as students marched into Sproul Hall and sat down. The police came in the middle of the night; almost 800 protesters were arrested. It was the largest mass arrest in California history.

On December 7, a desperate administration sponsored a mass meeting at the outdoor Greek Theatre. At the end of the event Savio walked to the microphone. Suddenly, campus policemen dragged Savio backstage. The crowd went wild. The symbolism was grotesque. A student advocate for free speech had been physically prevented from speaking.

The following day the faculty met and voted, 824–115, in favor of the FSM position. It was Savio's twenty-second birthday. For the first time during the crisis, he smiled. The administration gave in, and the university's regents adopted new regulations that implemented the FSM demands.

Although the FSM had won, its leaders paid a heavy price. Savio was sentenced to 120 days in jail for his role in the sit-in. In the spring of 1965, Savio married, left school, and quit the FSM.

Savio's political activity declined. An early opponent of the Vietnam War, he played only a modest role in that movement. Family responsibilities weighed heavily. He sold books, tended bar, and worked as a labor union organizer. Divorced and remarried, he became increasingly private.

In 1984 he returned to Sproul Hall to celebrate the FSM's twentieth anniversary. His oration, delivered to thousands of students who had no memory of the FSM, drew a standing ovation.

That same year he received a B.S. degree from San Francisco State University and was awarded a graduate fellowship to study physics. Later, he taught math at nearby Sonoma State College.

Bibliography

Cutner, Naomi. "Where the '60s Were Born," *Life* 7 (Dec. 1984): 142–48+.

Draper, Harold. *Berkeley: The New Student Revolt*. New York: Grove, 1968.

Eymon, Bret. "Community in Motion: The Free Speech Movement, Civil Rights, and the Roots of the New Left," *The Oral History Review* 17 (Spring 1989): 39–69.

Harrison, Thomas L. "Mario Savio," in *Political Profiles; The Johnson Years*, Nelson Lichtenstein, Eleanora W. Schoenebaum, and Michael L. Levine, eds. New York: Facts on File, 1976: 550–52.

Heirich, Max A. *The Spiral of Conflict: Berkeley 1964*. New York: Columbia University Press, 1971.

Hijiya, James A. "The Free Speech Movement and the Heroic Moment," *Journal of American Studies* 22 (April 1988): 43–65.

Lipset, Seymour Martin, and Sheldon S. Wolin, eds. *The Berkeley Student Revolt*. Garden City, NY: Anchor Books, 1965.

Miller, Michael V., and Susan Gilmore, eds. *Revolution at Berkeley; The Crisis in American Education*. New York: Dell, 1965.

Parshall, Gerald. "The Times They Are A-Changin'," *U.S. News and World Report* 101 (July 14, 1986): 5.

Rorabaugh, W. J. *Berkeley at War: The 1960s*. New York: Oxford University Press, 1989.

Rossman, Michael. *The Wedding within the War*. New York: Doubleday/Anchor, 1971. Rossman has been active in Berkeley politics from the 1960s into the 1990s.

W. J. Rorabaugh

DR. BENJAMIN SPOCK (1903–)

Celebrity author/pediatrician, peace advocate

The publication of *The Common Sense Book of Baby and Child Care* in 1946 made Benjamin Spock a household name. During the 1960s and early 1970s, he took on the additional role of peace advocate. Spock was featured in a 1962 advertisement for the National Committee for a Sane Nuclear Policy (SANE). A pensive Spock was next to a child; the ad was captioned, "Dr. Spock is Worried". He also became a prominent critic because of his 1968 indictment, trial, and conviction (later overturned) for conspiracy to counsel, aid, and abet resistance to the draft. Later, he was the presidential candidate of the People's party in 1972.

Spock was raised by traditional parents in New Haven, Connecticut. His father, an attorney for the New York, New Haven, and Hartford Railroad, praised Calvin Coolidge. When Benjamin cast his first vote in 1924 it was for Calvin Coolidge. From his mother, an independent and domineering woman, Spock fashioned a self-confident moralism that informed his later work and thought. Spock's migration to radicalism began late in the 1920s. When he transferred from Yale Medical School to Columbia's College of Physicians and Surgeons, he discovered medical students who were Democrats and even Socialists. He soon became a New Deal liberal. Spock's worldview was further shaped during the 1930s, while he began an office for pediatric medicine in New York City. In New York, psychiatric training introduced him to Freudian psychology and reinforced his belief in the aggressive nature of humanity and the value of sublimation. He became familiar with the democratic educational

Dr. Benjamin Spock protesting health care budget. Copyright *Washington Post*; Reprinted by permission of D.C. Public Library.

theory of John Dewey and William Heard Kilpatrick. He was also horrified by the hypocrisy of U.S., British, and French policies of "non-interference" during the Spanish civil war.

Spock was never a pacifist. He served as a lieutenant commander in the U.S. Naval Reserve during World War II. He believed that the war against Hitler was just; he approved the use of atomic bombs at Hiroshima and Nagasaki; and, over the years, he consistently supported the United Nations intervention in Korea. His opposition to the Vietnam War was based not on pacifism, nor was it grounded in opposition to American "imperialism," though he often used the term and believed that the United States was in Vietnam "to control Southeast Asia." At bottom, Spock opposed the war because he believed it had the potential to yield World War III and nuclear holocaust.

In this sense, his anti-war stance was an extension of his opposition to nuclear weapons. Spock's decision to join SANE in 1962 (he became co-chairperson in 1964) was an outgrowth of his work in pediatrics and his life-long concern for children. Despite his own hawkish tendencies in the 1950s, he contended that the cold war, and especially the atomic bomb, made children fearful and anxious. In addition, Spock believed that an effective ban on atomic testing was essential if children were to avoid the ravages of cancer and leukemia. Spock remained an advocate for SANE until 1967, when he resigned from the organization because it failed to participate with more radical groups in the April 15, 1967, Mobilization to End the War in Vietnam. "I believe in solidarity," he said in 1967.

Spock's conversion to peace advocacy was also linked to the feeling that he had been betrayed by politicians to whom he had given his trust. The first betrayal took place in 1961, when it became clear that the missile gap on which John F. Kennedy had campaigned did not exist; the second occurred when Lyndon Johnson, despite a promise to keep American boys out of an Asian war, escalated the conflict; the third was the revelation that Dwight Eisenhower and John Foster Dulles had broken "our government's promise" to support the Geneva Accords; the fourth was the betrayal of the American voter with the Tonkin Gulf resolution, which Spock believed had been approved under false pretenses. Spock was judging public officials by the standard of his mother, whose promises were inviolate.

Spock's sensitivity to betrayal was, in turn, related to his attachment to ideas about the rule of law and the democratic process. His legal emphasis was apparent in his interpretation of "A Call to Resist Illegitimate Authority." This 1967 statement was drafted by Spock and others; it became a centerpiece of the conspiracy charge against him. Although the statement brands the Vietnam War as immoral, Spock especially invoked its description of the conflict as "illegal and unconstitutional." As Spock later recalled, "I always based [my right to oppose the war] on rule of law. I never felt I had to differentiate between law and conscience or fall back on conscience." Moreover, the FBI's role in his conviction for conspiracy added to Spock's growing fear that the United States had become a police state. For several years after this, he spoke regularly on the theme of "Dissent and Social Change." He discussed the legal aspects of civil disobedience while raising money for the Civil Liberties Legal Defense Fund.

Just as *Baby and Child Care* rejected authoritarian parenting for democratic guidance and leadership, so did Spock utilize a democratic approach within the peace movement. During the conspiracy trial, Spock even claimed that he had intended his speeches, writings, and protest actions only as informational, not as persuasive, devices. People ought to make up their own minds about the war and the draft. This anti-authoritarian methodology may have impressed the Court of Appeals, which in 1970 reversed Spock's conviction on the grounds that his speech against the draft was protected by the First Amendment. Spock's growing appreciation for certain democratic forms was apparent in his attraction to the National Conference for a New Politics (NCNP). He co-chaired this organization after his departure from SANE. The NCNP not only favored immediate withdrawal from Vietnam and an end to the draft, but community control of schools and police, especially in black neighborhoods.

Spock gradually came to distrust and reject many aspects of American democracy. Disaffected with the sameness of the programs and ideals of the major parties, in 1972 Spock ran for president as a candidate of the People's party. Its platform stressed decentralized government, local control of essential services, worker and consumer control over matters of production and consumption, progressive taxation, a broad attack on discrimination, and an end to U.S. interference in the Third World. Convinced, too, that governments yielded only under extraordinary pressure, and following the example of Daniel and Philip Berrigan (*), the mild-mannered Spock turned increasingly to extralegal acts of civil disobedience. He was arrested more than a dozen times since October 1967. Many of Spock's acts of civil disobedience have involved nuclear weapons or reactors, though he has also been arrested while demonstrating on Capitol Hill against the plight of the homeless.

Spock's greatest contribution to the peace movement was the moral authority and integrity he carried by virtue of having assisted in the rearing of millions of American children. In addition, his pragmatic commitment to solidarity among protest groups functioned as an antidote to the divisiveness within the New Left in the late 1960s. One could argue, too, that the antinuclear grounding of his anti-war views held out the hope for a broad-based anti-war coalition. It did not require ordinary Americans to redefine the nation as an imperial aggressor.

Nonetheless, Spock's position was not without significant weaknesses. In early 1968, Spock's moral authority as author of *Baby and Child Care* was challenged by Rev. Norman Vincent Peale, who from his New York City pulpit charged that Spock's "permissive" child-rearing methods had produced "the most undisciplined age in history." Vice-President Spiro Agnew made a similar accusation during the congressional elections of 1970. Spock rightly insisted that he had never advocated permissiveness, and in *Decent and Indecent* (1969), he lamented the society's loss of "bearings" and "standards" even as it advocated new forms of censorship. But for some people Spock now became the problem, not the solution. Some feminists also attacked Spock; Gloria Steinem (3*) believed that he was "a major oppressor of women." Spock responded by making changes in the third edition of the baby book, published in 1976. Finally, his links to black issues, organizations, and leaders were often minimal, perhaps because he came to the peace movement through SANE rather than civil rights.

More follower than leader, Spock contributed his presence, support, and imprimatur to existing organizations and projects. While Spock deserves praise as a tireless opponent of the Vietnam War and the draft, his limitations may have prevented him from carrying out a project of which only he—and perhaps a few others—was capable: that of bringing to the peace movement the middle-class women who had raised their children on the advice of Dr. Spock.

Bibliography

Bloom, Lynn Z. *Doctor Spock: Biography of a Conservative Radical.* Indianapolis: Bobbs-Merrill, 1972.

Graebner, William. "The Unstable World of Benjamin Spock: Social Engineering in a Democratic Culture, 1917–1950," *Journal of American History* 67 (Dec. 1988): 612–29.

Mitford, Jessica. *The Trial of Dr. Spock: The Rev. William Sloane Coffin, Jr., Michael Ferber, Mitchell Goodman, and Marcus Raskin.* New York: Alfred A. Knopf, 1969.

Nyham, David. "A Prosecutor Praises 'Patriot' Spock," *Boston Globe,* Sept. 30, 1993, 15:1.

Spock, Benjamin. "The Conspiracy to Oppose the Vietnam War," in *It Did Happen Here: Recollections of Political Repression in America,* Bud Schultz and Ruth Schultz, eds. Berkeley: University of California Press, 1989: 90–100.

———. *Decent and Indecent: Our Personal and Political Behavior.* New York: McCall Publishing, 1969.

Spock, Benjamin, and Mary Morgan. *Spock on Spock: A Memoir of Growing Up with the Century.* New York: Pantheon 1989. Reviewed: *Nation,* Feb. 5, 1990, pp. 175–77; *New York Times,* Dec. 30, 1989, p. 20; *New York Times Book Review,* Nov. 5, 1989, p. 11; *Washington Post,* Nov. 27, 1989, B1, B4.

Spock, Benjamin, and Mitchell Zimmerman. *Dr. Spock on Vietnam.* New York: Dell, 1968.

Weiss, Nancy. "Mother, The Invention of Necessity: Dr. Benjamin Spock's Baby and Child Care," *American Quarterly* 29 (Winter 1977): 519–46.

Zuckerman, Michael, "Dr. Spock: The Confidence Man," in *The Family in History,* Charles Rosenberg, ed. Philadelphia: University of Pennsylvania Press, 1975: 179–207. See also Zuckerman's *Almost Chosen People: Oblique Biographies in the American Grain* (Berkeley: University of California Press, 1993).

William Graebner

PART THREE

SEXUALITY AND GENDER: LIBERATION FROM STEREOTYPES

Women have done much of the work for the movements included in this book, but they have often received little credit. In the civil rights struggles of the 1950s and 1960s, women were frequently crucial in local organizing, but men were almost invariably the public "leaders." In the anti-war coalitions, women were disproportionately represented in the drudge work that received little honor. It was considered natural that they would support the reputations of male leaders.

By the 1960s a growing number of women were not willing to accept this invisibility. More women had paid jobs outside the home; the civil rights movement had stimulated some feminist consciousness; and the rhetoric of President Kennedy's New Frontier had encouraged expectations of social reform. Liberal changes within the system, such as the Equal Pay Act of 1963 and Title VII of the Civil Rights Act of 1964, were followed by separate feminist groups to organize compliance and further progress. Liberal feminists such as Betty Friedan (*) and Gloria Steinem (*) became prominent. Liberal women politicians and administrators, however, remained rare, although they included Bella Abzug (*) and Eleanor Holmes Norton (*). The broader public became more aware of an emerging feminist movement (one which included both liberals and radicals) through such events as a demonstration at the Miss America contest in 1968. This featured the crowning of a live sheep as Miss America. One of the organizers, Robin Morgan, went on to compile the best-selling anthology *Sisterhood Is Powerful* (1970) and to help found *Ms.* magazine (1972).

Although conservatives have periodically declared that the movement is over, and that the United States has moved into "post-feminism," and radicals had once hoped for a "post-patriarchal" society, neither has yet happened. The 1990s saw high expectations among young women (even those who did not call themselves feminists); massive indignation against sexual harassment in the navy, Senate, and various businesses; major demonstrations in support of reproductive choices; rising numbers of women in the professions; and many more elected women officials. In 1971, women had earned only 6 percent of all professional degrees, such as in accounting, law, pharmacy, and business. In 1990, the percentage was more than one-third. By the early 1990s, women were about one-fifth of all representatives in state legislatures, and there were forty-seven in the U.S. House and six in the U.S. Senate.

Of course, by the standard of parity this was still inadequate. There continued to be widespread assumptions of the natural subservience of women. This was understandable in a culture with a male god, male military figures, male presidents, male church leaders, male executives, and male heroes. The educational system, from the earliest grades (usually taught by women) to the highest university classes (usually taught by men), implies male superiority. Numerous studies have demonstrated that teachers—whether men or women—have been conditioned to expect limited success from female students, favor male students, and channel students into subjects that are considered appropriate based upon sex. The general culture also encourages low self-esteem for women. As one high school woman complained: "A strong guy is a strong guy. A strong girl is a bitch" (*New York Times*, March 11, 1992, B8). Although there have been significant changes, often after considerable effort, further changes will be necessary if women are to have the same general freedoms and opportunities in life as men.

One remarkable change in sex roles since the 1960s has been the questioning of anti-homosexual beliefs. Some of the feminists of the 1960s had been taunted as lesbians, whether they were or not, because of their suppposedly mannish insistence on equality. Similarly, men who have supported such equality could be dismissed by some as "queer" (that is, not "real men"). Such stereotypes have become less common, certainly among the better educated classes. Already after World War II, Dr. Alfred Kinsey documented that some homosexual experiences were much more common in the general population than had been previously thought. *Sexual Behavior in the Human Male* (1948) and *Sexual Behavior in the Human Female* (1953) discussed what people actually did sexually, as opposed to public moralizing about what was proper or normal. The scientific study of sexuality continued in the 1960s with such works as *Human Sexual Response* (1966) by William Masters (*) and Virginia Johnson (*). The American Psychiatric Association removed homosexuality from its list of mental disorders in 1973, and few leading members of the medical profession, by the 1990s, characterized homosexual desires or behavior as intrinsically "sick." Although the Kinsey data has not been supplemented with modern scientific surveys of contemporary sexual practices—the federal funding for such projects having been blocked during the conservative presidencies of Ronald Reagan and George Bush—it is unlikely that homosexuality is rarer now than in the days of Dr. Kinsey. On the other hand, there is little evidence that homosexuality, as the basic orientation of an individual, is a lifestyle choice, any more than being born left-handed. Homosexuals appear to be a statistical minority found throughout history in widely different cultures.

The first major attempts in the United States to organize this minority, or to define it as a cohesive minority, came after World War II. Small urban gay subcultures had developed. Tiny organizations formed slowly, such as the Mattachine Society (1950), encouraged on the East Coast by Frank Kameny (*), and the Daughters of Bilitus (1955), long influenced by Del Martin (*) and Phyllis Lyon (*). By the mid-1960s, there was a tiny movement that described itself as "homophile." This grew and changed following the 1969 Stonewall Riot in New York City, where a police raid on a gay bar prompted resistance from the youthful "throwaways and runaways" (as one commentator described them) who were there. The times had changed; people were no longer as fearful and resigned. Soon there were larger organizations, publications, and demonstrations representing a movement now called "gay liberation."

By the early 1990s, there were several hundred significant gay organizations scattered throughout the United States, along with about 160 gay weeklies, biweeklies, monthlies, and quarterlies. Major advertisers had begun to patronize these publications, as noted in the *New York Times* (March 2, 1992, A1, D9). Politically, eleven states had executive orders or civil service rules forbidding discrimination in state employment based on sexual orientation, some local governments had similar laws, and politicians were more likely to support, or at least not hinder, such regulations. When the Republican National Convention in 1992 was suffused with anti-gay rhetoric (as part of the general theme of "traditional family values"), this produced more hostility than support when many people concluded that hate was not a traditional family value. Indeed, the Democratic presidential candidate, Bill Clinton, was notably willing to repudiate what was increasingly called homophobia and advocate various changes in government rules, such as one banning all gay men and lesbians from serving in the military forces of the United States, no matter what their personal abilities or behavior. In fact, by 1992, it was obvious that there were already gay men and lesbians in the military, and that they had always been there. It was also obvious that there were gay men and lesbians in education (at all levels), the churches (at all levels), and in all aspects of American life. These people were neither all saints nor all demons. This recognition, by many Americans, was a change. Gay men and lesbians were no longer invisible.

The March on Washington, in April of 1993, was a dramatic sign of this. Whether one believed the estimate of 300,000 participants (by the Park Service), 500,000 (by the D.C. police), or 1,000,000 (by the organizers), there had never been a larger national march for gay rights. It was not only one of the largest demonstrations ever held in the nation's capital, it was the largest pro-gay political demonstration in the history of the world. Many who participated were no longer apologetic about their identity, whether they were the quieter (and usually older) moderates or the more militant (and usually younger) activists who chanted "we're here; we're queer; get used to it."

Of course, many Americans had not gotten used to it. The placards of some counterdemonstrators ("God hates fags"/"Back into the closet"), along with commonly believed stereotypes about gay men and lesbians in the military as hormonal beasts, seemed to prove that homosexuals were one group that it was still widely acceptable to ridicule and hate. But was it possible to go back to the "good old days" before gay liberation? The subject was no longer taboo in public discussion; AIDS education encouraged more frank recognition of sexual practices; and homosexuals themselves were, in large numbers, no longer willing to hide. Indeed, many were not satisfied with toleration but insisted upon liberation: completely equal treatment and general public understanding of sexual differences.

The 1993 demonstration by gay men and lesbians, and the 1992 demonstration for women's reproductive rights (which brought perhaps 500,000 people to Washington, D.C.) indicated that the supposedly conservative Reagan-Bush years had not suppressed these powerful tendencies for social change. The women's movement and the gay liberation movement have both challenged basic cultural stereotypes that limit the potential humanity of all, men and women, heterosexuals and homosexuals. Although there were still many people who wanted to keep women "in their place" (whatever that might be) or scorned "faggots" (whether they "flaunted it" or were "respectable"), prejudices were now likely to be met with organized resistance.

SELECTED BIBLIOGRAPHY

Heterosexual Redefinition

Aptheker, Bettina. *Tapestries of Life: Women's Work, Women's Consciousness, and the Meaning of Daily Experience.* Amherst: University of Massachusetts Press, 1989.
———. *Woman's Legacy: Essays on Race, Sex, and Class in American History.* Amherst: University of Massachusetts Press, 1987.
Barber, James, and Barbara Kellerman, eds. *Women Leaders in American Politics.* Englewood Cliffs, NJ: Prentice Hall, 1986.
Bataille, Gretchen M., ed. *Native American Women; A Biographical Dictionary.* New York: Garland Publishing, 1992.
Boone, Joseph A., and Michael Cadden, eds. *Engendering Men: The Question of Male Feminist Criticism.* New York: Routledge, 1990.
Boston Women's Health Book Collective. *Our Bodies, Ourselves; Updated and Expanded for the '90s,* 3d rev. ed. New York: Simon and Schuster, 1992 (1970).

Breines, Wini. *Young, White, and Miserable: Growing Up Female in the Fifties*. Boston: Beacon Press, 1992.

Butterick, George F. "Diane di Prima," in *The Dictionary of Literary Biography*, vol. 16. Detroit: Gale Research, 1983: 149–60.

Caraway, Nancie. *Segregated Sisterhood; Racism and the Politics of American Feminism*. Knoxville: University of Tennessee Press, 1991.

Chafe, William H. *The Paradox of Change: American Women in the 20th Century*. New York: Oxford University Press, 1991.

Clatterbaugh, Kenneth. *Contemporary Perspectives on Masculinity: Men, Women, and Politics in U.S. Society*. Boulder, CO: Westview Press, 1990.

Costello, John. *Virtue under Fire: How World War II Changed Our Social and Sexual Attitudes*. Boston: Little, Brown, 1986.

Davidson, Harriet. "Adrienne Rich," in *Modern American Women Writers*, Elaine Showalter, Lea Baechler, and A. Walton Litz, eds. New York: Scribner's, 1991: 441–55.

Firestone, Shulamith. *The Dialectic of Sex: The Case for Feminist Revolution*. New York: Quill, 1993 (1970). Reviewed by Alice Echols in "Like a Hurricane: Shulamith Firestone's Wild Ride," [Village] *Voice Literary Supplement*, Oct. 1993, pp. 13–14.

Davis, Flora. *Moving the Mountain: The Women's Movement in America Since 1960*. New York: Simon and Schuster, 1992.

D'Emilio, John, and Estelle Freedman. *Intimate Matters: A History of Sexuality in America*. New York: Harper and Row, 1986.

di Prima, Diane. *Memoirs of a Beatnik*. San Francisco: Last Gasp, 1989.

Echols, Alice. *Daring to Be Bad: Radical Feminism in America, 1967–1975*. Minneapolis: University of Minnesota Press, 1989.

Evans, Sara. *Born for Liberty: A History of Women in America*. New York: The Free Press, 1989.

———. *Personal Politics: The Roots of Women's Liberation in the Civil Rights Movement and the New Left*. New York: Random House/Vintage, 1980.

Ferree, Myra Marx, and Beth B. Hess. *Controversy and Coalition: The New Feminist Movement*. Boston: Twayne Publishers, 1985.

Filene, Peter G. *Him/Her/Self: Sex Roles in Modern America*, 2d ed. Baltimore: Johns Hopkins University Press, 1986.

Fout, John C. and Maura Shaw Tantillo, eds. *American Sexual Politics: Sex, Gender, and Race since the Civil War*. Chicago: University of Chicago Press, 1993.

Friedman, Jean, and William G. Shade, eds. *Our American Sisters: Women in American Life and Thought*, 4th ed. Lexington, MA: D. C. Heath, 1987.

Garland, Anne Witte. *Women Activists: Challenging the Abuse of Power*. New York: The Feminist Press, 1988.

Garcia, Alma M. "The Development of Chicano Feminist Discourse, 1970–1980," in *Unequal Sisters: A Multi-Cultural Reader in U.S. Women's History*, Ellen Carol Dubois and Vicki L. Ruiz, eds., New York: Routledge, 1990: 418–31.

Giddings, Paula. *Where and When I Enter: The Impact of Black Women on Race and Sex in America*. New York: Morrow, 1984.

Gilmore, David G. *Manhood in the Making: Cultural Concepts of Masculinity*. New Haven: Yale University Press, 1990.

Goldin, Claudia. *Understanding the Gender Gap: An Economic History of American Women.* New York: Oxford University Press, 1989.

Gordon, Linda. *Woman's Body, Woman's Rights: A Social History of Birth Control in America,* rev. ed. New York: Penguin, 1990.

Griffin, Susan. *Made from This Earth: An Anthology of Writings.* New York: Harper and Row, 1982.

Hagan, Kay Leigh, ed. *Women Respond to the Men's Movement,* intr. by Gloria Steinem. San Francisco: HarperSan Francisco, 1992.

Harrison, Cynthia. *On Account of Sex; The Politics of Women's Issues, 1945–1968.* Berkeley: University of California Press, 1988.

Hartmann, Susan M. *From Margin to Mainstream: American Women and Politics Since 1960.* New York: Oxford University Press, 1989.

Hine, Darlene Clark, Elsa Barkley Brown, and Rosalyn Terborg-Penn, eds. *Black Women in America; An Historical Encyclopedia.* 2 vols. Brooklyn, NY: Carlson Publishing, 1992.

Hooks, Bell. *Ain't I a Woman: Black Women and Feminism.* Boston: South End Press, 1981.

Hull, Gloria, Patricia Bell Scott, and Barbara Smith, eds. *All the Women Are White, and the Blacks are Men, but Some of Us Are Brave.* Old Westbury, NY: Feminist Press, 1983.

Hunter College Women's Studies Collective. *Women's Realities, Women's Choices: An Introduction to Women's Studies.* New York: Oxford University Press, 1983.

Jones, Jacqueline. *Labor of Love, Labor of Sorrow: Black Women, Work, and the Family from Slavery to the Present.* New York: Basic Books, 1985.

Kaledin, Eugenia. *Mothers and More: American Women in the 1950s.* Boston: Twayne, 1984.

Kerber, Linda K., and Jane S. De Hart, eds. *Women's America: Refocusing the Past,* 3d ed. New York: Oxford University Press, 1991.

Kimmel, Michael S., and Thomas S. Mosmiller, eds. *Against the Tide: Pro-Feminist Men in the United States, 1776–1990; A Documentary History.* Boston: Beacon Press, 1992.

Lerner, Gerda. *The Majority Finds Its Past: Placing Women in History.* New York: Oxford University Press, 1982.

Linden-Ward, Blanche, and Carol Hurd Green. *Changing the Future: American Women in the 1960s.* New York: Twayne Publishers, 1992.

Lynn, Susan. *Progressive Women in Conservative Times; Racial Justice, Peace, and Feminism, 1945 to 1960s.* New Brunswick, NJ: Rutgers University Press, 1993.

McAdam, Doug. "Gender as a Mediator of the Activist Experience: The Case of Freedom Summer," *American Journal of Sociology* 97 (March 1992): 1211–40.

Matuz, Roger, Cathy Falk, Sean R. Pollock, and David Segal, eds. "Kate Millett, 1934–, American Nonfiction Writer," in *Contemporary Literary Criticism,* vol. 67. Detroit: Gale Research, 1992: 232–63.

May, Elaine Tyler. *Homeward Bound: American Families in the Cold War Era.* New York: Basic Books, 1988.

Morgan, Robin. *The Word of a Woman: Feminist Dispatches, 1968–1992.* New York: W. W. Norton, 1992.

———, ed. *Sisterhood Is Global: The International Women's Movement Anthology.* New York: Anchor/Doubleday, 1984.

————. *Sisterhood Is Powerful; An Anthology of Writings on the Women's Liberation Movement*. New York: Random House, 1970.

Morton, Patricia. *Disfigured Images: The Historical Assault on Afro-American Women*. Westport, CT: Greenwood Press, 1991.

Norton, Mary Beth, ed. *Major Problems in American Women's History*. Lexington, MA: D. C. Heath, 1989.

Offen, Karen, Ruth Roach Pierson, and Jane Rendall, eds. *Writing Women's History: International Perspectives*. Bloomington: Indiana University Press, 1991.

Piercy, Marge. "Active in Time and History," in *The Art and Craft of the Political Novel*, William Zinsser, ed. Boston: Houghton Mifflin, 1989: 91–123.

————. *To Be of Use*. Garden City, NY: Doubleday, 1973.

Pomeroy, Wardell B. *Dr. Kinsey and the Institute for Sex Research*. New Haven, CT: Yale University Press, 1982.

Raphael, Ray. *The Men from the Boys: Rites of Passage in Male America*. Lincoln: University of Nebraska Press, 1988.

"Rich, Adrienne," in *Contemporary Literary Criticism*, vol. 36. Detroit: Gale Research, 1986: 364–79.

Robinson, Paul. *The Modernization of Sex: Havelock Ellis, Alfred Kinsey, William Masters, and Virginia Johnson*, with a new preface by the author. Ithaca, NY: Cornell University Press, 1988.

Salem, Dorothy C., ed. *African American Women: A Biographical Dictionary*. New York: Garland Publishing, 1993.

Scott, Anne Firor. *Natural Allies: Women's Associations in American History*. Urbana: University of Illinois Press, 1992.

Scott, Joan Wallach. *Gender and the Politics of History*. New York: Columbia University Press, 1988.

Smith, Jessie Carney, ed. *Notable Black American Women*. Detroit: Gale Research, 1992.

West, Guida, and Rhoda Lois Blumberg. *Women and Social Protest*. New York: Oxford University Press, 1990.

Willis, Ellen. *No More Nice Girls: Countercultural Essays*. Middletown, CT: Wesleyan University Press, 1993.

Zophy, Angela, and Frances M. Kavenik, eds. *Handbook of American Women's History*. New York: Garland Publishing, 1990.

Lesbian and Gay Liberation

Adam, Barry. *The Rise of a Gay and Lesbian Movement*. Boston: Twayne, 1987.

Beam, Joseph, ed. *In the Life: A Black Gay Anthology*. Boston: Alyson Publications, 1986.

Berube, Allan. *Coming Out under Fire; Gay Men and Women in World War II*. New York: The Free Press, 1990.

"Boyd, Malcolm," in *Contemporary Authors*, vol. 26, New Revision Series. Detroit: Gale Research, 1989: 64–70.

"Brown, Rita Mae," in *Contemporary Literary Criticism*, vol. 43. Detroit: Gale Research, 1987: 80–86.

Bunch, Charlotte. *Passionate Politics: Essays, 1968–1986: Feminist Theory in Action*. New York: St. Martin's Press, 1987.

Cruikshank, Margaret. *The Gay and Lesbian Liberation Movement*. New York: Routledge, 1992.

D'Emilio, John. *Making Trouble; Essays on Gay History, Politics, and the University*. New York: Routledge, 1992.

———. *Sexual Politics, Sexual Communities: The Making of a Homosexual Minority in the United States, 1940–1970*. Chicago: University of Chicago Press, 1983.

DiBernard, Barbara. "Zami: A Portrait of an Artist as a Black Lesbian" [on Audre Lorde, who died in 1992], *The Kenyon Review*, n.s. 13 (Fall 1991): 195–213.

Duberman, Martin Bauml. *About Time: Exploring the Gay Past*, rev. and enl. ed. New York: New American Library/Dutton, 1991.

———. *Cures: A Gay Man's Odyssey*. New York: New American Library/Dutton, 1991.

———. "Reclaiming the Gay Past" (review article), *Reviews in American History* 16 (Dec. 1988): 515–25.

———. *Stonewall*. New York: Dutton, 1993.

Duberman, Martin Bauml, Martha Vicinus, and George Chauncey, Jr., eds. *Hidden from History: Reclaiming the Gay and Lesbian Past*. New York: New American Library, 1989.

Duggan, Lisa. "History's Gay Ghetto: The Contradictions of Growth in Lesbian and Gay History," in *Presenting the Past: Essays on History and the Public*, Susan Porter Benson, Stephen Brier, and Roy Rosenzweig, eds. Philadelphia: Temple University Press, 1986: 281–90.

Dynes, Wayne R. *Homosexuality: A Research Guide*. New York: Garland Publishing, 1987.

———, ed. *Encyclopedia of Homosexuality*, 2 vols. New York: Garland Publishing, 1990.

Faderman, Lillian. *Odd Girls and Twilight Lovers: A History of Lesbian Life in Twentieth-Century America*. New York: Columbia University Press, 1991.

Fee, Elizabeth, and Daniel M. Fox. "The Contemporary Historiography of AIDS," *Journal of Social History* 23 (Winter 1989): 303–14.

———, eds. *AIDS: The Burdens of History*. Berkeley: University of California Press, 1988.

Grahn, Judy. *Another Mother Tongue: Gay Words, Gay Worlds*, updated and expanded. Boston: Beacon Press, 1990.

Greenberg, David F. *The Construction of Homosexuality*. Chicago: University of Chicago Press, 1988.

Humphrey, Mary Ann. *My Country, My Right to Serve: Experiences of Gay Men and Women in the Military, World War II to the Present*. New York: HarperCollins, 1990.

Jay, Karla, and Allen Young, eds. *Out of the Closet: Voices of Gay Liberation*, 2d ed., intr. by John D'Emilio. New York: New York University Press, 1992 [1972].

Katz, Jonathan ed. *Gay/Lesbian Almanac*. New York: Harper and Row, 1983.

———. *Gay American History: Lesbians and Gay Men in the U.S.A.*, rev. ed. New York: Meridian Books, 1992.

Kleinberg, Seymour. *Alienated Affections: Being Gay in America*. New York: Warner Books, 1982.

Licata, Salvatore, and Robert Petersen, eds. *The Gay Past: A Collection of Historical Essays*. New York: Harrington Park Press, 1985.

Likosky, Stephan, ed. *Coming Out: An Anthology of International Gay and Lesbian Writings*. New York: Pantheon Books, 1992.

Lorde, Audre. *Zami: A New Spelling of My Name*. Watertown, MA: Persephone Press, 1982.

Marcus, Eric. *Making History: The Struggle for Gay and Lesbian Equal Rights, 1945–1990; An Oral History*. New York: HarperCollins, 1992.

Miller, Neil. *In Search of Gay America; Women and Men in a Time of Change*. New York: Atlantic Monthly Press, 1989.

Munt, Sally, ed. *New Lesbian Criticism; Literary and Cultural Readings*. New York: Columbia University Press, 1992.

Nelson, Emmanuel S., ed. *Contemporary Gay American Novelists: A Bio-Bibliographical Sourcebook*. Westport, CT: Greenwood Press, 1993.

Perry, Troy D., and Thomas L. P. Swicegood. *Profiles in Gay and Lesbian Courage*. New York: St. Martin's Press, 1991.

Pollack, Sandra and Denise D. Knight, eds. *Contemporary Lesbian Writers of the United States: A Bio-Bibliographical Sourcebook*. Westport CT: Greenwood Press, 1993.

"Rechy, John Francisco," in *Chicano Literature: A Reference Guide*, Julio Martínez and Francisco A. Lomelí, eds. Westport, Ct: Greenwood Press, 1985: 323–32.

Shilts, Randy. *The Mayor of Castro Street: The Life and Times of Harvey Milk*. New York: St. Martin's Press, 1983.

Rutledge, Leigh W. *The Gay Decades: From Stonewall to the Present, the People and Events That Shaped Gay Lives*. New York: Plume, 1992.

Timmons, Stuart. *The Trouble with Harry Hay: Founder of the Modern Gay Movement*. Boston: Alyson Publications, 1990.

Vaid, Urvashi. Margin to Center: *The Mainstreaming of Gay and Lesbian Liberation*. New York: Anchor Books, forthcoming, 1995.

Ward, Carol M. *Rita Mae Brown*. New York: Twayne Publishers, 1993.

BELLA ABZUG (1920–   )

Congresswoman, feminist, peace advocate

Bella Abzug's career exhibited both the opportunities and the liabilities of pursuing social activism within mainstream politics. A lifelong advocate of peace, feminism, and social justice, Abzug maintained her links with grassroots activism while serving in Congress, in the Democratic party, and in the Carter White House. She used her position as an insider to gain significant accomplishments, but her gender, ideological stance, and personal style frequently placed her on the margins of the political mainstream.

Bella Savitzky was born in 1920 and grew up in the Bronx, where her father operated a meat market. She traced her early interest in social justice to her grandfather, a Russian Jewish immigrant. A 1942 graduate of Hunter College, Abzug earned a law degree from Columbia University in 1947. She combined marriage and raising two daughters with a legal career focused on labor law and defense of civil rights activists and victims of McCarthyism. Issues of peace claimed much of her attention in the 1960s, when she helped found Women Strike for Peace (WSP) in 1962 and served as its Washington lobbyist. Originally committed to nuclear disarmament, WSP pioneered in the movement against the war in Vietnam with its demonstrations at the Pentagon and protests against the use of napalm. At the same time, Abzug worked with reform Democrats to deny Lyndon Johnson a second term in 1968.

In 1970, Abzug entered the political establishment, defeating the Democratic incumbent for the congressional seat representing the West Side of Manhattan. On her first day in Congress, she introduced a resolution calling for U.S. withdrawal from Vietnam. She remained a vocal anti-war activist until the last American left Vietnam in 1975.

Abzug's campaign slogan, "This woman's place is in the House," expressed her commitment to the goals of the newly resurgent feminism. During her six years in Congress, she carried with her a standard anti–sex-discrimination clause, which she sought to insert into every relevant piece of legislation. Although Abzug's fight for a federal child-care program and for the right of poor women to abortions under Medicaid failed, she helped win passage of bills promoting equal employment, education, and credit for women, as well as the inclusion of domestic workers under the minimum wage law. In addition to influencing national policy on women, Abzug challenged the masculine atmosphere and control of Congress and helped make the corridors of power more hospitable to women. She insisted on being addressed as "Ms.," and forced congressmen to allow women to use the congressional swimming pool, over resentful complaints that now they would have to wear swim suits.

Bella Abzug. *Source*: Library of Congress

With the large hats that became her trademark and her flamboyant style, Abzug attracted considerable media attention for herself and her causes. She was outspoken, scrappy, and impatient with traditional procedures and courtesies and with anyone who opposed her views. Mainstream representatives found these characteristics especially unacceptable in a woman. "Bellicose Bella," "abrasive," "overbearing," and "disruptive" were her enemies' words for her, but even some of Abzug's allies found her hard to work with and considered her personal style counterproductive.

Abzug worked tirelessly to open the political system to women. In 1971, she joined with Shirley Chisholm (1*), Betty Friedan (*), and Gloria Steinem (*) to establish the National Women's Political Caucus (NWPC), a broad-based organization that included not just visible feminists, but also women from organized labor, religious groups, traditional women's organizations, and diverse ethnic groups. Its composition reflected Abzug's insistence at the founding meeting that the NWPC was not intended "to replace the *male* white middle-class elite that runs this country with a *female* white middle-class elite."

With its purpose to combat sexism, racism, institutional violence, and poverty, the NWPC promoted party reform, worked for the election and appointment of women to public office, and supported women's issues and feminist candidates of both sexes and across party lines. Justifiably claiming a share of credit for the growing numbers of women policymakers, the NWPC maintained a national presence into the 1990s, and Abzug continued to be a featured speaker at its national conventions.

The year 1976 ushered in a period of political setbacks for Abzug. She gave up her House seat to run for the Senate, but in a five-way contest, she lost the Democratic primary by just one percentage point to Daniel Patrick Moynihan. In 1977, she entered the race for mayor of New York, but was defeated by Edward Koch in the Democratic primary. Attempting to return to the House in 1978, she lost once more, this time to the Republican candidate in the general election. She remained active in the Democratic party, where her greatest contribution was to transfer power from party regulars to women, racial minorities, the poor, working-class people, and similar underrepresented groups.

Before Abzug left the House, she sponsored a bill authorizing $5 million for a national women's conference to be held as part of the United Nations International Decade of Women. Appointed in 1977 by President Jimmy Carter as presiding officer of a commission to plan the conference, Abzug oversaw the planning of public meetings on women's issues in every state and the national meeting itself. More than 2,000 delegates attended the meeting in Houston, representing a cross-section of American womanhood and including some 20 percent anti-feminists. They adopted resolutions on a wide range of issues, including child care, reproductive freedom, welfare, and the Equal Rights Amendment, and on problems of such specific groups as racial minorities, lesbians, homemakers, and older women. This National Plan of Action became the first national agenda for policymaking on women's issues.

President Carter followed up his support of the national conference by establishing a National Advisory Committee for Women (NACW) in 1978. He selected Abzug to serve as co-chair along with Carmen Delgado Votaw. Abzug, however, was already at odds with Carter over his opposition to abortion rights. She viewed the NACW as the vehicle for translating the National Plan of Action into actual policy. But within six months, Abzug and the committee grew alarmed at Carter's plans to combat rising unemployment and inflation, plans which they believed would have a disproportionately adverse effect on women.

In January 1979, the committee issued a press release under the headline "President Carter Challenged on Social Priorities." The release noted that while Carter's proposed budget increased military spending, it included $15 billion worth of cuts in spending for employment, education, health and welfare, and other programs of importance to women. After a meeting between the NACW and Carter, Abzug was abruptly informed by a Carter aide that she was fired as co-chair. In response, twenty-six of the forty Committee members resigned in protest.

"We were . . . meant to advise, not just consent," Abzug insisted, reflecting her unfailing refusal to allow the attractions of being a political insider prevail over her commitment to principle. In addition to demonstrating Abzug's willingness to take on anyone over social justice issues, the NACW imbroglio reflected a maturation of the women's movement. Encouraged by Abzug and others, mainstream feminism had moved from a focus on individual rights and equal opportunity that were of greatest benefit to relatively privileged women to embrace the needs of diverse groups of women. Feminism, as it made the economy a women's issue, came to challenge not just sex discrimination but also the prevailing distribution of resources and power.

Lack of a political office did not stop Abzug's efforts to promote women's rights, peace, and social justice. In 1979, along with former Congresswomen Yvonne Braithwaite Burke and Patsy Mink, she founded Women U.S.A. to mobilize "grass-roots, Middle American women, who are not in organizations or involved in politics." The new organization sponsored lobbying, letter-writing campaigns, and boycotts, and it worked to get more women registered to vote.

Throughout the 1980s, Abzug continued to be active in the left wing of the Democratic party, pushing for progressive platform planks and pressuring Democratic presidential candidates to take strong stands on women's issues. With her longtime aide, Mim Kelber, she wrote a book, *The Gender Gap* (1984), which demonstrated that in many elections women supported the more progressive candidates and stands on issues by as much as 10 percentage points more than men. Through the book, speeches, and other writings, Abzug popularized the idea of a gender gap, warning politicians and party leaders that responsiveness to women's concerns was critical to their success at the polls.

Abzug played a central role in a small group of leading Democratic women pushing for a woman on the 1984 ticket. When presidential nominee Walter Mondale selected Geraldine Ferraro as his running mate, Abzug was ready with cigars bearing the tag, "It's a girl," and she worked for the ticket in New York. Throughout the decade, she attacked the Reagan policies of skyrocketing defense expenditures, slashes in social welfare programs, and military intervention in Nicaragua and elsewhere. In 1985, she attended the U.N. Decade for Women Conference at Nairobi, where she challenged the official U.S. position and delegation by supporting a petition demanding a cut in the defense budget, regulation of multinational corporations that adversely affected women, the right to full employment, and elimination of all forms of racism and discrimination against women.

In 1986, Abzug tried once more for elective office, this time a House seat from New York's Twentieth District in Westchester County, where she had earlier lived for fourteen years and recently established a law office. Even though her campaign was interrupted for three weeks at the death of her husband, she won a four-way Democratic party primary, but she failed to unseat the Republican incumbent in the general election.

Working within the establishment in Congress and in the Democratic party, Abzug contributed to reform, in part through her ability to gain national attention and through her uncompromising positions, which benefited the efforts of moderate reformers by making them appear more acceptable. Her leadership in the National Women's Political Caucus and on Carter's National Advisory Commission on Women helped to make feminism more inclusive and to connect it to broader issues of social justice. Shut out of the political establishment, Abzug refused to trim her sails to the rising conservative winds. She continued to speak out for peace and the needs of marginalized Americans.

Bibliography

Abzug, Bella. *Bella! Ms. Abzug Goes to Washington.* New York: Saturday Review Press, 1972.

———. "Martin, What Should I Do Now?" *Ms.* July/August 1990, pp. 94–96.

———. "'Morally Correct' Environmentalists," *Washington Post*, April 21, 1992, A19.

———. "Raising Our Voices," *The Unesco Courier* 45 (March 1992): 36–37.

Abzug, Bella, with Mim Kelber. *The Gender Gap: Bella Abzug's Guide to Political Power for American Women.* Boston: Houghton Mifflin, 1984.

Auletta, Ken. "'Senator' Bella—Seriously," *New York*, Aug. 11, 1975, pp. 27–34.

Brenner, M. "What Makes Bella Run?" *New York*, June 20, 1977, pp. 54–64.

Gertzog, Irwin N. *Congressional Women: Their Recruitment, Treatment, and Behavior.* New York: Praeger, 1984.

Hartmann, Susan M. *From Margin to Mainstream: American Women and Politics Since 1960.* New York: Knopf, 1989.

Susan M. Hartmann

TI-GRACE ATKINSON (1939–)

Radical feminist

Ti-Grace Atkinson was a major theorist and strategist of the radical feminists of the late 1960s and early 1970s. Genteel, sophisticated, and soft-spoken, she contradicted the stereotyped image of a revolutionary and an activist. College students flocked to her speeches, many of which she published in *Amazon Odyssey* in 1974. Other people tried to censor her. Her outspokenness in the movement, her attacks on the Catholic church, and her analysis of the oppression of women won her unprecedented notoriety and press coverage. The ideals that she espoused in her speeches during the turbulent 1960s and 1970s remained unchanged in the 1990s.

She was born in 1939 in Baton Rouge, Louisiana, and given a Cajun first name. She lived there until age five and again from ages nine to eleven. Her affluent Republican family traveled extensively. Her travels and her upbringing in a genteel southern home exerted a strongly formative influence. As a youth she had attended over fifteen different schools in Europe and the United States. Her travels provided cultural experiences that enabled her to appreciate people's differences. Unlike some feminists, she felt less threatened by such differences and was capable of perceiving people in less conventional ways.

She married at age seventeen and lived with her student husband in a campus community. When he entered the military service, she enrolled at the University of Pennsylvania, from which she received a Bachelor of Fine Arts degree. They later divorced. Thereafter, she pursued her interest in art, becoming a critic for *Art News* and one of the founders of the Institute of Contemporary Art in Philadelphia, where she was its first director in 1964.

In 1962 she read Simone de Beauvoir's *The Second Sex* and was moved to write to the author. De Beauvoir, in turn, suggested a correspondence with Betty Friedan (*). Atkinson, who had felt isolated in her problems, began to connect to other women. She also sought out broader interpretations by enrolling at Columbia University as a doctoral candidate in political philosophy. (She eventually completed all of her work except for the dissertation.) At the same time, Friedan encouraged her to become more active in women's rights. Friedan hoped that Atkinson's "Main Line accent and ladylike blond good looks would be perfect . . . for raising money from the mythical rich old widows which we never did unearth" (Echols, *Daring to Be Bad*, p. 167).

Atkinson first became an active participant in the National Organization for Women (NOW) in 1967. She rose rapidly in both the New York chapter and the national organization, becoming the president of the former and the national fund-raiser of the latter. She appeared to be an excellent choice considering her family connections and social experience. In early 1967 she was still a registered Republican.

She began to make some members of NOW nervous by insisting that the organization discuss sensitive issues like abortion and the inequalities of marriage. She also began to urge that NOW, if it was to be truly democratic and escape from male politics of domination, should rotate its officers on a regular basis and choose them by lot. While these positions gained her recognition by the *New York Times* as feminism's "haute thinker," many feminists found her style imperious and some of her ideas dubious.

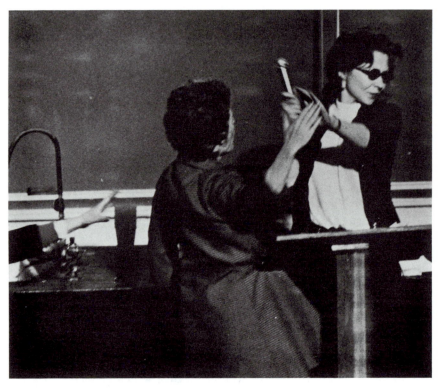

Ti-Grace Atkinson attacked at Catholic University. Copyright *Washington Post*;
Reprinted by permission of D.C. Public Library.

In 1968 she insisted on a vote to restructure the New York chapter of NOW.
She was defeated by a two-to-one margin and resigned all of her NOW offices.
She declared that the women's movement was divided between those women
who "want women to have the opportunity to be oppressors, too, and those
who want to destroy oppression itself" (Atkinson, *Amazon Odyssey*, p. 10). If
women rose to power in the existing society, they would not necessarily behave any better than men.

Atkinson moved on, in 1968, to help found the Feminists. Again, however,
there were internal conflicts. Many of the members believed in skills sharing,
which involved the rotation of both creative and routine work within the
group. When the group required that individual members not speak to the
press without collective consent, Atkinson resigned in 1971. In the same year,
she also quit the Daughters of Bilitis in New York City when her friend Ruth
Simpson was forced from the presidency. As she noted in her speech at Juniata
College in February of 1970, women could and did oppress other women
within the women's movement.

Her outspokenness brought her notoriety, as did her arrest for disorderly conduct and resisting arrest in October 1972. Atkinson, Florynce Kennedy, Ruth Simpson, Ellen Povl, and Merle Goldberg had demonstrated in front of a Nixon campaign office on Madison Avenue. Additional publicity came when she was banned from speaking at Catholic University by Clarence C. Walton, the president. He argued that she had blasphemed the church's doctrine on the Virgin Mary. Students took the issue to court, making it a free speech protest against the church's repression. A U.S. District Court judge ruled that she was constitutionally guaranteed access to a speaker's platform at the university. She addressed an audience of about 800 students in Maloney's Hall plus many viewers who watched on closed-circuit television. Meanwhile, small groups and individuals picketed her appearance while some 1,500 people attended benediction at the National Shrine of the Immaculate Conception. In the midst of her remarks on virgin birth and comments that Mary was "more used" than she would have been had she participated in sexual conception, she was attacked. Patricia Buckley Bozell, sister of Senator James F. Buckley, Jr., of New York, shouted "I can't let her say that," as she ran forward to slap Atkinson's face. This event was captured by the media. Atkinson later expressed her appreciation to the board of trustees of Catholic University and to the church for having provided evidence for her theory on the Catholic church versus feminism.

Her combined interest in feminism, art, aesthetics, and politics led her to new commitments in publishing and teaching. In 1974 she published *Amazon Odyssey*, which included commentaries on abortion, the myth of vaginal orgasm, lesbianism and feminism, prostitution and pornography, violence, and the treatment of older women as "the garbage of society." From 1976 to 1978 she taught women's studies at Western Washington University in Bellingham and for one year at the University of Washington, Seattle. Thereafter, she returned to New York City, where she was an adjunct faculty member for ten years at the Parsons School of Design. She also served on the faculty at the School of Visual Arts. At Columbia University she taught summer courses in aesthetics, feminism and political philosophy, art and politics, and contemporary civilization. In addition to her appointments in academia, she has written two hundred papers and participated with four other women in a project collecting data on radical feminism in the 1960s.

As an intellectual leader of such radical feminists, Atkinson has argued that male insecurity led to the creation of various institutions to control women. These institutions, broadly defined, included romantic love, sexual intercourse, marriage, and religion. All of these were created primarily by men to consolidate their own power. Romantic love, for example, is "the euphoric state of fantasy in which the victim transforms her oppressor into a redeemer." While love may be a means for women to attain their humanity, it has been perverted by giving up one's self and identifying with a man. Marriage, as Atkinson saw it, was unpaid prostitution between a superior, powerful male and a subservient woman. Women were locked into accepted roles. Reinforcing all of this was male religion. It adjusted women's consciousness to oppression. Since women are needed for population growth and indoctrination of the youth, and since churches cannot survive without this political condition, the churches sustain their existence through the oppression of women.

Atkinson's solution to men's oppression of women was the organization of women to actively change the political definition of the female role. Only then would women be free to be human. As one means of eliminating the politics of sex, Atkinson suggested the use of an extra-uterine device for prenatal development. This would reduce sex to a practice instead of a function. Women would be relieved of childbearing if they chose. Of course, the overall liberation of women would be complex since the denigration of women is implicit in the central institutions of our society.

While Atkinson's ideals remained constant, radical feminism suffered from considerable dissolution. She attributed much of this to the shrinking back of radical feminists from the full implications of their values. Nonetheless, Atkinson saw continuing feminist consciousness in some women and men, although sisterhood proved to be elusive. She continued to write and speak for her vision of an equal reality for both women and men.

Bibliography

Atkinson, Ti-Grace. *Amazon Odyssey*. New York: Links Publishers, 1974.
———. Interview, by Beatrice K. Reynolds, Aug. 18, 1990.
———. "An Interview with Ti-Grace Atkinson: Her Speeches and Speechmaking" (by Beatrice K. Reynolds), *Today's Speech* 21 (1973): 3–10.
"Contact," *New York Times*, March 14, 1981, D8.
Echols, Alice. *Daring to Be Bad: Radical Feminism in America, 1967–1975*. Minneapolis: University of Minnesota Press, 1989.
Johnston, Laurie. "Five Women Militants Held after Demonstration Here," *New York Times*, Oct. 24, 1972, p. 34.
Lear, Martha Weiman. "The Second Feminist Way," *New York Times*, March 10, 1968, VI:57.
Martin, Judith. "An Attack on Ti-Grace Atkinson," *New York Times*, March 11, 1971, B1.
Reynolds, Beatrice K. "Ti-Grace Atkinson," in *American Orators of the Twentieth Century: Critical Studies and Sources*, Bernard K. Duffy and Halford R. Ryan, eds. Westport, CT: Greenwood Press, 1987: 7–13.

Beatrice K. Reynolds

BETTY FRIEDAN (1921–   )

A founder of the second feminist movement

Betty Friedan was both a catalyst and a leader of the second feminist movement that grew larger and raised more issues than the pre–World War II movement that lead to the nationwide right of women to vote in 1920. Her analysis of women's lives and her actions as a founder of feminist organizations were of prime importance to the beginnings of feminism in the 1960s. Her description of the dissatisfaction that many white, middle-class women felt in the 1960s provided the ideological underpinnings of the major tendencies in this new feminism.

Born in Peoria, Illinois, Friedan graduated *summa cum laude* from Smith College in 1942. She then settled in New York City, where she met and married Carl Friedan. Although she was primarily a housewife raising three children from 1947 to 1957, she continued to work as a free-lance magazine writer. In 1957 she asked the members of her college class to describe their lives during the fifteen years since college. From the questionnaires and other research came her instant best-seller, *The Feminine Mystique*, published in 1963. The book sold three million copies, was excerpted in all the major women's magazines, and made Friedan a celebrity.

In 1966 she was one of the founders of the National Organization for Women and served as its first president until 1970. In 1969 she was a founder of the National Association for the Repeal of Abortion Laws (NARAL) and in 1971, the National Women's Political Caucus (NWPC). During the 1970s she served as a columnist and editor of *McCall's* magazine and a lecturer and visiting teacher at major universities across the country. She continued to be in great demand because of her impassioned message. In 1976 she published *It Changed My Life*, her reminiscences of the first years of the feminist movement. In 1981 she published her third book, *The Second Stage*, her view of the future direction of feminism.

Her first book had argued that suburban middle-class housewives were not fulfilled by homemaking and child bearing. Her thesis provoked hundreds of letters from unhappy and dissatisfied women who recognized their own situation in Friedan's description. Friedan pinpointed their "problem with no name" and gave it a name. This was "the feminine mystique," the belief that women's fulfillment could be found only in motherhood and the family. She criticized psychiatrists, social scientists, educators, and business people because they used the feminine mystique to encourage women to live segregated lives as mothers, housewives, and volunteers in the new suburban ghettos of the postwar world. She urged women to leave those ghettos and find meaningful work outside the home. While her analysis in *The Feminine Mystique* spoke directly and powerfully to middle-class white women, it had far less relevance for most minority and working-class women.

As president of the National Organization for Women (NOW) during its first three years (1966–1969), Friedan provided NOW with publicity, an increasing membership, a program, and an ideology. In 1966 she wrote the founding statement for NOW. She declared that "the purpose of NOW is to take action to bring women into full participation in the mainstream of American society now, exercising all the privileges and responsibilities thereof in truly equal partnership with men." The goal has been to make women the

Betty Friedan, 1968.
Copyright *Washington Post*;
Reprinted by permission of
D.C. Public Library.

equals of men and full participants in the existing society, not to radically transform that society.

In 1967 she led NOW to add an equal rights amendment and a call for legalized abortion to its Bill of Rights. Other provisions included enforcement of employment discrimination laws, maternity leave benefits, day-care centers, tax deductions for child care, integrated equal education, and equal opportunity in job training for impoverished women.

During her NOW presidency she traveled across the country publicizing the new feminist movement. When she stepped down from the presidency of NOW in March 1969, she suggested that NOW sponsor a strike to commemorate the fiftieth anniversary of the suffrage movement. As an attempt to broaden the feminist movement, August 26 succeeded far beyond her wildest dreams. She led the organizing efforts for the march and was one of the speakers at the New York rally which attracted 50,000 women. The initial impact of the day was an enormous spurt in prominence and membership for NOW and other feminist groups.

As a founder of the National Association for the Repeal of Abortion Laws in 1969, she insisted that NARAL recognize that abortion was a women's issue. This statement, while self-evident in later years, was controversial because the pro-abortion movement was led by doctors and clergymen. When Friedan stated that "only one voice needs to be heard on the question of whether a woman will or will not bear a child, and this is the voice of the woman herself," she was uttering words that, endorsed by millions of women, would reorient the abortion movement. Rallying support of many of the women at the conference, she led a fight that resulted in NARAL asserting in its founding statement that women have a right to choose to have a child.

Friedan continued to emphasize the need for a mainstream-oriented, broad-based concept of feminism. From the beginnings of the feminist movement, she was fearful of the influence of radical feminists and gay rights activists because she believed that feminism should appeal to a broader constituency of both women and men. Her leadership in the founding of NOW, NARAL, and NWPC, key organizations of mainstream feminism, fit in with this philosophy. Rather than viewing feminism as a revolutionary movement, she saw it as part of the ongoing movement of various minorities to gain their rightful place in democratic society. She did eventually include the emerging gay and lesbian movements, although she had once warned of a "lavender menace" that might diminish the public's support for feminism. In 1977 she offered a successful gay rights resolution at the International Women's Year conference in Houston, Texas.

In her third book, *The Second Stage* (1981), Friedan presaged the 1980s feminist issues related to a society where both spouses work and no one person is the primary caretaker and housekeeper for the family. Friedan and other feminists had initially criticized women's roles in the family because they believed that status and success were attained through work outside the home. By the 1980s Friedan said that both feminists and society needed to realize that women and men desire both the prestige and fulfillment that come from work outside the home and the love and identity gained through marriage and children. Feminism had moved away from concern with these issues in the 1970s as it had become too woman-centered and too sexual in its orientation. Rather than polarizing the relationship between the sexes, Friedan urged feminists to join with men and even with right-wing conservatives of both sexes to work on family issues. Her goal was to keep feminism within mainstream American politics by keeping it focused on issues that would appeal to a broad constituency of both men and women.

By the early 1990s, Friedan attacked a different set of limiting stereotypes, not those based on sex but those based on age (although older women suffered most from both sexism and ageism). In 1993, she published *The Fountain of Age*. This was thirty years after *The Feminine Mystique* had—in the words of social critic Alvin Toffler—"pulled the trigger of history" about feminism. Her new target was the youth mystique which considers youth to be the ideal and aging to be only a set of problems. She criticized gerontological studies that were based primarily on the institutionalized and she deplored most of those people and institutions that profited from treating the old as feeble and diseased. Friedan argued that older people needed to define a more positive present and future for themselves. As she noted in one interview: "This I learned in 30 years in the women's movement—the first step of any revolution is consciousness" (*Senior Beacon* [Washington, DC] 5 [Oct. 1993], p. 7). Although many reviewers found her book too lengthy (it was more than six hundred pages), somewhat redundant, and too limited in its examples to affluent white people, it was generally praised for its overall merits.

Friedan's own later years exemplified the positive themes of *The Fountain of Age*. She spent winters teaching such courses as "Women, Men, and Media" at the University of Southern California and worked as a visiting professor at New York University. She completed her book despite two heart operations. She continued to live a full social life with her friends, a daughter, two sons, in-laws, and grandchildren. She concluded *The Fountain of Age* by hoping that, "if I'm lucky, I'll die on the move, in the air, on the road."

Bibliography

"Betty Friedan," in *Current Biography* 50 (March 1989): 18–22.

Bowlby, Rachel. " 'The Problem with No Name': Rereading Friedan's *The Feminine Mystique*," *Feminist Review* no. 27 (Autumn 1987): 61–75.

Breines, Wini. *Young, White and Miserable: Growing Up Female in the Fifties*. Boston: Beacon Press, 1992.

French, Marilyn. "The Emancipation of Betty Friedan," *Esquire* 100 (Dec. 1983): 510–14+.

Friedan, Betty. "Back to the Feminine Mystique?" *The Humanist* 51 (Jan./Feb. 1991): 26–27.

———. "Fatal Abstraction," *New Perspectives Quarterly* 4 (Winter 1988): 14–19.

———. *The Feminine Mystique*. New York: Norton, 1963.

———. *The Fountain of Age*. New York: Simon and Schuster, 1993.

———. "How to Get the Women's Movement Moving Again," *New York Times Magazine*, Nov. 3, 1985, pp. 26–29+.

———. *It Changed My Life: Writings on the Women's Movement*, with a new introduction. New York: Norton, 1985 [1976].

———. "The New Traditionalism," *New Perspectives Quarterly* 7 (Spring 1990): 66; "On Prodigal Parents," *ibid.*, pp. 66–67.

———. "Preserving Family Values in a Changing World," *USA Today* 116 (Aug. 1987): 2–3.

———. *The Second Stage*. New York: Summit, 1981.

———. "Twenty Years after *The Feminine Mystique*," *New York Times Magazine*, Feb. 27, 1983, pp. 34–36+.

Furth, Jane. "Her Cause and Effect," *Life* 11 (Feb. 1988): 96–98.

Wandersee, Winifred. *American Women in the 1970s*. Boston: Twayne/G. K. Hall, 1988.

Yates, Gayle Graham. *What Women Want: The Ideas of the Movement*. Cambridge: Harvard University Press, 1975.

Frances Arick Kolb

FRANK KAMENY (1925–   )

*Gay activist, founder of the Mattachine Society of
Washington, D.C.*

Franklin E. Kameny was a champion of a new militancy in the fledgling homosexual rights movement of the early 1960s. As founder and president of
the Mattachine Society of Washington, Kameny showed that gays, like other
minority groups, could stand up for themselves and demand equal rights as
"homosexual American citizens." He adopted traditional reform movement
tactics—publicity, court suits, lobbying, public demonstrations—to launch the
first challenge to anti-gay policies adopted by the federal government during
the McCarthy era. By unabashedly proclaiming that homosexuality was neither
sick nor immoral, he helped move gays and lesbians out of the shadows of
1950s apologetic, self-help groups and into the sunlight of the civil rights
movement. He was, in many ways, America's first gay activist.

Kameny was born in Queens, New York, to a middle-class Jewish family.
A precocious child, Kameny took an early interest in science and by the age
of seven had decided on a career in astronomy. Upon graduation from Richmond Hill High School at the age of sixteen, he studied physics at New York's
Queens College. World War II interrupted Kameny's scientific education and
brought him to Europe, where he served as a U.S. Army mortar crewman and
unofficial translator for his unit. After the war he finished his undergraduate
education and moved on to Harvard, where he earned a Ph.D. in astronomy
in 1956.

Early on Kameny developed an absolute belief in the validity of his intellectual processes and a habit of challenging accepted orthodoxies. As a teenager, he announced to his parents that he was an atheist. As a teaching fellow
at Harvard, he refused to sign a loyalty oath without attaching qualifiers. "If
society and I differ on something, I'm willing to give the matter a second look.
If we still differ, then I am right and society is wrong," Kameny declared.
"And society can go its way so long as it doesn't get in my way." Consequently,
when he realized that he was attracted to men, he suffered little of the traditional guilt associated with "coming out." According to his philosophy, society's long-standing homophobia, not his sexuality, was at fault.

Upon graduation from Harvard, Kameny moved to Washington, D.C., to
accept a position as a research and teaching associate in the Astronomy Department at Georgetown University. In the 1950s the federal government,
engaged in an arms race with the Soviet Union, was sponsoring much of the
nation's scientific and technical research. Kameny transferred to the Army
Map Service, where cold war pressures promised fast advancement. Along
with the government's scientific patronage, however, came demands for po-

Frank Kameny picketing the White House. Copyright *Washington Post*; Reprinted by permission of D.C. Public Library.

litical and sexual conformity. In 1957, army security officials interrogated Kameny concerning alleged homosexual activity. When Kameny asserted that his private life was none of the federal government's concern, he was dismissed from his job and his scientific career ended. At the dawning of the space race, Kameny was jobless and depending upon charity.

According to U.S. Civil Service policy, his homosexuality made him "unsuitable" for federal employment. Hundreds of federal employees had been dismissed since the McCarthy era, which gratuitously linked homosexuality to communism as a threat to national security. Kameny was the first to challenge this policy. When administrative appeals failed and the U.S. Court of Appeals ruled against him, even his attorney abandoned the case. Forced to write his appeal to the Supreme Court himself, Kameny outlined a strategy that served him for most of the next two decades. He charged that the government's anti-gay policies were "no less illegal and no less odious than discrimination based upon religious or racial grounds." He asserted that because of his homosexuality he was being treated as a second-class citizen. Moreover, based on the

1948 Kinsey study finding that approximately 10 percent of the population is homosexual, Kameny charged that 15 million Americans were being subjected to the same treatment.

In 1961, when the Supreme Court refused to rule on his unprecedented claims, he decided to enlist others in the cause and founded the Mattachine Society of Washington (MSW). The idea of a gay organization was not new. The first Mattachine Society had been founded in California in 1951 as a kind of gay fraternal order. It borrowed its name from medieval court jesters who wore masks and were therefore allowed to articulate unpopular truths. But Kameny's group rejected the internal focus and secretive nature of the earlier group. It adopted political activism. The main goal of Mattachine of Washington was nothing less than changing the homosexual's place in society. It sought "to act by any lawful means to secure for homosexuals the right to life, liberty, and the pursuit of happiness." Kameny, elected the group's first president, was one of the few homosexuals in America willing to appear publicly and use his own name.

Kameny took inspiration from the black Civil Rights movement. He quickly redefined homosexuality, traditionally considered a moral or, more recently, a mental health problem, into a civil liberties issue. "It is time that considerations of homosexuality were removed from the psychoanalyst's couch and taken out of the psychiatrist's office," he argued. "The average homosexual . . . is far more likely to have employment problems than emotional ones." Kameny lobbied the local affiliate of the American Civil Liberties Union (ACLU), persuading it to take a stand against the federal government's anti-gay policies long before the national ACLU did so. He called his group the "NAACP of the homosexual minority."

Because they were fighting for basic American rights, Mattachine of Washington used traditional methods. They distributed press releases, testified before committees, and lobbied government officials. Earlier gay organizations had shunned publicity; MSW sought it. Earlier groups had brought in various authorities to speak to their membership; MSW sent out speakers to educate the non-gay population about homosexuality. Kameny, convinced that the prejudice they were facing was based primarily on emotion, not reason, put little faith in attempts to educate and persuade. As he wrote in 1964, "The Negro tried for 90 years to achieve his purposes by a program of information and education. His achievements in those 90 years, while by no means nil, were nothing compared to those of the past 10 years, when he tried a vigorous civil liberties, social action approach." So in the spring and summer of 1965 Kameny helped organize a series of gay pickets in front of the White House and other government buildings in Washington, D.C. He also launched a series of test discrimination cases in the courts, all signaling a new period of militancy.

Kameny was convinced that the success of the gay movement hinged on debunking the psychiatric profession's assertion that homosexuality was a mental illness. While earlier groups had sponsored debates by medical and religious authorities on the causes and problems of homosexuality, Kameny took strong pro-gay stands. He proclaimed, "there is no homosexual problem, there is a heterosexual problem." Kameny, as a scientist, pointed out the flaws in medical pronouncements based solely on the observation of psychiatric patients, not the millions of mentally healthy gays and lesbians beyond the medical gaze. In 1965, at the initial suggestion of member Jack Nichols, MSW was the first gay organization to declare that homosexuality was not a sickness but "a preference, orientation, or propensity, on a par with, and not different in kind from, heterosexuality." But with negative theories of homosexuality so pervasive, even among gay people, Kameny realized he needed a more positive approach. By 1968 he coined the slogan "Gay is Good." This was consciously inspired by the often-chanted motto that "Black is Beautiful."

Kameny spread his activist agenda by speaking across the country, radicalizing existing gay organizations (such as the Mattachine Society of New York), and helping a myriad of new groups get started in other cities. Kameny also succeeded in forming coalitions of gay organizations, first regionally and then nationally. He founded the East Coast Homophile Organizations (ECHO) in 1963 and was an active participant in the North American Conference of Homophile Organizations (NACHO), which in 1968 formally adopted "Gay is Good" as the motto for the movement. Within his own group, however, Kameny's uncompromising positions cost him support. He believed that MSW's purpose was to advance the cause of gays and lesbians as a class, not to serve the needs of individual members. His dominance of the group and his single-minded focus on the enemy failed to inspire broad-based participation. After 1970, MSW ceased to function as a group.

By the late 1960s and early 1970s, as the counterculture loosened moral strictures and general respect for authority, the gay rights movement entered a new stage. Its numbers grew dramatically and its demands became more radical after the Stonewall Riot in New York, where a routine police raid on a gay bar in June 1969 produced confrontation between gays and the police. With a new cultural climate the organizational and legal groundwork by Kameny and other early activists began to bring victories. Throughout the decade Kameny had orchestrated a series of test cases brought by fired gay civil servants, many of whom were members of MSW. Several early victories were overturned. But in 1969, in *Norton vs. Macy*, the U.S. Court of Appeals demanded a proven connection between the off-duty sexual conduct of federal civil servants and their suitability for employment. This case established the "nexus criteria" later invoked in many federal employment situations. By 1975, after several court defeats, the Civil Service Commission relented and modified its regulations. Homosexuality was no longer a disqualification for federal employment. Kameny's battle, inaugurated eighteen years earlier, had been won.

By the 1970s the American Psychiatric Association (APA) began to reconsider its definition of homosexuality as a pathology. After appearing on numerous television debates with professional psychiatrists, Kameny succeeded in getting the APA to sponsor a panel of openly gay men and women at its 1971 annual convention in Washington, D.C. Along with members of the Gay Liberation Front and anti-war protesters, Kameny stormed the convention, grabbed the microphone and declared, "Psychiatry is the enemy incarnate. . . . You may take this as a declaration of war against you." Under pressure from gay activists and a growing number of psychiatrists, the APA voted in 1973 to remove homosexuality from its *Diagnostic and Statistical Manual of Psychiatric Disorders.*

If the 1970s gave Kameny several victories, they also offered new venues for battle. Prior to that time, the District of Columbia, Kameny's adopted home, was governed by a presidentially appointed city council. With no local political life, Kameny's early activism naturally focused on the national level. But in 1971, when Congress permitted the District to elect a nonvoting delegate to the House of Representatives, Kameny ventured into local politics and became the first openly gay person to run for Congress. Although he came in fourth in the six-way race, he succeeded in using the election to increase publicity for his "personal freedoms" platform and to politicize the local gay community. In announcing his candidacy, Kameny declared, "I am a homosexual American citizen determined to move into the mainstream of society from the backwaters to which I have been relegated. Homosexuals have been shoved around from time immemorial. We are fed up with it. We are starting to shove back and we're going to keep shoving back until we are guaranteed our rights." This was the opening salvo in over twenty years of involvement in local politics.

After the election, Kameny's campaign committee reorganized into the Gay Activists Alliance (GAA), a nonpartisan group dedicated to securing "full rights and privileges" of citizenship for the gay and lesbian community of the District of Columbia through "peaceful participation in the political process." Kameny and GAA were instrumental in securing passage of the D.C. Human Rights Law in 1973, one of the nation's first laws to ban discrimination against gays and lesbians. With the advent of limited home rule in Washington, D.C., the Gay and Lesbian Activists Alliance (as it was later called) has been a powerful advocate for the gay community with local officials, the media, the police, and the school system. Kameny continued to be an active member and elder statesman to the group.

Since his unsuccessful congressional campaign, Kameny has served the city in a variety of appointed and elected positions. In 1975, after lobbying by GAA, he was appointed to the District's Human Rights Commission. He was the first openly gay mayoral appointee in the nation's capital. After serving for seven years, he was appointed to the city's Board of Appeals and Review, where he served six more years. As an outspoken advocate of statehood for the District of Columbia, he was elected a delegate to the D.C. Statehood

Constitutional Convention in 1981, where he helped draft a constitution for the proposed State of New Columbia. And since 1969 he has served intermittent terms on the executive board of the National Capital Area Civil Liberties Union.

After being fired from the federal government in 1957, Kameny held a number of temporary jobs using his scientific background, but he never again worked in the field of astronomy. Since 1968 Kameny has managed to integrate his full-time activism and need to make a living by serving as a paralegal, offering counsel to gay and non-gay military personnel, civil servants, and contractors having problems with the federal government. Pointing to a lack of evidence that homosexuals are any more likely to pose a risk to national security than heterosexuals, Kameny has accused the government of running a "sexual-conformity program rather than a security program." His basic advice to people being interrogated by government officials about their sexuality never varies: "Say nothing. Sign nothing. Get counsel. Fight back." In 1974, Kameny forced the Department of Defense to conduct the first public security clearance hearing. His gay client, Otis Tabler, was granted a clearance, marking a watershed in the Pentagon's program. Since then, gays may be subject to special scrutiny and harassment, but they are generally granted the necessary clearance. Kameny has succeeded in getting other federal agencies to liberalize their security clearance programs, including the National Security Agency (NSA), which first issued a security clearance to an openly gay man in 1980.

As the nation's foremost expert on homosexuality and the federal government, Kameny was also involved in the first legal steps to challenge the U.S. military's policy of automatically discharging gay and lesbian service members. This included the much publicized case of gay Air Force Sergeant Leonard Matlovich. Although this suit, initiated in 1975, eventually led to an out-of-court settlement in Matlovich's favor, the Pentagon responded by strengthening its ban on homosexuals in the military. For years, the Pentagon automatically discharged openly gay and lesbian soldiers. Kameny, often acting as counsel, helped ensure that they at least received honorable discharges. Changes of military policy in the early 1990s still had ambiguities that meant continued conflicts and litigation.

The influence of Kameny, one of the few gay leaders from the 1960s still involved in the movement, spans three decades. When Bruce Voeller and a group of fellow New Yorkers founded the National Gay Task Force (NGTF) in 1973, Kameny was one of two longtime national activists asked to sit on its board of directors, where he served until 1982. As a NGTF Board member, Kameny was among a group of gay rights leaders who met with officials of the Carter administration in 1977. This was the first such White House meeting in American history. Today, almost any issue involving the federal government or the District of Columbia and their approach to homosexuality also involves Kameny.

Despite his longevity in the movement, his philosophy and tactics have remained remarkably consistent. Although his brashness may have increased over the years, Kameny has always preferred to work through established legal and political channels. Rather than protest outside, Kameny goes inside and makes the bureaucracy work for him. His ability to use the court system was recognized in 1988 when he received the Durfee Award for his contributions to the "enhancement of human dignity through the law." As one creative attempt in the 1990s, at using existing structures, Kameny formed a corporation in Washington, D.C., under the name "Traditional Values Coalition," thereby preventing a California-based anti-gay organization of the same name from operating in the city.

Though he prefers to work on the inside, Kameny is not opposed to civil disobedience. His first dignified demonstration in front of the White House in 1965 has since led to numerous arrests defending the rights of homosexuals. In his fight to overturn the District of Columbia's statute outlawing consensual sodomy, he has advocated and participated in sit-ins and other organized harassment directed at specific members of the city council blocking the effort. (The law was repealed in 1993.) Ultimately he is a pragmatist. "If society becomes intransigent, you escalate the battle as necessary. You plan a strategy using 'small guns' before 'big guns' in a calculated fashion."

His ultimate goal has always been assimilation. Gays and lesbians should have the same rights and privileges enjoyed by all citizens. More radical elements in the gay movement have criticized him for being co-opted by a system they feel is fundamentally oppressive not just to gays and lesbians but to all minority groups. But Kameny feels he is helping to alter society, thereby giving gays and lesbians the choice of whether or not to participate in that society. They should make this choice for themselves. According to Kameny, the gay movement's ability to "get things done" rests on not becoming "isolated in ivory towers of unworkable ideologies." Kameny's ability to combine the enthusiasm of an activist with the pragmatism of a bureaucrat has lent a powerful force to that movement.

Bibliography

Bayer, Ronald. *Homosexuality and American Psychiatry: The Politics of Diagnosis*. New York: Basic Books, 1981: 81–111.

D'Emilio, John. *Sexual Politics, Sexual Communities: The Making of a Homosexual Minority in the United States, 1940–1970*. Chicago: University of Chicago Press, 1983: 150–75.

Kameny, Frank. "Gay is Good," in *The Same Sex: An Appraisal of Homosexuality*, Ralph W. Weltge, ed. Philadelphia: Pilgrim Press, 1969: 129–45.

———. "The Federal Government versus the Homosexual," *The Humanist* 29 (May/ June 1969): 20–23.

———. "Homosexuals as a Minority Group," in *The Other Minorities*, Edward Sagarin, ed. Lexington, MA: Ginn, 1971: 50–65.

———. "Gay Liberation and Psychiatry," in *The Homosexual Dialectic*, Joseph A. McCaffrey, ed. Englewood Cliffs, NJ: Prentice-Hall, 1972: 182–94.

———. Introduction to *Gay life and Maturity: Crises, Opportunities, and Fulfillment*, John Alan Lee, ed. Binghamton, NY: Harrington Park Press, 1991.

Marcus, Eric. *Making History: The Struggle for Gay and Lesbian Equal Rights 1945–1990: An Oral History*. New York: Harper Collins, 1992: 93–103.

Marotta, Toby. *The Politics of Homosexuality*. New York: Houghton Mifflin, 1981: 22–68.

Tobin, Kay, and Randy Wicker. *The Gay Crusaders*. New York: Paperback Library, 1972: 89–134.

White, Edmund. *States of Desire: Travels in Gay America*. New York: Bantam Books, 1980: 302–6.

David K. Johnson

DEL MARTIN (1921–   ) and PHYLLIS LYON (1924–   )

Co-founders, Daughters of Bilitis; lesbian-feminist activists and community leaders

The 1950s were generally a time of social conservatism and repression. Homosexuals suffered more than most other groups. The "witchhunts" of Senator Joseph McCarthy targeted gay men and lesbians as well as communists. Gay bars, the only places where homosexuals could meet publicly, were frequently raided. Patrons were arrested; their employers sometimes were notified.

Del Martin and Phyllis Lyon, two lesbians who met and began a long relationship during the 1950s, remember that the public then saw lesbians and gay men as "deviants" who were "illegal, immoral and sick." The two women found it difficult to meet other lesbians with whom to socialize.

In 1955, Lyon and Martin, along with six other women, founded a social club for lesbians that they dubbed the Daughters of Bilitis (DOB) after the French poem "Songs of Bilitis." They hoped to cloak their group in respectability by suggesting a resemblance to such organizations as the Daughters of the American Revolution.

Although many of the original founders of DOB had been interested primarily in creating a private social club, others—including Martin and Lyon—were more interested in social reform. They wanted to gain civil rights for lesbians, much as the already-existing Mattachine Society was doing for gay men. This reform movement, known as the homophile movement, was the forerunner of the gay liberation movement of the 1960s and 1970s. Del Martin and Phyllis Lyon, as the only two of the original DOB founders to lead their organization into an era of greater civil rights for lesbians and gay men, have

Del Martin *(right)/***Phyllis Lyon.** Copyright Joan E. Biren

been recognized and honored for well over thirty years as the leaders of the lesbian rights movement in this country.

Growing up in the 1930s and 1940s, neither Martin nor Lyon had a name for the physical and emotional attraction toward women that each was beginning to feel. In fact, Lyon became engaged to a man, and Martin married and had a child. Both were independent, college-educated women with experience in journalism. They both rejected society's prescribed roles for them as either passive, "domesticated" women (housewives and mothers) or "illegal, immoral and sick" lesbians.

Their role models as young women included such feminists as Amelia Earhart ("I spent a number of years wanting to be a pilot," confesses Lyon) and Eleanor Roosevelt. In their book, *Lesbian/Woman*, Martin and Lyon explain, "[Mrs. Roosevelt] taught us how to overcome fear, how to turn pain into strength and disappointment into purpose."

But, as young lesbians living in a repressive social climate, Lyon and Martin also were influenced by Franklin Roosevelt. "[His] statement, 'The only thing we have to fear is fear itself,' had a lot of influence on us in the 1950s," admits Martin (1990 interview with author). Thus, while DOB was conceived in part as a self-help organization for lesbians, it included among its goals "education of the public through acceptance first of the individual" (*The Ladder*, vol. 1, no. 1, Oct. 1956). Basic to their political philosophy, Lyon explains, "is the concept that all people should have the right to do what they want to do, without being discriminated against" (1990 interview).

For this reason, and because of the conservative times during which DOB was founded, it was not a militant or doctrinaire group. As Martin noted, "The Daughters of Bilitis was sort of a coming-out place. We dealt with a lot of women who were just becoming aware that they were lesbians and needed some answers and support, and to meet others like themselves. . . . That first step out is still a problem for a lot of people. . . . Everybody isn't at the same level of consciousness. There are always going to be new ones."

Lyon agrees. "You always have people in the group whose consciousness changes as they grow. They reach a 'higher plateau,' but you still have others just barely out to themselves, who need to learn how to cope" (1990 interview).

This attention to each woman's stage of political consciousness is characteristic of Martin and Lyon's view of the group as a collection of separate people rather than a monolith. As Martin commented, "We found that we were always geared to the individual as well as to the group. So that individual's needs also had to be served, so they could come out, they could become whole persons, and become self-accepting, and be able then to conquer the world."

This realization that people come into political consciousness in different ways is central to Martin and Lyon's reformist philosophy. In the same way, they feel that society reacts to change slowly, and that a combination of different policies is needed to effect such change.

"After Stonewall," Martin recalls, "there was the whole demonstration/genderfuck scene, all kinds of shock tactics. Men with beards dressed as women may have been trying to show their feminine side, but their message didn't come through. . . .

"You have to learn: What's the best way to communicate? What's going to further your movement?"

Martin illustrates her point by describing how 1970s gay liberation activists marched in front of San Francisco's Family Service Agency: "They had a bullhorn and they were carrying on about [how] we have families too and we should be represented. They scared the people inside to death! So a bunch of us went inside and sat down and talked. And we wound up with a lesbian and a gay man on their board. We were getting across to them that our families needed their services, too."

Martin concludes, "Sometimes it's good to have a group that will shock people, allowing others to go in and negotiate. This scenario often brings results" (1990 interview).

Martin and Lyon's perspective, centered on the individual and on rational discourse, was formed during an era when political activism could have dire consequences. "A lot of movement people [today] only think in terms of group actions and demonstrations," Martin believes. "In the space that we were in, in the 1950s, where everybody was in the closet and there was so much fear, we had to work towards a sense of selfhood. Nobody had it. We'd all been 'illegal, immoral and sick'; that's a lot to cope with! And then the way you were looked upon by society—the raids and the purges—we had to build a positive self-image. You couldn't have a movement until you did. We had to get our act together before we could really become activists. And that's something, I think, that a lot of today's historians don't understand, as they look back on what we did" (1990 interview).

Indeed, from the "gay lib" days of the 1970s through today's ACT-UP and Queer Nation activism, homophile groups such as DOB and Mattachine have been dismissed unfairly as quaint relics of the "bad old days" rather than as the groups which laid the foundations for later gay freedoms.

For example, while many gay activists regard the Stonewall Inn riot in New York City during June 1969 as the beginning of the modern gay civil rights movement, few are aware that Stonewall was predated by the homophile movement's California Hall incident on January 1, 1965.

The Daughters of Bilitis and other San Francisco homophile groups had joined with local religious leaders to form the Council on Religion and the Homosexual. This new organization sought to remove the "immoral" taint from gays. A New Year's Ball at San Francisco's California Hall was planned to raise funds.

At least fifty police officers also arrived at the Hall. They took pictures of everyone who went into the building. The religious representatives who were present found this a "shocking revelation of police power directed against a minority group for no apparent reason other than that of harassment" (Martin and Lyon, *Lesbian/Woman*). Seven clergymen held a press conference the next day to protest. A judge later dismissed all charges against those arrested at the Hall.

Another historically significant action by DOB was the publication of its newsletter, *The Ladder*. This was the first nationally distributed lesbian magazine. Its premier issue was published in October 1956, one year after DOB was founded. It brought such voluminous mail that, as Lyon and Martin recall in *Lesbian/Woman*, "As volunteers working for DOB after our regular jobs, and small in membership, we were hard put to read it all—let alone answer it!"

Some early correspondents feared being on the mailing list of a lesbian organization. In response to their concern, *The Ladder* published an article in its second issue promising readers that "Your Name Is Safe!" The editors cited a Supreme Court case that upheld the right of publishers to keep private the names of purchasers of their periodicals.

Other readers were pessimistic about the openness of DOB and its newsletter: "I must hesitate when such things as our way of life get down to a black and white state of things—in print yet!" worried a reader in *The Ladder*'s second issue.

But the letters of thanks and congratulations were rewarding: "I cannot tell you what a source of both inspiration and pleasure *The Ladder* contained for me within its pages"; "If we don't get up and speak our piece and stand up for ourselves, it's our own fault"; "I greatly admire each of you—not only for the stand you take, but for the fact that you have the courage to make that fact known publicly. Bravo, indeed!"; "[A] magazine basically by and for others in the same group as I am would be . . . helpful in overcoming the lost and lonesome feelings I seem prey to at times" (*The Ladder*, vol. 1, nos. 2, 5).

But *The Ladder*'s importance went far beyond the hope it gave to isolated lesbians during its more than fifteen years of publication. The magazine, like the organization that sponsored it, was recognized later as a foremother of lesbian liberation. *The New Woman's Survival Sourcebook*, published in 1975, notes that *The Ladder* evidenced "an incipient radical feminist consciousness which predates many of the same revelations made later on a mass-media scale by the (supposedly) heterosexual feminist movement."

Lesbian historian Joan Nestle, writing as co-editor of an anthology of lesbian fiction, states that a book such as hers "could not have happened without the courage and tenacity of a lesbian writing and publishing community that reaches back into the late fifties. When [*The Ladder* was published], a new literary tradition was born" (Afterword, *Women on Women*, p. 301).

Lesbian novelist Lee Lynch agrees, describing how she discovered *The Ladder* "in a magazine shop in Greenwich Village. . . . This small, rough periodical was not full of unhappy endings. . . . [It] allowed entry into a legitimate universe. . . . Most importantly, I had something, as a young writer, to which I could aspire" ("Cruising the Libraries," in Jay and Glasgow, eds., *Lesbian Texts and Contexts*, p. 45).

"One of the things that was wrong in the '70s was that the movement went all out politically and neglected education of the public," commented Martin in her interview with the writer of this entry. "Earlier, we had used professional people to validate us, because we needed validation in the 1950s. By the mid-1960s, *we* became the experts. We [sponsored] symposia for professional people who were going to do any kind of counseling with lesbians and gays. We figured they needed to have this knowledge. . . .

"We had psychologists, psychiatrists, ministers, lawyers, social workers, theology students, and the symposia were very successful. They started with small groups that had a lesbian and a gay man facilitating; then we had panels, followed by small-group discussion. We took them into lesbian and gay homes, bars, and restaurants. They really got the feel of who we were. By the time they finished, we were people; and some friendships developed out of it. . . .

"The point is, we've always felt like we were part of the human race, and that we were citizens. . . . [W]e didn't want to just be a separate group, and we still don't want to be."

When asked what they feel it is about their work, and their willingness to speak out and be visible, that has brought them such acclaim, Lyon modestly notes, "I think it has to do with being someplace at the right time. . . . [Also], once you start thinking about something like [DOB], you see all kinds of ways that you could do other things."

Martin adds, "Things just kept unfolding, and we just went along. Sometimes we provoked some of it, sometimes we just went along with it" (1990 interview).

Such self-effacement doesn't explain the list of honors bestowed upon Martin and Lyon, a list filling three pages each in their respective resumes. From the early 1960s, when each was recognized by DOB for her leadership role in the group, to the early 1990s, when they received the ACLU of Northern California's Earl Warren Civil Liberties Award, Martin and Lyon have been committed activists for social justice over nearly four decades.

Their work in the homophile movements of the 1950s and 1960s led Lyon and Martin to realize that lesbians are discriminated against as women as well as because they are gay. They subsequently became involved in the feminist movement of the 1970s, most notably through their association with the National Organization for Women (NOW). Martin became the first openly gay woman to serve on NOW's National Board of Directors.

Martin and Lyon also have been active in San Francisco politics since the 1950s. In 1972, they were among the co-founders of the Alice B. Toklas Memorial Democratic Club, the first lesbian and gay Democratic club in the nation. This political involvement led to government service. Among other appointments, Martin served as a member of the San Francisco Commission on the Status of Women from 1976 through 1979 (including a stint as chair from 1976 through 1977), and Lyon was a member of the San Francisco Human Rights Commission from 1976 through 1987 (chairing in 1982 and 1983).

Martin and Lyon, during their careers, have developed individual spheres of expertise. Phyllis Lyon earned a doctorate in education in human sexuality from the Institute for Advanced Study of Human Sexuality, and is a diplomate of the American Board of Sexology. She served as a professor and registrar at the Institute for Advanced Study of Human Sexuality from 1976 through 1987, and as associate director and co-director of the National Sex Forum from 1968 until 1987.

Del Martin authored the landmark book *Battered Wives* in 1976 and became a nationally known expert on the subject of battered women, serving on task forces and speaking at venues across the country. She is a co-founder of the Coalition for Justice for Battered Women, the La Casa de las Madres shelter for battered women, and the California Coalition against Domestic Violence.

Del Martin and Phyllis Lyon exemplify lives of activism and service. When asked the source of their longevity as activists, Martin notes, "I think what kept us going was the challenge. Also, we've always been political animals. . . . And we got a lot out of it. I think there's a lot of self-growth in the process. We learned a lot. . . . Maybe we weren't antagonistic enough, or confrontational enough, [for] some people, but our process worked for us. . . . Once you're involved with trying to beat those three issues [of homosexuals being "illegal, immoral and sick"], it takes you in lots of different directions" (1990 interview).

Martin and Lyon also attribute their continuing activism to the realization that change is not always favorable to progressive social reform. As Martin comments, "It's like anything that we've gained. . . . If you don't monitor it, it can go downhill again. . . . The whole thing about changes that we've gone through [is that] we could lose all that in another trend and another way. You always have to hang in there. You have to keep monitoring. It's never-ending."

Perhaps the life and work of Del Martin and Phyllis Lyon can be summed up by Martin's words from the first issue of *The Ladder* in 1956: "Nothing was ever accomplished by hiding in a dark corner."

Bibliography

Abbott, Sidney, and Barbara Love. *Sappho Was a Right-On Woman.* New York: Stein and Day, 1974 [1972].

D'Emilio, John. *Sexual Politics, Sexual Communities: The Making of a Homosexual Minority in the United States, 1940–1970.* Chicago: University of Chicago Press, 1983.

D'Emilio, John, and Estelle B. Freedman. *Intimate Matters: A History of Sexuality in America.* New York: Harper and Row, 1988.

Duberman, Martin Bauml, Martha Vicinus and George Chauncey, Jr., eds. *Hidden from History: Reclaiming the Gay and Lesbian Past.* New York: New American Library, 1989.

Faderman, Lillian. *Odd Girls and Twilight Lovers.* New York: Columbia University Press, 1991.

Jay, Karla, and Joanne Glasgow, eds. *Lesbian Texts and Contexts: Radical Revisions.* New York: New York University Press, 1990.

Katz, Jonathan. *Gay American History.* New York: Avon Books, 1978 [1967].

Kehoe, Monika, ed. *Historical, Literary and Erotic Aspects of Lesbianism.* New York: Harrington Park Press, 1986.

———. *Lesbians Over Sixty Speak for Themselves.* New York: Harrington Park Press, 1989.

The Ladder, newsletter of the Daughters of Bilitis, 1956–1972.

Lyon, Phyllis, and Del Martin. Interviewed by the author on Oct. 20, 1990. Interview tape and transcript at the Gay and Lesbian Historical Society of Northern California (GLHSNC), P.O. Box 424280, San Francisco, CA 94142.

———. "Reminiscences of Two Female Homophiles," from *Our Right to Love: A Lesbian Resource Book,* Ginny Vida, ed. Englewood Cliffs, NJ: Prentice Hall, 1978: 124–28.

Martin, Del, and Phyllis Lyon. "Anniversary," from *The Lesbian Path,* Margaret Cruikshank, ed.; revised and enlarged edition. San Francisco: Grey Fox Press, 1985 [1980]: 143–46.

———. "Lesbians—The Key to Women's Liberation," reprinted from *Trends,* July–August 1973 (Copy at GLHSNC).

———. *Lesbian/Woman: Twentieth Anniversary Edition*, updated and enlarged. Volcano, CA: Volcano Press, 1991 (1972).

———. "The Older Lesbian," from *Positively Gay*, Betty Berzon and Robert Leighton, eds. Millbrae, CA: Celestial Arts, 1979: 134–45.

Martin, Del. *Battered Wives*, rev., updated ed. San Francisco: Volcano Press, 1981 [1976].

Nestle, Joan, and Naomi Holoch, eds. *Women on Women*. New York: Plume/Penguin, 1990.

Sherman, Suzanne, ed. *Lesbian and Gay Marriage: Private Commitments, Public Ceremonies*. Philadelphia: Temple University Press, 1992.

Research assistance was provided by Paula F. Lichtenberg, MLS, and supporters of the Archives of the Gay and Lesbian Historical Society of Northern California.

Kate Brandt

WILLIAM H. MASTERS (1915–) and VIRGINIA E. JOHNSON (1925–)

Sex therapists

Masters and Johnson are best known for conducting research on the anatomy and physiology of human sexual response. They have done this research in their laboratory at the Reproductive Biology Research Foundation, under the auspices of Washington University's School of Medicine. (The Foundation later became the Masters and Johnson Institute.) They are authorities in the field of sexology, a multidisciplinary subject which involves research on sexuality. Their work benefitted from that of several predecessors. Dr. Alfred Kinsey pioneered the use of interviewing in sex research. Kinsey's work made Masters and Johnson's observations of sex the logical next step in understanding sexuality. Masters and Johnson's laboratory findings, published in their first book, *Human Sexual Response* (1966), built on the research of Joseph R. Beck, Ernst P. Boas, Ernst F. Goldschmidt, Abraham Mosovich, John B. Watson, and Robert L. Dickinson, among others. Instead of keeping their findings a secret as some academics had, Masters and Johnson replicated, speculated, and above all publicized their observations of orgasms and masturbation. The timing was right for the disclosure of their research. *Human Sexual Response*, which was the first book to record the anatomy and physiology of human sexual response, became a nonfiction best-seller despite its poor literary quality, sampling problems, and imprecise findings.

William H. Masters graduated from Hamilton College in 1938 and earned an M.D. from the University of Rochester in 1943. In 1947 he was an intern and then a resident at Barnes Hospital and Maternity Hospital at Washington University School of Medicine in St. Louis, Missouri. He also taught obstetrics

William H. Masters/Virginia E. Johnson. Copyright *Washington Post*; Reprinted by permission of D.C. Public Library.

and gynecology at Washington University's School of Medicine. In 1951 he received board certification in obstetrics and gynecology. He designed his laboratory to investigate human sexual response in 1954. Masters was director of the Reproductive Biology Research Foundation from 1964 to 1973, co-director of the Masters and Johnson Institute, 1973–1980, and chairman of its board from 1981. Virginia E. Johnson, who became his assistant at the original research foundation in 1957, attended Drury College in Springfield, Missouri, from 1940 to 1942 and the University of Missouri from 1944 to 1947. She was a research associate of the Reproductive Biology Research Foundation, 1964–1969; assistant director, 1969–1973; co-director, 1973–1980; president and director, 1981–1985; and co-chairman of the board from 1986. Masters and Johnson married on January 7, 1971. Both of them had been married previously, and each had two children from that previous marriage. Although they divorced in 1993, they remained together as a research team and continued to be referred to as one entity, Masters and Johnson.

During Masters's early phases of research, he interviewed prostitutes who shared various techniques for stimulating or controlling sexual tensions. Masters and Johnson would use some of these techniques in their work with couples who had sexual problems. That research led to their second book *Human Sexual Inadequacy* (1970). Masters did not use prostitutes, however, for his original physiological study. For that study, some 694 highly educated volunteers participated in the Masters and Johnson laboratory program. Of those, 276 were married couples. Only 11 couples were black. There were 34 married couples over fifty years of age. The participants experienced more than 10,000 orgasms under laboratory conditions during the twelve years of the laboratory research program. Scientific observers watched them while they engaged in masturbation and coitus. Masturbation by hand or fingers and sometimes, but only rarely, with a mechanical vibrator was observed as was sexual intercourse with the woman on her back and with the man on his back. Masters and Johnson also observed "artificial coition" with a transparent electronically controlled probe. They also recorded observations of genital responses with stimulation of the breasts alone.

They have been criticized for faulty sampling for their sex research. Their research group was neither a representative sample nor a random sample. They had an underrepresentation of poor people. They also were unrepresentative by age distribution (very few young people) and by sexual preference (they were clearly a heterosexual population). Along with underrepresentation of the poor, diverse races, the young, and homosexuals, the self-selection of volunteers, who were willing to be observed during sexual relations, meant that generalizations could be applied only to the people in this study. Masters and Johnson, however, generalized their findings for all men and women. The general reading public was little disturbed by these problems. Masters and Johnson received an eager reception to their work. More than 250,000 copies of *Human Sexual Response* were sold in the United States, and the book was translated into nine languages. Tens of millions of readers learned about their research from newspaper and magazine articles. Masters and Johnson had an impact far beyond their Institute and the verifiability of their conclusions.

There are many ironies inherent in their work. Masters and Johnson claimed scientific objectivity, but their findings often exuded ideology. For instance, in *Human Sexual Response*, they highlighted their research on what they called "the orgasmic platform" in order to dispute the Freudian distinction between the clitoral and the vaginal orgasm. In that book they also generalized optimistically about "geriatric sexual response" for those subjects over fifty years of age, but the physiological responses they recorded showed a substantial decrease in sexual functions. While their analysis contradicted some of their data, it is important to note that their work documented that sexuality extends throughout the life cycle. Older people could enjoy sex without having identical responses that they may have had in their youth. Masters and Johnson encouraged the potential of geriatric sex.

While they claimed, above all, to be researchers, some critics argued that other agenda influenced their conclusions. For instance, as historian Paul Robinson has pointed out, Masters and Johnson were interested in therapeutic results rather than strict research findings. This motivation was also obvious in their second book, *Human Sexual Inadequacy* (1970). Reporting on sexual problems, they gave suggestions for people who had not learned to experience enjoyable sex. They documented that sexual dysfunctions could be changed by knowledge and techniques. They reported success using exercises such as the "squeeze technique," and suggested more direct clitoral stimulation during intercourse. They also suggested using different positions during coition. A more comprehensive assessment of solutions for sexual dysfunction acknowledges that some sexual problems are not receptive to knowledge and techniques, for they are a result of the dynamics of the relationship and society.

In *Human Sexual Inadequacy*, Masters and Johnson's therapeutic programs were motivated by the goal of saving marriages. This book and their other writings have a definite marriage bias. They called the couples that they studied "marital units" or "family units" rather than "couples." They observed unmarried people sparingly, usually for studies of masturbation. According to Janice M. Irvine, a sex educator, Masters and Johnson are basically conservative. Their goal is to cure problems in the marriage by facilitating better sex and orgasms rather than to bring about social change. Their book *The Pleasure Bond* (1975), a popular version of their ideas, is mostly concerned with freeing women sexually. It reinforces the goal of marriage and monogamy.

Knowledge of their research has proved a mixed blessing for women. Masters and Johnson were opposed to the attitudes of repressed sexuality, especially of women, which carried over from the Victorian era. They insisted upon a woman's right to sexual pleasure. Working as a dual sex team validated a woman's voice in her sexuality. Their insistence on a woman's right to sexual pleasure led to their attention to and encouragement of masturbation and their research claim that woman's intense sexual release came from clitoral stimulation. Thus, they also opposed Freudian theory which focused on vaginal orgasms. The attention they paid to the clitoris was truly liberating to most women. Highlighting the clitoral orgasm as most desirable was tremendously important to those women who had never experienced a vaginal orgasm. Those women were relieved to think of themselves as normal. However, Masters and Johnson have been criticized for putting too much attention on the clitoral orgasm. Their analysis that all orgasms were clitoral in origin redefined the locus of sexuality for women. But popularizers of their work misinterpreted their studies to mean no vaginal orgasms. For a while after Masters and Johnson's work emphasizing the clitoris was published and accepted, very little was written on vaginal orgasms. Critics have said that the myth of the vaginal orgasm was replaced by the myth of the clitoral orgasm. This meant that those women who experienced a vaginal orgasm might feel inadequate.

Masters and Johnson have often been presented as freeing women. This assessment comes from the attention they paid to the clitoris and masturbation and their clear intention of liberating women to enjoy sex. But, as Irvine has pointed out, Masters and Johnson saw sex as a natural function; they were unable to see power differences within sexuality. They were part of the zeitgeist of the times which looked to technically based solutions. Their work supported a conservative ideology, stressing the traditional monogamous marriage. Their purpose was to help people improve sex. They argued that better sex would mean better marriages. They were not general marriage therapists. Thus, as Irvine has pointed out, Masters and Johnson's emphasis on saving marriages by facilitating better sex did not liberate women beyond bed. Prior to Masters and Johnson, little attention had been paid to female sexuality. They naively assumed that advocating sexual equality and sexual expression in the relationship would eliminate other aspects of inequality that would affect sexuality in the relationship. Their suggestions worked for many, but for others, identity and power issues were left unexamined.

Some have contended that Masters and Johnson obscured gender hierarchy by focusing more attention on woman's sexual responses than on man's, and also by claiming similarities between the sexual lives of women and men. Masters and Johnson contended that both the female and the male proceeded through four levels of arousal during sexual intercourse: excitement, plateau, orgasm, and resolution. Critics, such as Robinson, argued that while the distinction between orgasm and resolution is fairly straightforward, their division between excitement and plateau is almost "altogether groundless." Furthermore, using the woman as the model and trying to fit male stages into the same stages as the woman was particularly strained and unconvincing. Robinson documented what he considered a strong female bias in Masters and Johnson's works. In fact, their original book portrayed female sexuality as so central that Robinson suggested that *Human Sexual Response* should have been titled *Female Sexual Response*. So much attention was paid to male sexual dysfunction in *Human Sexual Inadequacy* that Robinson said it should have been titled *Male Sexual Inadequacy*.

Masters and Johnson's research on homosexuals included both physiological data and information about sexual dysfunction. They published that research in *Homosexuality in Perspective* (1979). The sampling problems that marred their other research were also evident in these studies. The subjects were mostly white, highly educated, and from upper socio-economic levels. The subjects had to be in a relationship for at least a year. Once again, Masters and Johnson's preference for monogamy prevailed. While Masters and Johnson claimed that homosexuality was an acceptable lifestyle, reports of their clinical programs to convert homosexuals into heterosexuals may have reinforced society's homophobia.

Their heterosexual bias prevailed in their controversial book on AIDS, *CRISIS: Heterosexual Behavior in the Age of AIDS* (1988), which was released seven years after AIDS was officially diagnosed in the United States. Irvine has argued that by focusing on heterosexuals who were only 4 percent of those infected by the dread disease, Masters and Johnson showed their disregard for homosexuals. Their sample study was once again flawed. It was mostly white, married, and college educated. Their alarmist conclusions called for abstinence and monogamy. At the time of their study, they estimated that three million Americans were infected with the AIDS virus, two times as many people as the Centers for Disease Control acknowledged. They stated that AIDS was "running rampant" among heterosexuals. Masters and Johnson also claimed, contrary to scientific studies, that AIDS could be spread by casual contact.

While the media found it perplexing that the supposed sexual radicals were espousing such conservative views, those who had followed Masters and Johnson's research over the years were not surprised. A mixture of radical and conservative thinking was evident in their work from the very beginning. It was present, for example, in their attitudes toward women. They took a radical stance on woman's need for and exercise of sexual satisfaction, and yet they consistently presented an uncritical acceptance of the institution of marriage. The norm throughout their studies was the monogamous heterosexual marriage. As Irvine has noted, in virtually all their work, Masters and Johnson have aimed to change the individual and not the society. Still they must be evaluated within the context of their times. When they began their work, they endured a conservative reaction which included physical threats to their safety and that of their children. Thus, even though they inadvertently supported the status quo and the traditional heterosexual marriage, they made major contributions by publicizing sex research and working against a past of sexual repression and ignorance. Their attention to the importance of the clitoris, masturbation, and woman's sexual pleasure placed woman at the center of sexual thought and dramatically changed views about woman's sexuality. Masters and Johnson's work exudes an egalitarian tone, whether they were discounting the assumed ecstasy of the vaginal orgasm as compared to clitoral excitement or refusing to accept a passive role for woman during sex. While they assumed a traditional view of marriage and monogamy, they also fostered what Paul Robinson has called a "democratic revolution." This may be their major contribution to sexual thought.

Bibliography

"Divorced, Yes, But Not Split," *New York Times*, March 24, 1994, C1, C6.

Irvine, Janice M. *Disorders of Desire: Sex and Gender in Modern American Sexology*. Philadelphia: Temple University Press, 1990.

Masters, William H., and Virginia E. Johnson. *Homosexuality in Perspective*. Boston: Little, Brown, 1979.

———. *Human Sexual Inadequacy*. Boston: Little, Brown, 1970.

———. *Human Sexual Response*. Boston: Little, Brown, 1966.

———. *The Pleasure Bond*. New York: Bantam Books, 1975.

Masters, William H., Virginia E. Johnson, and Robert C. Kolodny. *Ethical Issues in Sex Therapy and Research*, vol. 1. Boston: Little, Brown, 1977.

———. *CRISIS: Heterosexual Behavior in the Age of AIDS*. New York: Grove Press, 1988.

———. *Heterosexuality*. New York: Harper Collins, 1994.

———. *Human Sexuality*. Boston: Little, Brown, 1982.

———. *Textbook of Sexual Medicine*. Boston: Little, Brown, 1979.

———. *Masters and Johnson on Sex and Human Loving*. Boston: Little, Brown, 1986.

Masters, William H., Virginia E. Johnson, Robert C. Kolodny, and M. A. Briggs. *Textbook of Human Sexuality for Nurses*. Boston: Little, Brown, 1979.

Masters, William H., Virginia E. Johnson, Robert C. Kolodny, and S. M. Weems, *Ethical Issues in Sex Therapy and Research*, vol. 2. Boston: Little, Brown, 1980.

Robinson, Paul. *The Modernization of Sex: Havelock Ellis, Alfred Kinsey, William Masters and Virginia Johnson*, with a new preface. Ithaca, NY: Cornell University Press, 1988 [1976].

Sara Alpern

ELEANOR HOLMES NORTON (1937–   )

Congresswoman, government administrator, attorney, human rights activist

Eleanor Holmes Norton was born to Coleman and Vela Holmes in Washington, D.C., on June 13, 1937. Her college-educated parents imbued their children with the value of education. Eleanor and her sisters were also taught that their gender and race should not limit their aspirations. Any restrictions should be challenged and overcome. Eleanor graduated from Washington's prestigious Dunbar High School in 1955. She then attended Antioch College in Yellow Springs, Ohio, where she majored in history. She continued her post-graduate education at Yale where she earned a master's degree in American studies in 1963 and a law degree in 1964.

Norton's credentials as a social activist were well established at an early age. Perhaps she learned the value of cooperative endeavors by growing up in a nurturing community of family and friends in Washington, D.C., that sought both to create a niche for themselves in a segregated city and to transform its racially biased policies. Antioch College's cooperative work release and study program further cemented these beliefs and helped her to develop skills and strategies for her life's work.

It was during her college days at Antioch that she was captivated by the Civil Rights movement. She participated in sit-ins, joined the Student Nonviolent Coordinating Committee (SNCC), worked on the staff of the 1963 March on Washington, and founded the New Haven chapter of the Congress of Racial Equality (CORE) during her student days at Yale. In addition to this work, she became committed to protecting the First Amendment rights of free speech. She later provided legal counsel to anyone whose free speech had been infringed. Her career path as an attorney and government official permitted her to work toward achieving the goals of freedom and equality for every American and to support the individual's right to speech.

Eleanor Holmes Norton. *Source*: Library of Congress

After Norton graduated from Yale, she worked for the American Civil Liberties Union (ACLU), where she specialized in constitutional law and primarily handled First Amendment cases. Several of her defendants were renowned for their political activism and their cases received extensive media coverage. She was one of the attorneys who wrote the defense for Julian Bond (1*) when the Georgia legislature denied him his seat because of his opposition to the Vietnam War.

Norton's tenacity occasionally brought her into conflict with potential political allies. One such incident occurred when Norton took on a case defending George Wallace, a white supremacist who was running for president in 1968 as an independent. Wallace wanted to rent Shea's Stadium in New York to hold a political rally in 1969. Mayor John Lindsay and the city of New York opposed this. Although Norton won a victory for Wallace, New York appealed the decision and Wallace opted to move his rally to Madison Square Garden. Eleanor also listed other extremists, such as a klansman, among her defendants, arguing that a threat to any individual's free speech is a threat to everyone's. In October of 1968, she defended the National States Rights party, a white supremacist group, before the Supreme Court. This was her first case before the highest court, which resulted in upholding the party's right to hold a public demonstration.

Eleanor Holmes Norton also promoted women's rights during the 1960s. She brought a class action suit on behalf of women employees at *Newsweek* who claimed that the magazine used gender bias in both hiring and determining promotions. Some sectors of the black community questioned the value of becoming associated with the women's movement. Norton responded to critics by saying that "unless the black woman finds that she has been treated with total equality, she had better find the women's liberation movement relevant." In 1973, she was one of the founders of the National Black Feminist Organization, which proposed to attack racism, sexism, and economic exploitation. Norton always sought to interpret the events around her within some larger context, including how people in the United States should relate fairly to the rest of the world.

She had become well known enough to be appointed the chair of the New York City Human Rights Commission in 1970. This job, like her five-year stint as an ACLU attorney, provided another platform for her to articulate human rights principles and to protect the rights of oppressed groups. Norton researched, lobbied, and lectured widely about discrimination based upon race, gender, religion, and national origin. She urged businesses to counteract widespread job biases against racial minorities, women, veterans, and older employees by offering training programs and real opportunities for advancement.

She also urged changes in housing policies and education. Her Commission influenced the New York State legislature to enact the nation's strictest law prohibiting discriminatory real estate practice. In education, she was shocked to learn that only 9 percent of the faculty in the New York City public school system was of color, at a time when the student body comprised 55 percent. She held hearings on the board's hiring practices and called for recommendations for "immediate change and improvement in the way blacks and Puerto Ricans are treated by the educational system." Her investigation of the municipal government for possible racial and sexual discrimination resulted in the Commission's drawing up affirmative action guidelines and broadening maternity leave policy. The Norton Commission promoted the rewriting of outdated laws that regulated workmen's compensation and minimum wages, liberalized abortion rights, and established adequate day-care centers. She sought and won the approval of various women's rights groups. To maintain the Commission's effectiveness, Norton recommended that it be elevated to departmental status and that the reorganization include the substitution of paid hearings officers for the largely volunteer board. In 1974, Mayor Abraham Beame was so impressed by Norton's ability and tenacity that he asked her to stay on for a second term in his new administration. Her re-appointment was welcomed by several women's advocacy and civil rights groups.

In 1977, President Carter appointed her the first woman to head the Equal Employment Opportunity Commission (EEOC). Her major responsibility in this position was for the enforcement of Title VII of the Civil Rights Act of 1964 and the Equal Employment Act of 1972. She brought her considerable skills to Washington to tackle these issues to which she had dedicated her life. Confident in her abilities, Carter consolidated some eighteen civil rights enforcement agencies under her auspices to cut the gridlock that characterized so much of government efforts in this area. Norton won general high marks for her operation of the EEOC. The American Jewish Congress (AJC) praised her decision to hold hearings prior to devising guidelines for "reasonable accommodation" to the religious needs of employees. This was a response to the narrow ruling of the Supreme Court in *TWA v. Harison* in which the court decision influenced some employers to ignore employee requests for accommodation for religious beliefs. Leo Pfeffer, special counsel to the AJC, noted that Commissioner Norton's support of a Senate bill that would permit federal workers to work overtime in lieu of time off would make it possible for members of all religious denominations to observe holy days. She encouraged the House to enact similar legislation. Noting that affirmative action had enhanced the economic status of African-Americans and women, she continued to promote and to monitor such hiring practices. The Norton administration also reduced the enormous backlog of cases. With the defeat of the Carter administration in 1980, Eleanor Holmes Norton left office when her term expired. She became a professor at the noted law school of Georgetown University.

Although she continued her previous work for civil rights, her efforts in the 1980s may have had a more international dimension. She believed, for example, that racism and economic exploitation had stripped Africa of much of its resources and had relegated many of its people to poverty and ignorance. (As early as 1961 she had worked in Libreville, in Gabon.) Within the United

States, she helped to organize opposition against the white apartheid regime in the Union of South Africa. She was one of the prominent people arrested for demonstrating outside that country's embassy in Washington, D.C., along with Mary Frances Berry (1*), D.C. delegate Walter Fauntroy, political scientist Roger Wilkins, and Randall Robinson of TransAfrica. Their high visibility attracted widespread media attention and helped to jolt a torpid Congress and an indifferent White House.

In 1990, a coalition of civil rights and women's rights groups helped to elect Norton to the job of congressional representative for the District of Columbia. (She then resigned her tenured law school professorship.) The end of her campaign was marred by the revelation that she and her husband of twenty-five years, Edward Norton, a prominent Washington attorney, had not filed D.C. taxes for eight years. Although Norton placed the blame upon her husband (whom she later divorced), her credibility was tarnished, and she lost considerable support. Norton was nonetheless an active first-term congresswoman and served on key committees to allow her to address the needs of her constituency. She lobbied for D.C. statehood and served on the executive committee of the research and policy arm of the Democratic members of the House of Representatives. Her successful legislation included the Federal Payment Formula Bill in 1991. This was the most important change for the District of Columbia since Congress granted the District home rule.

Eleanor Holmes Norton has described herself as a "reform Democrat." She once noted: "I stand in politics as a political, radical activist, and I work for the militant causes that are advanced." She has been a staunch advocate of civil rights, free speech, women's rights, and economic advancement for the poorer classes. Although her pronouncements and actions placed her at the center of black progressive thought, she has had her critics. Some African-Americans have opposed her defense of free speech for racists. Others have questioned the overall merits of liberalism, which seems to rely largely upon moral persuasion and goodwill to produce slow change. Within liberalism, however, Eleanor Holmes Norton has been a persistent and responsible voice for greater justice in American society.

Her potential influence grew in January of 1993 when she convinced the Democratic majority of the House to allow the District and four U.S. possessions (American Samoa, Guam, Puerto Rico, and the Virgin Islands) the right to vote in most of the business conducted by the House. The District previously had a vote in committees of the House, but not in final decisions in the entire House. Since most final business is conducted in a "committee of the whole," it was agreed that the five jurisdictions that had been denied such voting rights would be given them. Because of unanimous opposition by Republican members, and by some Democrats, it was stipulated that when a bill passed by only a five-vote majority there would be an automatic second vote in which the five jurisdictions could not vote.

Although some people argued that this change was merely symbolic and did not give the D.C. delegate greater power, it was also true that many votes in the House were taken only by voice (and the Republicans, if they objected to a possible deciding edge given by the new voting members, would need to object before forcing a formal ballot), and that less than a half-dozen of the several hundred votes conducted in 1992 had such tiny margins of success. While a federal judge rejected the Republican lawsuit, asserting that the change was "meaningless," Norton may have been correct in noting that the House functions on relationships based on trading votes, and that if you have no vote, you are generally irrelevant.

Bibliography

Davis, Marianna W. *Contributions of Black Women to America*. Columbia, SC: Kenday, 1982: 1:473–74, 591; 2:146, 156, 192, 247, 251, 472.

"Eleanor Holmes Norton: A Tough New Sister at E.E.O.C.," *Black Collegian* 8 (March–April 1978): 124–26.

"For Norton, A Hill Vote with Historic Cast," *Washington Post*, Feb. 4, 1993, B1.

Lahmon, Jo Ann. "Eleanor Holmes Norton," in *Notable Black American Women*, Jessie Carney Smith, ed. Detroit: Gale Research, 1992: 809–12.

Lamson, Peggy. "Eleanor Holmes Norton Reforms the Equal Employment Opportunity Commission," in *Women Leaders in American Politics*, James David Harper and Barbara Kellerman, eds. Englewood Cliffs, NJ: Prentice-Hall, 1986: 340–44, 401.

"Norton, Eleanor Holmes," *Current Biography* 37 (Nov. 1976): 15–17.

Norton, Eleanor Holmes. ". . . and the Language Is Race," *Ms.* 2 (Jan./Feb. 1992): 43–45.

———. "Bargaining and the Ethic of Progress," *New York University Law Review* 64 (June 1989): 493–577.

———. "A Dialogue with Eleanor Holmes Norton," *Emerge* 1 (Aug. 1990): 11–13.

———. "Equal Employment Law: Crisis in Interpretation—Survival against the Odds," *Tulane Law Review* 62 (March 1988): 681–715.

———. "It's Not a 'Power Grab' by Democrats," *Washington Post*, Jan. 4, 1993, A21.

———. "Population Growth and the Future of Black Folk," *Crisis* 80 (May 1973): 151–53.

———. "Restoring the Traditional Black Family," *New York Times Magazine*, June 2, 1985, pp. 42–43+.

———. "The Role of Black Presidential Appointees," *Urban League Review* 9 (Summer 1985): 105–11.

"Women in Government: A Slim Past but a Strong Future," *Ebony* 32 (Aug. 1977):89–92.

Lillian Serece Williams

GLORIA STEINEM (1936–   )

A leader of the feminist movement

Born in 1936 in Toledo, Ohio, Gloria Steinem was a *magna cum laude* graduate of Smith College. She studied in India following college. Later, she worked for an organization in Cambridge, Massachusetts, that provided press services to foreign journalists. In 1960 she moved to New York City where she became a well-known free-lance writer.

When *New York* magazine was formed in 1968, Steinem became a contributing editor. As part of a writing assignment that year, she attended a radical feminist meeting. Not only did the resulting article win a journalism prize, but Steinem became a feminist. In writing the article, she realized that her problems as a woman in a largely male professional world were shared by many women. She turned from her role as observer and writer to that of feminist activist.

As a leader of the second feminist wave, she was central in establishing several major feminist organizations. In 1971 she was one of the founders of the National Women's Political Caucus and the Women's Action Alliance. In 1972 Steinem and others founded *Ms.*, the first mass market feminist magazine in U.S. history. She continued as its editor until 1987. She was a founding member of the Coalition of Labor Union Women in 1974 and a member of the International Women's Year Committee that sponsored the Houston Women's Conference in 1977. In 1972 she was a co-founder of the Ms. Foundation. She continued to be president of the Board of Directors of this foundation, one of the first devoted to women's concerns and projects. She has described herself as an "itinerant speaker and feminist organizer."

While her writings were usually for magazines, a collection of her work, entitled *Outrageous Acts and Everyday Rebellions*, was published in 1983. In 1986, her book on Marilyn Monroe (written with George Barris), entitled *Marilyn: Norma Jean*, was completed. For Steinem, Monroe was an icon for women's roles in the 1950s, illuminating the gender roles of that time. Monroe was not a doomed sex object, but an object lesson in gender and sexuality. Her insecurities were the insecurities of women of her time. A later book, *Revolution from Within: A Book of Self-Esteem*, continued her commentary on the problems of women developing a strong sense of personal worth in a society that belittles them.

Ms. magazine was instrumental in providing individuals with information about the second feminist movement and in helping to coalesce that movement. The 300,000 copies of the preview issue sold out on newsstands in its

Gloria Steinem. *Source*: Library of Congress

first eight days. The 1972 preview issue contained controversial articles on a typically wide range of feminist issues from sexuality to employment to marriage. Steinem, in an introductory essay entitled "Sisterhood," explained her own early reluctance to join the feminist movement because she had internalized society's "lack of esteem for women—black women, Chicana women, white women—and for myself." This first issue stimulated a deluge of mail. More than 20,000 letters poured in from women across the country. They wrote about how the magazine spoke to their own lives. Many of these women now realized that their problems were not unique but were shared.

During Steinem's fifteen years with *Ms.* magazine, life was reexamined from a feminist perspective. Some articles became major consciousness raisers. The magazine sought the moment of "the click" when some event or word awakens a woman's understanding. For *Ms.*, the ideal woman was not an unmarried "miss" or a married "mrs." but an autonomous individual.

Ms. editors also used the magazine to educate the advertising and business world to the sexist nature of much advertising. Every month sexist ads appeared in the magazine as a way of informing the public about sexism. Its staff also rejected paid advertising that they labeled sexist. *Ms.* staff tried to persuade advertisers that their advertising should reflect the new world of working women. Thus the magazine served as both a conduit for new, non-sexist advertising and as a critique of much that presently existed.

From its beginning the public responded to *Ms.* in a very personal way. Thousands of letters sent to the magazine have been donated to the Schlesinger Library. Some of them were compiled by Mary Thom into a book, *Letters to Ms.* It showed how feminism resonated with the readers of *Ms.* As an example, a long article on wife beating in 1976 brought a flood of letters from battered women. This, in turn, demonstrated the article's assertion that battering was far more widespread than many people believed.

Steinem tried to keep the magazine on the cutting edge of feminism, even though its appeal had to be a mainstream audience. This fit in with her feminist philosophy. She initially reacted against the National Organization for Women (NOW) as too middle class and white. Instead, she agreed with the radical feminist analysis that women are a subordinate caste whose purpose for the patriarchy is reproduction of the species. As she said, "If you aren't born white and male in America, you are statistically likely to end up as some sort of support system for those who are." While she continued her views into the 1990s, she came to speak more admiringly of the early NOW founders. She concluded that they were brave in their actions and much closer to her ideals than she once believed.

Steinem's 1992 book, *Revolution from Within*, summarized the journey of her life. She described a painfully unhappy childhood spent caring for her emotionally disturbed mother. Both as a child and as a young woman, she absorbed her society's expectation of women as quietly subordinate to men. When the second women's movement began in the 1960s, she first resisted supporting it. As the movement challenged traditional roles for women, Steinem's own understanding of herself began to change. People in the movement became her "chosen family." She overcame her self-doubts to become an editor of *Ms.* She developed the confidence to raise money for the magazine and various causes, and to speak before audiences and cameras.

For many years, her life was dedicated to this movement. She gave away most of her money and had little concern about where she lived. As she commented in one interview: "I had lived in my apartment for at least four or five years before I found out that the oven didn't work" (*Vanity Fair*, Jan. 1992). Eventually, she became depressed and exhausted. She felt that her public image as confident and sophisticated was not authentic. In *The Revolution from Within*, she disclosed that "what I felt like *inside* was a plump brunette from Toledo, too tall and much too pudding-faced, with . . . a voice that felt constantly on the verge of revealing some unacceptable emotion."

She briefly became involved in a romantic relationship and attempted to meet conventional definitions of beauty.

The Revolution from Within discusses her major conclusions. How can women overcome the dominant society's demeaning expectations? She talks about the potential value of everything from social protest to meditation, Yogic breathing, and journal writing. The feminist slogan that "the personal is political"—that much of what we are is stimulated by society's expectations—was interpreted to mean that the individual can transform her self-understanding and apply this to social change. Although the 1970s produced massive consciousness-raising, there still needed to be systemic institutional change to make women truly equal members of society. Redistribution of family power, lessened violence against women, and equal pay for comparable work would be necessary components of this new equality.

This 1992 book was criticized by many for its fundamental individualism, but Steinem was always more of a gadfly, publicist, and energizer than a person with a communal philosophy associated with a specific institution. *Revolution from Within* was full of pop psych jargon. It may not have been sensitive to the powerful molding forces of class and race, but it did present Steinem as an "emblematic" feminist who developed some of the potential within herself through participation in a nurturing movement. Steinem continued to advise women to support at least one demonstration a month "just to keep your blood tingling" (*Washington Post*, Feb. 1, 1992, p. 1). Deirdre English, a one-time editor of the leftist magazine *Mother Jones*, expressed both the uses and the limits of Steinem's emphasis on self-esteem in her review:

> To improve the lot of America's women, the pressing need is not an ever greater focus on the self. More good will come from swapping ideas about how to force employers to pay attention to women's needs, how to handle sex discrimination and harassment situations, how to get ahead despite the obstacles of sexism. Accomplishing any of these things will send women's spirits soaring and fuel further activism, and that does seem to be what Ms. Steinem would like to achieve. (*New York Times Book Review*, Feb. 2, 1992, p. 13)

Bibliography

Carmody, Deirdre. "Power to the Readers: *Ms.* Thrives without Ads," *New York Times*, July 22, 1991, D6.

The Decade of Women: A MS History of the Seventies in Words and Pictures. New York: G. P. Putnam's Sons, 1980.

"Gloria Steinem," *Current Biography* 49 (March 1988): 46–50.

Henry, Sondra, and Emily Taitz. *One Woman's Power: A Biography of Gloria Steinem.* Minneapolis: Dillon Press, 1987.

Hoban, Phoebe. "Big WAC [Women's Action Coalition] Attack," *New York* 25 (Aug. 3, 1992): 30–35.

Orenstein, Peggy. "Ms. Fights for Its Life," *Mother Jones* 15 (Nov./Dec. 1990): 4, 32–36+.

Povich, Lynn. "Gloria Steinem," *Working Woman* 17 (Jan. 1992): 66–68+.

Quilligan, Maureen. "Marilyn/Norma Jean," *The Yale Review* 77 (Winter 1988): 259–86.

Steinem, Gloria. "Bringing Changes Home" (interview), *Iris; A Journal about Women* (University of Virginia) no. 21 (Spring/Summer 1989): 20–23.

———. "Humanism and the Second Wave of Feminism," *The Humanist* 47 (May/June 1987): 11–15+.

———. *Outrageous Acts and Everyday Rebellions*. New York: Holt, Rinehart, and Winston, 1983.

———. *Revolution from Within: A Book of Self-Esteem*. Boston: Little, Brown, 1992. Reviewed: Beryl Lieff Benderly, *Washington Post Book World*, Feb. 23, 1992, pp. 3, 12; Deirdre English, "She's Her Weakness Now," *New York Times Book Review*, Feb. 2, 1992, p. 13.

Steinem, Gloria, and George Barris. *Marilyn: Norma Jean*. New York: New American Library, 1988.

Thom, Mary, ed. *Letters to Ms., 1972–1987*. New York: Henry Holt and Sons, 1987.

Frances Arick Kolb

PART FOUR

FOR A SAFE ENVIRONMENT

Is nature an inventory of assets to be sold for short-term profits or managed as a long-term business? Is nature something that humanity is superior to, and can totally dominate, or are people an inextricable part of nature? Will people suffer if nature suffers? Are these questions primarily moral or practical? Scattered writers of the 1800s, most of them ignored by the majority of Americans, began to raise such issues. These writers included Henry David Thoreau, Frederick Law Olmsted, and George Perkins Marsh. Tiny conservation groups also emerged, such as the Audubon Society (1888) and the Sierra Club (1892). By the beginning of the 1900s, there was wider concern because of the officially announced end of the frontier in 1890, fears of depleted resources, and anxiety about the rapaciousness of unregulated industrial capitalism.

The first large-scale conservation movement coalesced during the presidential administration of Theodore Roosevelt (1901–1908). He preached conservation (popularizing it to a large audience), encouraged protection of the federally owned lands, urged reclamation of damaged land, and secured the passage of various laws for public health and safety. As old government agencies grew, as new government agencies were established, and as private conservation societies developed, the conservation movement became an institutional part of American life. "The environment" now had lobbyists whose motives were diverse. There were sportsmen who sought to protect hunting grounds; businessmen and administrators (such as Gifford Pinchot) who interpreted conservation as a wise use of resources that insured future profits; and idealists who lauded the healing powers of nature, such as John Muir. After this founding period, public interest or funding for conservation might ebb (as in the 1920s and the 1950s), but it always retained some major support from individuals and institutions. In the 1930s, the New Deal accomplished much for conservation as a part of its make-work programs, which aided reforestation and soil protection. New private clubs, such as the Wilderness Society (1935), added their efforts.

Although World War II and the 1950s preoccupation with family life and material progress deflected the attention of most of the public from issues of conservation, by the 1960s there was significant enthusiasm for protecting the national parks from commercial intrusions, and growing opposition to testing nuclear weapons in the atmosphere and to contaminating food with pesticides and herbicides. Rachel Carson's powerful best-seller about poisons used in the environment, *The Silent Spring* (1962), and the Nuclear Test Ban Treaty of 1963 were signs of popular concerns. The term "ecology" became common, emphasizing how humanity fit within the overall web of life, the fundamental disruption of which could mean peril to humanity. Private organizations such as the Friends of the Earth (1968) sought to persuade the general public and the agencies of state power. Congressional responses to many pressures included the National Environmental Policy Act (1969) and the creation of the Environmental Protection Agency (1970). Another milestone in the formation of this contemporary movement was the successful organization of Earth Day, by Denis Hayes (*) and others, in 1970.

The center of gravity of this movement seemed to be less in special interest groups than in an emphasis on the pervasive interconnections of life. A central theme has been that we are inside nature, not outside of it. We cannot, without harm to ourselves, poison the air, water, plants, and animals. Without decisive coordinated actions to protect the local, national, and international environments we may be slipping into a slow motion catastrophe. Industrial emissions have eroded the protective ozone layer of our atmosphere that acts as the planet's sunscreen; this could allow damaging radiation to reach plant and animal life. Industrial emissions may also be trapping more of the sun's rays, acting like the glass panes of a greenhouse, raising the temperature of the atmosphere. In addition, groundwater has been threatened with contamination; forests are being rapidly cut down; the oceans are too frequently used as the world's largest garbage cans; petroleum will run out eventually; topsoil is being eroded or paved over; pesticides and herbicides are intensifying in the food chain; mountains of trash are accumulating; and 15–20 percent of all life forms may perish by A.D. 2000. Are there limits to the life support system of this planet? Where will we go if it fails? Is it alarmist to raise such concerns, or is it escapist to ignore them?

Most politicians have dismissed these issues as exaggerated, too complex, or too remote from their narrow constituencies. Some politicians have responded, but mainly with cheap talk. President George Bush (1988–1992) grandly styled himself "the environmental president." He illustrated this with his pledge that the Greenhouse Effect (on atmospheric warming) would be countered by "the White House effect." In practice, Bush avoided even the twentieth anniversary of Earth Day (which he spent fishing in Florida) and demagogically belittled Senator Al Gore, in the 1992 campaign, as Dr. Ozone. Little leadership could be expected from such leaders. They usually move ahead only when some determined groups push them.

Many of the activists of the environmental movement could be characterized as liberals. Men such as Lester Brown (*), Paul Ehrlich (*), and Ralph Nader (*) would not fundamentally change the structure of capitalist production. They want more social controls on it, or policies (such as population control) that would limit pressures on the environment. Most conventional leftists, whether socialist, communist, or independent Marxist, have also not rejected the definition of progress as pervasive industrial development. Some leftists, such as the democratic socialist Barry Commoner (*), do place a greater emphasis on genuine popular control of the means of production, not just some technocrats (whether capitalist or socialist) ruling "in the interests of the people."

Some of the most radical criticism has come from libertarian socialists and anarchists like Edward Abbey (*) and Murray Bookchin (*). Abbey commented that "growth for the sake of growth is the ideology of the cancer cell." Although most of these critics seek to create new socio-economic orders, some, like the advocates of "deep ecology" in Earth First! (1980), virtually dismiss humanity as a hopeless blight on nature. Further perceptive critiques were developed by the 1990s, by some feminists (ecofeminism), independent Marxists (ecomarxism), native Americans, members of People for the Ethical Treatment of Animals, and some people of color ("environmental equity" vs. "environmental racism"). The major environmental groups have long been controlled by affluent white men who were little interested in the health and housing problems of inner cities and the poor. This was slowly changing by the 1990s, both within the old organizations, and through the environmental platforms of such people as Representative Ron Dellums (6*), Jesse Jackson (6*), and most of the Congressional Black Caucus (*New York Times*, Jan. 11, 1993, B7).

If the coming crises are too great, will there be a call for rigid, state-oriented social engineering? Will society be fundamentally restructured? Will ecology become virtually a new religion, or will it be mainly "good business?"

SELECTED BIBLIOGRAPHY

Allen, Thomas B. *Guardian of the Wild: The Story of the National Wildlife Federation, 1936–1986.* Bloomington: Indiana University Press, 1988.

Belasco, Warren. *Appetite for Change: How the Counterculture Took On the Food Industry, 1966–1988.* New York: Pantheon Books, 1990.

Biehl, Janet. *Rethinking Ecofeminist Politics.* Boston: South End Press, 1991.

Bramwell, Anna. *Ecology in the 20th Century; A History.* New Haven, CT: Yale University Press, 1989.

Brooks, Paul. *Speaking for Nature: How Literary Naturalists from Henry David Thoreau Have Shaped America.* Boston: Houghton Mifflin, 1980.

Brower, David. *For Earth's Sake: The Life and Time of David Brower.* Salt Lake City: Peregrine Smith Books, 1990.

———. *Work in Progress.* Salt Lake City: Peregrine Smith Books, 1991.

Bullard, Robert D., ed. *Confronting Environmental Racism; Voices from the Grassroots.* Boston: South End Press, 1992.

Callicott, J. Baird, ed. *Companion to San County Almanac; Interpretive and Critical Essay: Capitalism, Nature, Socialism; A Journal of Socialist Ecology* (quarterly). Madison: University of Wisconsin Press, 1987.

Carson, Rachel. *Silent Spring,* 25th anniversary edition. Boston: Houghton Mifflin, 1987 (1962).

Davis, John, ed. *The Earth First! Reader: Ten Years of Radical Environmentalism,* foreword by Dave Foreman. Salt Lake City: Peregrine Smith Books, 1991.

Dobson, Andrew. *Green Political Thought: An Introduction.* London: Unwin Hyman, 1990.

———, ed. *The Green Reader: Essays toward a Sustainable Society.* San Francisco: Mercury House, 1991.

Dunlap, Thomas R. *Saving America's Wildlife: Ecology and the American Mind, 1850–1990.* Princeton, NJ: Princeton University Press, 1991.

Foreman, Dave. *Confessions of an Eco-Warrior.* New York: Harmony Books, 1991.

Foreman, Dave, and Murray Bookchin. *Defending the Earth: A Dialogue between Murray Bookchin and Dave Foreman.* Boston: South End Press, 1991.

Fox, Stephen. *The American Conservation Movement: John Muir and His Legacy.* Madison: University of Wisconsin Press, 1986.

Gaard, Greta, ed. *Ecofeminism: Women, Animals, Nature.* Philadelphia: Temple University Press, 1993.

Gabriel, Trip. "If a Tree Falls in the Forest, They Hear It" (on Earth First!), *New York Times Magazine,* Nov. 4, 1990, pp. 24, 58–59, 62–64.

Graf, William L. *Wilderness Preservation and the Sagebrush Rebellions.* Savage, MD: Rowman and Littlefield, 1990.

Hays, Samuel P. *Beauty, Health, and Permanence: Environmental Politics in the United States, 1955–1985.* New York: Cambridge University Press, 1987.

Hynes, H. Patricia. *The Recurring Silent Spring.* New York: Pergamon Press, 1989.

Koppes, Clayton R. "Efficiency/Equity/Esthetics: Toward a Reinterpretation of American Conservation," *Environmental Review* 11 (Summer 1987): 127–46.

Lancaster, John. "The Green Guerilla: 'Redneck' Eco-Activist Dave Foreman Throwing a Monkey Wrench Into the System," *Washington Post,* March 20, 1991, B1, B4.

Lewis, Martin W. *Green Delusions: An Environmentalist Critique of Radical Environmentalism.* Durham, NC: Duke University Press, 1992.

McCay, Mary A. *Rachel Carson.* New York: Twayne Publishers, 1993.

McCormick, John. *Reclaiming Paradise: The Global Environmental Movement.* Bloomington: Indiana University Press, 1989.

McKibben, Bill. "David Brower" (interview), *Rolling Stone,* June 28, 1990, pp. 59–62+.

McMurray, Emily J. "Jeremy Rifkin," in *Contemporary Authors,* vol. 129. Detroit: Gale Research, 1990: 362–68.

Manes, Christopher. *Green Rage: Radical Environmentalism and the Unmaking of Civilization*. Boston: Little, Brown, 1990.

Mayer, Robert N. *The Consumer Movement: Guardians of the Marketplace*. Boston: Twayne, 1989.

Meines, Curt. *Aldo Leopold: His Life and Work*. Madison: University of Wisconsin Press, 1988.

Melosi, Martin V. *Coping with Abundance: Energy and Environment in Industrial America, 1820–1980*. New York: Alfred A. Knopf, 1985.

Merchant, Carolyn, ed. *Major Problems in American Environmental History: Documents and Essays*. Lexington, MA: D. C. Heath, 1992.

Nash, Roderick. *The Rights of Nature: A History of Environmental Ethics*. Madison: University of Wisconsin Press, 1989.

———. *Wilderness and the American Mind*, 3d ed. New Haven, CT: Yale University Press, 1982.

———, ed. *American Environment: Readings in Conservation History*. 3d ed. New York: McGraw-Hill, 1989.

Norwood, Vera L. "The Nature of Knowing: Rachel Carson and the American Environment," *Signs* 12 (Summer 1987): 740–60.

Paehlke, Robert C. *Environmentalism and the Future of Progressive Politics*. New Haven: Yale University Press, 1989.

Parfit, Michael. "Earth First!ers Wield a Mean Monkey Wrench," *Smithsonian* 21 (April 1990): 184–86+.

Pertschuk, Michael. *Revolt against Regulation: The Rise and Fall of the Consumer Movement*. Berkeley: University of California Press, 1982.

Petulla, Joseph M. *American Environmental History*, 2d ed. Columbus, OH: Merrill Publishing Company, 1988.

Rifkin, Jeremy. *Biosphere Politics: A New Consciousness for a New Century*. New York: Crown, 1991.

Rosner, David, and Gerald Markowitz, eds. *Dying for Work: Workers' Safety and Health in Twentieth-Century America*. Bloomington: Indiana University Press, 1987.

Roszak, Theodore. *The Voice of the Earth*. New York: Simon and Schuster, 1992.

"Sale, Kirkpatrick," in *Contemporary Literary Criticism*, vol. 68. Detroit: Gale Research, 1991: 342–61.

Sale, Kirkpatrick. *The Green Revolution: The Environmental Movement, 1962–1992*. New York: Hill and Wang, 1993.

Scarce, Rik. *Eco-Warriors: Understanding the Radical Environmental Movement*. Chicago: Noble Press, 1990.

Scheffer, Victor B. *The Shaping of Environmentalism in America*. Seattle: University of Washington Press, 1991.

Shabecoff, Philip. *A Fierce Green Fire: The American Environmental Movement*. New York: Hill and Wang, 1993.

Silber, Norman. *Test and Protest: The Influence of the Consumers Union*. New York: Holmes and Meier, 1983.

Strong, Douglas H. *Dreamers and Defenders: American Conservationists*, 2d ed. Lincoln: University of Nebraska Press, 1988.

Telgen, Diane. "Amory B. Lovins," in *Contemporary Authors*, vol. 32, New Revision Series. Detroit: Gale Research, 1991: 269–70.

Terrie, P. G. "Recent Work in Environmental History" (review article), *American Studies International* 27 (Oct. 1989): 42–65.

Udall, James R. "Prophets of an Energy Revolution" (in Amory B. Lovins and L. Hunter Lovins), *National Wildlife* 30 (Dec. 1991/Jan. 1992): 10–13.

White, Richard. "Historiographical Essay on American Environmental History: The Development of a New National Field," *Pacific Historical Review* 54 (Aug. 1985): 297–335.

Whorton, James C. *Crusaders for Fitness: The History of American Health Reformers.* Princeton, NJ: Princeton University Press, 1982.

Worster, Donald. *Nature's Economy: A History of Ecological Ideas.* New York: Cambridge University Press, 1985.

———. *Turning to the Land: Environmental History and the Ecological Imagination.* New York: Oxford University Press, 1993.

———, ed. *The Ends of the Earth: Perspectives on Modern Environmental History.* New York: Cambridge University Press, 1988.

Nuclear Power

Ball, Howard. *Justice Downwind: America's Nuclear Testing Program in the 1950s.* New York: Oxford University Press, 1985.

Boyer, Paul. *By the Bomb's Early Light: American Thought and Culture at the Dawn of the Atomic Age.* New York: Pantheon Books, 1985.

Cantelon, Philip L., Richard G. Hewlett, and Robert C. Williams, eds. *The American Atom; A Documentary History of Nuclear Policies from the Discovery of Fission to the Present,* 2d ed. Philadelphia: University of Pennsylvania Press, 1992.

Clarfield, Gerald H., and William M. Wiecek. *Nuclear America: Military and Civilian Power in the United States, 1940–1980.* New York: Harper and Row, 1984.

Holsworth, Robert D. *Let Your Life Speak: A Study of Politics, Religion, and Antinuclear Weapons Activism.* Madison: University of Wisconsin Press, 1989.

Katz, Milton S. *Ban the Bomb: A History of SANE, The Committee for a Sane Nuclear Policy, 1957–1985.* Westport, CT: Greenwood Press, 1986.

McCrea, Frances B., and Gerald E. Markle. *Minutes to Midnight: Nuclear Weapons Protest of America.* Newbury Park, CA: Sage Publications, 1989.

Powaski, Ronald E. *March to Armageddon: The United States and the Nuclear Arms Race, 1939 to the Present.* New York: Oxford University Press, 1987.

Price, Jerome Brian. *The Antinuclear Movement,* 2d ed. Boston: Twayne, 1989.

EDWARD ABBEY (1927–1989)

Ecological provocateur

Edward Abbey was one of the more influential ecological writers of late twentieth-century America. "Cactus Ed" was the inspiring figure, both as writer and archetype, for the Earth First! Movement, founded in 1980. Both he and this movement promoted a fervent libertarian defense of wilderness, civil disobedience, and sabotage of technological development, especially in the West.

Abbey, who was raised on a hardscrabble farm in the hill country of Pennsylvania, was an army draftee for several years at the end of World War II. He then moved to the desert and mountain West. After completing two degrees in philosophy at the University of New Mexico (with his M.A. thesis being on the ethical issues of anarchism and violence in the late nineteenth century), and a Fulbright year at the University of Edinburgh, he worked as a U.S. Forest Service fire-lookout and as a Park Ranger in the mountain-desert states. (His other jobs included that of social caseworker in New York City.) He finally settled permanently in the U.S. West, except for travels to wilderness areas in Alaska, Mexico, and Australia. He married several times, fathered four children, and taught in his later years at the University of Arizona. He viewed his main vocation as literary defender of wilderness and freedom.

He early identified with socially rebellious fiction, which he defined as including Dreiser, Steinbeck, Celine, B. Traven, Tolstoy, Nietzsche, Kropotkin, Whitman, Thoreau, and many later nature writers. His first significant publication was a novel about adolescence, *Jonathan Troy* (1954). This was a rather awkward tale of the struggle to manhood in Pennsylvania poverty. It was marked by disillusionment with mainstream social attitudes, especially those identified with the East, as well as with leftist politics and with what he later characterized as "chicken-shit liberalism."

His more interesting second novel, *The Brave Cowboy* (1956), received greater attention. It became the basis for an unusual Western movie called *Lonely Are the Brave*, starring Kirk Douglas and Walter Matthau. The movie, subtitled "An Old Tale in a New Time," was dedicated to "the outlaws." It intentionally combined the anachronistic with the contemporary political. The nuclear issue is posed by a veteran who refuses, on libertarian principles, to re-register under the 1948 Selective Service Act. He goes public about his refusal, is convicted of willful defiance, and suffers a two-year prison sentence. (There were, in fact, hundreds of related situations during 1948–1950.) This draft-resister, Jack Bondi, is little developed or dramatized, which weakens the story. The focus is mostly on his non-intellectual best friend and alter ego, the quixotic late-twenties Jack Burns, who goes to jail to help Bondi escape.

When Bondi refuses, Burns does escape and is pursued by the authorities. This provides most of the story. Abbey admired the militant civil disobedience of Burns. Similar themes occur in his later work, including his final novel.

Burns is an earlier Western man-on-horseback. He is a brawling, drinking, and sweet-natured guy who loves wilderness freedom and heroically escapes by shooting down a helicopter with his carbine. He outwits a sheriff's posse, eludes the thuggish military, and scales near-impossible mountain ridges with his horse. He is finally struck down while crossing a highway on horseback by a speeding eighteen-wheeler loaded with toilets.

Such personal stories were part of Abbey's larger ethos of craft, with doing things directly and well. This included someone making camp; shooting a deer; cooking a traditional breakfast; following a trail; preserving a waterhole; climbing an escarpment; and personally fighting the inherently brutal authorities and "technotyranny." The craftsman ethic is at the center of his style and sensibility. The enemy is not only the authorities of raving urban-technological civilization—"the fury of men and women immersed in engines"—but the loss of autonomous craft to sensitively engage the natural reality that defines the authentically human.

Such poignancy appears in related conflict in the too-thin novel *Fire on the Mountain* (1962; also made into a movie). Western natural-anarchism is expressed by a twelve-year-old boy (the narrator, with rather improbable language and perceptions) and an old, somewhat inchoate cattle rancher. The latter is a lover of the land who pyrrhically battles the government to save, without regard for profit, his family place from being absorbed into a U.S. military-missile range. (This draws upon actual New Mexico events.) The story tends toward mere pathos, with a manipulated ending that includes an irrelevant fatal heart attack and then a portentous ritual cremation in the beloved primal mountains. Some larger intelligence is suggested by an inexplicable character in the story who points up various paradoxes. This brave old rancher's supposed sacral sense of the land had not stopped him from destroying it by overgrazing, and his supposed principle of private property sanctions his grandfather's earlier thievery from the Indians over the later thievery by the military bureaucrats.

A later novella, *Black Sun* (1971), has vivid descriptions of the natural Western scene and of physical sensation, this time adding romantic-erotic sex, but again lacking complex characters and plots. The fated romance is the short love affair of an educated but inarticulate and reclusive older forest-fire lookout (Will Gatlin) and a summering, pretty, and virginal nineteen-year-old upper-middle-class college girl. She inexplicably disappears in the wilderness. The action is often sentimental, abbreviated, and understated. A bit of intellectual range is added, with arch awkwardness, by the letters and talk of a philosophy teacher who is Will's buddy, a wisecracking womanizer who variously proposes sacred community whorehouses and a libertarian vision of communal childrearing and free erotic relationships.

Good News (1980) uses a favorite modernist form, the dystopia. Unfortunately, the report on life-in-the-ruins is undercut by an often trite style and the ranting caricature figures which demand it: a fancy fascistic general compensating for his sexual impotence; a stock-sadistic sergeant- torturer and his motorcycle gang; a good-hearted whore who helps save the real men; a clichéd young cowpoke initiated into revolution; Robin Hoodish student guerrillas led by a quaint radical professor; a brave Indian who is both a practicing tribal shaman and a philosophical Harvard Ph.D; and a quick-draw, forever rebellious, one-eyed old rancher. Despite this fractured comic-strip plotting, there are suggestive touches. For example, there is the positive utopianism, the gospel news, that lurks within most dystopias, including the contrary affirmations of endless resistance to authority and retreat to the pastoral edges of the wilderness. But no larger ideas, such as what it takes to resist, no fuller experience, such as the craft of living among the ruins, is adequately presented.

So Abbey attempted other literary ways. His most ambitious personal fiction, and the last published in his lifetime, was *The Fool's Progress: An Honest Novel* (1988). It is partly a redoing of episodes from his first works, including some personal essays. This book dramatizes an Abbey-like character on pilgrimage for his roots. An aging and ailing macho failure (a disgusted social caseworker) journeys from a Tucson suburb, after being dumped by his umpteenth young wife. He travels to an Appalachian family farm in an ailing pickup with an ailing dog. On that narrative string are beaded some colorful episodes of impoverished origins on a family farm, experiences as a draftee, adventures as a bohemian graduate student, work as a park ranger, several marriages, and meetings with assorted eccentrics. Between the episodes with people there is camping out on the margins of a lavishly alienating America, with its good life of increasing phoniness and destructiveness. The rebellious comic energy and defiant marginal's acuteness get swamped (and the truck and much else literally) in pathos, with the overemphasized sick dog but of the symptoms of too much self-pity. The dying all-American fool's guilty progress, a final Abbey piety, is a return to simple living and brotherly compassion.

Social critique and defiance are always part of Abbey's novels. This is certainly true of his best-known handbook of trouble-making, *The Monkey-Wrench Gang* (1975), and its posthumously published continuation, *Hayduke Lives!* (1990). Abbey's purpose was to incite. As Abbey wrote: "Society . . . is like a stew—if you don't keep it stirred up you get a lot of scum on top." Abbey's people, however, are caricatures. There are Doc Sarvis, a philanthropic middle-aged surgeon whose hobby is destroying billboards; Connie Abbsug, a hip-educated Brooklyn-Jewish female campfollower; Seldom Seen Smith, a rather trite Mormon river-guide-farmer-polygamist; and the dominant figure of George Washington Hayduke, a Vietnam combat vet, reverse redneck-style outlaw, inverted Lone Ranger, and ecologically driven saboteur. The "gang," bohemia in the wilds, operates mostly in the Grand Canyon area.

The Western decor encompasses intense river and canyon camping scenes, hairy pickup escapes and near-lethal shoot-outs, wry and outrageous confrontations with a variety of officials, and an array of monstrous machines such as bulldozers, helicopters, coal trains, and other "development" paraphernalia which are often ingeniously disabled, battered, burned, and blown up. The wilderness bohemians are nurtured by a radical conservationist-conservatism (under the slogan of "keep it like it was") which separates them from progressive leftists.

The eco-activism of the rogues has some lovely humor and physicality, along with savaging wit. It is also a handbook for "ecoteurs." It tells the reader how to cut down a billboard, overheat a 'dozer, and fuse explosives. (This function is also fulfilled by the more modest Abbey-inspired and prefaced *Ecodefense: A Field Guide to Monkeywrenching*, by Dave Foreman and Bill Haywood.) Abbey has elements of traditional anarchism such as affinity groups and consensus decisions; machine-breaking and other "creative destruction"; and equality and maximized freedom. The macho-individualist gestures toward a "counter-industrial revolution" and there is a mythical upbeat ending. Hayduke, a rogue who is thought to be finished by the authorities, reappears, on horseback, with a one-eyed Lone Ranger (Jack Burns again). Hayduke is apparently planning to blow up the biggest damn dam of them all, Glen Canyon. Rebellion is never finished.

But what is destroyed, with Rabelaisian gusto, in the sequel, *Hayduke Lives!*, is the "world's largest mobile land machine," *Goliath*, out to stripmine the desert. While eco-protests by Earth First! are sympathetically and poignantly presented by Abbey, the central incitement is to the "Code of the eco-warrior." He/she "hurts no living thing," and, unlike the civil disobedient, avoids capture, cost-consciously discouraging the ravagers of "our native and primordial home." Doc Sarvis calls for a "felonious conspiracy to commit non-felonious misdemeanors against the perimeters of the techno-industrial *ordnung*." The eco-warrior, "operating strictly on anarchic principles of democratic decentralism," "does not fight people" but discouragingly heightens the costs to the institutions of "the planetary Empire of Growth and Greed." The "monstrous megamachine" of a "runaway technology, an all devouring entity that feeds on humans, on all animals, on all living things, and even finally . . . on the earth itself, on the bedrock basis of universal being?" Comic-mythic Hayduke is the vulgar and manic personification of the eco-warrior.

There are obvious disproportions between the romantic eco-warrior code of resistance and the immense power of megamachines, and the economic argument seems insufficient. Technocracy is not just a matter of convenience and profit, to be undermined by inconvenience and high costs caused by sabotage. For example, the nuclear and space technologies (Abbey wrote positively about the latter) may be systemic dementias which aggrandizingly go on despite real unprofitability and human suffering. Faith in technological

overdevelopment is like millennial religion; it may thrive regardless of economic costs and human and earthly degradations. Yet ecodefense and related
radical resistance are some of the few pertinent responses and may have significant larger effects in changing ideology and sensibility. Such acts can be
therapeutic, too: "One single act of defiance against power, against the State
that seems omnipotent but is not, transforms and transfigures the human personality" (*Down River*).

Though dedicated to his role as novelist, Abbey wrote more nonfiction, such
as travel and nature-description essays, reportage, polemics, journals, and even
a final collection of epigrams. These writings were collected into several volumes. The first, *Desert Solitaire* (1968), perhaps most enduringly rooted his
reputation. Abbey in his personal essays, can be sharply tendentious and richly
responsive. By contrast, his fictional characters are less various and persuasive
than his more casually revealed personal character.

He said that the central impetus of his writing and resistance was passion:
"anger and love . . . each implies the other." The anger is against the "megamachines" and "all big social organizations [which are] ugly, brutal, inhuman"
(*Desert Solitaire*). Their dominant ideology is the endless growth of power,
and the power of growth. Or, as he put it in a later essay, if real progress is
the development of human and social quality, "*growth is the enemy of progress*" (*One Life*). He often repeated the metaphor that "growth for the sake of
growth is the ideology of a cancer cell" (*Journey Home*). A natural antithesis
comes with Abbey's love for the deserts and mountains of the less trammeled
west. His overall view was not nature mysticism, although he sometimes used
the world-organicist metaphors of deep ecology. The ultimate intensity of nature experience is "not God—the term seems insufficient—but something
unnameable, and more beautiful, and far greater, and more terrible" (*Abbey's
Road*). Because of such experience, "I find myself equally opposed to the
technological mania of the West and the occult morbidity of the East: Both
are the enemies of reason, and of life, and of the earth." Thus: "loyalty to the
earth . . . the only home we shall ever know, the only paradise we ever need"
(*Desert Solitaire*). Again mocking nature mysticism, he repeats, "Why Wilderness?" He offers many reasons, including senses of beauty, refreshment,
basic order, and difference. Especially he lauds difference, which, for him, is
the deep evolutionary (genetic) "salvation of variety, diversity, possibility and
potentiality." We are now too disconnected from nature, and our "contempt
for the natural world implies contempt for life" (*Beyond the Wall*).

Nature offered alternatives to the present human strife. Even when he
watched desert buzzards at work, Abbey was reminded of "the principle of
evolutionary success: mutual aid." Not "power," as in our technocracy, "for
that does not lead to wisdom, even less to understanding. Sympathy, love,
physical contact—touching—are better means." And that requires an appropriate order of human ways, instead of power which is always "the natural
enemy of truth" (*River*). Instead, we need "some sort of steady-state economy,

some sort of democratic, wide-open society" (*Journey*). As he summarized in "Theory of Anarchy," that should be "democracy taken all the way," which demands practical ways of "how to keep power decentralized, equally distributed, fairly shared" in a society consisting of "a voluntary association of self-reliant, self-supporting, autonomous communities" (*One Life*). Improbable? He asserted that "in social affairs, I'm an optimist. I really do believe that our military-industrial civilization will soon collapse" (*A Voice Crying in the Wilderness*). He hoped that it would be replaced by a neopastoral society "keeping true to the earth and remaining loyal to our basic animal nature" (*One Life*).

He concluded that our maniacal growth was the greatest enemy, not only in indiscriminate technology and monstrous power organization, but "most important" in population growth. For him, there was no justice, sense, or decency in mindless global breeding. One of his most notorious essays urged no more immigration into the United States. He especially dismissed what he characterized as authoritarian and religion-diseased Latin Americans. He suggested that each turned-back alien be given a gun and ammunition to straighten out his or her own unjust country. Liberal critics charged him with ethnocentrism, wild-west posturing, statist policing, and reaction.

Abbey was committed to fusing art and sedition. He once described his occupation as criminal anarchy. His distinctive anarchism has attracted many admirers and many critics.

Bibliography

Abbey, Edward. *The Best of Edward Abbey*. San Francisco: Sierra Books, 1988.

———. *Black Sun*, rev. ed. Santa Barbara, CA: Capra Press, 1990.

———. *The Brave Cowboy*. Albuquerque: University of New Mexico Press, 1977 [1956].

———. *Fire on the Mountain*. Albuquerque: University of New Mexico Press, 1978 [1962].

———. *The Fool's Progress: An Honest Novel*. Boston: Little, Brown, 1988.

———. *Good News*. New York: NAL-Dutton, 1991.

———. *Hayduke Lives!* Boston: Little, Brown, 1990.

———. *One Life at a Time, Please*. New York: Henry Holt, 1988.

———. *A Voice Crying in the Wilderness*. New York: St. Martin's Press, 1990.

Berry, Wendell. "A Few Words in Favor of Edward Abbey," *Whole Earth Review* no. 45 (March 1985): 38–44.

Earth First! Journal (Tucson, Arizona; 1980–).

Foreman, Dave. *Confessions of an Eco-Warrior*. New York: Harmony Books, 1991.

Foreman, Dave, and Bill Haywood, eds. *Ecodefense: A Field Guide to Monkeywrenching*, 2d ed., introduction by Edward Abbey. Tucson: Ned Ludd Books, 1987.

Hepworth, James, and Gregory McNamie, eds. *Resist Much, Obey Little: Some Notes on Edward Abbey*. Salt Lake City, UT: Green Garden Press, 1985.

Hoagland, Edward. "Edward Abbey: Standing Tough in the Desert," *New York Times Book Review*, May 7, 1989, pp. 44–45.

McKibben, Bill. "The Desert Anarchist," *New York Review of Books*, Aug. 18, 1988, pp. 42–44.

Manes, Christopher. *Green Rage: Radical Environmentalism and the Unmaking of Civilization.* Boston: Little, Brown, 1990.

Obits. *Audubon* 91 (July 1989): 14+; *Mother Earth News* 120 (Nov./Dec. 1989): 56–57; *National Parks* 63 (May/June 1989): 100–101; *New York Times Biographical Service* 20 (March 1989): 254; *New York Times Book Review* 94 (May 7, 1989): 44–45; *Newsweek* 113 (March 27, 1989): 76; *Sierra* 74 (May/June 1989): 100–101; *Time* 133 (March 27, 1989): 85; *Utne Reader*, July/August, 1989, pp. 36–37.

Ronald, Ann. *The New West of Edward Abbey.* Albuquerque: University of New Mexico Press, 1982.

Scarce, Rik. *Eco-Warriors: Understanding the Radical Environmental Movement.* Chicago: Noble Press, 1990.

Slovic, Scott. *Seeking Awareness in American Nature Writing: Henry Thoreau, Annie Dillard, Edward Abbey, Wendell Berry, Barry Lopez.* Salt Lake City: University of Utah Press, 1992.

Kingsley Widmer

MURRAY BOOKCHIN (1921–   )

Anarcho-ecologist

Murray Bookchin was born in New York City on January 14, 1921, of Russian Jewish immigrant parents who had been active in the revolutionary movement of Tsarist Russia. He grew up in the highly politicized milieu of New York's immigrant community of the 1920s and 1930s. He entered the Communist youth movement in the early 1930s, but became increasingly disillusioned with its authoritarianism by the latter part of the decade. He was outraged above all by what he saw as the disgraceful role of the Communists in the Spanish civil war and the Moscow Trials. In 1939, not surprisingly, he was expelled for "Trotskyist-anarchist deviations." He then worked for several years in the Trotskyist movement, but ultimately broke with it also over issues of authoritarianism and centralism.

After returning from military service in the 1940s, he worked as a foundryman, organized for the CIO in industrial areas of northern New Jersey, and later was an auto worker active in the UAW. He became increasingly skeptical of the orthodox Marxist conception of the industrial working class as a vanguard class. He began working with dissident Marxists as a libertarian socialist, writing numerous articles for the journal *Contemporary Issues*. It was at this time that he began introducing ecological issues to the Left. His series of articles, "The Problem of Chemicals in Food" was published in *Contemporary*

Murray Bookchin. Photo
courtesy of Murray Bookchin.

Issues at the strikingly early date of 1952, and was later published as a book
in German translation in 1955.

By the 1960s, Bookchin had begun elaborating the first fully developed
ecological politics in a series of works that established him as an important
voice in the American ecology movement and as a major critic of technology.
His first book to be published in this country, *Our Synthetic Environment,*
was called by René Dubos "the most comprehensive and enlightened book
on the environmental crisis." Appearing in 1962, this was a pioneering work,
preceding even Carson's *Silent Spring* in posing crucial issues concerning ecological degradation. In 1965, he published *Crisis in Our Cities,* which began
his extensive analysis of urbanism and the decline of the city.

It was also during the 1960s that Bookchin wrote the first of a long series
of essays that established his place as an influential radical social theorist.
"Ecology and Revolutionary Thought" (1963) and "Toward a Liberatory Technology" (1964) were epochal in uncovering the far-reaching implications

of ecology for a social theory and practice, and in showing the possibilities for alternative, emancipatory courses of technological development. Perhaps the most notable essay of this period was "Listen, Marxist!" (1969), a devastating critique of traditional Marxism and its recycled versions of the 1960s. This work was widely reprinted and translated into many languages, and it exerted considerable influence on the development of a non-Marxist New Left, rooted in the anarchist, utopian, and communitarian traditions.

The 1960s were also a time of intense political activity for Bookchin. In 1963, he founded the Citizens Committee on Radiation Information, a group to fight the construction of the Ravenswood Reactor in the New York Metropolitan area. He edited the group's publication, *Radiation Information*, and authored a pamphlet that was instrumental in achieving the rejection of the project by the New York City Council. During 1964, he worked with the Congress on Racial Equality, and was arrested with CORE at the New York World's Fair protests. In 1965, he helped form the East Side Anarchists, a group active in the developing Lower East Side counterculture community, and the Torch Bookstore, a center for left libertarian literature. He also founded Ecology Action East, one of the first radical ecological organizations, and wrote its manifestos, including the widely reprinted "The Power to Destroy, the Power to Create." In 1967, he helped form the Anarchos group, and was the major writer for its publication, also called *Anarchos*. One of Bookchin's most important contributions at this time was the introduction to the American New Left of the concept of the "affinity group." This organizational form was developed over many decades by the Spanish anarchist movement. Rejecting the hierarchical militantism typical of the Left, it proposed a revolutionary political movement based on small, intimate groups of friends who shared values and commitments and practiced mutual aid. In 1969, in line with this and other libertarian decentralist principles, Bookchin formed the Radical Decentralist Project (RDP) an anarchist and libertarian socialist faction within Students for a Democratic Society. The RDP became an important tendency and sent about 300 delegates to the 1969 SDS convention.

During the 1970s and 80s, Bookchin continued his political activity, but began focusing increasingly on the project of developing an ecological social theory, and on propagating the message of social ecology through education. From 1974 to 1983 he was Professor of Social Theory in the School of Environmental Studies at Ramapo College in New Jersey. In 1974 he founded the Institute for Social Ecology at Goddard College in Plainfield, Vermont, and Served as its director until 1980, after which he became director emeritus. Most important, he developed the principles of social ecology in a series of important works in philosophy and social theory, most notably, *Post-Scarcity Anarchism, Toward an Ecological Society, The Ecology of Freedom* (his magnum opus), and *The Rise of Urbanization and the Decline of Citizenship*.

In these works, Bookchin develops social ecology into a comprehensive ecological philosophy, based on the fundamental ecological principle of organic unity-in-diversity, and on a dialectical approach that sees all of reality as a process of self-development and self-transcendence. Social ecology, in affirming such a dialectical holism, rejects both the social divisions and the dualistic ideologies that have been central to the history of domination. In opposition to the dualism of hierarchical society, social ecology proposes a principle of *ecological wholeness* that sees the entire course of planetary evolution as a process aiming at increasing diversity and emergence of value. Social ecology thus forms part of a long teleological tradition extending from the ancient Greeks to the most advanced twentieth-century process philosophies. Bookchin avoids the term "teleology" because of its deterministic connotations and its association with a hierarchical worldview. Yet, what is affirmed is that the entire process of development of life and mind has "directiveness," and is a movement toward the greater unfolding of value. There is a tendency (or *nisus*) within substance toward life, consciousness, and self- consciousness.

The evolutionary view presented by social ecology is above all a *developmental* one. For Bookchin, as for Hegel and other dialectical thinkers before him, there is an important sense in which each phenomenon consists of its own history. Each stage of evolution is seen as "grading" into the next, and each successive level as including within it all that has preceded it. "Mind" and "body" are thus seen as mutually developing at every level of evolution, so that each human being incorporates within himself or herself the entire history of mind and body. Social ecology, as a dialectical naturalism, demonstrates that mind, like all phenomena, must be understood as rooted in nature and in history.

Bookchin sees the major obstacle to social and natural evolution to be the long history of human attempts to dominate others and to conquer even nature itself. One of the most distinctive theories advanced by Bookchin is his view that the human urge to dominate nature (a futile, but nonetheless powerful impulse) results from human domination of other humans. He traces the roots of domination to a long history of hierarchy, beginning with the domination of women by men, young by old, and of early communities by political, economic, and religious elites. To the Marxist and traditional leftist focus on economic exploitation as the source of all evils, he counterposes a highly elaborated analysis of a complex system of hierarchy and domination. To the reduction of the problem of ecological crisis by some (though not all) "Deep Ecologists" to a question of "anthropocentrism" and a generalized human exploitation of nature, he offers an analysis of the basis of that exploitation in hierarchical social and political institutions and in human relationships based on domination.

Bookchin counterposes to the long history of domination and hierarchy a submerged and often forgotten "history of freedom" that serves to inspire his utopian vision. Bookchin discovers—in the democratic Greek *polis*, in radical heretical and millennarian movements, and in modern revolutionary movements in their most anti-authoritarian moments—the "forms of freedom" that can give direction to a liberatory future. In pursuing such liberation, social ecology proposes the most positive conception of freedom. "Freedom" signifies for Bookchin not the mere "being left alone" of the liberal tradition, but rather self-determination in the richest sense. As such, it is found to some degree at all levels of being: from the self-organizing and self-stabilizing tendencies of the atom to the level of the entire universe as a vast sphere of evolutionary development. Bookchin finds freedom present in the directiveness of all life, and sees it as reaching its highest development in the self-conscious self-determination of human beings. As nature achieves its highest self-expression in a free human community in harmony with the rest of the natural world, what was seen as "brute" nature finally becomes "free nature."

Bookchin's social ecology sees this planetary evolution as a holistic process, rather than merely as a mechanism of adaptation by individual organisms or species. It sees evolution, not as a process of adaptation by individual organisms, or even by species, but rather as a process that can be understood only by examining the interaction between species and by studying "eco-systems" as complex, developing wholes. Such an examination reveals that the progressive unfolding of freedom (as self-determination and self-directed activity) depends on the existence of symbiotic cooperation at all levels—as Kropotkin pointed out almost a century ago. We can therefore see a striking degree of continuity in nature, so that the free, mutualistic society that is the goal of social ecology is found to be rooted in the most basic levels of being.

According to Bookchin, social ecology's holistic, developmental understanding of organic wholes and their evolution has enormous importance for ethics and politics. Indeed, only if the place of humanity in nature and natural processes is understood can we adequately judge questions of value. We then see our own experience of valuing and seeking the good as part of the vast process of the emergence and development of value in nature and human society. Social ecology sees the biosphere as a whole of which all beings are parts, and a community of which all are members. The common planetary good can be conceptualized only in a nonreductionist, holistic manner.

A basic question that Bookchin poses is the place of humanity in attaining this good. He argues that, in view of the vast transformations of the biosphere already wrought by humanity, our role in the future can hardly be underestimated. But he does not see our function as merely reversing the damage we have already done, as some ecological thinkers would suggest. Rather, humanity's role in nature results from its inextricable interrelationship to the biospheric whole, and from its character as the most richly developed realm of being to emerge thus far in the earth's evolutionary self-realization. We cooperate with natural evolution through our own self-development.

To say this is not to adopt an "anthropocentrism" that makes humanity the final or even the only end of nature. But neither does it imply a narrow "biocentrism" that would ignore evolutionary developments for the sake of "biosphere egalitarianism." Bookchin insists, rather, that we must reject all "centrisms" and attempt instead to seek our place within the whole, to situate our good within the larger context of the developing planetary good, and to transform our often narrow rationality into truly planetary reason. In accepting the responsibilities implied by our being "nature rendered self-conscious," we can begin to reverse our presently anti-evolutionary and ecocidal direction, and begin to contribute to the continuation of planetary natural and social evolution.

Bookchin argues that success in this endeavor requires that a new ecological sensibility pervade all aspects of our social existence. This sensibility will consist of a nondominating, nonhierarchical outlook toward other beings and toward nature. What Bookchin has called "the epistemology of rule" is thus replaced by a perspective which he has likened to "a new animism." This outlook recognizes a pervasive subjectivity throughout nature that is latent even within matter itself, and which reaches highly developed form in the self-conscious biosphere. As we attain such a new ecological sensibility, the mutualism found throughout nature attains its highest development in a mutualistic system of values and perceptions. This sensibility will give direction to all the processes of regeneration that are necessary: the regeneration of nature, the regeneration of true human community, and the regeneration of authentic selfhood.

Thus, ecological regeneration is inseparable from social regeneration. Consequently, Bookchin calls for the creation of eco-communities and eco-technologies that restore the balance between humanity and nature, and which reverse the accelerating processes of degradation of the biosphere. Such communities will be a carefully integrated part of their ecosystems (which are themselves natural "eco-communities") and will practice true "economy," the careful attending to and application of "the rules of the household." The extent to which humans can have a desirable impact on the ecosystem can be decided only through careful determination of our abilities to act on behalf of nature and of the detrimental effects of our disturbances of natural balances.

Bookchin argues that all this requires a radical rethinking of the political. Mechanistic organization based on "statecraft" (he refuses to concede the term "political" to conventional, authoritarian politics) and capitalist economic power must be replaced by an organic community regulated through common ecological values and a commitment to a common life. The "post-scarcity" society advocated by Bookchin does not transcend the "realm of necessity" through vastly increased production (as Marx advocated) or by increased consumption of commodities (as capitalism promises). Rather, the eco-community is to achieve abundance through a critical analysis and reshaping of its system of needs (thus overcoming our present "fetishism of needs"). The eco-community will reject the consumption for its own sake typical of capitalist mass society, while multiplying the true social wealth of the community, in such forms as aesthetically pleasing surroundings, edifying work, creative play, fulfilling interpersonal relationships, and the appreciation of nature.

The social forms that will emerge from such a culture will themselves embody the ecological ideal of unity-in-diversity. Bookchin argues that the fundamental social unit in the ecological society must be the "commune" or basic community. His approach is authentically communitarian, in that it sees this level of community, in which humans can develop fully as social beings, as the most essential social, political, and, indeed, ethical sphere. In this, Bookchin carries on the deepest insights of classical politics, which were implicit in the democratic Greek *polis* and in the most profound dimensions of Aristotle's ethics. While Bookchin's ecological anarchism is a scathing critique of all conventional politics, it is also a heroic effort to regain the political in its deepest sense, to re-create an authentic public space, and to recover our long-obscured nature as *politikon zoon*.

Within the eco-community, as depicted by Bookchin, cooperative institutions in all areas of social life will begin to emerge. These will include mutualistic associations for child care and education, for production and distribution, for cultural creation, for play and enjoyment, for reflection and spiritual renewal. Organization in an eco-community is based, not on the demands of power, as is inevitable under capitalist and statist institutions, but rather on the requirements for people's self-realization as free social beings, and for a nondominating human interaction with nature. Such a conception of the political requires that institutions be humanly scaled, decentralized, nonhierarchical, and based on face-to-face interaction.

In such a community, it becomes possible to re-create authentic citizenship and to establish meaningful "grassroots democracy." While consensus, the ideal form of decision making, may be possible for small groups, Bookchin stresses that other participatory forms will be necessary within most cooperative institutions, and certainly at the level of eco-communities. What is essential is that participatory democracy be pervasive and authentic, and that ultimate authority be retained at the level of the local community—the level of lived experience. For Bookchin, "representative democracy" is not only a contradiction in terms, but more important, a dangerous ideological concept.

For this reason, a political form that is of crucial importance is the town or neighborhood assembly. This assembly gives the citizenry an arena in which to publicly formulate its needs and aspirations. It creates a sphere in which true citizenship can be developed and exercised in practice. The community assembly creates a forum through which a highly valued multiplicity and diversity can be unified and coordinated. It thus allows each citizen to conceive vividly of the good of the whole community. Much of Bookchin's work in recent years has been dedicated to the development of a "libertarian municipalism" not only at the level of theory, but also as a political actuality. The municipalist political strategy is, first, to work for ecological and decentralist institutions (such as neighborhood assemblies) wherever possible, then to establish a growing number of libertarian municipalities, and ultimately, as their number multiplies, to reach a condition of "dual power" in which authoritarian institutions can effectively be challenged at the societal level. The long-term goal is the replacement of hierarchical capitalist and statist organization by a confederation of ecological communities. This would be a true ecological democracy.

Bookchin has always insisted that such a possibility depends on a renewal at the most personal level: that of the self. As he has formulated it, social ecology sees the self as a harmonious synthesis of "reason, passion, and imagination." It affirms an ideal of a many-sided self, in which diverse aspects are not repressed, but rather attain a mutually compatible development. The self is seen as an organic whole, yet as a whole in constant process of self-transformation and self-transcendence. On the one hand, there are a respect for the uniqueness of each person and a recognition of individuality: the striving of each toward a good that flows in large part from his or her own nature. But personal development is incomprehensible apart from dialectical interaction with other persons, with the community, and with the whole of nature. The goal is thus the maximum realization of both individuality and social being. The replacement of the "hollowed-out" ego of consumer society with such a richly developed selfhood is one of the preeminent goals of social ecology.

In the 1990s, Bookchin vigorously continued his development of the principles of social ecology and dialectical naturalism. Indeed, his later works (for example, *The Philosophy of Social Ecology: Essays in Dialectical Naturalism*) present many of these ideas in their most philosophically sophisticated form. In addition, he continued work on some of his most important projects, including *The Politics of Cosmology*, a comprehensive critique of the history of the philosophy of nature that promised to be a landmark in its field. Furthermore, he has been an increasingly important voice in the American Green movement helping to shape the principles of Left Green Network and the Youth Greens.

Murray Bookchin's legacy lies above all in his enormous contribution as a visionary thinker. He will be remembered as the foremost theorist in the anarchist tradition since Kropotkin, as one of this century's major exponents of utopianism, as an important theorist of technology, and as a bold innovator in a highly developed ecological social theory.

Bibliography

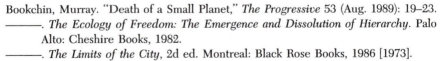
Bookchin, Murray. "Death of a Small Planet," *The Progressive* 53 (Aug. 1989): 19–23.
———. *The Ecology of Freedom: The Emergence and Dissolution of Hierarchy*. Palo Alto: Cheshire Books, 1982.
———. *The Limits of the City*, 2d ed. Montreal: Black Rose Books, 1986 [1973].
———. *The Modern Crisis*. Philadelphia: New Society Books, 1986.

————. *The Philosophy of Social Ecology: Essays in Dialectical Naturalism*. Montreal: Black Rose Books, 1990.

————. *Post-Scarcity Anarchism*, with a new introduction, 2d ed. Montreal: Black Rose Books, 1986.

————. *Remaking Society*. Boston: South End Press, 1989.

————. *The Rise of Urbanization and the Decline of Citizenship*. San Francisco: Sierra Books, 1984.

————. *Toward an Ecological Society*. Montreal: Black Rose Books, 1980.

————. "Will Ecology Become the Dismal Science?" *The Progressive* 55 (Dec. 1991): 18–21; responses, *ibid.* 56 (March 1992): 5–8.

Bookchin, Murray, and Dave Foreman. *Defending the Earth*. Boston: South End Press, 1990.

Bookchin, Murray, and Demitrios Roussopoulos, eds. *The Anarchist Papers*. Montreal: Black Rose Books, 1986.

Clark, John. "The Social Ecology of Murray Bookchin," in *The Anarchist Moment: Reflections on Culture, Nature and Power*, by John Clark (Montreal: Black Rose Books, 1984).

Eckersley, Robyn. "Divining Evolution: The Ecological Ethics of Murray Bookchin," *Environmental Ethics* 11 (Summer 1989): 99–116; discussion, *ibid.* 12 (Fall 1990): 253–74.

John Clark

LESTER BROWN (1934–)

Founder of Worldwatch Institute, environmental activist

Lester Brown worked throughout the 1960s in a series of governmental and organizational positions related to agriculture and foreign agricultural policies. He stood out as a person who was able to see global perspectives. He had a low-key and informative activism that sought to educate a broad public about problems in the global environment. In 1963, Brown wrote an extended report on the state of the world's natural resources while he was working for the U.S. Department of Agriculture (USDA). This report made the cover of *U.S. News and World Report* and became one stimulus for the emerging environmental movement. He went on to become an advisor to the secretary of agriculture on issues of foreign agricultural planning. After that, he worked for the International Agricultural Development Service (IADS) and continued to speak out on the depletion of resources and on the need for change. His most important achievement probably has been the founding of the Worldwatch Institute (WI) in 1974, an organization which he continued to direct.

Brown was born in 1934 and grew up on farmland in New Jersey near the Delaware River. He remembers being influenced by a "great man" series of books, in large print, that was designed for children. He was pleased that so

Lester Brown. *Source*: Library
of Congress

many of the founding fathers had been active in agriculture. At an early age
he decided to spend his life growing tomatoes. At the age of fourteen he and
a brother began a tomato-growing business with a used tractor and some
leased land. The operation eventually became one of New Jersey's largest. He
was growing and selling 1.5 million pounds of tomatoes a year, and now had
visions of being the biggest tomato farmer in the world. Even in the 1990s,
he proudly displayed photos of twelve-foot-high tomato plants. He later recalled that "farming is all I ever wanted to do with my life. You have to know
soils, weather, plant pathology, entomology, management, even politics. It's
the ideal interdisciplinary profession."

Following his graduation from Rutgers in 1956, with a B.A. in agricultural
science, he spent six months in India through an exchange program developed
by the 4-H Clubs. His experiences in Indian villages changed his life. Although he went back to growing tomatoes when he returned to the United
States, this no longer seemed like exciting work. Soon he took a job at the

"foreign section" of the USDA. He began to develop a global view of food resources. At the same time, he got an M.A. at the University of Maryland in agricultural economics.

After only four years with the USDA, he assembled a famous study on world resources. The secretary of agriculture for President Lyndon Johnson, Orville Freeman, pulled Brown out of the lower bureaucracy and elevated him to the policy councils, saying that "you sketched the problems. Now you have to do something about them." Brown became the USDA's resident specialist on global issues. He advised the secretary of agriculture on his overseas agricultural policies. He worked for the International Agricultural Development Service throughout the late 1960s and early 1970s, while earning an M.A. in public administration from what is now called the Kennedy School of Government, in Cambridge, Massachusetts. His job was to increase food production in underdeveloped countries.

Brown was then enthusiastic about the possibilities of a Green Revolution, where better seeds and cultivation practices could solve the problems of poverty and hunger. He asserted that this technology was the most crucial historical event since the steam engine. (Later, he admitted that population growth devoured most of the gains.) Brown left the federal government in 1968, after Richard Nixon's election. He wrote several important works and, in 1974, received $500,000 from the Rockefeller Brothers Fund. He used this award to establish the Worldwatch Institute, located in the District of Columbia. He gathered a staff of young idealists just out of college. They were expected to be "professional generalists," rather than narrow specialists with advanced degrees.

The institute became a generally respected think tank on environmental issues and a clearinghouse for environmental information. WI educates about problems and recommends specific changes. It avoids all political affiliations and steadfastly refuses to lobby. Brown has asserted that "the world is filled with specialists who dig deep burrows into the earth and bring up these nuggets of insight, but there's no one up on top pulling it all together. That's our job." WI has published many occasional papers and books, including (since 1984) an annual "state of the world" checkup on the planet's vital signs. This latter volume regularly sold more than 200,000 copies a year, being distributed in a dozen languages in more than 120 countries. It became a major source of revenue for the institute.

Brown has been described as one of the world's most influential thinkers and was given a $250,000 "genius award" by the MacArthur Foundation in the late 1980s. As a man also renowned for his "conspicuous frugality," it was not surprising that when he was asked what he intended to buy for himself, he responded: "I am thinking of maybe buying a 10-speed bike."

Although the work of the institute has commanded a wide audience across the globe, it has not been without controversy. The late Julian Simon, a conservative economist and advocate of population growth, stated flatly that agricultural economists have disdain for Lester Brown's writing. Brown has admitted that he often uses sources that may not be academically acceptable, but which he believes give clues to the nature or extent of a problem. These odds and ends of information help him to make predictions about world food production, patterns of global hunger, and environmental problems.

Despite this controversy, Brown's audience has included policymakers. He regularly makes reports to the World Bank on issues of environment and Third World development. Television magnate Ted Turner annually buys copies of the *State of the World* and gives them to the country's top political and business leaders.

Brown's farming background and his experience in India led him to develop concepts of the environment, beginning with human food production and expanding outward in logical patterns until it encompassed the entire biosphere. This starting point is important when trying to understand his work and its widespread acceptance. This is a conservative route to fairly radical ideas of societal change. Whenever possible, Lester Brown points to simple changes in lifestyles and priorities which can create huge changes in resource usage if taken in the aggregate. When all of these simple changes are taken together, however, they create a picture of a fundamentally new society, a conserving and austere world of caring people. It is a modest approach to revolution, and Brown's most effective weapon has been education.

His basic beliefs and philosophies have changed little except to broaden and include issues which overlap. His basic goal is the achievement of a sustainable society, one which could maintain itself at a steady state indefinitely. This means that energy and resource usage could not increase and must rely on renewable sources. Population growth must slow to little or nothing and the entire global community must accept the task of providing for the maintenance of the biosphere.

Brown points to current trends in energy and resource use, and in population growth. He extrapolates these trends to show how a change in direction is required if a crash is to be avoided. The "vital signs" of the planet are interrelated. A negative trend in one often impacts on or exacerbates others. His work, for example, has investigated how increased energy usage in the West has depleted the world supply of fossil fuel to the point that the Third World cannot expect development based on this resource. There isn't enough fossil energy to increase the living standards of all those people by basing their economies on those fuels. This example points to the size of the population in the "developing" world and the speed at which it is increasing. The two seemingly disparate trends of energy and population synergistically affect Third World development.

Brown's analysis points to several steps or subgoals toward the broader ideal of a sustainable society. Each of these subgoals has a host of issues and problems which are associated with it and which must be addressed as part of the greater problem. In a 1982 Worldwatch Paper, Brown and Pamela Shaw out-

lined the six most crucial steps toward the achievement of a sustainable society. All of these are recurring themes in his work and will be considered
briefly below.

One theme which frequently recurs is the need for the stabilization of world
population. In the introduction to his 1978 book *The Twenty-Ninth Day*,
Brown pointed to the rampant increase in human population and its interference with the natural systems that humans require to sustain themselves. He
emphasized four major biological systems on which humans depend for food
and raw materials: oceanic fisheries, grasslands, forests, and croplands. All but
the last of these are natural systems which humans have barely altered. In
large areas of the world the pressures of increasing human demand on these
biological systems have reached the "carrying capacity" of these systems. In
other words, the productive capacity of these vital systems is impaired. The
increasing population will have a smaller and smaller food resource base.

The answer to this problem is (as always) education; the further problem,
however, is getting the knowledge to the people who are making the babies.
Reprioritizing foreign aid monies, insisting on family planning, focusing on
birth control and sex education, and making clear the problems of population
growth to everyone are the means toward stabilizing the human population.
He pulls no punches in his assessment, asserting that without family planning
and population control most countries are unlikely to avoid depressed living
standards, and it will be impossible to avert such disasters as famine and mass
migration.

One of the steps toward sustainability, to which WI and Brown give great
credence, is the protection of the world's croplands. Perhaps the emphasis on
this problem has something to do with Lester's agricultural background, but
he argues the point with great eloquence and instills one with a sense of
urgency with respect to the issue. Soil erosion, desertification, and urban
sprawl are the primary reasons he sees for the loss of cropland and the depletion of topsoil, which he says can be seen in every country. This reduces
the capacity of the earth to support the number of humans and increases the
amount of land needed for food production, thus exacerbating the pressures
humans are placing on the biosphere. In addition, the loss of topsoil has
changed the nature of the aquatic ecosystems adjacent to the cropland, clogging them with silt and decreasing the depth to which sunlight can permeate,
creating new and less diverse systems than would exist there without human
intervention.

In the introduction to the 1991 *State of the World* Brown notes that since
the first Earth Day in 1970, the world has lost over 200 million hectares of
tree cover, roughly the area of the United States east of the Mississippi River.
Reforesting the world is central to the achievement of a sustainable society.
The planet's forests are important links in planetary climate systems and car-
bon and oxygen cycles, and the treasure troves of species diversity. In addition, forests serve to trap rainwater so that it can percolate down to aquifers.

In areas where the forests have been depleted, runoff during rains has caused massive soil erosion, clogging streams with silt and wasting topsoil, while the aquifers often continue to decline even in wet years. WI has tracked the decline of forests on all continents, especially in places where the population uses fuelwood as a primary energy source. He points to a need for massive governmental intervention and reforestation efforts to stem the tide in all countries.

Essential to the very idea of a sustainable society is the concept of a conserving and austere humanity, which uses less "stuff" and reuses or recycles most of what it does use. This new society must establish much lower levels of waste production than are currently present, especially in the industrialized world. Brown sees this as the only means by which the limited resources of our small planet could possibly continue to sustain us indefinitely.

Here again this relatively simple assertion points to a host of simple—and a few painful—lifestyle changes which, taken in the aggregate, present an entirely new society. The act of separating one's garbage is simple and may not take a great deal of time, but a society of people who separate and recycle their garbage and decrease the amount of waste in their production and distribution processes, is one that understands its place in the biosphere.

One of the main reasons for recycling and reusing materials is that of conserving energy. The conservation of energy is another step toward a sustainable society. The key here is efficiency. If a society uses what it has in the most efficient manner, it can do much more with it. The more efficient a society becomes, the closer it moves toward sustainability. Brown notes that the potential for conservation in both the Third World and the industrialized world is immense. Most of the change required for sufficient energy conservation is at the household level. It is a long list of small, medium, and large changes which must add up to a drastic decline in energy use.

The last of the six steps to a sustainable society which appear in Brown's writing is the development of renewable energy sources. Renewable energy is energy derived from sources which do not suffer depletion if managed well. This step seems almost obvious to Brown due to the depletion of the energies upon which our current economies are built. Oil will be gone in only a few decades at current extraction rates. Reliance on coal could alleviate some of the pressure for renewables, but the greenhouse gases and other pollution associated with the burning of coal make it an unlikely candidate, and eventually it will be used up as well. Renewable energy sources are the only route to sustainability.

These are the steps needed to reach a sustainable society. If one were to look at the changes needed just to make these steps achievable (much less to achieve them in reality), these could be boiled down to three which recur in Brown's writings: (1) governmental reprioritization; (2) redefinition of security in environmental terms, which would lead to a decrease in military spending to free the needed capital for the transition; and (3) the alteration of personal lifestyles and values. These are all so interrelated that it is difficult to see any occurring without the others. It is only a change in personal values which will allow for a redefinition of security and force governments to reprioritize toward more environmentally sound, sustainable options.

Lester Brown's method for achieving the changes required for a sustainable society has always been education. He believes that if people understand the extent of the problems and the changes needed to alleviate those problems, the job is half done. Worldwatch Institute is a facilitator for that knowledge and toward that change. Brown's genius lies in his ability to tell what needs to be done and what will happen if it isn't done. He tracks what is happening so that when the information is needed, it is available.

Brown's style has been reflected in the Worldwatch Institute. It is learned and learning, powerful because of the force of facts, but relaxed in its presentation, and yet serious about change. Lester Brown's assertions are not very different from those of other environmentalists. It is his quiet activism, combined with his broad knowledge, that led to his acceptance in circles where environmentalists are not often heeded.

Bibliography

Brown, Lester. *Building a Sustainable Society.* New York: W. W. Norton, 1981.

Brown, Lester, Christopher Flavin and Sandra Postel. *Saving the Planet: How to Shape an Environmentally Sustainable Global Economy.* New York: W. W. Norton, 1991.

Brown, Lester, et al. *State of the World* (an annual volume). New York: W. W. Norton, 1984-present [11 vols. 1994].

Brown, Lester, Hal Kane, and Ed Ayres. *Vital Signs, 1993: The Trends that Are Shaping Our Future.* New York: W. W. Norton, 1993.

Flavin, Christopher, and Sandra Postel. "A Planet in Jeopardy," *The Futurist* 26 (May/June 1992): 10–14.

Hackman, Sandra, and Mark S. Miller. "The State of the World: An Interview with Lester Brown," *Technology Review*, July 1988, p. 50+.

Pacher, Leo. "Lester Brown" (interview), *The Mother Earth News*, Sept./Oct. 1986, pp. 96–105.

Sean M. Enright

BARRY COMMONER (1917–   )

Environmental activist, professor, biologist

If the term "radical" has strong overtones of "outsider" for many of those profiled in this volume, that connotation may not be appropriate for Barry Commoner. Indeed, he could be considered a pillar of the establishment.

Barry Commoner. Copyright
Washington Post; Reprinted
by permission of D.C. Public
Library.

Commoner published in journals and magazines ranging from *Science* to the
New Yorker to *Field and Stream*. He appeared on the cover of *Time* in 1970.
He ran for president on the Citizen's party ticket in 1980. By 1992 he had at
least eleven honorary degrees, eight literary or public service awards, and was
founder, board member, or advisor to twenty organizations and five publications. Although he has been a persistent critic of federal environmental
policies, he once received a standing ovation after castigating an audience of
Environmental Protection Agency officials.

These accomplishments are not bad for a son of Russian immigrants. Indeed, Commoner has been an exemplar of the American dream. He overcame
considerable early problems. His parents lost their savings in the Great Depression, and his father, a tailor, worked until he was blind. Barry enrolled at
Columbia University with enough money to attend for one semester. He then
worked his way through college. There was considerable student activism
during those years. There were campus rallies for the radical government then

fighting for its survival in Spain, protests against lynchings in the South, and Socialist and Communist meetings to support various causes allied with union movements. As Commoner later remembered: "I'm a child of the Depression." The period either radicalized him or made him at least unusually sensitive about social problems.

In 1937, he graduated with honors in zoology from Columbia University. He continued his studies at Harvard University, receiving his doctorate in biology in 1941. After naval service in World War II, he spent most of his teaching career, from 1947 to 1981, at Washington University, in St. Louis. He established there the Center for the Biology of Natural Systems, which in 1981 moved with him to Queens College in Brooklyn, New York. But it was in St. Louis, out in the heartland of America, that he began to change the way that people think about the natural environment. Washington University was often unhappy about the impact of his work on some of the school's financial contributors. Commoner reported that his environmental activism, combined with his criticisms of the war in Vietnam, often got him stopped on the campus by Chancellor Thomas Eliot. The chancellor was likely to open his remarks this way: "I want to tell you how much of our endowment we have lost this week because of you."

While Commoner's early work focused on conventional biological research, already by then mid-1950s his long-standing attachment to progressive causes had brought him to be concerned with radioactive fallout and a nuclear test ban. He was a founder of the St. Louis Committee for Nuclear information. This "public interest" science organization developed a nationwide baby tooth survey that proved the human ingestion of radioactive Strontium 90 nationwide, helping to promote an atmospheric test ban treaty. The organization put out a mimeographed newsletter, titled at first *Information*, and then *Nuclear Information*. Its subsequent changes symbolized Commoner's own development. It became *Scientist and Citizen* in 1964 under the auspices of the Scientists Institute for Public Information, for which Commoner served on the board of directors. In 1968 it became the well-known glossy magazine *Environment*, put out by the Helen Dwight Reid Foundation. At each step, the magazine's critical focus broadened along with Commoner's. By 1970, Commoner appeared on the cover of *Time* magazine as the Paul Revere of ecology, a founding father of the contemporary environmental movement.

There is a paradox here. Commoner's goal of social transformation driven by environmental concerns places him both in the establishment and with the radicals. "The environment" has become a mainstream issue, and extensive bodies of law and regulation seek to protect it. Commoner has insisted, however, that environmental quality cannot be assured by incremental, regulatory efforts. He claims it requires fundamental changes in the political and economic systems not only of the United States but of the world. This conviction of the necessity for radical reform is what allows him to remain a critic of many of the very policies and movements which his work has, in significant ways, inspired.

How did Commoner, unlike so many of his radical colleagues, gain such a wide audience, even if all of his message was not acted on? As we will see, the answer to this question points to the heart of Commoner's thinking. While the environmentalism that formed in the 60s was often accused by its critics of being Luddite or technophobic, Commoner has been an eloquent spokesman for modern technology. This optimism accounts both for his dissatisfaction with the political and economic world as it is, and for the willingness of that world to heed much of his message. To understand this phenomenon, we must expose the three layers of Commoner's argument: from the scientific, through the normative, to the technocratic.

Commoner's books often begin with the enunciation of certain scientific principles, be they the laws of ecology or of thermodynamics, and proceed to examine in light of those laws, and of scientific research, specific areas of environmental concern, such as energy policy or water pollution. Having established that a problem exists, he proceeds to discuss what to do about it, again looking to the lessons of science. Thus, readers of his books, if reviews are any indication, often come away with the impression that Commoner, speaking with the authority of a professional trained scientist, has presented an *essentially* scientific analysis of the causes and cures of environmental ills. Where earlier conservationists may have appealed primarily to morality, aesthetics, or economics, Commoner enlisted science to defend the environment. His work has been vital to giving science a prominent place in environmental discussions.

Yet this first impression is not entirely accurate. At least since *Science and Survival*, his first book addressed to a broad public, Commoner has emphasized both the power and limits of science in solving environmental problems. Science, Commoner says, can describe the risks and benefits of what we are doing, or would like to do, but it cannot tell us what balance of risk and benefit we should prefer. Science can tell us the consequences of living in a polluted environment, but it cannot tell us that we ought not want to live in such an environment, or how much we should want to alter those circumstances. The most pressing questions of what to do are based on value judgments. Science cannot help us in this realm. Indeed, Commoner has alleged that science itself is ultimately based on value commitments whose truth it cannot establish. On this basis he has articulated some interesting doubts about the possibility of there being an objective scientific assessment of *any* situation.

While Commoner's wholehearted assertion of the distinction between facts and values would have put him at odds with some of his fellow radicals, his attacks on scientific objectivity were very much part of the 1960s radical ethos. Yet *Making Peace with the Planet* contains what appears to be a defense of scientific objectivity against a Reagan administration EPA that was doing the kind of risk-benefit analyses that Commoner once seemed to think appropriate to environmental decision making. He says these EPA reports are "masquerading as objective science." Is Commoner most disturbed by the alleged lack of scientific objectivity of the EPA, or because his value commitments differ? He had, after all, justified a central place for values in decision making. Perhaps this makes it possible for critics to charge him with being a better ideologue than a scientist.

In any case, since Commoner strives to turn our attention from science to values, if we are to understand him, we must enquire into those values he believes should inform our understanding of environmental issues. This second layer of his thinking, the normative, points us to what Commoner has called "the S word: Socialism."

Since the early 1970s, Commoner's books have argued that it is the quest for profits by private industry that has brought us ever more polluting technologies. This link is crucial to his critique of the free enterprise system. So long as decisions about what to produce and how to produce it are governed by profitability, there will be powerful incentive for polluting technologies. Hence it is necessary to govern these decisions not privately, but publicly, not for the good of owners and investors but for the good of society as a whole.

Called variously "social thrift," "the right of political governance," or "the social governance of production decisions," Commoner's socialism is not a completely worked out political philosophy. While *The Poverty of Power* interpreted the energy crisis with fairly orthodox Marxist categories, and argued that the long delayed crisis of capitalism was finally in full flower, Commoner has not been dogmatic about the content of his socialism. He early admitted that existing socialist regimes were hardly ecological paradises. (After the virtual collapse of communism, and the full public revelation of ecological horrors that were once only known or suspected by specialists, he came to blame this situation in part on the importation by the East of flawed Western technologies.) Because of the failures of most socialist regimes, he recognized that his notions of social governance needed more work. He hoped that "wholly new political forms" would spring from "the inherent impulse to extend democracy."

What is the basis of his faith? Commoner has no illusions about the forces that block social transformation. His hope partly rests on his ability to convince people of the seriousness of ecological problems. While Commoner remains unsatisfied with what has been done about environmental problems, it must be some comfort to him that they occupy center stage in so many people's concerns. Another element of his faith in our ability to transform our relationship with nature has to do with his long-standing attempt to link the environment with other progressive causes such as disarmament and ending discrimination. Hence his 1980 presidential campaign for the Citizen's party, his 1984 support for the Jesse Jackson (6*) Rainbow Coalition, and his later work with progressive elements within the Democratic party. But both of these factors pale in comparison to his expectations for the rationalization of life that modern technology could create.

While Commoner is known, among other things, for popularizing the notion that "nature knows best," he has never meant that phrase in any romantic sense of a return to a less technologically sophisticated way of life. Indeed, with the rise of so-called radical or deep ecology, he has been unrelentingly critical of the tendency to read human beings and their achievements out of the world. Instead, he has taught that human productive technologies need to mimic and accommodate themselves to natural constraints and cycles. Nature recycles; human technologies must recycle. The waste of cities could fertilize the countryside; industrial by-products could be reclaimed. Nature is sun driven, so our economy should be predicated on solar power, the ultimate renewable resource. The extraordinary rearrangement of American life called for in *The Politics of Energy*, Commoner's blueprint for a solarized technology and economy, is testimony to how Commoner's socialism is less about equality, liberty, or fraternity than about the redesign of everything from power plants to streetlamps to create efficient energy production and consumption.

And yet, in another sense, is this vision so radical? Americans have long been technological optimists. While napalm and the drug culture made "better living through chemistry" a problematic slogan in the 1960s, isn't Commoner promising a similar progressivism? To see the distinctive character of his outlook, we must note one final aspect of his thought. Commoner has approved sometimes the decentralized political institutions of the United States. But his thinking overall favors a highly centralized, planned, and expertise-driven governance that might be described as technocratic. Commoner understands that something about American democracy makes it inappropriate to call in the experts to make decisions, but that may limit American democracy's ability to deal well with the environment. As he notes in *The Closing Circle*, the problem with existing socialist regimes is that they do bad central planning. The theoretical advantages of such planning for dealing with environmental problems are, for Commoner, too obvious to require elaboration.

Or again, take his interpretation of the so-called NIMBY (not in my backyard) syndrome that hinders the siting of waste facilities and power plants. Commoner argues that, contrary to appearances, people are not really concerned first about their own backyards. Such an outlook might suggest both the need for and the limits of decentralized decision making. Instead Commoner suggests that the NIMBY syndrome shows a social concern about "the environment that they share with the rest of society." If that were true, then people would presumably be happy with authoritative decisions made centrally with the whole of society in mind.

One of Commoner's most powerful metaphors for understanding his view of an environmental crisis comes from *The Closing Circle*. There, in good Enlightenment fashion, he likens nature, with its delicate balances and complex relationships, to a watch. He turns the metaphor around by suggesting that our present interactions with nature are like trying to improve the watch by poking a pencil in its works. But there is an unexpressed side to the likeness. If we are to live properly with nature, we must presumably know it with all the precision that we know watches, which are artifacts of our making. Human beings can learn to make nature serve our ends by obedience to her. Perhaps Commoner is a radical in a literal sense. His work brings to our attention the often obscured rationale for modern technology begun long ago by thinker like Francis Bacon and René Descartes. The flaws he sees in society today, and the potential that technology has to eliminate them, serve as reminders of unfulfilled promises.

Bibliography

Anderson, Alan. "Scientist at Large," *New York Times Magazine*, Nov. 7, 1976, pp. 58–76.

Commoner, Barry. *The Closing Circle: Nature, Man, and Technology*. New York: Alfred A. Knopf, 1971.

———. "Ending the War against Earth," *The Nation*, April 30, 1990, pp. 589–92.

———. *Making Peace with the Planet*. New York: Random House, 1990. Reviewed: *In These Times*, May 2–8, 1990, p. 20; *New York Times*, April 14, 1990, p. 16; *New York Times Book Review* 95 (April 22, 1990): 15–16.

———. *The Politics of Energy*. New York: Alfred A. Knopf, 1979.

———. *The Poverty of Power*. New York: Alfred A. Knopf, 1976.

———. *Science and Survival*. New York: Viking Press, 1966.

Ehrlich, Paul R., and John P. Holdren. "Critique [of *The Closing Circle*]," *Bulletin of the Atomic Scientists*, May 1972, pp. 16–27. (See also Commoner's response in the same issue.)

Krier, James E. "The Political Economy of Barry Commoner," *Environmental Law* 20: 11 (1990): 11–33.

Lens, Sidney. "The Commoner Touch," *The New Republic*, Aug. 23, 1980, pp. 15–17.

Nixon, Will. "Barry Commoner: Earth's Advocate," *In These Times*, July 10–23, 1991, pp. 4–5.

Paehlke, Robert C. *Environmentalism and the Future of Progressive Politics*. New Haven: Yale University Press, 1989.

Rubin, Charles T. "Environmental Policy and Environmental Thought: Ruckelshaus and Commoner," *Environmental Ethics* 11 (Spring 1989): 27–51.

Strong, Dennis H. *Dreamers and Defenders: American Conservationists*, 2d ed. Lincoln: University of Nebraska Press, 1988: 221–45.

Charles T. Rubin

PAUL EHRLICH (1932–   )

*Population biologist, professor, author,
environmental activist*

Dr. Paul Ehrlich began his career as a prominent American activist in 1968 with the publication of his first book written for the general public, *The Population Bomb*. The book was monumental in its content, its message, and the breadth of its reception among the American people. It quickly gained recognition as one of the all-time greatest ecological best-sellers. By 1990 it sold over three million copies. It was not long before the author himself, and all that he stood for, gained in both popularity and infamy. But, before exploring the message in and uniqueness of *The Population Bomb*, let us temporarily digress so that we may first understand Paul Ehrlich's personal history and how he came to formulate the philosophy and worldview that make him notorious today.

Paul Ralph Ehrlich was born in Philadelphia on May 29, 1932, the son of William Ehrlich, a salesman, and Ruth Rosenberg Ehrlich, a public school Latin teacher. During his childhood the family moved to Maplewood, New Jersey, and it was here that Ehrlich attended high school. During approximately the same time, naturalists were increasingly replacing economists as society's doomsayers, and these same individuals dominated the conservation movement of the time. In 1948 two renowned naturalists authored their own best-selling books to forecast the coming environmental crisis. They were Fairfield Osborn, then president of the New York Zoological Society, who wrote *Our Plundered Planet*, and William Vogt, an ornithologist, who wrote *Road to Survival*. The latter of these writers had a particularly important influence on the young Ehrlich's life. Vogt introduced him to the interrelated issues of population, resource depletion, and famine.

As a high school student, Paul Ehrlich was already forging ahead as a naturalist, researcher, and writer. He spent much time at the Museum of Natural History, where he was encouraged by a mentor to study butterflies, conduct research, and publish papers, despite the fact that Ehrlich was only a high school student at the time. In 1953 Ehrlich graduated with an A.B. from the University of Pennsylvania, and shortly thereafter on December 18, 1954, he married Anne Fitzhugh Howland. Ehrlich continued his studies in biology, graduating with his master's degree from the University of Kansas in 1955, and his Ph.D. from the same institution in 1957. The title of his dissertation was "The Morphology, Phylogeny and Higher Classification of The Butterflies (Lepidoptera: Papilionoidea)."

As an entomologist, or insect biologist, Ehrlich received a post-doctoral

Paul Ehrlich. Photo courtesy of Paul Ehrlich.

fellowship from the National Institutes of Health to study at the Chicago Academy of Sciences, the genetics and behavior of parasitic mites. After this project, in 1959, Ehrlich was hired by Stanford University as an assistant professor of biology. In 1962 he was made associate professor, in 1966 a full professor in the Department of Biology; and in 1967, Bing Professor of Biology. During these early years of his career Ehrlich did fieldwork in Jasper Ridge Biological Experimental Area, the Rocky Mountain Biological Laboratory in Crested Butte, Colorado, and as far away as Africa, Alaska, Australia, Mexico, Southeast Asia, and the South Pacific. The fruits of his labor included numerous articles, many presentations, and several books. For example, in 1960 Ehrlich authored the book *How to Know the Butterflies*, and Anne H. Ehrlich illustrated the guide. In 1963 Ehrlich wrote a textbook entitled *The Process of Evolution* with colleague Richard W. Holm. Ehrlich had become a well-respected scientist.

Paul Ehrlich experienced a turning point in his life and career in 1966. As a long committed naturalist and engaged student of science, his head and intellect understood the problems of world population growth and resource depletion. However, it was only on a trip to India (with his wife Anne and their only daughter, Lisa Marie) that Ehrlich understood these global issues in human, personal, and emotional terms. He writes:

> One stinking hot night in Delhi, [we] were returning to our hotel in an ancient taxi. The seats were hopping with fleas. The only functional gear was third. As we crawled through the city, we entered a crowded slum area. . . . The streets seemed alive with people. People eating, people washing, people sleeping. People visiting, arguing and screaming. People thrusting their hands through the taxi window, begging. People defecating and urinating. People clinging to buses. People herding animals. People, people, people, people. . . . the dust, noise, heat, and cooking fires gave the scene a hellish aspect. (*The Population Bomb*, p. 1)

It appears that this incident ignited a fire in Ehrlich, inciting him to apply his knowledge of science for the benefit of humanity.

Ehrlich intensified his frequent lectures on world population growth, the inherent and interrelated dilemmas therein, and what needed to be done. It was on one such occasion that David Brower, then executive director of the Sierra Club, heard Ehrlich's speech on population problems and urged him to put his thoughts into print for the general public before the 1968 presidential election. Brower introduced Ehrlich to a contact at Ballantine Books. The resulting book, *The Population Bomb*, rose on the best-seller list. Ehrlich's career as a scientist became coupled with his newfound roles as population control advocate and environmental activist.

Ehrlich's new status became further solidified when he appeared with Johnny Carson on "The Tonight Show" to discuss *The Population Bomb*. The two previous guest appearances were short and disappointing. Ehrlich saved the show by prompting questions to Johnny during commercials and answering them in a monologue-like manner with great finesse between the breaks. What was originally scheduled to be a standard interview turned into a nearly one-hour-long discussion about the information and assertions contained in Ehrlich's book. His performance generated more than 5,000 letters to the television network. Ehrlich personally received between 20 to 25 letters per day for some time afterwards. This unprecedented "Tonight Show" coverage of an author and his book, combined with the provocative message Ehrlich was conveying, skyrocketed Paul Ehrlich into the public spotlight. Although this new activist-advocate role was not actively sought by Ehrlich, he did not retreat into the polite and quiet world of academia. It is for this reason that we have not lost sight of him since his emergence in 1968.

What was the controversial message in *The Population Bomb* that caused such a literary, environmental and political furor? Simply stated, Ehrlich warned that if we continued, on our current (1968) trajectory of growth and consumption, the world would soon face unprecedented disease, famine, destruction, and death. Painting with a broad brush dipped in elementary scientific principles, Ehrlich told his readers a sorrowful story about humanity's future, while simultaneously inciting his audience to respond on a personal level.

Ehrlich introduced the problem by explaining that in UDCs (underdeveloped countries) population was increasing as food production was decreasing. Growing hunger, misery, and death seemed imminent. At the same time, explained Ehrlich, the population in ODCs (overdeveloped countries) was expanding, consumption was increasing, environmental quality was declining, and resources were becoming depleted. Ehrlich also pointed out that the number of years it takes to double the world population was decreasing ominously. From 8000 B.C. to A.D. 1968 the doubling time for the world population went from 1,000,000 years to 1,000 years to 200 years to 80 years, and finally to a terrifyingly brief 35 years.

Overpopulation was defined by Ehrlich by two simple criteria: if you cannot produce enough food to adequately feed all of the people, and you cannot adequately dispose of all the wastes those people create, then humanity has reached a state of overpopulation.

He eloquently reminds his readers that one cannot rationally and dispassionately discuss the scientific causes of a given phenomenon, namely, population growth, without concurrently considering the human dimension. For this reason, he further stated that "overpopulation occurs when numbers threaten values" (*The Population Bomb*, p. 9). After all, his definition of overpopulation utilizes consumption patterns as a key variable which sets the maximum number of people who can live without creating a problem of overpopulation. This introduces the issues of international growth and development, racism, colonialism and transnational equity. Further, Ehrlich identifies the relationship between birth and death rates as most critical to understanding overpopulation. He provides two solutions to overpopulation: a lower birth rate or a higher death rate.

Ehrlich advocates population control; in fact, he promotes the long-term goal of zero population growth. He vociferously warns that not dealing with these difficult and interrelated issues today will result in nature forcing death upon humanity to solve our problems for us. Thus, not paying heed to his warnings and avoiding difficult decisions is equivalent to choosing increased suffering and early death for large portions of humankind. It became clear to many readers that the growing number of humans was becoming a severe threat to the health of the planet and the health of humanity, and that each individual is responsible for a part of the problem.

Ehrlich actively promoted the idea that population growth must be halted and environmental protection must occur if we are going to save ourselves and our habitat. He went further by stating that the United States has a responsibility as the most powerful superpower and the largest consumer per capita to clean its house first, and then administer the appropriate aid worldwide. He states, "Remember that above all, more than half of the world is in misery now. That alone should be enough to galvanize us into action, regardless of the exact dimensions of the future disaster now staring Homo Sapiens in the face" (p. 180). In this same vein, he proposed an analogy to Pascal's famous wager which held that we should believe in God, because if there is a god we will gain everything, and if there isn't we will have lost nothing. It is the same with environmentalism. When it comes to protecting the planet, we can never be too careful, because the stakes are too high. If we successfully curtail population, quality of life for the whole of humanity is likely to increase and the environment will flourish, but if we do not and Ehrlich proves correct, we lose it all. For this reason, Ehrlich calls for a new culture which emphasizes human values and foresight instead of material values and short-term vision.

Ehrlich tells the readers of his 1968 landmark book what people can do to help diffuse the population bomb, and in so doing help the environment and secure their own quality of life. His entire last chapter is dedicated to this endeavor. Ehrlich recommends the following: join ZPG (zero population growth—the national organization Ehrlich himself founded) and other activist groups, write letters to officials, organize action groups, and proselytize friends and relatives. Ehrlich hopes that people will take responsibility for their own future. They need the vision, tools, and knowledge necessary to empower them to take action. This unique feature is introduced in *The Population Bomb*, and it returns as a trademark in each of Ehrlich's later books. In *Earth* (1987) he and Anne Ehrlich even remind readers that our problems are not caused by an uncontrollable "Planet Mongo" on a destruction course with Earth, but that we cause our own problems and the solutions to them are, therefore, within us. For Ehrlich, understanding the often complex web of blame for global problems is the first step to solutions. He encourages his readers to look to their own behavior, society, culture, and politics to understand these intricate connections. He consistently emphasizes the importance of looking to the future.

Thus, in *The Population Bomb* Ehrlich set the tone and themes which frequently reappear in his later writings. Specifically, he educates readers in all of the basic principles related to the issue being discussed by writing in an understandable manner and frequently using short stories, scenarios, analogies, and real global examples to illustrate his points and convey his message. Ehrlich also masterfully combines scientific tenets with political criticism, social critique, and values clarification, while resisting the use of dogma. This combination characterizes Ehrlich's writings for the general public; and it also parallels his own personal development from pure scientist to social scientist, political critic, and environmental activist. He and co-author Richard L. Harriman state (1971):

> Scientists in our society are often criticized for being too narrow, but when they step outside the narrow field of training they are invariably told they should stick to their specialty. We prefer to risk the latter criticism. In many areas . . . we have gone beyond the boundaries of our formal training to try to seek solutions to human problems. We see no other course than for scientists in all fields to do the same—even at the risk of being wrong.

Again, this theme permeates his writing. He is vigilant about reminding his readers that much of what he says does not fall into the rubric of population biology, and that science cannot be correct all of the time.

Ehrlich has set tremendous goals for himself. He maintains his high stature as an accomplished biological scientist, while also acting as a dedicated advocate for population control, environmental protection, scientific literacy, and technological control. He summarizes the bulk of his activist work by explaining to his audience that three factors influence the quality of life and integrity of the environment. They may be summarized as follows:

$$\text{Total Env. Destruction} = \text{(population levels)} \times \text{(amount of affluence per person)} \\ \times \text{(technologically induced damage)}$$

This equation embodies a whole host of domestic and international issues, none of which Ehrlich shies away from in his role of activist.

Ehrlich works to achieve his goals primarily by writing books. He also lectures frequently, is active in ZPG, participates in government hearings, speaks at world conferences, and appears regularly on television. In each forum, he attempts to discuss issues in their entirety. That is, he embraces a holistic or systems approach. This gives his work an international dimension, and it expands the breadth of his advocacy beyond the immediately obvious issues of population and environment, to species extinction, nuclear war, issues of race, and immigration.

Ehrlich is convinced that the basic principles of ecology would forever change our worldview. We will come to see all life as interrelated and interdependent parts of nature upon which we humans depend for survival. Implicit in this message is the fact that all interactions between people, cultures, governments, and the like are also interrelated, and therefore not exempt from scrutiny or blame.

Finally, his arguments for action are vaguely leftist. Ehrlich advocates decentralization, community cohesion, grassroots activism, and direct political action. He reprimands the political, economic, and religious systems alike for their role in sustaining inequality, avoiding meaningful discussions about and action to improve population problems, and sacrificing other sentient beings and the environment in "the spirit of folly" surrounding growth-mania. He has called those in industry, government, energy leaders and spokespersons the "worst and dullest." Ehrlich has denounced resource-based imperialism, encouraged public vigilance to insure democracy, and even published a list of Senate and House good guys and bad guys. Despite such criticisms, Ehrlich has for the most part avoided marginalization and maintained his status as respected scientist.

The central problem with Ehrlich's work today is that the doom and gloom forecasts for the 1980s that he enumerated in *The Population Bomb* were not fulfilled. By some standards he has been proven blatantly wrong. For example, contrary to his original predictions, global life expectancy has increased, infant mortality has decreased, and more of humanity lives better today than in 1968. However, Ehrlich looks at things differently. He sees acid rain, topsoil erosion and depletion, increasing food shortages (as of 1988, the United States no longer is able to feed itself, let alone all those worldwide depending on our exports), deforestation, species extinction, and perhaps most ominously, global warming and the Greenhouse Effect. Ehrlich's response to critics is simple: he admits that his time frame was off, but he points out that given the afore-mentioned global problems, some things have gotten worse faster than he had anticipated. He had not envisioned the depth and breadth of current problems in 1968.

Let me share with you an interesting story. In 1980 Ehrlich agreed to a $1,000 bet proposed by Julian Simon, pitting the philosophies of the "doom-ster and boomster" against one another. Simon, an economist, had for years attacked the claims made by Ehrlich regarding population, environment, re-sources, and growth mania. Thus, in 1980, Simon made an open offer to Mal-thusians to bet on the future price of five metals on the assumption that if population increased and resources became scarce, prices would rise. Ehrlich seized the opportunity, and with colleagues John Harte and John Holdren, bet $1,000 on the future cost of chrome, copper, nickel, tin, and tungsten. During the decade, world population increased by more than 800 million and the store of metals did not expand. Yet, when the bet came due in October 1990, the value of all five metals had declined and Simon had won. However, there is no indication that this embarrassed Ehrlich. He had even anticipated this possibility in his books. You see, the value of the metals dropped because of more efficient mining practices and the advent of improved technology. Ehrlich has repeatedly agreed that technology can be beneficial in the short-term, but that reliance on technology to save humanity from itself in every case is nothing other than frivolity.

Ehrlich's 1990 book, authored with his wife, Anne, was entitled, *The Pop-ulation Explosion*. In it, the Ehrlichs contend that the population bomb has detonated. More than 200 million people have died of hunger and related diseases since 1968, human population is still increasing, and consumption is on the rise. The world has hundreds of billions fewer tons of topsoil and 100 trillions fewer gallons of water than in 1968. Famine and plague are possible, and seemingly unrelated problems are intimately tied to population, such as homelessness, crime, drugs, global warming, war, acid rain, racism, and sexism.

While most of Ehrlich's arguments, pleas, and warnings have not evolved much over the last twenty-three years, they have expanded, become more urgent, and in some ways more sophisticated. His activism and writings have, however, maintained their clarity, educational theme, and goal of empowering readers to become personally involved and responsible. The one new principle that has clearly emerged since 1968 is that of mindset. In his 1989 work, *New World New Mind*, co-authored with Robert Ornstein, they develop the intriguing idea that the human mental system is failing to comprehend the modern world due to a tragic mismatch between our human nervous systems and the ever-changing realities of the world in the late twentieth century. The result of this cultural, biological, and evolutionary lag is the inability to comprehend the multiplicity of related crises facing humankind and the incapacity to rationally and effectively deal with them. According to Ornstein and Ehrlich, this amounts to nothing less than a human loss of control over our own future.

Thankfully, this has not occurred for Paul Ehrlich. He has lectured on more than 150 campuses, testified before Congress numerous times, and written hundreds of scientific articles, a series of textbooks, and more than twenty books for the general public. In addition, he is a Fellow with California Academy of Science, the American Academy of Arts and Science, and the American Association of Advanced Science. Ehrlich is a member of countless organizations, among them the National Academy of Science, the Society for the Study of Evolution, Society of Systematic Zoology, American Society of Naturalists, the Lepidopterists Society, and an Honorary life member of the American Museum of Natural History. Finally, Ehrlich has been the recipient of numerous awards and honors, the most notable of which are Sierra Club's John Muir Award, the 1987 World Wildlife Federation Medal, his position as president of the Center for Conservation Biology in 1988, his appointment as an NBC News Correspondent in 1989, the award of a five-year MacArthur Foundation Grant for $345,000 in 1990, and finally, he was co-recipient of the Crafoord Prize in 1987, which is the ecologist's equivalent of a Nobel Prize.

Over the years, Paul R. Ehrlich has become perhaps the nation's most respected and outspoken advocate on population and environmental issues. Throughout, he has sustained himself and his activism by remaining at Stanford University as Bing Professor of Biology. He has shed the stereotype of "narrow academic" and resisted a full-time commitment to activism. It is precisely for this reason that Ehrlich has not only survived twenty-three years of part-time activism and advocacy, but thrived on it. He has admirably combined the traits necessary to pursue a "life of the mind" in the world of scientific academia with the personal characteristics and charisma required of a "life of the heart and hand" in the realm of advocacy and activism. Further, it is primarily due to his combined proficiencies in science and social science (sociology, political science, philosophy, history, anthropology, and economics) that Ehrlich's books and messages have been so widely received, discussed, and regarded.

Nonetheless, it may be somewhat frustrating for Paul Ehrlich to be so well respected, outspoken, and famous, and yet remain powerless in the face of skyrocketing population figures, escalating consumption, and spiraling environmental destruction. Perhaps he sometimes identifies with Cassandra, the prophet of doom in Greek mythology. Cassandra reneged on a promise to Apollo, who then cursed her with the gift of prophecy that no one would heed. In 1987, Ehrlich was a prominent figure in the Cassandra Conference which was called to celebrate the human potential to avert tragedy. We can hope that Dr. Ehrlich will fight the curse of Cassandra and continue his good work.

Bibliography

Bailey, Ronald. "Doomsday Rescheduled," *Forbes* 145 (April 2, 1990): 81+.

Berreby, David. "The Numbers Game," *Discover* 11 (April 1990): 42–43+.

Boyce, James K. "The Bomb Is a Dud," *The Progressive* 54 (Sept. 1990): 24–25.

"Ehrlich, Paul," in *Contemporary Authors*, vol. 8, New Revision Series. Detroit: Gale Research, 1983: 152–53.

Ehrlich, Paul R. *The Cold and the Dark: The World after Nuclear War*. New York: W. W. Norton, 1984.

———. *The Machinery of Nature*. New York: Simon and Schuster, 1986.

———. *The Population Bomb*, rev. and expanded. New York: Ballantine Books, 1978 (1968).

Ehrlich, Paul. R., and Anne H. Ehrlich. *Earth*. New York: Franklin Watts, 1987.

———. *Healing the Planet: Strategies for Resolving the Environmental Crisis*. Reading, MA: Addison-Wesley, 1991. Reviewed: *BioScience* 42 (April 1992): 301–2; *New York Times Book Review* 96 (Dec. 15, 1991): 23; *Technology Review* 95 (April 1992): 68–70; *Washington Monthly* 23 (Nov. 1991): 42–46.

———. *The Population Explosion*. New York: Simon and Schuster, 1990. Reviewed: *BioScience* 40 (Nov. 1990): 778–79; *Ecologist* 20:6 (1990): 238–39; *New York Times Book Review* 95 (April 1, 1990): 27.

Ehrlich, Paul R., and Richard L. Harriman. *How to Be a Survivor*. New York: Ballantine Books, 1971.

Ehrlich, Paul R., John P. Holdren, and Earl Ferguson Cook. *The Cassandra Conference*. College Station, TX: Texas A & M University Press, 1988.

Mann, Charles C. "How Many Is Too Many?" *The Atlantic Monthly* 271 (February 1993): 47–50, 52–53, 56, 59, 62–64, 66–67.

Ornstein, Robert, and Paul R. Ehrlich. *New World New Mind: Moving toward Conscious Evolution*. New York: Doubleday, 1989.

"Too Many People; The Population Bomb Keeps Ticking," *Washington Post*, Aug. 23, 1992, C3.

Kathryn Wald Hausbeck

DENIS HAYES (1944–   )

Earth Day organizer, environmentalist

In April 1970 Denis Hayes, acting upon a proposal made by Senator Gaylord Nelson of Wisconsin, organized the first Earth Day in order to raise American environmental consciousness. Hayes became a leading environmental advocate and in 1990 helped celebrate Earth Day's twentieth anniversary.

The son of a paper mill worker and a beautician, Hayes was raised in the small town of Camas, Washington, where sulfide aromas marred the pristine Northwest. Restless, he left home and, after spending three years hitchhiking around the world, attended Stanford University, where he served as student body president.

Following graduation, he attended Harvard Law School and originally worked on Earth Day 1970 as a class project. Hayes, however, quickly concluded that the effort, if it was to succeed, needed a full-time organizer. Accordingly, he quit law school and moved to Washington, where he lived cheaply in a sparsely furnished apartment.

Devoting almost all his time and energy to Earth Day, Hayes drew attention with his creativity and wit. On his office wall a sign read, "Earth—love it or leave it." Asked why his group did not distribute bumper stickers, he explained that automobiles polluted.

Hayes tapped a large reservoir of goodwill. Environmentalists were excited by the prospect of increasing public awareness for what they saw as the major problem facing humanity. "The problem isn't technological," said Hayes. "The problem is a matter of values." He added that the issue was "specie-cide."

Businessmen contrasted the wholesome and good-natured Hayes with militant blacks, anti-war radicals, and hippies. Even if corporate executives did not entirely share his outlook and worried about the high cost of cleaning up the environment, they saw no harm in joining a celebration of the earth.

Activist students, frustrated by the anti-war movement's failures, turned to Earth Day with relief. The media, played shrewdly by Hayes, were fascinated by Earth Day, but they also developed, as Hayes had hoped, more concern for the environment.

On Earth Day, April 22, 1970, the public marched in parades, listened to songs and speeches, and enjoyed a number of clever publicity stunts. Around the country an estimated twenty million people participated. The most immediate consequence of Earth Day was congressional passage of the Clean Air Act.

Hayes moved to channel Earth Day's energy into a larger and more robust environmental movement. This effort was unsuccessful, because the excite-

Denis Hayes. Copyright *Washington Post*; Reprinted
by permission of D.C. Public Library

ment at the novelty of Earth Day could not be repeated. Attempts to celebrate
later Earth Days were mostly ignored.

From 1975 to 1979 Hayes represented the Worldwatch Institute, a Wash-
ington-based environmental research and policy group. Focusing his attention
on developing alternative sources of energy, he wrote frequently for the press
and came to advocate solar power, especially in his book *Rays of Hope* (1977)
and through the celebration of Sun Day, May 3, 1978.

In 1979 President Jimmy Carter named Hayes to head the Solar Energy
Research Institute in Golden, Colorado. He directed a budget of $90 million.
After the Reagan administration took office, with its free market, oil-based
philosophy, Hayes was dismissed in 1981. He moved to the San Francisco
Bay Area, finished law school, practiced as a corporate attorney, was president
of Green Seal, and, by the early 1990s, a director of a multi-million-dollar
foundation in Seattle.

Hayes, although somewhat mellowed and less confident of immediate drastic improvement in the world's environment, retained his faith. In 1990, he helped to organize the twentieth anniversary of Earth Day. The Earth Day committee established a national headquarters and fifteen regional offices, raised perhaps $4 million, and stimulated events during April 16–22 in about 3,600 U.S. cities and in more than 140 countries. Activities were supported by a broad coalition that included Greenpeace, the Rainbow Coalition, the National Education Association, the Sierra Club, and Planned Parenthood. Hayes urged the creation of a "citizens' army" that could push individuals, corporations, and the world's governments toward a "decade of the environment." He restated his own credo: "I have always felt that there is something to be offered by the environmental movement, by ecology as a science, that would transcend psychology and really transform in an almost religious way the ongoing principles of society."

Critics like Kirkpatrick Sale characterized the Earth Day in 1990 as either naively individualistic (ignoring the profound structural bases for environmental degradation) or excessively reliant upon corporate and governmental experts and regulations. Earth Day, for Sale, was primarily a "one-time splash" that left behind no permanent grassroots organizations or networks. Supporters of Earth Day, even if they conceded its limits, were likely to argue that the 1970 and the 1990 events had contributed to fundamental shifts in the environmental values of the general public. This was reflected in the rapid growth in conservation groups (from 200 in 1975, according to the National Wildlife Federation, to 350 in 1990, with more than twelve million members), a proliferation of environmental lawyers (from several hundred in the 1960s to about 20,000 in 1990), more than $100 billion a year spent by public and private agencies to reduce pollution, broader environmental concerns by most of the old-line conservation societies, and considerable struggle to pass and enforce higher environmental standards. The basic question, of course, remained. Was this enough?

Bibliography

Cahn, Robert, and Patricia Cahn. "Did Earth Day Change the World?" *Environment* 32 (Sept. 1990): 16–20+.

"Ecotopia" Greene by $85 million," *Los Angeles Times*, March 3, 1993, AS:1 (on the creation and management of the Bullitt Foundation in Seattle).

Gilbert, Bill. "Earth Day Plus 20, and Counting," *Smithsonian* 21 (April 1990): 46–52, 54, 56.

Hayes, Denis. "Earth Day 1990: Society's Challenge," *Environmental Science and Technology* 24 (April 1990): 403–4.

———. "Earth Day 1990: Threshold of the Green Decade," *Natural History*, April 1990, pp. 55–58+.

———. "Looking Back, Looking Ahead—Earth Day: One View," *EPA Journal* 16 (Jan./ Feb. 1990): 24–26.

———. *Rays of Hope: The Transition to a Post-Petroleum World*. New York: W. W. Norton, 1977.

Lewis, Thomas A. "A New Day Must Dawn," *National Wildlife* 28 (Feb./March 1990): 4–7.

Reed, Susan K. "Twenty Years After He Mobilized Earth Day, Denis Hayes is Still Racing to Save Our Planet," *People Weekly* 33 (April 2, 1990): 96–97+.

Sale, Kirkpatrick. "The Trouble with Earth Day," *The Nation* 250 (April 30, 1990): 594–98.

Shabecoff, Philip. "Veteran of Earth Day 1970 Looks to a New World," *New York Times Biographical Service* 21 (April 1990): 366–67.

Steinhart, Peter. "Bridging the Gap," *Audubon* 92 (June 1990): 20–23.

W. J. Rorabaugh

RALPH NADER (1934–   )

Founder of the Center for Study of Responsive Law, campus-based Public Interest Research Groups, Public Citizen, Congress Watch; author of Unsafe at Any Speed; *public interest activist*

Ralph Nader burst into the American consciousness in 1965 with the publication of his book on automobile safety, *Unsafe at Any Speed*. This book, a passionate attack on the American automobile and its makers, detailed the tendency of General Motors' Corvair to swing out of control on curves. Nader's work shook the auto industry in general and GM in particular. After GM admitted in congressional hearings that it had hired a private investigator to follow Nader and attempt to uncover compromising information about his personal life, Ralph Nader became a household name and his book a bestseller. The $425,000 GM paid Nader for invasion of privacy enabled him to launch his Washington, D.C.–based Center for Study of Responsive Law. This group was instrumental during the late 1960s and 1970s in getting legislation through Congress designed to protect the American consumer. By the end of the 60s, Nader had single-handedly launched a nationwide consumer protection movement spearheaded by college students, known as Nader's Raiders, and the campus-based Public Interest Research Groups, known as PIRGs.

Born on February 27, 1934, of Lebanese parents in Winsted, Connecticut, Ralph Nader graduated from Princeton University in 1955, and Harvard Law School in 1958. The years between graduation from law school and the publication of *Unsafe at Any Speed* were somewhat inchoate ones. Nader served six months as an army cook; established, and neglected, a law practice in Hartford; published his first article on auto safety in *The Nation*; traveled in Europe, the Soviet Union, Africa, and Latin America as a free-lance journalist; and eventually wound up in Washington, D.C., as a consultant to Assistant Secretary of Labor Daniel Patrick Moynihan. For a year, Nader immersed

Ralph Nader. *Source*: Library of Congress

himself in arcana of the federal highway and traffic safety program, which led to his ground-breaking book on GM's criminal negligence in 1965. His skillful use of the media, combined with his Don Quixote–like attack against a corporate megalith, established him as the modern-day champion of the little person.

The central thesis of *Unsafe at Any Speed*—that car manufacturers make big profits from the sale of vehicles they know to be unsafe—was not an idea original to Nader. It was pursued, however, with his own brand of doggedness and unjaded outrage. The origins of Nader's preoccupations are somewhat obscure and he is reluctant to discuss "influences." His immigrant parents were unusually active and aware citizens who imbued in Nader an intense patriotism and a mistrust of power. Both of these, combined with Nader's own passion to see justice done, led him to attend courtroom hearings as a five-year-old, and peruse the pages of the *Congressional Record* as a teenager.

When Nader was twelve he read Upton Sinclair (author of *The Jungle*, the 1906 exposé of the federal meat inspection system), and Lincoln Steffens, two of America's most renowned muckrakers. As a student at Princeton, he was mystified by campus-wide indifference to heavy spraying of the pesticide DDT, which left students wiping their faces and dead birds littering the sidewalks. Nader began to focus on cars after years of hitchhiking in which he would come upon accidents, including one in which a little girl had been decapitated by a glove compartment door which flew open upon impact. By the time he began to focus as a law student on the crimes committed by corporations against consumers, he had developed a desire "to give voice to voiceless people." As he put it, "I got an intellectual and almost an aesthetic pleasure from it."

As one of Nader's biographers, Charles McCarry, has written, "All the legislation in which Nader has interested himself has to do with the protection of the human body." According to McCarry, Karl Marx's writings had a tremendous appeal for Nader, particularly Marx's ability to sensitize workers to the harm being done them by factory bosses in the early stages of the industrial revolution. By the mid-1960s, at any rate, Nader had found his life's work in taking on the "bosses." It remains largely unchanged, although its scope has grown, and the methods for pursuing it have evolved.

True to his somewhat paradoxical nature, Nader can be described as a radical reformer. He aims, not to overthrow capitalism per se, but to effect a democratic revolution whereby citizens are empowered and corporations made their tools rather than vice versa. Nader seeks a cleaner, safer, and ultimately saner American society of full-time citizens. His quest has led him to champion legislation regulating highway safety, public health, food additives, industrial pollution, congressional reform, and federal pay. He was the major force behind passage of the Occupational Health and Safety Act (1970) and the Freedom of Information Act (1975). He also has taken his campaigns away from Washington, to the states; he played a central role in passing a California initiative that rolled back the cost of auto insurance. Overseas, he has been to various Eastern European countries and the former Soviet Union, states which he feels are ripe for consumer and environmental protection movements.

Nader's methods have changed during three decades of his activism. After his success against GM in the late 1960s gave him a media and financial base from which to operate, he established the Center for Study of Responsive Law. This set out to investigate and reform governmental agencies like the Federal Trade Commission, and push wave after wave of legislation through Congress. During this early period, Nader demonstrated a gift for taking esoteric subjects out of the hands of government and corporate experts and turning them into public causes. Although he was skillful at getting legislation through Congress, Nader became disillusioned by the frequency with which the new laws were watered down and congressional allies lost interest in causes that he felt were critical to the survival of average Americans.

By the end of 1971, Nader had created a dozen mechanisms, including the Public Interest Research Group, the Center for Auto Safety, and Public Citizen, to deal with issues ranging from clean water to corporate responsibility to the antitrust system. He began to move away from relying solely on Congress to advance his goals (in fact, Nader turned his investigative powers against Capitol Hill in the early 70s), and focused instead on finding ways to build, as he put it, an "organized consumer constituency to provide a functioning counterpoise to industry-backed priorities." Nader found the average American asleep in the early 70s, and citizen action at a "primitive" stage. To awaken the giant, he formed a nationwide organization of students to lobby for the reform of society. Campus-based Public Interest Research Groups (PIRGs) are now familiar entities at colleges and universities across the country.

Nader also forayed into the world of union politics through his 1969 efforts to elect Jock Yablonski the president of the United Mine Workers. Yablonski's candidacy, which was encouraged by Nader, ended tragically in the murder of him and his wife and daughter after Tony Boyle was re-elected. Nader and two of his colleagues also agitated against Union Carbide's polluting of a small West Virginian town and forced the company to clean up its operations.

Nader's frustration with the inertia and corruption of government institutions led him to try to strengthen "noninstitutional sources of power" via the efforts of committed student activists, but also to an active use of the courts, which he views as the most effective, least iniquitous branch of government. Nader has championed the use of class-action and private liability suits as a way of dealing with the damage caused by unsafe cars, pharmaceuticals, fabrics, and construction materials. When questioned about the danger of an overly litigious society, Nader denied that such a society exists: "only a fraction of those injured by negligence or worse ever get a lawyer, much less a settlement, much less a verdict, much less get it upheld on appeal. The few that do break through show companies that they'd better be more careful. And why," Nader goes on, "do you think it's bad to channel conflicts through the courts of law? Otherwise they're suppressed, as they were in Eastern Europe, or they come out in vigilante ways."

With the departure of Ronald Reagan in early 1989, Washington's perfervid anti-regulatory spirit dimmed a little. Nader enjoyed a corresponding upswing in attention and respect from the public and the media and, in his fourth decade of activism, showed no signs of slowing his pace. He had a regular column in *Mother Jones* magazine, and received favorable and unfavorable publicity in journals ranging from *The Economist* to *Vanity Fair* to *Forbes*. He became less reclusive and more overtly populist. He was more willing to sign autographs and go on the stump for the myriad causes that he championed. Nader relished the role of protest politician, going on TV and radio talk shows, drumming up support for public financing of congressional elections or opposition to congressional pay hikes. Nader's speaking fees have steadily amounted to a quarter of a million per year. Funding for Nader's organizations comes from members, foundations, door-to-door canvassing, labor unions, subscriptions, and book sales.

By the early 1990s, there were twenty-five PIRG state chapters on ninety college campuses. The effectiveness of these groups varied, as did the issues which each addressed, but they had become a permanent presence on campuses and had helped politicize members of several generations of students. As this decade began, Nader's Critical Mass Energy Project had its hands full fighting the pro-nuclear support building in response to fears about global warming. The Occupational Safety and Health Law Center was busy defending workers' rights and employee suits. Public Citizen was working with Greenpeace on toxic waste and nuclear energy. And Nader's colleagues were circulating a treatise called the Corporate Decency Act in Warsaw, and helping to organize, train, and fund fledgling East European public interest movements.

In the 1960s, Nader, with his revulsion against materialism and his hunger to right the causes of social injustice, struck a nerve with white middle-class youth who were driven out of the Civil Rights movement by the end of that decade. In the 1990s, although he still did not expound a political philosophy to give meaning to his particular causes, the underlying questions that Nader addressed were profound ones relating to democracy and the exercise of political power. He illustrated these questions (and his answers) in 1992 by both his write-in campaign for the presidency and by the publication of an unusual civics textbook.

Some supporters in New Hampshire convinced him to enter the 1992 presidential primary there, although he believed that no one personality, making promises, could accomplish much. Instead, the American political system required fundamental change. Nonetheless, he traveled in New Hampshire, making various points. First, there should be public funding of candidates such as in Canada, with definite spending limits. Corporate and wealthy donations are really legalized bribery. Even if you don't buy such politicians, you can at least rent them. Second, candidates should have free prime-time radio and TV advertising. The airwaves are, after all, publicly owned, licensed and regulated by the government. Third, ballots should automatically include an option marked "none of the above." This would allow voters to express their displeasure. Nader, during this campaign, sometimes introduced himself in the following manner: "I'm none of the above. I'm running for president. Vote for me" (*New York Times*, Feb. 18, 1992, A17). Fourth, pay increases for the White House and Congress since 1988 should be repealed. The federal government is becoming more and more elitist—plutocratic rather than democratic. The government is cheap with the poor (cutting programs and limiting the minimum wage), while being generous to themselves, savings and loan banks, the military establishment, and (especially through tax cuts) the rich.

Fifth, there should be limits on how long politicians can "serve," such as twelve years.

Since politics should be more than a spectacle, like a parade, he offered various programs that he hoped would allow "new horizons of possibility to spread across the land." He praised the Canadian health care system, which offered comprehensive choices and security "from cradle to nursing home." He urged greater stockholder power in corporations, pro-consumer legislation, cuts in military spending, and "reconversion" of the American economy to civilian needs. To accomplish any of this, he insisted that it was necessary to do more than vote for Nader as a way to send a message to Washington; it was necessary to build a movement. He wanted to be different from most politicians who "leave nothing behind but crushed coffee cups and torn posters on the floor. All that money and effort, and the day after: poof!" (*Washington Post*, Feb. 16, 1992, A33).

As one means to create a new generation of activists, Nader encouraged changes in the school system. In 1992, the Center for the Study of Responsive Law published *Civics for Democracy*, by Katherine Isaac. This criticized textbooks that had abstract charts about politics but no advice about how to become involved. For example, too many civics books ignored or minimized labor, consumer, women's, and environmental movements. Nader argued that teaching civics without teaching activism was like "teaching chemistry without a chemistry lab." Students should be active in local efforts for a safer environment and a more responsive government. Although Nader conceded that local school authorities might be nervous about using such a book, especially since he admitted that "we are determined to make this a movement," he received praise from the head of the National Education Association and the state superintendent of schools in California (*Washington Post*, Dec. 2, 1992, A24).

Ralph Nader has had a long track record fighting for the average American. For him, the nineties promised to be a time when pent-up consumer and citizen frustration might break forth in "a new political movement for real democracy."

Bibliography

Brimelow, Peter, and Leslie Spencer. "Ralph Nader, Inc.," *Forbes* 146 (Sept. 17, 1990): 117–22+; discussion, *ibid.* 146 (Oct. 29, 1990): 128–30.

Brobeck, Stephen. *The Modern Consumer Movement: A Guide to References and Resources*. Boston: G. K. Hall, 1990.

DeParle, Jason. "Eclipsed in the Reagan Decade, Ralph Nader Again Feels the Glare of the Public," *New York Times Biographical Service* 21 (Sept. 1990): 850–51.

Griffin, Kelley. *Ralph Nader Presents More Action for a Change*. New York: Dembner Books, 1987.

Holsworth, Robert D. *Public Interest Liberalism and the Crisis of Influence*. Cambridge, MA: Schenkman Publishing, 1981.

Kelley, Kevin J. "A Party for the Ages," *In These Times*, Feb. 5–11, 1992, pp. 12–13.

Litwak, Mark. *Courtroom Crusaders*. New York: Morrow, 1989: 203–47.

McCarry, Charles. *Citizen Nader*. New York: Saturday Review Press, 1972.

Mayer, Robert N. *The Consumer Movement: Guardians of the Marketplace*. Boston: Twayne, 1989.

Nader, Ralph. *The Big Boys: Power and Position in American Business*. New York: Pantheon Books, 1986.

———. "How Clinton Can Build Democracy," *The Nation* 255 (Nov. 30, 1992): 649, 652–53.

———. "Knowledge Helps Citizens, Secrecy Helps Bureaucrats," *New Statesman* 111 (Jan. 10, 1986): 12–13.

———. "Nader's Nineties," *Mother Jones* 15 (July/August 1990): 24–27.

———. "Passing on the Legacy of Shame," *The Nation* 250 (April 2, 1990): 444–46.

———. "Ralph Nader" (interviewed by William Greider), *Rolling Stone*, Nov. 5–Dec. 10, 1987, pp. 115–16+.

———. "Rip-Off, Inc.," *Mother Jones* 16 (May/June 1991): 16–17.

———. "To Promote Democracy, Bring Pressure on the Media," *USA Today* 120 (March 1992): 89–90.

———. *Unsafe at Any Speed*. New York: Grossman, 1965 (expanded ed., Grossman, 1972).

———. "The World According to Nader" (interviewed by Claudia Dreifus), *The Progressive* 48 (July 1984): 58–61.

"Nader, the Non-Candidate, Presses His 'None of the Above' Campaign," *Washington Post*, Feb. 16, 1992, A33, A36.

"Rallying the Raiders; Nader's Consumer Corps Celebrates Its 20th," *Washington Post*, Oct. 28, 1989, C1. See also Christopher Hitchens, *The Nation*, Nov. 20, 1989, p. 590.

"Ralph Nader," *Current Biography* 47 (April 1986): 35–38.

"Ralph Nader Up Close" (New Day Films, New York, New York).

Sifry, Micah L. "Nader's Progress," *The Nation*, Feb. 17, 1992, p. 185.

———. "The 'None of the Above' Candidate," *The Nation*, Dec. 23, 1991, cover, 800, 801, 816.

Stewart, Thomas A. "The Resurrection of Ralph Nader," *Fortune* 119 (May 22, 1989): 106–8+.

"There Ought to Be a Law; Why Ralph Nader Still Loves to Pick on the Big Guys," *The Washingtonian* 25 (July 1990): 53–59.

Jennifer Scarlott

PART FIVE

RADICAL CULTURE

We learn, when we are children, the accepted patterns of behavior that become central to who we are. We learn what kind of family is "normal." We learn proper roles for male children and female children. We learn whether people with "white" and "nonwhite" skin colors are treated differently. We learn whether English is the only civilized language. These messages, from parents, television, literature, or peers, need not be explicit. If you are black, for example, and the media do not include you, it is like looking into a mirror and not seeing yourself. The message: you don't count.

A child does have a self-image, whether fundamentally positive or negative, by the time formal education begins. This section includes some critics of U.S. education, such as John Holt (*) and Jonathan Kozol (*), while mentioning others, such as Ivan Illich and Herbert Kohl. These critics argue that conventional education does not encourage the student to think independently, but to passively absorb data. This information is biased in favor of ruling elites and may not serve the interests of most people. Furthermore, such education or indoctrination occurs in a setting of educational apartheid. At a prep school, children receive an inside-track ruling-class education. At a crumbling ghetto school, rooms are crowded, social problems severe, and funding minimal. One environment establishes a pattern of success, the other a pattern of failure.

Unequal funding within the public school system has been challenged, along with stultifying racial, sexual, and class biases in textbooks and teachers' assumptions. As a result, it could be argued that public schools have become more integrated (racially, sexually, and culturally) than U.S. society overall, such as churches, neighborhoods, and businesses.

The youth and adults who participated in the progressive movements of the 1960s frequently drew upon the official ideals of this society that they had been taught. Some were angry because reality did not match these ideals; others were optimistic that these ideals could be achieved. Such contradictions were sometimes displayed, for example, in the popular music of this era. Joan Baez (*), Bob Dylan (*), Phil Ochs (*), and Pete Seeger (*) drew upon the fervent morality of civil rights struggles. Some rock music, such as by Country Joe McDonald (*) and John Lennon, expressed critical themes.

The 1960s also brought to wider popularity some of the earlier cultural critics, such as William S. Burroughs, Allen Ginsberg (*), Paul Krassner, and Kenneth Rexroth (*). Some popular writers turned more to social criticism, including Norman Mailer, as in *Armies of the Night* (1968), and Gore Vidal (*).

The cultural ferment that was expressed in literature, music, drugs, and the "underground press" convinced some people that a higher consciousness was evolving that would transform American society. This view was expressed in such popular books as *The Making of Counter Culture* (1969), by Theodore Roszak, and *The Greening of America* (1970), by Charles Reich. Instead, much of it was either defeated or turned into marketable items, such as records, drug paraphernalia, clothes, videos, jewelry, posters, and advertising images. Some critics renounced their earlier views, such as Jerry Rubin (*) and the writing team of Peter Collier (*) and David Horowitz. Some appear to have been co-opted, such as the film star Jane Fonda (*). Others, such as Abbie Hoffman, are dead. A few are relatively isolated within specific racial groups, such as Maulana Karenga (*), or have experienced highly idiosyncratic changes, such as the conversion, by Julius Lester (*), to Judaism. Many, of course, continued their work, such as Irving Howe (*) and his democratic socialism.

SELECTED BIBLIOGRAPHY

General Cultural Criticism

Angus, Ian, and Sut Jhally, eds. *Cultural Politics in Contemporary America*. New York: Routledge, Chapman and Hall, 1989.

Arney, William Ray. *Experts in the Age of Systems*. Albuquerque: University of New Mexico Press, 1991.

Basil, Robert, ed. *Not Necessarily the New Age: Critical Essays*. Buffalo, NY: Prometheus Books, 1988.

Brown, Norman O. *Love's Body*, new edition. Berkeley: University of California Press, 1990 (1966).

Casale, Anthony M., and Philip Lerman. *Where Have All the Flowers Gone? The Rise and Fall of the Woodstock Generation*. Kansas City: Andrews and McMeel, 1989.

Dickstein, Morris. *Gates of Eden: American Culture in the Sixties*, new edition. New York: Penguin, 1989 (1977).

Didion, Joan. *Slouching Toward Bethlehem*. New York: Farrar, Straus and Giroux, 1968.

Gilbert, James B. *Writers and Partisans: A History of Literary Radicalism in America*. New York: Wiley, 1968.

Illich, Ivan. *Deschooling Society*. New York: Harper and Row, 1971.

Kennedy, Liam. "Precocious Archeology: Susan Sontag and the Criticism of Culture," *Journal of American Studies* 24 (April 1990): 23–39.

King, Richard. *The Party of Eros:Radical Social Thought and the Realm of Freedom*. Chapel Hill: University of North Carolina Press, 1972.

Kohl, Herbert. "The Politics of Education," *Z Magazine*, April 199 4, pp. 19–24.

———. "The Politically Correct Bypass: Multiculturalism and the Public Schools," *Social Policy* 22 (Summer 1991): 33–40.

Leigh, Nigel. *Radical Fictions and the Novels of Norman Mailer*. New York: St. Martin's Press, 1990.

Louvre, Alf. "The Reluctant Historians: Sontag, Mailer, and the American Culture Critics of the 1960s," *Prose Studies* 9 (1986): 47–61.

Mogan, Ted. *Literary Outlaw: The Life and Times of William S. Burroughs*. New York: Henry Holt, 1988.

Olendorf, Donna. "Ehrenreich, Barbara," in *Contemporary Authors*, vol. 16, New Revision Series. Detroit: Gale Research, 1986: 104–5.

Passaro, Vince. ' 'William S. Burroughs," in *American Critics: A Collection of Literary Biographies*, supplement three. New York: Scribner's, 1991: 91–110.

Pinsker, Sanford. "Lenny Bruce: Shpritzing the Goyim/Shocking the Jews," in *Jewish Wry: Essays on Jewish Humor*, Sarah B. Cohen, ed. Bloomington: Indiana University Press, 1987: 89–104.

Randall, Margaret. *Albuquerque: Coming Back to the U.S.* Vancouver, Canada: New Star Books, 1986.

———. "Forbidden Utterances: Reason Enough for Exclusion," in *It Did Happen Here: Recollections of Political Repression in America*, Bud Schultz and Ruth Schultz, eds. Berkeley: University of California Press, 1989: 183–94.

———. *Gathering Rage: The Failure of 20th Century Revolutions to Develop a Feminist Agenda*. New York: Monthly Review Press, 1992.

———. *Walking to the Edge: Essays on Resistance*. Boston: South End Press, 1991.

———. "When the Imagination of the Writer Is Confronted by the Imagination of the State," in *Freedom at Risk: Secrecy, Censorship and Repression in the 1980s*, Richard Curry, ed. Philadelphia: Temple University Press, 1988: 169–77.

Randall, Margaret, and Ruth Hubbard. *The Shape of Red: Insider/Outsider Reflections: Ruth Hubbard and Margaret Randall*. Pittsburgh: Cleis Press, 1988.

Reich, Charles. *The Greening of America*. New York: Bantam, 1970.

Rollyson, Carl E. *The Lives of Norman Mailer: A Biography*. New York: Paragon House, 1991.

Roszak, Theodore. *The Cult of Information: The Folklore of Computers and the True Art of Thinking*. New York: Pantheon Books, 1986.

———. *The Making of a Counter Culture: Reflections on the Technocratic Society and Its Youthful Opposition*. Garden City, NY: Doubleday, 1969.

———. *Person/Planet: The Creative Disintegration of Industrial Society*. Garden City, NY: Anchor/Doubleday, 1978.

———. *Unfinished Animal: The Aquarian Frontier and the Evolution of Consciousness*. New York: Harper and Row, 1975.

———. *The Voice of the Earth*. New York: Simon and Schuster, 1992.

———. *Where the Wasteland Ends; Society and Transcendence in Postindustrial Society*. Garden City, NY: Doubleday, 1972.

————, ed. *The Dissenting Academy*. New York: Pantheon Books, 1968.

————. *Sources: An Anthology of Contemporary Materials Useful for Preserving Sanity While Braving the Great Technological Wilderness*. New York: Harper and Row, 1972.

Roszak, Theodore, and Betty Roszak, eds. *Masculine/Feminine: Readings on Sexual Mythology and the Liberation of Women*. New York: Harper and Row, 1969.

Sayres, Sohnya. *Susan Sontag: The Elegaic Modernist*. New York: Routledge, 1990.

Schor, Esther H. "Sontag, Susan," in *Modern American Women Writers*, Elaine Showalter, Lea Baechler, and A. Walton Litz, eds. New York: Scribner's, 1991: 471–83.

"Sontag, Susan," *Current Biography* 53 (Feb. 1992): 51–55.

Sontag, Susan. *Against Interpretation*. New York: Farrar, Straus and Giroux, 1966.

Stone, Albert E. *The Return of Nat Turner: History, Literature, and Cultural Politics in Sixties America*. Athens: University of Georgia Press, 1992.

Thomas, William Karl. *Lenny Bruce: The Making of a Prophet*. Hamden, CT: Archon Books, 1989.

Von Hoffman, Nicholas. *We Are the People Our Parents Warned Us Against*. Chicago: Ivan R. Dee, 1989 (1968).

Wald, Alan. *The New York Intellectuals: The Rise and Decline of the Anti-Stalinist Left from the 1930s to the 1980s*. Chapel Hill: University of North Carolina Press, 1987.

Whitfield, Stephen J. *A Critical American: The Politics of Dwight Macdonald*. Hamden, CT: Archon Books, 1984.

Wolfe, Tom, ed. *The Purple Decades: A Reader*. New York: Farrar, Straus and Grioux, 1982.

Wresin, Michael. *A Rebel in Defense of Tradition: The Life and Politics of Dwight Macdonald*. New York: Basic Books, 1994.

Zinn, Howard. *The Politics of History*, 2d ed. Urbana: University of Illinois Press, 1990.

Communes; Counterculture

Berger, Bennett. *The Survival of a Counterculture*. Berkeley: University of California Press, 1981.

Charters, Ann, ed. *The Portable Beat Reader*. New York: Penguin, 1992.

Fairfield, Richard. *Communes USA: A Personal Tour*. Baltimore: Penguin, 1972.

Fellowship for Intentional Community, and Communities Publications Cooperative. *Directory of Intentional Communities: A Guide to Cooperative Living*. Rutledge, MO: Sandhill Farm, 1991.

Grogan, Emmett. *Ringolevio; A Life Played for Keeps*. New York: Carol Publishing Group/Citadel Press, 1990 (1972).

Hoffman, Abbie. *The Best of Abbie Hoffman*, Dan Simon, ed. New York: Four Walls Eight Windows Press, 1989.

Jezer, Marty. *Abbie Hoffman, American Rebel*. New Brunswick, NJ: Rutgers University Press, 1992.

Johnson, Anne Janette. "Hunter S. Thompson," in *Contemporary Authors*, vol. 23, New Revision Series. Detroit: Gale Research, 1988: 421–24.

Kanter, Rosabeth Moss. *Commitment and Community: Communes and Utopias in Sociological Perspective*. Cambridge: Harvard University Press, 1972.

McKeen, William. *Hunter S. Thompson*. Boston: Twayne Publishers, 1991.

Miller, Timothy. *American Communes, 1860–1960: A Bibliography*. New York: Garland Publishing, 1990.

———. *The Hippies and American Values*. Knoxville: University of Tennessee Press, 1991.

Mungo, Ray. *Beyond the Revolution: My Life and Times Since Famous Long Ago*. Chicago: Contemporary Books, 1990.

———. *Famous Long Ago* (a one volume reprint of *Famous Long Ago* [1970], *Total Loss Farm* [1970] and *Return to Sender*]1975]). New York: Carol Publishing Group/Citadel Press, 1990.

Perry, Charles. *The Haight-Ashbury*. New York: Random House, 1984.

"Ram Dass," in *The New Age Encyclopedia*, J. Gordon Melton, Jerome Clark, and Aidan A. Kelley, eds. Detroit: Gale Research, 1990: 373–74.

"Sanders, Ed," in *Contemporary Literary Criticism*, vol. 53. Detroit: Gale Research, 1989: 303–10.

Sanders, Ed. *Tales of Beatnik Glory* (two volumes in one). Secaucus, NJ: Citadel Press, 1990 (1975).

———. *Thirsting for Peace in a Raging Century: Selected Poems, 1961–1985*. Minneapolis: Coffee House Press, 1987.

Sturgeon, Tony. "An Interview with Edward Sanders," *Contemporary Literature* 31 (Fall 1990): 263–80.

"Thompson, Hunter S.," in *Contemporary Literary Criticism*, vol. 64. Detroit: Gale Research, 1986: 425–31.

Veysey, Laurence. *Communal Experience: Anarchist and Mystical Counter- Cultures in America*. New York: Harper and Row, 1973.

Wagner, Jon, ed. *Sex Roles in Contemporary American Communes*. Bloomington: Indiana University Press, 1982.

Wavy Gravy [Hugh Nanton Romney]. *Something Good for a Change: Random Notes on Peace Thru Living*. New York: St. Martin's Press, 1992.

Whitfield, Stephen J. "The Stunt Man: Hoffman (1936–1989)," *Virginia Quarterly Review* 66 (Autumn 1990): 565–84.

Whitmer, Peter O., with Bruce Wyngarden. *Aquarius Revisited: Seven Who Created the Sixties Counterculture That Changed America*. New York: Citadel Press, 1991 (1987).

Yinger, Milton. *Countercultures: The Promise and the Peril of a World Turned Upside Down*. New York: Free Press, 1982.

Drugs

Bloom, Fred. "Marijuana Culture," *The Antioch Review* 42 (Summer 1984): 277–90.

Furst, Peter T. *Hallucinogens and Culture*. San Francisco: Chandler and Sharp, 1976.

Gaskin, Stephen. *Haight Ashbury Flashbacks*, 2d ed. Berkeley: Ronin Publishers, 1990.

Horowitz, Michael, Karen Walls, and Billy Smith. *An Annotated Bibliography of Timothy Leary*. Hamden, CT: Archon Books, 1988.

Leary, Timothy. *Changing My Mind, Among Others: Lifetime Writings*. Englewood Cliffs, NJ: Prentice-Hall, 1982.

———. *Flashbacks: A Personal and Cultural History of an Era*. Los Angeles: Jeremy P. Tarcher, 1990.

——. *The Politics of Ecstasy*. Berkeley, CA: Ronin Publishing, 1990 (1968).

——, Robert Anton Wilson, and George A. Koopman. *Neuropolitique*, rev. ed. Scotsdale, AZ: New Falcon Press, 1991.

Lee, Martin A., and Bruce Shlain. *Acid Dreams: The CIA, LSD, and the Sixties Rebellion*, 2d ed. New York: Grove Weidenfeld, 1992.

Miller, Richard Lawrence. *The Case for Legalizing Drugs*. New York: Praeger, 1991.

O'Brien, Geoffrey. *Acid Dreams: Chapters from the Sixties*. New York: Viking, 1988.

Stevens, Jay. *Storming Heaven: LSD and the American Dream*. New York: Atlantic Monthly Press, 1987.

Szasz, Thomas. *Our Right to Drugs: The Case for a Free Market*. New York: Praeger, 1992.

Walker, William O., III, ed. *Drug Control Policy: Essays in Historical and Comparative Perspective*. University Park, PA: Pennsylvania State University Press, 1992.

Wolfe, Tom. *Electric Kool-Aid Acid Test*. New York: Farrar, Straus and Giroux, 1968.

Fiction; Poetry

Bloom, Harold, ed. "Gary Synder," in *Twentieth-Century American Literature*. New York: Chelsea House, 1987. 7: 3715–23.

Corso, Gregory. *Mindfield*. New York: Thunder's Mouth Press, 1989.

Gitlin, Todd, ed. *Campfires of the Resistance: Poetry from the Movement*. Indianapolis: Bobbs-Merrill, 1971.

Johnson, Anne Janette. "Synder, Gary," in *Contemporary Authors*, vol. 30, New Revision Series. Detroit: Gale Research, 1990: 416–20.

"The Literature of the Beat Generation," in *Twentieth Century Literary Criticism*, vol. 42. Detroit: Gale Research, 1992: 50–102.

Neal, Larry. "The Black Arts Movement," in *Afro-American Writers After 1955*, ed. Thadious M. Davis and Trudier Harris, vol. 38 of *The Dictionary of Literary Biography*. Detroit: Gale Research, 1985: 293–300. (There is a separate entry on Neal, pp. 225–30.)

Smith, David L. "The Black Arts Movement and Its Critics," *American Literary History* 3 (Spring 1991): 93–110.

Music

Anderson, Terry. "Pop Music and The Vietnam War," *Peace and Change* 11: 2 (1986): 51–65.

Aquila, Richard. *The Old Time Rock and Roll: A Chronicle of an Era, 1954–1963*. New York: Schirmer Books, 1989.

Bindas, Kenneth J., and Craig Houston. " 'Taking Care of Business': Rock Music, Vietnam and the Protest Myth," *Historian* 52 (Nov. 1989): 1–23.

Denisoff, R. Serge. *Great Day Coming: Folk Music and the American Left*. Urbana: University of Illinois Press, 1971.

——. *Sing a Song of Social Significance*. 2d ed. Bowling Green, OH: Bowling Green Popular Press, 1983.

Draper, Robert. *Rolling Stone Magazine: The Uncensored History*. New York: Doubleday, 1990.

"Frank Zappa, Musical Iconoclast, Guitarist and Restless Innovator, Dies at 52," *New York Times*. Dec. 7, 1993, B12.

"Garcia, Jerry," in *Current Biography Yearbook 1990*. New York: H. W. Wilson, 1990: 264–67.

Garofalo, Reebee, ed. *Rockin' the Boat: Mass Music and Mass Movements*. Boston: South End Press, 1992.

Guthrie, Arlo, interviewed by Lauren Kessler in *After All These Years: Sixties Ideals in a Different World*. New York: Thunder's Mouth Press, 1990: 163–71.

Hampton, Wayne. *Guerilla Minstrels: John Lennon, Joe Hill, Woody Guthrie, and Bob Dylan*. Knoxville: University of Tennessee Press, 1986.

Hotchner, A. E. *Blown Away: The Rolling Stones and the Death of the Sixties*. New York: Simon and Schuster, 1990.

Lemisch, Jesse. "Pop Front Culture: I Dreamed I Saw MTV Last Night," *The Nation* 243 (Oct. 18, 1986): 36+.

Lieberman, Robbie. *"My Song Is My Weapon": People's Songs, American Communism, and the Politics of Culture*. Urbana: University of Illinois Press, 1989.

Makower, Joel. *Woodstock: The Oral History*. New York: Doubleday, 1989.

Omolade, Barbara. "Bernice Reagon Wedding Political Action and Music," *The Black Scholar* 16 (May/June 1985): 2–9.

Reagon, Bernice Johnson. "African Diaspora Women: The Making of Cultural Workers," *Feminist Studies* 12 (Spring 1986): 77–90.

Weiner, Jon. *Come Together: John Lennon in His Time*. Urbana: University of Illinois Press, 1991.

"Zappa, Frank," in *Current Biography Yearbook 1990*. New York: E. H. Wilson, 1990: 633–38.

Press

Armstrong, David. *Trumpet to Arms: Alternative Media in America*. Boston: South End Press, 1984.

"From Some 2,000 Alternative Magazines, a Digest" (on the *Utne Reader*), *New York Times*, Jan. 4, 1993, D12.

Glessing, Robert J. *The Underground Press in America*. Westport, CT: Greenwood Press, 1984 (1970).

Goldstein, Richard. *Reporting the Counterculture*. Boston: Unwin Hyman, 1989.

Kessler, Lauren. *The Dissident Press: Alternative Journalism in American History*. Beverly Hills, CA: Sage, 1984.

———. "Sixties Survivors: The Persistence of Countercultural Values in the Lives of Underground Journalists," *Journalism History* 16 (Spring/Summer 1989): 2–11.

Krassner, Paul. *Confessions of a Raving Unconfined Nut*. New York: Simon and Schuster, 1993.

"Krassner, Paul," in *Contemporary Authors*, vol. 11, New Revision Series. Detroit: Gale Research, 1984: 310–11.

"Les Freaks, C'est Chic" (Gilbert Shelton in France), *Washington Post*, Sept. 19, 1993, F1.

Peck, Abe. *Uncovering the Sixties: The Life and Times of the Underground Press*. New York: Pantheon Books, 1985.

Seeger, Arthur. *Berkeley Barb: Social Control of an Underground Newsroom*. New York: Irvington Publishers, 1987.
Von Hoffman, Nicholas. *We Are the People Our Parents Warned Us Against*. Chicago: Ivan R. Dee, 1989 (1968).
Wachsberger, Ken. *Voices from the Underground*, 2 vols. Tempe, AZ: Mica Press, 1993.

Theatre

Blau, Herbert. *To All Appearances: The Ideology of Performance*. New York: Routledge, 1992.
Davis, R. G. "Deep Culture: Thoughts on Third World Theatre," *New Theatre Quarterly* 6 (Nov. 1990): 335–42.
————. "The Politics, Packaging, and Potential for Performing Art," *New Theatre Quarterly* 4 (Feb. 1988): 17–31.
————. Review of "Berkeley in the Sixties" (documentary), *Film Quarterly* 44 (Fall 1990): 58–60.
————. *The San Francisco Mime Troupe: The First Ten Years*. Berkeley: Ramparts Press, 1975.
Jasper, Lawrence. "San Francisco Mime Troupe," in *American Theatre Companies, 1931–1986*, ed. Weldon B. Durham. Westport, CT: Greenwood Press, 1989: 470–78.
Trousdell, Richard. "The Director as Pacifist-Anarchist: An Interview with Judith Malina," *Massachusetts Review* 29 (Spring 1988): 22–38.
Van Erven, Eugene. *Radical People's Theatre*. Bloomington: Indiana University Press, 1988.

JOAN BAEZ (1941–   )

Most prominent of female folk singers, peace activist

Born in Staten Island, New York, on January 9, 1941, Joan Baez moved around the country with her family until finally landing in Boston in the 1950s. The Kingston Trio had just helped to launch the folk music revival. When Joan was a student at Boston University, she began performing in Cambridge at Club Mt. Auburn 47 (Club 47), and she cut her first record with two friends. Her break came during the summer of 1959, first with an engagement at the Gate of Horn in Chicago. This was followed by a guest appearance at the Newport Folk Festival. She gained immediate popularity with her haunting voice and store of traditional ballads. Her first album for Vanguard, *Joan Baez*, was released in 1960, and her many concerts quickly propelled her to the forefront of the folk music revival. Other successful albums followed in quick succession, defining for the burgeoning youth culture the female folk sound. Her crowning as the queen of folk music came with a cover story in *Time* on November 23, 1962.

But Baez was also a political activist, partially because of her Quaker heritage. She joined the boycott in 1963 of the "Hootenanny" TV show because of the television blacklist of Pete Seeger (*). She was attracted to Bob Dylan's offbeat style, lyrical substance, and initial political sensitivities. She introduced him during her concerts during the summer of 1963, and she performed his topical songs. "Bob's songs seemed to update the concepts of justice and injustice," she later wrote in *And a Voice to Sing With* (1987). "And if the songs were not about justice, he made you think they were, because of his image, his rejection of the status quo, set against the mounting turbulence in the country" (p. 92). Justice was becoming her passion.

Her first direct involvement was in the Civil Rights movement. In 1962, she committed herself to a tour in the South that included four black colleges, integrated audiences, and a close association with Dr. Martin Luther King (1*). Her concerts, now filling 10,000- and 20,000-seat halls, were permeated with "We Shall Overcome," "Oh, Freedom" and other civil rights songs. She performed with Dylan, the Freedom Singers, and Peter, Paul, and Mary at the 1963 March on Washington. She joined the Selma to Montgomery, Alabama, march two years later. For Baez, as for many others, the Civil Rights movement introduced her to other political struggles by mid-decade. While not a student, she was present during the beginnings of the Free Speech movement at the University of California at Berkeley in the fall of 1964. Her soaring voice and luminous image captured the spirit of the developing campus revolts.

Joan Baez. Copyright *Washington Post*; Reprinted by permission of D.C. Public Library.

By 1965 her popularity was fueled by her political commitments. Her marriage of style and substance reached a peak just as Dylan, and others, changed direction and launched folk rock, a more cultural than political musical challenge to the status quo. Her brief tour with Bob in the spring, oddly, drew small crowds. Their subsequent trip to England was a disaster for her and ended their personal relationship, although she continued to perform his songs. Her two-disc 1968 album *Any Day Now* included only Dylan tunes. Her commitment to pacifism, combined with the escalating war in Vietnam, soon led her into the growing anti-war movement. The start of a ten-year tax protest and numerous interviews in the mass media were the most visible aspects of her controversial peace commitment. Her Institute for the Study of Non-Violence, founded in 1965 in the Carmel Valley under the inspiration of Ira Sandperl, promoted the intense study of "the concept, theory, history and application of nonviolence in all its aspects, from use in personal relationships to internationally organized methods of fighting oppression" (*And a Voice to Sing With*, p. 126).

Her anti-war activities increased, resulting in a few jail terms for supporting draft resistance and her marriage to David Harris, later imprisoned for his anti-draft stance. Her appearance at the Woodstock musical festival in the summer of 1969, the symbolic end of the decade, was somewhat odd, given the prevalent rock, drugs, and sex atmosphere. "Woodstock? Hell, I was already pushing my luck," she later wrote. "I'd been on the music scene for ten years and still didn't take dope or use a backup band. But Woodstock was also me, Joan Baez, the square, six months pregnant, the wife of a draft resister, endlessly proselytizing about the war. I had my place there. I was of the sixties, and I was already a survivor" (*And a Voice to Sing With*, pp. 163–164).

For the next two decades she continued to combine music and activism. Her albums and performances mixed the old and new, with a country and western twist here and there, and increasingly her own introspective compositions. Her singles were rare, but "The Night They Drove Ol' Dixie Down," surprisingly reached number five on the pop charts in 1972. She became involved with Amnesty International, publicizing the plight of political prisoners throughout the world, but while it lasted the Vietnam War plagued her life. Her trip to Hanoi during the 1972 Christmas bombing was a frightening ordeal, resulting in an album, *Where Are You Now, My Son?*," including the sirens, the bombs, Phantoms, B-52's, anti-aircraft, the children laughing, Monti talking, the Vietnamese singing, myself singing in the shelter" (*And a Voice to Sing With*, pp. 224–225). She participated, of course, in the "War Is Over" concert, organized by Phil Ochs (*), in Central Park in 1975.

In the mid-1970s Joan once again toured with Dylan, and many others, in the Rolling Thunder Review. This also included the filming of *Renaldo and Clara*. They would continue to have a bumpy relationship. Her past stayed with her into the 1980s, partially through a reunion concert in 1985 for Club 47 alumni. Her appearance at the spectacular Live Aid concert the same year, a political Woodstock for the eighties, refurbished her image for a new generation. She continued to perform concerts.

Baez's natural image and powerful voice, appeared at the close of the 1950s. She punctuated the end of the stultifying Eisenhower years and marked the beginnings of Camelot. While the previous decade had more heterogeneity than is often recognized—the beats and rock-and-roll were not alone in challenging the status quo—Kennedy's victory symbolized to many, then and subsequently, a stimulating breeze blowing through the land. Youthful icons were increasingly in demand, partially by a rapidly growing youth market and, therefore, the commercial purveyors of taste and style. There developed a confluence of demand and supply. Baez, with a wealth of style and talent, combined with the skills of her manager Manny Greenhill and the marketing ability of Vanguard Records, was able temporarily to personify the new age.

There was style, but there was also substance. As the young, particularly the increasing numbers of college students, began searching for authenticity and understanding, they became attracted to folk music. It was certainly not new, even as popular music. There had been previously the commercial success of Burl Ives, The Weavers, Harry Belafonte, and many others. But folk music now became, for a few years in the late 1950s and early 1960s, immensely appealing. Baez was following on the heels of the successful Kingston Trio, launched in 1958, and her appearance at the 1959 Newport Folk Festival was more than fortuitous.

Unlike the Kingston Trio, the ongoing Weavers, and other groups and many individuals, who performed a mixture of traditional and topical songs, she initially preferred older English and American ballads. On her first album, for example, she included "Silver Dagger," "Wildwood Flower," and "Mary Hamilton," followed by "Barbara Allen" and "Banks of the Ohio" in *Joan Baez Vol. 2*. These were stories about love and death, fidelity and infidelity, work and play, potent themes for many young people searching for authenticity as well as romance, a heady combination unfilled by the pop and rock-and-roll music of the time. Ballads had been the staple of both popular and traditional folk performers of previous decades, but were fading by the late 1950s. Baez, and a few others, helped keep alive the ballad tradition, at least temporarily. Her subtle acoustic accompaniment added to the force of the music, encouraging a do-it-yourself attitude among her listeners that marked the folk revival. Indeed, the sale of guitars, banjos, and other folk instruments quickly escalated. Guitar-playing young women in long hair and peasant dresses, as well as their male counterparts, were ubiquitous on college campuses and in coffeehouses.

Another element of her repertoire was the occasional foreign-language song, such as "El Preso Numero Nueve" on *Joan Baez*, followed by "Plaisir d'Amour" in the next album. Pete Seeger and the Weavers had also included an international component in their concerts, common among many performers since World War II. Baez would continue the practice, revealing both her own ethnic background as well as her ongoing belief in world peace through mutual cooperation and understanding. With the rise of Dylan and other singer-songwriters in the early 1960s, however, with their introspective styles, this international folk flavor temporarily lost popularity. Ethnic music later made a comeback, featuring performers from around the world.

Baez, however, never abandoned her eclectic musical tastes. In *Joan Baez/5*, she included songs by Phil Ochs, Richard Farina, and Dylan, two Child ballads, as well as "O Cangaceiro." As she began to add her own compositions to her performances, as well as more of Dylan and other contemporaries, there was necessarily less time for her older songs, but they were never absent. By the end of the 1960s she was including poems, readings, and a variety of other presentations. Her concerts and albums were always noted by their variety.

During the 1960s, a time of much flamboyance and creativity, Joan Baez made her mark through style and example. She was perhaps more the symbol than the instigator of change in both musical taste and political consciousness, although her personal involvements in the Civil Rights and nonviolence/anti-war movements surely motivated others. While a heroine to those on the left, she naturally had her detractors among those fearing dissent, including the federal government. Her voice and conscience continued to speak the idealism of the decade.

Bibliography

"Active Voice: Baez Is Back," *Washington Post*, Nov. 17, 1989, p. 27.

"Baez, Joan," in *The Encyclopedia of Folk, Country and Western Music*, Irwin Stambler and Grelun Landon, eds., 2d ed. New York: St. Martin's Press, 1984: 28–31.

"Baez, Joan," in *The Penguin Encyclopedia of Popular Music*, Donald Clarke, ed. New York: Viking, 1989: 60.

Baez, Joan. *Daybreak: An Autobiography*. New York: Avon Books, 1968.

———. *And a Voice to Sing With: A Memoir*. New York: Summit Books, 1987.

Denselow, Robin. *When the Music's Over: The Story of Political Pop*. Boston: Faber and Faber, 1989.

Goldsmith, Barbara. "Life on Struggle Mountain," *New York Times Biographical Service* 18 (June 1987): 603–4.

Heylin, Clinton. *Bob Dylan behind the Shades: A Biography*. New York: Summit Books, 1991.

"Joan Baez, the First Lady of Folk," *New York Times*, Nov. 29, 1992, H25.

Loder, Kurt. "Joan Baez." *Rolling Stone*, October 15, 1992, p. 105+.

Spitz, Bob. *Dylan: A Biography*. New York: McGraw-Hill, 1989.

von Schmidt, Eric, and Jim Rooney. *Baby, Let Me Follow You Down: The Illustrated Story of the Cambridge Folk Years*. Garden City, NY: Anchor Books, 1979.

Ward, Ed, Geoffrey Stokes, and Ken Tucker. *Rock of Ages: The Rolling Stone History of Rock & Roll*. New York: Summit Books, 1986.

Ronald D. Cohen

PETER COLLIER (1939–) and DAVID HOROWITZ (1939–)

Radical writers who became conservatives

Peter Collier and David Horowitz established a collaborative presence in American political and social criticism during the 1960s and early seventies that they maintained into the 1990s. They first became visible especially as editors and writers for *Ramparts*. This journal began in 1962 as an essentially literary and intellectual enterprise with Roman Catholic associations. It then evolved into a forum for left commentary. The two men, in later years, joined the conservative opponents of the left and, in effect, to their former selves. This effort became a significant intellectual event in 1987 when they held a Second Thoughts Conference in Washington, D.C. This was a discussion by a group of 1960s activists who were still politically diverse but all skeptical about their earlier commitments.

The different backgrounds of the two men define the polarities within American culture. David Horowitz was a "red diaper baby" whose parents believed in the Soviet Union. His father was a Jew who had strayed from much of the Jewish heritage and eventually discovered the perfidies of the Communist party, but lived his final days in brokenhearted loyalty to the Communist idea. The young Horowitz resolved never to adopt ruthless and unexamined beliefs such as those which had entrapped his parents' generation. He was determined to be a humane and unillusioned radical. David never converted to the left; by birth and upbringing he was already there. Much of his early work on the left was for peace and anti-imperialism. He was employed by the Bertrand Russell Peace Foundation for some time in the 1960s. He also published extensively on foreign policy, contributing to the revisionist thesis that the West was the initiator of the cold war and the Soviet Union was the defensive party.

Peter Collier, raised in California, was of older conservative stock. His father, raised in a South Dakota sod hut, was a simple believer in the nation's basic ways and institutions. Peter's father was the sort of American who later would draw the easy scorn of the New Left. The son's introduction to the politics of the New Left was apparently gradual, encouraged by events in Berkeley and the Civil Rights movement.

By early 1967 Collier appeared on the masthead of *Ramparts* as a staff writer, followed soon after by Horowitz as contributing editor from London. In March 1968 Horowitz gained listing as a senior editor, and two months later Collier joined him among senior editors. As late as June 1973, both were on the editorial board. Thereafter, until the final issues in the summer of 1975, the two had occasional associations with the journal.

Ramparts escapes any simple characterization. Some of its work was in investigative reporting. The journal gained much attention by its proof of the CIA's contacts within the Michigan State University and the National Student Association. The diversity within its covers included Martin Luther King, Jr. (1*), Jean-Paul Sartre, and Che Guevara. It drew upon the editorial or other talents of such activist writers as Noam Chomsky (6*). It maintained wide intellectual curiosity even when more hysterical segments of the left had lapsed into paranoid sloganeering. Yet the contributions to the journal seemed individually and collectively suspended between a sophisticated radical criticism and a surrender to the excitements of its day. An article for May 1968 achieved a detailed and, on its own terms, quite intelligent analysis of the Maoist Cultural Revolution. Its main flaw was that it accorded too much respect to that historical absurdity. The editors for the issue of May 1974, when Horowitz and Collier had no position on the journal, also lengthily and eloquently condemned the Symbionese Liberation Army for confusing murder with revolutionary justice. They strongly lectured against lethal enthusiasms that thought themselves to be serious politics. But the piece also suggested that executions such as those in Cuba were legitimate acts of revolutionary movements. In the end, the editorial statement was at odds with its own better nature.

The difficulty of judging *Ramparts* is illustrated by the case of Horowitz and Collier. If the two were taken seriously in their memory of what they once were, they represented that essential portion of the New Left that gave the whole a bad name. They indicted the left—old, new, and recent—in *Destructive Generation: Second Thoughts about the Sixties*, published in 1989. They deplored a totalitarianism of mind and of practice, compounded of egotism and illusion. This life-crushing moralism would even justify, Collier now claimed, the killing of informers within a revolutionary organization. Horowitz said that he had been guilty of a moral totalitarianism similar to the Communist variety that had earlier crushed the Soviet peoples and betrayed the hopes of his parents' comrades. He had substituted a more romantic and colorful form of the same death-dealing. The conversion that the two underwent to conservatism was the product both of a growing skepticism and of the murder of a friend by the Panthers. A later leftist may resent the Collier and the Horowitz who, in their radical phase, contributed to bringing scandal to radical politics. A later leftist might also question the pronouncements on "the left" of two converts to conservatism. It is therefore a surprise to turn from *Destructive Generation* to their contributions to *Ramparts* and elsewhere, and find instances of measured judgment by Horowitz and of serious reportage by Collier that belie what they now say of themselves and the New Left.

Collier was at his best, for instance, when he wrote in the early 1970s on the plight of Indians under federal regulation. If the writing is inflammatory, it is not because it is thick with slogans. It is inflammatory because the facts are painful. Horowitz on the cold war argued a case that was perfectly compatible with the author's condemnation of Moscow's oppression of its own and its satellite peoples. He claimed that the self-interest of the USSR prompted that empire to be defensive rather than expansionist. This claim is vulnerable, but not for reasons of naïveté about the moral character of the Communist regime. Horowitz in a *Ramparts* article for June 1974, when the author's commitment to the left was doubtless weakening but still alive, scolds fellow radicals who were uncomfortable with Alexander Solzhenitsyn's questioning of Soviet repression. Although Horowitz's concentration is on the history of the Soviet Union, the essay calls for the left to stand by its humane convictions and its championship of free personal integrity. Yet Horowitz, a critical observer who never apologized for the Soviet Union, was also capable of a wholly puzzling admiration for North Korea.

So Collier and Horowitz in their radical days were an enigma. Their retrospective self-condemnation is partially though not completely contradicted by their better writings of the time. In addition, there are major elements of their earlier characters in their later conservatism.

Most obviously, they remained conscious of an Enemy: not a host of partial wrongs and evils, but a single Enemy. Once it was imperialist capitalism; now it is the Left. Both Collier and Horowitz concede that leftists sometimes disagree among themselves, and that each generation of radicals can perceive the faults of its ideological elders. But they dismiss these differences as twists and turns of a deluded leftism trying by one strategy or another to sustain itself. Horowitz in "Letter to a Political Friend," a chapter in *Destructive Generation* that bears his own name, explained that he now recognized human fallibility and the precariousness of improvement. A critic of Horowitz could argue that this conclusion need not justify conservatism, but a skeptical liberalism, withholding itself from any final program but committed to particular reforms at home and abroad, intolerant alike of rule by commissars and rule by rightist death squads. But the appeal to the fallibilities of human nature for Horowitz, provides an excuse for the vicious regimes American foreign policy has adopted, just as utopianism allowed some Western radicals to excuse repression within Communist countries.

Closely akin to this reduction of individual enemies to an abstract Enemy is an investigative reporter's urge to find connections and to assume that when you have found them you have found everything. Horowitz on the left was diligent at this. An instance is "The Making of America's China Policy," an article of October 1971 that traces the influence of American corporate interests in the development of that policy. All other factors are missing. The character or even the existence of anti-Communist ideology gets no serious consideration. The reader is deprived of quarreling with our China policy on its own intellectual and moral grounds or agreeing with it. *Destructive Generation* continues the task of finding connections. Part of a chapter, "The Fifth-Column Left," spends time finding Cuban and Sandinista influence in groups critical of Washington's Central American policy. It reads very much like its opposites on the left that delight in showing which diversified companies held shares in Vietnamese tungsten.

Collier and Horowitz once broke away from cold war clichés to embrace various shallow formulations on the Left. Later they rejected leftist principles that they thought had enthralled them. What they present is confessional. It is the report of a conversion. Collier and Horowitz discovered human imperfection, but this did not make them humble. Instead, they insisted, with an aggressive self-righteousness, that everyone should be judged by their new standards. Those who disagreed were presumably fools and/or dupes. Even if the reader is not convinced, however, the book does illustrate something about the uses of critical introspection in the forming of a politics that is at once personal and responsible.

Bibliography

"The Changelings," *The Nation* 240 (April 6, 1988): 388–89.

Churcher, Sharon. "Radical Transformations," *New York Times Biographical Service* 20 (July 1989):686–88.

Collier, Peter. *Crisis*. New York: Harcourt, Brace and World, 1969.

———. *Dilemmas of Democracy*. New York: Harcourt Brace Jovanovich, 1976.

———. *Downriver*. New York: Holt, Rinehart and Winston, 1978.

———. *The Fondas: A Hollywood Dynasty*. New York: Putnam, 1990.

———. *When Shall They Rest?* New York: Holt, Rinehart and Winston, 1973.

Horowitz, David. *Empire and Revolution: A Radical Interpretation of Contemporary History*. New York: Random House, 1969.

———. *The Fate of Midas and Other Essays*. San Francisco: Ramparts Press, 1973.

———. *The Free World Colossus: A Critique of American Foreign Policy in the Cold War*. New York: Hill and Wang, 1965.

———. *Shakespeare: An Existential View*. New York: Hill and Wang, 1965.

Horowitz, David, and Peter Collier. *Destructive Generation: Second Thoughts about the Sixties*. New York: Summit Books, 1989.

———. *Deconstructing the Left: From Vietnam to the Persian Gulf*. Lanham, MD: University Press of America/Madison Books, 1991.

———. *The Fords: An American Epic*. New York: Summit Books, 1987.

———. *The Kennedys: An American Drama*. New York: Summit Books, 1984.

———. *The Rockefellers: An American Dynasty*. New York: Holt, Rinehart and Winston, 1976.

———, eds. *Second Thoughts: Former Radicals Look Back at the Sixties*. Lanham, MD: Madison Books, 1989.

"Panthers, Contras, and Other Wars" (an exchange between Paul Berman, Peter Collier, and David Horowitz), *The New Republic*, June 26, 1989, pp. 38–42.

Thomas R. West

BOB DYLAN (1941–   )

Most influential singer-songwriter-performer

First folk music, then rock and roll, served to entertain, define, and motivate the burgeoning population of young people during the 1960s. Exploding onto the music scene in 1963, Bob Dylan quickly became the prime exponent of folk protest songs, leading an emerging group of politically motivated singer-songwriters who challenged the social, cultural, musical, and political status quo. They were involved with issues of race, war and peace, rebellion and love. These were the concerns chiefly of high school and college students. Just as folk protest began to reach a crescendo, however, Dylan switched to a more introspective style, examining his own psyche and intensely personal problems. He was also now influenced by the revival of electric rock-and-roll music, and so quickly exemplified what became known as folk rock, his basic style for the remainder of the sixties and afterward, although he also developed a more mellow country sound and a variety of other voices over the years. For the next two decades Dylan would continue to change styles, usually keeping one step ahead of the critics, still influential although occasionally fading from the public eye. He is called by one reference book "the most important figure in white rock music."

Born Robert Allen Zimmerman in Duluth, Minnesota, on May 24, 1941, he soon moved with his family to the smaller town of Hibbing, where Bob lived until settling briefly in Minneapolis to attend the state university. He was interested in a wide range of music, including rock and roll, country and western, as well as (black) rhythm and blues. He played the piano, then guitar, and performed locally. His stay at the university was brief, but he managed to fall in with the local folk music crowd, then growing because of the popularity of the Kingston Trio, among many others, and the music's somewhat rebellious tinge. And here he first heard Woody Guthrie on records, quickly to become his prime influence.

Dylan, arriving in New York City in January 1961, headed straight for Greenwich Village and Izzy Young's Folklore Center, the heart of the country's growing folk music scene. He soon found an audience and his own unique voice and style. Following local concerts and increasing regional popularity his first record (1962) contained little that was new, but the next release, *The Freewheelin' Bob Dylan* (1963), including "Blowin' In The Wind," marked his artistic and political birth. Next appeared *The Times They Are a-Changin'* which featured the title song and "With God on Our Side." In addition to his music, heavily topical, he became temporarily involved in the Civil Rights movement and was quickly considered the musical poet of the student-organized New Left. He was also paired with Joan Baez (*); they quickly became the king and queen of folk music. But a restless Dylan soon switched gears.

His last acoustic album, *Another Side of Bob Dylan*, appeared in 1964, followed in March 1965 by *Bringing It All Back Home*, the first to include a backup band, and then in the fall by *Highway 61 Revisited*. The songs were now becoming highly personal, often poetic allegories, sometimes embarrassingly intimate, and he introduced electric instruments. His biographer Bob Spitz has called *Highway 61* "as unequivocally rock as any album ever made," with its inclusion of "Like a Rolling Stone" and the title song (*Dylan: A Biography*, p. 297). During the summer, between the two albums, Dylan intro-

Bob Dylan. Copyright *Washington Post*; Reprinted by permission of D.C. Public Library.

duced his new style at the Newport Folk Festival, to a decidedly mixed reaction. While the folk crowd was temporarily unsettled by his transformation, the larger youth market, conditioned by the Beatles-inspired rock-and-roll revival then spreading throughout the country, and attracted to the developing rock counterculture, enthusiastically responded. Folk rock captured the headlines and Dylan's songs were widely performed, while many folk performers formed rock groups. The growing drug culture welcomed the new Dylan, whose lyrical and mystical style was now epitomized in *Blonde on Blonde*, a double album appearing in mid-1966 and characterized by Spitz as "a near-perfect collaboration of music, lyrics, and performance" (*Dylan: A Biography*, p. 342).

As the youth movement, and the country generally, during the late 1960s assumed a more frenetic pace, with urban violence, anti-war activism, and the mushrooming drug-influenced counterculture, Dylan again changed, catching his fans off guard. *John Wesley Harding*, appearing in late 1967, marked a mellower, somewhat religious artist; and the same year he appeared at a Woody Guthrie memorial concert. Two years later *Nashville Skyline* exhibited a country Dylan. He had by now experienced one metamorphosis after another, a trait that would last another twenty years as album followed album, some to critical acclaim, while others were poorly received. He would continue to record, perform throughout the world, and experiment with various religious, political, and artistic persuasions, as his audience coalesced into a loyal following of young and aging fans. His concerts often combined the old and the new, a mélange of songs and styles with something, generally, for everyone.

Dylan's iconoclastic and mysterious personality, combined with his obvious musical genius, marked the parameters of his influence during the 1960s. When he felt secure with his own voice and style, he proceeded to capture the hopes and frustrations of the emerging youth movement, including the burgeoning New Left. Dylan's musical reach and influence has been worldwide, with perhaps more of a cult following in Europe and Japan than in the United States. There are Dylan newsletters and festivals on both sides of the Atlantic, and a continuing market for both his new releases and re-releases including the ubiquitous bootleg albums starting with his earliest performances in Minnesota. Columbia Records initiated an "official bootleg series" of previously unreleased live and studio recordings in 1991. Indeed, Dylan originally inspired the bootleg album craze, for his audience desired considerably more than was commercially available. There has been an unending stream of books, articles, and dissertations dissecting his every word, style, and inflection, much less the never-ending transformation of his political, religious, and personal life, usually shrouded in obfuscation and secrecy. While his politically activist period was essentially over by 1965, he has continued to appear in politically oriented megaconcerts, such as Live Aid in 1985. The release the same year of *A Biography*, a five-record reprise of his career, elicited considerable attention among old and new fans.

Dylan's influence on and representation of the 1960s, particularly the revolt of the young, was highly significant, although his biographer Bob Spitz, voicing a popular view, elevates him to a higher plane, surely transcending that particular decade: "He created a musical standard against which everything that evolved must be measured. And a body of music that lifts our hearts, reminding us of all the passion and desire and frustration and sacrifice and pity and pride which mold our lives" (*Dylan: A Biography*, p. 546). Clinton Heylin concludes his rich biography of Dylan on this note: "His life and work will continue to fascinate and intrigue, and like an artistic Rorshach test he will continue to mean different things to each and every fan. And though the worn lines and scruffy beard suggest he is unlikely to stay forever young, long may he endeavor to paint his masterpiece" (*Bob Dylan behind the Shades*, p. 440).

Just considering the 1960s, however, the passions and frustrations of youth were succinctly captured by "The Times They Are A-Changin'," as was the hypocrisy of the Vietnam War in "With God on Our Side." Others, such as Phil Ochs (*), had strong lyrics, political consciousness, and obvious musical appeal, but Dylan's combination of style and substance were unmatched. For rock superstar Bruce Springsteen, "Dylan was a revolutionary. Bob freed your mind the way Elvis freed your body. He showed us that just because the music was innately physical did not mean it was anti-intellectual. He had the vision and the talent to make a pop song that contained the whole world. He invented a new way a pop singer could sound, broke through the limitations of what a recording artist could achieve and changed the face of rock and roll forever" (Heylin, *Bob Dylan behind the Shades*, pp. 401–2). The tried-and-true Tin Pan Alley formula for popular music had always concentrated on dreams and abstractions, hardly touching real-life issues of suffering and death, sex (rather than ethereal love), politics, war and peace, and the like. Even rock and roll had basically shied away from such topics, although other musical styles, particularly country and the blues, had confronted the personal as well as the political.

But Dylan, first and foremost, made both the personal and the political respectable topics, although often couched in poetic images and abstractions that have puzzled his critics and followers. He was not reticent about expressing his raw emotions, sometimes annoyingly so. Concerning a number of the songs on *Another Side of Bob Dylan*, biographer Clinton Heylin has remarked that they were "embarrassingly self-conscious," while others "sounded forced and unconvincing . . . .The inconsistency in the material on *Another Side* was precisely because Dylan was too close to the experiences he was drawing upon" (*Bob Dylan behind the Shades*, p. 107). Whether embarrassing or not, however, and most were not as his lyrics became more poetic and visionary, his songs captured the growing need among the young for authenticity and validation, connecting the personal and the political in new and often subtle ways. His medium was not books and speeches—where he was often seemingly inarticulate—but the ever-changing tempo and word images of his songs, whether subtle or powerful, brutally frank or apparently inexplicable. Countless other performers, including the Beatles, adopted his style and often his songs, with great success. The Byrds' version of "Mr. Tambourine Man" became very popular in mid-1965, introducing Dylan to an even wider audience. Dylan has been a vital musical, cultural, and social influence, starting in the early 1960s.

Bibliography

Bauldie, John, ed. *Wanted Man: In Search of Bob Dylan*. Secaucus, NJ: Carol Publishing Group/Citadel Underground, 1991.

Current Biography 52 (Oct. 1991): 26–30.

Dunaway, David K. "No Credit Given: The Underground Literature of Bob Dylan," *The Virginia Quarterly Review* 69 (Winter 1993): 149–55.

Dylan, Bob. *Tarantula*. New York: Macmillan, 1970.

Foorland, Tor Egil. "Bringing It All Back Home or Another Side of Bob Dylan: Midwestern Isolationist," *Journal of American Studies* 26 (Dec. 1992): 337–55.

Gilmore, Mikal. "Bob Dylan at Fifty," *Rolling Stone*, May 30, 1991, pp. 56–57+.

Hampton, Wayne. *Guerilla Minstrels: John Lennon, Joe Hill, Woody Guthrie, Bob Dylan*. Nashville: University of Tennessee Press, 1986.

Heylin, Clinton. *Bob Dylan Behind the Shades: A Biography*. New York: Summit Books, 1991.

Kramer, Daniel. *Bob Dylan: Portraits of the Singer's Early Years*. Secaucus, NJ: Carol Publishing Group/Citadel Underground, 1991.

McGregor, Craig, ed. *Bob Dylan—The Early Years: A Retrospective*. New York: DeCapo Press, 1990.

Marsh, Dave. "Out of the 60s into His 50s," *New York Times Biographical Service* 22 (May 1991): 494–96.

Shelton, Robert. *No Direction Home: The Life and Music of Bob Dylan*. New York: William Morrow, 1986.

Spitz, Bob. *Dylan: A Biography*. New York: McGraw-Hill, 1989.

von Schmidt, Eric, and Jim Rooney. *Baby, Let Me Follow You Down: The Illustrated Story of the Cambridge Folk Years*. Garden City, NY: Anchor Books, 1979.

Ronald D. Cohen

JANE FONDA (1937–)

Celebrity publicist and fund-raiser for progressive causes

Although Jane Fonda was known as an actress in the 1960s, she first made headlines around the world by her 1972 trip to North Vietnam while the United States was still at war with that country. Critics belittled her as "Hanoi Jane" and a "Commie slut." Leftists praised her commitment to anti-war and radical politics. In the years that followed, she continued her work through movies that she made. In addition, she raised money, made speeches, hosted rallies, demonstrated, and boycotted various products. The causes that she supported included rent control, energy conservation, and women's rights. Such radical advocacy was surprising given her sheltered and privileged early life.

Jane Seymour Fonda was born the first child of Henry Fonda and Frances Seymour Fonda in New York City on December 21, 1937. She grew up in Brentwood, a wealthy area on the west side of Los Angeles, California, where she attended the Brentwood Town and Country School. Because of her father's starring Broadway role in *Mister Roberts*, the family moved East again when Jane was ten. Henry deliberately sheltered his children from the pressures placed on celebrity children. Jane later commented that this also meant that she and Peter had little contact with children their own age.

Jane Fonda. *Source*: Library of Congress

At twelve, Jane was devastated when her mother, who suffered from repeated bouts of depression, committed suicide in 1949. Jane's father then sent
her and Peter to live with their maternal grandmother at his home in Greenwich, Connecticut. Less than a year later, Henry married Susan Blanchard,
the stepmother of Oscar Hammerstein II. Jane was to remember her as a
marvelous woman who provided a good home for her and Peter.

Jane continued her education at the Greenwich Academy and, later, at the
Emma Williard School in Troy, New York. She discovered that she was drawn
to the theatre. Her father neither encouraged nor discouraged this interest.
She made her acting debut at Williard playing the male lead in Christopher
Fry's *Boy with a Cart*. She made her first formal stage presentation with her
father in 1955, playing in *The Country Girl*. That fall, Jane took freshman
courses at Vassar College in Poughkeepsie, New York. She spent most of her

time outside of the library and the classroom. She went to parties, dated, and disregarded most school restrictions. She finally pleaded with her father to let her withdraw. When he refused, she attempted to get herself expelled but was unsuccessful.

After another year, Jane dropped out. She convinced her father that she wanted to be a painter. She persuaded him that she should go to Paris to study art, the languages, and music. He reluctantly agreed to send her to the Sorbonne. There, she lived with a French family, worked at the office of the *Paris Review*, and did little studying. Henry, unhappy about her behavior, summoned her home after just a few months. Back home in New York, she studied art at the Art Students League, music at the Mannes College of Music, and French and Italian at the Berlitz School. She also worked at the New York office of *Paris Review* and began doing some modeling.

A friend of Jane's persuaded her to apply for lessons at the Actor's Studio. Alumni of the Studio included Joanne Woodward, Paul Newman, Marlon Brando, Montgomery Clift, and Maureen Stapleton. Jane began lessons in the fall of 1958. Lee Strasberg, the director of the studio, told Jane that she was highly talented. He encouraged her to be more positive about acting and enhanced her confidence as an actress.

Afterwards, director Joshua Logan offered her a screen test. Logan was an eminent director and producer as well as her godfather and one of her father's oldest friends. After the screen test, Logan offered Jane a five-year contract. Under Logan, she appeared on Broadway in *There Was a Little Girl* (1959–1960) and made her film debut as a cheerleader in 1960 in *Tall Story*. Neither production won critical acclaim but Jane received the New York Drama Critics Award as "the most promising new actress of the year" for her performance in *There Was a Little Girl*. Her stage and screen performances over the next two years received mediocre reviews.

Jane decided to go to Paris in the fall of 1963 to make René Clement's *Joy House*. She believed that she could make a name for herself in Europe. Jane was quickly dubbed "La BB Américaine," the American Brigitte Bardot. Bardot, with the help of her husband Roger Vadim, had been the French screen's major sex symbol since the mid-1950s. When Vadim directed Jane in *La Ronde* (Circle of Love), they became lovers. He subsequently divorced Bardot and married Jane on August 15, 1965. Vadim later directed Jane in *La Curée* (The Game Is Over, 1965), *Barbarella* (1968), and *Spirits of the Dead* (1969). In addition, Jane made well-received movies in the United States: *Cat Ballou* (1965), *The Chase* (1966), *Any Wednesday* (1967), and *They Shoot Horses Don't They?* (1969).

Nineteen hundred sixty-eight was a momentous year. In France, many students and workers held massive demonstrations in May which paralyzed the city. The Tet offensive in Vietnam and the assassinations of Dr. Martin Luther King, Jr. (1*), and Robert Kennedy also occurred in that year. There were violent racial and political riots throughout the United States. In August, some protesters outside the Democratic National Convention in Chicago were brutally beaten and arrested.

Nineteen hundred sixty-eight was also a pivotal year for Jane. She came to identify herself with the anti-war movement and decided that she wanted to participate in it. Jane recalled that she felt betrayed by her government. She was angry and wanted to help stop the war.

Jane and Roger were expecting their first child in 1968. During Jane's second trimester, a case of the mumps confined her to bed. She spent much of her time reading and watching the television coverage of U.S. race riots, anti-war demonstrations, and damage to Vietnamese villages from bombs. Like many Americans, Jane originally defended the American presence in Vietnam. As she learned more, however, she began to think about the social and political upheavals occurring in the world. Jane met with American military deserters who confirmed the war atrocities for her.

She began to make donations to their anti-war work. She slowly came to believe that the war reported on the television and in the press was different from the actual war that was taking place in Vietnam. She was impressed, in addition, by meeting anti-war student activists in the United States. They were willing to be beaten and jailed for their beliefs.

Jane's most controversial film directed by Vadim, *Barbarella*, was released two months after Vanessa's birth in 1968. Vadim described this erotic science fiction fantasy as a "kind of sexy Alice in Wonderland of the future." It was a box office hit where it was not banned. She defended her role, stating that it was fun and that she was glad that she had done it.

After this movie and her childbirth, Jane was exhausted. She accepted a friend's invitation for a vacation in India in1969. The results were more educational than relaxing. Encounters with starvation and poverty sensitized her further about pervasive injustices in the world. She added this to her understanding of problems within the United States, especially for native Americans, women, workers, and blacks.

After reading articles in *Ramparts* about American Indians who had occupied Alcatraz Island, Jane asked one of the authors, David Collier (*), to accompany her on a trip there. She was fascinated by the Indians, who accused the Bureau of Indian Affairs of mismanaging their resources. In March of 1970, she went to Fort Lawson in Washington State to encourage militant Indians who were trying to claim federal property so that they could establish an Indian cultural center. She also went to the Fort to distribute invitations to the GIs to meet her at a local coffeehouse for radical GIs. She was arrested, held, and then escorted off the base. Jane later stated that this incident was significant for her. She had been arrested for doing nothing more than exercising her constitutional rights. It contributed to her radicalization. Moreover, she realized that her participation in this protest had attracted far more attention to it from the press.

Jane continued working with other activists and raising funds. For instance, in 1970 she joined Dr. Benjamin Spock (2*) in a thirty-six-hour fast for peace. She entered Fort Carson where three members of the Black Panthers were allegedly being held, to give out political literature. Once again she was arrested for trespassing, detained, and released.

Jane managed to increase her activism while working on another film project, *Klute*. Jane was later awarded the Oscar for best actress for her performance as Bree Daniels, a prostitute. Jane had wanted to do this film because Bree represented "the inevitable product of a society that places ultimate importance on money, possession, and competition." Bree was an example of the sexual exploitation of women. Jane's decision to make this movie as a statement about a particular issue gave rise to a form of activism which she found to be effective.

Jane used her fame as an actress to engage overtly in political activities. One example was her involvement in the anti-war/anti-establishment traveling theatre show called Free the Army or Free Theatre Association (FTA). Jane Fonda, Dick Gregory (*), Donald Sutherland, Peter Boyle, and others presented FTA at GI coffeehouses situated near military bases. The show was a series of anti-military skits, songs, and scripts.

Some of Jane's other activities included visiting Angela Davis (6*) in the Marin County jail, walking a picket line to support Cesar Chavez's national boycott of non-union grapes, and speaking at a rally to support a group of nuns and priests who had been accused of plotting to kidnap Henry Kissinger.

Jane met Tom Hayden (6*) during a peace rally at Ann Arbor, Michigan, in February of 1971. He was familiar with her movies and her activities, and she was aware of his accomplishments as a member of the Chicago Seven, a group of men convicted for starting a riot outside the 1968 Democratic National Convention in Chicago. Hayden was well known as one of the founders of the Students for a Democratic Society (SDS) and for authoring the *Port Huron Statement* which served as the constitution for SDS. He was an accomplished speaker, a veteran demonstrator, and a protest organizer.

Early in 1972, Jane began planning a trip to Hanoi, the Communist capital of North Vietnam. Jane wanted to see for herself how the war was affecting North Vietnam. She also went on to film any evidence of Nixon's increased bombing. Jane, Hayden, and Herbert Aptheker, a member of the Communist party, went to Hanoi in July of 1972. Jane toured areas where villages and hospitals had been destroyed. She was appalled by the American bombing raids on the North Vietnamese dike system. She spoke with prisoners of war. Having seen the death and destruction of the war, Jane decided to use Radio Hanoi to appeal directly to the American men dropping the bombs. She accused U.S. pilots of "betraying everything that American people have at heart, betraying the long tradition of freedom and democracy."

Jane's presence in Hanoi made headlines in many newspapers. Congressmen Fletcher Thompson and Richard Ichord, along with others, argued that charges of treason should be brought against Jane. She welcomed such an investigation since it would have been an opportunity to testify. She could have made what she learned in Hanoi a permanent part of the congressional record. She did not believe that the North Vietnamese government had simply used her for anti-American propaganda, but that she represented Americans who justifiably condemned the war.

Some Hollywood friends argued that Jane was taking unnecessary risks. Her political activism was sure to hinder her acting career. The Nixon administration placed her on its "enemies list" and she was watched by the FBI. Her film career also suffered restrictions. She received considerably fewer scripts. Her next five films *F.T.A.* and *Steelyard Blues* in 1972, and *Tout Va Bien* and *A Doll's House* in 1973 were not very successful. However, Jane returned from Hanoi more committed than ever to the anti-war movement and more confident as an activist. Her trip established her as an outspoken critic of the war. While Jane later admitted that she sometimes used poor judgment about some of her activities in Hanoi, she did not regret making the trip.

In the fall of 1972, Jane continued to protest the war, denounce the Nixon administration, and share her views with reporters and on talk shows. She and Tom Hayden established the Indochina Peace Campaign (IPC) to raise funds for medical aid to North Vietnam, bring pressure on Congress to cut off economic support to the capitalist regime in South Vietnam, and to demand the release of political prisoners of war in South Vietnam. IPC offices were established in Cambridge, Massachusetts, and Los Angeles.

November of 1972 was significant for Fonda. On the negative side, Richard Nixon was re-elected president, which seemed to offer little hope for the future. More positively, the seventh Circuit U.S. Court of Appeals reversed the Chicago conspiracy conviction against Hayden and his co-defendants. Jane and Tom Hayden decided to marry, which they did in January of 1973. During 1973–1975, they concentrated their political energies on insisting that the 1973 cease-fire agreement be carried out and that U.S. troops totally withdraw from Vietnam.

In April of 1974, Jane returned to Hanoi with Hayden, their son Troy, her mother-in-law, and cinematographer Haskell Wexler. They filmed a documentary, entitled *Introduction to the Enemy*, which highlighted their journey from Hanoi to the liberated section of Quous Tri Province, and documented the rebuilding of Vietnam. This film was not widely distributed.

In 1976, Hayden ran against incumbent John Tunney in the Democratic primary for the U.S. Senate. Jane invested $500,000 of her own money and campaigned heavily for Hayden. Although Hayden lost the race, he received 40 percent of the votes. His political influence was maintained by founding, in that year, the Campaign for Economic Democracy (CED), which ultimately became Campaign California. CED was founded as an egalitarian grassroots organization which promoted middle-class causes such as rent control, government-sponsored day care, a safe and clean environment, and energy conservation. The group has sponsored several statewide ballot initiatives and helped elect over fifty candidates running for local offices.

Jane resumed her career as an actress with the 1977 film *Fun with Dick and Jane*. Most of her salary from the film was invested in CED and their ranch at Santa Barbara, California, where they established a summer camp for underprivileged children. In 1978, Bruce Gilbert became a partner in IPC. It was renamed the International Pictures Corporation. IPC would eventually produce several major films including *On Golden Pond*.

CED relied heavily on Jane's income as an actress. When additional money became necessary, Jane decided to invest in something that she knew about, physical fitness. She established the Jane Fonda Workout Studio in Beverly Hills, California, in 1979. After two years, the *Jane Fonda Workout Book* was published by Simon and Schuster. As the popularity of the workout spas and books increased, Jane decided to market her exercise routine as a videotape. The business prospered. Jane finally bought the workout business from CED and continued to contribute a significant portion of the profits to CED.

Jane received an Academy Award for best actress for her performance in *Coming Home* in 1979. She and Tom participated in a march on Washington to demonstrate against the building and activating of nuclear power plants. Jane and Tom joined the picket lines to support the United Farm Workers. This was part of a fifty-city tour in which they campaigned for rent control, corporate control by employees, energy alternatives, and health care improvements. They continued speaking out against nuclear power, unfair working conditions, and environmental pollution.

Jane continued acting in message movies such as *The Electric Horseman*. This made a statement against big business and the amorality of advertising. *Nine to Five*, another tremendous success for IPC films, addressed how management treated secretaries and other women working in corporations. Her next film, *On Golden Pond*, carried a strongly personal message about family relationships. In addition to uniting two great film stars, Katharine Hepburn and Henry Fonda, the movie allowed Jane and Henry to mend their father-daughter relationship. Henry's performance earned him his first Academy Award. Shortly afterwards, after eight operations and a long bout with heart disease, Henry Fonda died on August 11, 1982.

Jane's exercise business and Hayden's political career continued to prosper. She released her first workout video in 1982 and a year later co-authored *Women Coming of Age*. She supported Hayden in his successful campaign against Republican Bill Hawkins for the Forty-Fourth District State Assembly seat. Both candidates spent more than two million dollars, making it the most expensive race for a California Assembly seat.

Jane experienced another significant year in 1986. Jane and her family, including Shirley Fonda, participated in Hands Across America, a nationwide event to raise funds for the poor. IPC was renamed Fonda Films, and Lois Bonfiglio, a New York producer, became Jane's partner. CED continued to grow and to help elect candidates to office. Hayden won his bids for re-election, each time by a wider margin. Jane also assisted in the release of Ida Nudel, a Soviet refusenik.

Less successful was her marriage. Tom and Jane had begun to grow apart. By 1988, family time was made by appointment. She and Hayden had conflicting schedules. Moreover, Tom had a public affair with Vicky Rideout, a woman he had met while working for the presidential campaign of Michael Dukakis. Jane and Hayden separated and divorced in 1989.

Jane's next two films, *Old Gringo* and *Stanley and Iris*, were not well reviewed but could be considered significant. When *Stanley and Iris* was being filmed in Winterberry, Connecticut, local Vietnam veterans did not welcome Jane or her film crew. They attempted to prohibit the production of the film because of Jane's action in Hanoi. Jane met with the veterans to discuss her trip to Hanoi and their feelings about it. Some veterans remained angry with Jane, while others chose to forgive her.

Jane later married Ted Turner, cable TV magnate. They had been seen around the world together—at a White House dinner, the Cannes Film Festival, the Oscar show, the 1991 World Series, and visiting Mikhail Gorbachev. Her 1990s film projects included plans to produce a film based on Neil Sheehan's award-winning *A Bright Shining Lie* (on the Vietnam War) and an American version of the Pedro Almadovar film *Women on the Verge of a Nervous Breakdown*. Jane continued to generate money and publicity for causes and organizations that she supported. She remained motivated by the belief that her work was improving the lives of others.

Bibliography

Anderson, Christopher. *Citizen Jane: The Turbulent Life of Jane Fonda*. New York: Henry Holt and Company, 1990.

Carroll, Peter N. *Famous in America: Jane Fonda, George Wallace, Phyllis Shafley, John Glenn; The Passion to Succeed*. New York: Dutton, 1985.

Collier, Peter. *The Fondas: A Hollywood Dynasty*. New York: Putnam, 1990.

Fonda, Henry, with Howard Teichmann. *Fonda: My Life*. New York: New American Library, 1981.

Guiles, Fred Lawrence. *Jane Fonda, The Actress in Her Time*. Garden City, NY: Doubleday, 1982.

Haddad-Garcia, George. *The Films of Jane Fonda*. Secaucus, NJ: The Citadel Press, 1981.

Hayden, Tom. *Reunion: A Memoir*. New York: Collier Books, Macmillan Publishing Company, 1989.

Olson, James S., ed. *Dictionary of the Vietnam War*. Westport, CT: Greenwood Press, 1988.

Spada, James. *Fonda, Her Life in Pictures*. Garden City, NY: A Dolphin Book, Doubleday and Company, 1985.

Vadim, Roger. *Bardot, Deneuve, Fonda*. New York: Simon and Schuster, 1986.

Zeidler, Jeanne. "Speaking Out, Selling Out, Working Out: The Changing Politics of

Jane Fonda," in *Women and American Foreign Policy: Lobbyists, Critics, and Insiders*, Edward P. Crapol, ed., 2d ed. Wilmington, DE: Scholarly Resources, 1992: 137–51.

Regina T. Akers

H. BRUCE FRANKLIN (1934–   )

Venceremos organizer, radical professor

In the late 1960s H. Bruce Franklin, a tenured associate professor of English at Stanford University, became a radical Marxist-Leninist. He helped organize a revolutionary group called Venceremos. In 1971 he was involved in several campus protests, including one that led to the university's computer center suffering considerable damage. As a result, in 1972 Franklin became the first tenured professor fired by a major American university in many years.

Franklin's life was filled with juxtapositions. Born into a poor, white- collar family in Brooklyn, New York, he attended Amherst. He worked on a tugboat, served three years as an officer in the U.S. Air Force, and received his Ph.D. from Stanford. His brilliance led Stanford, in an unusual move, to hire him for its own faculty. The leading scholar on Herman Melville in his generation, he received tenure at a younger age than any other person in the history of his department.

Between 1964 and 1967 Franklin turned left. Morally offended by racism, by the excesses of American society, and especially by the Vietnam War, Franklin saw in Fidel Castro and Mao Tse-tung revolutionary heroes worthy of respect and imitation. He was, at the root, a romantic.

Franklin recruited students for Venceremos, a multiracial, gun-toting group that preached violent revolution. Defying the American government's ban on travel to Cuba, the organization sent students to cut sugar cane as an act of solidarity with the Cuban people. For Franklin, Venceremos proved that people could shape their own lives.

By 1971 opposition to the Vietnam War had engulfed the Stanford campus. Many students protested, and Franklin frequently attended demonstrations. Critics charged that he stimulated student militance but that when the police came, he carefully avoided arrest, which fell upon the students.

Prior to a crucial sit-in at the university's computer center, Franklin spoke publicly to the demonstrators. He did not join the sit-in. Before or during the inevitable arrests, considerable damage was done to the center's equipment. At this point the university administration decided to fire Franklin.

To dismiss the radical professor, a panel of seven distinguished faculty members was assembled to hear testimony in a proceeding resembling a court trial.

H. Bruce Franklin. Copyright *Washington Post*. Reprinted by permission of D.C. Public Library.

Franklin's antics at the hearing did not help his case; he kept a portrait of Stalin at the defense table.

After sessions costing $180,000 and lasting six weeks, the faculty members voted, 5 to 2, to fire Franklin. One of the two dissenters was Donald Kennedy, later president of the university.

Although Franklin lost his battle for reinstatement in the courts, he had better luck with intellectuals. Many scholars saw the issue as one of free speech. Stanford University's claim that he had been dismissed not for his politics but for advocating illegal or destructive acts generated less and less support over time.

Harassed by the FBI and rejected for a position at the University of Colorado for political reasons, Franklin in 1975 was hired by Rutgers University in Newark, New Jersey.

Unrepentant, although no longer a Maoist, he said in 1978, "The main thing that has happened since 1968 is not that those of us who had certain views that were considered radical in '68 have changed our views, but that the majority of American people now hold the views I held. They don't seem now to be so radical."

Franklin went on to publish important books on the "mythology" of U.S. prisoners of war in Vietnam, science fiction (a long-term interest), and on prison literature, which he called one of the few forms of authentic American literature.

Bibliography

Franklin, H. Bruce. *American Prisoners and Ex-Prisoners, Their Writings: An Annotated Bibliography of Published Works, 1798–1981.* Westport, CT: Lawrence Hill, 1982.

———. *Back Where You Came From: A Life in the Death of the Empire.* New York: Harper's Magazine Press, 1975.

———. *From the Movement toward Revolution.* New York: Van Nostrand Reinhold, 1971.

———. *Future Perfect: American Science Fiction of the Nineteenth Century,* rev. ed. New York: Oxford University Press, 1978.

———. *M.I.A.; or, Mythmaking in America,* expanded and updated edition. New Brunswick, Rutgers University Press, 1993.

———. "The POW/MIA Myth," *The Atlantic* 268 (Dec. 1991): 45–47+.

———. *Prison Literature in America: The Victim as Criminal and Artist,* expanded ed. New York: Oxford University Press, 1989.

———. *Robert A. Heinlein: America as Science Fiction.* New York: Oxford University Press, 1980.

———. *The Wake of the Gods: Melville's Mythology.* Stanford: Stanford University Press, 1963.

———. *War Stars: The Superweapon and the American Imagination.* New York: Oxford University Press, 1988.

Levinson, Sandra and Carol Brightman, eds. *Venceremos Brigade: Young Americans Sharing the Life and Work of Revolutionary Cuba.* New York: Simon and Schuster, 1971.

W. J. Rorabaugh

ALLEN GINSBERG (1926–   )

Poet, teacher

Allen Ginsberg's *Howl*, published in 1956, is one of the most important poems written in the second half of the twentieth century. After the San Francisco police arrested Lawrence Ferlinghetti and Shig Murao for selling this book, the media pushed Ginsberg into the spotlight. A sensational trial lasted throughout the summer. Finally, Judge Clayton Horn ruled that *Howl* was not obscene; it had redeeming social value. After this event, Ginsberg used his celebrity to focus public attention on the views of himself and his friends. The 146,000 copies of *Howl* that were in print by 1967 suggest that he sometimes reached a wide audience.

Nearly all of the social themes that animate Ginsberg's work were articulated in *Howl*: sexual liberation, harsh criticism of predatory business and bureaucratic government, the open declaration of subterranean feelings, antiwar and pro-working-class sentiments, "one world" values, and spiritual enlightenment. He spoke about and acted on these issues throughout the sixties. Despite various controversies, the rewards of the Establishment did not elude him. He has been Distinguished Professor of English at Brooklyn College, a Guggenheim fellow, recipient of a National Book Award, and member of the American Academy and Institute of Arts and Letters. But he continued to urge his audiences to take the world into their own hands and oppose war, famine, tyranny and repression with love, cooperation, and compassion. Even though he wore a suit and tie in the 1980s, he did not compromise his essential values. Instead, he turned Herbert Marcuse's contention—that society accommodates, superficially absorbs, and dissolves dissension—to his own use. He made himself acceptable for subversive reasons.

Ginsberg's parents were Russian immigrants who settled in New Jersey. His father, Louis, was a socialist, schoolteacher, and poet whose work would appear in Louis Untermeyer's anthologies, Alfred Kreymborg's *The Others*, Max Eastman's *The New Masses*, and *The New York Times*. His mother, Naomi Levy, was a Communist, and both families objected when Louis and Naomi married in 1919. Their first son, born in 1921, was named Eugene, after Eugene Debs, the labor organizer and Socialist party candidate for U.S. president five times between 1900 and 1920. Their second son, Irwin Allen, was born five years later, and named in honor of his great-grandfather. Allen attended local public schools and experienced anti-Semitism. The summers that he spent in camps run on socialist principles acquainted him with another dimension to being "other." He also confronted the steady deterioration of

Allen Ginsberg with Ishmael Reed, 1974. Copyright *Washington Post*; Reprinted by permission of D.C. Public Library.

Naomi's mental health. Her intense paranoia and bouts of depression eventually landed her in the psychiatric ward of various institutions. Throughout his childhood, Allen directly observed madness in a beloved one. And in high school he felt his first strong homosexual longing. The boy who he desired would be attending Columbia University. Ginsberg vowed to himself that he would be an "honest revolutionary labor lawyer" if he, too, were admitted (See "Kaddish," Ginsberg's elegy to Naomi). When Allen won a scholarship to attend Columbia in 1942, he dreamed that he might become a senator or president.

Ginsberg was graduated from Columbia in 1948. Although he submitted to the required dose of great books, he discovered that he could be severely punished for bucking the system. His friendship with Jack Kerouac and William Burroughs began during these years, and their escapades (some rather sordid) with drugs, booze, and sex got Ginsberg into so much trouble that he was suspended from the college. He was required to seek psychiatric counseling before he could return. In the interim, he worked as a merchant seaman, laborer, and market researcher. By the early fifties, he was seriously searching for his poetic voice. He claimed to have heard the spirit of William Blake talking to him in his East Harlem apartment. He left for San Francisco, a hotbed, according to a sensational *Harper's* article, of sex and anarchy, with Henry Miller and Kenneth Rexroth (*) the leaders. There Ginsberg recited *Howl* for the first time at the famous Six Gallery Reading with Gary Snyder, Michael McClure, and Philip Whalen. Soon after, Ginsberg embarked on a series of trips to North Africa, Central America, India, Japan, and Southeast Asia. He was searching for both spiritual enlightenment and good times. As part of that quest, he became involved in the drug scene, including Timothy Leary's experiments with LSD. Ginsberg has said that he "stupefied himself" from 1948 to 1963 to find consciousness.

During the sixties Ginsberg set the pace of his lifestyle. As an activist and a poet, he seemed to be constantly making tracks across the United States. He attended an October 1963 protest rally at San Francisco's Sheraton Palace Hotel against "Dragon Lady" Madame Nhu; participated in a spring 1964 ACLU demonstration to protest the shutdown of Bay Area poetry coffeehouses that did not meet cabaret standards; testified with Susan Sontag in the defense of Jonas Mekas, who was charged with obscenity for screening films by Jean Genet and Jack Smith; staged with Ed Sanders a LeMar demonstration to legalize marijuana at the Department of Welfare on New York City's Lower East Side in December 1964; gave an anti-war teach-in at Columbia University; chanted mantra in what he erroneously hoped would be a nonviolent demonstration for peace, the 1968 Yippie Festival of Life; and testified at the Chicago Conspiracy trial during which time he recited "Going to Chicago" (1968), "Howl" (1955–1956), "Love Poem on a Theme by Whitman" (1954), "The Night Apple" (1950), and "In Society" (1947). The prosecution, in particular, was determined to discredit Ginsberg's credentials as a witness by implying that anyone who wrote overtly homosexual poems, as some of these are, could not be trusted to tell the truth. Apparently the U.S. government concurred. The FBI had already started a file on Ginsberg. An entry in 1968 notes that he was observed chanting "unintelligible poems" in San Francisco's Grant Park. (Lewis Hyde tells us that Ginsberg was reciting Blake's "The Grey Monk.")

Throughout the sixties, Ginsberg developed a public persona that seemed impervious to assault. He was an iconoclastic mix of wise and wild man, of satyr and ascetic, of priest and clown, a poet of daring and discipline who did not separate his art from his politics. His style of writing reflected his determination to break down oppressive convention and nurture the sense of personal responsibility and personal freedom that inform both creative and political actions. "Wichita Vortex Sutra" is frequently cited as Ginsberg's best known and "most heartfelt artistic response to the horror of the Vietnam War," according to Barry Miles, whose biography of Ginsberg appeared in 1989. Part of its success has to do with the skill with which Ginsberg juxtaposes hawkish messages from the government-controlled media with the miseries of war. (For a fine discussion of Ginsberg's use of language in this poem, see Laszlo Géfin's *Ideograms: History of a Poetic Method*.) Ginsberg himself is on the page, with reminiscences about friends' sexual encounters, exhortations for Buddhist wisdom, descriptions of life on the road, and finally, and painfully, a mourning of his mother, whose mental breakdown and death he blames on the same "vortex of hatred that defoliated the Mekong Delta." Other poems like "Pentagon Exorcism" and "War Profit Litany" would deliver political messages in more obvious ways. Sexual poems like "Please Master" and "On Neal's Ashes" may be shocking for some readers. The humor in a poem like "Kiss Ass" could offend many. Nevertheless, in these sixties poems, Ginsberg makes his emotions and perceptions palpable, not exclusively for the sake of self-expression but to create a better world.

In the following decades, Ginsberg steadfastly matched his rhetoric and action. He became both famous and rich, but he sometimes rejected lucrative offers—as large as $100,000 from a prospective publisher in 1970—or gave away whatever sums he received for poetry readings and other public appearances. His home continued to be a railroad apartment in the East Village. The money went to both political and artistic causes. In the late sixties, he founded the Committee on Poetry and distributed thousands of dollars to needy writers and underground publications. He always spoke up for those poets whose work he admired but who had not yet been embraced by the academy as he was. Ginsberg had vivid memories of being excluded from poetry anthologies in the fifties along with poets like Denise Levertov, Robert Duncan, Robert Creeley, Gary Snyder, and Charles Olson because they were "shaggy" poets rather than "combed" ones. In the seventies and eighties he was still praising writers like Gregory Corso and Philip Whalen, while lambasting authors who were sent abroad by the CIA as cultural ambassadors because they never uttered anything critical about the United States. He helped William Burroughs, when he was broke, get a lecturer's position at City College. There were countless unrecorded deeds of goodwill. He also created with Anne Waldman the Jack Kerouac School of Disembodied Poetics at the Naropa Institute in Boulder, Colorado. The Institute itself was founded by his guru Chogyman Trungpa. Ginsberg was instrumental in securing funds for the school through organizations like the National Endowment for the Arts. He also gave numerous benefit readings for the school.

As E. Klingenberg once put it, Ginsberg is an "anarchist hostile to any regime or regimentation, a revolutionary par excellence who says exactly what he thinks and feels [who] can be a nuisance to any state." Ginsberg demonstrated this perspective in January 1965 when he was invited to attend a writers' conference in Cuba. Although he was told on numerous occasions that Cuba was chiefly concerned with building schools, hospitals, and housing, he called for legalizing marijuana and ending the persecution of homosexuals. He lectured on spontaneous composition and mantra singing, and discussed with a journalist a sex fantasy that he had about Che Guevara. Ginsberg was soon expelled from Cuba. In Czechoslovakia, he evoked the same response from authorities because they feared that he was a drug addict and a sexual deviant. Although he was selected as the King of May by college students for the medieval festival that they had revived during a wave of Communist liberalism, his behavior in Prague was regarded as provocative. He was arrested three times before being deported.

Ginsberg's commitment to personal freedom did not waiver over the years. However, he spoke later from a position of power and influence, and with a better understanding of the problems of the world. Still, the mature Ginsberg did not become stuffy. His collaboration with musicians like Bob Dylan (*) in 1975 and the British punk rock band the Clash in 1982 showed that he was still hip. He did not censor himself in his art or his talk although on occasion he admitted that he said more than he knew. He could still shock an audience by stating that erotic relationships between student and teacher should be institutionally encouraged. His political demonstrations continued, typified now perhaps by Ginsberg, Peter Orlovsky, and three young women meditating on the railroad tracks outside Rockwell Corporation's plutonium bomb trigger factory in Colorado, and, as a result, halting a trainload of waste materials. On the day of this event (July 14, 1978), Ginsberg completed his poem "Plutonian Ode."

Ginsberg's barometer for human rights violations has been finely tuned. He joined the Freedom to Write Committee of PEN in 1966 when he helped gather support for Amiri Baraka (1*) whose writings were being used against him in an assault case. He also supported Reza Baraheni, the expatriate Iranian poet, after he was imprisoned and tortured by SEVAK during the regime of the Shah. He remained an active member, opposed to censorship of any kind anywhere in the world. In December 1990, he performed at Symphony Space to raise money for an emergency fund for writers and editors with AIDS. Philip Glass played the piano while Ginsberg recited "Wichita Vortex Sutra" and part of a chamber opera, "Hydrogen Jukebox," which they had collaborated on in 1989 at the Spoleto Festival. Throughout the seventies and eighties, Ginsberg maintained his pacifist, anti-authoritarian position. He was supremely aware that the release of the Iranian hostages coincided with the inauguration of Ronald Reagan, and that the U.S. government was giving military aid to the death squads in El Salvador while ignoring requests for aid from the Sandinistas in Nicaragua. He participated in UNESCO War on War readings in Italy, traveled to Tel Aviv in 1988 to read poetry at a demonstration protesting the treatment of Palestinians on the West Bank, and compiled data on thirty-five Palestinian journalists who were being detained without trial or charges.

Allen Ginsberg's massive *Collected Poems* was published by Harper and Row in 1984. The volume was as unorthodox as Ginsberg's lifestyle and politics. He personally oversaw the assembly of his published and unpublished poems. He wrote extensive notes that not only elucidated the poems but provided an underground guide to their literary, historical, and political contexts. He included illustrations by his friends, and photographs of his gurus and of protest happenings. He supplied the cast of characters who appear in his poems, and appended to them the prefaces, epigraphs, dedications, introductions, and jacket copy from the first printings. Furthermore, his acknowledgments included not only those who helped create this hefty volume, but also the people who participated in the original publication. He redefined a whole category in the publishing business by making the book a historical document of his life and times, as well as a definitive record of his accomplishments. He took pride in his work, and expressed his debt and gratitude to all those who helped him. In other words, he brought an intense kind of personal responsibility to this project, the same perspective that if practiced truthfully by us all, might eradicate much of the suffering that exists in this world. Reviews in such publications as *Time*, *Commentary*, and *New Republic* were either negative or out of focus. Nonetheless, 20,000 copies were sold within the first two years of publication. As Kenneth Rexroth testified at the "Howl" trial in 1957, Ginsberg's voice is like that of "the prophets of the Bible . . . in purpose and in language, and in subject matter . . . .The theme is the denunciation of evil and pointing the way out." The visionary Ginsberg continued to startle, anger, and inspire.

Bibliography

Allen, Donald, and Warren Tallman, eds. *The Poetics of the New American Poetry*. New York: Grove, 1973.

Ginsberg, Allen. *Collected Poems*. New York: Harper and Row, 1984.

———. *Empty Mirror*. Corinth, NY: Totem, 1961.

———. *The Fall of America*. San Francisco: City Lights Books, 1972.

———. *The Gates of Wrath*. Bolinas, CA: Grey Fox, 1972.

———. *Howl*. San Francisco: City Lights Books, 1956.

———. *Kaddish*. San Francisco: City Lights Books, 1961.

———. *Mind Breaths*. San Francisco: City Lights Books, 1977.

———. *Planet News*. San Francisco: City Lights Books, 1968.

———. *Plutonian Ode*. San Francisco: City Lights Books, 1982.

———. *Reality Sandwiches*. San Francisco: City Lights Books, 1963.

Gray, Richard. *American Poetry in the Twentieth Century*. London and New York: Longman, 1990.

Hyde, Louis, ed. *On the Poetry of Allen Ginsberg*. Ann Arbor: University of Michigan Press, 1984. (This volume contains reprints of essays by E. Klingenberg, Laszlo Géfin, and Hayden Carruth that are cited in the text.)

Kramer, Jane. *Allen Ginsberg in America*. New York: Random House, 1969.

"The Life and Times of Allen Ginsberg" (1992 film directed and produced by Jerry Aronson, 83 minutes). Available from Jerry Aronson, P.O. Box 897, Boulder, CO 80306.

Merrill, Thomas F. *Allen Ginsberg*. New York: Twayne, 1969.

Miles, Barry. *Ginsberg*. New York: Simon and Schuster, 1989. Reviewed: Andrei Codrescu, "The Beat Gone On," *The Nation*, Dec. 25, 1989, pp. 798–800.

Milosz, Czeslaw. *Visions from San Francisco Bay*. New York: Farrar, Straus and Giroux, 1982.

Morgan, Bill, and Bob Rosenthal, eds. *A Tribute to Allen Ginsberg*, Part 1 and Part 2. New York: Lospecchio, 1986.

Schumacher, Michael. *Dharma Lion: A Critical Biography of Allen Ginsberg*. New York: St. Martin's Press, 1992.

Linda Hamalian

DICK GREGORY (1932–   )

Civil rights activist; cultural critic

In name and rise in fortune, Richard Claxton Gregory matches his namesake hero Ragged Dick of Horatio Alger's nineteenth-century boys' stories boosting truth, justice, and the American way. Gregory's two installments of autobiography, *Nigger* (1964) and *Up from Nigger* (1976), describe his transformation from an impoverished welfare case to an affluent success. By 1990 he had established himself as a businessman who marketed a Slim-Safe Bahamian Diet based on a powdered drink mix. His new image as a conservative capitalist fit Gregory no better, however, than his 1960s' stock comic image. Those who then found his wit too telling may have wanted to call him a simple comedian rather than a social critic championing fundamental change in American life. But Gregory's life and work resist simplistic dichotomy or the single-dimensional label.

Gregory rose to prominence as a comedian. His successful nightclub acts earned him as much as $5,000 a week during the 1960s. But he was never a clown or extravagantly boisterous. He was not engaged in farce. He never talked nonsense. His comedy was classic, not slapstick; that is to say, it was serious. As Gregory put it in the early 1970s, he wasn't "just whistlin' Dixie." He worked to move blacks and whites, North and South, to meet basic social needs.

To understand the man and his message requires understanding Dick Gregory's concern about the dignity of human life, particularly among blacks in America. His earnest approach from the start has emphasized basics, perhaps because he was born into a life with early brutal experience. A child of the Great Depression, he was born on October 12, 1932, in St. Louis, Missouri, the second of six children. He learned from his mother, Lucille, that "man has two ways out in life—laughing or crying." Gregory has done much of both.

As a child he cried a lot. He learned the harsh reality of a system that saw

[PUBLIC CITIZEN #1 - PRESIDENT OF THE UNITED STATES IN EXILE - INAUGURATED 3-4-69]

Dick Gregory. *Source*: Library of Congress

his mother as a welfare cheat because she got a meager relief check while working as a domestic for whites so that she could keep her children from starving or being homeless. He cried at school, where he learned hate and shame. He felt sorry for himself, but he did not wallow long. He started making money shining shoes and selling newspapers; he lied about his age to get better summer jobs and factory work.

He was never the proverbial good boy who studied hard (unlike Horatio Alger). He learned less in school than in the streets. There he realized the power of a joke. He got kids off his fatherless, raggedy, skinny back by making jokes instead of running home, hiding, and crying.

Schooled by his childhood poverty, Gregory learned a key principle of comedic social criticism. "Once you get a man to laugh with you," Gregory realized, "it's hard for him to laugh at you." Once an audience expected to hear funny things, he explained, "I could say anything I wanted. I got a reputation as a funny man. And then I started to turn the jokes on them."

Joking helped Gregory survive the streets while athletic running helped him survive school. He found something he could do; he could run as fast as anyone in St. Louis. Running gave him social meaning and inner purpose. He ran in high school to fight being poor. He ran in college at Southern Illinois University, which gave him an athletic scholarship. In running, he learned himself. He learned self-respect.

Running also brought recognition. By Gregory's senior year at St. Louis's segregated Sumner High School he was a schoolboy champion at cross-country and on the track. People knew who he was. He was SIU's outstanding athlete of 1953. He was the first black to win the award in the school's eighty-four-year history.

Gregory's self-improvement was linked with self-discovery. While he was learning about himself, he was learning about others and the world. His personal struggle with being poor and black became bitter lessons in a broader education. For example, when snubbed during college at a Carbondale movie theatre that permitted blacks to sit only in the balcony, Gregory staged a personal sit-in to desegregate. He learned that asking was not enough. Anger needed direction. Change required direct action. He learned the society-wide dimensions of his personal struggle.

His personal struggle carried Gregory to the struggle for civil rights. He marched and sat-in both in the South and in the North, in city and countryside. He was shot in 1965 during the rioting in Los Angeles's Watts section while appealing for calm and trying to get folks off the streets. He opposed the war in Vietnam. He went to jail. He went to the U.S. Supreme Court. And his case, *Gregory v. City of Chicago* (394 U.S. 111 [1969]) made a bit of law as the nation's highest court overruled the Illinois Supreme Court in reversing disorderly conduct convictions of Gregory and his fellow peaceful civil rights demonstrators. Gregory also ran in 1967 as an independent write-in candidate against incumbent Richard Daley, Sr. for mayor of Chicago. Then in 1968 he was an independent write-in candidate for U.S. president, opposing former Vice President Richard M. Nixon.

Following the example of Martin Luther King, Jr. (1*), Gregory explored the nonviolent philosophy of the Indian nationalist leader and social reformer Mahatma Gandhi. Again following a personal approach to the broader struggle, Gregory became committed to fasting as the definitive act of nonviolent protest. He initiated his new approach in 1967. He announced a thirty-two-day water-only fast, from Thanksgiving to Christmas, to protest the war in Vietnam.

The fast, or "hunger strike," as some called it, changed Gregory's life. Under the direction of nutritionist Dr. Alvenia Fulton, who operated the Fultonia Health Food Center in Chicago, Gregory developed a scientific fast from which he experienced profound physical and mental transformation. As he remembered it, "What began as a protest against the war was later to become a way of life, a whole new understanding of the functioning of the human body and the laws of Mother Nature."

He became a vegetarian. Nonviolence required him to renounce all killing and destruction. He accepted nonviolence as a creed to live by, rather than as a mere tactic to maneuver against segregation. Since nonviolence meant living in harmony with nature, killing animals to eat them was a crime against nature.

As was typical of Gregory, his personal approach had developed into an engagement with broad social problems. His personal battles with poverty and racism moved him to a concern for human dignity and civil rights and carried him to oppose the war in Vietnam. Fasting carried him to see hunger as the ultimate attack on human rights. Protesting world hunger moved him in 1974 to a 900-mile run from Chicago to Washington, D.C., via Gary, Indiana, Detroit, and Cleveland, to focus attention on the nation's and world's food crisis.

He now wanted to live in a less urban and polluted environment. He left Chicago's South Side for Plymouth, Massachusetts. Gregory, his wife, Lillian, and their ten children left a four-bedroom apartment in 1974 for a seven-bedroom house on a 400-acre farm overlooking Long Pond Lake. He lived there for many years.

Gregory's concern with healthful living resulted in *Dick Gregory's Natural Diet for Folks Who Eat: Cookin' with Mother Nature* in the 1970s. In the 1980s he began Dick Gregory Health Enterprises, which marketed his weight-loss powdered drink mix titled the Slim-Safe Bahamian Diet. This product offered to reduce dieters by five-to-ten pounds per week. It was sold in sixteen ounce cans for $19.95 and became the basis for Gregory's temporary rise to capitalist stature. His diet sought to reduce the cholesterol and saturated fats connected with heart attack, high blood pressure, obesity, and other diseases that particularly ravaged African-Americans. By 1989 the financial press was referring to Gregory's "diet empire" as he developed Dick Gregory's Diet and Health Resort and Beachmark Inn. This was a five-building, 117-suite luxury hotel complex in Florida's Fort Walton Beach. Despite later business reverses, he retained remarkable gifts as a self-promoter.

Gregory also continued to see himself as an advocate of fundamental change. His diet pressed for transforming nutrition habits. The same man who titled his two installments of autobiography *Nigger* and *Up from Nigger*, the man who wrote *No More Lies: The Myth and the Reality of American History* and *The Shadow That Scares Me* became an entrepreneur. But he was not exploiting weakness. He was trying to encourage health. In 1987 he went on a forty-four day fast to fight drugs in Atlanta. When President George Bush confronted Iraq in October 1990 Dick Gregory marched alone outside the White House in Washington, D.C., bearing a placard that read: "Dear Mr. President, before you veto the Civil Rights Bill, please think about the number of Black African-Americans you have sent to the Persian Gulf willing to die for someone else's human rights." Dick Gregory was still a perpetual-motion man.

Bibliography

Barry, Thomas. "Dick Gregory Uses His Wit to Awaken Young Whites," *Look*, June 25, 1968, pp. 69–78.

Coleman, Sandy. "Gregory Launches Fast for Gulf Peace with Plymouth Vigil," *Boston Globe*, Nov. 23, 1990, p. 49.

"Comedy Awards Show Honors Arsenio Hall, Salutes Dick Gregory," *Jet* 76 (June 18, 1989): 53.

"Dick Gregory Comes to the Rescue of 1,000-pound Walter Hudson," *Jet* 73 (Nov. 9, 1987): 17–18.

"Dick Gregory Is Arrested at NW Park," *Washington Post*, Oct. 13, 1993, D7.

"Dick Gregory Returns to Nature," *Ebony* 30 (Nov. 1974): 37–40.

Gregory, Dick. "And I Ain't Just Whistlin' Dixie," *Ebony* 26 (Aug. 1971): 149–50.

———. *Dick Gregory's Natural Diet for Folks Who Eat: Cookin' with Mother Nature.* New York: Harper and Row, 1974.

———. *Dick Gregory's Political Primer*, James R. McGraw, ed. New York: Harper and Row, 1972.

———. *From the Back of the Bus*, Bob Orben, ed. New York: Avon Books, 1962.

———. *Nigger: An Autobiography.* New York: Dutton, 1964.

———. *No More Lies: The Myth and Reality of American History.* New York: Harper and Row, 1971.

———. *The Shadow That Scares Me*, James R. McGraw, ed. Garden City, NY: Doubleday, 1968.

———. *Up from Nigger.* New York: Stein and Day, 1976.

Gregory, Dick, and Mark Lane. *Code Name "Zoro": The Murder of Martin Luther King, Jr.* Englewood Cliffs, NJ: Prentice-Hall, 1977.

"Gregory Says Court Freezes $2 Million Owed Him as He Faces Eviction and Creditors," *Jet* 78 (Aug. 27, 1990): 52–53.

"Humor, Integrated," *Time* 17 (Feb. 1961): 67.

Leavy, Walter. "A Comedic Look at the Black Middle Class," *Ebony* 42 (Aug. 1987): 68.

McGreevy, Brian. "Activist Dick Gregory Praises Civil Rights Gains," *Atlanta Constitution*, Nov. 8, 1990, XI:3.

Nash, Jonell. "Vibing Vegetarian," *Essence* 20 (July 1989): 69–72.

"New Book Reveals J. Edgar Hoover's Hatred of Dr. King, Dick Gregory and the Black Panthers," *Jet* 83 (March 23, 1993): 34–7.

Schwartz, John. "Funny Man, Serious Money," *Newsweek* 112 (Oct. 17, 1988): 61.

Thomas Joseph Davis

JOHN HOLT (1923–1985)

Educational critic, activist, and writer

With the 1964 publication of *How Children Fail*, John Holt emerged as one of the leading figures in the educational reform movement of the 1960s. "Nobody starts off stupid," wrote John Holt in 1964. Yet, as he saw it, the American educational system was schooling children in stupidity. Holt's writing fit within a new genre of educational critique presented as first- person accounts by radical school teachers. *How Children Fail*, along with James Herndon's *The Way It Spozed to Be* (1965), Herbert Kohl's *36 Children* (1967), Jonathan Kozol's *Death at an Early Age* (1967), and George Dennison's *The Lives of Children* (1969), depicted the day-to-day repression and inanity experienced in schools, and rapidly became the classic texts for the educational activists of the 1960s. The voices of these "new critics" of education were attractively anti-authoritarian and served to inspire the establishment of a wide variety of "free," "alternative," and "open" schools and classrooms. Within this context, John Holt's work became enormously influential because it appealed to progressive teachers and administrators in the schools as well as middle-class and counterculture parents. It helped set the agenda for a decade of educational activism that was to eventually disappear amid a splintering of reformist educational strategies and the conservative "back to basics" backlash of the mid-seventies. As the movement dissolved, and the other new critics in education continued their struggles in different arenas, John Holt came to the conclusion that the reform of public education was hopeless. By 1978 he was advising the American parent to abandon the school and "teach your own."

John Holt's own educational experience took place in the elite private schools of the well-to-do. John Caldwell Holt was born into a wealthy family in New York City on April 14, 1923. His parents, Elizabeth Crocker Holt and Henry Holt, moved to a prosperous Connecticut suburb during his early childhood. He was sent to school in Switzerland and then to Phillips Exeter Academy in New Hampshire. Although Holt proved to be a good student, he recalled that he was bored and alienated during his school years. Nevertheless, he went on to college at Yale University and graduated with a degree in engineering in 1943. He then joined the U.S. Navy and spent the remainder of World War II aboard a submarine. In 1978 when he looked back at this time of his life in *Never Too Late: My Musical Life Story*, he eulogized his war experience as the most meaningful education he had ever received.

After the war Holt, like many veterans, found it difficult to find a place for himself. He worked as a lecturer and lobbyist for an organization based in New York City called the World Federalists, USA, that hoped to promote world peace through the formation of a united world government. Although this work might have helped him to understand some of the processes involved in lobbying for social change, it also frustrated and overwhelmed him. As a result, when he was twenty-nine, he took a year off to travel in the United States and Europe. This personal quest finally ended and his career in education began when he took a job as a cook at a private school in Colorado in 1953.

Holt did not remain a cook for long. He soon became a teacher of secondary language and mathematics at the Colorado Rocky Mountain School. During the next fifteen years he remained in teaching; moving from Colorado to the Shady Hill Elementary School in Cambridge, Massachusetts, in 1958; the Leslie Ellis Elementary School in Cambridge in 1959; and the Commonwealth Secondary School in Boston in 1965. By 1968, Holt's book and articles had won him a wide audience, and he left full-time teaching to concentrate on his writing. Then, during 1968 and 1969, perhaps the most turbulent and creative years of the 1960s, he accepted visiting lectureships at the Harvard Graduate School of Education and the University of California at Berkeley. He was now clearly at the center of the growing debate on educational reform.

In his early writing Holt's major thesis, based on his experiences as a student and teacher, was essentially Rousseauian. For Holt as well as Rousseau, social institutions serve to thwart and corrupt the healthy development of human nature. Holt maintained that the child "is by nature and from birth not only loving and kind but serious and purposeful." She or he is a natural explorer, a natural learner, who, if left alone, will set the most appropriate educational goals and pursue them in the most appropriate way. When it forces children to conform and learn "what we and not they think they ought to know" through standardization, competition, and the administration of reward and punishment, the school succeeds only in humiliating, confusing, frightening, and oppressing the child's true nature.

In 1967 in *How Children Learn* Holt began to suggest ways in which schools could become "places where children learn what they most want to know" and teachers could become nondirective and trusted learning guides. This book, along with a series of articles published as *The Underachieving School* in 1969 and *What Do I Do on Monday?* in 1970, were intended to serve as resources for radical parents and teachers who wanted to transform schools and classrooms from the inside.

It's easy to see why Holt's critique became so popular with members of the counterculture. It rejected traditional authority relations and the cultural agenda embedded within the public schools' standard curriculum that were increasingly being seen as a covert preparation for American racism and imperialism. It advocated self-directed, experientially based, and relevant educational processes that were seen as capable of fostering human creativity and freeing self-expression. And finally, it offered the hope that schools, if reformed from the bottom up, just might serve to liberate rather than oppress.

Holt's critique of the schools, however, did not delineate a more inclusive philosophy for social change. It failed to develop any obvious or thoroughgoing political vision. Unlike his peers whose writing had emerged from the experience of teaching poor and black children in the inner cities, Holt confined his attention to describing the coercive manipulation of middle-class white children. This focus may have prevented him from seeing the complexity of structural constraints on educational reform. As a result, he grounded the possibility for the transformation of the school in a change of consciousness in teachers, parents, and administrators and neglected to address what changes in the social and political context might be necessary. He did not, except parenthetically, address the issues of race, sex, and class. His interest was primarily confined to the psychological results, rather than the racial, sexual, or economic sources of school oppression. The seemingly apolitical nature of Holt's critique may have been why his writings became so popular within middle-class educational communities by the end of the 1960s. It may also explain why other educational activists, while praising his portrayal of the school child, began to find Holt's analysis simplistic and naive.

Ironically, as Holt's work gained in popularity and he traveled around the country to present his ideas, he began to recognize his own naivete. He kept encountering adults who he felt "actively distrust and dislike children," and he began to doubt his earlier optimism about the possibility of school reform. However, these doubts did not cause him to broaden his focus and look at the impact of the larger social structure on the educational system. Instead he now seemed to understand educational oppression and injustice as a product of personal choice. He concluded that schools were "doing what most people want them to do, and doing it very well."

The shape John Holt's analysis took after his disillusionment with the reform movement was influenced in part by his connection to an international community of radical scholars at Ivan Illich's Intercultural Center of Documentation in Cuernavaca, Mexico. Holt began attending educational institutes at the Center in 1969 just as Illich was focusing his attention on compulsory state systems of education and developing an argument for the "deschooling" of society. Thus in 1971 Holt began to explore private and individual alternatives to public institutions. During this period he wrote about children's rights in *Freedom and Beyond* (1972) and *Escape from Childhood* (1974). Then in 1976 in *Instead of Education* he offered his own version of deschooling. Compulsory Schools were to be challenged by noncompulsory resource centers that would become "doing places for children."

Instead of Education was really Holt's final break with the educational activists, parents, and teachers who had considered themselves his colleagues during the 1960s. In the book's chilling final paragraph he asserted, "Education—compulsory schooling, compulsory learning—is a tyranny and a crime against the human mind and spirit. Let all those escape it who can, any way they can." Following 1976, Holt continued to maintain that compulsory schooling was "perhaps the most authoritarian and dangerous of all the social inventions of mankind," and he turned his attention to promoting the cause of "home schooling." In 1978 he began to publish *Growing without Schools*, a newsletter for parents who were educating their children at home. His later work, *Teach Your Own: A Hopeful Path for Education*, which was published in 1981, grew out of his work with homeschoolers and was intended as an argument for the inauguration of a nationwide home schooling movement.

There are some common threads in John Holt's development from *How Children Fail* in 1964 to *Teach Your Own* in 1981. Throughout he maintained a romantic libertarianism in which the individual, the child as noble savage, was necessarily seen as the victim of coercive social institutions. From the beginning of his career as an educational commentator, John Holt advocated the establishment of contexts that would maximize the potential for self-realization, personal autonomy, and individual independence. While this position was compatible with the classic conservatism of laissez-faire individualism, in the context of the educational activism of the 1960s it appeared to support a radical critique of the school's dehumanization and manipulation of students. However, it really offered no hope for cooperative social frameworks or collectivist strategies for school reform. Holt was frustrated and discouraged by his involvement in a movement that included a diversity of constituencies in which some consensus, some surrender of personal autonomy, was necessary to the statement of goals and the formation of group solidarity. In effect, Holt grew to distrust group association. In *Teach Your Own* his contempt for the "group," "the people at large," and "the general public" was finally made explicit. In any extended social group, he argued, "the very worst are very likely to make it to the top." Thus, the only people who could be trusted to educate children were the child's own parents. However, in this misanthropic view he estimated the number of parents who "love and trust" their children enough to educate them at home at "no more than one percent of the population."

In some ways, John Holt's loss of faith in educational reform and his acceptance of a world in which we would be socially responsible only for our *own*, characterizes the story of the sixties' educational reform movement itself. It began with outrage at injustice and an expansive, energetic, and somewhat naive optimism, and it ended—for some—in disenchantment, cynicism, and retreat. John Holt's *How Children Fail* will endure however, as a particularly insightful and sensitive portrayal of how children experience their schooling that served to raise the consciousness of the parents and teachers of the 1960s.

Bibliography

Dennison, George. *The Lives of Children*. New York: Random House, 1969.
Franzosa, Susan D. "The Best and Wisest Parent: A Critique of John Holt's Philosophy of Education," *Urban Education* 19 (Oct. 1984): 227–44.
Friedenberg, Edgar. *Coming of Age in America*. New York: Random House, 1963.

Goodman, Paul. *Compulsory Miseducation*. New York: Vintage, 1964.

Herndon, James. *The Way It Spozed to Be*. New York: Simon and Schuster, 1965.

Holt, John. *Escape from Childhood*. New York: E. P. Dutton, 1974.

———. *Freedom and Beyond*. New York: E. P. Dutton, 1972.

———. *How Children Fail*. New York: Pitman Publishing, 1964.

———. *How Children Learn*. New York: Pitman Publishing, 1967.

———. *Instead of Education*. New York: E. P. Dutton, 1976.

———. *Learning All the Time*. Reading, MA: Addison-Wesley, 1989.

———. *Never Too Late: My Musical Life Story*. New York: E. P. Dutton, 1978.

———. *Teach Your Own: A Hopeful Path for Education*. New York: Delacorte Press, 1982.

———. *The Underachieving School*. New York: Pitman Publishing, 1969.

———. *What Do I Do Monday*. New York: E. P. Dutton, 1970.

Holt, John, and Susannah Sheffer. *A Life Worth Living: Selected Letters of John Holt*. Columbus: Ohio State University Press, 1990.

Postman, Neil, and Charles Weingartner. *Teaching as a Subversive Activity*. New York: Delacorte Press, 1970.

Silberman, Charles. *Crisis in the Classroom*. New York: Random House, 1970.

Susan Douglas Franzosa

IRVING HOWE (1920–1993)

Socialist literary critic, editor of Dissent

In the 1960s, Irving Howe achieved renown as the most widely read socialist literary critic in the United States, and as a controversial figure within the noncommunist left. He was a popular reviewer and essayist in periodicals such as *New York Review of Books*, the *New York Times Book Review*, and *New Republic*. He was also an aggressive polemicist against young militants and, with Michael Harrington (1928–1989), a founder of the Democratic Socialists of America, a liberal socialist grouping within the Democratic party. Howe subsequently achieved even wider fame for his best-selling history of Jewish-American immigrant life, *World of Our Fathers* (1976), and an eloquent political-intellectual autobiography, *A Margin of Hope* (1982).

He was born Irving Horenstein into a New York Jewish immigrant family in 1920. A teenage recruit to the Trotskyist wing of the Young Peoples Socialist League (YPSL) in the mid-1930s, he began using the name Howe soon after. He began his career as a talented left-wing writer even as he was an undergraduate at the City College of New York and a graduate student at Brooklyn College.

Prior to the spring of 1940, he was associated with the Socialist Workers party until it suffered a major split over Soviet policy in Eastern Europe.

Thereafter he was a member of the Workers party and the independent Socialist League, until resigning in the fall of 1952. These latter organizations were led by Max Shachtman (1904–1972), a youth leader of U.S. communism in the 1920s who became one of the founders of American Trotskyism in 1928.

In the 1940s, Howe was mainly influenced by the Shachtman version of Trotskyism. This approach, popularly known as "bureaucratic collectivism," held that the Russian Revolution and Lenin's Bolshevik policies were progressive for the USSR in their time, but that the ascendancy of Stalin's faction established a new ruling class vitiating social and economic achievements. Thereafter, revolutionary socialists must build a "Third Camp" movement, independent of either the United States or the USSR.

Internationally, in the 1940s and 1950s, this meant refusing to support any government in World War II or the Korean War. Domestically, the Shachtman group was sympathetic to the Walter Reuther–led wing of the United Auto Workers. This labor orientation became the subject of Howe's first book *The UAW and Walter Reuther* (1949), co-authored with his comrade B. J. Widick.

Howe participated in Shachtman's organizations primarily in a literary capacity, editing the YPSL's *Challenge of Youth* and the Workers party's *Labor Action*. He also frequently contributed to the *New International*, the theoretical organ of both the Workers party and the Independent Socialist League. His most prolific writings were on literature and issues of concern to radical intellectuals, but he also published on international events and theoretical questions.

The roots of many of Howe's later ideas about politics and culture can be found in these early debates, essays, and reviews, some of which appeared under pseudonyms such as "R. Fahan" and "R. Fangston." By the late 1940s he also began to publish in several intellectual journals with editors and staff members who themselves once held Trotskyist sympathies, such as Dwight Macdonald's *Politics* (where Howe was employed as a part-time assistant and some of his work appeared under the name Theodore Dryden), Philip Rahv's *Partisan Review*, and Elliott Cohen's *Commentary*.

Howe became disaffected from the Shachtman group with the onset of the cold war, resigning just before accepting a teaching position at Brandeis University. He felt that the Third Camp orientation was a failure and that U.S. socialism should undergo a phase of rethinking. Along with two close cothinkers, Emmanuel Geltman and Stanley Plastrik, Howe also concluded that democratic socialists should give critical support to the "West" against Stalinism.

A short time later, the sociologist Lewis Coser, himself a one-time sympathizer of the Shachtman group, proposed a new magazine to carry out this perspective. *Dissent* was founded in mid-1953 and has appeared regularly ever since, although the journal has changed its political identification from "socialist" to "radical" to "democratic left."

Throughout the 1950s Howe and *Dissent* struggled to maintain a radicalism to the left of traditional social democracy but free of any taint of "left-wing authoritarianism." This was a term he regularly applied not only to supporters of official Communist parties, but also to such individuals as Paul Baran, Paul Sweezy, and even Isaac Deutscher who defended progressive features that they felt existed in post-revolutionary societies, including Cuba. Howe's insistence on this formula provoked breaks with one-time allies such as the radical pacifist A. J. Muste, the militant trade unionist and author Sidney Lens, and the New Left theoretician C. Wright Mills.

Howe's publications in the 1950s included book-length studies of Sherwood Anderson and William Faulkner, as well as *Politics and the Novel*. He also co-authored with Lewis Coser and Julius Jacobson *The American Communist Party: A Critical History*, plus collections of his own essays and translations of Yiddish stories. By 1961, Howe was well established as a literary critic and moved to California to teach at Stanford University. In 1963 he returned to New York City where he became Distinguished Professor of English at the City University of New York.

Although Howe first responded sympathetically to the early stirrings of the New Left, he rapidly became disenchanted with the refusal of leaders of Students for a Democratic Society to share his principled anti-communism. Moreover, while Howe had once condemned French socialists who refused to demand complete withdrawal of French troops from Vietnam, he now supported the "negotiations" position against the "immediate withdrawal" wing of the movement against the war in Vietnam. By the late 1960s, Howe and *Dissent* were seen as opponents of the New Left. Howe published essay after essay denouncing the tactics of radical students, African-American militants, supporters of Palestinian self-determination (caricatured as "anti-Semites"), and even the new feminism expressed by Kate Millett's *Sexual Politics* (1970).

In retrospect, Howe's role in the 1960s was more modulated than it appeared to many militants at the time. Many of his criticisms of the New Left such as its failure to study history and develop strategies that could relate to the working class, its idealization of Third World regimes and its exaggeration of prospects for immediate transformation in the United States, proved to be accurate. In addition, his commitment to working within the Democratic party became more acceptable to leftists in the 1970s and 1980s, especially after Jesse Jackson (6*) organized the Rainbow Coalition and waged several campaigns for the U.S. presidency.

Moreover, as the student and African-American rebellion waned in the late 1970s and 1980s, Howe became less rigid in excoriating the excesses of the left. Earlier he had broken his ties with the rightward moving *Commentary* and vigorously denounced the neoconservatism of one-time allies. In the 1980s, he opened his mind to the new feminism and even became more critical of the Israeli state.

His close association with Michael Harrington (6*) continued until the latter's death. For example, in the early 1960s after Shachtman and Harrington (who had entered Shachtman's Independent Socialist League two years after Howe left it) led the majority of their followers into the Socialist party. There was a time when the three of them collaborated on projects. But when Shachtman revealed himself to be a "Hawk" on Vietnam, and even appeared to give tacit support to Richard Nixon in the 1970 election, Howe joined Harrington in forming the new Democratic Socialist Organizing Committee. When Harrington brought this organization into a fusion with the New Left group called New American Movement, Howe reluctantly cooperated.

Howe's effort to create a "democratic socialism," free of the defects of European social democracy as well as all forms of Leninism, played a contradictory role within U.S. radicalism. On the one hand, he helped to give the general idea of socialism a wider currency among intellectuals. On the other hand, his vision of socialism was divested of the militancy that historically inspired oppressed and exploited sections of the population to fight for a better world. On a moral and cultural plane, Howe gave the idea of socialism a sophistication and depth not evident in the work of earlier U.S. socialist writers, but strategically he offered nothing superior to conventional social democracy. His political orientation was certainly to the right of Eugene V. Debs and even Norman Thomas.

As a literary critic, Howe seemed to have been without major influence on the left, or, in fact, on the entire younger generation of literary scholars. His writings are sensitive and craftsman-like, but, despite a historical sensibility, eschew theory in the modern sense. Although he had a large following among educated East Coast readers, his topics were usually conventional and canonical figures. While some people may have seen him as a cultural radical, he never was.

In this regard, even in the 1980s Howe faithfully continued to carry out the original literary program of the group known as "the New York Intellectuals" and first associated with *Partisan Review* magazine. That program began with a defense of modernist literature as the cultural counterpart to the revolutionary politics of (anti-Stalinist) Marxism-Leninism. Over the decades, literary modernism became institutionalized in the universities as virtually the status quo, as did the *Partisan Review* writers. Culturally, Howe participated in this institutionalization and stood apart from contemporary developments in Marxist literary theory as well as the new explorations of writers of color, women, post-colonial society, and mass culture. At his death, he was warmly remembered by many liberals and moderate socialists for his lifelong commitment to a socialism that would be the fulfillment of equality and democracy. Quite another interpretation was expressed by Alexander Cockburn, who concluded that Howe's "prime function, politically speaking, in the last thirty years of his life was that of policing the left in behalf of the powers that be" (*The Nation*, June 14, 1993, p. 822).

Bibliography

Bloom, Alexander. *Prodigal Sons: The New York Intellectuals and Their World.* New York: Oxford University Press, 1986.

Cain, William. "An Interview with Irving Howe," *American Literary History* 1 (Fall 1989): 554–64.

Howe, Irving. *The American Communist Party: A Critical History,1919–1957*, with Lewis Coser and the assistance of Julius Jacobson. Boston: Beacon Press, 1957.

———. *Decline of the New.* New York: Harcourt Brace and World, 1970.

———. *Leon Trotsky.* New York: Viking, 1967.

———. *A Margin of Hope: An Intellectual Autobiography.* San Diego: Harcourt Brace Jovanovich, 1985.

———. *Politics and the Novel.* New York: Horizon, 1957.

———. *Selected Writing: 1950–1990.* New York: Harcourt Brace Jovanovich, 1990.

———. *Socialism and America.* San Diego: Harcourt Brace Jovanovich, 1985.

———. *Steady Work: Essays in the Politics of Democratic Radicalism, 1953–1966.* New York: Harcourt, Brace and World, 1966.

———. *The UAW and Walter Reuther*, with B. J. Widick. New York: Random House, 1949.

———. *World of Our Fathers.* New York: Harcourt Brace Jovanovich, 1976.

Jumonville, Neil. *Critical Crossings: The New York Intellectuals in Postwar America.* Berkeley: University of California Press, 1990.

Krupnick, Mark. "Irving Howe," in *Modern American Critics Since 1955*, Gregory S. Jay, ed.; vol. 67, *Dictionary of American Literary Biography.* Detroit: Gale Research, 1988: 167–75.

Obits: E. J. Dionne, Jr., *Washington Post*, May 11, 1993, A19; Ted Solotaroff, *The Nation*, June 7, 1993, p. 761; Michael Weinstein, *New York Times*, May 10, 1993, A18; Michael Walzer, *Dissent*, Summer 1993, pp. 275–76; and Leon Wieseltier, *New York Times Book Review*, May 23, 1993, p. 31.

Pinsker, Sanford. "Lost Causes/Marginal Hopes: The Cultural Elegies of Irving Howe," *Virginia Quarterly Review* 65 (Spring 1989): 215–30.

"Remembering Irving Howe," *Dissent*, Fall 1993, pp. 515–49.

Wald, Alan. *The New York Intellectuals: The Rise and Decline of the Anti-Stalinist Left from the 1930s to the 1980s.* Chapel Hill: University of North Carolina Press, 1987.

Alan Wald

MAULANA KARENGA (1941–)

Activist and intellectual; black cultural nationalist (Afrocentrist)

Maulana Karenga burst onto the national scene after the Watts uprising in Los Angeles in August of 1965. He quickly emerged as a principal architect of an influential and controversial black cultural nationalism. His commitment to cultural nationalism persisted, although the emphases and content of his beliefs periodically shifted. By the 1990s, his vision of cultural nationalism fit comfortably within the rubric of Afrocentrism. This was an analytical and historical framework that stressed the significance of African developments to an understanding of the histories and cultures not only of African peoples worldwide, but of various non-African peoples as well, such as Europeans.

Prior to the 1965 Watts uprising, Karenga had been involved in the "Movement" in a variety of student and community empowerment organizations in Los Angeles. After Watts, he assessed that apocalyptic event as part of the growing radicalism of the black liberation insurgency. He became convinced of the necessity for cultural revitalization as the essential next step. This realization led him to create his own organization, US (variously signifying "us" as in "us versus them" or "US" as in "United States"). He developed a highly eclectic ideology that drew upon various streams of diasporan and continental African nationalist beliefs. These were filtered through his reading of what they meant for African-Americans in the United States. The nationalist thought and leadership of Marcus Garvey and Malcolm X (1*) were especially important for Karenga.

In the context of the Black Power movement of the late 1960s and early 1970s, cultural nationalism blossomed. From the Black Arts movement with its emphasis on grassroots, revolutionary, and political art, to concurrent developments in popular music, notably free jazz and soul, the issue of black identity politics became more and more important. Karenga's ideology continually tapped into this wellspring of cultural reassertion and offered highly revealing ideas about how to define and structure this process.

Unfortunately, Karenga's clarion call for cultural nationalism publicly collided head on with the more political and economic brand of revolutionary nationalism espoused by the Oakland-based Black Panther party led by Huey Newton and Bobby Seale (1*). Exacerbated by official U.S. government efforts to destroy both his organization and the Black Panthers, this awful internecine battle took its toll on both groups and its leaders. Furthermore, in 1971 Karenga was convicted of assaulting a woman within his organization. As a result, he began a four-year sentence as a "political prisoner." Despite that regrettable turn of events, Karenga continued to preach the gospel of cultural nationalism, even as his US organization disbanded in 1974 and he adamantly rejected allegations that he had been a government agent.

As the seventies wore on and the liberation struggle assumed a less militant stance, the influence of revolutionary cultural nationalism dwindled. Indeed, the dominant stance of both the larger black liberation struggle and its cultural nationalist wing had been consistently more liberal and inclusive than the more narrow and doctrinaire vision of Karenga's brand of cultural nationalism. From the mid-seventies, the latter acquired several new elements as Karenga endeavored to remain intellectually flexible and viable. A critical overview of Karenga's ideological development and leadership reveals much about the

Maulana Karenga. Photo
courtesy of Maulana Karenga.

strengths and weaknesses of revolutionary, or oppositional, theory and practice
in the recent black liberation struggle.

Born Ronald McKinley Everett on July 14, 1941, in Parsonburg, Maryland,
he grew up in what he has characterized as a peasant background. Organized
religion left an impression because his father preached. Joining an older
brother in Los Angeles in 1959, he attended Los Angeles City College before
he attended UCLA. There he received a B.A. (1963) and a M.A. (1964) in
political science. The African studies specialization of his M.A. signaled an
expanding Pan-African sensibility which undergirded his evolving cultural nationalism. Between 1959 and 1965, in addition to his formal academic training,
he was deeply involved in student politics at Los Angeles City College, where
he became the first black president of the student body, and at UCLA, where
he was active in promoting a black student union. His student organizing
encompassed efforts to forge links between Africans and African-Americans

and further revealed his Pan-African concerns. Similarly, his work to promote various coalitions among all peoples of color evidenced his growing identification with an incipient Third World consciousness.

Concurrent with his involvement in student politics, he became an integral part of several black study groups emphasizing black history and culture generally and the contemporary black freedom struggle specifically. Roughly between 1963 and 1965, he was a prime mover in the Los Angeles branch of the Bay Area–based Afro-American Association. This group supported local civil rights activities. It also sponsored study sessions, tutorials, language and history instruction, and street speaking (that is, taking their messages directly to the people by open-air soapbox oratory).

Karenga consistently sought to join his intellectual work with his political activism: to merge theory and practice. Participating in sixties boycotts, sit-ins, and protests led by groups like CORE and SNCC, he was deeply influenced by the philosophy and tactics of the mainstream nonviolent direct-action wing of the Civil Rights movement. This influence could be seen most broadly in Karenga's acceptance of the ends of that movement even as he increasingly dissented from its means. Likewise, this fundamental commitment to freedom, equality, and justice was a critical basis for Karenga's belief in operational unity. As a result, throughout his years as an activist-scholar, he attempted to work closely with a variety of groups on specific issues and projects.

Even before the emergence of black nationalism after the mid-sixties, Karenga embraced a cultural nationalist perspective. Symbolic of that fundamental commitment is his name change. He reinvented himself as the Maulana, the master teacher. This change symbolized his creative reworkings of an African-American cultural identity. From the early 1960s on, his cultural nationalist vision has grown out of efforts to discern the best tactics and strategies to advance the black liberation struggle. His studies in history, political theory, and nationalist struggles and their leadership have helped to shape that position. He found activist-intellectuals like Garvey, Malcolm X, Kwame Nkrumah (Ghana), Sékou Touré (Guinea), Amilcar Cabral (Guinea-Bissau), and Frantz Fanon (Martinique) especially appealing. His intellectual development mirrored the influence of continental and diasporan African liberation movements and many of the major thinkers of those movements. Consequently, it reflected deep Pan-African and nationalist roots.

The historical sources of Karenga's nationalism can be traced back at least to the nineteenth century and pioneering African-American activist-intellectuals like David Walker, Martin R. Delany, Henry Highland Garnet, and Henry McNeil Turner. They helped to articulate the complicated yet compelling vision of blacks as "a nation within a nation" and the corresponding need for black self-definition, self-determination, pride, and unity. Karenga has acknowledged his major twentieth-century influences; Garvey and Malcolm X. Both men stressed the importance of grassroots or mass involvement in nationalist struggle and led significant social movements themselves. Both, especially Malcolm X, displayed little of the middle-class elitism of earlier black nationalists. Likewise, their separatist, anti-integrationist, pro-black thrust excited Karenga. His reading of Garveyism, an extraordinary mass movement which peaked in the early 1920s, led him to ask, like Garvey, where was the black man's world? Also like Garvey, not seeing that world around him, he dedicated himself to helping to realize it.

Malcolm X was clearly the most significant domestic influence on Karenga's ideological development. Karenga recalled his discussions with Malcolm X as provocative and inspiring. In many ways, he saw Malcolm X as a prophet. He admired Malcolm's boldness, clarity, rhetorical style, and organizational ability. Malcolm X challenged him to realize his best self. In addition to Malcolm X's concern for the black masses, Karenga absorbed his emphasis on self-defense, the critical importance of history (African as well as African-American) to the liberation struggle, and religion as an instrument for social change. The latter was also a key aspect, of course, of the civil rights strategy of the southern movement led by Martin Luther King, Jr. Nevertheless, Malcolm X was Karenga's hero. Indeed, Karenga was a prime mover in a Los Angeles ceremony on February 22, 1965, to honor the memory of the recently slain Malcolm X. In a similar vein, Malcolm X's birthday, May 19 (Kuzaliwa), was seen as integral to the series of distinctive African-American holidays that Karenga promoted.

Karenga's ideological influences outside of the U.S. are revealing. Essentially, they reinforced and deepened critical elements of his evolving belief system. Nkrumah's writings helped him to understand better the salience of struggle waged from the bottom up. Fanon's powerful writings illuminated several things for Karenga, among them the centrality of identity politics for oppressed peoples of color and the need for a comprehensive approach to liberation. The latter had to be subjective and objective, theoretical and practical. Cabral's works fortified Karenga's belief that culture and history were basic necessities in overcoming alienation and reconstituting a positive and viable black sense of self and community.

The mid-sixties confluence of the Watts uprising, the Black Power movement, the War on Poverty, and unparalleled social ferment framed the unfolding of Karenga's cultural nationalism. From his perspective, the "cultural crisis" confronting blacks took priority (and continued to do so) and demanded an all-out attack. The primary strategy of this continuing cultural war has been to win "the minds of the people" through massive grassroots re-education led by an elite vanguard personified by Karenga and his followers and supporters. Cultural nationalism is the necessary first step toward revolution because it prepares the people for the exigencies of systemic change. Karenga reasons that before the black liberation struggle can proceed logically to political and economic radicalism, not to mention any kind of armed rebellion, blacks must be unified behind a resonant vision rooted in their cultural ethos and historical experience. The daunting challenge of that vision has animated Karenga's continuing odyssey of ideological and practical struggle.

Vital elements of the appeal of Karenga's cultural nationalism are its aura of simplicity, coherence, viability, and authenticity. Using Swahili, an East African lingua franca, as a source of nomenclature because of its nontribal and Pan-African qualities, he fashioned a philosophy structured around seven interlocking principles: Umoja (Unity); Kujichagulia (self-determination); Ujima (Collective Work and Responsibility); Ujamaa (Cooperative Economics); Nia (Purpose [community- and nation-building]); Kuumba (Creativity); and Imani (Faith). This "consistent and well-planned ideology" (according to its creator) builds upon the energy of the dialectical tension between culture and politics. These same principles constitute the ideological basis of the increasingly popular Kwanzaa (December 26 to January 1), an African-American holiday developed by Karenga to commemorate community and nationhood as well as the spirit of past, present, and future achievements.

Karenga labored hard to institutionalize continental and diasporan African studies. He has been a key figure since the late sixties in the often difficult efforts to establish and legitimate Black and Ethnic Studies Departments and programs. He continued to lecture and teach around the world, and has chaired the Department of Black Studies at the California State University at Long Beach. In addition to his noteworthy efforts to make black studies an essential component of the academic curriculum, especially at the college-university level, he published prolifically. His *Introduction to Black Studies* (1980) is a popular text. He also writes for a lay audience and has done so since the early sixties. A publisher as well, he has been responsible for the production and dissemination of much of his written work.

His commitment to institution-building informed his efforts to help plan and to co-convene a series of national Black Power conferences in the late sixties. On the local level, from the mid-sixties to the early seventies, he was a key organizer of the Watts Summer Festivals. These major productions endeavored to educate as they provided entertainment. Critics charged they simply exploited the cultural fixation on singing, dancing, and big-name entertainers. For Karenga, however, these events were important attempts to take his message of cultural resuscitation to a wide audience: Kwanzaa, Kuzaliwa, Uhuru Day (the anniversary of the Watts Revolt, August 11), Kuanzisha Founder's Day (the anniversary of the US organization's founding, February 1966), Arusi (an African-American wedding ceremony), Akiki (a nationalization ceremony for children), and Maziko (an African-American funeral ceremony). These "invented traditions," as Eric Hobsbawm would call them, are integral features of Karenga's vision of cultural revitalization. These events and their attendant rituals are seen as a way to reconstitute a meaningful black sense of self and community.

Roughly speaking, the development of Karenga's cultural nationalism can be divided into two overlapping phases. From the early sixties to the early seventies, it evolved as the ideological basis of the US organization and Karenga's wide-ranging activist pursuits. It heavily influenced the concurrent cultural nationalist scene, including political artists like Chicago-based poet Don L. Lee (Haki Madhubuti) and, for a time. the highly influential Harlem- and Newark-based writer LeRoi Jones (Amiri Baraka [1*]). During the early seventies, Karenga's belief system became Kawaida. Within this expanded ideology, Karenga stressed seven interrelated areas of culture: religion, history, social organization, creative production, psychology, economics, and politics. In a sense, Kawaida signified a shift toward a more socialist and a more gender-sensitive posture. His cultural nationalist system also became increasingly Afrocentric as the ideological battle against Eurocentric hegemony heated up.

The shifts toward socialism and gender sensitivity are especially revelatory. As with other cultural nationalists, such as Baraka, the economics of liberation has necessitated increasing attention from Karenga. Heavily influenced by proponents of African socialism, like Cabral and Touré, Karenga has adopted a socialism that has been critical and flexible rather than dogmatic. This shift has given his ideology a materialist edge and greater analytic depth, but the lack of theoretical detail and programmatic emphasis means that his nationalism remains far more cultural than economic.

That the turn toward a less overtly patriarchal perspective apparently transpired as Karenga was serving time for the felonious assault of a woman within his organization is instructive. The debate surrounding the truth of the charges and the justice of the conviction notwithstanding, the incident opened his eyes to the blatant sexism of his ideology, especially given the growing black feminist movement. The intensely patriarchal "House System" outlined in *The Quotable Karenga* (1967) gave way by 1975 to a ringing defense of woman's right to self-defense and a more implicit and ambivalent endorsement of gender equality. He used the occasion of the mid-seventies JoAnne Little case (wherein she claimed self-defense in the murder of a white male jailer whom she argued attempted to rape her) as a platform to denounce the sexual abuse of women, especially black women at the hands of white men. Not surprisingly, however, he joined the black chorus condemning Michele Wallace's *Black Macho and the Myth of the Superwoman* (1978) as both a diatribe against black men and a failed look at black female-male relations. In Karenga's discussion of the book, the reality of the sexist oppression of black women, notably at the hands of black men, was obscured and thus went largely unexamined. While in other places he has spoken out more forcefully against sexism, typically his cultural nationalism has failed to grapple adequately with the profound challenges posed by feminist developments.

Ultimately, the construction of an African-American national culture has been seriously compromised by the inextricable ties between the African-American and the broader American cultures and histories. Karenga's vision conflates the often different and conflicting realities of race, culture, gender, class, and nation for the exceedingly diverse African-American population into a racial universe. Shunning nuance and complexity, this vision consists essentially of a set of common and relatively inoffensive cultural denominators behind which a significant, hopefully influential, number of blacks can unite and act. Within this racialist worldview, notably in the late sixties and early seventies, race functions as a historical reality and an analytic category of far greater significance than class, economics, and politics. Similarly, this worldview is fundamentally patriarchal, even when it occasionally nods toward a black feminist agenda. The appeal of Karenga's philosophy of cultural nationalism is undercut, then, by its inability to grapple with the complexity of identity formation: the myriad and tangled ways in which people actually define themselves and their interests. Race is obviously a salient aspect of this process in the United States. Nevertheless, a singular emphasis upon race as the explanation for the problems of black identity has seldom been wholly sufficient, even when necessary, even at the height of black power politics and black nationalist enthusiasms.

It is not surprising, therefore, that given the lack of effective black control over the cultural apparatus of black communities—not to mention that of the larger society—important elements of the cultural nationalist agenda have been co-opted and even commodified. Paradoxically, Karenga's leadership kept the cause of cultural nationalism alive while it helped to unleash forces and popularize ideas which the capitalist marketplace and its hegemonic cultural ethos have marginalized, neutralized, and co-opted. Kwanzaa has become a big business, despite the noncommercial intentions of its founder. Similarly, in late 1992, the commercialization of the image of Malcolm X, Karenga's nationalist hero, pointedly illustrated how a once threatening cultural icon could be sanitized and rendered mass marketable. As diversity and multiculturalism advanced, the richness of black culture was exploited increasingly to sell both the ostensibly black as well as the ostensibly nonracial product.

By the 1990s, Karenga and his cultural nationalist, or Afrocentrist, cohorts continued to face an awesome struggle to win "the minds of the people." Not only had untold numbers of Americans, especially African-Americans, suffered greatly during the Reagan-Bush years, but the contradictions of American life, particularly for African-Americans, became more obvious. This unacceptable situation contributed to what many saw as a resurgence of grassroots black nationalism. Karenga remained dedicated to cultural nationalism. His significance, therefore, resided not merely in his invention of the increasingly popular Kwanzaa holiday. It derived from his continuing efforts, mostly outside the cultural mainstream, to help African-Americans as a people to clarify who they are and who they might become.

Bibliography

Baraka, Imamu Amiri. *Kawaida Studies: The New Nationalism*. Chicago: Third World Press, 1972.

Halisi, Clyde, and James Mfume, eds. *The Quotable Karenga*. Los Angeles: US Organization, 1967.

Karenga, Maulana. *The Book of Coming Forth by Day: The Ethics of the Declarations of Innocence.* Los Angeles: University of Sankore Press, 1990.

———. "Culture, Politics, and Common Ground; A Review Essay," *The Black Scholar* 21 (March/May 1990): 57–61.

———. Interview, in *African Commentary* 1 (Oct. 1989): 61–64.

———. *Introduction to Black Studies.* Inglewood, CA: Kawaida Publications, 1982. Reviewed: Harold Cruise, *The Black Scholar* 15 (May/June 1984): 41–47.

———. "Kawaida and Its Critics: A Sociohistorical Analysis," *Journal of Black Studies* 8 (Dec. 1977): 125–48.

———. *Kawaida Theory: An Introductory Outline.* Inglewood, CA: Kawaida Publications, 1980.

———. *Kwanzaa: Origin, Concepts, Practice.* Inglewood, CA: Kawaida Publications, 1977.

———. "Political Culture and Resurgent Racism in the United States," *The Black Scholar* 16 (May/June 1985): 21–35.

Van Deburg, William L. *New Day in Babylon: The Black Power Movement and American Culture, 1965–1975.* Chicago: University of Chicago Press, 1992.

Waldo E. Martin, Jr.

KEN KESEY (1935–)

Novelist; notable personality in the California psychedelic and counterculture movements

Ken Kesey became prominent during the sixties both as a successful novelist and as a charismatic trend-setter in the psychedelic movement that transformed the Beats into the Hippies. Kesey had been a creative writing student at Stanford University. Beginning in 1958, he discovered the Beat culture in San Francisco. When he was a volunteer for government drug experiments, in 1961, at the Menlo Park Veterans' Hospital, he was introduced to mind-altering drugs, including LSD. These experiences launched his quest for new forms of consciousness and expression involving all the senses. After the 1962 appearance of his famous novel *One Flew over the Cuckoo's Nest*, a group calling themselves the Merry Pranksters gathered around him. They influenced patterns of the emerging counterculture movement through drugs, rock music, Day-Glo paint, strobe lights, and uninhibited communal living. Kesey and his friends were renowned especially for their 1964 trip across the country in an old bus painted in psychedelic colors and patterns. These adventures and Kesey's likable personality were painted vividly in Tom Wolfe's widely read *The Electric Kool-Aid Acid Test* (1968). This book elevated Kesey's status as a counterculture hero and drug guru.

Born September 17, 1935, in La Junta, Colorado, Ken Elton Kesey grew

Ken Kesey. *Source:*
Library of Congress

up near Eugene, Oregon, where his family had a creamery business. His father was an avid outdoorsman and his family loved physical competition. Ken early developed a fascination with magic and ventriloquism and a flair for performing. These boyhood interests continued into his college years at the University of Oregon, where he played football, excelled as a wrestler, and participated in theatre productions. He learned radio and television writing as a major in speech and communication. He also tried his hand at fiction. He spent two summers in Hollywood seeking parts in films. When he graduated from college, a Woodrow Wilson Fellowship enabled him to enter the creative writing program at Stanford. He went to California accompanied by his wife, Faye Haxby Kesey, the high school sweetheart he married in 1956. Faye, a mild but determined woman, remained a loyal source of strength for him.

San Francisco in the late fifties was a center of social-cultural experimentation. The Beat culture, especially, was a Bohemian life characterized by beards, sandals, wine, drugs, guitar strumming, and readings of experimental poetry. Nearby Stanford had been stirred by this movement, and Kesey was drawn into the cultural turbulence. He was influenced more by his relationships with other students in Perry Lane, a small housing area near campus, than by any of his classes. Perry Lane had become a haven for what became considered typical of hippy culture: drugs (such as LSD and other psychedelics), flowery clothing, mystical religion, colorful art, long hair, and sexual freedom.

While living at Perry Lane, Kesey completed his first two novels: *One Flew over the Cuckoo's Nest* and *Sometimes a Great Notion. Cuckoo's Nest* (published in 1962) is the story of a joking and fast-talking nonconformist who subverts the repressive order of a mental ward and restores a measure of hope and sanity to its inmates. It was a powerful success, becoming one of few works to achieve acclaim in three forms: novel, play, and film. It criticized an American society of organizational men who were offered affluence only if they lived within social straightjackets. This novel fit the mood of rebellion germinating during the early sixties. Its apparent message was that we needed to get back in touch with nature, open new doors of perception, enjoy spontaneous sensuous experience, and resist the manipulative forces of a technological society. This vision was particularly appealing to the young, but not just to them. During the late sixties and into the seventies, the book was one of the most frequently taught on American campuses, in disciplines as varied as literature, sociology, psychology, medicine, and law.

Sometimes a Great Notion (1964) is a larger and more ambitious novel. It is complex in point of view, narrative techniques, and motifs drawn from America's frontier experience and popular culture. It may be a greater artistic achievement than *Cuckoo's Nest*, but since it requires several readings to be understood and appreciated, it never achieved as large an audience. It tells the story of a family of fiercely independent wildcat loggers who are living on the coast of Oregon. Their resistance to a labor union causes conflict with their community. Many of Kesey's friends in the counterculture were bewildered by the novel's negative treatment of unionism and by its glorification of violent self-reliance.

In 1963, developers bought most of Perry Lane and bulldozed the cottages. The Keseys bought a place in La Honda and were joined by the friends who became the Merry Pranksters. Their experiments with drugs, self-expression, and behavior were guided by the slogan "go with the flow." For Kesey these experiments were not primarily social protest or rebellion, nor were they a simple pursuit of hedonism. He was seriously committed to discovering radically new forms of artistic expression. He invested much of his earnings from *Cuckoo's Nest* in these experiments. The drug-oriented Prankster activities enabled him to indulge his theatrical tendencies and his interests in expressive media other than the written word. Although he stated his intention, as late as 1963, of devoting his life to writing, he began to say that his goal was to move beyond writing to more "electrical forms." He asserted, "I'd rather be a lightning rod than a seismograph." He talked of new forms of expression in which he and the audience would be joined in a singular way: "It would be all one experience, with all the senses opened wide, words, music, lights, sounds, touch—*lightning*."

The first major expedition in this direction was the bus trip of 1964. The bus was a 1939 International Harvester converted into a camper. It had been painted luridly in a spontaneous and reckless array of primary colors. The destination sign on the front said "Further" and a sign on the back read "Caution: Weird Load." The ostensible reason for the trip was to visit the World's Fair and be in New York when *Sometimes A Great Notion* was published. More important reasons were to experiment as a group with drugs and make a movie of the experience as it happened. The trip was a communal psychedelic version of Kerouac's *On the Road*. Kesey spent considerable money for sound and film equipment and had high hopes that the Movie, as it was known, would be a ground-breaking and marketable achievement. Portions of the forty hours of film have been used for various purposes, but the bulk of it remains in storage. It is part of what is called the Prankster Archives.

Kesey's drug activities resulted in two arrests for possession of marijuana. He feared a harsh sentence for the second offense, and fled with friends in the famous bus to Mexico in 1966. He returned after six months and was arrested in San Francisco. After serving sentences totalling about five months in a county jail and a rural prison, he moved to a farm near Eugene, Oregon, where he remained.

Because of his notoriety, many young people made pilgrimages to the farm during his first years there. There were sometimes several hundred in a weekend. Many wanted to live there or at least get stoned with the master. The Keseys discouraged this, however, and turned their attention to the farm and their children. Both Ken and Faye came from close families and were very family oriented. While they maintained their friendships from the sixties, and Ken continued to write, teach, and participate in a variety of mixed media presentations, the family had first priority.

Living on the farm heightened his awareness of some negative aspects of the counterculture. Actually, he was never wholly in tune with that revolution, particularly with some of its collective and political aims. The revolution that interested him had been one of individual consciousness: "You work from the heart out; you don't work from the issue down." He once remarked in an interview, "I know more about my brother's creamery than I do about the revolution." But he wasn't silent on issues that concerned him, issues such as community and state environmental problems, highway safety, and reform of marijuana laws. On the question of drugs, he favored marijuana and LSD but adamantly opposed cocaine and heroin.

The sixties formed Kesey. He styled himself an "archivist" for an incandescent period of American history. Although his admirers waited decades for another major novel, he did publish collections of sixties-related materials in *Kesey's Garage Sale* (1973), *The Demon Box* (1986), and a half dozen sporadically appearing issues of the magazine *Spit in the Ocean*. He collaborated with thirteen students of his creative writing course at the University of Oregon to produce a novel titled *Caverns* (1990). One publication, *The Further Inquiry* (1990), was a filmscript (actually written in 1979) of the 1964 bus trip. It is abundantly illustrated from "the Movie" filmed during that trip. To promote this book, Kesey drove a near duplicate of the famous bus to a number of cities in the West. Some of the original passengers were on the bus, along with their children and relatives. This time, however, no freaking out on drugs was allowed. There was an element of sixties nostalgia that appealed to many as the nineties began. Kesey's friends Paul Perry and Ken Babbs also used "the Movie" to present a version of the bus trip in *On the Bus* (1990). These books joined a growing number of books and television documentaries reviewing the sixties. Some items by Kesey that were not directly related to the sixties also came out in the 1990s: two children's stories, *Little Tricker the Squirrel Meets Big Double the Bear* (which Kesey has performed accompanied by several orchestras around the country) and *Shoola and the Sea Lion*, along with *Sailor Song*, a novel set in Alaska.

Bibliography

"Kesey, Ken," in *Contemporary Literary Criticism*, vol. 64. Detroit: Gale Research, 1991: 206–44.

"Kesey, Ken," in *Twentieth-Century American Literature*, Harold Bloom, ed. New York: Chelsea House, 1987: 4: 2079–92.

Kesey, Ken. *Demon Box*. New York: Viking, 1986.

———. *The Further Inquiry*. New York: Viking, 1990.

———. *Kesey*, Michael Strelow, ed. Eugene, OR: Northwest Review Books, 1977.

———. *Kesey's Garage Sale*. New York: Viking, 1973.

———. *One Flew over the Cuckoo's Nest*. New York: Viking, 1962.

———. *The Sailor Song*. New York: Viking, 1992.

———. *Sometime A Great Notion*. New York: Viking, 1964.

Leeds, Barry H. *Ken Kesey*. New York: Frederick Ungar, 1981.

McClanahan, Ed. "Ken Kesey's Latest Trip," *Esquire* 115 (Feb. 1991): 26–27.

Perry, Paul and Ken Babbs. *On the Bus: The Complete Guide to the Legendary Trip of Ken Kesey and the Merry Pranksters and the Birth of the Counterculture*. New York: Thunder's Mouth Press, 1990.

"Sometimes a Great Commotion; Take a Deep Breath, Ken Kesey's Back with the Bus," *Washington Post*, Sept. 9, 1992, C1.

Tanner, Stephen L. *Ken Kesey*. Boston: Twayne, 1983.

Wolfe, Tom. *The Electric Kool-Aid Acid Test*. New York: Farrar, Straus and Giroux, 1968.

Stephen L. Tanner

JONATHAN KOZOL (1936–   )

Educator, author, social activist, gadfly

Kozol burst onto the scene in 1968 by winning the National Book Award with the publication of *Death at an Early Age: The Destruction of the Hearts and Minds of Negro Children in the Boston Public Schools* (1967). The book is based on his year as a fourth-grade teacher in the Christopher School in Roxbury, a predominantly black neighborhood of Boston. He was fired from his teaching position just before the end of the school year because he used a poem that was not on the approved list of readings. The poem, "Ballad of the Landlord" by Langston Hughes, is a call to revolution rather than the standard fourth-grade material. In his book, Kozol laid bare the abuses of the Boston urban school system. *Death at an Early Age* helped focus, for the sixties generation and open-minded adults, the public schools' hidden purposes, that is, socialization, inculcation, and indoctrination. More important, he did not stop at exposing the inequities in the schools. He vigorously protested the economic, political, and social system that allowed the Boston schools to exist. During the next twenty-five years Kozol wrote books and essays on the education of children and adults, as well as health issues and living conditions of the economically disenfranchised.

Jonathan Kozol was born September 5, 1936, in Boston, the son of Harry and Ruth. He attended the Noble and Greenough School in Dedham, Massachusetts. In 1958 he graduated from Harvard (B.A., *summa cum laude*), and spent almost a year as a Rhodes scholar, Magdalen College, Oxford. Kozol resigned the scholarship and moved to Paris to finish his second novel. His first, *Fume of Poppies* (1958), was received with critical acclaim. However, confused and scared, he returned to Boston during 1963 and drifted for about a year trying to discover "life." He found a purpose to his existence in 1964 when he signed up as a CORE worker and directed a successful rent strike. Kozol taught in the Boston public schools 1964–1965, and the Newton public schools, 1966–1968. He was a trustee to the Store Front Learning Center, 1968–1971. In addition to writing books and numerous articles, he was a correspondent for the *Los Angeles Times* and *USA Today*, 1982–1983; contributor to the *New York Times Book Review*, 1968–1985; reporter-at-large, the *New Yorker* magazine, 1988; trustee, New School for Children, Roxbury, Massachusetts; and a member of the Board of Directors National Literacy Coalition, 1980–1983. He received numerous awards including the National Book Award, for *Death at an Early Age*, 1968; and the Robert Kennedy Book Award, for *Rachel and Her Children*, 1989. Kozol was the recipient of a Guggenheim fellowship in 1970, 1984, and 1990; and he was a Field Foundation

Fellow, 1972; Ford Foundation Fellow, 1974; and Rockefeller Foundation Senior Fellow in 1978 and 1983. He has been a member of the Fellowship of Reconciliation and American PEN.

He was a child of upper-middle-class privilege; his father was a well-known Boston psychologist. He was raised by caring and loving parents who taught him about fairness and gave him the strength and wisdom to seek answers to his questions about racism, poverty, and equity in a democratic society.

Kozol was radicalized by his work with CORE and his year in the Boston school system. His first three books were, in order of publication, an attempt to create a climate for change in the operation and outcomes of the educational system; a plea to the founders of the free school movement to clarify and focus their goals; and an attempt to help the children of the economic, political, and social elite to recognize that they were also victims of an educational system that socialized them to feel helpless to change society.

He recognized that U.S. society was racist, materialist, and structured to guard vested interests. Education was a key institution to maintain these realities. *Death at an Early Age* described the long-entrenched and deep-rooted racism of the white teachers in the Boston public schools. The political scene in the United States during the 1960s was one of rebellion against the status quo. In the Boston ghetto, this rebellion met strong resistance. The Boston School Committee (Boston's name for its school board) was trying to maintain, as it had since the 1840s, a segregated school system. Boston, once a bastion for the abolition of slavery, hung out the "Do Not Disturb" sign when it came to eliminating segregation. *Death at an Early Age* helped a generation of radicals address such hateful purposes of public schooling as passivity and indoctrination.

Kozol's second book, *Free Schools* (1972), attempted to envision a place that would educate children and not blind them. Education meant giving children the skills to form their own view of reality, to become independent beings. Since the public schools were not about to educate the child, Kozol felt that we must create an environment that would teach the children to understand the world on their terms, not as it was presented by the school. Thus educated, the child could ask questions, could see through his or her own eyes, and could frame answers not necessarily based on the official version of truth. Free schools would provide that political consciousness to empower individuals to control their destiny. If the public schools trained the person to accept his or her lot, then the free school would focus on the individual's understanding the issues of control, direction, success, and most important, power to gain individual freedom.

Kozol also raised the issue of how we were defining free or alternate schools. White middle-class suburbanites perceived free schools, he believed, as places to learn basket weaving. The philosophy that education was to be happy and become liberated from some middle-class values was interfering with the wants and needs of the urban poor, whose views were, in general, quite different. Kozol stressed that the philosophical undergirding of the free or alternate schools was not a monolithic concept to be uniformly applied. It was to be structured by those who were directly affected by their schools. In fact, it was those who were affected who would run the schools. Kozol was keenly aware that by imposing a single definition on free schools, we would deny the very purpose of their original establishment. Turning urban free schools into cathartic experiences for the guilt-ridden white middle class was not what Kozol had in mind; neither was the co-optation by suburban youth.

If the public schools would not reform their curriculum to reflect an ethical reality, and if the middle class turned the free school movement into an obscene characterization of his vision, he would focus his next book on the children of the managers of society, the rich and powerful. In *The Night Is Dark and I Am Far from Home* (1975), Kozol attempted to reach the future policymakers. Victims, he noted, need victimizers; both must learn their societal roles and believe that they have no power to alter them. Schools can break the will of the victim and create an acceptance of the status quo. The victimizers also were taught that the world is not changeable. Neither group learned how to ask the right questions to begin the process of altering the world. Future decision makers were taught that it was not the institutions' fault that the majority of people lived stunted lives. It was the individual's fault. The official mythology is that all children have the same opportunity; the playing field is level for all in society. Since the decision makers are taught to accept the status quo, they are educated (trained) to lead but not to see or understand the ethical consequences of their actions. The issue then becomes one of convincing them that they, the victimizers, are also victims of the schools, and that the political and economic systems that hold the poor in place also keep them in bondage.

When he was writing *The Night Is Dark and I Am Far from Home*, Kozol spent many hours listening to and learning from Paulo Freire, who was a visiting professor at Harvard. It was Freire who introduced him to the literacy programs in Latin America, especially the most successful effort during the 1960s, the Great Campaign in Cuba. Perhaps Kozol felt that if the schools were not to be the vehicle of change, or that if the children of the middle class were seeking an escape from reality in the alternate schools, or that if the decision makers' children saw themselves as helpless in changing the status quo, then the best approach would be to ethically educate individuals who were lost to the society, the millions of individuals who were illiterate. At least these people were not victimized by the very schools that he had tried to reform.

The book *Children of the Revolution* (1978) was a narrative of the Cuban Great Campaign to eradicate illiteracy. It was also an indictment of the United Nations (UN) of the 1960s which was, at that time, under the control of the industrial nations of the world. Kozol described the attempt by the UN to downplay its failure to improve literacy around the world, and the effort to censor a positive report written by a UN-commissioned person about the overwhelming success of the Cuban project. The key concept, as noted by Kozol, that guaranteed the success of the Cuban experiment was its linking of nonreaders to their economic, political, and social circumstances, and reforming all of them at the same time. Kozol also noted that the failure of the UN-sponsored literacy campaigns could be traced to their not linking these concepts, thus assuring failure. Many argue that this idea of educating the person for the status quo has been the driving force in American education since the 1840s, when Horace Mann, a conservative lawyer, began his great crusade for free, compulsory education.

Over the next few years Kozol attempted to challenge Americans who believed that there was no hidden agenda within American education. He knew that education was state controlled. It was not freeing the individual to see that only a few percent of the population had money, power, and status. From 1978 to 1982, Kozol revisited the Boston schools and saw a marked improvement in the attitudes and environments of the students, parents, teachers, and administrators. Society had partly caught up with Kozol and his criticisms of the public schools. While the schools were not teaching radical revolution, they were trying to practice equality of educational opportunity. Instead of imposing the good society on Boston's minorities, he recognized that, to a degree, the schools were responding to what the African-American and Hispanic citizens defined as the good life.

In the early 1980s, Kozol took a slightly different approach to the problems of the disenfranchised parent and teacher. He addressed the issue of adult illiteracy in *Prisoners of Silence: Breaking the Bonds of Adult Illiteracy in the United States* (1980). In his book *On Being a Teacher* (1981), he offered many helpful insights that teachers could use to educate, as opposed to train, students in the public schools. His idea in *Prisoners of Silence* was to bring a Cuban-style plan of attack to solving the problem of the urban poor and illiterate, giving them the power to see the world as it is, and most important, to believe that they have the power to change the institutions that have defined how the poor, either urban or rural, and the powerless, were to be participants in this society. Perhaps we needed to ask why policymakers are often indifferent to the problem of illiteracy. If society is structured to protect vested interests, then one method, among many, to keep the status quo in place would be to look the other way in coping with the estimated sixty million people that are functionally illiterate. Thus we are creating future classes of nonreaders, ensuring a permanent underclass for cannon fodder, creating a voting block that can be swayed by demagogues, and, finally, developing a class of individuals that will supply the jobs for the social workers and the adult educators of the twenty-first century.

Kozol also addressed this issue from a social class perspective, in terms of the separation of classes by high- and low-brow culture. *Illiterate America* (1985) addressed the vast gap between the study of the humanities by the few who could appreciate them and the millions of individuals who lacked the skills and motivation to benefit from such education. Taking a cue from the Cuban program, Kozol began the education of nonreaders by introducing to them the words they used in their everyday life. Power over their environment is important in demonstrating to them that they can be in control. Kozol hoped to contribute to a situation that could lead to the elimination of poverty, of the body as well as the mind, if society so wished.

Consistent with trying to solve the problem of teaching the humanities, Kozol next attempted to bring the teacher to a state of understanding the world from a nonsocietal perspective. In *On Being a Teacher*, Kozol addressed the role teachers could play in educating as opposed to training the child. Since we educate the citizen and not the person, a dedicated teacher has the power to inject into the curriculum the truth (real belief, he called it) as opposed to the sanitized version of reality the textbooks and curriculum guides have supplied to the teachers. He believed that the truth would protect the teacher from the authorities. Kozol asked several key questions in this book: What does it mean to be free? How can we educate the person as well as the citizen? Why do the school, the principal, and the curriculum continue to be accepted by the citizens as sacred and not critically examined?

How have the critics responded to Mr. Kozol? They have accused him of being unscholarly in his writings. They noted that his books lack documentation, footnotes, and the objective perspective of a researcher. The irony of such comments is lost on the reviewers who are caught up in the legitimation issue; they often focus on details rather than the broader perspective. Critics also dismiss his writings as shrilly polemical. They also ask for detailed solutions. Despite such criticisms, his books remained popular with the general public. Kozol's writings have alerted many people to the systemic problems of this society. His books raised the consciousness of the American public. Whether they promoted permanent changes remains to be seen.

Kozol has been a 60s radical who embarked on the journey of life searching for the solutions to the problems of racism, inequality of educational opportunity, classism based on different cultural values, and middle- and upper-class myopia to the plight of the poor, the illiterate, and the homeless. His trek began with the racism in the Boston public schools. It carried him to writing about the homeless. In his books *Rachel and Her Children* (1988) and *Savage Inequalities: Children in America's Schools* (1991), he has, in one sense, come full circle in his personal and public journey. He began his writings with the children of the urban ghetto, whose education was stopped by racism. In 1991, he wrote about families who existed in the most dire of circumstances in a homeless shelter, and the systemic problems of the urban school brought about by the inequitable methods used to fund public education. When these homeless families sent their children to the public school, they were stigmatized because they were poor. And as we know, people who are poor must be dumb because if they were smart they would not be poor.

Each step that Kozol took along this path could be construed as a logical progression in trying to find the best solution to the preceding problem: from the 1960s inequality of educational opportunity he moved to the organization of alternative schools, and then to the consciousness-raising of the children of the policymakers. Kozol kept searching for solutions to these problems. To stop the schools from intellectually killing the children, he sought ways to educate the illiterate parents, since parents who were enlightened would break the cycle of ignorance. He realized that none of this could be accomplished without the family's living in dignity, and with hope and confidence that they have control over their lives. Finally, to accomplish this education, the concept of equalizing the funding of public schools became a critical issue regarding society's ability to level the playing field to allow urban children the same life chances as their suburban counterparts.

The first step to wisdom is knowing that you do not know. Since 1968, Kozol informed his readers of their collective lack of knowledge about the deadening role of schools. Has he accomplished any good? Some of his critics argued that he began to mellow in the late 1980s. I would argue that this is not so, and that, instead, society began to awaken to some of his perceptions of reality.

Bibliography

"Author Attacks Policies Used in Funding Schools," *Atlanta Constitution*, Feb. 25, 1993, XA7:1.

Burns, Robert E. "It's Time to Stop This Savage Neglect," *U.S. Catholic* 57 (March 1992): 2.

Donohue, John W. "Lazarus' Schools," *America* 166 (April 11, 1992): 301–3.

Glazer, Nathan. "The Real World of Education," *The Public Interest* no. 106 (Winter 1992): 57–75.

"Kozol, Jonathan," in *Current Biography* 47 (Jan. 1986): 22–26.

Kozol, Jonathan. *Alternative Schools: A Guide for Educators and Parents*. New York: Continuum, 1982.

———. *Children of the Revolution: A Yankee Teacher in the Cuban Schools*. New York: Delacorte Press, 1970.

———. *Death at an Early Age: The Destruction of the Hearts and Minds of Negro Children in the Boston Public Schools*. Boston: Houghton Mifflin, 1967.

———. *Free Schools*. Boston: Houghton Mifflin, 1972.

———. *Illiterate America*. New York: Doubleday, 1985.

———. *The Night Is Dark and I Am Far from Home*. rev. ed. New York: Simon and Schuster, 1990 (1975).

———. *On Being a Teacher*. New York: Continuum, 1981.

———. *Prisoners of Silence: Breaking the Bonds of Adult Illiteracy in the United States*. New York: Seabury Press, 1980.

———. *Rachel and Her Children: Homeless Families in America*. New York: Crown, 1988.

———. *Savage Inequalities: Children in America's Schools*. New York: Crown, 1991.

Mitchell, Emily. "Do the Poor Deserve Bad Schools?" *Time* 138 (Oct. 14, 1991): 60–61.

Nore, Gordon W. E. "Jonathan Kozol," *The Progressive* 55 (Dec. 1991): 34–36.

Peter Andre Sola

JULIUS LESTER (1939–)

Black cultural critic; convert to Judaism

Julius Lester became known in the 1960s for such books as *Look Out Whitey! Black Power's Gon' Get Your Mama* (1968), *Revolutionary Notes* (1969), and *Search for a New Land* (1969). He also began to publish essays and poems in a wide range of "alternative" and establishment journals, to work in film and photography, to make records, and to write fiction. Lester, like his literary predecessor Langston Hughes, was skilled in many genres and became a significant literary figure on the American scene. He made two major attempts at interpreting his own life: *All Is Well: An Autobiography* (1976) and *Lovesong: On Becoming a Jew* (1988). By the 1990s, he had become a controversial professor in the Department of Judaic and Near Eastern Studies at the University of Massachusetts.

Lester begins *All Is Well* with his Kansas City childhood. Although he was the son of a Methodist minister and middle class, he was not completely isolated from the tensions of racial segregation and white oppression that sometimes threatened violence. In his early youth he witnessed a system of enforced inferiority that assured economic and personal failure for most southern blacks. He knew that the fate of homeless blacks could await him if he had not enjoyed the status of being a minister's son, or if he made the wrong future career choices. His father's position created both strains and possibilities. Lester was also aware of a complex family history that included a maternal great-grandfather who was Jewish.

Although Lester did have an adolescent rebellion against his father's religion, announcing that he was an atheist, closer examination reveals a longing, on Lester's part, to rise above the formality of ritualistic religion and approach genuine spiritual integrity. He later saw this time in his life as part of a pattern:

> My atheism . . . was not only an act toward self definition, but part of a reassessment of humanity's relationship to itself then occurring in the West. I was not the only one who looked upon the world and found no nourishment. It was no longer possible to believe there was a God; it was no longer possible to praise humanity and glorify it as being only a little lower than the angels. (*All Is Well*, p. 33)

Julius Lester. Photo courtesy of David Leviatin

When Lester attended Fisk University in Nashville, Tennessee, he was influenced both by his teachers, such as the poet Robert Hayden, and by other students, such as Stokely Carmichael, the head of the Student Nonviolent Organizing Committee at Fisk. Carmichael easily persuaded Lester to participate in demonstrations to integrate local lunch counters, to join in Freedom Rides to integrate transportation, and to help rural people to register to vote.

After college, Lester worked as a social caseworker. He saw misery and poverty in home visits. Later, he returned South to work in civil rights struggles in Mississippi. All of his experiences drew Lester toward finding spiritual explanations for these experiences in the secular world. Outwardly he was a revolutionary radical thinker and activist; inwardly he was on a religious quest. Not only did this activity bring Lester to national attention, but Lester recorded these events in his first serious nonfiction which brought him to the attention of many who would not otherwise have known him. His personal life, however, remained the unspoken backdrop to the public man. There was his first marriage; two children; divorce; a second interracial marriage; and a third child. It is the first autobiography that reveals this private Lester. Beneath the external political behavior which appeared so simple and clearcut there were difficult personal choices.

His work experiences varied widely in these years. He recorded several blues records with the Vanguard label, was the director of the Newport Folk Festival (Newport, Rhode Island) during 1966–1968, was a producer of the New York radio show "The Great Proletarian Cultural Revolution" (1968–1975), edited and wrote several books, did television work for WNET (New York), and joined the Afro-American Studies Department at the University of Massachusetts, Amherst, in 1971. Some of his actions attracted widespread comment, such as his repeated inclusion in his radio program of a poem by a New York student that outraged many people as anti-Semitic.

By the 1970s he seems to have left radical politics and become deeply immersed in a re-evaluation of his own life. In 1979 he published "The Uses of Suffering," which was later included as the introduction to *Lovesong*. His colleagues at the Afro-American Studies Department criticized him for (in their estimate) giving greater weight and loyalty to Jewish suffering than to African-American suffering. He felt rejected by his associates. His conversion to Judaism may have accelerated with this break, although Lester referred to his search for his long-lost Jewish maternal relatives in *All Is Well*. His eventual 1983 conversion almost divided him from his second wife and his children until his wife voluntarily consented to her own conversion. The children never agreed.

Lovesong, then, describes his final resolution, his complete conversion to Judaism. This final resolution is expressed in joyous terms by Lester. In fact, when Lester finally made the decision, his words glow from spiritual fulfillment. From Lester's youthful impatience with the over-thirty generation voiced in his earliest work through the midlife *Lovesong*, questions of integrity and political morality had risen continually in his writings. Just as he had to cope with the distinctions between the outer and the inner man, he questioned whether there existed the same public versus private dichotomy in political figures about whom he wrote. Did each figure sustain a genuine commitment to larger human goals or merely to the self? He criticized Martin Luther King (1*), for example, as a person "who did not exist except as an object, a leader, a public person and on his tombstone are inscribed the words 'Free at last! Free at last! Thank God almighty! I'm free at last.' " Was King merely a pawn in a vast drama who was swept involuntarily into importance by external forces? Additionally, Jesse Jackson's public statements were held up against what Lester considered Jackson's private narcissism. Although Jackson (6*) galvanized the black vote far more than any other black politician, and despite the fact that he articulated the hopes and fears of millions of poor and oppressed, Lester accused Jackson of primarily articulating Jackson. Angela Davis (6*) was also questioned for the reductionism of her Marxist beliefs, which were not deemed likely to change either the world or the individual. Perhaps Lester's movement from radical youth to moderate middle age tempted him to test the strength of others' political gods.

James Baldwin, for example, came under his scrutiny. Baldwin was given high praise for not succumbing to bitterness as he struggled out of poverty and ignorance. Baldwin, of four people discussed, comes closest to gaining Lester's unrestrained approval. That approval quickly dissolved, however, when Baldwin delivered a talk critical of Jewish merchants in Harlem.

The 1960s produced intellectuals like Julius Lester who would sustain, to one degree or another, portions of the idealism of that era throughout their work and their lives. Lester sought a steadying emblem or linkage with a spiritual-historical community to help him reconstitute the fragments of his past and present experiences. His colleagues at the University of Massachusetts, however, as well as many black people throughout America who knew of Lester's career, believed his conversion too extreme for their understanding. His act seemed alien to them; in many cases, they viewed the Jewish community as one in which they found themselves alien. Nevertheless, his conversion was the culmination of his own psychological and spiritual self's attempts to find coherence. It resolved his own inner conflicts. A fragmented self had become apparently whole.

Bibliography

Butterfield, Stephen. *Black Autobiography in America*. Amherst: University of Massachusetts Press, 1974.

"Don't Believe the Hype . . . " [a critique of Lester], *The Black Scholar* 19 (Nov./Dec. 1988): 27–43.

Garvey, John. "Pilgrims of the Absolute," *Commonweal* 115 (March 25, 1988): 167–69.

Lester, Julius. "Academic Freedom and the Black Intellectual," *The Black Scholar* 19 (Nov./Dec. 1988): 16–26.

———. *All Is Well: An Autobiography*. New York: William Morrow, 1976.

———. "Ambush at Amherst," *The New Republic* 198 (June 27, 1988): 9–10.

———. "Black and White—Together," *Salmagundi* no. 81 (Winter 1989): 174–81.

———. *Falling Pieces of the Broken Sky*. New York: Arcade Publishing, 1990.

———. *Look Out, Whitey! Black Power's Gon' Get Your Mama*. New York: Dial Press, 1968.

———. *Lovesong: On Becoming a Jew*. New York: Henry Holt, 1988. Reviewed: *Partisan Review* 57 (Spring 1990): 321–25.

———. "Malcolm," *New York Times Book Review* 96 (Nov. 24, 1991): 11–12.

————. "Man in the Mirror: Hero Worship in the Jackson Campaign," *The New Republic* 198 (1988): 20–22.

————. *Revolutionary Notes.* New York: Richard Baron Publishing, 1969.

————. *Search for a New Land: History as Subjective Experience.* New York: Dial Press, 1969.

————. "Some Tickets Are Better: The Mixed Achievement of James Baldwin," *Dissent* 33 (1986): 189–92, 214.

————. "You Can't Go Home Again: Critical Thoughts about Jesse Jackson," *Dissent* 32 (Winter 1985): 21–25.

Priscilla Ramsey

COUNTRY JOE McDONALD (1942–   )

Singer, guitarist, composer

"The most revolutionary thing you can do in this country is change your mind," Country Joe once pointed out. McDonald survived the sixties, and the two ensuing decades, in part because of his ability to change his mind, explore new opportunities as they presented themselves, and roll with the changing times while still remaining on the cutting edge. Country Joe and the Fish first achieved limited West Coast fame as part of the San Francisco scene of the middle sixties: a politically left psychedelic band, the group played area coffeehouses, demonstrations, the Avalon Ballroom, and the Fillmore with area groups like the Grateful Dead, the Doors, the Jefferson Airplane, Big Brother and the Holding Company. McDonald had developed a black humor, anti-war song titled "Feel-Like-I'm-Fixin'-to-Die Rag" (in which, to the up-tempo Dixieland tune of "Muskat Ramble," Joe invited Wall Street to quick invest in this go-go War Thing, and urged parents to become the first on their block to have their son sent home in a box). The group usually prefaced this song with some version of an audience participation "Fish Cheer": "Give me an F . . . ." Sometimes the word spelled out was *fish*, sometimes another four-letter F word. The cheer was a great crowd-pleaser, and the group gained a tremendous following on the West Coast almost exclusively word-of-mouth.

The *Feel-Like-I'm-Fixin'-to-Die* album sold over 500,000 copies (the number required for a gold record) on virtually no advertising. Country Joe and the Fish performed at the Monterey Pop Festival and at Woodstock (in person and in the films) and gained a national reputation. A fluid group in the West Coast style, with frequent personnel additions and subtractions, the Fish pretty much disbanded after Woodstock, to be briefly reconstituted in 1976. During the interim, McDonald produced several solo albums, scored films, toured Europe repeatedly, got himself into and ultimately out of serious booze and drug problems, divorced, remarried, redivorced, remarried. He toured with Jane Fonda (*) and Donald Sutherland on their FTA Review (Free/Fuck the Army), played benefits for various Vietnam veterans organizations, and campaigned for Greenpeace and Save the Whales. His political independence and extreme musical eclecticism brought criticism at one time or another in his career from just about every segment of musical and political culture, but have in the end resulted in the respect due any individual of strong and independent convictions.

Joe McDonald was born in El Monte, California. His grandfather was a Presbyterian minister and a farmer from Oklahoma. His parents were organizers for the local Communist party and named their son after Joseph Stalin. Although presently a well-developed suburb of Los Angeles, El Monte was still largely rural when Joe was young, and country music was popular, live, on the radio, and in McDonald's home. McDonald did grow up country. By the time he entered high school, however, his affections had shifted toward rock and roll, with a typically 1950s American admiration for Elvis Presley. In high school he became sports editor of the Arroyo High School *Knights' Banner*, covered high school sports for the El Monte *Herald*, formed a band (the Nomads), and wrote his first song, "I Seen a Rocket," for a friend's campaign for student body president. Not particularly politicized at seventeen, McDonald joined the navy, serving four years before returning home on the verge of a nervous breakdown. ("I fell in love with a Japanese girl, and I tried to marry her. I met a lot of stupid resistance from the Navy.") After a semester in college at Pomona, McDonald dropped out to work four months as a migratory worker in central California and Washington, playing guitar and singing. Finally he returned to California and got a job packaging breaded shrimp and scallops; he was fired for having a bad attitude, not taking his work seriously enough.

McDonald spent a year at Los Angeles City College, where he became involved in civil rights activities. Impelled by national and international events, he began writing protest songs and gravitated toward Berkeley, where the climate and audience were more hospitable. "I felt the call to come to the San Francisco Bay area, like I think a lot of people did—sort of like lemmings to the sea," McDonald later recalled. "I became obsessed with the concept of becoming Bob Dylan . . . I listened to 'Masters of War' a couple of times a day." In Berkeley he began his own underground magazine, *Et Tu, Brute*; formed a jug band (named the Berkeley String Quartet); began singing for radio station KPFA (anyone who wanted to could sing late at night), and playing the coffeehouse circuit, especially the Jabberwock and the Drinking Gourd. Country Joe was in change of music for the October 15 and 16, 1965, March on Oakland.

In Berkeley, too, McDonald met guitarist Barry Melton, who—with Country Joe, 'Chicken' Hirsh, and David Cohen—comprised the core of the Fish. The jug band became the Fish and turned electric "by buying an amplifier." "Fixin'-to-Die Rag"—first published in 1965 in a magazine called *Rag Baby* created by a former staff member of *Sing Out!*—provided the group a strong identity amid the plethora of Bay Area music groups, as did the group's politically overt lyrics (if the anti-war movement had an anthem, "Fixin'-to-Die" was it). By 1966, the group was playing at love-ins and political rallies up and down the coast, at the Jabberwock, the Avalon, and the Fillmore. For a couple of bucks, you got several hours of Country Joe and the Fish, the Grateful Dead, the Airplane, Big Brother and the Holding Company, with a light show thrown in gratis. With his usual sense of ambiguities, McDonald frequently showed up at love-ins in an army jacket emblazoned with political pins and at political rallies with amps and speakers covered with stick-on hippie daisies. Denison became the group's manager, and it self-recorded a record for local distribution.

In 1966 Vanguard signed the group (part of the national acknowledgment of the San Francisco sound). *Electric Music for the Mind and Body* appeared in 1967 (containing many of the songs from the group's home-grown album), to be followed by *I-Feel-Like-I'm-Fixin'-to-Die* in 1968. "Fixin'-to-Die Rag," "Superbird" (Lyndon Johnson), and "Not So Sweet Martha Lorraine" (sex) became underground classics, the one a political chant, the second a political satire, the third a psychedelic, Dylanesque extravaganza. The group toured Europe in 1967 with great success, and returned three times in 1968 and 1969. It played Monterey and Woodstock and woke up famous.

Things happened very quickly in the second half of the 1960s. McDonald and the band blasted through musical stages and influences one after the other (Burl Ives, Harry Belafonte, acoustic Dylan, Joan Baez (*), Mike Bloomfield, John Cage), rehearsing six to eight hours a day, assimilating, assimilating, assimilating. *Electric Music* was recorded three months after the Fish first formed. The group was barely a child when it became suddenly an adult: the San Francisco scene barely came together before it was exploited commercially, sent out in component parts on promotional tours literally all over the world. "Well, there was childhood's end, which came about 1968," McDonald recalled. "Everyone had left the San Francisco Bay Area and discovered the horror of the road. Work, that's what happened, work and work and work and work. It took creativity and smashed it to pieces. There came contracts—one record every six months—and then one-nighters and airplanes." Looking back to San Francisco from New York in 1968, road manager Sandy Loring spoke for all the San Francisco groups: "One thing we all miss is seeing each other. . . . I miss those days. I miss the feelings, the trust that was there. Everybody seems to have become a lot more serious."

Woodstock (1969) McDonald remembers as another calling, like going to San Francisco in 1965: "I get kind of mystical about my solo performance at Woodstock. I think I was fated to do it." The band was a late hire, but the F-cheer was a great success, as was the "No More Rain" chant. "When the electricity went out, the kids were bored. Having played a lot of demonstrations, we knew that people would respond to some kind of nonamplified noise-making." They banged pots and pans and cowbells and started chanting "No more rain." The audience picked it up immediately.

One thing that did not happen for Country Joe and the Fish was Chicago, 1968. The group had been scheduled to perform as part of the Yippie Festival of Life scheduled to coincide with the Democratic National Convention of 1968, but McDonald pulled his group at the last minute. Testifying at the Chicago Conspiracy Trial, he said, 'The vibrations were so incredibly vicious that I thought it was impossible to avoid violence on the part of the police. . . . there would be a possibility that people would follow us to the Festival and be clubbed and maced and tear-gassed."

The stress of late sixties repression and life on the road began to tell on Country Joe and the Fish. In Worcester, Massachusetts, the group was arrested for inciting the audience to lewd behavior. "We were met in Boston by one police captain, three lieutenants, 75 uniformed patrolmen with clubs, guns and mace, police squad cars, 25 plain clothes detectives and a paddy wagon, and we were informed that we couldn't do that thing which we had done in Wooster, but no one would articulate what it was we had done because I imagine they were just waiting for us to do it again," reported McDonald. He considered this an unconstitutional act by authorities who were really responsible for immoral acts against the environment.

In mid-1969, Vanguard issued a *Greatest Hits* album, and a live album was developed out of the fourth European tour. McDonald scored and performed the music for a Danish film based on Henry Miller's *Quiet Days in Clichy*. Following the lead of Bob Dylan, and catching the mood of 1970 America, McDonald returned to his own country roots on two solo albums titled *Thinking of Woody Guthrie* (1970) and *Tonight I'm Singing Just For You* (1971). Some of Nashville's best sessions men accompanied him on both albums, and songs and performances are both high-quality country. He set to music a collection of Robert Service World War I poems for an album titled *War, War, War* (1971). He toured with Fonda and Sutherland's anti-war show. Then, again catching the mood of the nation, he headed for Europe with the All-Star Band (Peter Alvin, Tucki Bailey, Dorothy Moscowitz, Anna Rizzo): "I wanted to make a feminist band and write material that I felt was reflective of what was happening at the time." *The Paris Sessions* was released by Vanguard in 1973, containing songs on the oppression of women and the power of media, including the music industry.

The seventies were hard on Country Joe, as they were for many other sixties people. He had turned from rock to folk music and was playing small houses for small fees a decade after the golden age of folk music. His personal life was in a shambles, and his debts were heavy. "Disillusioned isn't the right word," he told *Rolling Stone* magazine in January 1975. "My personal life is totally messed, I'm in debt up to my ass, I'm turning into a fascist." He had returned from the financially ruinous All-Star Band tour to a divorce suit from his second wife ("the great feminist seeking spousal support") which pushed his indebtedness to more than $100,000. In response, McDonald burrowed further into drugs and alcohol, and threw a million-dollar lawsuit at Vanguard Records. "I got burned," he said. "I've been a pacifist all my life, but now I'm going to fight."

Although his 1978 album *Rock 'n' Roll Music from the Planet Earth* contained a song titled "Bring Back the Sixties, Man," McDonald refused to live in memory or illusion: "People want to pretend that what they're hearing is really good music, that they're surrounded by a radical culture, that they're living a free, happy, groovy life. The reality is that we are leading a very conservative, boring life right now. And there isn't a hell of a lot of good music to hear."

McDonald moved to France. He toured Europe (three times) to work off his debts. He moved back to the States, to Washington's Puget Sound area, bought a house, and opened a small music store. He changed from Vanguard to Fantasy records. He fell in love and married again. ("You can't make really good music if your life is in a shambles, and if you're so untogether in your mind that you can't discipline yourself to work at your craft.") The newer, happier Country Joe produced *Paradise with an Ocean View* (its cover depicted a tropical paradise of water and palm trees, bulldozer encroaching from the left, and a sign advertising "Model Homes" erected on a sand bar), which got very good reviews, and *Love Is a Fire*, an album of pseudo-disco tunes that was not very well received. Despite feeling plagued during the early seventies with his reputation as a protest singer, McDonald engineered a reunion of the Fish in 1977: a series of performances, and an album—*Reunion*—on Fantasy Records. In the 1980s, McDonald was engaged in ecological concerns like the Greenpeace Foundation ("Save the Whales—Save the Earth" was bannered across the inside of *Paradise with an Ocean View*) and veterans' rights, mostly "offshoots of Vietnam Veterans against the War—the radical veterans." His song "A Vietnam Veteran's Still Alive" became a kind of anthem for radical vets, the way "Fixin-to-Die Rag" was an anthem for the anti-war protesters of the sixties.

Through the changes, McDonald retained the macabre sense of life's absurdity which made early Country Joe and the Fish albums some of the best absurdist protest. In his musical eclecticism, he mirrored the multifaceted personality of the whole sixties generation. "Our audience is a collectivization of all the disaffiliated people," Fish co-founder Barry Melton once told *The New Yorker*, "The only thing we can do is build up our corporation—make peace a nice, marketable product and sell it to the country." This is essentially what McDonald did with his political songs, with the psychedelic songs, with the women's liberation and the save-the-whales songs, with his love songs, and with his filmscores and his homage to Woody Guthrie. In many cultural respects, the sixties found one of its most representative embodiments in Country Joe McDonald.

Records

Electric Music for the Mind and Body (Vanguard, 1967).
I-Feel-Like-I'm-Fixin'-to-Die (Vanguard, 1967).
Greatest Hits (Vanguard, 1969).
Thinking of Woody (Vanguard, 1970).
War, War, War (Vanguard, 1971).
Life and Times of Country Joe and the Fish (Vanguard, 1971).
Paris Sessions (Vanguard, 1973).
Paradise with an Ocean View (Fantasy, 1975).
Reunion (Fantasy, 1977).
Rock'n'Roll from Planet Earth (Fantasy, 1978).

David Pichaske

PHIL OCHS (1940–1976)

Folksinger and composer

For one brief and shining moment in the early sixties, Phil Ochs was considered the equal of Bob Dylan (*) and one of the inner circle of Greenwich Village "children of Woody" that included Dylan, Ochs, Joan Baez (*), Peter Paul and Mary, Dave Van Ronk, and others. At the 1964 Newport Folk Festival he and Dylan led, together, a workshop in topical song writing, and in Sis Cunningham's *Broadside* magazine, that mimeographed repository of Village protest songs, Ochs out-published Dylan by a considerable margin. When Dylan clearly captured the title of "King of Protest," Ochs was regarded as heir apparent. However, Ochs took the road less traveled, opting consistently for personal appearances on the coffeehouse and demonstration circuit over work in the recording studio, and while his melodies were subtle, moving, and memorable, his lyrics were often too vitriolic for even FM radio. Not one of his albums ever sold over 50,000 units, although Ochs built a fanatical underground following in the high sixties. A founding member of the Youth International Party (the Yippies), Ochs alone among members of the musical establishment participated in the Festival of Life held in Chicago in 1968 to coincide with the Democratic National Convention. His testimony a year and a half later at the conspiracy trial was inspired: "The Court: 'You are a singer, but you are a smart fellow, I'm sure.' Ochs: 'Thank you. You are a judge, and you are a smart fellow.'" With the disintegration of the Movement and the passing of the sixties themselves, Ochs lost his sense of purpose and direction, singing only occasionally on the coffeehouse circuit and unwilling, or unable, to confront the new decade on terms acceptable to himself and it. At the moment of his suicide, Ochs had virtually disappeared from the observable

Phil Ochs. Copyright *Washington Post*; Reprinted by permission of D.C. Public Library.

universe, although his name, and his work, was a powerful memory in the minds of a dedicated and happy few, and when shared with the younger generation, continued to win converts. The response of one New York editor to a 1976 proposal for a Phil Ochs biography was, "America didn't want Phil Ochs when he was alive; we can't sell them Phil Ochs now that he's dead."

Ochs was born in El Paso, Texas, spent some of his childhood in his mother's native Scotland, but lived most of his formative years in New York, in Far

Rockaway and Perrysburg, watching movies, listening to Elvis Presley, and playing clarinet, a self-described "American nebbish." When Phil was a teenager, the Ochs family moved to Columbus, Ohio. Phil spent his last two years of high school at Staunton (Military) Academy in Virginia, where he played in the band and quickly became, in the words of his buddies, "Mr. Universe." In 1958 he enrolled at Ohio State University, wearing a red jacket similar to that worn by James Dean in *Rebel without a Cause*. That spring he dropped out of the university, telling his mother he was wasting her money and his time. He headed to Florida in search of singing jobs, worked washing dishes and selling shoes, spent fifteen days in jail (vagrancy), and took the Greyhound bus home. The following fall he returned to Ohio State intent on a journalism major. There he met Jim Glover, who was also interested in music. Glover introduced Ochs to the work of the Weavers, Pete Seeger (*), and the Legendary Woody Guthrie. Glover's father was a Marxist, and the friendship reinforced the music of Guthrie, the Weavers, and Seeger to turn Ochs's thoughts to the plight of exploited workers and the evils of capitalism. Glover and Ochs became a folk duet, the Sundowners, singing traditional folk songs and topical songs Ochs composed himself. Although Phil was writing extensively for the Ohio State newspaper, *The Lantern* (columns and musical reviews), he grew quickly dissatisfied with its studied neutrality on hard political and social issues, and founded his own paper, *The Word*. He also published letters to the editor in commercial newspapers, including the Cleveland *Plain Dealer*. When *The Lantern* decided he was too controversial to make a good editor, he left Ohio State, one semester short of graduation, for New York City.

In New York he gravitated naturally to Greenwich Village, to Gerde's Folk City with its Monday talent night. In March 1963 Ochs opened at Gerde's for John Hammond, who also introduced him to *Broadside* magazine, for which he began to write as he had written for *The Word*: prolifically and with spirit. "There was no question that Phil was major, from the very outset," Dave Van Ronk recalled. The Bleecker Street apartment of Phil and Alice Ochs became a meeting place visited regularly by virtually every significant Village musician and most visitors to the Village. When folk music achieved national popularity in 1963, Ochs expected—and was expected by others in the Village—to ride its popularity to national fame. But when the popular ABC television program "Hootenanny" passed over Peter Seeger and the Weavers because they "wanted better folk singers," first Joan Baez refused to appear on the program, and then Phil Ochs and Tom Paxton (against the advice of Seeger, who understood better than they the politics of the possible) organized a formal boycott of the program. "Hootenanny" was ultimately cancelled by ABC, thereby aborting the folk flowering on national television and cutting Ochs, and others, off network TV.

In 1963 Ochs, Dylan, and others toured Hazard County, Kentucky, publicizing the plight of striking miners there and further identifying themselves with left-leaning causes. The next year Ochs and others left the Newport Folk

Festival for the still segregated South, forming "the Mississippi Caravan of Music." They had been in the state only two days when the bodies of three civil rights workers were found buried in the Mississippi swamps. Such trips gave Ochs currency in East Coast folk circles and material for songs, which he churned out like sports articles. By late 1964 Ochs was a headliner in Village coffeehouses and had his first album, released by Elektra: *All the News That's Fit to Sing*. The album, with its title adapted from the *New York Times* motto "All the News That's Fit to Print," was conceived as a musical newspaper, complete with editorial pages, from which Ochs could fire his "barbed musical shafts" at all the traditional opponents of left-liberals.

The year 1965 brought an official separation from Alice, distance from Phil's daughter Meegan, and a second album from Elektra, *I Ain't Marching Any More*. The album contained more topical protest songs, and liner notes in which Ochs reproduced some of his salty on-stage patter: "This borders between pacifism and treason, combining the best qualities of both"; "Scenes and images of the riots last summer in Harlem. As is usually the case, the loudest bursts of outrage came from those most responsible for the debacle." Bruce Jackson's liner notes attempted to distinguish the work of the new Children of Woody from other folk music by creating a new category, "urban folk music," an issue which, though academic at best, provoked heated argument during the mid-sixties, and underlay the folk community's rejection first of Dylan and later of Ochs. Dissatisfied with playing second fiddle to Bob Dylan, Ochs replaced Albert "Dear Landlord" Grossman as his manager, with Arthur Gorson, a political activist associated with Americans for Democratic Action and Students for a Democratic Society. Gorson, who had organized the Hazard County crusades, knew politics, but he did not know music the way Grossman knew music. While Gorson reinforced Ochs ideologically, this kind of support was not what Phil Ochs the musician needed: spring saw Ochs breaking commercial engagements to participate in the Jerry Rubin–organized teach-in at Berkeley. Fired with the excitement of being on the cutting political edge and playing for people who appreciated his music, Ochs left Berkeley for a similar teach-in at Haverford College, then to Ohio State for the Free Speech Front rally, then to demonstrations all over the country throughout the late sixties. It is arguable that commitment to Movement rallies, where he sang to hundreds or even thousands at a time, cost Ochs time which might more profitably have been invested in promoting his work through electronic media, which would have reached millions.

With Gorson, Ochs formed Barricade Music, a private publishing corporation designed to retain royalties on Ochs's songs. He played a sell-out concert at Carnegie Hall (a hall Grossman had refused to book), which— supplemented with material taped at a Boston concert and at a private session in New York's Judson Hall—resulted in *Phil Ochs in Concert* (1966). Phil's editorializing introductions to his songs and the reaction of a live audience make this his most successful protest album: "In every community there are varying shades of political opinion. One of the shadiest of these is the liberal." Instead of jacket notes, Ochs printed English translations of poems by Mao Tse-tung above the caption "Is This the Enemy?" Although Elektra asked him to reconsider, he insisted. Half the country's record distributors refused to carry the album.

After some initial successes like the Carnegie Hall concert, Gorson did not work out as Phil's manager: Phil was constantly on the edge of poverty, despite the fact that he and other singers in the Gorson stable were performing constantly. Ochs replaced Gorson with his brother, Michael Ochs, the one manager who did, finally, make Phil some money. Ochs also broke from Elektra, and after a disastrous negotiation with Columbia, signed with A&M Records of Los Angeles, whose curiously eclectic list included the Procol Harum and soft pop singers like Burt Bacharach and Liza Minnelli. Ochs prepared his first A&M record, *Pleasures of the Harbor*, while A&M prepared a cross-country promotional tour.

While in Los Angeles recording *Pleasures of the Harbor*, Ochs conceived of the idea for a "The War Is Over" rally, which he staged with great success on the West Coast and then, later, in New York: "We are going to celebrate the end of the war. . . . Everyone who comes should try to do something creative on his own—make up a few signs like 'God Bless You Lyndon for Ending the War,' wear clothes appropriate to the re-enactment of VE day, wave a flag and mean it, invite a soldier along, form a brass band to play 'When Johnnie Comes Marching Home,' bring extra noisemakers and confetti, drink beer, kiss girls, and give thanks this weekend that the war is over."

Also in Los Angeles Phil became close friends with Britisher Andrew Wickham, elegant, elitist, the opposite pole from Ochs on virtually every social and political issue. The net effect of this friendship, which lasted several years, was to deradicalize Ochs, or at least to confirm him into a new, artsy direction already apparent in cuts on *Pleasures of the Harbor*, which got scathing reviews in *Broadside*, brought charges of an Ochs sell-out similar to those leveled previously at Bob Dylan, and effectively estranged Ochs from his folk audience. Ochs stopped writing for *Broadside*, and he was not invited to participate in a Carnegie Hall tribute to Woody Guthrie. The concert brought Dylan out of a year-and-a-half seclusion, showcased everyone who was anyone and others who were not, and produced, finally, a very handsome two-record album on which Ochs is conspicuous by his absence.

Ochs, his brother, and Wickham pressed ahead with plans for a songbook (March 1968), featuring songs, articles, essays by Phil, Ron Cobb cartoons, and tastefully antique photographs of scantily clad women. Ochs pressed ahead with a second A&M album, *Tape from California*, which combined art songs with some of his best protest lyrics, most of them against the war in Vietnam. And Ochs prepared for the Democratic National Convention in Chicago, where he helped purchase and nominate for president of the United States a large pig, and watched "the fog roll in and the gas roll out" as Mayor

Daley's police pummeled delegates and demonstrators alike. The experience destroyed Ochs almost as much as it destroyed Hubert Humphrey and the Democratic party: friends had warned him the Yippie demonstrations might be a trap, and they had proven correct. The net result of Chicago was broken bodies and Richard Nixon, president by a whisker. And the promise only of more Vietnam war. Out of Ochs's Chicago experience came a third A&M album, *Rehearsals for Retirement*, his last major attempt at the market. He wrote all the songs—some of his finest—in the space of two weeks, including the title cut: "The days grow longer for smaller prizes . . . ."

After Chicago, Ochs played another concert at Carnegie Hall, perhaps the last unqualified success of his life. Then he returned to Los Angeles, where he and Wickham attended one of Elvis Presley's "comeback tour" concerts. Ochs was transfixed with Presley's gold lamé suit, and his old admiration for Presley was rekindled. If folk was dead and art rock would not sell, Ochs would do old-time rock and roll (a not entirely preposterous idea, as groups like the Sha-na-na would demonstrate). He ordered a gold Presley suit, recorded a rock and roll album and planned a promotional tour. The album (*Greatest Hits*, with a very posed photo of an overweight Phil in the golden suit on front, another photo of overaged Phil in a black leather jacket and sun glasses on the back, below the slogan—by then only slightly ironic—"50 Phil Ochs Fans Can't Be Wrong!") did not make its production costs, even though only two days of production were involved. The rock-n-roll tour opened at Carnegie Hall to a very small house; Ochs, nervous, played less than an hour for the first performance, then overcompensated at the second, rambling incoherently on until 3:00 A.M. when management turned off the electricity.

By the 1970s, Ochs was drinking heavily, estranged from former wife and friends, and usually broke. He and Jerry Rubin (*) visited Chile in search of Salvador Allende. He visited Australia. He visited Africa, where he was mugged by several natives and, in trying to scream for help, ruptured his vocal cords. The Watergate hearings briefly rekindled Ochs's interest in politics: he reissued "Here's to the State of Mississippi" as "Here's to the State of Richard Nixon" (a single which went nowhere); played a series of concerts across the East Coast, Chicago, and Los Angeles (his most popular material was the early sixties work, making him a museum piece in his early thirties); and produced another rock and roll album, *Gunfight at Carnegie Hall* (1975; side two ended in an Elvis Presley medley). It disappeared into a black hole. After the overthrow of the Allende regime, Ochs set to organizing a benefit concert at Madison Square Garden's Felt Forum. A week before the concert less than a quarter of the tickets had been sold; only Dylan's announcement, the day before the concert, rescued the concert from absolute disaster. But Ochs had been saved only to be destroyed: Ochs was devastated to realize that Dylan could sell out in a single day the concert he had been unable to move in months of work. And when, two years later, Dylan's Rolling Thunder Review, which the two had discussed together on the evening of the Chile benefit, rolled without Ochs, and when Dylan's *Blood on the Tracks* album showed just how much Dylan still had, and by contrast just how little remained in Ochs, Phil was finished.

At the end, Ochs turned heavily to pills, alcohol, movies, and a long suicide trip which consumed what remained of his money and estranged all remaining friends. He assumed a new name, John Butler Train, and a new personality: angry, drunken, aggressive, abusive. Train, he claimed, had murdered Ochs out of political necessity. The drunken Train-Ochs became persona non grata at all his old hangouts, was frequently in jail, walked out of Gracie Square Hospital after Jerry Rubin finally convinced him to enter treatment, and washed up, finally, at the home of his older sister Sonny in Far Rockaway, New York. In the bathroom of that home he hanged himself with his own belt.

A memorial celebration was held at Madison Square Garden's Felt Forum, and a two-record memorial album titled *Chords of Fame* was released by A&M under an agreement with Elektra Records in 1976.

Phil Ochs's significant work (his Elvis Presley is to be taken about as seriously as Elvis's own comeback tour) divides into two categories: topical protest songs and art songs, with some degree of overlap, because Ochs's art songs, like Simon's "The Boxer" and Dylan's "Desolation Row," usually contain an element of protest in the largest sense. With conspicuous exceptions, the topical protest songs came early in Ochs's career on the Elektra records (although "Ten Cents a Coup" appeared on the *Greatest Hits* album) with the art songs being concentrated on the late sixties A&M albums (although his first album contained a sung version of Poe's "The Bells," and his second album a sung version of Noyes's "The Highwayman").

"Every newspaper headline is a potential song," wrote Ochs in a *Broadside* editorial, "and it is the role of an effective songwriter to pick out the material that has the interest, significance, and sometimes humor adaptable to music." The effective songwriter, he argued, must reject superfluous and trite phrases for "the cogent powerful terms." Ochs was a master of the topical protest song, a journalist-folksinger since his Ohio State days. Ochs had been writing topical protest lyrics for the Sundowners even as a college student. Sis Cunningham mentioned "30 or 40 Phil Ochs songs" printed in *Broadside*, and probably as many more scattered around the office awaiting publication. Most of Ochs's topical protest songs are now as dated as old journalism and died with the causes which gave them birth. William Worthy (convicted of illegal re-entry into the United States after visiting communist Cuba in the early 1960s), the USS *Thresher* and the USS *Scorpion* (submarines lost at sea), Billie Sol Estes (an aide to Lyndon Johnson involved in shady deals), even the Cuban Missile Crisis, Medgar Evers, Hazard, Kentucky, and Birmingham, Mississippi, require footnotes today. The matter of these and other Phil Ochs topical protest lyrics has not endured as has, say, the story of the Edmund Fitzgerald. And in his telling, Ochs never really achieved the dramatic, compelling simplicity Dylan managed in some of his topical songs like "The Lonesome Death of Hattie Carroll."

In treating material, Ochs often took an easy moralizing stance which reinforced the prejudices of those already converted, alienated those not in the fold, and slightly unnerved anyone able to see subtleties and nuances. Ochs's facile rhymes, his facility with alliteration, and his wit save some songs, especially later songs from the A&M albums. The melody of "Bracero" (on migrant workers) is haunting, as are many other Ochs melodies. In introducing his material to a relatively intimate audience, Ochs was magnetic, better than Dylan, better than most of the Village crowd: 'The other night a voice came to me. Turned out it was God. Said, 'Ochs, wake up, this is God here. Over.' I said, 'You're putting me on, of course, Dylan.'" Of the earlier topical protest songs, "Too Many Martyrs" (on the death of Medgar Evers), "I Ain't Marching Any More," and "Draft Dodger Rag" (general anti-war songs), "I'm Going to Say It Now" (student rights), "Bracero," "Santo Domingo" (the invasion of Santo Domingo), and "Love Me, I'm a Liberal" are major-league performances. In addition, "Power and the Glory" (a celebration of America similar in many respects to Guthrie's "This Land Is Your Land") and "Bound for Glory" (a celebration of Woody Guthrie) are memorable songs.

In some of his protest songs Ochs exhibited a sharp visual imagery more suggestive of the poet than the journalist. "Santo Domingo," for example, begins with a close-up of crabs scuttling across the sandy beaches in front of the advancing marines—a stroke of genius on Och's part. In "White Boots Marching in a Yellow Land" Ochs attacked the Vietnam War with color imagery, metaphors (mountains of machinery; old whores following tired armies), and his usual alliteration and rhetoric. The song is a rich fabric of images and sounds, equal (except for the clear moralistic stance) to Dylan at his best. In another anti-war song, "The War Is Over," Ochs moved beyond imagism into surrealism: through a landscape dotted with cardboard cowboys, tattooed sons of tattooed widows, one-legged veterans mowing their lawns, a mad movie made by a mad director, Ochs pressed ahead, whistling a march of his own, warning that the gypsy fortune teller had told him we have been deceived, and concluding that even treason might just be worth a try.

In his later songs, Ochs often used allusions. "The Harder They Fall" incorporated the witches of *Macbeth*, elements of nursery rhymes (Jack and Jill looking for a thrill, Mary making it with a lamb), and allusions to stand-up comic Lenny Bruce in depicting a war become black comedy and a nation turned from sexual, political, and social revolution to sexual, political, and social perversion. "William Butler Yeats Visits Lincoln Park and Escapes Unscathed" weaves a whole lyric from materials borrowed, quite effectively and very much to the point of the song, from the Irish nationalist-poet-revolutionary William Butler Yeats. "The Doll House" refers to an Ibsen play. "I Kill, Therefore I Am" was built around Descartes' famous bedrock philosophical dictum melded with the familiar American adage, "Shoot first and ask questions later."

In these later art-protest songs, Ochs achieved a certain depth of psychological analysis, suggesting insecurity (usually sexual) as the root of American violence. In "Pretty Smart on My Part," Ochs created a John Birch Society narrator terrified of switchblade-wielding burglars, dominating women (with large breasts), sinister foreign agents, and subversive hitchhikers. His response is to take his car, his rifle, his NRA buddies, and blast away at innocent and guilty alike.

Ochs approaches allegory in many of his songs. "The Scorpion Departs But Never Returns" transforms the disappearance of a U.S. nuclear submarine into the departure of a new Lost Generation. They turned their backs on the war and the nation and disappeared. "Pleasures of the Harbor" celebrates, specifically, sailors on shore leave, but this is a port call in the journey of life, when we take a break from straining at the oar. Ochs's most ambitious allegory, however, was "Crucifixion," with the death of Christ becoming an allegory for the assassination of John Kennedy and the death of any handsome hero who is sacrificed by followers who both love and hate him. Ochs may have seen a little of himself in this story of the hero reaping the fruits of affection and the penalty of hate from the fickle masses. An experimental arrangement for full orchestra put "Pleasures of the Harbor" on a par with such Beatles' experiments as *Sgt. Pepper* and Van Dyke Parks's *Song Cycle* as a high water mark of sixties art rock.

In pursuing rock as art, Ochs was following the natural development of the sixties, and the natural progression of many sixties artists, who began in the relative musical and philosophical simplicities of either rock and roll or folk protest, then exploded into the infinite explorations (of self, of musical potentialities, of artistic form, of social and political arrangements) that marked the late sixties, and then returned, almost to an individual, into something familiar, formalist, socially and artistically conservative. Ochs's remaining fans rejected his Elvis material no less viciously than Dylan's fans rejected Dylan's post–*John Wesley Harding* country material and born-again Christian songs. Dylan had the self-confidence or arrogance to sustain himself. Ochs did not.

Phil Ochs was one of the lucky few who write their own epitaph. In fact, he did so several times. His first epitaph was the song "When I'm Gone," written in the middle sixties when he was a famous protest singer. Phil Ochs, singer-composer, realized that one day he would not be around to delineate right from wrong, and he committed himself to making a statement while he could. The song is a haunting credo of the artist as protest singer. Ochs's second epitaph appeared on the cover of *Rehearsals for Retirement* (1968). There were yellow flowers beside a black tombstone featuring a photograph of Ochs, gun across his shoulders, standing in front of an American flag. The inscription read: "Phil Ochs (American), Born: El Paso, Texas 1940; Died: Chicago, Illinois 1968." Ochs, as true an American as Henry Thoreau, died at the Democratic National Convention in Chicago in 1968. The third epitaph was a song called "Chords of Fame," in which Ochs the sage took a hard look at Ochs the protest singer.

Finally, there was "No More Songs." This was the final cut on the disastrous *Greatest Hits* album. The burned-out singer lamented the ashes of the sixties dream. He apologized to what remained of his public when he admitted candidly "there are no more songs." When Ochs was no longer around to perform live, and his albums disappeared, his work vanished.

Bibliography/Discography

Eliot, Marc. *Death of a Rebel*, rev. ed. New York: Franklin Watts, 1989.
Ochs, Phil. *All the News That's Fit to Sing* (Elektra Records, 1964).
————. *I Ain't Marching Any More* (Elektra Records, 1965).
————. *Chords of Fame* (A&M, 1976).
————. *Greatest Hits* (A&M, 1970).
————. *Gunfight at Carnegie Hall* (A&M, 1975).
————. *Phil Ochs in Concert* (Elektra Records, 1966).
————. *Pleasures of the Harbor* (A&M, 1967).
————. *Rehearsals for Retirement* (A&M, 1968).
————. *Tape from California* (A&M, 1968).
————. *The War Is Over* (songbook) (Barricade Music, 1968).
Pichaske, David R. *A Generation in Motion*. Granite Falls, MN: Ellis Press, 1989.
————. *The Poetry of Rock: The Golden Years*. Granite Falls, MN: Ellis Press, 1981.
Stambler, Irwin, and Grelun Landon, eds. *The Encyclopedia of Folk, Comedy and Western Music*, 2d ed. New York: St. Martin's Press, 1983: 527–29.

David Pichaske

KENNETH REXROTH (1905–1982)

Anarchist, poet, and critic

In *The Nation* of June 2, 1960, Kenneth Rexroth published an essay he called "The Students Take Over." It is the earliest and clearest forecast of the social weather that was to envelop the following decade. Youth all over the world, Rexroth wrote, were no longer just "turning their backs and walking away. Today they are striking back.... Hardly a person over thirty in our mass societies believes it is possible to strike back, or would know how to go about it if he did." Rexroth had taken a shrewd look over his shoulder and seen that "during the past couple of years, without caring about the consequences, making up their techniques as they went along, organizing spontaneously in the midst of action, young people all over the world have intervened in history."

The range of recent events Rexroth's synoptic glance took in was wide: the

Kenneth Rexroth *(right)* with Ogden Nash. Copyright *Washington Post*; Reprinted by permission of D.C. Public Library.

swelling ranks of the "Ban the Bomb" movement, opposition to ROTC training and the draft, sit-ins in the South initiated by students, youth demonstrations against capital punishment and the witchhunting of the House Un-American Activities Committee, student marches and organizations of similar thrust in Korea, Japan, France, and Latin America, and even the simple refusal of high school kids in New York to sign loyalty oaths or accept prizes offered them by the American Legion. The young were rejecting major institutions of the adult world not because these seemed reactionary but because they were "morally contemptible." It was "a kind of mass vomit. Everybody in the world knows that we are on the verge of extinction and nobody does anything about it." Rexroth saw that young people, stirred by disgust at the vast chasm between the ideals taught them in school and the horror of a universal chaos and emergency awaiting them just beyond the school gates, were beginning to do something about it. And he agreed with them that "what matters is the immediate realization of humane content, here, there, everywhere, in every fact and relationship of society. Today the brutal fact is that society cannot endure without the realization of humane content. The only way to realize it is directly, personally, in the immediate context."

Rexroth imagined that the greatest danger the young would face would be "all these eager helpers from the other side of the age barrier, all these cooks, each with a time-tested recipe for the broth." Therefore, past fifty himself, Rexroth refused the temptation to speak for the young. He was inclined to think they would fail. "But that isn't the point. You might as well be a hero if society is going to destroy you anyway. There comes a time when courage and honesty become cheaper than anything else."

Soon after this essay appeared, one academic critic momentarily bubbled up from oblivion to reject Rexroth as "mad" for "announcing a nationwide revolution among students on behalf of national and international integrity." Certainly, many of his kind agreed, at least at first. But in 1969, Robert Stock, also writing in *The Nation*, pointed out more accurately that "what is most viable in the so-called New Left is in large part the creation of Rexroth and Paul Goodman whether the movement knows it or not." Rexroth and Goodman both were poets. Poets in America have seldom had influence over social movements. How did Rexroth come to have his money on the right horses? Or better still, how had he come to whisper in the horses' ears?

At poetry readings during the sixties and beyond, Rexroth liked to tell approvingly of the evening he had asked an audience whether they wanted poems about sex, mysticism, or revolution and was answered seductively by a blond woman in the front row, who asked back, "What's the difference?" He might have added to the list his other great subject, wilderness, without leaving the current his young audiences found appealing. What made Rexroth so congenial to the young was his ability to project a personal presence— compounded of dramatic engagement with the world, great learning, lyrical praise and satirical condemnation, and humor high and low—which made it tangible that one could lead a life built on the conviction that all these subjects really were mutually reflective of one another. But by the sixties, Rexroth also had lived a busy life full of activities that, in fact, had prepared the ground in which the characteristic passions of the new youth had taken root and begun to grow. He had helped create a world climate in which he had become one version of the exemplary person.

Despite this, Rexroth often spoke of himself as an envoy from the time before, a kind of cultural dinosaur misthrown in a world past hope, "the lot of this tenth-rate Russian movie called 'The Collapse of Capitalist Civilization' onto which somehow we all seem to have wandered." Rexroth was born just short of ten years before the Great War. He believed the war marked both the death of a widespread revolutionary hope that sprang from "a moral confidence in the future" and the advent of "the struggle of our civilization to suppress its own potential." Until the war was over, everyone in the radical movement believed everything from clothing design to the game of chess to race relations and the relations between the sexes was going to change for the better. On the other side, "nobody in what they used to call the master class . . . not the Pope, not J. P. Morgan, not Calvin Coolidge, had any belief that the capitalist system would outlast the century, or even that it would last another generation." The huge primary disappointment of Rexroth's young manhood was that both groups turned out to be wrong.

Rexroth was born in South Bend, Indiana. His father was a wholesale pharmacist, given somewhat to high living and high-minded drinking companions. His mother had dropped out of Oberlin College and gone into business with a suffragist friend before marrying. After marriage, she channeled her artistic temperament into educating her son, more or less according to the principles of Maria Montessori. As the family's fortunes rose and finally fell, they shuttled back and forth between Elkhart, Indiana; Europe; Battle Creek, Michigan; Chicago; and Toledo, Ohio. Rexroth's mother died of tuberculosis in 1916. His father died of alcoholism in 1918. Rexroth was then shipped back to Chicago to live with his aunt, and Chicago remained his home base for the next ten years. By age sixteen, he had dropped out of Englewood High School and was living independently and very much at the center of Chicago's bohemia, where artists, bizarre underworld characters, and political radicals all crossed paths that entered his life.

Rexroth had grown up among people full of "an awareness of the need for social change." He enjoyed saying his parents had descended from a long line of "Schwenkfelders, Mennonites, German revolutionaries of '48, Abolitionists, suffragists, squaws and Indian traders, octoroons and itinerant horse dealers, farmers in broad hats, full beards and frogged coats." From this heritage, Rexroth soaked in a permanent attitude of *noblesse oblige* some mistook for arrogance. His parents, grandparents, and their widely extended family taught "that I was different from irresponsible people, that it was up to me to be better mannered, more courteous, more concerned, as the Quakers say, in all social relationships." This early training in the responsibilities of privilege also made him a lifelong political radical. He remembered that as a boy he had on his wall a picture of a high-society ball where elegantly dressed men and women were dancing. "Supporting the floor like half-prostrate caryatids were workers, men, women, and children, kneeling, bowed, crawling figures in a shallow cellar under the black and white tile floor. . . . In the center of the picture a worker had thrust his clenched fist up through the floor and all the nearby revelers were staring at it aghast."

After leaving high school, Rexroth sporadically attended classes at the University of Chicago and the Chicago Art Institute. He learned to paint in the constructivist and cubist manners, and he began translating poetry. These were practices he continued throughout his life. When he was sixteen, he began work on his first long poem, *A Homestead Called Damascus*. The poem, finished when he was twenty but not published until 1957, is a philosophical and dramatic meditation on politics, history, anthropology, sex, and the evolution of human personality. Rexroth systematically studied the subjects that went into the poem, both alone and with friends. At the same time, at Chicago clubs like the Dill Pickle and the Green Mask, he performed in and directed avant-garde plays and read poetry to jazz. He was a founder of the Chicago Dadaist movement, the Escalator, and learned to be a soapbox orator and reader of populist poetry at both the Bug Club in Washington Park and in Bughouse Square next to the Newberry Library. Much of Rexroth's activity in the Chicago of the twenties was later mirrored in the pursuits of similar youth during the fifties and sixties in New York, San Francisco, and other big American cities. Paradoxically, the later manifestations of bohemianism were both more highly publicized and more marginal to the overall cultural life of the country.

Late in his teens, Rexroth began traveling. He spent several winters working in the western mountains as cook, horse wrangler, trail sweep, and fire patrolman. He enjoyed the work and the company of the men who did it, and the mountains afforded him both the occasions for contemplation and the new subject matter for poetry he needed. For the next forty years, he spent as much time as he could in the mountains, and he never stopped writing about them. In his late teens, he also began his first serious love affair with a social worker several years older than he. He eventually followed his lover east to New York and Massachusetts. In Boston, he joined the demonstrations for his anarchist heroes, Sacco and Vanzetti. For many years after this, he would write a poem every August 22, commemorating their deaths.

In New York, Rexroth spent two Lenten months in contemplation at the Holy Cross Monastery, painting, writing, doing the work of a monk, participating in liturgical offices, and considering whether he wanted to become a postulant. He finally decided against it, realizing he lacked entirely the monastic vocation. What he did gain from the experience was a deepening of his commitment to contemplation as the source of universal communion and to "ethical activism . . . the only valid conservation of values . . . the assumption of unlimited liability." These were also tendencies that led him to an expanding interest in "the pure religious empiricism" of Buddhism during the thirties. By the end of the forties, the Buddhist content of his poetry weighed almost as heavily as the Christian. By the sixties, the Buddhist influence was pervasive. In fact, it was Rexroth's wide knowledge of Eastern poetry and of Buddhist texts and history that drew many younger poets with similar interests to him all through the fifties and until his death.

Nonetheless, Rexroth considered himself a kind of Catholic to the end. For him, Catholicism was "an anthropological religion . . . linked to the realities of life . . . the turning of the year and the changing seasons, and the rhythms of animal and human life." But Rexroth was no seeker after visions or religious experiences. Over and over again, he wrote of his detestation of religious antinomianism and sensationalism. He liked to quote St. John of the Cross: "Visions are a measure of the defect of vision." And vision itself, for Rexroth, was habitude and love, "an ever-increasing capacity for recollection and transcendence . . . developed by a kind of life rather than by manipulation." The illuminated, he learned, live in light as birds live in air and fish live in water.

From New York, Rexroth worked his way to Europe and traveled there, meeting everyone interesting he could find. When he returned to Chicago, he fell in love with and married Andrée Dutcher, a young painter who shared his political convictions, his tastes in the arts, and his appetite for adventure. Together they traveled west into the mountains, finally winding up in San Francisco. Soon after they arrived, they learned Sacco and Vanzetti had been executed. "A great cleaver cut through all the intellectual life of America. The world in which Andrée and I had grown up came forever to an end." Despite this crushing blow, Rexroth and Andrée felt they had found their perfect environment in San Francisco. They "decided to stay and grow up with the town."

The thirties for Rexroth were a time of intense political activity. Although he never became a member of the Communist party, he was a chief organizer in the West of the Party's literary arm, the John Reed Clubs. In later years, he loved to boast that he still had his party application across the top of which Earl Browder had scrawled, "Comrade Rexroth is a very valuable comrade, but he is entirely too much of an anarchist to be good party material." At Party writers' conferences, he argued against Party-line art and all other efforts to constrain literary genius for doctrinal or propaganda purposes. Instead, he made the claim that throughout modern times, "the poet, by the very nature of his art, has been an enemy of society,that is, of the privileged and the powerful." The task of the poet was to learn to speak for and to the under-privileged and the weak without any compromise of his art. Rexroth looked forward to a time, coming soon, when "if not interrupted by Fascism . . . every working stiff will be lots eruditer than E. Pound if he cares to be and folks will read Dante's Canzioni often for fun." He did his part to clear the way— and had his kind of fun—by writing poems over the next forty years that were by turns satirical, protesting, and philosophical. His elegies and lyrics fre-quently achieved an astonishing classical purity.

Rexroth helped agitate for and obtain money to pay writers and artists for their work through the WPA and the Federal Writers Project. He worked among the painters who decorated the Coit Tower on Telegraph Hill with a mural he called "the Diego Rivera funny papers." He also worked with the writers who produced the *WPA Guide to California* and anthologies like *American Stuff*. In addition he wrote two other books for the WPA which never were published, *A Field Handbook of the Sierra Nevada* and *Camping in the Western Mountains*. In the latter, he wrote, "The ideal camp is a miniature anarchist community straight out of Kropotkin. Each goes about his appointed task quietly and efficiently, the functions of the group are shared with spon-taneous equality, problems are settled by consultation rather than controversy, and whatever leadership exists is based solely on experience and ability."

Passages like these were not likely to win the approval either of Party appa-
ratchiks or the federal government.

Rexroth was also active helping to organize farm workers in the field and
seamen on the San Francisco waterfront. He even claimed to be responsible
for writing *"The Waterfront Worker* . . . all of the goddamn thing, week after
week after week." Through all this, he continued to write poetry, producing
the cubist poems of *The Art of Worldly Wisdom*, whose publication was delayed until 1949, and the poems of more direct address that made up the bulk
of his first published book, *In What Hour*. Notable in this book, and in much
of the poetry Rexroth wrote after it, is his twofold vision of nature as the
source of patterns and principles against which all human activity must be
measured and nature as itself the victim of the same evil human impulses that
divide, impoverish, and oppress people and lead ultimately to war. By 1940,
Rexroth's poetry had begun to foreshadow the eco-politics that erupted among
the young late in the sixties and the eco-poetics made popular then by younger
writers like Gary Snyder.

As the thirties ended, Rexroth's marriage unraveled along with his confidence that any of his activity would lead to lasting change. The Hitler-Stalin
Pact and his increasing knowledge of the Moscow show trials and Party purges
moved him from distrust of Bolshevism and the machinations of the American
party to outright loathing and aversion. The inevitability of America's participation in the world war drove him to be all the more confirmed in both his
anarchism and his pacifism. After 1940, the only organized political groups to
which he had ties were the Fellowship of Reconciliation, during the early
years of World War II, and Resist, the elders' support group for draft resisters
during the Vietnam War.

As World War II began and the government started to move Japanese
citizens on the West Coast to prison camps, Rexroth and his second wife,
Marie, became active in personally evacuating many Japanese to safety at the
center of the country and in organizing efforts to keep the personal property
of the evacuees secure. Throughout the war, Rexroth and Marie regularly
visited the Nisei camps, bringing food, company, and other necessary goods.
Rexroth applied to become a conscientious objector, and as such he went to
work in a psychiatric hospital. He and Marie also began to hold weekly pacifist
meetings in their home. They called the group the Randolph Bourne Council
in honor of the literary radical who, twenty years before in *The War and the
Intellectuals*, had condemned American writers for betraying their vocation to
support World War I. Word of Rexroth and his activities spread among conscientious objectors living in the Civilian Public Service Camps, especially
those at the camp in Waldport, Oregon, whose numbers included an unusually
high concentration of writers, craftsmen, and artists. On their furloughs, many
of these men would travel down to San Francisco where they would seek
Rexroth out for counsel and interesting conversation. A large number of these

pacifists, and many other men and women with similar attitudes and outlook, moved permanently to the Bay Area once the war was over.

Through Rexroth, the newcomers soon were in touch with compatible people already in town, including members of the Randolph Bourne Council and the artists and writers who attended Rexroth's Friday night at-homes as well as the older Jewish, Spanish, and Italian anarchists with whom Rexroth had kept up contact over the years. Together all these people became the San Francisco Libertarian Circle. Before long, space for regular Wednesday meetings was rented, and frequently as many as two hundred would attend. Rexroth, who sometimes arrived in a dramatic, long black cape, led discussions and provided contacts with speakers and connections to other similar groups in New York and England that had sprung up around people like Paul Goodman, George Woodcock, and Herbert Read. Rexroth also supplied the reading lists which included materials on social movements, ecology, philosophy, political theory, and poetry by authors like Lao-tse, Plato, Aristotle, Proudhon, Tolstoy and Kropotkin. By 1947, the Libertarian Circle had even attracted unwanted national notoriety when it became a focus of interest for a scurrilous piece published in *Harper's* and called "The New Cult of Sex and Anarchy."

The purpose of the group, as Rexroth saw it, was not to organize politically, but to rethink the fundamental principles of the radical movement and then radiate out into the cultural and communal life of the city with a humane philosophy as guide. Members of the group did just that, following a pattern very much like Rexroth's own tendencies. They were personalist and political, avant-garde and classicizing, religious and practical, regionalist and internationalist, street smart and learned. Members liked to boast, "We don't proselytize, we don't have any agenda, and we don't have a chairman." And yet the meetings were orderly, exciting, and productive.

Many of the members were students who went on to become professors, psychiatrists, social service workers, and engineers. The group also spawned three little theatres, several art galleries, and at least two literary magazines, *The Ark* and *Circle*. These magazines published poets involved in the group, including Robert Duncan, Philip Lamantia, Robin Blaser, Jack Spicer, William Everson, and poet-filmmaker James Broughton, as well as other writers with congenial inclinations. The poets were all very different from one another, but they had enough in common so that eventually they were identified as the First San Francisco Renaissance. Ultimately, they became the core of the San Francisco Poetry Center which, finally, was absorbed by San Francisco State College and set the national trend for large public poetry readings through the fifties and sixties and beyond.

Perhaps the single most important product of the Libertarian Circle was the first cooperatively organized and run, listener-sponsored FM radio station, KPFA, in San Francisco. The idea came originally from Lewis Hill, a member of the Circle and a former conscientious objector, who took responsibility for raising funds and setting the station up. His idea was that such a station could continue the Circle's discussions for a far wider audience. After a few years, Alan Watts was delivering the Sunday morning sermon, speaking on Zen and other Eastern religions; Pauline Kael was handling the film criticism, and Ralph Gleason did the same for jazz. Jaime de Angulo recorded his *Indian Tales*, and for many years Rexroth contributed a weekly book review program right off the top of his head. Elsa Knight Thompson coordinated and reported on public affairs. By the time she was preparing programs on local demonstrations against the execution of Caryl Chessman and hearings of the House Un-American Activities Committee, KPFA had inspired the birth of sister-stations, KPFK and WBAI, in Berkeley and New York City. Together the three stations became the Pacifica Network. Their coverage of the Civil Rights movement, the Vietnam War, and the movement against the war were heard by thousands and won awards. By the middle sixties, the stations not only continued their reporting at a very high level, but they also became points of coordination for the counterculture and the politics of the movement. During this later period, Rexroth taped for the stations a long series of popular talks recalling his youth among radicals, cast-offs, and the avant-garde. These were published in 1966 as *An Autobiographical Novel*, a labor of compelling self-dramatization Rexroth hoped would demonstrate to the movement young of the sixties their own participation in a long tradition of rebellion.

Late in 1947, Rexroth abruptly left San Francisco to travel, on a Guggenheim grant, across America and on to Europe. By the time he returned to stay at the end of 1949, the diffusion of the Libertarian Circle into the wider life of the city was complete. The group had disintegrated and abandoned its meeting hall. Rexroth's travels, along with all the thinking he had done in relation to the Libertarian Circle, went into his fourth long poem, *The Dragon and the Unicorn*. The poem is the fullest exposition of Rexroth's anarchism and pacifism. It is a rich structure of narrative, social protest, culture criticism, philosophical analysis, and lyrical realization. For Rexroth, the real is at base "the concourse of persons," each mutually reflecting and reflected by all the others. The source of evil is the reduction of persons to mere integers. History is the forlorn effort to creep from quantity back to quality. All that stands against the collectivity's exploitation of persons as objects is the creative act and the community of lovers and of friends who share work and the administration of things. Reality, "their infinite conversation," is ethical at its core. All else is illusion.

In the sections of social protest, Rexroth seizes on virtually all the issues that were to become critical to the movement during the sixties. He attacks the huge disparity between rich and poor, the exploitation of class and race hatreds, sexual repression and the bureaucratization of human association, and the tendency of the industrial mechanism to destroy human relations, natural process, and the beauty of the world. He also derides the Marshall Plan and all forms of local and international development, pursued at the expense of every human good. At the center of Rexroth's attack in his scorn for the pendulum swings—boom and bust—of an economy that rides back and forth between the twin poles of blind consumerism and blinder warfare and that depends upon all the other ills Rexroth catalogs.

The poem ends with a long series of lyrics, recapitulating in religious and contemplative terms the abstract philosophy of the earlier sections. Fundamental is the image of mutually reflecting crystals. This image continued to appear in varying guises all through Rexroth's poetry. Thirty years later, in his next to last long poem, *On Flower Wreath Hill*, it appears again, and Rexroth names it there as what it is, the Jewel Net of Indra, "the compound infinities of infinities," in which each jewel is uniquely differentiated as itself yet is identical to every other jewel it reflects. Despite its complexity, *The Dragon and the Unicorn* is the clearest and most accessible long poem written by an American during this century. Ironically, it has been little read. Yet, in one form or another, most of what it says has been repeated over and over by others who have set themselves in opposition to the wastes and shames of our civilization.

Late in the forties, Rexroth also edited a selection of D. H. Lawrence's poetry. The essay he wrote to introduce the book, "Poetry, Regeneration and D. H. Lawrence, " was the first of hundreds of essays on literature, art, politics, and culture he wrote over the next thirty years and collected in six separate books. Many of these essays sort through the work of contemporaries—Martin Buber, Simone Weil, Samuel Beckett, Morris Graves, and many others—to find what is of durable value. Most of them try to show just what is great in the great traditions, ancient and modern, of the East and West. All of them are written in a colloquial language brisk enough to capture the attention of any nonfrivolous and moderately educated reader. Rexroth preferred to think of these essays as highbrow journalism, jobs he was compelled to do to feed his family.

Through all this work, Rexroth seriously and cogently argued, with great wit and vitality, that there existed a long and still usable tradition of revolt. His view of this tradition was expansive: "All important works of art, from the middle of the eighteenth century on, have rejected all the distinguishing values of the civilization which produced them." The dominant civilization had always been responsible for what Rexroth called "The Social Lie," the rationalization of evil by appeal to transcendental causes and by denial of both the political facts and the facts of life. In modern times, it was also responsible for the underlying social malaise, the alienation of people from the products of their work, from each other and, finally, from themselves.

Rexroth's tradition of *aliénés* and *revoltés* included writers like Rousseau, Restif de la Bretonne, Blake, Hölderlin, Stendahl, Baudelaire, Whitman, Twain, Tolstoy, and Chekhov, among many others. The populist and anarchist social movements the dominant society had spit forth from its agony were also members of this tradition. Together, the two strands formed "the subculture of the alienated." Rexroth argued that "from the beginning capitalism secreted, as a kind of natural product, a small, slowly growing class of people who flatly rejected its alienation and lack of meaning." The artists, bohemians, and revolutionaries Rexroth admired were people who wrote, painted, and lived "as if the revolution were over." It was they who had kept vital, and had attempted to sow widely, the values and quality of experience which in earlier times had been available only to the very privileged and at devastating cost to all the rest. It was this tradition Rexroth believed the disaffiliated youth of the sixties were striving to enter through their insistence on face-to-face relations, their politics of social justice and nonviolent direct action, and their enthusiasm for song, crafts, and communalism.

Throughout the fifties, young artists and writers and their camp followers made their way to San Francisco. Some, like poets Philip Whalen and Gary Snyder, came to seek out Rexroth in particular because of a shared affinity for wilderness and Eastern thought and poetry. But most were drawn by the general cultural ambience of the town, very much the enduring product of the old Libertarian Circle. San Francisco seemed to them a real alternative to New York, the putative cultural center of the country. Taking advantage of the renewed climate of this Second San Francisco Renaissance, Rexroth sponsored and introduced two important events at the Six Gallery, a converted garage on Fillmore Street. The first was a poetry reading by Walter Lowenfels, a radical poet of Rexroth's generation who had all but disappeared during the anti-communist hysteria. The second was a reading of Robert Duncan's play, *Faust Foutu*. Both events were so enthusiastically attended that the owner of the Six Gallery asked Rexroth to organize and introduce a group reading of younger poets. Reading that night, in October of 1955, were Snyder, Whalen, Philip Lamantia, Michael McClure, and Allen Ginsberg (*). Jack Kerouac, who had just recently arrived in town, roved the crowd, noisily collecting funds for jugs of wine and shouting encouragement to the readers, much to Rexroth's everlasting annoyance. The most electrifying passage of the evening was Ginsberg's reading of *Howl*, a poem in part modeled after Rexroth's own earlier social blast in the form of an elegy for Dylan Thomas, "Thou Shalt Not Kill."

The national media were attentive, and almost at once the Beat Generation was born, at least in the popular mind. Rexroth himself wrote a series of articles heralding the birth of a new art and attitude of "disengagement." Many of his harshest critics missed the fact that he almost at once began making distinctions of better and worse among the members of the new movement and disavowed whole elements of it. Despite this and his frequently repeated terse disclaimer, "An entomologist is not a bug," Rexroth was saddled for the rest of his life with epithets of disdain, "Daddy-o" or "Father Figure of the Beats." Many of the poets Rexroth promoted most during this period and afterwards, Ginsberg, Lawrence Ferlinghetti, Michael McClure, Duncan, Everson, Snyder, Whalen, and Denise Levertov, became the major literary voices of protest during the Vietnam War. Many of them were only tangentially associated with the Beats. Some like Duncan, Everson, and Levertov were never Beat at all.

After the early sixties, Rexroth wrote no directly political poems. He did continue to write essays on politics, social currents, and the ecological and youth movements. In 1968, fed up with the increase of drugs and crime in San Francisco, the hate-mongering of the Black Panther party in his own predominantly black neighborhood, and the decline of the city's cultural life, Rexroth moved permanently to Santa Barbara. There he took his first formal academic job at the University of California, where he taught poetry until forced into retirement in 1973. He encouraged his students to write songs, and he insisted on sitting in the back rows or in the circle "among the people." This new contact with the young informed his social and political essays of the period, most of which were collected as *The Alternative Society* in 1970. Two years later, he published his only book-length historical study, *Communalism: From Its Origins to the Twentieth Century*. Rexroth hoped the book would reach young people who were living communally and would help them to distinguish the best of their tradition and evade the snares of cultists, drugged-out crackpots, and unsanitary crash pads. He was disappointed that the book was never issued in paperback at a price young communalists could afford.

Soon after this, Rexroth came to feel that the movement had collapsed into futile rhetorical posturing and the kind of violence produced either by utter misery or utter self-hatred. In a postlude for the republication of *An Autobiographical Novel* in 1978, he wrote, "After . . . the betrayal of the French revolt in 1968, the failure of 'The Movement' by 1970, there wasn't very much revolutionary hope left, and it was largely confined to crazy people. . . . For me, today, life is better. For the Indian peasant or the herdsman in the sub-Sahara or the inhabitants of the slums of Rio de Janiero, it is not." Rexroth's sense of universal responsibility never lapsed.

Bibliography

Gibson, Morgan. *Revolutionary Rexroth: Poet of East-West Wisdom.* Hamden, CT: Archon Books, 1986.

Hamalian, Linda. *A Life of Kenneth Rexroth.* New York: W. W. Norton, 1991.

Knabb, Ken. *The Relevance of Rexroth.* Berkeley, CA:Bureau of Public Secrets, 1990.

Parkinson, Thomas. "Reflections on Kenenth Rexroth," *Sagetrieb* 2:3 (Winter 1983): 37–44.

Rexroth, Kenneth. *The Alternative Society.* New York: Herder and Herder, 1970.

———. *Assays.* New York: New Directions, 1961.

———. *An Autobiographical Novel,* expanded ed. New York: New Directions, 1991 (1966).

———. *Bird in Bush: Obvious Essays.* New York: New Directions, 1959.

———. *The Burning Heart: Women Poets of Japan.* New York: Seabury Press, 1977.

———. *Classics Revisited.* Chicago: Quadrangle Books, 1968.

———. *The Collected Longer Poems of Kenneth Rexroth*. New York: New Directions, 1968.

———. *The Collected Shorter Poems of Kenneth Rexroth*. New York: New Directions, 1967.

———. *Communalism: Its Origins to the Twentieth Century*. New York: Seabury Press, 1974.

———. *The Elastic Retort: Essays in Literature and Ideas*. New York: Seabury Press, 1973.

———. *Poems from the Greek Anthology*. Ann Arbor: University of Michigan Press, 1962.

———. *With Eye and Ear*. New York: Herder and Herder, 1970.

Rexroth, Kenneth, Lee Bartlett, and James Laughlin. *Kenneth Rexroth and James Laughlin: Selected Letters*. New York: W. W. Norton, 1991.

Smith, Larry R. "Kenneth Rexroth," in *The Dictionary of Literary Biography*, vol. 48. Detroit: Gale Research, 1986: 350–68.

Weinberger, Eliot. "At the Death of Kenneth Rexroth," *Sagetrieb* 2:3 (Winter 1983): 45–52.

Woodcock, George. "Rage and Serenity: The Poetic Politics of Kenneth Rexroth," *Sagetrieb* 2:3 (Winter 1983): 73–84.

Geoffrey Gardner

JERRY RUBIN (1938–   )

Founder of Youth International party, defendant in Chicago Seven Conspiracy Trial

Jerry Rubin gained notoriety in the sixties as founder of the Youth International party (Yippies) that preached an international revolt of youth against all forms of traditional authority. He was renowned also as a defendant in the Chicago Seven Conspiracy Trial in which seven white activists and Black Panther leader Bobby Seale (1*) were indicted on federal charges of crossing state lines to incite a riot in Chicago on the eve of the Democratic National Convention in 1968. Rubin attracted publicity as much for the flamboyance of his political gestures, such as throwing dollar bills from the ledge of the New York Stock Exchange or attempting an exorcism of the evil spirits in the Pentagon, as for the threat that these gestures posed to the status quo (the stock market continued to function and the Pentagon remained moored to its foundations).

Rubin's childhood status and health anxieties made him sensitive to issues irrelevant to most of his peers and shaped his subsequent political development. Born in Cincinnati in 1938, Rubin grew up in a Jewish home buffeted by conflict because his intellectual mother had wed an uncouth New Yorker

Jerry Rubin. *Source*: Library of Congress

who drove a bread truck for fourteen years to support his family and who never achieved the affluence of her brothers who were able to move their families to segregated suburbs while Rubin's family remained trapped economically in their old neighborhood. As a result, Rubin became aware of racial injustice prior to the emergence of a strong Civil Rights movement. He learned through his father's civic and union activities that one can enhance self-esteem and gain power by successfully organizing others. His mother's five-year fatal bout with cancer, followed by his father's premature death eleven months later, shaped Rubin's subsequent preoccupation with issues of health and his willingness to follow a variety of health gurus.

Rubin credited the landslide defeat of Adlai Stevenson in the presidential election of 1952 for his subsequent political commitment to radicalism. Rubin worked as a sports reporter for the Cincinnati *Post and Times Star* for five years while simultaneously attending the University of Cincinnati. His disillusionment with newspaper work and with American materialism caused him to spend a year and a half in Israel because of his attraction to a socialist society of love built by fellow Jews. His subsequent discovery in Israel of the very materialism, oppression, and racism that he had sought to escape in the United States led him to journey to Berkeley, California, and enroll as a graduate student in sociology, dropping out six weeks later to become a full-time radical. Rubin participated in an illegal trip to Castro's Cuba and in the Free Speech movement that protested university restrictions on student political activities and the bureaucratized nature of the university. Rubin helped to organize Vietnam Day, a marathon teach-in on the Vietnam War that drew twenty thousand students and marched on the Oakland Army Terminal in a failed attempt to block troop trains for Vietnam. When, as a result of these protest activities, Rubin was subpoenaed to appear before the House Un-American Activities Committee, he appeared in the garb of a Revolutionary War soldier and handed out copies of the Declaration of Independence.

Back in Berkeley Rubin began to experiment with marijuana and LSD in an effort to expand his consciousness and on a whim ran for mayor of Berkeley on a pro-marijuana and anti-war platform, finishing second in a field of four. His interest turned to creating acts of guerrilla theatre that would mobilize public opinion against American capitalism and imperialism. Rubin joined Abbie Hoffman in an assault on the New York Stock Exchange. A band of hippies successfully stopped the market by throwing dollar bills down from the visitors' balcony. On October 21, 1967, Rubin joined in a nonviolent assault on the Pentagon whose aim was to surround the building and to exorcise its evil spirits. Rubin was among 832 protesters arrested and received a thirty-day jail sentence.

Rubin next associated himself with an audacious attempt to steal media attention in Chicago during the week of the Democratic presidential convention in 1968. On New Year's Eve, 1967, Rubin met with six others in Abbie Hoffman's Greenwich Village apartment to found the Youth International party to promote an international youth revolution. The Yippies believed that they could expropriate the mythmaking power that the media had exploited to sustain the status quo and transform it into a revolutionary tool.

However, by the time of the Chicago convention Lyndon Baines Johnson had renounced any intention to run for a second term as president and Robert Kennedy had been assassinated. Only five thousand radicals came to Chicago to protest, and Chicago responded with a police riot witnessed nationwide on television. Rubin was among eight radicals indicted as conspirators to riot in a five-and-a-half month trial that itself became a major media event as the presiding judge, Julius Hoffman, became a national media symbol of judicial prejudice, even ordering the gagging and chaining of Bobby Seale to prevent his demanding the right to serve as his own attorney. The defendants and their attorneys disrupted the trial proceedings so often that they were sentenced for contempt of court. The jury found the defendants innocent of conspiracy but guilty of crossing state lines with intent to riot, but two years later the Appeals Court invalidated the initial trial and reprimanded Hoffman for his judicial misconduct. A new trial resulted in a guilty sentence but no jail term for Rubin.

Rubin viewed the trial as the highlight of his life since he had won media attention and public sympathy for his victimization by government repression. He became a media superstar, traveling from campus to campus and on the general lecture circuit. He donated much of his earnings from these lectures and from his books *Do It* and *We Are Everywhere* to support movement activities and to finance legal expenses associated with his plethora of court trials. During the seventies Rubin became heavily involved in a variety of consciousness-raising and growth philosophies, including est, psychic therapy, and Arica training, hoping that enhanced spirituality would improve his effectiveness as a political revolutionary.

By the eighties Rubin had joined the Wall Street brokerage house of John Muir and Company, where he held the position of director of business development. Later, he left the company to form his own private money management firm. He and his wife, Mimi Leonard, also ran a series of networking salons in which tens of thousands of ambitious people paid for the privilege of attending parties at which they hoped to contact other individuals who might advance their career. Ironically Rubin justified his metamorphosis into a Wall Street entrepreneur in Yippie rhetoric: "Until me, nobody had really taken off their clothes and screamed out loud, 'It's O.K. to make money!' "

Rubin's transformation from Yippie into Wall Street entrepreneur was not as anomalous as it might initially appear. Rubin's politics always were eclectic, borrowing insights from sources as diverse as Karl Marx, Ernesto ("Che") Guevara, Timothy Leary, Bernardine Dohrn, Marshall McLuhan, Eldridge Cleaver (1*), Lenny Bruce, and Allen Ginsberg (*) with scant attention to issues of incompatibility. Rubin's motivation consistently included concern for issues of personal growth as they related to his political commitments. He was a genius at seizing media attention and he understood the value of networking to build a movement. It is not surprising that these concerns and skills shaped his successful adaptation to a career on Wall Street.

As a Yippie, Rubin had endorsed the vision of an international revolution that would destroy all nations and national boundaries to establish worldwide communism based upon the sharing of all material goods and services. The revolution would spell the end of Christian, capitalist culture and would replace it with a counterculture that fostered free sexual expression and experimentation with psychedelic drugs. The Yippies viewed white middle-class youth as a revolutionary class fighting its personal oppression in order to achieve freedom. Despite the arguments of intellectuals that revolution never has occurred in an affluent industrial nation, Yippies argued that the alienation that permeated American society made it ripe for revolution. The goal of Yippie revolution was to eliminate all intellectuals and to create a society that recognized no distinction between intellectual and physical work, that destroyed the university and abstract critical thought in favor of action and experience.

A highly gregarious individual, Rubin needed a sense of community to support his political visions. Thus, he quickly associated himself with the Free Speech movement in Berkeley, the Yippies, the national anti-war movement, and other counterculture groups. He was able to support himself financially from insurance money from the death of his parents, from advances and royalties from his books, from the proceeds of his lecture tours, and from donations to the movement, which peaked at the time of the Chicago Seven Conspiracy Trial.

Rubin used a variety of newsworthy tactics to achieve his goals. He initially believed in nonviolent direct action and engaged in acts of civil disobedience. He tried to stop the troop trains from the Oakland Military Terminal by blocking the tracks and promoted educational efforts like the Vietnam Day teach-in at Berkeley. However, his deepest affinity was for the dramatic gesture that would capture media attention, whether it was the defendants donning judicial robes to mock Judge Hoffman at the Chicago Conspiracy Trial or the decision to hold a youth festival of rock music, psychedelic drugs, mysticism, and sexual ecstasy in Chicago on the eve of the Democratic national convention in order to dramatize the youth revolution as public theater. He identified with Viet Cong guerrillas, outlaws, and the Weather Underground, even dedicating *We Are Everywhere* to Weatherperson Bernardine Dohrn, who was wanted by the Federal Bureau of Investigation for mob action, riot, and conspiracy. Rubin, however, did not engage in violent acts; he preferred guerrilla theater to sabotage or armed conflict.

Rubin remained committed to a vision of political liberation that would promote personal liberation. He sustained his New Left friendships even when he became a Wall Street entrepreneur, but during the seventies he moved increasingly toward a variety of approaches to individual salvation via such examples of the consciousness movement as est, psychic therapy, and Arica training. His initial scorn for homosexuality was replaced by greater tolerance, and he exhibited great guilt with respect to his male chauvinism while a movement superstar and became an ardent advocate of women's rights.

Rubin's social significance lay in his intuitive realization of the power of the media to shape public consciousness and in his understanding that capitalist oppression is not purely a political or economic phenomenon. Capitalism pervades consciousness and sexuality and must be combated personally as well as politically. He and his cohorts were able to dramatize the oppressive nature of Mayor Richard Daley's Chicago on the eve of the Democratic convention, the inexorable power of the American war machine, and the seeming viability of a counterculture based upon love and sharing as in the Woodstock Nation. However, many of the leaders of the New Left like Tom Hayden (6*) faulted Rubin and the Yippies for their lack of seriousness and for their failure to organize workers and other dissidents by imposing a revolutionary discipline.

Right-wing critics like William F. Buckley condemned Rubin for his willingness to defy laws created by a democratic majority while lamenting the repression that resulted from such defiance.

Rubin's work was flawed by its simplicity and naïveté. His concern for the personal and the psychological often blinded him to wider social issues. He never considered the question of whether a complex industrial society could be organized without any significant repression, or whether the return to the land and a system of barter that might facilitate the coming of his communist utopia was an impossible dream for the bulk of mankind. Rubin remained unaware of the way in which power relations continued to cloud the sexual liberation of the sixties, creating a situation in which women felt compelled to be sexually available to movement men. It remained difficult for those who were not socially empowered to exercise complete freedom of sexual choice. This became increasingly clear with the later proliferation of cases of date rape, sexual harassment on the job, and child abuse. Rubin's celebration of North Vietnam and Cuba exhibited no awareness of the political repression practiced by both regimes, and his penchant for using trials of New Left figures to expose the corruption of the American system left the movement drained of personnel and resources needed for more fundamental and permanent organizing activities. Nor did Rubin deal with the problems attendant upon transforming revolutionary outlaws bred in a culture of disruption into citizens of a communist utopia that needed cooperation to survive. Nevertheless, Rubin and his fellow Yippies left their mark on the wider society by promoting a politics of ecstasy and personal fulfillment that could be assimilated into a dominant culture committed to consumption and pleasure.

Bibliography

"Chicago," *Time* 131 (Jan. 11, 1988): 26–27.

Dellinger, David T. *The Conspiracy Trial*. Indianapolis: Bobbs-Merrill, 1970.

Farber, David. *Chicago '68*. Chicago: University of Chicago Press, 1988.

Feiffer, Jules. *Pictures at a Prosecution: Drawings and Texts from the Chicago Conspiracy Trial*. New York: Grove Press, 1971.

Ginsberg, Allen. *Chicago Trial Testimony*. San Francisco: City Lights Books, 1975.

Hayden, Tom. *Trial*. New York: Holt, Rinehart and Winston, 1970.

Hoffman, Abbie. *Revolution for the Hell of It*. New York: The Dial Press, 1968.

———. *Woodstock Nation: A Talk-Rock Album*. New York: Random House, 1969.

Kinoy, Arthur, Helen E. Schwartz, and Doris Peterson. *Conspiracy on Appeal: Appellate Brief on Behalf of the Chicago Eight*. New York: Center for Constitutional Rights, distributed by Agathon Publication Services, 1971.

Mailer, Norman. *Miami and the Siege of Chicago: An Informal History of the Republican and Democratic Conventions of 1968*. New York: World Publishing Company, 1968.

Martin, Douglas. "Jerry Rubin Is 50 (Yes 50) Years Old," *New York Times Biographical Service* 19 (July 1988): 798–99.

Rubin, Jerry. *Do It! Scenarios of the Revolution*, intr. by Eldridge Cleaver. New York: Simon and Schuster, 1970.

———. *Growing (Up) at Thirty-Seven*. New York: M. Evans and Company, 1976.

———. *We Are Everywhere: Written in the Cook County Jail*. New York: Harper and Row, 1971.

Rubin, Jerry, and Mimi Leonard. *The War between the Sheets*. New York: R. Marek, 1980.

Seale, Bobby, Abbie Hoffman, David Dellinger, Jerry Rubin, John Froines, Lee Weiner, William Kunstler, and Leonard Weinglass. *Contempt: Transcript of the Contempt Citations, Sentences, and Responses of the Chicago Conspiracy Ten*; foreword by Ramsay Clark; intr. by Harry Kalven, Jr. Chicago: The Swallow Press, 1970.

Leslie Fishbein

PETE SEEGER (1919–   )

Folksinger and song writer

"If I've got a talent it's for picking the right song at the right time for the right audience. And I can always seem to get people to sing with me." This is how Pete Seeger summed up his musical abilities in a 1964 *Life* magazine close-up of "A Minstrel with a Mission." He was known then for inspiring some of the young stars of the folk revival, including Bob Dylan (*), Joan Baez (*), and Peter, Paul and Mary. His mission and talents had not changed much since he began singing professionally twenty-five years before, nor would he change significantly in the twenty- five years that followed. The motto on his banjo, "This machine surrounds hate and forces it to surrender," symbolized his commitment to using folk music for such causes as labor, civil rights, civil liberties, peace, and the environment. Despite numerous attempts to intimidate him—including the infamous Peekskill riot in 1949, when the American Legion physically attacked both performers and audience—Pete Seeger spent more than fifty years singing out on local and global issues.

Pete Seeger was born in New York to a New England WASP professional family. His parents were both musicians. His father, Charles Seeger, had a central influence on Peter's career and outlook. Charles was a musicologist with left-wing ties in the 1930s. He later changed his focus from proletarian art music to collecting, composing, and promoting folk music. Pete Seeger was aware of the relationship between art and politics from an early age. There were family discussions at the dinner table, and Pete also read the left-wing cultural journal *New Masses*, especially the commentary by Mike Gold, a communist.

Seeger came of age during the Popular Front period of the late 1930s. This

Pete Seeger. Copyright *Washington Post*; Reprinted by permission of D.C. Public Library.

was a time when the whole country seemed to be looking for its roots. It was also a time when liberals and communists worked together to defend democratic rights at home (such as the rights of working people to organize unions and the rights of black people to be treated equally), and to fight against fascism abroad. During the Popular Front period, it seemed natural to identify folk music with left-wing politics. Pete Seeger became one of many who were dedicated to spreading the music and the message.

In 1937 he joined the Young Communist League at Harvard. He increasingly saw himself as a participant in change, rather than as a journalist. His excitement about folk music developed further when he worked with folk song collector Alan Lomax at the Library of Congress in 1938. It was Lomax who brought Huddie Ledbetter (better known as Leadbelly) and Woody Guthrie to record their songs in Washington. Seeger was deeply affected by traveling and singing with Woody Guthrie in 1940. Seeger now realized that he could make a living from his music. For more than five decades Seeger sang to all sorts of audiences and recorded numerous albums.

From 1940–1941 Seeger was a member of the Almanac Singers, one of the first urban folksinging groups. The Almanacs held weekly "hootenannies"— the term for a song festival that Seeger and Guthrie had brought back from their cross-country trip. These popular gatherings enabled the Almanacs to pay the rent on their Manhattan townhouse, while increasing the audience for folk and topical songs. Seeger entered the army in 1943, and sang for the troops on Saipan where he was stationed. After World War II, Seeger was the moving force behind the organization of People's Songs, Inc. This was a national organization that served as a clearinghouse for folk and topical songs. He hoped to create a "singing labor movement," picking up where Joe Hill— the bard of the Industrial Workers of the World—had left off. People's Songs dissolved after three years as the connections between labor and the left were severed due to the polarization of the cold war. Though People's Songs had no direct connection to the Communist party, many of its members were part of the broader Communist movement. In any case, the organization's focus on songs of the American past, world freedom songs, and topical songs (labor, civil rights, civil liberties, and peace) was seen as subversive in a nation seized by paranoid anti-communism. People's Songs may have wanted to spread the "true, democratic message" of the songs, but it was hard for people to accept this on face value. The Communist-oriented left had been neither true nor democratic over the years.

One of the highlights of the People's Songs years was Henry Wallace's 1948 Progressive party campaign for the presidency. Music played an integral part in Wallace's campaign. Seeger toured with Wallace, even in the South, where the Progressives were attacked for defying segregation. To have Pete Seeger challenge an angry Southerner to sing "Dixie" may now seem humorous, but it was not funny at the time.

The popularity of folk-style music was greatly enhanced by the success of the Weavers, a group that was composed of Pete Seeger, Fred Hellerman, Lee Hays, and Ronnie Gilbert. Their recording of one of Leadbelly's songs ("Goodnight, Irene") was number one on the charts in 1950. But their success was cut short by the blacklist of entertainers who were attacked for past or present left-wing connections. Pete Seeger was blacklisted longer than most other artists. His opportunities to sing what he wanted and where he wanted were restricted throughout the 1950s and most of the 1960s. When Seeger was called to testify before the House Un-American Activities Committee in 1955, he chose to appeal to his First Amendment rights. Also he told the committee: "It is improper to ask about my associations and opinions. I have said that I would be voluntarily glad to tell you any song, or what I have done in my life." Seeger was sentenced to a year in jail for contempt of Congress, but he appealed his case successfully. This fight lasted until 1962.

By the 1960s, Seeger had an international reputation. He had demonstrated his commitment to many causes. He sang, for example, for the Civil Rights movement in Alabama, Georgia, and Mississippi, along with concerts in the

North, and in his travels abroad. Seeger's ability to get audiences to sing along with him was legendary. Not only did he inspire live audiences to sing, but he played a central role in sparking people's interest in playing music themselves. The huge increase in sales of guitars, banjos, and do-it-yourself manuals in the 1960s owed something to Seeger's spirit. His belief that there was a connection between making music for yourself and thinking for yourself was expressed, among other places, in his regular column in *Sing Out!*, the folk music magazine he helped found. Younger musicians always benefited from Seeger's encouragement. The formation of the Freedom Singers, four young singers committed to civil rights, was Seeger's idea. Joan Baez (*) said of young folk singers in the 1960s: "Most of us owe our careers to Pete." Finally, some of the songs he wrote traveled far and wide. "If I Had a Hammer" (written in 1950 as "The Hammer Song") became a hit when Peter, Paul and Mary recorded it. "Where Have All the Flowers Gone?" became a standard anti-war song. And it was Seeger who helped rearrange and spread the song that became the anthem of the Civil Rights movement, "We Shall Overcome." This song is still heard all over the world.

Despite his reputation and successes, Seeger could not get on network television for most of the 1960s. When ABC started a show called "Hootenanny," the producers did not invite Seeger. One producer had the gall to claim that Seeger "can't hold an audience." Everyone knew that the real obstacle was Seeger's politics. When Seeger finally appeared on prime time, it was 1967. Even then, the producers of CBS-TV's "Smothers Brothers Show" cut out a song that questioned U.S. involvement in the Vietnam War. After protests, Seeger was invited back in 1968 to sing his allegorical song "Waist Deep in the Big Muddy" for a prime-time audience.

In the late 1960s, Seeger launched a campaign to clean up the Hudson River near his hometown of Beacon. The "Clearwater" Festival, named after the sloop Seeger helped to build, continued as an annual event in upstate New York.

Though Seeger focused on many issues throughout his career, a few ideas remained constant. For example, in the 1980s, Pete Seeger still said that "Socialism is still the only hope for the human race." Seeger held tightly to his Popular Front beliefs in equality and democracy, even if his overall philosophy seemed elusive. In 1989, he declared that "Truth is a rabbit in a bramble patch. You can circle around and point that it's somewhere in there, but you can't put your hand on it. So I sing songs that seem to contradict each other. I try to persuade people to sing themselves, not just listen." Seeger had a basic faith in humanity that was hard to shake. Despite adversity, he maintained his commitment, his optimism, and his stage presence.

Pete Seeger continued to write, to sing, to travel. He had great ambivalence about money and commercial success. He probably did more benefit performances than any other artist. And doubtless he was unsure of what to make of the more than 100 recorded versions of "If I Had a Hammer." No one has thoroughly answered the question of what happens to folk-style music when it becomes popular. Does commercial success dilute the meaning of a song, or does the message spread further? Seeger, the great popularizer, was disappointed that people were not taught to appreciate folk music that was more rough than that of the popularizers.

Pete Seeger was not an easy person to be around, one on one. He seemed more at ease in front of a large audience. He was never physically attractive, as people came to expect of "stars." (In 1980 the *Washington Post* described him as "fraily skinny, fidgety.") He was sometimes naive or self-righteous. Yet he will be remembered for his contributions to his country and the world. He attempted to spread tolerance and basic ideas about equality and democracy. He will be remembered for encouraging people to participate in making music and, by extension, making the world which we all live. Perhaps no other person has taught us more about using music to transform society. This is Pete Seeger's legacy.

Bibliography

Cantwell, Robert. "He Shall Overcome: Pete Seeger," *New England Review* 15 (Winter 1993): 205–19.

Dunaway, David King. *How Can I Keep from Singing: Pete Seeger*. New York: Da Capo, 1990 (1981).

Erwin, Michael. "Pete Seeger's Homemade Music," *The Progressive* 50 (April 1986): 35–37.

"400 Honor Seeger's Folk Protests," *New York Times* (metro issue), March 19, 1990, B3.

Lomax, Alan, compiler. *Hard Hitting Songs for Hard Hit People*; music transcribed and edited by Pete Seeger. New York: Oak, 1967.

Seeger, Pete. *American Favorite Ballads*. New York: Oak, 1961 (songbook).

———. *How to Play the 5-String Banjo*. New York: Oak, 1962.

———. *The Incompleat Folksinger*, Jo Metcalf Schwartz, ed. Lincoln: University of Nebraska Press, 1992.

———. "Johnny Appleseed, Jr." Column in *Sing Out!*, beginning with Vol. 4, No. 7 (Fall 1954).

———. *Oh Had I a Golden Thread*. New York: Sanga Music, 1968 (songbook).

———. Records: *American Industrial Ballads* (Folkways, 1956); *The Essential Pete Seeger* (Vanguard, 1978); *Pete Seeger's Greatest Hits* (Columbia, 1967); *Sing Out with Pete!* (Folkways, 1961); *Strangers and Cousins* (Columbia, 1965); *Waist Deep in the Big Muddy* (Columbia, 1967); *We Shall Overcome* (Columbia, 1963); *The World of Pete Seeger* (Columbia, 1974).

———. Testimony before the House Un-American Activities Committee, 1955; reprinted in *Thirty Years of Treason*, Eric Bentley, ed. New York: Viking, 1971: 686–700.

———. "Thou Shalt Not Sing," in *It Did Happen Here: Recollections of Political Repression in America*, Bud Schultz and Ruth Schultz, eds. Berkeley: University of California Press, 1989: 13–21.

Seeger, Pete, Ronnie Gilbert, Lee Hays, and Fred Hellerman. *The Weavers at Carnegie Hall.* Vanguard records, 1955.
Ware, Leslie. "Pete Seeger: Keeping the Dream," *Sierra* 74 (March/April 1989): 82–86+.

Robbie Lieberman

JOHN SINCLAIR [legally changed to Omowale John Sinclair in 1975] (1941–   )

Poet-performer, leader in marijuana law reform, manager of MC5 rock band, chairman of the White Panther party, cultural activist, music producer

John Sinclair became a powerful symbol of injustice and repression in late July 1969, when Judge Robert A. Colombo of the Detroit, Michigan, Recorders Court sentenced him to serve nine and a half to ten years in prison for possession of two marijuana cigarettes. Sinclair was also well known as the manager of MC5, a high-energy Detroit rock band, and as chairman of the White Panther party, whose goal was cultural revolution led by youth.

Born in Flint, Michigan, John Alexander Sinclair, Jr. was raised by middle-class parents in the nearby town of Davison. There, by age eleven, he had developed a fondness for rhythm and blues. As a teenager, Sinclair worked in clothing stores and record shops, sported the pegged pants and "Mr. B" collars that marked him, in his own words, as an "incipient hoodlum." He served as a disc jockey, under the name Frantic John, for high school dances. Sinclair was further exposed to black and beat culture at Albion College in Albion, Michigan (1959–1961). When he was at college, deeply affected by the poetry of Jack Kerouac, Lawrence Ferlinghetti, Gregory Corso, and Allen Ginsberg (*), he began to write his own verse. After earning a bachelor's degree from Flint College of the University of Michigan in January 1964, Sinclair enrolled in the graduate program in American literature at Wayne State University in Detroit. He wrote a thesis on William Burroughs's *Naked Lunch*.

In November 1964, Sinclair and others founded the Artists' Workshop in Detroit. This was the forerunner of Trans-Love Energies, which was at once a hippie commune, a music-promotion business, and a propaganda agency for cultural change and revolution. Members of these groups smoked marijuana, frequently took LSD and peyote, and played an active role in what Sinclair calls the "mimeograph revolution." Inspired by *Fuck You* magazine editor-publisher Ed Sanders, Artists' Workshop published more than twenty mimeo-graphed books of poetry, including three books of Sinclair's poems, a mimeographed magazine called *Work*, and an avant-garde jazz magazine

John Sinclair. Copyright *Washington Post*; Reprinted by permission of D.C. Public Library.

called *Change*, which focused on the music of Sun Ra, Cecil Taylor, and John Coltrane. At the same time, Sinclair became the Detroit correspondent for *Downbeat* magazine (1964–1966), wrote music criticism for *Jazz* magazine in New York and *Coda* magazine in Toronto, and contributed to underground Detroit newspapers, including the *5th Estate* and the *Warren Forest Sun*. From 1964 through 1979, Sinclair lived in a series of small communes in Detroit and Ann Arbor (1968–1969), earning a minimal income by selling poetry books, maintaining a building he lived in, and managing musicians.

Although Sinclair strongly opposed the Vietnam War, he was not particularly active in the anti-war movement. Indeed, by the mid-1960s he had rejected politics, petitions, demonstrations, and appeals to government as useless efforts to bring change by appealing to those who were responsible for problems in the first place. From Malcolm X (1*), the Black Muslims, and especially C. Eric Lincoln's *Black Muslims in America*, which he read as a college freshman, Sinclair developed an oppositional perspective that emphasized distance and withdrawal from the dominant culture—or "dropping out," in the phrase popularized by Timothy Leary. This posture was made possible, Sinclair believed, by a post-scarcity, post-industrial economy that had made traditional modes of work obsolete.

MC5 was assembled in 1963 by working-class teenagers from the Detroit suburb of Lincoln Park. By mid-decade the band had decided to court the developing hippie scene, and for this purpose sought the aid of Sinclair, whose contacts among local "beatniks" were known to be extensive. Under Sinclair, who managed MC5 after August 1967, the band's free-form psychedelic music was focused, hardened, energized, increased in volume, politicized, and combined with a wild performance style that Sinclair termed "guerrilla/street theatre." During its regular performances at Detroit's Grande Ballroom and at area high schools and teen clubs, MC5 often ran afoul of local police, who objected to the obscene lyric employed in the band's opening number and anthem, "Kick Out the Jams, Motherfucker." On June 7, 1968, the band scandalized some elements of the community—and exhilarated others—by tearing the American flag to shreds and raising in its stead a "Freek" flag emblazoned with a circled marijuana leaf.

For Sinclair, the band's performance transcended the frame of music and entered that of politics, working—like drugs—to transform "American honko plastic culture" and a passive, low-energy, consumer-focused, "television consciousness" into something invigorating and real. In an April 1969 letter to the *Village Voice*, Sinclair contrasted the revolutionary rock and roll of MC5 with effervescent pop music. Sinclair may have overstated the band's knowledge of radical social thought, but MC5 was the only prominent American band to play at the Festival of Life during the Chicago Democratic Convention in August 1968. And historians of rock music agree that the band was a formative influence in the "power rock" tradition that would yield both heavy metal and punk. Noteworthy, too, is that power rock developed simultaneously in Michigan and California, where students on state university campuses at Ann Arbor and Berkeley pioneered the student movement.

The politicization of MC5 corresponded in time with Sinclair's growing desire to merge the "cultural revolution" with the "political revolution." Although "rock and roll, dope, and fucking in the streets" remained the core of Sinclair's revolutionary methodology, he now believed that this cultural program had to be made explicitly political. To pursue this goal, on November 1, 1968, Sinclair joined Lawrence R. "Pun" Plamondon, Genie Johnson, Leni Sinclair, Skip Taube, Bob Rudnick, Dennis Frawley, Gary Grimshaw, Jesse Crawford, and a few others in creating the White Panther party. The organization was inspired by admiration for the Black Panther party and, especially, by the admonition of Black Panther leaders that whites could best contribute to change by working with their own people. The White Panthers spent much of their time promoting MC5. Grimshaw did the artwork for *Back in the USA*, their first album for Atlantic. Sinclair's wife, Magdalene (Leni) Arndt, served as the band's photographer. And Genie Johnson Plamondon handled the group's correspondence. Although the White Panther party provided individuals in other communities with White Panther buttons and other materials and was reputed to have some thirty chapters, the group had little organizational strength beyond Ann Arbor and Detroit.

Perhaps because Sinclair was central to both the band and the White Panthers (he managed and promoted MC5 and served as minister of information and chairman of the White Panthers), the band and the party shared a common ideology. At its core was the sense that competitive capitalism had produced a distended society of lonely, alienated, and profoundly separated Americans, lodged in nuclear families and suburbs, and desperately in need of some sort of social bonding. Through MC5 and its own White Panther News Service, the White Panther party offered its vision of a revolution driven by music and carried out by youth, who were enjoined to remain distant from the war, drop out of school, refuse to take the work offered by the mainstream society, abstain from consumerism, and in other ways maintain an alternative sensibility. From novelist Kerouac, poet Ginsberg, the culture of jazz, Buddhism, and Malcolm X's letter writings and teachings, Sinclair, MC5, and the White Panthers developed a strong sense of one-world unity, as well as a commitment to "driving people out of their separate shells and into each others' arms." "We had a vision of the future," Sinclair recalls, "of a multi-racial, multi-cultural, communalistic society."

Sinclair attributes his radicalization in the sixties in part to his harassment by law enforcement agencies. Most of his troubles with the law involved drugs. Sinclair believed that marijuana, and especially LSD, had provided the hip subculture with an alternative vision of life and transformed rock and roll from a rebellious into a revolutionary music. By the late 1960s he had become a prominent proponent of the catalytic and subversive qualities of these and other "good" drugs. Arrested in October 1964 and August 1965 for selling marijuana, Sinclair served six months in the House of Corrections in early 1966. On January 24, 1967, Sinclair was among fifty-six persons arrested during a raid at the Artists' Workshop. He was charged with giving (equivalent, under the law at that time, to selling) two joints of marijuana to an undercover policewoman, a crime that under Michigan law carried a mandatory minimum sentence of twenty years and a maximum of life imprisonment. While Sinclair was challenging the constitutionality of the statute, he was convicted of the lesser charge of possession and sentenced, without bond (despite his pending constitutional case) to nine and a half to ten years in prison. While he was in prison, the manifest injustice of the sentence made Sinclair a cause celebre, prompting Abbie Hoffman to mount the stage at Woodstock (August 1969) on his behalf and bringing some 15,000 demonstrators, including John Lennon and Yoko Ono, to a University of Michigan protest rally (December 1971).

Several days after the rally, and after serving two and a half years of his sentence, Sinclair was released on bond pending his appeal. In mid-March 1972, a six-person judicial panel overturned his conviction, some members holding that his sentence was "cruel and unusual punishment." Publicity surrounding the case prompted the Michigan legislature to approve a new drug law that removed marijuana from the "hard drug" category and significantly reduced penalties for marijuana-related offenses.

While in prison on the marijuana charge, Sinclair was charged along with John W. Forrest and White Panther party founder Plamondon with conspiracy in the September 25, 1968, bombing of a CIA-recruiting office in Ann Arbor. Apparently two sticks of dynamite were detonated in the middle of the night on the steps of the building housing the office; no one was injured. Sinclair insists that he was not involved and believed he was charged in order to demonstrate that he was a danger to society. Attorneys Leonard Weinglass and William Kunstler, along with local counsel Hugh M. "Buck" Davis, agreed to represent the defendants in the case to heighten its political visibility. When defense lawyers demanded access to wiretap evidence gathered against Plamondon, the Justice Department, apparently fearing the revelation of wiretaps on the Oakland, California, headquarters of the Black Panthers, refused. In February 1971 the trial was postponed indefinitely while the wiretap issue went through the courts. Charges were dropped altogether in 1972 when the U.S. Supreme Court, in a 8–0 decision, ruled that domestic security surveillance conducted solely within the discretion of the executive branch (i.e., without judicial warrants) violated the protections of the Fourth Amendment to the Constitution (*U.S. vs. U.S. District Court*).

These encounters with the authorities convinced Sinclair that his cultural revolution was, on the one hand, threatening to the dominant culture and, on the other hand, unachievable in the absence of a larger political struggle. This perception produced the White Panther party and led Sinclair and his followers to the extremist and apocalyptic rhetoric ("off the pig," "smash the state") typical of 1969 and 1970. Still another turn occurred in 1971, when, threatened by the violence at Kent State and against Black Panther groups in several cities, and aware that their name invited accusations of racism, the White Panthers metamorphosed into the Rainbow People's party.

At about the same time, Sinclair and Plamondon, their thinking politicized by prison reading of Mao, Lenin, and other communists, decided to focus the organization's energies on developing Ann Arbor into a socialist community and revolutionary base. Sinclair also wanted to promote local culture as an alternative to the rootless values offered by the dominant culture of the marketplace. Hence the Rainbow People's party became involved in local politics and formed a coalition, the Ann Arbor Tribal Council, with other community activists. Among the results were a free clinic, a refuge for runaway youths, and a People's Food Co-op.

The Rainbow group disbanded in 1974, the victim of a recession caused by the Arab oil boycott and of political infighting. Sinclair returned to Detroit, where in the late 1970s he wrote grants for Detroit jazz musicians, produced concerts, and, in 1977, convinced of the futility of securing changes in the state's marijuana laws, retired from political activism. In a *Newsweek* interview that same year, Sinclair appeared both ambivalent about and disenchanted with his activist past, on the one hand critical of the programless politics of Tom Hayden (6*) and Jerry Rubin (*) and of his own rejection of Hubert Humphrey's candidacy in 1968, on the other hand convinced that "the shit I believed in and went to jail for is starting to happen."

In 1982, his spirits rising, Sinclair fashioned his first poetry since the late 1960s and began managing and promoting a dance band, the Urbations, which broke up in 1987. Between September 1988 and December 1990, he edited Detroit's fine arts magazine, *City Arts Quarterly*. Sinclair has been adjunct professor of music history at Wayne State University, teaching courses in blues history and the roots of rock and roll, and producing and hosting a weekly FM radio program, "Blues Sensations." He often performed his poetry with a musical ensemble, the Blues Scholars. Sinclair planned to move to New Orleans, where, he noted, "black culture was not suppressed as it was elsewhere."

Bibliography

Allen, Ron, and Stella Crews, eds. *Hipology*. Detroit: Broadside Press, 1990.

Leni and John Sinclair Collection, Bentley Historical Library, University of Michigan, Ann Arbor.

Sinclair, John. "The Devil's Music," *Playboy*, June 1990 (Part 1 of *Playboy*'s "Illustrated History of Jazz and Rock").

————. *Fire Music: A Record*. Detroit: Artists' Workshop Press, 1966.

————. *Guitar Army: Street Writings/Prison Writings*. New York: Douglas Book Corporation, 1972.

————. Interview, by William Graebner, Jan. 19, 1991.

————. *Meditations: A Suite for John Coltrane*. Detroit: Artists' Workshop Press, 1966.

————. *The Poem for Warner Stringfellow*. Detroit: Artists' Workshop Press, 1966.

————. *This Is Our Music*. Detroit: Artists' Workshop Press, 1965.

————. "*We Just Change the Beat*": Selected Poems. Roseville, MI: Ridgeway Press, 1988.

Sinclair, John, and Robert Levin. *Music and Politics*. New York: Jazz Press, 1971.

Weiner, John. *Come Together: John Lennon in His Time*. Urbana: University of Illinois Press, 1991: 187–96.

William Graebner

GORE VIDAL (1925–   )

Political novelist, playwright, and essayist

Gore Vidal, one of the most widely known American literary figures of the post–World War II generation, has been a best-selling novelist, script writer, and pop-media celebrity as well as a political intellectual. He has been identified with dissenting views for many decades.

Vidal came from a somewhat patrician political and social background. His first name came from the last name of his admired grandfather, Thomas P. Gore. Thomas Gore, a populist, had been twice a U.S. Senator from Oklahoma. His father, Eugene Vidal, Sr., was a West Point officer and instructor who became an aviation official under Franklin Roosevelt. Gore's mother was embedded in the social upper class. Gore was raised in a Washington political ambience and fancy private schools, graduating from Phillips Exeter in 1943. Political connections allowed him to escape service in the U.S. infantry in 1943. Instead, he performed small duties in Alaska and was discharged as a warrant officer in 1946.

Although Vidal's primary commitments have been to his writing roles, he has repeatedly been a political activist in other ways. He unsuccessfully ran as a liberal Democrat for U.S. Congress in upstate New York in 1960. He was active in dissident party efforts for some years from 1968 on, acting as co-chairman of the People's party from 1970 through 1972. For decades, he has been widely recognized in his roles as public political lecturer, witty liberal essayist, and intermittent pop-television performer.

Vidal's slight first novel, *Williwaw* (1946), drew upon his experiences on a noncombatant army ship in the Aleutians during World War II. It was written in a rather conventional style that centered on the ship's officers during a storm. The plot turns on a semi-accidental death. There is a mildly contemptuous mockery of the military and its petty authority. Nature seems to be indifferent and society is an arbitrary collection of narrowly unaware commonplace people.

Vidal was early identified as one of the promising new novelists of the World War II generation. He energetically played this career role, publishing seven more novels in the following eight years, plus three detective novels under the pseudonym Edgar Box. The range of material, from religious history through medieval romance and Central American Revolution to contemporary war and gay subcultures, was remarkable.

His second novel, *In a Yellow Wood* (1947), takes a day in the life of an aspiring young stockbroker who rejects more unconventional possibilities. it is a slightly satirical documentary by one in a position to choose upper-

Gore Vidal. Copyright
Washington Post; Reprinted
by permission of D.C.
Public Library.

bohemianism. Vidal's marginality, his early liberation from an establishment background, was partly sexual. The early novel that had the largest role,
both as best-seller and as social document, was his third, a study of homosexuality, *The City and the Pillar* (published in 1948 and revised in 1965). It
portrays a Virginia adolescent tennis player with a sexual fixation on his boyhood chum. He later becomes a rather self-tormented part-time male prostitute. The protagonist's forays provide an early candid commentary on
American homosexual mores and styles in the slick purlieus of Hollywood and
New York. Vidal published several short stories about homosexual dilemmas
(such as *A Thirsty Evil* in 1956), and the subject insistently appears in a number of his novels.

The treatment is somewhat problematic. While many commentators viewed

The City and the Pillar as treating the subject "sympathetically," that should be understood by the standards of the day. The protagonist is guilt-ridden, manipulative, unintelligent, and rather nasty. Vidal admitted, elsewhere, that the novel was weakened by his having made the central character a "dumb bunny." Again, the condescension leaves an aftertaste of inadequacy. The "bunny" brutally force-sodomizes his now anti-homosexual buddy when they get together years later. (In an earlier version of the novel, the buddy is murdered.) Vidal also inserts into the revision his later doctrine—apparently arrived at in the early 1960s—that there are "no homosexuals," just homosexual acts by usual persons capable of varied sexual behavior. His protagonist, however, is incapable of ever engaging sexually or emotionally with women, or of any equal and enduring relationships or purposes.

Vidal's reasonable and appealing view, expressed in a number of later essays, holds that fundamentally "we are bisexual," and that "there is no such thing as a homosexual or heterosexual person. There are only homo- or heterosexual acts." Most people are a mixture of impulses if not practices. Practices are primarily a matter of circumstances, along with background repressions and ideologies.

The Season of Comfort (1949) is apparently semi-autobiographical. It offers impressionistic fragments of the history of an upper-political family. There are a meanly domineering mother and an uncertainly discontented and emotionally inadequate young American of the war generation. Vidal then turned to historical-political fiction. *A Search for the King: A 12th Century Legend* (1950) centers on Blondel, devoted troubadour-companion of England's Richard I. Curiously, this rather floridly written experiment mixes stock romance elements, such as fighting dragons, with standard history and an appropriately cynical view of the famous but hardly deserving king. *Dark Green, Bright Red* (1950) takes an almost contemporaneous form of political exoticism, a standard Latin American "revolution"—Vidal was then living in Guatemala—centering on a vaguely presented American adventurer and the mild satire of various leaders, right and left, in their manipulations and viciousness. The early Vidal displayed a variety of political disenchantments.

The Judgment of Paris (published in 1952 and revised in 1965) is a rather brittle modern-dress retelling of a Greek myth which has the young American abroad unpersuasively choose Aphrodite's love. (Vidal rarely pretended to believe in love as an enduring state or adequate value.) It also displays cynical political power as one of the dominant attractions. A generation later Vidal was to bluntly put the fundamental principle he had arrived at: "power, not sex, is true motor to human life." Oddly, he does not always recognize sex as power-play.

Power is also at the center of what is perhaps his most interesting early novel, the fable *Messiah* (1954). This is the fictional memoir of an old American writer, Eugene Luther. Luther, like Vidal, is a cultivated skeptic. Decades earlier, he had become fascinated by a simple but hypnotic prophet who spoke of a joyous "acceptance of death." The earlier Luther wrote down the doctrines, drawing on theological history and aiming to popularize a libertarian ethic which is anti-repressive and anti-family. The new doctrine, battling Christianity, becomes institutionalized by a manipulative advertising tycoon. This new Paul, aided by an ambitious Jungian psychiatrist and a power-mad maternal witch, defeats Christianity in America and Europe. The sincere messiah is killed by Paul in order to Christ-heroize the doctrine. Luther is not only exiled but written out of history. The doctrine is authoritatively modified into ritualized worship; dissent is repressed; anti-life Christianity is repeated. Most of the characters are driven by power motives which are rather arbitrarily reinforced by making the main characters sexually impotent.

Some of the ironies, including the self-referential ones, may be seen as too manipulated, including the smugly cynical presence of a two-millennia-old goddess who has set up the religious game, and the double-play of the skeptical intellectual who was really a fanatical believer. But this salutary religious-political dystopia has the virtues, over earlier Vidal, of not only a large vision but a more sophisticated, though sententious, style.

With a declining income after *The City and the Pillar* (which supported his traveling abroad for several years), and with a bitter sense (he later wrote) that he had been "blacked out" of mainstream commercial novel acceptance because he had been candidly responsive to homosexual subjects, and with the intellectual quickness, and connections, to change literary genres, Vidal gave up writing novels for the decade from 1954 on and took up television, movie, and Broadway stage scripts. Well aware of the artistic and ideological restrictions that entailed, he hoped, he later wrote, to bridge "the commercially profitable and the seriously meaningful." He was commercially quite successful. At its literary best, the result was pertinent though rather mild political satire within popular modes and manners.

Vidal's breadth and variety included the adaptation of a Durrenmatt play about late Rome (*Romulus*), a cinematic redoing of buddy Tennessee Williams (*Suddenly Last Summer*), television versions of James and Ferber, Faulkner and Kaufman, Crane and Du Maurier, and original though formulaic television dramas and pop-current-affairs Broadway plays and movies. Skilled high-hackery with intermittent more serious purposes.

Visit to a Small Planet (in its post-TV, Broadway comedy, version, 1956) acknowledges (in the Preface) that commercial considerations modified the presentation of the ideas and political angers. It is a fantasy-farce, with a mocking UFO visitor to earth and easy contemptuous put-downs of a TV commentator, a U.S. Army general, upper-suburban romance and family, and American anti-communist war manias. The drawing-room scene, dramaturgy, and caricaturizations are stock. Some of the detailing, such as telepathy with a cat, is intolerably cute. The neat plotting, a Vidal expertise, probably makes a consoling circle of concerned unchange for the standard audience. The form and manner undercut Vidal's claim in an essay on his uncongenial role as a playwright that my "only serious interest is the subversion of a society that bores and appalls me." The self-neutering of subversion in the mannering suggests that the scripts be seen, in the idiom of the sixties, as literature of liberal co-option.

The later long-running political play *The Best Man* (1960; also a movie) uses standard drawing-room comedy pattern and patter to satirize the personal politics of American presidential nomination. The more decent figure, drawn partly on Adlai Stevenson—a mid-liberal icon of the fifties—battles in manipulation with a righteously ruthless opportunist, partly drawn on Richard Nixon. Smear and countersmear, with the nice guy having undergone tabooed psychiatric treatment, and the nasty guy apparently having been involved with even more tabooed homosexual action while in the military, which later is double-played with his having been a vengeful spy against homosexuality, the real immorality. After some waffling, the nice guy renounces personal-smear politics and, certain to be defeated by the opposing smear, throws his presidential delegates to a non-entity, who is nominated in the usual politics of mediocrity. That, we may grant Vidal (later in "Political Melodramas"), is "realistic," given long-prevailing American politics (though he says shrewd J. F. Kennedy told him that explicit candor is uncommon). But this sub-ideological melodrama is both reductive and mild, as even Vidal grants later in writing of his political plays that "I am struck [in 1973] by the tameness of my work."

That also applies to his *An Evening with Richard Nixon* (1972). Employing a more persuasively interesting though less popular form, the fanciful stage documentary, it brings on as speaker the historical figure, using Nixon's actual words, plus undercutting asides by other figures (Washington, Eisenhower, Kennedy, et al.) In line with the prevailing radical-liberal but pre-Watergate perspective of the early 1970s, it emphasizes the persisting American dedication to empire, which was to become a dominant theme of Vidal's writing and politics. In his later political essays (*Reflections*, 1980s), Vidal was even to half-defend Nixon, ostensibly for some of his foreign policy ploys, a standard mod-liberal irrelevancy. But he put it in the context of the "cavalcade of mediocrity" which has constituted the presidency since imperialist-master F. D. Roosevelt. (Vidal had lost his early admiration for friend Kennedy, whom he reasonably viewed as not much of a reformer and considerably a militaristic adventurer.) By then, Vidal had read widely in American political history, and may have been speaking from a wider disenchantment with the venality of Washington politicians, so often Nixon-like opportunists, and the viciousness of American imperial ambitions.

In the 1950s (as one can see in the early political pieces in *Homage to Daniel Shays*), Vidal's politics included a moderate advocacy of civil rights, and his always persisting concern with civil liberties. He has been strong on anti-censorship, and on rejection of the anti-communist manias. But then in the rather complacent context of improved "social and moral legislation" which would "aid in the tying up of the loose ends in our own society." That assumes a rather positive view of the American fabric which his reading of history, his political and media activism, and the critical ferment of the sixties was to partly pull open.

There are a number of curious divergencies in Vidal's roles and writings as the political and literary sophisticate cum radicalized liberal. This is not just in the Washington and Hollywood insider alternating his witticisms in high-brow journals with wisecracks on meretricious TV talk shows, and the earnest historical novelist diverting to partly pornographic transsexual parody fictions, but in some of his political positionings. For example, in essays, speeches, historical novels, and satires, he has been insistent on the mediocrity and venality of American politicians, their dominant role as political hacks for the propertied and other greedy manipulators, and their long-term furthering of our "predatory empire." Yet he expresses shock, in reporting on his political speeches around the country ("The State of the Union," 1975), that his college and other audiences "expressed constant hatred of government." Contradicting the lack of democracy which he has labored in writing to show, he insists that this "is of course hatred of ourselves." His sometimes admired rebels, in the tradition of Shays, knew something else.

Many of Vidal's political pronouncements have been mainstream liberalism, with greater "social justice" by governmental reforms and decrees and financing, such as national health service and subsidized public transport. He advocated better education (though as outsider to the academic, he has shown skepticism about some of the schoolism ideology, and later expressed disgust at the "academization . . . of everything" from ordinary careers to literature and history). He supported reformist environmental laws; restrictions on advertising (consumerist and political); drastic reduction of the military (and elimination of the service academies); and less dominance by the rich. He has also been a strong advocate of individual liberties—for sexual behavior (very few restrictions), on drugs (only direct control to be honest labeling), for more freedom from religion (equally tax all churches, philanthropies, and schools). He advocated maximum individual liberties, but in the unquestioned context of a centrally directed, reformed but still hierarchical, mass-technological society. There is little sense of alternative institutions and decentralized ways and a radically different society. Vidal is no utopian.

Within the standard context, Vidal strongly held to freedom, except on some crucial issues. For example, from the mid-1950s on he had sensibly held that overpopulation was a crisis issue (*Messiah*, where a religion of suicide was his answer). In the early 1960s he came to the grim conclusion that "if the human race is to survive, population will have to be drastically reduced." In a "Manifesto" (1968) he insisted on personal liberties but also on a central authoritarianism to necessarily control environment and population. Rightly enough, he later summarized that "too many people destroy not only the biosphere which supports us but the society which sustains us." In the mid-1970s, he drastically proposed that "we ought to try by the next century to reduce our numbers by half." No one is to add a child to the community "without permission." A decade later he has no specific proposal but still an insistence that "as we get more people, we lose 'amenities' of every sort."

Vidal's rhetoric, and some crucial perceptions, have often been more radical than his essentially reformist proposals and activism. "I do not think that the American system in its present decadence is worth preserving" (1973). And a dozen years later he foresees America's accelerating "economic and moral collapse." More recently he announced (PBS interview, 1990) that it would be "no bad thing" to "shut down the government" of the United States—and then went on to talk about hopes of possible electoral modifications from discontent in part of the exploited population. Vaguely irrelevant piety.

Essentially more radical was his prolific return to his "first allegiance," the novel, after a decade hiatus. This took several rather different directions. The one that produced some notoriety was the pastiche-parody-farce—*Myra Breckinridge* (1968), *Myron* (1974), *Kalki* (1978), and *Duluth* (1983). *Myra* could be said to have an earnest purpose in its concern with overpopulation, which is black humorishly presented through anal-dildoing a representative American adolescent stud, "terrifying and humiliating him . . . to change his view of what is proper masculine behavior. To keep him from breeding, and so adding to the world's overpopulation." That works less even in the fiction than serves as the revenge of transsexual Myra on macho males. It also provides Vidal an excuse for some homosexual pornography. The context for the revenge farce and its *"destruction of . . . traditional manhood"* in its crude harshness as well as fertility, carried out in contemporary Hollywood, depends on the knowing cultism of 1930s–1940s movie mythology (taking off on Parker Tyler) with some contemptuous satire also of the pop-culture of the 1960s. The mocking pastiche is erudite, clever, jokey, and rather too synthetically and arbitrarily overdone to be very effective. The final apparent joke is that an accident turns Myra back into Myron, who marries and settles down in the Valley with a sweet young female and a fast food business, which seems appropriate metaphor also for the style. The real black joke may be suggested in the passing reflection that for the impossibly overdone human race, especially in its recent American form, "extinction is not only inevitable but . . . desirable."

The continuation in *Myron* a few years later consisted of quick snacks of topical satire and misanthropy. While it more or less continues the outraged gestures "to shatter the false machismo of the American male," and the demand that the U.S. population be reduced by two-thirds, the fantasy mechanism of entrapment on the set of a bad earlier movie overburdens with Hollywood trivia, as do the schizy Myra/Myron double-plays. A typical stylistic cuteness is to use Supreme Court Justices' names (of those who voted a mildly regressive obscenity decision) in place of standard obscenities. But the whole fiction seems hysterically coy.

Kalki, perhaps the most competently controlled of his fantasy fictions (and partly a revisit of *Messiah*), is mostly a first- person account by a mid-thirties bisexual woman test pilot and journalist of the events leading up to the end of the human world. With usual erudition, Vidal scenarios Hindu religion by way of a resentful-fanatic American become guru-Kalki, acting out both Vishnu and Siva, and under pop-cultist cover uses a U.S. Army biological weapon to wipe out the world's people, leaving only his immediate coterie. The satire savages pop-media events, the usual American corrupt and opportunistic politicians, governmental/criminal double-agents, religious dupes, and a generally overpolluted and overpopulated civilization. Egomaniac Kelly-Kalki is jealously power-tricked out of becoming the Adam of a new Golden Age humanity. Monkeys are replacing the human in a renewed nature. But the arch play with pop-clichés remains trite, as does the unpersuasive overplotting of the clever misanthropy.

Vidal tried again a few years later in his efforts to be an *au courant* satirist with *Duluth*. A parody of the popular television serial "Dallas," of easy Gothic romance and sci-fi conventions, and other stockly inverted stock materials, it is a brittle bunching of wisecracks and media in- and out-jokes. It burlesques a wide splay of stock roles, from midwestern Babbitts (his caricatures sometimes old-fashioned) through blacks, browns, and what have you—realtors, militants, police, pop novelists, and others. Free-floating bits, sometimes quite literally, such as the ghost of Hubert Humphrey in a spaceship, are political satire, including funhouse images of Nixon and Reagan, and the usual American statesmanlike hypocrisy and corruption. In a low-scale Swiftian ending, bugs from outer space take over all.

With mock ponderousness, *Duluth* also parodies avant-garde literary theory (such as in the French "new novel," and from the pompous professors of English, both of whom Vidal has mocked in essays). Right enough, but also part of a Vidalean confusion. He mixes pop mythologies with intellectual manners, grand historical erudition with glitzy current fads, easy burlesque with hard satire. This confusion of realms, intellectually, also confuses audiences, which are not, and cannot be, all one. As intellectual-journal commentator Vidal knows even if pop-media performer Vidal refuses to admit it in his drive for the power of popularity. (In his literary criticism, another of his prolific modes, he is quite good on popular novels, and other glad fools, but rather less interesting in his traditionalist taste—James, Howells, Wharton, et al.—and in his commemorations of social and sexual friends.) One admires, if responsive, only this or that bit of Vidal satire or bizarreness or wisecrackery in his literary acrobatics.

Other Vidal writings as well display the forced-and-mixed acrobatics, which may be viewed as contemptuous denigrations. *Two Sisters; A Memoir in the Form of a Novel* (1970), is, for a long and slow part, neither but a playscript on classical materials, centering on that early nihilist Herostratus who made his mark by burning down the great Temple of Diana. No doubt outrageousness-for-fame, and the connected though involuted incest theme, provide oblique comment on the memoir (bits of 1948 and 1970), brittle anecdotes of a hack writer reflecting back. At the gossip level, it should have been more interesting than it skittishly, unprobingly, is. After all, Vidal has publicly announced his erotic relations with quite a range of celebrities, from Anais Nin through Jack Kerouac to some variety of less celebrated hustlers—his own Herostratus gestures.

Vidal's more systematic pursuit of political hustlers, and their power-for-its-own-sake, in novels took two more directions, classical and American. *Julian* (1964), a lavishly and earnestly researched historical novel, is one of his better performances. This fourth century (C.E.) chronicle seems to be "accurate in detail," and effectively dramatized. It uses a favorite Vidal form, a fictional memoir based closely on the historical "record," plus later addenda and commentary for skeptical distance and enlargement—in *Julian* by two partly fictionalized actual fellow Hellenists. In the sympathetic treatment of the most liberal major ruler of the late Roman era—Julian decreed in A.D. 362 that "anyone could worship any god in any way he chose"—who betrayed his efforts at religious freedom, and pagan restoration, by his imperialist mania, Vidal shows several poignancies of culture versus power.

Emperor Julian, an impassioned highbrow and last classical attempt at the philosopher-king, made a good case in the post-Constantine empire against the cultural and political dominance of the anti-life "Galilean" bigots. Christianity was treated with knowledgeable contempt but political fairness (disestablished, including of the yet continuing tax exemptions). But Vidal's Julian was also caught up in the ancient mystery religions, and in the far more horrendous magic of reincarnating Alexander on the imperial road. His very talents led him to military expansionism (including a power- hungry rejection of peace with the Persian Empire), and to the conditions which allowed a servant of Christian conspirators to murder him after less than two years as Roman emperor. Hellenistic reform, and religious tolerance, went under to the Dark Ages.

Vidal's liberal fable is sensibly modified by skeptical complexities and human pathos, but his focus on intellectual power-seekers, mainline but partly dissenting, seems set. He turned to an ancient version of its history in the ironically titled *Creation* (1981). Again dramatized memoir, set in the fifth century B.C., it is by a part-Greek part-Persian grandson of the prophet Zoroaster, a far-traveler who spends ideological time with Buddha, Confucius, and high prophets for Jainism, Taoism, Greek philosophy, and other pathetic attempts to explain creation. Vidal attempts skeptical exploration of religious views in their great generating era. Somewhat implausibly, his believing Cyrus keeps discovering unbelief, such as at the core of Buddhism "is perfect atheism," and behind the tradition and rule-ridden Confucius is also an "atheist," though desperately avoiding facing up to it. Near the end, a Greek follower summarizes Cyrus's lesson: "Matter is all. All is matter."

And rather inconsequential and humanly meaningless matter at that, for the blind old Cyrus's final reflections in Periclean Athens. Politics are also anti-human matter. Using an insider-become-outsider disenchanted perspective (as in some of his other fictions), Vidal gives us a deflating view of the supposed golden age of Athens, with statesman Pericles pretty much a blowhard in a corrupt and bigoted society. Politics is seen as a ruthless gaming of those who "preferred power to pleasure," or, anyway, whose main pleasure is power.

Novelistically, the trouble is that such arguments are embedded in a relentless exotica of places, dynasties, religions, unto a wearying packrat pedantry. Vidal's historical fiction is certainly more intelligently informed than most but that relentless pedantic purpose sometimes takes over and de-novelizes, tiresomely denaturing the individual imagination, and the issues.

Vidal seems to have rather backed into the other, and major, direction of his historical fictions, an American political "chronicle." After the classical history of *Julian*, he did a single novel combining near-contemporary American political history, from the late 1930s through the early 1950s, with a fictional family saga in *Washington, D.C.* (1967). The emphasis is on the afterwash of F. D. Roosevelt, who turned the country, by mixing "cant with shrewdness in such a way as to inspire his followers and confuse his enemies," until he "had managed to transform an isolationist republic into what no doubt would be the last empire" to dominate the earth. But Vidal's omniscient account is more psychologically probing than his other political accounts. It centers on two young men, one a ruthlessly ambitious and sexually ambiguous figure who rises to be a nasty McCarthy-like senator, the other (and rather Vidalean surrogate), the scion of a powerful political-publishing family, considerably fictional, who becomes an alienated and disenchanted liberal intellectual. Incest, homoeroticism, promiscuity, and abuse of women play considerable part, as do old-fashioned vanity and greed. Vidal also poignantly draws on his grandfather, the blind and conservative senator, and other shrewdly observed Washingtonia.

Iconoclastic fascination with the history of Washington and national politics, and with the family of journalists he had created, and probably with the book's popular success, led Vidal back to another, and then another, until he had six linked volumes ending (so far) in the immediately preceding period to the first, *Hollywood, A Novel of America in the 1920s* (1990). The American drive for empire and politics as power for its own sake, along with hardly varied corruption, had become thematic in the unusually knowledgeable survey.

The second published, *Burr* (1973), probably the most praised of the series, takes up early American history. Parallel to *Julian*, the entitling figure's imaginary memoir draws carefully on the documentary record, with a recording narrator (Burr's unacknowledged illegitimate son-litterateur-journalist, ancestor of the fictional media-Sanfords in the later volumes) as a frame for broadening and ironic perspective. It also centers again on a problematically fascinating figure sometime at the center of mainstream political power yet sardonic dissenter to many of the conventional currents of his time. The art of the informed turnaround, and political double-play.

The conventional image-breaking applies not just to rehabilitating Aaron Burr, who may have done the country a democratic favor in killing Hamilton in a duel, for he provides an aptly cynical perspective on American political iconography, including Washington as pompous fool. Perhaps the most liberal-disturbing of the other deflations is that of Thomas Jefferson, who is considerably presented as a sly madman. In the Afterword, Vidal defends the denigration by the left-handed claim that, for historical accuracy, "the novel's viewpoint must be Burr's" of the Jefferson who cheated him of more than the presidency. In an essay apparently written while working on *Burr* (title piece in *Shays*), Vidal rather ingeniously argued that there were *two* Jeffersons, one the famous democratic liberal, the other, as we may now recognize along with Burr, a notorious early American political manipulator and imperialist. It may be countered that here, and elsewhere, Vidal partly fudges issues of why American liberalism and imperialism have so often been yoked together—manipulative- hierarchical expansionary ideologies.

Lincoln (1984, a best-seller also made into a TV network miniseries) took up some of the American issues of political power versus human decency. Again closely deploying the factual historical records, Vidal tells the Lincoln story from multiple contemporaneous views such as that of the young presidential secretary John Hay. Thus Lincoln is only presented externally, especially (and excessively) in rather Dickensian quirks and tics, and remains somewhat ambiguous. Still, the dominant emphasis is on political power manipulations, concluding with Hay's analogizing Lincoln to hyper-realist-nationalist Bismarck. Lincoln as primarily power-player rather than man of liberal principle, however granted brilliance at it, certainly deflates the reigning hagiography. But, as Vidal reasonably reflected later (to Jon Wiener, 1988), Lincoln re-created himself as "dictator," brutally advanced conscription, caused loss of liberties and the centralized militaristic state, and forced a long murderous war which "didn't need to take place."

Harshly petty attacks on Vidal by those he aptly called "scholar-squirrels" followed (for examples, C. Vann Woodward, Richard N. Current, Harold Holzer, in *New York Review of Books* 87 and 88, with Vidal rebuttals). The larger ideological issues include whether or not anti-abolitionist Lincoln remained a racist who wanted to export ex-slaves. I take it, with Vidal, that the clever dictatorial politico did but made it somewhat ambiguous because of political and logistical problems. Clearly, skeptical Vidal sees Lincoln as also illogical and morally dubious as he became "mystical about the union," which he used as justification for vicious repression and totalitarian war. Vidal's Lincoln seems to be a wily "re-creator" of the country into a centralized empire, for motives of personal power-glory to be the most famed American president.

Is rather old-fashioned historical fiction the best vehicle for this iconoclastic purpose? A choral character in *1876* (1976) says, "We *cannot* know any history, truly. . . . what we think to be history is nothing but fiction." In that piece of the Washington political story, the double irony of the bicentennial fictionalizing of the centennial "low point in our republic's history," has the literary journalist-narrator-descendant of *Burr*, now an old returned expatriate, report, in his rather tiresomely conventional responses and Vidal's competent but flat style of historical realism, the end of the corrupt Grant administration. Externally seen, Grant is also a somewhat ambiguous figure. We also have in detail Hayes stealing the presidency from the more admirable Tilden, and knowledgeably more of such mean records.

Empire (1987) creates fictional journalistic and dynastic links to the earlier parts of the chronicle, and historically documents the imperial semi-culmination in the 1898–1904 political scene. William Randolph Hearst and Teddy Roosevelt seem aptly scored off as vulgarly ambitious and viciously imperialistic power and propaganda players. McKinley comes off rather better. Sympathetically handled historical characters such as Henry Adams and, especially, John Hay seem less persuasively positive, as does the too shifting point of view in a record lacking the primary focus of *Burr* and *Lincoln*. The fictional newspaper dynasty (Sanfords), which provides continuity through the series, and nets for gossip about the wealthy and powerful, seems rather trite in conception. To finger American politics as considerably the sagas of the celebrated rich and powerful may have its popular novel utility, and insider-sophisticate advantage for Vidal, but is quite limiting. Conventional criminality, as with the greedy well-born, is usually humanly thin stuff. Lesser breeds only appear in passing, such as influential dissidents (a paragraph on Ingersoll in *1876*, a couple of sentences on Goldman in *Empire*, a naive little more on a government-insider Marxist in *Washington*). The other nation, socially, only appears in somewhat archly descriptive paragraphs. Rather old-fashioned in novelistic manner, Vidal's history is also rather vulgarly celebrity centered. But the sophisticate has always had a somewhat patronizing disdain for real outsiders.

Commenting on his *Hollywood* (1990), Vidal naively says of his historical fictions that he has no ruling theory or scheme, only disillusioning "exhibits of what I find." However, in the same context he notes that he finds that "the United States has always been militaristic." Elsewhere, he repeatedly insists that the propertied oligarchy which has mostly ruled America has culminated in our present "national security state," which will only be changed by its economic calcification and world-destructive effects. The pattern of his chronicles certainly puts emphasis not only on the rich but on imperial ideologies. And on his insistence on the dominance of power-for-its-own-sake motives. Certainly some iconoclasm about conventional political admirations of presidents, and other powers, is pervasive. But he may have had in mind his historical openness to small discoveries, such as that the little-remembered but literate James A. Garfield was "the most civilized of all our presidents." Or, in *Hollywood*, the detailed case that Warren G. Harding, who is usually treated with contempt, was a genial fool, controlled by his wife and greedy hacks, but a rather decent one. (Reagan, he notes elsewhere, was rather like Harding, "handsome, amiable, ignorant," though given the circumstances, rather more dangerous.) Intellectual Woodrow Wilson is treated somewhat more ambiguously. Vidal, as usual, makes intelligently skeptical political observations.

Less persuasive may be his fictional media-Sanfords in *Hollywood* since, for example, he makes the central female not only beautiful, intelligent, ambitious, cultivated, rich, and financially and socially brilliant, but both a successful silent-movie star and then producer, and a successful Washington journalist and publisher. She also as variously screws around. The pop-novel acrobatics aims nonetheless at the serious exposure of the fusion of popular media and national politics, and endless Hollywoodish reeling and unreeling of American political reality.

Much of *Hollywood* seems a divergence from the imperialist theme, though not historically inappropriate for the effects of the quite unnecessary Great War. But only a temporary divergence since the media-propaganda role established around World War I has become a dominant controlling political force for the empire. In interviews Vidal has promised a seventh novel for his Washington chronicle, the immediate post–World War II period, whose politics he sees as an absurd extension of American imperialism, and whose culture he sees (perhaps rather self-congratulatorily) as a Golden Age before the great decline. As a political activist, Vidal still mockingly defends a variety of liberties, and insists (as in a speech, "The Tree of Liberty," *Nation*, August 27, 1990) that the most crucial politics for America would be to "abandon all military pretensions," which would also drastically limit the powers of the ruling rich oligarchy. Otherwise, says the still radicalized if rather pessimistic liberal, the tree of liberty, as Jefferson said, "must still be nourished with the blood, if necessary, of tyrants and of patriots."

But that is the rhetoric of one who perhaps thinks too much in perspectives of figural history and in terms of political power. Historical processes and, especially, chance, may be undervalued. And the role of politicians, from Cyrus and Julian through Lincoln and Roosevelt to the later mediocrities, may be overvalued. Vidal's iconoclasm only rarely goes beyond the assumptions of power motives. Although he recognizes that politicians are often playing charades for the social and economic forces that they mostly serve, alternatives are not clear. And, finally, our history may be trivial. Siva the Destroyer (*Kalki*) awaits our overpolluted and overpopulated human world.

Bibliography

Dick, Bernard F. *The Apostate Angel: A Critical Study of Gore Vidal.* New York: Random House, 1974.

Parini, Jay, ed. *Gore Vidal: Writer against the Grain.* New York: Columbia University Press, 1992.

Pease, Donald E. "Citizen Vidal and Mailer's America," *Raritan* 11 (Spring 1992): 72–98.

Vidal, Gore. "The Agreed-Upon Facts," in *Paths of Resistance: The Art and Craft of the Political Novel.* William Zinsser, ed. Boston: Houghton Mifflin, 1989: 127–52.

———. *At Home: Essays, 1982–1986.* New York: Random House, 1988.

———. *The Best Man; A Play about Politics.* Boston: Little, Brown, 1960.

———. *Burr: A Novel.* New York: Random House, 1973.

———. *The City and the Pillar.* New York: E.P. Dutton, 1948; rev. ed., 1965.

———. *Creation.* New York: Random House, 1981.

———. *Dark Green, Bright Red.* New York: E.P. Dutton, 1950.

———. *Duluth.* New York: Random House, 1983.

———. *1876: A Novel.* New York: Random House, 1976.

———. *Empire.* New York: Random House, 1987.

———. *An Evening with Richard Nixon.* New York: Random House, 1972.

———. *Hollywood: A Novel of America in the 1920s.* New York: Random House, 1990.

———. *Homage to Daniel Shays: Collected Essays, 1952–1972.* New York: Random House, 1972.

———. Interview, conducted by Jon Weiner, *Radical History Review* no. 44 (1989): 109–137.

———. *The Judgment of Paris.* New York: E.P. Dutton, 1952; rev. ed., 1965.

———. *Julian: A Novel.* Boston: Little, Brown, 1964.

———. *Kalki: A Novel.* New York: Random House, 1978.

———. *Lincoln: A Novel.* New York: Random House, 1984.

———. *Live from Golgotha.* New York: Random House, 1992.

———. *Matters of Fact and Fiction: Essays 1971–1976.* New York: Random House, 1977.

———. *Messiah.* New York: E.P. Dutton, 1954; rev. ed., 1965.

———. *Myra Breckinridge.* Boston: Little, Brown, 1968.

———. *Myron: A Novel.* New York: Random House, 1974.

———. *Reflections on a Sinking Ship.* Boston: Little, Brown, 1969.

———. *Rocking the Boat.* Boston: Little, Brown, 1962.

———. *Screening History.* Cambridge: Harvard University Press, 1992.

———. *A Search for the King: A Twelfth Century Legend.* New York: E.P. Dutton, 1950.

———. *The Second American Revolution.* New York: Random House, 1987.

———. *Two Sisters, A Memoir in the Form of a Novel.* New York: Ballantine Books, 1987 (1970).

———. *United States: Essays 1952–1992.* New York: Random House, 1993.

———. *Visit to a Small Planet: A Comedy akin to Vaudeville.* Boston: Little, Brown, 1957.

———. *Washington, D.C.: A Novel.* Boston: Little, Brown, 1967.

———. *Williwaw.* New York: E.P. Dutton, 1946; rev. ed. 1965.

Kingsley Widmer

PART SIX

VISIONS OF ALTERNATIVE SOCIETIES

A map of the world that does not include Utopia is not worth even glanc-
ing at, for it leaves out the one country at which Humanity is always
landing. And when Humanity lands there, it looks out, and seeing a better
country, sets sail. Progress is the realization of utopias.

—Oscar Wilde

In the 1950s some intellectuals described "the end of ideology." It supposedly
had been replaced by realism or pragmatism, which rejected any general systems of reform or revolution. In the early 1990s, some intellectuals spoke
about "the end of history" and the death of all "utopian" ideologies. Historians
are likely to dismiss all such predictions as naive. We all have some notion of
the ideal society whether we are conscious of it or not. Models of community
provide meaning not only for individuals and minority groups but for the
general society. A society always has certain-basic assumptions. The question
is whether they best serve our interests. Advertisers, for example, have a vision
of a good society of avid consumers. Is this our ideal? Do we find perfection
at the Mall? Is our vision of the ideal world found at world's fairs? Is Dis-
neyland our utopia?

Without alternative visions of society we may not be conscious of our assumptions, nor of other possibilities. Carlyle wrote that history is "an imprisoned prophecy," but people do have the ability to transcend what is called
realism and common sense (that is, the dominant prejudices of the day) toward
new images of potentiality that light up the entire intellectual and social landscape. In the past, "impractical" people may have dreamed of equality for
women, racial justice, influence for organized workers, or many other subjects

that demonstrated the truth of Victor Hugo's dictum that "utopia is the truth of tomorrow."

The individuals in this section all have some broad vision of community. Some advocate a society where individuals have direct control over their own lives through such institutions as unions, co-ops, and voluntary associations, rather than being "represented" by elected officials. Some call this ideal society anarchism, such as Noam Chomsky, Dorothy Day, and Paul Goodman. Others advocate forms of democratic or libertarian socialism, such as Heather Booth, Ron Dellums, Michael Harrington, Tom Hayden, Sidney Lens, I. F. Stone, Staughton Lynd, and James Weinstein. Some, like C.L.R. James and Herbert Marcuse, spoke for a non-party form of Marxism; some have been members of the Communist Party USA, such as Angela Davis and Dorothy Healey. Others have been idealistic liberals (like Jesse Jackson) or champions of specific groups like the aged (in the case of Maggie Kuhn).

One of the conventional cartoons of the 1960s was of shabby people living in squalid communes. This ridicule obscures many basic issues. Why should individuals live isolated in individual apartments, condominiums, and houses? Rising unemployment and low wages increased the number of people with roommates, or people who continued to live with their parents. While this was often seen as an affliction, it could be done positively. Rather than each person having his or her own small room, several people could pool their income and buy a much larger place, while also dividing up the laundry, cooking, cleaning, and child care. In theory, such an arrangement would hold great opportunities for the flexible sharing of time, energy, and income. This option, seriously considered, could apply to many people. The 1970s saw the publication of essays on "communiums" (communes and condominiums), articles in journals like *Redbook* on unrelated families living together, discussions of "communes for old folks" in *Life* magazine, *U.S. News* reporting on "Group Living Catches On and Goes Middle Class" and "Communes: A More Businesslike Way," or such commentary in a small journal like *The Futurist* as "Communes: A Way to Beat the High Cost of Living."

Average individuals have little power. It is only by working with others that people can hope to have some major control over their own lives and to more fully develop their potential.

See also, for anarchism: Edward Abbey (4*), Murray Bookchin (4*), and Kenneth Rexroth (5*); for black nationalism: Imamu Amiri Baraka (1*), James Forman (1*); for Catholicism: Philip Berrigan (2*); for the counterculture: Jerry Rubin (5*); for ecotopia: Edward Abbey (4*), Murray Bookchin (4*); for Islam: H. Rap Brown (1*), Louis Farrakhan (1*), Malcolm X (1*); for Pan-Africanism: Maulana Karenga (5*); for Protestantism: Rev. William Sloane Coffin, Jr. (2*), Rev. Martin Luther King, Jr. (1*); for Democratic Socialism: Irving Howe (5*), Staughton Lynd (2*), David McReynolds (2*), and Bayard Rustin (1*).

SELECTED BIBLIOGRAPHY

Anarchism

Avrich, Paul. *Anarchist Portraits*. Princeton, NJ: Princeton University Press, 1986.

Benello, C. George. *From the Ground Up: Essays on Grassroots and Workplace Democracy*, with commentaries by Len Krimerman, Frank Lindenfeld, Carol Korty, and Julian Benello. Boston: South End Press, 1991.

Bookchin, Murray, et al. *The Anarchist Papers*. Montreal: Black Rose Press, 1986.

De Leon, David. *The American as Anarchist: Reflections on Indigenous Radicalism*. Baltimore: Johns Hopkins University Press, 1978.

Ehrlich, Howard, Carol Ehrlich, David De Leon, and Glenda Morris, eds. *Reinventing Anarchy: What Are Anarchists Thinking These Days?* London and New York: Routledge and Kegan Paul, 1979.

Nursey-Bray, Paul, ed. *Anarchist Thinkers and Thought: An Annotated Bibliography*. Westport, CT: Greenwood Press, 1992.

Perlin, Terry, ed. *Contemporary Anarchism*. New Brunswick, NJ: Transaction, 1979.

Reichert, William O. *Partisans of Freedom: A Study in American Anarchism*. Bowling Green, OH: Bowling Green University Press, 1976.

Sonn, Richard D. *Anarchism*. New York: Twayne, 1992.

Veysey, Laurence. *The Communal Experience: Anarchist and Mystical Communities in Twentieth Century America*. Chicago: University of Chicago Press, 1978.

Woodcock, George. *Anarchism*, with a new preface. New York: Penguin, 1986.

Communism

Bart, Philip, Theodore Bassett, William W. Weinstone, and Arthur Zipser, eds. *Highlights of a Fighting History: Sixty Years of the Communist Party, USA*. New York: International Publishers, 1979.

Brown, Michael E., Randy Martin, Frank Rosengarten, and George Snedeker, eds. *New Studies in the Politics of Culture of U.S. Communism*. New York: Monthly Review Press, 1993.

Chernin, Kim. *In My Mother's House*. New Haven: Ticknor and Fields, 1983.

Crossman, R.H.S., ed. *The God That Failed*. New York: Bantam, 1965.

Dennis, Peggy. *The Autobiography of an American Communist: A Personal View of a Political Life, 1925–1975*. Westport, CT: Lawrence Hill, 1977.

Gornick, Vivian. *The Romance of American Communism*. New York: Basic Books, 1977.

Green, Gil. *Cold War Refugee: A Personal Story of the McCarthy Years*. New York: International Publishers, 1984.

Haynes, James Earl. *Communism and Anti-Communism in the United States: An Annotated Guide to Historical Writings*. New York: Garland, 1987.

Haywood, Harry. *Black Bolshevik: Autobiography of an Afro-American Communist*. Chicago: Lake View Press, 1978.

Howe, Irving. *The American Communist Party: A Critical History*. New York: Praeger, 1962.

Hudelson, Richard H. *The Rise and Fall of Communism*. Boulder, CO: Westview Press, 1993.

Hudson, Hosea. *The Narrative of Hosea Hudson: His Life as Negro Communist*, Nell Irvin Painter, ed. Cambridge: Harvard University Press, 1979.

Isserman, Maurice. *If I Had a Hammer: The Death of the Old Left and the Birth of the New Left*. New York: Basic Books, 1987.

———. "Three Generations of Historians View American Communism" (review article), *Labor History* 26 (Fall 1985): 517–45.

———. *Which Side Were You On? The American Communist Party and the Second World War*. Middletown, CT: Wesleyan University Press, 1982.

Klehr, Harvey, and John Earl Haynes. *The American Communist Movement: Storming Heaven Itself*. Boston: Twayne Publishers, 1992.

Kraditor, Aileen S. *"Jimmy Higgins": The Mental World of the American Rank-and-File Communist, 1930–1958*. Westport, CT: Greenwood Press, 1988.

Lewy, Guenter. *The Cause That Failed: Communism in American Political Life*. New York: Oxford University Press, 1990.

"Maoists Hope to Show L. A. Latinos the 'Shining Path' to Revolution," *Washington Post*, Nov. 12, 1992, A3.

Nelson, Steve, James R. Barrett, and Rob Ruck. *Steve Nelson: American Radical*. Pittsburgh: University of Pittsburgh Press, 1981.

New York Times (on CPUSA), Aug. 31, 1991, p. 10; Oct. 29, 1990, D8.

"Panhandling the Kremlin: How Gus Hall Got Millions," *Washington Post*, March 1, 1992, A1.

Richmond, Al. *A Long View from the Left: Memoirs of an American Revolutionary*. New York: Delta, 1972.

Starobin, Joseph. *American Communism in Crisis, 1943–1957*. Cambridge: Harvard University Press, 1972.

Community Organizing

ACORN (Association of Community Organizations for Reform Now), 1024 Elysian Fields Ave., New Orleans, LA 70117.

Bobo, Kim, Jackie Kendall, and Steve Max. *Organizing for Social Change: A Manual for Social Activists in the 1990s*. Cabin John, MD: Seven Locks Press, 1990.

Boyte, Harry C. *CommonWealth: A Return to Citizen Politics*. New York: Free Press, 1989.

Boyte, Harry C., and Sara Evans. *Free Space: The Sources of Democratic Change in America*, 2d ed. Chicago: University of Chicago Press, 1992 (1986).

Boyte, Harry C., Heather Booth, and Steve Max. *Citizen Action and the New American Populism*. Philadelphia: Temple University Press, 1986.

Brecher, Jeremy, and Tim Costello, eds. *Building Bridges: The Emerging Coalition of Labor and Community*. New York: Monthly Review Press, 1990.

Breines, Wini. *Community and Organization in the New Left, 1962–1968: The Great Refusal*. New Brunswick, NJ: Rutgers University Press, 1989.

Brobeck, Stephen J. *The Modern Consumer Movement: A Guide to the Sources*. Boston: G. K. Hall, 1990.

Carroll, Andrew. *Volunteer America*. New York: Ballantine/Fawcett, 1991.

Delgado, Gary. *Organizing the Movement: The Roots and Growth of ACORN*, intr. by

Richard A. Cloward and Frances Fox Piven. Philadelphia: Temple University Press, 1986.

Driver, David. *Defending the Left: An Individual's Guide to Fighting for Social Justice, Individual Rights, and the Environment.* Chicago: The Noble Press, 1992.

Erickson, Brad, ed. *Call to Action: Handbook for Ecology, Peace and Justice,* with a preface by Rev. Jesse Jackson. San Francisco: Sierra Club Books, 1990.

Fellowship for Intentional Community and Communities Publications Cooperative. *Directory of Intentional Communities: A Guide to Cooperative Living,* rev. ed. Rutledge, MO: FIC/CPC, 1991.

Fisher, Robert. *Let the People Decide: Neighborhood Organizing in America.* Boston: Twayne, 1984.

Goldberg, Robert A. *Grassroots Resistance: Social Movements in Twentieth Century America.* Belmont, CA: Wadsworth, 1991.

Griffin, Kelley. *Ralph Nader Presents More Action for a Change.* New York: Dembner Books; distributed by W. W. Norton, 1987.

Hedemann, Ed, ed. *War Resisters League Organizer's Manual,* rev. ed. New York: War Resisters League, 1986.

Horwitt, Sanford D. *Let Them Call Me Rebel: Saul Alinsky—His Life and Legacy.* New York: Alfred A. Knopf, 1989.

Industrial Areas Foundation (founded by Saul Alinsky), 36 Hyde Park Road, Franklin Square, New York, NY 11010.

Kahn, Si. *Organizing: A Guide for Grassroots Leaders,* rev. ed. Silver Spring, MD: NASW Press, 1991 (1982 1st ed. by McGraw-Hill).

Kann, Mark. *Middle Class Radicalism in Santa Monica.* Philadelphia: Temple University Press, 1986.

Knipe, Judy. *Stand Up and Be Counted: The Volunteer Resource Book.* New York: Fireside/Simon and Schuster, 1992.

La Botz, Dan. *A Troublemaker's Handbook: How to Fight Back Where You Work— and Win!* Detroit: Labor Notes, 1991.

Melvin, Patricia Mooney. *American Community Organizations: A Historical Dictionary.* Westport, CT: Greenwood Press, 1986.

Naison, Mark, and Ronald Lawson. *The Tenant Movement in New York City, 1904– 1984.* New Brunswick, NJ: Rutgers University Press, 1986.

Oppenheimer, Martin. *A Manual for Direct Action.* Chicago: Quadrangle Books, 1965.

Piven, Frances Fox, and Richard A. Cloward. *Poor People's Movements: Why They Succeed, How They Fail.* New York: Random House/Vintage, 1979.

Rabinowitz, Alan. *Social Change Philanthropy in America.* Westport, CT: Quorum Books, 1990.

Richan, Willard C. *Lobbying for Social Change.* New York: Haworth Press, 1991.

Walls, David. *The Activist's Almanac: The Concerned Citizen's Guide to the Leading Advocacy Organizations in America.* New York: Fireside/Simon and Schuster, 1993.

West, Guida. *The National Welfare Rights Movement: The Social Protest of Poor Women.* New York: Praeger, 1981.

Wigginton, Eliot, ed. *Refuse to Stand Silently: An Oral History of Grass Roots Social Activism in America, 1921–1964.* New York: Doubleday, 1992.

Woliver, Laura R. *From Outrage to Action: The Politics of Grass-Roots Dissent.* Urbana: University of Illinois Press, 1993.

Democratic Socialism

Anderson, Jervis. *A. Philip Randolph: A Biographical Portrait.* Berkeley: University of California Press, 1986.

Blackburn, Robin, ed. *After the Fall: The Failure of Communism and the Future of Socialism.* London: Verso, 1992.

Cantor, Milton. *The Divided Left: American Radicalism, 1900–1975.* New York: Hill and Wang, 1978.

Conroy, W. J. *Challenging the Boundaries of Reform: Socialism in Burlington* [Vermont]. Philadelphia: Temple University Press, 1990.

Diggins, John R. *The Rise and Fall of the American Left.* New York: W. W. Norton, 1992.

Harrington, Michael. *The Long-Distance Runner: An Autobiography.* New York: Henry Holt, 1988.

———. *Taking Sides: The Education of a Militant Mind.* New York: Holt, Rinehart, and Winston, 1985.

Howe, Irving. *A Margin of Hope; An Intellectual Autobiography.* New York: Holt, Rinehart, and Winston, 1985.

———. *Socialism and America.* San Diego: Harcourt, Brace, Jovanovich, 1985.

Hyfler, Robert. *Prophets of the Left: American Socialist Thought in the Twentieth Century.* Westport, CT: Greenwood Press, 1984.

Johnpoll, Bernard K. *The Impossible Dream: The Rise and Demise of the American Left.* Westport, CT: Greenwood Press, 1981.

———. *Pacifist's Progress: Norman Thomas and the Decline of American Socialism.* Westport, CT: Greenwood Press, 1987 (1970).

Klehr, Harvey. *Far Left of Center: The American Radical Left Today.* New Brunswick, NJ: Transaction, 1988.

Laslett, John H., and Seymour Martin Lipset, eds. *Failure of a Dream? Essays in the History of American Socialism,* rev. ed. Berkeley: University of California Press, 1984.

Pfeffer, Paula. *A. Philip Randolph: Pioneer of the Civil Rights Movement.* Baton Rouge: Louisiana State University Press, 1990.

"Sanders, Bernard," *Current Biography Yearbook 1991.* New York: H. W. Wilson, 1991: 494–98.

Soifer, Steven. *The Socialist Mayor: Bernard Sanders in Burlington, Vermont.* New York: Bergin and Garvey, 1991.

Swanberg, W. A. *Norman Thomas, the Last Idealist.* New York: Scribner's, 1976.

Libertarianism

Baker, James T. *Ayn Rand.* Boston: Twayne, 1987.

Branden, Nathaniel. *Judgment Day: My Life with Ayn Rand.* Boston: Houghton Mifflin, 1989.

Gladstein, Mimi Reisel. "Ayn Rand," in *Contemporary Authors,* vol. 27, New Revision Series. Detroit: Gale Research, 1989: 394–99.

Hess, Karl. *Community Technology.* New York: Harper and Row, 1979.

———. *Dear America.* New York: Morrow, 1975.

————. *Neighborhood Power; The New Localism*. Boston: Beacon Press, 1975.

Machan, Tibor, ed. *The Libertarian Reader*. Lanham, MD: Rowman, 1982.

Narveson, Jan. *The Libertarian Idea*. Philadelphia: Temple University Press, 1989.

Neuman, A. Lin. "Interview with Karl Hess," *Reason* 14:1 (1982): 44–48.

Newman, Stephen L. "The Chimeras of 'Libertarianism': What's Behind This Movement?" *Dissent* 34 (Summer 1987): 308–16.

O'Neil, William F. *With Charity toward None: An Analysis of Ayn Rand's Philosophy*. New York: Philosophical Library, 1971.

Peikoff, Leonard. *Objectivism: The Philosophy of Ayn Rand*. New York: Dutton, 1991.

"Rand, Ayn (1905–1982)," in *Contemporary Literary Criticism*, vol. 30. Detroit: Gale Research, 1984: 291–305.

"Rand, Ayn," *Current Biography Yearbook 1982*. New York: H. W. Wilson, 1982: 331–35.

"Rothbard, Murray Newton," in *Contemporary Authors*, vol. 6, New Revision Series. Detroit: Gale Research, 1982: 436–37.

Rothbard, Murray. *The Ethics of Liberty*. Atlantic Highlands, NJ: Humanities Press, 1982.

————. *For a New Liberty: The Libertarian Manifesto*. Lanham, MD: University Press of America, 1985 (1978).

Slavin, P. "Karl Hess Eludes the System, Again: An Interview," *Business and Society Review* 18 (Summer 1976): 24–30.

Telgen, Diane. "Nathaniel Branden," in *Contemporary Authors*, vol. 27, New Revision Series. Detroit: Gale Research, 1989: 62–66.

Marxism

Alexander, Robert J. *International Trotskyism, 1929–1985: A Documented Analysis of the Movement*. Durham, NC: Duke University Press, 1991.

Bell, Daniel. *Marxian Socialism in the United States*. Princeton, NJ: Princeton University Press, 1967.

Buhle, Paul. *Marxism in the USA: Remapping the History of the American Left*, rev. ed. London: Verso, 1991.

Callinicos, Alex. *Trotskyism*. Minneapolis: University of Minnesota Press, 1990.

Chasin, Barbara H. "C. Wright Mills, Pessimistic Radical," *Sociological Inquiry* 60 (Fall 1990): 337–51.

Cunningham, George P. "W.E.B. DuBois," in *African American Writers*, Valerie Smith, Lea Baechler, and A. Walton Litz, eds. New York: Scribner's, 1991: 71–86.

"DuBois, W.E.B.," in *Contemporary Literary Criticism*, vol. 64. Detroit: Gale Research, 1991: 101–35.

Fields, A. Belden. *Trotskyism and Maoism: Theory and Practice in France and the United States*. New York: Praeger, 1988.

Gorman, Robert A. *Biographical Dictionary of Marxism*. Westport, CT: Greenwood Press, 1986.

————. *Biographical Dictionary of Neo-Marxism*. Westport, CT: Greenwood Press, 1985.

————. *Yankee Red: Non-orthodox Marxism in Liberal America*. Westport, CT: Greenwood Press, 1989.

Gottlieb, Roger S. *Marxism 1844–1990; Origins, Betrayal, Rebirth.* New York: Routledge, 1992.

Horowitz, Irving Louis. *C. Wright Mills: An American Utopian.* New York: Free Press, 1983.

Johnpoll, Bernard, and Harvey Klehr. *Biographical Dictionary of the American Left.* Westport, CT: Greenwood Press, 1986.

Marable, Manning. *W.E.B. DuBois: Black Radical Democrat.* Boston: Twayne, 1986.

Ollman, Bertell, and Edward Vernoff, eds. *The Left Academy.* Vol. 1 (New York: McGraw-Hill, 1982); vol. 2 (New York: Praeger, 1984); vol. 3 (New York: Praeger, 1986).

Robinson, Cedric J. *Black Marxism: The Making of a Black Radical Tradition.* London: Zed, 1983.

Tilman, Rick. *C. Wright Mills: A Native Radical and His American Intellectual Roots.* University Park: Pennsylvania State University Press, 1984.

Wohlforth, Tim. *The Prophet's Children.* Atlantic Highlands, NJ: Humanities Press, 1993.

HEATHER BOOTH (1945–   )

Community organizer

Heather Tobis Booth was born in 1945, participated in SNCC and several student movement organizations, and helped found the Chicago Women's Union, all before the end of the 1960s. Within "the Movement," she was recognized as an able activist who had paid her dues in the South and was one of the New Left women who gave birth to women's liberation.

Both the pattern of her activism in the 1960s and its trajectory since show Heather Booth to be a leading representative of the New Left's optimistic democratic strain. Her work remained rooted in the belief that full democracy has not been achieved in the United States, but that it could be if people organized responsibly. Her approach has been characterized by an informed optimism: a hope that southern black people could stand up to the power structure; a belief that students, women, and communities could organize to make change, if they had the proper tools; an expectation that local and state governments could be made to perform more responsibly; and most recently, even hope that the Democratic party can be realigned to advocate progressive issues.

Others represented in this volume have expressed more fundamental criticisms of, and less hope for, U.S. democracy. But few could deny that the politics represented by Heather Booth's life of activism have helped keep alive, legitimize, and develop the values articulated by the New Left in the early 1960s.

Heather Booth grew up in a liberal Jewish family in Bensonhurst, New Jersey. She acknowledges the influence of her family traditions, and the early Civil Rights movements, on the political path she chose during her undergraduate years at the University of Chicago.

At college, Booth tutored, protested, and was involved in movement-sponsored community service projects. She joined SNCC in Chicago and, in the summer of 1964, went to Mississippi to teach in Freedom Schools, and support the Mississippi Freedom Democratic party.

This Freedom Summer was a transforming experience for Booth. She saw American racism in full force, but more important for her, she saw the heroism of everyday people standing up for their own lives. As she has said in several interviews, she gained immense respect for the bravery of regular people who lived for freedom. Booth, unlike those who were disillusioned by the realities of American injustice, came away with a conviction that organized people could change government, social structures, and history.

As one of the women in SNCC, Booth also learned that women must define freedom struggles for themselves and must question their own place in society and in the movements for change. This led her to help found the earliest campus women's organization in the country, in 1965. She aided the early women's liberation movement in Chicago, played an important role in "Jane," Chicago's underground abortion movement, and was a founder of the Chicago Women's Union, one of the most influential women's liberation organizations of the early seventies.

Booth's politics since that time incorporated women's concerns into an emphasis on "citizen action." Booth has worked to promote women's leadership and to support abortion rights and other feminist issues since. Married and with children before the end of the 1960s, she said that being a parent grounded her in the real world. This helped explain why her politics kept returning to the practical questions of achieving necessary changes, rather than toward more abstract theorizing.

Booth founded the Midwest Academy (centered in Chicago) in 1972. This institution became a major source of training and strategic development for community, labor, and citizen's action groups. Her base in the Midwest Academy allowed her to meet, train, and learn from a wide range of organizers. As natural outgrowths of contacts made at Midwest, Booth founded, supported, and led a number of other organizations. The most long-lasting and influential of those is Citizen Action, a national organization of 2.5 million dues-paying members in thirty-two states, which supports grassroots political action for economic and political democracy. By 1980, she became more involved in electoral as well as more issue-oriented politics. She worked with Walter Washington's campaigns in Chicago and founded the State and Local Leadership Project to help support progressive leadership in running for political office. In 1990, she became director of the Coalition for Democratic Values, a new national organization founded, under the leadership of Senator Howard Metzenbaum, to hold the Democratic party to progressive standards.

While Booth's goals evolved since the 1960s, her goal was essentially the same: organizing for democratic change. She viewed the development of national and local organizations as essential to a process of grassroots politics catalyzed by skilled leaders imbued with democratic values. She always argued for staying within and changing the systems that control life in America—and for looking toward long-range change, as well as immediate victories.

Booth has long differentiated herself from, but not opposed, self-defined socialist groups. For her, "socialism" was either an unclear abstraction or a designation for systems that failed the test of democracy. Booth's energies went toward building a broad base for achievable change, with attention to both democratic processes and organization building.

The organizations Booth has founded and led have always supported organizing that builds upon connections among fundamental values, whether the issue is environmental waste, abortion, or urban reform. She has never taken what she calls an "armageddon view" of political change, but has seen one struggle leading to another with the fundamental values remaining dignity and "small 'd' democracy."

Booth has always been an organizer, concerned about defining and building the forces that support more than one kind of governing. Her work has been to bring people together to form programs, tactics, and actions. Early on, Booth was influenced by Saul David Alinksy's methods, but has always been more focused on attaining substantive as well as process values than he was. Booth has consistently portrayed herself as supporting movements for "majoritarian change," always seeking ways to "build a better majority."

While her participation in SNCC, Jane, and in the Chicago Women's Union was critical in setting core values, probably the defining organizational context for Heather Booth's political development and impact was the Midwest Academy.

Although Booth had been building organizations for years, she started Midwest, in her words, "to cure an ill, not just build an organization." Her view was that many activists from the sixties were dispirited and lacking both the skills to handle long-run organizing campaigns and the confidence to seek new directions. So the Academy began as a place to nurture, support, and energize old activists, as well as to train new organizers. Groups and organizations from across the country sent staff to be trained in an ongoing series of courses and programs. Conferences and meetings were held where winning organizing strategies for the seventies were hammered out. Booth was in contact with organizers from around the country as organizations like "Fair Share" or "9 to 5" formed and struggled for direction.

Out of this period of activism came a more coherent philosophy, the renewal of a broad-based populism, tied to economic democracy and citizen action. While others have written about the development of this new tendency, especially in the mid-seventies, Booth has written little herself, except for one book with Harry Boyte and Steve Max, *Citizen Action and the New American Populism*, published in 1986. But she has helped create and lead several national organizations—like the Citizen/Labor Energy Coalition, the Citizens Leadership Foundation, and Citizen Action—that attempted to sharpen and carry out this "populist" approach to politics.

Booth's role in all these groups was that of behind-the-scenes organizer and up-front leader. As one observer commented, "she knew everybody, and kept things going—sometimes by inspiration, often by arm twisting. Even those who disagreed with her, respected her commitment."

What organizational methods has she used? Booth has been involved in struggle, but is not viewed as sectarian, even by those who disagree with her. Instead, the criticisms, when they occur, center around whether the approach she promotes organizationally and theoretically is an overly romantic version of majoritarian democracy, and is too unmindful of ideological, class, race, and gender conflicts that cannot be collapsed into "democratic" struggles. Opponents have characterized the Midwest Academy as too tied to Alinksy models of organizing, as too willing to settle for organizing the widest coalitions of citizens effectively, so that poor people's concerns, or those of other minorities with less "winnable" demands, are neglected.

In response, Booth and her associates stressed the need for real-world results, for making connections among people, for both broadening the public conception of democracy and making it work. Booth has always emphasized the importance of human relationships in making change, of treating people well and avoiding the bitterness of Left politics. Indeed, she most often has questioned whether it is useful in an American context to focus attention on socialism, given its anti-democratic record. Instead she has argued that a radical definition of democracy has a greater chance of changing minds and political practice in the United States. Similarly, while Booth placed race and gender as central components of training, organizing, and strategyzing, she has not been a part of the ongoing debates within feminism and the Left about how to reframe our whole direction in non-Eurocentric, gender-sensitive ways.

Booth's politics evolved over the years as she tried to take advantage of the opportunities for real change that emerge in this society. From a focus on grassroots and issue organizing she has developed an increasing concern with electoral politics, at all levels. The 1990s found her moving further into mainstream politics with her work, in Washington, D.C., for the Coalition for Democratic Values. Through this group, and its attempt to bring the Democratic party back to progressive politics, Booth could be seen as seeking an ever-wider national political base to effect change.

Heather Tobis Booth is an important representative of sixties activists who have not burned out. She and others brought the values and strategies of the New Left to the dominant society. She never gave up hope that U.S. citizens could change. She struggled continuously against what she viewed as pessimistic politics. She represents that part of the movement that was not, above all, interested in the socialist project, but in democratically achieving economic and social justice, by whatever name.

When asked about the most difficult aspects of her work over the years, Booth answers that "understanding the ways in which division and fear by race can undercut a progressive economic populism" has been the toughest challenge. She also cites the struggle to achieve programs for economic growth that balance environmental concerns. She still talks about the need to spread democracy within the United States and to keep energy alive for organizing. Ever the feminist, Booth attempts to keep personal relationships alive while working for change.

It has been her continuing belief in the defining issues of the sixties that made Booth's influence important for the rest of the Left. Even as others of us chose, or were forced, to move farther to the margins of political discourse,

Booth fought for a place in mainstream America for progressive ideas. She thereby served to legitimate the values, if not the methods and language, of those more marginal than she. During an era of conservative ascendancy, this alone was a critical achievement.

Bibliography

Behrens, Leigh. "Activist Voice: A Passion for Justice Fuels Heather Booth's Life," *Chicago Tribune*, July 23, 1989, 6, 3:1.

Booth, Heather. "Planning a New U.S. Agenda," *Social Policy* 18 (Fall 1987): 2–5.

————. "Seize the Moment," *The Progressive* 54 (Nov. 1991): 19–20.

Booth, Heather, and Janet Kelsey. "Citizen Power Finds Its Voice," *The Progressive* 48 (June 1984): 24–25.

Boyte, Harry, Heather Booth, and Steve Max. *Citizen Action and the New American Populism*. Philadelphia: Temple University Press, 1986. Reviewed: *Christianity and Crisis* 47 (Feb. 2, 1987): 22–30; *The Oral History Review* 15 (Fall 1987): 204–6; *Journal of the American Planning Association* 53 (Summer 1987): 399–401.

Evans, Sara. *Personal Politics: The Roots of Women's Liberation in the Civil Rights Movement and the New Left*. New York: Random House, 1979.

Fisher, Robert. *Let the People Decide: Neighborhood Organizing in America*. Boston: Twayne Publishers, 1984.

Lilienthal, Steve. "Heather Booth: No Dem Fatale," *In These Times*, Oct. 2–8, 1991, p. 4.

Van Gelder, Lindsay. "The Jane Collective: Seizing Control," *Ms.* 2 (Sept./Oct. 1991): 83–85.

"Where to from Here?" *The Progressive* 54 (Nov. 1990): 17–32+.

Ann Withorn

NOAM CHOMSKY (1928–   )

Founder of RESIST; radical critic of American foreign policy; anarchist social thinker, political analyst, and activist

Noam Chomsky first became a prominent dissident with the publication of his famous and widely translated essay "The Responsibility of Intellectuals" in the *New York Review of Books* (February 23, 1967). A few months later he was a sponsor of the "Call to Resist Illegitimate Authority," signed by thousands, that was printed in the *New York Review of Books* on October 12. This initiative led to the founding of RESIST, a national organization that focused on issues of imperialism abroad and repression at home. He soon figured prominently in the conspiracy trial of Dr. Spock and the other Boston

Five. Chomsky, indeed, was an unindicted co-conspirator. On the weekend of October 19–21, 1967, he was a widely-reported member in demonstrations at the Justice Department and the Pentagon. This was depicted by Norman Mailer, who was his jail cellmate on the latter occasion, in *The Armies of the Night*. Chomsky is portrayed as "a slim sharp-featured man with an ascetic expression, and an air of gentle but absolute moral integrity."

"The Responsibility of Intellectuals" was reprinted during the following year in Theodore Roszak's *The Dissenting Academy*. Soon after, in 1969, Chomsky published his first book on a nonlinguistic subject, *American Power and the New Mandarins*. This collection of historical and political essays was hailed by *The Nation* as "the first significant work of social and political thought to come out of the Vietnamese catastrophe" and "the first draft of a declaration of intellectual independence." The book displayed Chomsky's awesome gifts as a debater and his uncanny ability to dissect the logical flaws in rival views. Chomsky soon became internationally known as an eloquent anti-war speaker, social critic, and activist. He was sometimes referred to as a hero or "guru" of the New Left.

By then, Chomsky had also gained another sort of worldwide intellectual fame. He was known as the initiator and undisputed prime mover of a conceptual revolution in the field of linguistics ("transformational generative grammar"). This was the outcome of work he had carried out, in almost complete isolation, in his early twenties. His great achievement has been a theory of language which, "with unprecedented originality," as Robert Freidin has written, "fuses three major strands in the history of the field into a powerful scientific research program": "the tradition in the formal analysis of natural language," "the search for explanatory models in historical linguistics," and "the tradition of philosophical grammar." This theory proved to be a central strand in the dramatic change in perspective in the history of psychology that was to become widely known as the "cognitive revolution" of the mid-1950s. This was the starting point of current work in the cognitive sciences. In the late 1950s Chomsky went on to become the founder of algebraic linguistics (a new branch of abstract algebra sometimes referred to as "mathematical linguistics") "and by far the best man in this exciting new field," in the words of one of its most eminent practitioners, Israeli logician and mathematician Yehoshua Bar-Hillel.

Since the mid-sixties Chomsky lectured and wrote extensively, continuously, and indefatigably about the social and political problems of the day. His audiences at universities and local communities have been large and enthusiastic. Between *American Power* (1969) and *Deterring Democracy* (1991) he published some twenty "nonprofessional" books (including massive volumes) and countless articles in many periodicals, becoming a regular contributor to *Z* magazine and to *Lies of Our Times*.

This productivity did not slow his extensive, deep, and original investigations in cognitive psychology and philosophy. This work continued unabated. It was

Noam Chomsky. Photo
courtesy of Donna Coveney/
MIT.

followed with sustained interest, and often eagerness, by readers from many
walks of life. Chomsky may be the only linguist whose works are widely read.

His professional career, which has unfolded in its entirety at the Massachusetts Institute of Technology (MIT), was meteoric. He advanced to the
rank of associate professor at twenty-nine and full professor at thirty-two. He
quickly went on to hold an endowed chair at thirty-seven and to become an
Institute Professor (a rank reserved for a dozen scholars of special distinction,
most of them Nobel Prize winners) at forty-seven. In June of 1988 he was
awarded the Kyoto Prize in Basic Sciences, one of the three "Japanese Nobel
Prizes." This was perhaps the most obvious sign of his success in turning the
study of language into a natural science. In the course of his career, he has
received many honors, both in the United States and abroad. His eminence
has been unique within linguistics.

Beyond that, he has been described in the *New York Times* as "arguably
the most important intellectual alive" when "judged in terms of the power,

range, novelty and influence of his thought," and as "one of the most powerful thinkers who ever lived." He is, in any case, one of the few major figures in the history of the natural sciences who have thought and written extensively about the nature of human beings and human society. He has been a rare instance of a major intellectual who is nevertheless a committed activist and an undeterred social analyst and critic. (In this respect he has been likened to the late Bertrand Russell.)

The sources of his activism are to be found in his childhood. He was born on December 7, 1928, in "Quaker, egalitarian Philadelphia," where he grew up in the alien culture of the immigrant community (in a sense) of the Jewish-Zionist cultural tradition. He attended an experimental (essentially Deweyite) progressive private school. His parents, both teachers, were deeply involved in mainstream Zionism, a cultural movement inspired in the West European Enlightenment. They were particularly influenced by one of its most gifted and dedicated exponents, Asher Ginsburg (1856–1927), a prominent Hebrew writer and stylist who pointedly used the pen name Ahad Ha-am, meaning "one of the people" (prefiguring Chomsky's egalitarian stand). The next range of family, such as uncles and cousins, was in part Jewish working class. He gravitated toward the most assimilated and radical of his relatives. Some of them worked in sweatshops and were heavily involved in the politics of the depression period. A few were or had been on the fringes of the Communist party.

One of these relatives, a man who had never gone beyond the fourth grade, was to greatly influence Chomsky. This was his mother's sister's husband, who had already been through several varieties of Marxist sectarian politics. These included Stalinist, Trotskyite, and non-Leninist sects, even semi-anarchist ones. He became a successful lay psychoanalyst. Chomsky respected the advice of this extraordinarily gifted and sophisticated revolutionary who ran a newsstand in New York. The gifted nephew managed to learn, as a teenager, a good deal about Marxism and Freudianism that was in sharp contrast with many conventional ideas on the left.

Amazingly, Chomsky's basic social and political perspectives did not appreciably change since he wrote his first political article for a school newspaper a few weeks after his tenth birthday. Its topic was the fall of Barcelona, which signaled the end of the Spanish civil war. Neither has the root of his concern changed. Already as a child and as a teenager he was vitally concerned about the Jewish community in Palestine. This involvement continued to be at the core of his existence.

His father's influence is easier to trace than that of his mother, née Elsie Simonofsky, who was more left oriented than her husband. William Chomsky (1897–1977) had essentially fled from his native Russia to the United States in 1913. It was then unlikely that the *New York Times* would eventually describe William Chomsky as "one of the world's foremost Hebrew grammarians" (July 22, 1977). William became known not only for his work on medieval

Hebrew grammar and for one of the most popular books about the Hebrew language, but also for his writings on education. He was a professor of Hebrew and Jewish education, for many years, at Gratz College and at Dropsie University.

Shortly before his death, William Chomsky described the major objective of his life as "the education of individuals who are well integrated, free and independent in their thinking, concerned about improving and enhancing the world, and eager to participate in making life more meaningful and worthwhile for all" (*Contemporary Authors*, Detroit, MI: Gale Research, 1978). It is hard to improve on this as a description of Noam Chomsky. William Chomsky's work in historical linguistics may also have suggested to his son, quite early in life, what was to become a view of language theory as an explanatory science ("generative grammar") by providing the historical analogy which inspired his trail-blazing linguistic investigations. Both wings of this crucial relay that his father supplied (the ideas of cultural Zionism and scientific explanation as a starting point) were of key importance. It's fair to guess that the cultural gap he was to open between himself and his father was smaller than that between his father and his grandfather.

Chomsky attended Central High School in Philadelphia, and after graduating in 1945 he entered the University of Pennsylvania. At the end of two years, when he had just turned eighteen, he was planning to drop out to pursue his own interests, which were then largely political. He was fascinated by "radical politics with an anarchist or left-wing (anti-Leninist) Marxist flavor and even more deeply involved in Zionist affairs and activities—or what was then called 'Zionist,' though the same ideas and concerns are now called 'anti-Zionist.'" He was particularly seeking for socialist, binational options for Palestine, particularly "efforts at Arab-Jewish cooperation within a socialist framework, opposed to the deeply antidemocratic concept of a Jewish state" (*Chomsky Reader*, p. 7). He was impressed by the kibbutzim and the whole cooperative labor system that had developed in the Jewish settlement in Palestine (the Yishuv). Chomsky considered going there, perhaps to a kibbutz, and with this in mind he studied Arabic.

It was through these interests that he happened to meet Zellig Harris, an extraordinary person with a coherent understanding of this whole range of issues who happened to be one of the leading figures, perhaps the leading figure, in modern linguistics. Harris was without question the most rigorous practitioner of the methodology that Chomsky was to overthrow. The encounter led to a decisive change of course for Chomsky. He returned to college to continue his formal education. He plunged into the study of philosophy, mathematics, and linguistics. He took his B.A. as a member of Phi Beta Kappa in 1949, after supporting himself by teaching Hebrew at the Mikve Israel School in Philadelphia. He completed his Ph.D. in 1955, after spending the years 1951–1955 as a member of the Society of Fellows at Harvard. There, he wrote his first *magnum opus*, *The Logical Structure of Linguistic Theory*, a monumental work of close to one thousand pages which has changed the course of intellectual history.

When Chomsky arrived in Cambridge in 1951 the human sciences were being reconstructed on the basis of the concepts developed in the technological approaches to human behavior, such as electronics, cybernetics, acoustics, the mathematical theory of communication, and computers. These concepts were closely connected with behaviorist concepts of human nature, which were essentially manipulative and coercive. Like the Bolsheviks and other authoritarians, the behaviorists conceived of the brain as a blank tablet upon which a particular type of consciousness could be imprinted by foresighted leaders ("liberal" in Cambridge, "Leninist" in Moscow). Not surprisingly, the young radical was disturbed by these developments, in part for political reasons. This whole complex of ideas seemed to justify authoritarian and manipulative systems.

His concern intensified when he started teaching at MIT in 1955. He discovered that everyone there was convinced that a certain type of abstract finite automata would solve everything that remained to be solved, in particular having to do with language. It was for this reason that Chomsky began working on the mathematical properties of automata in the fall of 1955. It had seemed obvious to him even when he was a student at Harvard that this idea was extremely naive and was unlikely to work. He began to prove his argument.

He succeeded in doing this by showing that a generalized form of finite automata that he developed for the purpose was much too narrow to serve as a model for human language. An adequate model would have to make use of abstract "nonterminal" symbols, which cannot be characterized in terms of observed behavior. He presented his proof at a symposium on information theory, which is another name for the mathematical theory of communication, held at MIT on September 11, 1956. This date has been proposed as the birthdate of the cognitive sciences. Chomsky's version left ample room for the traditional notions of individual freedom and creativity while the so-called behavioral sciences intended to consign such notions as freedom and dignity to the junkyard.

Hidden in this discussion of the properties of mathematical automata is the much debated question of the respective contributions of "nature" (biological endowment) and "nurture" (environment) to our knowledge. This is a question full of political implications which is at the root of the centuries-old controversy between the rationalist philosophers (Plato, Descartes, Leibniz, Kant, and Chomsky) and the empiricist philosophers (Aristotle, Hobbes, Locke, Hume, Wittgenstein, Quine, and Donaldson). Suffice it to say that racism or sexism is a logical impossibility under the dualist conception advocated by Chomsky and earlier rationalists (a creature is human or it is not—there are no "degrees of humanness"), but not under the empiricist conception. Here is then a point of contact between his philosophy, rooted in his linguistic psychology, and his politics.

More generally, both Chomsky's cognitive psychology and his libertarian social thought developed from a common ground of assumptions and attitudes, a particular conception of human nature that inspires each. At the core of this conception are the notions of self-development directed from within and freely undertaken creative work, notions that are also central in his conception of language acquisition and language use.

As emphasized in the rationalist tradition, a crucial part of language is the creative aspect of language use and the elements of human nature which make it essential to our lives. The use of language is creative in the sense that it lies beyond the bounds of mechanical explanation. It is free from control by identifiable stimuli of the behaviorist type, novel and innovative, appropriate to situations, coherent, and engendering in our minds new thoughts and ideas. Normal use of language can be distinguished from the ravings of the insane or the output of a computer with a random element. This is then a typical case of free rule-governed behavior, which is not realizable by even the most complex automata, hence it cannot be accounted for by any empiricist theory, least of all by radical behaviorism, an extreme form of empiricism.

It is reasonable to think that this essence of language is also essentially true of other dimensions of human behavior. Humans, then, are not the malleable and hapless product of either the invisible hand of the market or the blind forces of history. Rather, they are richly endowed biological organisms constrained by their own built-in capacities and should not be restrained by external controls. Moral constraints can spring only from within in a tenable naturalistic ethics.

It should be no surprise that Chomsky has always vehemently opposed the empiricist assumptions of the intelligentsia (the blank slate model) and has always passionately advocated the responsibility of intellectuals, and more generally the responsibility of human agents who are presumably endowed with an innate moral faculty, as opposed to nonhuman animals. This is at the root of his egalitarianism and his uncompromising rejection of the elitist attitudes of both capitalist liberals and noncapitalist Bolsheviks, which for him have much in common. He agrees with Bakunin that "liberty without socialism is privilege, injustice; socialism without liberty is slavery and brutality." A society partitioned into a minority of privileged leaders and a majority of dispossessed followers will always fall short on the scale of justice. Moreover, social democracy is not likely to lead to true socialism, just as the Leninists argued, and Bolshevism could never lead to true democracy, just as the social democrats argued.

Chomsky advocates libertarian socialism, and more precisely a socialist anarchism based on his perceptions of human nature. His understanding of human needs leads to a vision of a future society based on individual self-realization in solidarity with others, rather than liberal acquisitiveness and wage slavery, and on the common appropriation of capital required for economic democracy rather than capitalist private expropriation. The appropriate strategy would produce a popular cultural transformation, rather than an elitist political coup, and would be organized as an industrial syndicalism. The guiding principle has been reiterated to the point of cliché: "From each according to his abilities, to each according to his needs." (See the last two chapters of *For Reasons of State* and "Equality" in the *Chomsky Reader*.)

Unlike other anarchists, Chomsky has spent little time speculating about his vision of a future society. His work has centered on analyzing the nature of power and oppression in the world in which we live. In a society that has attained a certain degree of democracy the people rule, at least in principle, but in present-day societies the actual power of making decisions over central areas of life is in the hands of a few. This fact has large-scale effects throughout the social structure; in other words, the people's democracy is undermined by the overarching oligarchy of the privileged.

It is immediately obvious that there are two ways of resolving the tension: in favor of the few or in favor of the many. The only way to resolve the tension in favor of the many would then involve a libertarian extension of democracy to the economic realm, or socialist anarchism. A way to resolve the tension in favor of the few is by eliminating public interference from the exercise of power. In today's advanced industrial societies the problem is typically solved by measures which reduce democratic political structures to hollow frauds. As Chomsky shows, ideological institutions channel thoughts and attitudes within acceptable bounds, deflecting any potential challenge to established privilege before it can take form and gather strength. This is thought control, as conducted through the elite-controlled media and related elements of the ruling intellectual culture. (See *Necessary Illusions* and *Manufacturing Consent*.)

Thousands of pages of Chomsky's nontechnical writings are dedicated to applying this interpretation to foreign policy. His choice reflects an ethical judgment. Even if the United States were responsible for only a small percent of the violence in the world, an American citizen would be responsible primarily for that small percent.

However, the terror and violence carried out by the U.S. government happens to be the largest component of international terror. This is Chomsky's second reason for concentrating on the foreign policy of the U.S. government. The impact of U.S. foreign policy on millions of people throughout the world is enormous, and furthermore these policies substantially increase the probability of conflict and catastrophe. In addition, he feels that while many Americans do excellent and important work concerning crucial domestic issues, very few concern themselves in the same way and with the same depth of commitment to foreign policy issues. There are also personal factors involved such as his gifts and limitations, his class background, his training, his interests and preferences, and his place in the society.

In his critical analysis Chomsky is basically concerned with two major and interrelated themes. One is the subservient role that elite intellectuals have often had toward established power, especially toward their own state. The other is the specific contribution of the American intelligentsia (which he called the "new mandarins" of his first nontechnical book) to the untrammeled exercise of U.S. power.

The reasons that he has spent considerable time and effort on the role of intellectuals in modern industrial society are basically two. One reflects a judgment of importance, by the criteria already mentioned; another is simply that these are the circles in which he lives and works. These considerations have led him to concentrate on how ideological institutions, such as schools, the media, and journals of opinion, serve to indoctrinate and control the population. The intelligentsia have become, in the modern era, a kind of "secular priesthood." Although this term was arbitrarily restricted by Isaiah Berlin to the commissars of the old USSR, most intellectuals in most societies are apologists for the dominant institutions of power.

Chomsky has become an accomplished master of insightful political analysis; few people have been more consistently enlightening. He has sought to "discover the institutional and other facts that block insight and understanding in crucial areas of our lives and ask why they are so effective" (preface to *Knowledge of Language*). A comparison with Marx may be useful here. If Marx was the pioneering theoretician and analyst of the nature of mid-nineteenth-century capitalism, Chomsky is the pioneering theoretician and analyst of the ideological underpinnings of the capitalist global system of over a century later. Since Chomsky has learned from the work of Marx and later thinkers (such as Freud), it is reasonable to conclude that Chomsky's analysis is more comprehensive. Much of what has happened in the last century escaped Marx's expectations. Although Marx did see the revolutionary more as a frustrated producer than a dissatisfied consumer, it is Chomsky who has given new meaning and wider application to the producer's "instinct" for freedom and creativity, or the "species character" on which Marx based his critique of alienated labor.

Since the 1960s, Chomsky has been one of the foremost critics of the institutions and policies of the most powerful empires in history and of its client states. The strength of the evidence that he has gathered and the force of his argumentation are without parallel in the history of class struggle and have been as painful to the powerful and privileged as they have been rewarding to those sharing his sense of moral responsibility. Confirmation of the powerful effect of his work comes from the range of reactions it has triggered, including his name on President Nixon's "enemies' list." Perhaps the most direct evidence of his impact is provided by the international campaign of derogations and vilification mounted against him, both at home and abroad. When he has not been slandered, he has been ignored, whether in journalistic political commentary or in the writings of academics and other "professional experts," particularly in his own country.

Bibliography

Chomsky, Noam. *American Power and the New Mandarins*. New York: Pantheon Books, 1969.

———. *The Chomsky Reader*, James Peck, ed. New York: Pantheon Books, 1987.

————. *Chronicles of Dissent*. Monroe, ME: Common Courage Press, 1992.

————. *Deterring Democracy*. London: Verso, 1991.

————. *The Fateful Triangle: The United States, Israel and the Palestinians*. Boston: South End Press, 1983.

————. *For Reasons of State*. New York: Pantheon, 1973.

————. Interview, by Charles Young. *The Rolling Stone*, May 28, 1992, pp. 42–43+.

————. *Knowledge of Language: Its Nature, Origin, and Use*. New York: Praeger, 1986.

————. *Language and Politics*, C. P. Otero, ed. Montreal: Black Rose, 1989.

————. *Letters from Lexington: Reflections on Propaganda*. Monroe, ME: Common Courage Press, 1993.

————. *Language and Problems of Knowledge: The Managua Lectures*. Cambridge, MA: MIT Press, 1988.

————. *Necessary Illusions: Thought Control in Democratic Societies*. Boston: South End Press, 1989.

————. *On Power and Ideology: The Managua Lectures*. Boston: South End Press, 1987.

————. *The Prosperous Few and the Restless Many*. Berkeley, CA: Odonian Press, 1993.

————. *Radical Priorities*, C. P. Otero, ed. Montreal: Black Rose, 1984 [1981].

————. *Towards the New Cold War*. New York: Pantheon Books, 1981.

————. *Turning the Tide: U.S. Intervention in Central America and the Struggle for Peace*. Boston: South End Press, 1985.

————. *What Uncle Sam Really Wants*. Berkeley: Odonian Press, 1992.

————. *Year 501: The Conquest Continues*. Boston: South End Press, 1992.

Chomsky, Noam, and Edward Herman. *Manufacturing Consent: The Political Economy of the Mass Media*. New York: Pantheon Books, 1988.

George, Alexander, ed. *Reflections on Chomsky*. London: Basil Blackwell, 1988.

Jacoby, Russell. "The Responsibility of Intellectuals?" *Grand Street* 8 (Summer 1989): 185–95.

"Noam Chomsky: Manufacturing Consent" (film). Part one: 95 mins; part two: 70 mins. Canada: Necessary Illusions/Film Board of Canada 1992.

Parini, Jay. "Noam Is an Island," *Mother Jones* 14 (Oct. 1988): 36–41.

Salkie, Raphael. *The Chomsky Update: Linguistics and Politics*. London: Unwin Hyman, 1990.

Carlos P. Otero

ANGELA DAVIS (1944–   )

African-American communist, feminist, social activist

As a sixties radical and an African-American communist, Angela Davis captured hearts and minds nationally and internationally. She became the most famous political fugitive of the United States when she was placed on the FBI's Ten-Most-Wanted list charged with murder, kidnapping, and conspiracy in the summer of 1970. The charges stemmed from an attempt by seventeen-year-old Jonathan Jackson to rescue two prisoners from a San Rafael, California, courthouse. In the process, the judge died, the prosecutor was wounded, and both the prisoners and Jonathan were killed. An FBI investigation of the weapons used by Jonathan found that some had been legally purchased by Angela Davis. There was a nationwide dragnet for her as an accomplice in what was described as a "terrorist" takeover of the courthouse.

Angela had been passionate earlier about her prison support work and its significance for the liberation struggle. As she observed in her autobiography, "under the hostile glares of jail guards I became convinced that there were impending explosions behind the walls, and that if we did not begin to build a support movement for our sisters and brothers in prison we were no revolutionaries at all."

A close relationship had developed between Angela and Jonathan and his family when Angela worked to raise public consciousness about his brother, George Jackson. George was one of the most prominent of the Soledad brothers, and a close ally of Angela's, because of his revolutionary writings and challenges to unjust prison practices. George was a perfect example of racism in the criminal justice system. He had been arrested at age eighteen for being in a car while, unknown to him, an acquaintance robbed a service station of seventy dollars. When Angela first heard of his case, he was then serving the tenth year of a one year to life sentence. George Jackson, along with his prison comrades, Fleeta Drumgo, and John Cluchette, became known as the Soledad brothers.

At George's suggestion, she had incorporated his talented brother in prison solidarity work. Jonathan sometimes served as her bodyguard. Like everyone in the support group, she was stunned by the events at the courthouse. She felt that this would give an excuse to police authorities, who had been harassing her and other black revolutionaries, to claim her guilt, smear her name, and perhaps kill her. She went underground so that she could live to tell her side of the story.

She eluded FBI agents for two long months. It seemed like ages for her political allies and many ordinary people who viewed her as a victim of a governmental conspiracy. She was finally arrested and faced the possibility of the death penalty. This was before an unrelated California State legislative initiative eliminated the death penalty while she was imprisoned. The eyes of the world were on her as a political prisoner.

This was the historical period a little more than a decade after Senator Joseph McCarthy had led a vicious campaign to weed out suspected communists from public life. Many public officials in the sixties and seventies still waged political attacks against registered Communist party members and black radicals using laws, intelligence agencies like the FBI, and local police authorities to harass and even murder radicals. Angela had already felt the sting of then-Governor Ronald Reagan when he led a campaign to fire her from

FREE ANGELA DAVIS NOW!

NEW YORK COMMITTEE TO FREE ANGELA DAVIS · 29 WEST 15th ST. · 7th FLOOR
NEW YORK, N. Y. 10011 · 929 2010

Angela Davis. *Source*: Yanker Collection, Library of Congress

UCLA because she was a communist. She mobilized many academics who viewed this as an issue of academic freedom, and temporarily retained her job, but she was finally fired by the Board of Regents because of her support for the Soledad brothers.

Hate mail, bomb threats, harassing phone calls, and shoot-outs between political rivals and with the police dominated black radical politics just before the court takeover. This political climate led her and many other activists to legally purchase guns for protection.

Print and electronic media flashed pictures of her as dangerous and armed. Her image as a black communist with a gun loomed in the establishment media's imagination. President Richard Nixon fueled this fiery image by labeling her a "terrorist."

Angela became a symbol of African-American pride and revolutionary activism. Angela Davis Defense Committees were organized nationally and internationally by communists, progressive forces, and neighborhood community workers. The chant "free Angela Davis and all political prisoners" rang out at solidarity rallies throughout the world.

After twenty-two months of hiding, imprisonment, and trial, Angela was acquitted of all charges by a majority white jury on June 4, 1972.

The seeds of Angela's political commitments were present in her childhood years. Her parents, particularly her mother, were politically involved in the Civil Rights movement. Her mother had been politically active even in the 1930s and 1940s. Angela, as a child growing up in fairly middle-class but segregated circumstances in Birmingham, Alabama, was keenly conscious of racism and violence against black people by vigilante whites and police. Her neighborhood was referred to as "dynamite hill" because of the many bombings against her African-American community.

Angela's first encounter with socialist thought occurred when she was fifteen, while attending a Greenwich Village prep school as a visiting teenager. For the first time her high school classes examined socio-economic relations and the advantages of socialism as a utopian ideal. Angela recalled her intellectual development during those teenage days: "My ideas about Black liberation were imprecise, and I could not find the right concepts to articulate them; still, I was acquiring some understanding about how capitalism could be abolished." As she was exploring these new ideas, she was invited by another teenager to attend a youth-led study group with links to the Communist Party. She spent time with the children of intellectual giants within the Communist party such as Herbert Aptheker, William Patterson, and James Jackson. Her attendance at lectures and study group discussions enabled her to sharpen her understanding of social justice. And the group did more than study. They participated in demonstrations and pickets that supported freedom fighters in the South as well as anti-nuclear protests. Her own recollection of this period is one of emotional ambivalence. She wanted to be part of the civil rights struggle in the South, yet she felt some apprehension about completing her high school studies in the North as her parents wished.

She eventually went to Brandeis for her undergraduate studies. Her interest in philosophy and social issues sharpened in her last two years at Brandeis. It was here that she was mentored in the classics by the great philosopher Herbert Marcuse. By the time she attended graduate school in Frankfurt, Germany, the rebellion in the Watts section of Los Angeles was taking place in 1965. Angela recounts in her autobiography the mental turmoil she felt as the struggle escalated in the United States while she studied philosophy in Germany: "The more the struggles accelerated, the more frustrated I felt at being forced to experience it all vicariously. I was advancing my studies, deepening my understanding of philosophy, but I felt more and more isolated. I was so far away from the terrain of the fight that I could not even analyze the episodes of the struggle. I did not even have the knowledge or understanding to judge which currents of the movement were progressive and genuine and which were not. It was a difficult balance I was trying to maintain, and it was increasingly hard to feel a part of the collective coming to consciousness of my people."

By the summer of 1967 Angela arrived in San Diego, California, to renew her doctoral studies with her former professor Herbert Marcuse. She also wanted to search for, as she said, her place among the "collective consciousness" of her people. She wore her hair in a large natural as a symbol of her allegiance to the Black Power movement. She actively searched for radical black community activists and she began participating in the anti–Vietnam War demonstrations. She became one of the organizers of the Black Student Council and the Third World Educational Center at the University of San Diego. But these campus activities, however significant, did not satisfy Angela's desire to be part of the black liberation struggle.

Although Angela's contemporary image has been that of a radical public speaker who "tells it like it is," she spent considerable time learning the lessons of mass organizing and grounding herself in an activist collective during the 1960s. She felt that she had to be part of a political collective or she would float from activity to activity. Angela did not immediately see the Communist Party USA (CPUSA) as the context for her collective work, although she is often presented in the literature as a product solely of the CPUSA. She recalled in her autobiography that her international experiences had exposed her to criticisms of Communist party formations. This may have been one source of her hesitancy. She also knew that it would be a big decision to join such an officially reviled group.

In 1967 she became a member of a Los Angeles collective that called itself the Black Panther party, although it was unrelated to the Black Panther party for Self-Defense that was led by Huey Newton. Tensions between the two organizations began to fragment the collective. At the suggestion of James Forman (1*), a leader of the Student Nonviolent Coordinating Committee (SNCC), Angela and others assumed the leadership of the Los Angeles wing of SNCC. Some of her most serious organizing experiences occurred during this period. Her understanding of the contradictions within the Black Power movement also grew. She and many other progressives had ideological, political, and work-style differences with other members of the group. Most of these critics (including Angela) eventually left SNCC. Angela was particularly chagrined that a SNCC representative was apprehensive about registered Communists being associated with SNCC. She later acknowledged that she needed to be a member of a disciplined revolutionary party. Ad-hoc groups were too unstable to make long-term change.

In July 1968 Angela joined the Communist party. Participating in the Che Lumumba Club, a black collective of the Communist Party USA, she was influenced by people like Charlene Mitchell, who founded and led the club, and Franklin and Kendra Alexandra, as well as Dorothy Healey (*), a noted white communist. Che Lumumba members focused their energies on community uprisings against police brutality as a way of building mass consciousness. The most visible contradictions were between the criminal justice system and the black community. Angela and other Che Lumumba members worked to raise political consciousness and to organize people by leafleting, door-to-door mobilizing, public speaking, publishing radical publications, and creating a liberation school.

This was a period of repression, led by the FBI, local police, and undercover agents, against black radical groups. Not only were militant individuals in the Panthers forced into shoot-outs with police, but revelations during the 1980s revealed that this campaign, under the code name COINTELPRO, was designed and led by the FBI to destroy the burgeoning radical organizations in the black community.

After her lengthy trial in 1972, Angela moved to the Bay Area of California and focused on completing her autobiography. She did not do this to magnify herself as a unique person: "I attempted to utilize the autobiographical genre to evaluate my life in accordance with what I consider to be the political significance of my experiences."

In the mid-seventies and eighties she spent considerable time nationally and internationally speaking about social justice, capitalism, and imperialism. Her political work style, which got little publicity, has been to organize study groups on campuses and in prison settings. In 1980 and 1984 she ran on the CPUSA electoral ticket for vice president of the United States.

During the 1980s, she was a revered radical but was viewed warily by some African-American activists because of her political allegiance to Marxism. She answered this concern in the popular African-American woman's magazine *Essence*: "The notion that to be a communist is to be associated with European ideas is, unfortunately, used against the interests of Black people, because even though as African-Americans we should affirm our cultural heritage, at the same time we should be aware of the kind of system that oppresses us. If Marxism helps us to recognize how it is we're being oppressed, then certainly we should make use of that" ("Davis Talking Tough," Aug. 1986).

In her academic life, she was awarded honorary doctoral degrees from Lenin University in what was then the Soviet Union and the Doctor of Political Science from the University of Leipzig, Germany. She was a professor of philosophy at Moscow University and of political science at Havana University in Cuba. She was also a lecturer at a variety of leading California schools such as Claremont College (1975); Stanford University (1976); California College of the Arts and Crafts (1983–1985); University of California at Santa Cruz (1984); and San Francisco State University (beginning in 1978 and continuing for many years). By 1993, she was a full professor at the University of California at Santa Cruz.

If one is to understand this extraordinary young woman of the sixties, one must appreciate that her history emerged from the struggle of her people and her effort to be loyal to their cause. By the mid-seventies the women's movement, particularly the feminist debate within the academy, was a prominent forum for intellectual struggle. She wrote two important books that projected new conceptual angles into the debate in the eighties. *Women, Race and Class* presented an insightful history on the intersection of these factors and their implications for forging a stronger women's movement. Using women's activism in historical moments, she demonstrated the ways that race and class separation weakens and distorts the challenge to capitalism. Her later book, *Women, Culture and Politics*, offered further insights. One especially interesting analysis by Angela is the contradiction that emerged between Western and Third World women at the International Decade of Women conference in 1985. White feminists were seeking to place on the international agenda one of the more brutal aspects of growing up female in some African countries, genital mutilation. The primacy of this issue as a way of defining the political reality of African women was challenged by Egyptian women while Angela visited their country. Angela's internal intellectual debate between the reality of this crime against women and understanding why her intellectual counterparts viewed imperialism as the primary contradiction is informative both personally and politically. Angela has not been afraid of questioning herself and exploring self-criticism. Yet, as one reviewer of this book commented, she never critiqued socialism or communism.

An observer of her life could comment that her way of living, as a political activist and a scholar, is a metaphor for the central ideological issues of her time. A catalyst for her ideological struggle in the nineties emerged when socialism in Eastern Europe collapsed in the eighties. With the rejection of communism by the Soviet leadership and upheavals in other East European countries, some U.S. Communist party members began to have debates about the central tenets of the strategy and tactics of the Party. Led by Charlene Mitchell, Angela's earliest mentor and longtime comrade, the effort to force such a debate was futile at the Twenty-Fifth National Convention of the CPUSA. Although Angela could not attend, she sent a letter that supported change: "I was one of the original signers of the Initiative because I believe that the communist Party will become ever more rapidly obsolescent . . . if it is afraid to engage in rigorous self-evaluation, radical restructuring and democratic renewal." The Initiative, written by eighteen leading members of the CPUSA, including Angela, also expressed concern that the Party minimized the significance of popular struggles such as the women's movement, antiracist struggles, and black-led labor struggles. For the first time, Angela publicly criticized the CPUSA. She withdrew from the Party and joined the Committee of Correspondence, a group largely consisting of former CPUSA members.

Angela, like most radicals with an ideological focus and a history of activism, did not give up because her organization failed to be a catalyst for change.

She and her political allies continued their work with the National Black Women's Health Project, the National Political Congress of Black Women, and the National Alliance against Racist and Political Repression. Yet these activities did not negate her long-standing commitment to socialism. In her words: "I still passionately believe in the quest for justice and equality. And even though I may be involved in a different way today than I was in 1968 or 69, that commitment to see that struggle through to the end is unshaken, utterly unshaken." Although Angela changed with the times, her fundamental principles were not abandoned. For her, the United States still needed the radical democracy that could be found only in socialism.

Bibliography

Aptheker, Bettina. *The Morning Breaks: The Trial of Angela Davis*. New York: International Publishers, 1975.

Churchill, Ward, and Jim Wall. *Agents of Repression*. Boston: South End Press, 1988.

Cummins, Eric. *The Rise and Fall of California's Radical Prison Movement*. Stanford, CA: Stanford University Press, 1993.

Davis, Angela. *Angela Davis: An Autobiography*. New York: International Publishers, 1988.

———. *If They Come in the Morning: Voices of Resistance*. New York: Third Press, 1971.

———. "Meditations on the Legacy of Malcolm X," in *Malcolm X in Our Own Image*, Joe Wood, ed. New York: St. Martin's Press, 1992: 36–47.

———. "Nappy Happy: A Conversation with Ice Cube and Angela Y. Davis," *Transition* no. 58 (1992): 174–92.

———. *Women, Culture and Politics*. New York: Vintage Books, 1990.

———. *Women, Race and Class*. New York: Random House, 1981.

Elbaum, Max. "Upheaval in the CPUSA: Death and Rebirth?" *CrossRoads* 17 (Jan. 1992).

Greene, Cheryll Y. "Davis Talking Tough," *Essence Magazine* 17 (Aug. 1986): 62–64+.

Hooks, Bell. *Black Looks: Race and Representation*. Boston: South End Press, 1992.

Jackson, George. *Soledad Brother: The Prison Letters of George Jackson*. New York: Bantam Books, 1970.

Kessler, Lauren. *After All These Years: Sixties Ideals in a Different World*. New York: Thunder's Mouth Press, 1990: 7–14.

Newman, Debra. "A. Y. Davis," in *The Encyclopedia of World Biography: 20th Century Supplement*, Jack Heraty, ed. Palatine, IL: Heraty and Associates, 1987: 354–55.

Smith, Jessie Carney. *Notable Black American Women*. Detroit: Gale Research, 1992.

Sylvia Bennett Hill

DOROTHY DAY (1897–1980)

Editor of The Catholic Worker, co-founder of Catholic Worker movement

For Dorothy Day, the socially conscious decade of the 1960s brought new attention and new followers to the Catholic Worker movement that she had founded with Peter Maurin during the depths of the Great Depression in 1933. While many younger people were attracted by this old woman's fierce integrity and longtime social activism, few at the time fully understood or appreciated the Catholic Worker movement's comprehensive spiritual radicalism, or realized the complex ways that Dorothy Day had blended the ancient traditions of Catholic social thought with her own American radical sensibility. To those who knew of her extraordinary life and work, Day's orthodox Catholic faith and social radicalism had long seemed a paradox or even a contradiction.

In many respects, Day's life and career define a central strand of twentieth-century native American radicalism, from the "lyrical left" of World War I–era Greenwich Village to the political and cultural rebellions of the 1960s. Yet Day's was hardly a typical story or outlook. Her differences with most American radicals are perhaps as significant as her strong affinities with them.

Day was born in 1897 in Brooklyn into a thoroughly conventional American family of nonpracticing Protestants. Her father, John Day, was a sports writer whose career with a number of newspapers took the family to the Bay Area and then to Chicago, where the precocious Dorothy grew up and attended Lincoln Park High School. For two years she attended the University of Illinois, where she associated with literary students and developed an intense social consciousness. When her parents moved to New York, Day also moved to Manhattan. She began writing vivid muckraking articles for the socialist *Call*. Dorothy soon fell in with the young intellectuals and radicals of Greenwich Village—Eugene O'Neill, John Reed, Malcolm Cowley, Mike Gold, and many others—and adopted most of their rebellious political and cultural outlook. In 1917 Day ended up working as an assistant to Floyd Dell on *The Masses* just before its demise. Although Day was often described later as an "ex-socialist" or "ex-communist," and sometimes used such phrases herself, she was never a member of either the Socialist or the Communist party. The formative social outlook she acquired from her early leftist days is best described as a "native American radicalism." Her views might be described by such words as egalitarian, libertarian, non-Marxist, anarchist, anti-statist, and eclectic.

Although her radical social commitments never wavered, Day became

Dorothy Day. Copyright
Washington Post; Reprinted by
permission of D.C. Public
Library.

deeply disillusioned with the bohemian moral outlook and what she came to
see as its spiritual aimlessness. A disastrous love affair, an abortion, and a
failed rebound marriage left her adrift and discontented with social protest as
a basis for life. She explored these doubts in her autobiographical novel *The
Eleventh Virgin* (1924). In the early 1920s, while many of her radical friends
became literary expatriates or joined Marxist parties, Day looked beyond politics for fundamental meaning in life. Increasingly drawn to religion, she resisted it as a sign of "weakness" in herself. But a love affair with naturalist
Forster Batterham and the birth of her daughter Tamar Teresa produced a
conversion to Catholicism in 1927.

Day was now cut off from most of her old radical friends. She was propelled into a new and totally unfamiliar world that she assumed was completely "bourgeois" and reactionary. The depression increased her longing to act on her social convictions, but it was only after meeting the itinerant French peasant philosopher Peter Maurin in 1932 that she became aware of the traditions of Catholic social thought. Day produced the first issue of *The Catholic Worker* on May Day, 1933. It quickly became a depression era phenomenon with a circulation near 200,000. The Catholic Worker movement soon followed the paper, with over forty Houses of Hospitality providing free food and shelter to the poor in northern and eastern cities by 1940. (There were also a number of short-lived rural farming communes, which failed as agricultural experiments but survived as retreat centers for the movement.)

The Catholic Worker movement was, and is, a complex ideological blend. It has been compared often with the "perpetual stews" that bubbled on Catholic Worker stoves; anyone could contribute ingredients. The core stock was Day's and Maurin's fervent Catholicism, and their attempt to "blow the dynamite" of the radical Christian Gospel within contemporary American society. Further ingredients included "voluntary poverty," an anarchist communitarianism that nevertheless allowed for "private property with responsibility," and absolute nonviolence. Day incorporated the outlook of native American radicalism into the Catholic Worker movement, but she also drew freely on the rich traditions of Catholic Christian social thought, ancient and modern. The Gospels, the communitarian anarchism of the Book of Acts, the church fathers, the saints, the religious orders, and the liturgical movement led by Father Virgil Michel were all important influences. From Maurin and others Day also acquired the spiritual and social perspectives of many Catholic and orthodox writers and intellectuals: Emmanuel Mounier, the English Distributists, Dostoevsky, Nicholas Berdyaev, Romano Guardini, and Jacques Maritain.

The Catholic Worker became the forum for presenting these and many other views. While only a few hundred people completely adopted the Catholic Worker way of life in the Houses of Hospitality, many thousands of both religious and nonreligious people read and admired the paper or heard Day speak on her constant travels across the country. Many young working-class Catholics who joined the movement subsequently went on to careers in the Catholic labor movement, Catholic journalism, and the church itself, where they carried Day's sense of urgency about the social implications of Christian faith. The movement was financially sustained primarily by contributions from the paper's readers. Some Catholic Workers also held part-time jobs and contributed from their earnings.

The goal of the Catholic Worker was, and is, "to realize and practice the teachings of Christ in ourselves and in society." The Catholic Worker aimed, Day constantly said, to express the ancient doctrine of the Mystical Body of Christ by bringing about "a correlation between the material and the spiritual, and, of course, recognizing the primacy of the spiritual. Food for the body is not enough. There must be food for the soul." The specific means were the practice of the "corporal works of mercy" in the Houses of Hospitality; propaganda and nonviolent agitation for unions, racial justice, cooperative production, pacifism, and the like; and the spiritual disciplines of prayer, worship, and retreats. (Religious practices were pervasive but voluntary in all Catholic Worker houses.) As co-founder and editor, Day had immense personal authority within the movement, and sometimes used it. For the most part, however, the Workers attempted to live by their belief that "the only authority in a House of Hospitality is the cook."

The Catholic Worker retained a stylistic affinity with other radical movements, and Day cooperated with them in particular actions or demonstrations, while constantly retaining and emphasizing her own independent outlook. The Workers could not accept the materialism, atheism, authoritarianism, and politicized morality of most socialist and Marxist groups. The movement had the strongest affinities with the various tiny anarchist, pacifist, and communitarian movements such as the Peacemakers and Committee for Non-Violent Revolution that developed after World War II. Figures like A. J. Muste, Dwight Macdonald, and Martin Buber crossed Catholic Worker paths. There were also many international connections with Catholic pacifist and other European groups, with Gandhian communities in Asia, and with pacifist Buddhists in Japan and Vietnam. Day always acknowledged the final spiritual authority of the Roman Catholic church, but she constantly appealed to the church to return to its own deepest faith and Christian ideals. Many priests, bishops, and ordinary Catholics chafed at the movement's social criticism, but they could find no good ground for suppressing such a free-lance movement of pious Catholic lay people. Although the movement was originally condemned as a "communist front" within the church, Day lived to see the Catholic Worker increasingly respected if not valued by the church.

The movement and paper both slumped from 1945 to 1955. Most commentators began to describe it as a leftover depression curiosity. But the movement revived with its anti-nuclear activism in the late 1950s, gained notoriety with the publication of Catholic Worker alumnus Michael Harrington's *The Other America* (1962), and expanded greatly with the rise of the movement against the war in Vietnam. Day and her co-workers such as Martin Corbin, James Forest, and Tom Cornell were especially important to the thousands of young Catholics who became suddenly drawn into civil rights and anti-draft positions, but who saw nothing in their official church to bolster their position. Especially from about 1962 to 1968 the Catholic Worker was a vital influence in drawing young Catholics (and others) into anti-war and social justice activities. Houses of Hospitality grew; Day was in widespread demand as a speaker on campuses and elsewhere (where she often faced fierce opposition); and many new voices like Thomas Merton and the Berrigans paid tribute to her pioneering role. Day participated in numerous anti-war rallies and demonstrations in New York and elsewhere, and gave particular support to those who were engaged in draft resistance and community and labor organizing (such as Cesar Chavez and Martin Luther King). By the late sixties there had emerged an unprecedented American phenomenon, a Catholic Left. It had a complex relationship to other elements of the New Left and the general radicalism of the times.

Dorothy Day was clearly connected to the birth of this Catholic Left, yet as in her relations with other varieties of radicalism, those who assumed they could easily pigeonhole her often turned out to be wrong. She was absolutely opposed to all forms of violence or coercion, even when used by those who espoused goals she shared. And for all her fervent political radicalism, Day remained equally committed to the spiritual, doctrinal, and moral teachings of the whole church in a way that many younger Catholic rebels (not to mention more secular types) found quaint, incomprehensible, or dangerously "reactionary." With her long life and vast experience in radical and bohemian communities, Day saw nothing new and much that was dangerous in young people's "liberated" discoveries of sexual, chemical, and behavioral rebellions against inherited moral norms. This was not, as some supposed, because she was old-fashioned or secretly authoritarian. It was because her own life, and the ideology of the Catholic Worker, was based on belief in human existence as a gift of divine grace to be used in the service of others, rather than as a personal possession to be exploited for one's own satisfaction. Day was neither a prude nor a killjoy (she had an immense appreciation of friendship, nature, and the arts). But she saw both politics and personal life *sub specie aeternitatus* (under the aspect of eternity). Her deep piety was profoundly out of tune with the immediatist, sensualist, and apocalyptic side of the sixties.

In the 1970s, Day became less active, particularly as her once-robust health began to decline. She continued to live in Catholic Worker Houses of Hospitality and farms, and wrote her regular *Catholic Worker* column, but made few public appearances. She died in New York on November 27, 1980.

It is impossible to assess Day's importance by studying the sixties alone. One's judgment of her influence in American society will be affected by an assessment of the whole course of twentieth-century American social, political, intellectual, and religious history. Day had a substantial though variable impact on American Catholicism. The 1983 Catholic bishops' pastoral letter on nuclear war, *The Challenge of Peace*, cited Dorothy Day and Martin Luther King, Jr. (1*), as exemplars of Christian nonviolence. A few Protestants, such as the evangelicals in the Sojourners community in Washington, D.C., looked to Day as one of their inspirations. In the "secular" left, Day's name and that of the Catholic Worker have been well known and generally respected, although her ideas are little understood and perhaps regarded as a curiosity. Her autobiography, *The Long Loneliness* (1952), is widely read as a contemporary classic of religious literature. Finally, *The Catholic Worker* continued to reach a greater audience than perhaps any other radical publication in the United States. After Day's death, the Catholic Worker movement remained alive with over one hundred Houses of Hospitality and a vast network of "alumni" and fellow travelers.

Can we call this success? Most of the things that Day spent her life working for—concern for the poor, social justice, nonviolence, the honor of labor, and the care of creation—seem as far from realization as when she began. It remained true, as in a rabbinical saying quoted by a Catholic Worker publication, that "the rich will throw coins over a wall to the poor but will not pay to have the wall torn down" (*Washington Post*, April 17, 1993, A23). Most religious people still did not see the full social implications of their faith, and many people committed to social justice still regard religion as a hindrance. Day's achievement, like that of many who work for justice, may lie primarily in showing us how far we have to go.

Bibliography

The Catholic Worker, 1933–   .

Coles, Robert. *Dorothy Day: A Radical Devotion*. Reading, MA: Addison-Wesley, 1987.

Coy, Patrick, ed. *A Revolution of the Heart*. Philadelphia: Temple University Press, 1989.

Craig, Robert H. *Religion and Radical Politics: An Alternative Christian Tradition in the United States*. Philadelphia: Temple University Press, 1992.

Day, Dorothy. *By Little and by Little: The Selected Writings of Dorothy Day*, Robert Ellsberg, ed. New York: Knopf, 1983.

———. *The Long Loneliness*. New York: Harper and Row, 1952.

———. *On Pilgrimage: The Sixties*. New York: Curtis Books, 1972.

"In a Changing World, the Catholic Workers Hew to Their Course," *New York Times*, Oct. 6, 1992, B3.

Klejment, Anne, and Alice Klejment. *Dorothy Day and the Catholic Workers: A Bibliography and Index*. New York: Garland, 1986.

McCarthy, Colman. "The Catholic Worker's Long Mission," *Washington Post*, April 17, 1993, A23.

Merriman, Brigid O'Shea. *Searching for Christ: The Spirituality of Dorothy Day*. South Bend, IN: University of Notre Dame Press, 1994.

Miller, William. *A Harsh and Dreadful Love: Dorothy Day and the Catholic Worker Movement*. New York: Liveright, 1973.

———. *Dorothy Day*. New York: Harper, 1982.

O'Connell, Mary. "The Light's Still on at the Catholic Worker House," *U.S. Catholic* 57 (March 1992): 28–34.

Piehl, Mel. *Breaking Bread: The Catholic Worker and the Origin of Catholic Radicalism in America*. Philadelphia: Temple University Press, 1982.

Troester, Rosalie Riegle, ed. *Voices from the Catholic Worker*. Philadelphia: Temple University Press, 1994.

Wills, Garry. "The Saint of Mott Street," *New York Review of Books*, April 24, 1994, pp. 36, 45–48.

Mel Piehl

RONALD V. DELLUMS (1935–   )

Democratic Socialist congressman

Unlike most activists of the 1960s who became well known as a result of work outside the formal institutions of government, Dellums has been best known for his leadership role in Congress. For a time that stretches beyond two decades, he has been a leading representative in Congress of the forces of peace, nuclear arms control, and progressive social and economic reforms. He brought the energy and insights of social movement activism into the corridors of power in Washington, D.C.

Dellums is a product of the radical political culture of the San Francisco Bay Area. Born and raised in Oakland, he spent two years in the Marine Corps before he returned to complete his undergraduate education at San Francisco State University and a Master's in Social Work at the University of California at Berkeley. Specializing in psychiatric social work, he was employed for several years as associate director and later director of the Hunter's Point Bay View Community Center in San Francisco. This organization, inspired by Lyndon Johnson's anti-poverty initiative, brought him into direct contact with urban poverty and racism. It became clearer to him that fundamental change was necessary.

The San Francisco Bay Area was at the cutting edge of 1960s movement activism. In 1964 the Free Speech movement at the University of California, Berkeley, sparked a wave of campus activism. The Civil Rights movement, with its legislative victories of 1964 and 1965, was beginning to shift its focus to the urban ghettos. The Black Power movement emerged in 1966 and quickly found its most radical expression in the Oakland-based Black Panther party; black and Third World students at Berkeley, San Francisco State, and other Bay Area campuses were engaged in protracted struggles to establish ethnic studies programs. Mass demonstrations against the war in Vietnam were routine events on the campuses and in the streets of Oakland and San Francisco. The feminist movement's consciousness-raising groups were becoming well organized on area campuses and in the community. And the youthful movement for a counterculture in terms of life styles and mores had made the Bay Area its West Coast headquarters. Dellums's leadership role in American politics emerged out of the convergence of these varied streams of radicalism in American life.

In 1967 he was elected to the Berkeley City Council and three years later to the U.S. House of Representatives. In both elections a coalition of blacks (the congressional district was about 25 percent black in 1970), students, and upper-income voters provided the core of support that made Dellums the first

Ronald V. Dellums. *Source*: Library of Congress

black congressman elected from a majority white district. The district, described by *The Almanac of American Politics* as the most "self consciously radical" in the country, provided fertile ground for the transformation of 1960s movement activism into an effective electoral coalition. The 1970 election was in a sense a referendum on the Vietnam War. The incumbent liberal Democratic congressman opposed the war, but his opposition was viewed by many as timid. Dellums's more militant stance allowed him to garner 55 percent of the vote in the primary and 57 percent in the general election. He went to Congress with a reputation as a militant "peacenik" and radical reformer.

Dellums lived up to his reputation. During the long struggle to end the Vietnam War by congressional resolution he was an outspoken leader. Once the war ended, Dellums turned his attention to the twin problems of militarism and economic justice. For more than twenty years these two concerns shaped his work in the House.

These concerns are part of the unfinished agenda of Dr. Martin Luther King, Jr. (1*). King, during his brief time as leader of the black freedom struggle, articulated three overarching goals: (1) the elimination of racial segregation and the vindication of Afro-American citizenship rights, (2) an end to the war in Vietnam and more generally militarism in U.S. foreign policy, and (3) an attack on poverty and its consequences through a government policy that would insure a full employment economy. At the time of his death the Civil Rights Acts of the 1960s had eliminated the legal basis of segregation, and Dr. King's attention was increasingly focused on the war and militarism and the problems of joblessness and poverty. These two issues have been the abiding themes of Congressman Dellums's career. In his view, militarism and economic justice are interrelated because the nation's huge military expenditures deprive it of the resources to provide jobs and social security at home. Thus, reducing military spending and demilitarizing U.S. foreign policy are not ends in themselves but means to convert the economy from "warfare to welfare."

In pursuit of these goals Dellums went directly into the "hawk's nest." Most liberals and progressives in Congress have shunned service on committees dealing with military affairs. Dellums, to the surprise of his supporters and opponents, sought membership on the Armed Services Committee. This was a strategic judgment on his part. Although his assignment was opposed by the conservative leadership of the committee, he was elected (during his second term) with the help of his colleagues in the Congressional Black Caucus (CBC). From this vantage point he became a leading spokesman on defense issues for the CBC and the Democratic party's left.

During the Reagan administration, the CBC developed its own budgets as progressive alternatives to the conservative budget proposed by the administration and the neoconservative one proposed by the Democratic party leadership. As the only black member of the Armed Services Committee, Dellums was responsible for developing and presenting in floor debate the CBC's defense alternatives. When the Armed Services Committee refused to hold hearings on his proposals, Dellums and his CBC colleagues raised their own funds and sponsored a six-day series of hearings on the domestic and national security implications of the Reagan defense buildup. The results of these hearings was a CBC budget alternative that addressed the "problems of structural unemployment which affects such a large segment of the black population in America." The budget included a multi-billion-dollar job creation program and substantial increases in spending for infrastructure improvements and for health, education, and welfare programs. To pay for these initiatives, while moving toward a balanced budget the CBC proposed reforms in the tax code. Dellums's alternative military budget involved substantial reductions in military outlays (in 1981 from $264 to $196 billion), including the elimination of Reagan's entire strategic weapons buildup—the MX missile, the Trident-2 submarine, the sea and ground launched cruise missile, the Pershing 2 missile, and the B1 bomber. Although the CBC budgets received relatively little support in the House (69 votes in 1981), they did provide a blueprint of what a peace budget would look like if a progressive coalition would enact it into law.

Dellums actively worked to build such coalitions, in alliance with the Democratic Socialists of America (he is one of only two declared socialists in the Congress), the National Black Political Convention (he briefly considered becoming the convention's presidential candidate in 1976), civil rights, peace, environmental, and women's groups. An early supporter of Jesse Jackson's Rainbow Coalition presidential campaigns, Dellums has also written and lectured on peace, full employment, and the need for a multi-ethnic, multi-class progressive coalition in American politics.

Dellums paid a political cost for his outspoken radical activism. Conservatives in California and elsewhere never reconciled themselves to his election. As a result, he consistently faced well-financed opponents in the primary and/or the general election. This is unusual. After a member has won several elections to the House he seldom faces more than token opposition. This has been the case with black members of the House, who often run unopposed or win with an average of 80 percent of the vote. By contrast, Dellums generally had an opponent and won with about 60 percent, a comfortable but not necessarily safe margin. This meant that every two years he had to raise a substantial campaign budget. By the 1990s, this meant about a million dollars compared to about $300,000 for the average Democratic incumbent and $200,000 for the average black Democratic incumbent. And virtually all of his contributions came from individuals rather than Political Action Committees (PACs). Incumbent congressmen, black and white, generally receive about half their campaign funds from PACs. Dellums, however, usually gets no more than 10 percent from these sources. Dellums's reputation for radicalism apparently costs him support from organized political interests in the United States, even from labor and liberal groups. Consequently, he built and maintained an extensive network of individuals in California and elsewhere who are willing to contribute to his re-election efforts.

After twenty years in Congress Dellums has become a senior and respected member of the House. Although his views on most issues have never commanded anywhere near a majority in the Congress, he is no longer viewed, as he was in the 1970s, as some far-out Berkeley "peacenik." As testimony to his high regard, in 1986 the House and Senate overwhelmingly passed his bill imposing sanctions on the South African government and then overrode President Reagan's veto.

Yet he remained controversial. For example, his appointment in 1991 to the House Committee on Intelligence (which reviews the operations of the Central Intelligence Agency [CIA] and related espionage organizations) elicited cries of outrage from conservative Republicans in the House and the conservative press. But his appointment to this sensitive and secretive committee by the Democratic party leadership in the House was further evidence of his influence in that body and the respect he had earned among his colleagues. This was no small achievement for a 1960s activist who remained true to the ideas of radical change that animated that turbulent era in American history.

His opportunities to express those ideas expanded in January of 1993 when the House Democratic Caucus elected him the chairman of the House Armed Services Committee. The man who had once led an anti-war demonstration on the steps of the Capitol, and who had been initially blocked, in 1973, from membership on the committee, was now leader of this powerful military panel. He argued that it was time to "reorder our national priorities, convert our economy, and restructure our armed forces" (*In These Times*, March 22, 1993, p. 17). More than forty years of permanent war against communism—an enemy that Dellums had believed was exaggerated by American elites—was now ended. It was time to spend American money to help average Americans. Dellums, like most of those in the Congressional Black Caucus and the House Progressive Caucus, urged massive cuts in military spending (up to $1 trillion from 1993 to 2000), with most of the money being spent to demilitarize the American economy. Dellums promoted a bold plan for immediate help to those who suffered (advocating extended unemployment benefits and a broader GI bill), assistance to businesses, worker retraining, and a comprehensive vision of a productive civilian economy. If the military budget was cut without planning for the consequences, millions of people would be harmed. The future could be better if enough people had the imagination, the determination, and the organization to make it better.

Bibliography

Dellums, Richard V. "A Challenge to Congress," *EPA Journal* 18 (March/April 1992): 30–31.

———. Introduction to *Black Socialist Preacher*, Philip Foner, ed. San Francisco: Synthesis Publications, 1983.

———. "A New, Improved World Order," *In These Times*, March 22, 1993, p. 17.

———. "Peace, Justice and Politics," in *The New Black Vote*, Rod Bush, ed. San Francisco: Synthesis Publications, 1984.

———. "Warfare State vs. Welfare State: The Legislative Struggle for Full Employment," *Urban League Review* 10 (Summer 1986): 49–60.

Dellums, Ronald V., Richard H. Miller, H. Lee Halterman, and Patrick O'Hefferman. *Defense Sense: The Search for a Rational Military Policy*. Cambridge, MA: Ballinger, 1983.

"Dove to Head Armed Services Committee? Despite Opposition to Arms Buildup, Rep. Dellums Widely Viewed as a 'Pragmatist'," *Washington Post*, Dec. 23, 1992, A15.

Kesey, Ken. "Dellums: The East Bay's Preeminent Political Leader," *East Bay Express*, May 26, 1989.

McCarthy, Colman. "A Radical Approach to Military Planning," *Washington Post*, Jan. 26, 1993, D18.

Nathan, Harriet, and Stanley Scott. *Experiment and Change in Berkeley: Essays on City Politics, 1950–75*. Berkeley: Institute of Governmental Studies, University of California, 1978.

Scheer, Robert. "Ronald Dellums," *Los Angeles Times*, April 11, 1993, M3:1.

"War Foe to Oversee Military in House," *New York Times*, Dec. 24, 1992, A12.

Robert C. Smith

PAUL GOODMAN (1911–1972)

Anarchist social critic

Paul Goodman's years of public prominence coincided with the youth movement in America. From *Growing Up Absurd* (1960) to *New Reformation* (1970) the young were his subject, his audience, and his troops. But if youth provided perspective, his angry eye ranged the entire social order. His proposals for more fulfilling ways of growing up covered not only schooling, work, and family life, but also religion, psychotherapy, the standard of living, media, community planning, racial justice, and political activism.

Growing Up Absurd came at the right moment to heighten the consciousness of a new political constituency. He told the young that they were right to rebel against a society that failed to give them meaningful work, sexual freedom, a community to be proud of, and food for the spirit. While he criticized the present, he also harked back to positive alternatives from the past: splendid ideas and works of art, stirring acts, and glorious heroes. Goodman was able to arouse both indignation against injustice and hope for a better future.

The alienated recognized that Goodman was not a member of the establishment. He was a scruffy interloper who had somehow gotten hold of the microphone and was "telling it like it is." Some hostile reviewers were scandalized by his sympathy for roughnecks making free with other people's property, or his championing of sexual freedom for teenagers, but these were the things that also won him disciples. The young needed an adult world adequate to their growing up, but also—and this was what Goodman gave them— permission to *be* young and enjoy it. Many older readers, however, were shocked that Goodman justified this liberation by appeals to traditional values. Again and again he was described as "old-fashioned" and even quaintly moral because he spoke of honor and faith and a sense of vocation. Indeed, the values he loved such as prudence, thrift, honesty, patriotism, and temper-

Paul Goodman. Photo courtesy of Heka Davis.

ance—sounded like the Boy Scout Oath, except that he included lust, curiosity, and a readiness to break the rules for the sake of an evident good.

These were Goodman's own habits and ideals. They were the fruit of fifty years of bohemian life in his beloved New York City. Raised fatherless in a home full of women (his father abandoned them before he was born, and his brother Percy left at thirteen), Goodman had been a pampered and brainy kid. The family was Jewish, but not part of the wave of immigration from Eastern Europe. On the mother's side—and it was the matriarchal line that always held things together—they were Sephardim, from the low countries. His ancestors had already been in the United States for over a century, and relatively prosperous before his father ran off. Despite their poverty they had petty bourgeois values and a proprietary air as they walked the streets of Washington Heights.

After Paul graduated from City College in the early years of the depression, he lived with his older sister, who supported him while he attempted a literary career. He published a few stories, poems, essays, and a play. He won a small prize and even got some fan mail, but he made little money.

In 1936 he was offered an assistantship at the University of Chicago, where he began work on his doctorate in philosophy. He also married and had his first child. But Goodman was bisexual, and he continued to cruise the parks and bars for young men. Although his wife did not object, university officials finally did. He was fired when he would not promise to keep his amorous pursuits off campus.

By 1939 Goodman was homesick, and quite ready to return to Manhattan, where the literary avant-garde had "discovered" him. He rapidly finished his dissertation (which was published fourteen years later as *The Structure of Literature*) but he could not find a teaching job to support his little family.

Then came Pearl Harbor. When the editors of *Partisan Review* realized that their new film critic was not only a flagrant "queer" but also advocated draft-dodging, his work stopped appearing in their pages. He was soon relying on friends with little presses of their own to bring out his books. By 1950 *The Dead of Spring*, which he considered his best single work of fiction, had to be printed by subscription in David Dellinger's anarchist shop. Meanwhile, his wife had left him; he had remarried and fathered another child. (Neither of these marriages was legally ratified by the state.) They lived below the poverty line on his wife's wages as a secretary, augmented by what he made teaching in the night school at NYU and one summer at Black Mountain College.

Goodman's anti-militarism brought him in touch with the anarchist groups of New York. He wrote for *Why?* and *Retort* as well as for Dwight Macdonald's *Politics*, the most important of the radical magazines grappling with the disintegration of the Old Left. Parts of both *Communitas* and "The May Pamphlet," Goodman's major political writing of the forties, first appeared in these tiny magazines. During this period he also had his fleeting contact with Wilhelm Reich, which launched him on his own self-psychoanalysis. His article on Reich in *Politics* brought him into contact with Frederick and Lore Perls. Their friendship led to the founding of the Gestalt therapy movement. It was Goodman rather than Perls who wrote the theoretical portion of *Gestalt Therapy* (1951), though it was a genuine collaboration of ideas—just as *Communitas* (1947) had been with his brother Percival, who furnished the architectural expertise.

Goodman still considered himself primarily an artist, not a social critic. Stories and poems poured out of him faster than they got published. Although he had a dedicated little audience and was nominated (by W. H. Auden) for an award from the American Academy of Arts and Letters, Goodman became discouraged. He gave up trying to blast his way into New York's literary establishment and turned to psychotherapy as a way of making a living. He took private patients for the next decade, ran groups, and held training sessions for the Gestalt Therapy Institutes.

Despite this work, he also wrote. Four of Goodman's plays were produced in the fifties by the Living Theatre, for whom he was a kind of guru. *The Empire City*, a long comic epic, was the greatest achievement of his thirty years as a novelist. The book found a mainstream publisher in 1959 through the efforts of two young editors, one of whom lost his job because of those efforts. But none of this brought Goodman money or fame. Meanwhile, he contributed to such new political magazines as *Dissent* and *Liberation*, as well as to various student publications. By the end of the decade he had become an unofficial editor of *Liberation*, welcomed by A. J. Muste, David Dellinger, Bayard Rustin (1*), and other pacifist and civil rights leaders. Then came the invitation to write the book on juvenile delinquency that became *Growing Up Absurd*.

At the same time that his new book appeared, Goodman's publishers brought out a paperback edition of *Communitas*, the decentralist manual of community planning that he and his brother had written in the forties. It expressed his revulsion against America's commodity-obsessed standard of living, and called for rethinking the balance of urban and rural values, along with an insistence that decisions about technology be made on other than commercial criteria.

Goodman's anarchism of the forties began to be recognized as the "new left" politics demanded by the young of the sixties. He reissued "The May Pamphlet" under the title *Drawing the Line*, while adding an assessment of the "Crisis and New Spirit." These fifteen-year-old essays, written when he faced the draft during World War II, wrestled with questions that faced the young during the Vietnam War. At what point must the free citizen resist the violence of the state? Should moral law take precedence over the laws of society? What was the duty of the citizen when there was a crisis of legitimacy?

Henceforth Goodman would publish at least a book a year—sometimes two or three—and he spoke on several campuses every week. It took four or five publishers to keep up with his social commentary and to drain the backlog of fiction, poems, diaries, plays, and literary criticism. Although he continued to give his work to *Liberation*, *Dissent*, and the "little magazines," he could now be read in mainstream publications catering to liberal opinion. He was making money; his wife quit work; and the couple had a baby.

He became the first visiting fellow of the Institute for Policy Studies, a radical think tank founded in 1963 to lobby policymakers in Washington. After that he made several semester-long visits to various universities, where he acted as gadfly-in-residence. When the Free Speech movement erupted on the Berkeley campus, Goodman flew out to see it for himself. He quickly was invited to speak at a mass meeting. He was surprised by the anarchist character of the movement. There was a grassroots communication network, a "leaderless" steering committee, and sophisticated use of the general strike. Berkeley seemed to be genuinely revolutionary. For several months he was likely to receive phone calls at 4:00 A.M. from his "crazy young allies" wanting to discuss tactics with him. But even at this point in the movement, in early 1965, there were signs that his love affair with the students would not last. There can be little doubt that the "free university" experiments, at Berkeley and elsewhere, drew inspiration from Goodman's *Community of Scholars* (1962), just as his book on elementary-level schooling, *Compulsory Miseducation* (1964), influenced the free school movement. Yet his harping on the historical lessons to be found in the medieval university, and his badgering students to create alternative institutions on that model instead of simply "bringing down" the Ivory Tower, raised suspicions, in some quarters, of bourgeois individualism. Nonetheless, in the spring of 1966 he became the first student-hired professor in the Experimental College at San Francisco State.

Goodman summed up the case for decentralized counter-institutions in the book he wrote at the Institute for Policy Studies, *People or Personnel* (1965). This was a compendium of practical proposals for down-scaling and humanizing the Organized System. He was no social Luddite, and there was nothing doctrinaire about his utopia. "Decentralization is not lack of order or planning, but a kind of coordination that relies on different motives from top-down direction, standard rules, and extrinsic rewards like salary and status." Yet his argument was not based on a romantic view of human nature. On the contrary, "My experience is that most decentralists are crotchety and skeptical and tend rather to follow Aristotle than Rousseau. We must avoid concentration of power precisely because we *are* fallible. . . . Democracy, Aristotle says, is to be preferred because it is the 'least evil' form of government, since it divides power among many."

By the middle of the sixties the Vietnam War had escalated. Rebelling students were in direct confrontation with the government. Goodman's next book was *Like a Conquered Province: The Moral Ambiguity of America* (1966), which originated as a series of lectures for the Canadian Broadcasting System. Goodman never focused exclusively on the cold war or the conflict in Southeast Asia, but raised questions about the society that made such things possible. For Goodman, both capitalism and communism dehumanized people. He believed that especially young people, because they were not yet fully indoctrinated, realized the emptiness of conventional ideology.

By the spring of 1967 the radical young on the campuses had become the shock troops of the anti-war movement, which now included thousands of adult activists. Goodman's fellow editor at *Liberation*, Dave Dellinger, was coordinator of a series of protest marches and demonstrations. In April at a huge rally in New York's Central Park the first mass burning of draft cards took place. It was organized by a group of Cornell University students that included Goodman's son Mathew. Goodman joined Grace Paley and Karl Bissinger in forming the New York branch of Resist, which gave adult support and counsel to draft refusers. One of the five indicted for such activity (in the famous Dr. Spock case) was his friend Marc Raskin at the Institute for Policy Studies. Goodman prepared himself for a similar fate.

Mathew, his son, seemed likely to be prosecuted for draft refusal. Mathew had never registered, and the FBI was investigating his case. Paul and his son went to an old farmhouse in northern New Hampshire which Goodman had bought with the first proceeds from *Growing Up Absurd*. They talked about the future. Paul hoped that Mathew would escape to Canada, as many draft resisters were doing. That seemed unlikely, however, because his son had a very stubborn character. Then, on August 8, during a hiking and blueberry-picking party on a local mountain, Mathew fell and was killed. His father was shocked. A new recklessness entered his anti-war work. He seemed to be courting arrest and jail through "aiding and abetting" the draft resisters.

As the 1968 elections approached, Goodman spoke of a "crisis of legitimacy." He sensed a wave of disgust sweeping over ordinary people, not only the young or the blacks or the poor. This "new populism," he believed, would "throw the rascals out!" Perhaps so, though the country elected Richard Nixon. But it was not just the mood of the common man that was getting ugly. Many young radicals now called for violence to meet violence.

Goodman still hoped the "populist" masses were moving toward a new humane consensus. He tried to use his leverage in the media to encourage the Jeffersonianism that was America's native anarchist tradition. Movement vanguardists ridiculed this as a liberal ploy to blunt revolutionary zeal. His speeches began to be heckled and his writings vilified. When the *New York Times* published Goodman's little survey called "The Black Flag of Anarchism," distinguishing anarchist and Leninist strands in the SDS protests at Columbia, Murray Bookchin (4*) snapped at him, "How long do we have to endure . . . your senile posturing as the Establishment's 'spokesman' for anarchism in the United States?" (Bookchin later apologized.)

Goodman usually delighted in ad hominem polemics. He was seldom unnerved by heckling, but he was depressed when he saw the movement whipping itself up into romantic fantasies of insurrection. Goodman resigned from *Liberation* magazine when it adopted such desperate rhetoric. Aside from Dellinger (and Sid Lens [*] in Chicago), none of the original editors was left. When Goodman walked into its office, no one in the production collective even recognized him. They were busy pasting the next issue together, and when Goodman said he wanted his name off the masthead someone handed him a razor blade and told him to do it himself!

However deluded the young were about the "revolutionary situation," Goodman did not cease hectoring them about their historical potential. From the very beginning he had spoken of the movement as a religious phenomenon, in the tradition of Luther's denunciation of the Whore of Babylon. Goodman's last book of social commentary bore the title *New Reformation: Notes of a Neolithic Conservative* (1970). Once again he deplored the failure of scientists and professionals to live up to their responsibilities, but the young too were at fault. Their apocalyptic struggles to bring down the heavens were not justified by the times. He ended by telling the story of his son's brief pacifist career. His son had been modest, earnest, and practical, unlike the ambitious new cadres of violence. Goodman was nearing the end of his life. He seemed to know this even before his first heart attack in 1971. His final books ended with a little *apologia pro vita sua*. He was summing up.

His last book brought such personal testimonies to their climax. *Little Prayers and Finite Experience* (1972) printed a series of short poems on the verso and on the recto pages facing three essays on "how I think." The "little prayers" were poems he had written for himself in moments of crisis over thirty-five years, as he coped "with the despair, horror, joy, or confusion of my existence." The essays distilled for others the lessons of that existence.

His "peasant anarchism," as he now called it, seemed to lie deep within his character. He hadn't changed his political ideas from his youth. He continued to denounce the idolatry of power, the stifling arrogance of centralized planning, the intellectual anesthesia of ideology. He believed that the small things of life were most important: a little property, enough food, and available sex. The murderously grand schemes of the twentieth century—whether conservative, liberal, or radical—were rejected. He finished his last book in April 1972, but it did not appear until after his final heart attack in August.

Goodman was working on his *Collected Poems* when he died. He had published four volumes of poetry during the sixties, as well as two books of stories, a novel, three plays, and his journals. Of these only the novel and about half of the poems were actually written during the decade, but even so, combined with ten books of social thought, it was a tremendous output. Of all this, it will be the poems, a few of the stories, and *The Empire City* that future generations will read. These are major works that will hold their own against time and fashion. Most of his social commentary, excepting *Communitas* and *Growing Up Absurd*, went out of print, even though it read as fresh in the nineties as it did in the sixties. Goodman's name quickly dropped out of consciousness after his death. He could never be neatly packaged as a commodity, and his work later resisted nostalgia as much as it did co-optation while he was alive. His celebrity was peculiar. Although he was a brilliant talker, his platform style was not charismatic. His public manners kept him out of the mass media, where he was likely to speak the unspeakable. Yet much of his influence depended on his actual presence through hundreds of campus appearances. His death removed his presence, but not his principles. Goodman's solutions did not win the day, but his utopia, unlike those of communism and the brutal free market, remained an attractive vision of full human potential.

Bibliography

Carruth, Hayden. "Paul Goodman and the Grand Community," *American Poetry Review* 12 (Sept./Oct. 1983): 22–32.

Dennison, George. "The Ways of Nature," *Inquiry Magazine* 1 (March 6, 1978): 20–

22. (This issue also contains pieces on Goodman by Michael Rossman, Lewis Perry, and Emile Capouya.)

Gardner, Geoffrey. "Citizen of the World, Animal of Nowhere," *New Letters* 42 (Winter/Spring 1976): 216–27. (This is a special issue devoted to Goodman.)

Goodman, Paul. *Collected Poems*. Taylor Stoehr, ed. New York: Random House, 1973.

———. *Collected Stories and Sketches*, 4 vols. Taylor Stoehr, ed. Santa Barbara, CA: Black Sparrow Press, 1978–1980.

———. *Community of Scholars*. New York: Random House, 1962.

———. *Compulsory Mis-education*. New York: Random House, 1964.

———. *Creator Spirit Come! Literary Essays*, Taylor Stoehr, ed. New York: Free Life Editions, 1977.

———. *Drawing the Line: Political Essays*, Taylor Stoehr, ed. New York: Free Life Editions, 1977.

———. *Empire City*. Indianapolis: Bobbs Merrill, 1959.

———. *Growing Up Absurd*. New York: Random House, 1960.

———. *Like a Conquered Province*. New York: Random House, 1967.

———. *Little Prayers and Finite Experience*. New York: Harper and Row, 1972.

———. *Nature Heals: Psychological Essays*, Taylor Stoehr, ed. New York: Free Life Editions, 1977.

———. *New Reformation: Notes of a Neolithic Conservative*. New York: Random House.

———. *People or Personnel: Decentralizing and the Mixed System*. New York: Random House, 1965.

Goodman, Paul, and Percival Goodman. *Communitas*, with a new preface by Paul Goldberger and a new postscript by Percival Goodman. New York: Columbia University Press, 1990 (1947).

Goodman, Paul, Fritz Perls, and Ralph Hefferline. *Gestalt Therapy*. New York: Julian Press, 1951.

Horowitz, Steven P. "An Investigation of Paul Goodman and Black Mountain," *American Poetry* 7 (Fall 1989): 2–30.

King, Richard. *The Party of Eros: Radical Social Thought and the Realm of Freedom*. Chapel Hill: University of North Carolina Press, 1972: 78–115.

Nicely, Tom. *Adam and His Work: A Bibliography of Sources by and about Paul Goodman*. Metuchen, NJ: Scarecrow Press, 1979.

———. "Adam and His Work: A Bibliographical Update," in *Artist of the Actual: Essays on Paul Goodman*, Peter Parisi, ed. Metuchen, NJ: Scarecrow Press, 1986.

Raditsa, Leo. "On Paul Goodman—and Goodmanism," *Iowa Review* 5 (Summer 1974): 62–79.

Stoehr, Taylor. "Adam and Everyman: Paul Goodman in His Stories," in *Words and Deeds: Essays on the Realistic Imagination*. New York: AMS Press, 1986: 149–64.

———. "*Growing Up Absurd*—Again: Rereading Paul Goodman in the Nineties," *Dissent* 37 (Fall 1990): 486–94.

Widmer, Kingsley. *Paul Goodman*. Boston: Twayne, 1980.

Wieck, David. "Paul Goodman: *Drawing the Line*," *Telos* 35 (Spring 1978): 199–214.

Taylor Stoehr

MICHAEL HARRINGTON (1928–1989)

Champion of democratic socialism

"If you consider your country capable of democratic socialism," Michael Harrington often told his North American audiences, "you must do two things. First, you must deeply love and trust your country. You must sense the dignity and the humanity of the people who survive and grow within your country despite the injustices of its system. And second, you must recognize that the social vision to which you are committing yourself will never be fulfilled in your lifetime." In his lifetime, this extraordinary successor to Eugene Debs and Norman Thomas exemplified the difficult combination of qualities he urged were necessary to keep the vision of democratic socialism alive in the United States. He did not claim, as Debs and Thomas did before him, that his movement was building "socialism in our time." With a dedication that equalled his two great predecessors, however, and an intellectual proficiency that far surpassed them both, he helped to keep alive for three decades the vision of a democratized social order in the United States.

Michael Harrington was born in St. Louis, Missouri, in 1928 into a securely middle-class, Irish Catholic family. His father was a patent lawyer who fought in World War I, his mother a teacher who later earned a graduate degree in economics, "I grew up in a pleasant Irish Catholic ghetto," he later recalled, "which made the death of God particularly poignant for me."

He was educated by the Jesuits at St. Louis University High School and Holy Cross College. He was trained in a scholasticism that had more than a coincidental resemblance to his own later Marxism. Harrington understood the connection. "I have long thought that my Jesuit education predisposed me to the worst and best of Marx's thought," he explained. His political education took place in New York in the early 1950s as a member of a Young Socialist League faction led by the theorist of "democratic Marxism" and former associate of Trotsky, Max Shachtman. The tiny Young Socialist League behaved like the political and cultural exiles they were, strenuously debating abstruse points of Marxist doctrine in sessions which often lasted through the night. They were "determined, but unhysterical anticommunists," Harrington later recalled, "engaged in seemingly Talmudic exegeses of the holy writ according to Karl Marx." Harrington's major works of the 1970s bore the distinctive imprint of this scholastic training.

He thus learned his Marxist theory and history in the radical movement, rather than in the classroom. When Shachtman gave one of his stem-winding three-hour speeches on the evils of communism and reeled off the names of socialist leaders murdered by Stalin, Harrington recalled, "it was like hearing the roll call of revolutionary martyrs who were bone of our bone, flesh of our flesh." This background in the intensely anti-communist faction of the radical and trade-union movements shaped Harrington's conception of the socialist mission.

It also limited his relations with the leaders of the New Left during the early 1960s. In 1960, the old socialists in the League for Industrial Democracy tried to regenerate their youth division by funding a new student organization, later named Students for a Democratic Society (SDS). Having spent the past two years lecturing at colleges and universities across the country, Harrington was to be their bridge to the student generation. He met several times with Tom Hayden (*) and the other leaders of the student movement, trying to convert them to democratic socialism. Most of them resisted taking up what seemed to them the unnecessary historical baggage of Harrington's socialism. They felt that a new American radicalism needed to invent its own language and politics, shorn of the anti-communism and statism of the Old Left, and shorn, as well, of the Old Left's alliance with trade union and Democratic party liberalism. "They were in favor of political realignment," Harrington later commented, "but dismissed the liberals who were essential to it." For a brief period following the drafting of the *Port Huron Statement* (the founding manifesto of the SDS), Harrington advised the League for Industrial Democracy to stop funding SDS. Though he later effected a partial reconciliation with Hayden and the other leaders of SDS, Harrington's conflicts with them damaged his reputation in the student movement at the very moment that his own work was beginning to reach a mass audience.

The Other America was the product of Harrington's speaking tours and his earlier experiences living at the Catholic Worker house in New York's Bowery. In direct opposition to the reigning celebrants of the affluent society and the classless American melting pot, Harrington vividly described the conditions under which fifty million poor Americans worked and lived. With few hard numbers to cite and virtually no sociological studies to draw upon, the book described the "invisible" poor. They were the other side of America's celebrated affluence. "Until these facts shame us, until they stir us to action, the other America will continue to exist, a monstrous example of needless suffering in the most advanced society in the world," he declared.

With the help of a forty-page review by Dwight Macdonald in *The New Yorker*, the book became a best-seller. It even won the attention of President Kennedy, who ordered a federal war on poverty three days before his assassination. When an organizing group was appointed the following year by President Johnson to devise a federal anti-poverty strategy, Harrington was asked by Sargent Shriver to join their deliberations. He was stunned by the sudden fame which his book thrust upon him, but Harrington harbored no illusions about the anti-poverty effort he had partly inspired. During one of his meetings with Shriver's team, he remarked that given the dimensions of American poverty, the expenditures they were discussing amounted to nickels and dimes. Shriver archly replied, "Well, I don't know about you, Mr. Harrington, but I've never spent a billion dollars before." Harrington admired Shriver, but he nonetheless later insisted that this exchange explained why the Johnson administration lost its war on poverty. As he noted frequently, the increases in government spending between 1965 and 1968 were devoted not to anti-poverty programs, but to pay for the war in Vietnam and such largely middle-class entitlement programs as Social Security and Medicare. Social spending dramatically increased during the war on poverty years, but not for the war on poverty. For the rest of his life, despite the fifteen books that followed it, Harrington was almost invariably introduced—somewhat to his chagrin—as the author of *The Other America*. It was described as the book "which sparked the war on poverty."

Throughout the 1960s, while opposing American intervention in Vietnam, Harrington also vehemently criticized the New Left's tendency to romanticize the Vietnamese revolution. The forced collectivization of North Vietnam in the 1950s left him with no illusions about the consequences of a communist victory. In a series of articles in *The Village Voice* and later in his major work, *Socialism*, Harrington argued that those who waved Vietcong flags were forced to ignore a great deal of North Vietnamese history: "They ignored, for instance, the fact that Ho Chi Minh had by his own admission carried out a bloody collectivization in the North over the dead bodies of some tens of thousands of 'his' peasants." He later noted that those who disrupted peace rallies by waving their Vietcong flags never tried the same theatrics at less tolerant meetings, such as those of the American Legion.

Many of Harrington's friends in the Socialist party supported the American war in Vietnam. Shachtman and others argued that the war should be judged on political rather than moral grounds. What mattered was the political outcome, which, in this case, meant a communist victory. Harrington argued in reply that American intervention in Vietnam was legitimizing communism as a political force and recruiting Vietnamese peasants to its ranks. The Vietnamese revolution had been overtaken by Stalinists in response to popular resentment toward French colonialism, the corruption of Vietnamese governments, and American imperialism—all of which the communists successfully exploited. American intervention only gave propaganda victories to the communists, he argued, and secured their credibility as proponents of national liberation. He did not share, moreover, the Shachtmanites' denigration of the moral issue or their revulsion toward the American anti-war movement.

These disagreements were played out in two successive conventions of the Socialist party. Harrington later recalled of the 1972 convention, "I listened in stunned amazement as an old friend and comrade announced that she hoped Nixon would smash McGovern." It was a pivotal moment. This friend has been a colleague of Harrington's in the civil rights movement. On Marxist grounds, she was now arguing that Nixon's re-election would serve the interests of American workers and of the socialist movement. Upon realizing that this was what the party of Debs and Thomas had come to, Harrington led a dissident faction out of the party and, the following year, formed a new organization, the Democratic Socialist Organizing Committee (DSOC).

Under Harrington's leadership, this multi-tendency association became the largest democratic socialist organization in the United States in many decades. DSOC worked primarily as a socialist caucus in the left wing of the trade union movement and the Democratic party. Though it never exceeded 7,000 members, DSOC attracted intellectuals and activists from a wide range of social democratic, unionist, New Left, feminist, anti-imperialist, Marxist, religious, and other progressive currents, building a leadership base that included William Winpisinger, Bogdan Denitch, Irving Howe (5*), Gloria Steinem (3*), Rosemary Ruether, Robert Lekachman, Ron Dellums (*), and Jim Chapin. A further step toward healing and moving beyond the generational Old Left–New Left split occurred in 1982, when DSOC merged with a predominantly New Left organization, the New American Movement, to form Democratic Socialists of America (DSA). This merger brought such figures as Barbara Ehrenreich, Stanley Aronowitz, and Manning Marable into the new organization and reversed the long-standing American socialist tradition of splintering into ever-smaller sects. Until Harrington's death in 1989, he was the chair or co-chair of DSA. He came to respect the feminist, ecological, and New Left currents within his organization and to reconceptualize his own socialist vision.

The major theme of Harrington's work, which he expounded in eleven books during the 1970s and 1980s, was that modern industrialized societies were moving inevitably toward collectivism. The question was not whether economic planning would take place, but in what form would it take place? The trend under modern capitalism, he argued, was toward an increasingly top-down, command-model "bureaucratic collectivism" in which huge oligopolies administered prices, controlled the process of investment, and defined cultural tastes and values while obtaining protection and support from the state. Under modern capitalism, effective control over investment, credit, and social planning was increasingly vested in the hands of small unelected elites holding their own class interests and their own class-determined notions of the public good.

For Harrington, democratic socialism was primarily a vision of an alternative future in which an inevitably collectivized society was effectively democratized. The mission of democratic socialism was to democratize the inherently collectivist logic of modernity. He concluded that "the issue of the twenty-first century and of the late twentieth century is, can that collective tendency be made democratic and responsible? Can it be made compatible with freedom?" He answered that freedom could only survive the onslaught of increasing collectivization if it took the form of decentralized democratic socialism. Harrington opposed economic nationalization on both philosophical and programmatic grounds. Unlike the various authoritarian forms of collectivization, including state socialism and monopoly capitalism, his form of socialism promoted decentralized worker and community ownership and regionally based economic planning. His increasing emphasis on decentralized forms of socialization reflected the influence of the "green" movements on his thinking throughout the 1970s and 80s. Although some leftists then criticized his socialism as insufficient, he replied that he had learned as much from the failures of socialism as from its successes.

In his conception, the purpose of democratic socialism was to empower ordinary people and thus preserve and extend democratic freedom. Modern society, in all its forms, had too much reliance on bureaucracy. He relied upon the liberating aspects of liberalism, rather than its regimenting tendencies, to move toward democratic socialism. For Harrington, the road to democratic socialism ran through liberalism. His strategy was to work on what he called "the left wing of possibility," within the institutions in which most U.S. citizens actually lived. He organized within the Democratic party and the more progressive U.S. trade unions. He declared himself in solidarity with "actually existing" unionists rather than with the nonexistent proletariat typically fantasized by sectarian Marxists. He pointed to the Meidner Plan in Sweden and to other experiments in worker ownership as examples of a decentralized democratic socialism.

Harrington never kidded himself that this socialism was likely in the U.S. during his lifetime. In his last book, *Socialism: Past and Future*, he expounded a "visionary gradualist" strategy. He wanted movement toward democratic self-determination. "I insist that the political, social, and economic development of modern society points socialism toward an ethical, multiclass, and decentralized conception of its goal based on the democratization of the workplace and the creation of new forms of community, both within and throughout the world." Modern socialism, he believed, could fulfill the "republican values that derive from both the French and the American revolutions."

He admitted that he could hear the ghost of Karl Marx mocking his prescription as little more than warmed-over utopian socialism of the 1840s. But the failures of twentieth-century "socialisms" bearing Marx's name had undercut this criticism. Socialism was no longer innocent. It could not afford to ignore the errors in Marx's predictions. Marx mistook the rise of capitalism for its decline and he mistakenly assumed that the middle-classes in industrialized societies would become proletarianized. Moreover, his conception of socialism was thoroughly utopian. Harrington insisted that the core of his own socialism was Marxist, but in his case, it was a highly revised Marxism that had responded to the horrors of twentieth-century communism and the failures of state socialism. Harrington declared, at the end of his last book, that if the socialist movement could learn from the failures of its past about how to create the future, "then there is hope for freedom, solidarity, and justice. And perhaps there will be a visionary gradualism equal to the challenge of the 'slow apocalypse' in which we live."

He died of cancer in 1989, carrying on until the end with a full calendar of lectures, organizing, and writing. Irving Howe later remarked that Harrington's gentleness seemed almost a flaw. Even his critics attested that there was not a trace of meanness in Harrington. He lacked the hardness of the typical political leader and was extremely reluctant to criticize a comrade. When my own book on democratic socialism strongly criticized some of his arguments, I anxiously waited for his reaction. "So you think I don't know how to read Marx, do you?," he teasingly asked. "Well, you're in good company. Of course, you people are all wrong—it looks like I'm never going to set you straight. But that stuff is fair game." What especially delighted him, he said, was that his organization had learned to engage in mutual criticism and debate without engendering the acrimony or factionalism that characterized socialist movements of the past. It was, in large part, a personal achievement.

Bibliography

Carnoy, Martin, and Derek Shearer. *Economic Democracy: The Challenge of the 1980s.* White Plains, NY: M. E. Sharpe, 1980.

Dorrien, Gary. "The Vision of Michael Harrington," *The Democratic Socialist Vision.* Totowa, NJ: Rowman and Littlefield, 1986: 98–135.

Harrington, Michael. *Decade of Decision: The Crisis of the American System.* New York: Simon and Schuster, 1980.

———. *Fragments of the Century.* New York: Saturday Review Press/E. P. Dutton, 1973.

———. *The New American Poverty.* New York: Holt, Rinehart and Winston, 1984.

———. *The Next Left: The History of a Future.* New York: Henry Holt, 1986.

———. *The Other America: Poverty in the United States.* New York: Collier/Macmillan, 1993 (1963).

———. *The Politics at God's Funeral: The Spiritual Crisis of Western Civilization.* New York: Penguin Books, 1983.

———. *Socialism: Past and Present.* New York: Little, Brown, 1989.

———. *Taking Sides: The Education of a Militant Mind.* New York: Holt, Rinehart and Winston, 1985.

———. *Toward a Democratic Left: A Radical Program for a New Majority.* New York: Macmillan, 1968.

———. *The Twilight of Capitalism.* New York: Simon and Schuster, 1976.

Howe, Irving. "In Honor of Mike: Thirty Years after *The Other America*," *Dissent,* Summer 1993, pp. 340–44.

Jacoby, Tamar. "A Life at the Barricades," *Newsweek* 112 (Aug. 8, 1988): 30.

Lieber, Nancy, ed. *Eurosocialism and America: Political Economy for the 1980s.* Philadelphia: Temple University Press, 1982.

McKibben, Bill. "The Other America?" *Mother Jones* 13 (July/August 1988): 40–41+.

Gary Dorrien

TOM HAYDEN (1939–   )

---

*Organizer of the Students for a Democratic Society (SDS),
anti–Vietnam War activist, California Assemblyman*

Tom Hayden played a significant role as an activist who moved from domestic reform to anti-war activity and then back to domestic issues in the aftermath of the end of Vietnam. As the initial author of the *Port Huron Statement* (1962) and first president of SDS, Hayden attracted considerable recognition on campus. When Hayden shifted to anti-war activity in 1965, he gained national media attention culminating in his reputation as the movement's unofficial secretary of state and co-organizer of the Chicago protest in 1968. After 1975 Hayden maintained a significant profile in California as a leader of grassroots reform.

Hayden emerged as an activist after his arrival at the University of Michigan in 1957. Hayden came from a middle-class, Catholic family and exhibited little political consciousness beyond a nonconformist attitude as a high school student. By joining the student newspaper, the Michigan *Daily* in 1957, Hayden entered his first community of friends, and as editor he became a leading critic of the university. After a visit to Berkeley in the summer of 1960, Hayden participated in the Civil Rights movement as field secretary for SDS in Atlanta. The Student Nonviolent Coordinating Committee strongly attracted Hayden as another community of dedicated and sharing activists. As a symbol of the new student radical, Hayden went on the road as an SDS organizer to recruit campus activists.

The most significant intellectual influence on Hayden was C. Wright Mills, who shaped Hayden's rejection of the cold war and elitist liberal reform on the domestic scene. As a graduate student at Michigan, Hayden completed a study of Mills that endorsed Mills's thesis that a power elite, held together by the cold war, blocked reform and democracy. Although Hayden rejected Mills's pessimism and individualistic stance, he drew inspiration from Mills for his rejection of the cold war as a major barrier to dealing with issues of civil rights and poverty and for his advocacy of participatory democracy, of energizing people at the grassroots to come together and deal with their problems. Hayden also drew upon extensive reading in political philosophy, existentialism, and the ideas of a Michigan teacher, Arnold Kaufman.

In the *Port Huron Statement* Hayden offered the most influential statement of his goals which shaped his career long beyond the sixties. Although participatory democracy had different meanings to different activists, Hayden combined two concepts within it. First, Hayden viewed this approach as one of a sharing community of friends which he had experienced in Ann Arbor and

Tom Hayden. Photo courtesy
of the office of California State
Senator Tom Hayden.

with SNCC in Atlanta. Second, Hayden considered participatory democracy
as an experimental collective committed to new, challenging activities.
Through the method of participatory democracy, Hayden hoped to transform
domestic civil rights, poverty, and the corporate economy and undermine the
basic dimensions of cold war strategy. Instead of deterrence, military alliances,
aid to right-wing regimes, and CIA opposition to leaders such as Fidel Castro
in Cuba, Hayden called for negotiations with Moscow and China leading to
disarmament, aid for development, and toleration of new socialist regimes.

Hayden pursued his first objective, domestic reform, initially through SDS
and the vehicle of participatory democracy. In 1964 he moved to Newark,
New Jersey, to help initiate an SDS Economic and Research Project. This
was an effort by SDS to enter urban areas and organize people at the grassroots level. Through a community of activists with limited funding from SDS,
Hayden participated in the successful organization of tenants and welfare re-

cipients with the goal of turning them into community organizers. After creating the Newark Community Union Project (NCUP), Hayden's community launched a program similar to the community action dimension of Washington's poverty program. NCUP, however, stressed participatory democracy versus the official welfare bureaucracy and administrative management. "We developed a deserved reputation as the city's most dedicated and aggressive organization," Hayden recalled in *Reunion: A Memoir*, "taking up countless small but effective struggles against slumlords, city inspectors, the welfare office, judges, police and City Council members." Yet Hayden discovered that working outside the system imposed limits on what NCUP could accomplish. The emergence of Black Power and the Newark riot in 1967 reduced Hayden's role, and his community organizers moved into the system of social agencies and manpower programs.

After the end of the Vietnam War in 1975, Hayden immediately returned to domestic reform with a new version of participatory democracy functioning within the system. After an unsuccessful campaign for the U.S. Senate in California, Hayden directed a new progressive political movement, the Campaign for Economic Democracy (CED), which called for a shift away from big corporations and big government with greater consumer, employee, and community representation on corporate boards. CED aimed at local organization, running candidates for city councils and engaging in voter registration. With Hayden as chair, CED gradually grew to 7,000 members by 1979 in thirty chapters and successfully supported candidates for city councils in Santa Monica, Bakersfield, Berkeley, and Chico.

Although Hayden continued to address national issues on the economy, solar energy and environmentalism, and the cold war, he lowered his political ambitions by 1982 to run for the State Assembly. With expanding financial support from Jane Fonda's films and exercise business, Hayden successfully entered the Assembly and had (by the early 1990s) served five terms during which he emphasized environmental issues and education. In 1986 CED was replaced with a new Campaign California which reflected Hayden's shift to support entrepreneurial activity as well as anti-toxic initiatives against oil and chemical companies.

Hayden's pursuit of his second central objective, ending the cold war with Vietnam as the main battleground, accelerated dramatically when he visited North Vietnam in November 1965. National Liberation Front officials and Hanoi overwhelmed Hayden with their friendly spirit and dedication, and the American activist believed that he had found another participatory community similar to Ann Arbor and Newark. Upon his return to the United States, Hayden moved to the forefront of the anti-war movement with a book on the trip, *The Other Side*, and a coast-to-coast campus lecture tour. With new revenue from this activity, Hayden maintained contacts with Vietnamese officials through visits to Paris, North Vietnam, and Cambodia and organized a conference in 1967 to promote solidarity among American activists and the Vietnamese. Hayden also used his contacts with the North Vietnamese to offer unofficial mediation of the conflict in discussions with Robert Kennedy and Averell Harriman.

As a second method to bring the Vietnam War to an end, Hayden helped organize the anti-war protest at the Democratic convention in Chicago in 1968. Hayden pushed for a mass protest to confront the war machine and heighten the consciousness of anti-war protesters. By 1968 Hayden had shifted with other radicals toward an acceptance of violence and a romantic belief that the revolution was coming. When radical students at Columbia seized a building, Hayden joined their effort, viewing it as a movement toward the creation of liberated areas. After Mayor Richard Daley's police went out of control in Chicago, Hayden achieved his confrontation but also intensified the growing criticism of his stance from pacifist and moderate leaders in the anti-war movement and especially from the nation's media. In moving to Berkeley after the Chicago protest, Hayden moved deeper into the boiling cauldron of revolutionary fantasies and away from leadership of the anti-war movement. As new anti-war leaders and organizations moved to restrain the Nixon administration, Hayden battled with police and university authorities in Berkeley, drew up a "Berkeley Liberation Program," backed the Black Panthers in Oakland as "embryonic Vietcong," and flirted with joining the Weatherman's resort to violence.

After the Chicago trial on charges of conspiracy to incite a riot and after being kicked out of the Red Family commune in Berkeley, Hayden turned to a third approach to end the Vietnam War. Instead of burning out and moving on, Hayden bounced back and turned to teaching, writing, and trying to mobilize a new organization of students against the war. As the 1972 election approached, Hayden launched the Indochina Peace Campaign (IPC) with financial resources from Jane Fonda (5*) and a network of veteran activists. The IPC distributed Hayden's pamphlet on the Pentagon Papers, his slide show on Vietnam, and a multimedia exhibition prepared in his classes. In October and November, Hayden and IPC went on the road, visited ninety cities before the election, and aimed at middle America at state fairs, churches, and local auditoriums. Hayden returned to working within the system and IPC continued its mainstream efforts in 1973–1974.

Yet Hayden found it difficult to work completely within the system. Hayden, for example, didn't trust liberal Democrats and held back from an endorsement of Senator George McGovern. In *The Love of Possession Is a Disease with Them*, Hayden broadened his critique of U.S. policy in Vietnam to "genocidal wars toward the oppressed outside white American structures," most notably wars against Indians and "racist impositions" against many Americans. Finally, Hayden found it difficult to discard his sense of solidarity and community with Hanoi. Another visit to Paris by Hayden, Fonda's visit to Hanoi, and a joint trip to North Vietnam to make a film in 1974, brought intensified and lasting criticism from the media. After 1975 Hayden resisted a reassessment of his emotional ties with Hanoi and blamed Washington for the problems that continued to trouble the area.

Hayden's shift to working within the system increased the criticism that he faced from all perspectives. Moderates and pacifists especially resented his flirtations with violence and his prominence in the movement. When he ran for the U.S. Senate in 1976, some radicals denounced him as an opportunist pursuing his own ambitions.

Even more significant was the lasting impact of his Vietnam activities in curtailing his domestic reform activities and political ambitions. By 1980 Hayden thought he had overcome the memories and animosities over Vietnam, and many observers expected him to run again for the Senate in 1982. In *The American Future: New Visions beyond Old Frontiers* Hayden offered a fully developed manifesto of CED domestic reform and post–cold war foreign policies. The conservative resurgence, however, prompted Hayden to retreat to the California Assembly, and even there he had to combat criticism and efforts by conservatives to remove him because of his Vietnam activities. When Hayden backed a Big Green environmental initiative in the 1990 election, the opposition welcomed his involvement and used memories of Hayden as a "Vietnam-era radical" to defeat the initiative. Hayden also stayed away from public protests against U.S. involvement in Central America in the eighties and the public opposition to President George Bush's willingness to use force against Iraq.

Tom Hayden's pursuit of domestic reform through participatory democracy and an end to the cold war through opposition to the Vietnam War left a mixed, ironic legacy. Although Hayden had the least visible accomplishment on the domestic side, his advocacy of participatory democracy and his continuing reform activity had a positive impact. He demonstrated far more persistence in the face of adversity in Newark and California than most of his contemporary activists. Despite ultimate success on Vietnam, Hayden made a number of costly mistakes. Hayden did provide an anti–cold war perspective that enabled students to challenge Washington's policies in Vietnam which, despite claims to the contrary, never brought the United States anywhere close to a successful resolution of the conflict. Yet Hayden went too far in dismissing the cold war containment strategy and its substantial benefits to the United States and its allies. Furthermore, Hayden weakened the anti-war movement and undermined his own career through his excessive emotional identification with Hanoi and the NLF and his flirtation with revolutionary fantasies at Chicago and Berkeley. His 1994 run to be governor of California was weighed down by his great historical baggage.

Note

Professional address, 1994: State Senator, California State Senate, Sacramento, California (member of committees on Energy and Public Utilities, Housing and Urban Affairs, Natural Resources and Wildlife, Toxics and Public Safety Management, and Transportation).

Bibliography

Berman, Paul. "At the Center of the 60s," *New York Times Book Review*, June 12, 1988, p. 7.

Branch, Taylor. " 'If I Had a Hammer . . . '," *The Washington Monthly* 20 (May 1988): 51–54.

Bunzel, John H. *New Force on the Left: Tom Hayden and the Campaign against Corporate America*. Stanford, CA: Hoover Institution Press, 1983.

Burke, William K. "Solar Senator Tom Hayden Keeping Going and Going and . . ." *E: The Environmental Magazine* 4 (May/June 1993): 14–7.

Chaze, William L. "Still Idealists after All These Years," *U.S. News and World Report* 102 (June 15, 1987): 60–62.

DeBenedetti, Charles. *An American Ordeal: The Antiwar Movement of the Vietnam Era*. Syracuse, NY: Syracuse University Press, 1990.

Farber, David. *Chicago '68*. Chicago: University of Chicago Press, 1988.

Gitlin, Todd. *The Sixties: Years of Hope, Days of Rage*. New York: Bantam, 1987.

Greider, William. "California's Big Green Brings the Law to Earth," *Rolling Stone*, Aug. 23, 1990, p. 53+.

Hayden, Tom. *The American Future: New Visions beyond Old Frontiers*. Boston: South End Press, 1980.

———. Interview, in *After All These Years: Sixties Ideals in a Different World* by Lauren Kessler. New York: Thunder's Mouth Press, 1990: 61–70.

———. *The Love of Possession Is a Disease with Them*. New York: Holt, Rinehart and Winston, 1972.

———. "Our Finest Moment," *New Perspectives Quarterly* 4 (Winter 1988): 20–25.

———. *Rebellion in Newark: Official Violence and Ghetto Response*. New York: Random House, 1967.

———. *Rebellion and Repression*. New York: World Publishing Co., 1969.

———. *Reunion*. New York: Random House, 1988.

———. "Tom Hayden" (interview), *San Francisco Chronicle*, Jan. 24, 1993, IMA, 18:1.

Hayden, Tom, and Staughton Lynd. *The Other Side*. New York: New American Library, 1966.

Hayden, Tom, et al. *The Port Huron Statement: The Founding Manifesto of Students for a Democratic Society*. Chicago: C. H. Kerr, 1990.

Miller, James. *"Democracy Is in the Streets": From Port Huron to the Siege of Chicago*. New York: Simon and Schuster, 1987.

"Populist Challenge in California Race," *New York Times*, Feb. 11, 1994, A14.

Sale, Kirkpatrick. *SDS*. New York: Vintage, 1973.

Viorst, Milton. *Fire in the Streets: America in the 1960s*. New York: Simon and Schuster, 1973.

Zaroulis, Nancy, and Gerald Sullivan. *Who Spoke Up? American Protest against the War in Vietnam, 1963–1975*. Garden City, NY: Doubleday, 1984.

Thomas R. Maddux

DOROTHY HEALEY (1914–   )

*Dissident leader of the Los Angeles Communist party, radio
commentator, vice chair of Democratic
Socialists of America*

Dorothy Ray Healey already had three decades of intense political activism
behind her at the start of the 1960s. She was by then well known in Los
Angeles as the chairman of the Southern California District of the Communist
party, and as a commentator on the weekly radio show "Communist Currents"
broadcast over KPFK, the local Pacifica FM station. In the 1960s she remained a prominent activist in civil rights, civil liberties and anti-war struggles, despite a time-consuming five-year legal battle to overturn her conviction
under the McCarran Act. (The McCarran Act, passed in the McCarthy era,
required Communists to register with the federal Subversive Activities Control Board as agents of a foreign power.) Among other political ventures, she
ran a spirited campaign for Los Angeles county tax assessor in 1966, winning
over 86,000 votes (5.6 percent of the total cast in the election). Throughout
the 1960s she found herself opposed to the policies of Communist party general secretary Gus Hall, particularly over issues of the Party's relationship with
the Soviet Union. Her opposition to the Warsaw Pact invasion of Czechoslovakia in 1968 led to her resignation from Party leadership in 1969 and her
departure from the Party in 1973. She later became a leader in the New
American Movement and its successor organization, the Democratic Socialists
of America (DSA).

Healey was born on September 22, 1914, in Denver, Colorado, as Dorothy
Harriet Rosenblum. Both of her parents were Jewish immigrants from Hun-
gary: her father made a precarious living as a traveling salesman and her
mother was a Socialist party activist who became a charter member of the
American Community party in 1919. Her family moved to California in the
1920s, settling in Berkeley, where Healey attended high school. It was there,
in December 1928 at the age of fourteen, that she joined the Young Communist League (YCL). A natural-born organizer, Healey threw herself whole-
heartedly into the Communist movement's political work. Her first arrest for
political activity came on May Day, 1930, at a Communist-organized demonstration of the unemployed in Oakland; she was sent to the juvenile deten-
tion home in Oakland for two weeks, where she adopted the pseudonym
Dorothy Ray to protect her father's job.

Healey dropped out of high school shortly before she would have graduated
to take a job organizing cannery workers in San Jose. She then moved to Los
Angeles as a YCL organizer in 1931. In January 1934 she went to the Imperial

Dorothy Healey. Photo courtesy of Dorothy Healey. Photographer: Bernard Rosser, 1942.

Valley in southern California as an organizer for the Communist-led Cannery and Agricultural Workers Industrial Union (CAWIU) to help organize a strike among 10,000 Mexican lettuce pickers. The strike was smashed by police and vigilante attack, and Healey was arrested and sentenced to six months in county jail. In later 1930s, she served as organizer for the United Cannery, Agricultural, Packing and Allied Workers of America (UCAPAWA), one of the new CIO unions, which led to her involvement in many dramatic strikes.

In 1940 Healey took a position as a state deputy labor commissioner, based in San Francisco and charged with enforcing California's progressive state labor codes. She remained in the position for three years, despite attacks by conservative state legislators, finally resigning in 1943 to move to Los Angeles where she gave birth to her son. By then she had taken the name of her second husband, and was known as Dorothy Ray Healey.

In the aftermath of World War II, when the Communist Party USA (CPUSA) was shaken by charges of "revisionism," Healey took over as county organizer for the Los Angeles Communist party, and in 1949 was promoted to the top local position as county chairman. The Communist party came under heavy political attack in those early cold war years, and Healey was rarely out of legal hot water. In 1949 she went underground for six months to avoid being called before a grand jury; on surfacing, she was held in contempt for refusing to hand over membership lists of the Los Angeles Communist party to the grand jury (the conviction was eventually overturned by the Supreme Court). In 1951 she was indicted under the Smith Act (a 1941 law which made it a crime to conspire to teach or advocate the desirability of the overthrow of the federal government). After a lengthy trial she and her co-defendants were convicted and sentenced to five years in prison. This case too went all the way to the Supreme Court. In the landmark *Yates* decision in 1957, Healey's conviction was overturned and the Smith Act was effectively gutted.

By this time Healey had begun to establish her reputation as a Party dissident. Shocked by the "secret speech" delivered by Nikita Khrushchev at the Twentieth Soviet Party Congress in 1956 (in which Khrushchev denounced his predecessor Stalin as a bloody tyrant), Healey joined with those Communists who pushed for a fundamental re-examination of the Party's political theory, organization, and practice. Like many others, she felt that "democratic centralism" had in practice been all centralism and no democracy, and that the American Communist party had to break with its habit of loyally obeying Soviet directives if it were ever to have a chance of gaining influence in American political life. In time, many of Healey's closest friends and associates in the California Communist party decided to quit the Party. Healey decided to stay. She no longer regarded the Party as the fount of all political wisdom, but still saw it as a valuable organizational tool, which could not be easily refashioned outside its ranks. In the course of the next decade she turned the Southern California District of the CP into a freewheeling activist center (sometimes referred to as the Yugoslavia of the American Communist party). She became a well-known figure as an invited speaker on California campuses, breaking bans against Communist speakers at schools like UCLA. Unlike much of the rest of the country, where the Party was indifferent or hostile to the emerging New Left and black liberation movements in the 1960s, Healey worked to keep the links open between the old and new generation of radical activists. Her efforts helped attract some younger activists into the Party, including Angela Davis (*).

Healey's mother, Barbara Nestor, was one of the strongest influences over her political ideas and evolution. As Healey's younger sister recalled in an interview in the 1980s:

> Mama used to quote Shelley . . ."Strike to earth the chains that bind you/Ye are many, they are few." That was one of her favorites. These democratic, humanist ideals were the best part of what my mother had. . . . I think Dorothy inherited that. At one time we used to have very bitter arguments about the Party, and the reason Dorothy stopped and thought about them . . . was because she was Mama's daughter.

While in junior and senior high school, Healey read widely, and found herself affected by the novels of Upton Sinclair, the historical writings of Charles and Mary Beard, and other books. As she later recalled:

I had started reading Marx and Lenin, but at that point I think Walt Whitman and Henry David Thoreau had more effect on me. What I responded to in my readings were emotional rather than theoretical questions. I was developing a hatred of the brutality of the existing economic system, a hatred of the impersonal degradation of human beings. That's what moved me as a teenager, and stayed with me.

In the 1930s, through trial and error, she learned to approach workers in union organizing without preconceived notions of what they "should" believe. Often she found that issues of personal dignity were as important as bread-and-butter issues in moving workers to action. On one occasion in the 1930s at a walnut-packing plant in Los Angeles she had been trying to organize a strike around the issue of wages and had not met with much success:

What finally brought about a spontaneous walkout on the part of the workers was the fact that as they stood at the tables sorting the nuts, splinters from the legs of the tables would tear their stockings. They were just infuriated by this. It was not the kind of issue that I would have thought up to organize around. In order to be successful as an organizer you first had to acquire the ability to listen to what the workers had on their minds, and then you had to learn to articulate coherently back to them what they already felt in a disconnected or fragmented way.

Within the Party Healey tried to adhere to the democratic vision that had drawn her into the movement, though that was not always easy. She later acknowledged that in the 1940s and 1950s she was sometimes a "little Stalin" like other Party leaders. But she never had the taste for "inner-Party" intrigue that was characteristic of so many others who rose to influence within the movement; she was always concerned with the Party's "public face," and spoke out in public forums like Los Angeles CIO Council as an openly self-identified Party member. In the early 1950s she resisted Party pressure to close down public activities in favor of a purely "underground" existence during the worst of McCarthyism. And in 1959 she jumped at the opportunity when it was offered to go on KPFK as a radio commentator.

Healey's militance, candor, and high profile in Party activities guaranteed that she would be a favorite target of California newspapers and local witch-hunters: before she had turned twenty reporters had taken to referring to her as "ninety pounds of dynamite." During the 1950s she was called the "Red Queen of Los Angeles" by the tabloids, "hard as nails and with the vocabulary of a longshoreman." In time, she won a kind of grudging respect for her independence and persistence. The fiercely anti-Communist Los Angeles *Mirror*, for example, defended her editorially against "national Commie bosses" critical of her policies. "Mrs. Healey happens to be one of the very few female

Reds who doesn't look like an irrefutable argument for celibacy," the *Mirror* declared in a peculiar expression of local boosterism. An agent from the Federal Bureau of Investigation (FBI) offered a portrait of Dorothy in a secret report in 1969, calling her

> a decisive and logical thinker. . . . An excellent speaker with an extensive vocabulary and good diction. . . . She has considerable appeal to intellectuals and young people. . . . She speaks plainly on her stand on Party issues, a trait which has evoked criticism from other Party leaders.

The agent reported with evident disappointment that "her political views are too deeply based to expect them to be changed in any fundamental way," which was to say she could not be recruited as an FBI infiltrator.

Within the Left, she provided an inspirational example to many young activists in the 1960s, and particularly to women. Bettina Aptheker, one of the leaders of the Berkeley Free Speech movement in 1964, recalled:

> I had seen many women in the Party who worked very hard, and were intelligent, and developed theoretically and politically, but I hadn't seen anyone with quite Dorothy's energy and charisma. . . . She'd barge into these circles of men [at Party conventions] conversing on something or other, whatever caucus it was, she'd barge in there, and I just loved it. I thought that was great, just great. I didn't care what she said.

Angela Davis, destined to be the best known young Communist of the sixties, was attracted to the all-black Che Lumumba Club set up by the Los Angeles Party (a violation of Party policy, which opposed all-black groups as a capitulation to "black nationalism"). Davis wrote in her memoirs that in the months before she finally decided to join the Party she had

> long, involved discussions—sometimes arguments—about the Party, its role within the movement, its potential as the vanguard party of the working class [with Dorothy]. . . . I immensely enjoyed these discussions with Dorothy and felt that I was learning a great deal from them, regardless of whether I ultimately decided to become a Communist.

Healey's influence extended well beyond the Party's ranks. One young Los Angeles Communist remembered the experience in the later 1960s of going to a rally at UCLA, and listening to a speech by a leader of the Black Student Union:

He gave a harangue against the Soviet Union, and against the Communist Party, against the Communist youth on campus, he quoted Stalin, I think he even mentioned Dorothy by name as a revisionist. . . . Afterward I went over to Dorothy's house to talk over with her what had gone on, and there he was. He was getting advice from her, asking her what to read. She was his teacher too.

Healey's views changed in some important ways in the 1950s and 1960s. During the McCarthy era she had been impressed by the willingness of groups like the ACLU, Quakers, Unitarians, and others to speak out in defense of the Communists' political rights. In the mid-1950s she opened a dialogue with others on the Left, including socialists like Dave McReynolds (2*), and Shachtmanites like Michael Harrington (*). She also kept a close eye on debates within foreign Communist parties over questions of political theory and organization. A trip to the Soviet Union and Bulgaria in 1961 reinforced many of her doubts about the shortcomings of Soviet-style socialism. A critical turning point came in 1967 when she visited Czechoslovakia. There she met with some of the Czech Party intellectuals who within a year would be shaping the Prague Spring. The overthrow of the Dubcek government in 1968 through Soviet intervention completed her disenchantment with the Soviet bloc's version of socialism. In the 1970s she identified herself with Eurocommunism, particularly as developed by the Italian Communists, and in the 1980s she was a strong supporter of Mikhail Gorbachev's calls for "glasnost" and "perestroika" in the Soviet Union.

When Healey resigned from the CP in 1973, she declared on KPFK that she remained "a communist, as I have been all my life, albeit without a party." She soon returned to organizational activities, joining the New American Movement (NAM) in 1974. In NAM she grew impatient with New Leftists' stress on process (often achieved over any consideration of results), but also absorbed the lesson that the "personal is political." She developed a new sympathy for women's liberation, and the gay and lesbian movements, which she sought to integrate with her long-standing interest in civil rights, antiwar, and working-class struggles.

In the 1980s Healey supported the merger of NAM with Michael Harrington's Democratic Socialist Organizing Committee (DSOC), accepting a position as vice-chair of the Democratic Socialists of America (DSA). As the Soviet bloc collapsed at the end of the 1980s, throwing socialists around the world into a crisis of belief and identity, Healey remained committed to her vision of democratic socialism. Socialism, she declared, would be based on "modified market principles and coordinated (rather than 'central') planning to guide decision making." A future socialist society in the United States, she argued, would have to guarantee free elections, free press, and a system of checks and balances to guard against the abuse of power. In Healey's view, true socialism would consist of "government of, by and for the people."

At the start of the 1990s Dorothy Healey continued to make her views on current events known through a weekly one-hour radio program on Pacifica station WPFW in Washington, D.C. Her son Richard also carried on the family activist tradition as executive director of the Institute for Policy Studies in Washington.

Bibliography

Buhle, Mari Jo, Paul Buhle, and Dan Georgakas, eds. *The Encyclopedia of the American Left*. New York: Garland, 1990: 300–301.

Healey, Dorothy. "Dorothy Healey: The Great Purge of 1973," *Ramparts Magazine* 12 (Dec. 1973): 27–31.

Healey, Dorothy, and Maurice Isserman. *Dorothy Healey Remembers: A Life in the Communist Party*. New York: Oxford University Press, 1990. Reviewed: *The American Spectator* 24 (Jan. 1991): 44–46; *Monthly Review* 42 (Feb. 1991): 59–63; *The Nation* 251 (Dec. 31, 1990): 847–48. This book was also reprinted as *California Red: A Life in the American Communist Party* (University of Illinois Press, 1993).

Johnpoll, Bernard, and Harvey Klehr. *The Biographical Dictionary of the American Left*. Westport, CT: Greenwood Press, 1986: 195–97.

Maurice Isserman

JESSE JACKSON (1941–   )

African-American champion of a "rainbow coalition"

Of all the black heroic figures of the halcyon days of the sixties, Jessie Jackson was one of the few who endured and became more significant with the passage of time. His public service career was essentially local in the sixties, regional in the first part of the seventies, and national by the eighties. He had become one of the most visible personalities in America's civic life by the late twentieth century.

Jesse Louis Jackson was born in Greenville, South Carolina, in 1941, the son of Noah Louis Robinson and Helen Burns, next-door neighbors. Three generations of black males contributed to his name. His first name is that of his paternal grandfather, the Reverend Jesse Robinson. His second name is that of his father, Noah Louis Robinson. His surname is that of Charles Henry Jackson, who married his mother on October 2, 1943, six days short of Jesse's second birthday. Jesse's childhood was a constant effort to "be somebody," to establish a strongly positive identity.

Jesse rejected the racial mores of Greenville almost as soon as he became aware of them, although he was somewhat protected by his middle-class family and his abilities. A top student and athlete at Greenville's Sterling High School, Jackson attracted professional bids in both baseball and football but

Jesse Jackson. *Source*: Library of Congress

on racially discriminatory terms. He rejected such offers, preferring a football scholarship from the University of Illinois. After enrolling, however, he was told that he could not repeat his high school role of quarterback. This was a "white only" position.

After one year in Illinois, Jesse left the Midwest and entered predominantly black North Carolina Agricultural and Technical University in 1961. He blossomed as the school's star quarterback, the head of his fraternity, and the president of the student government. He was also the leader of the campus chapter of the Congress of Racial Equality (CORE), a national group founded in 1942 and committed to tactics of nonviolence in the desegregation struggle. Jackson came to anticipate deference as a matter of merit. Publicly, unexpectedly, and imperiously he told Jacqueline Lavina Davis of Fort Pierce, Florida, that she was going to marry him. This announcement was met, at first, with amused disbelief, but ended in a 1962 wedding in the Jackson family home in South Carolina. In time Jesse and Jacqueline became the parents of five children.

While Jackson was a student at North Carolina A & T, he discovered his dual career: preacher and politician. This was not a new combination for an African-American. Perhaps because blacks had been excluded from many centers of power for so long, black ministers, until recently, were the expected and preferred political and civic spokespersons for African-Americans. By 1963 his notable leadership of the Greensboro CORE had earned him a full-time position at the national headquarters of the Southern Christian Leadership Conference (SCLC), a group organized to support Dr. Martin Luther King, Jr. (1*). Jackson was a young man in a hurry; he left CORE with hardly a glance backward.

Buoyed by the energy of the Civil Rights movement, the SCLC remained true to the black tradition of otherworldly spirituality but promoted secular and civic activism as a Christian responsibility in an imperfect world. King's urban Baptist civic fundamentalism was not unlike that which attracted Jesse: the belief that the highest form of Christian service was the promotion of social justice, especially as related to the black presence in the United States. But unlike King, Jesse was reared in a ruder and smaller town than Atlanta, and also unlike King, he did not carry out his formal education plans. Hence, from the beginning, his handling of both mission and career reflected a rougher style than King's, qualities which may have been assets in northern ghettos suspicious of bookishly educated individuals.

In electing to enter the ministry while in college, then, Jackson could employ not only the training received in his sociology major, but also the tradition of service that almost automatically comes to those African-Americans professing the "call to Christian leadership." Jackson could not have selected a more propitious time to enter the southern black Baptist ministry. The SCLC, founded in 1957 when Jesse Jackson was a high school sophomore, represented the largest quasi-political organization of black preachers the nation had ever seen. It was regionally southern, functionally urban, deeply Baptist, and overwhelmingly black. After almost a century of near silence in matters clearly political, the southern black church found its voice for secular change in that of Martin Luther King. Going beyond simply furnishing meeting places for a variety of black local interest groups, literally hundreds of black churches participated in the Civil Rights movement on the basis of an agenda developed by the national body of the SCLC under the influence of Dr. King and his close associate, Ralph D. Abernathy.

If, as has been reported, Martin Luther King was pulled into the Civil Rights movement via the Montgomery (Alabama) Improvement Association, Jesse Jackson pushed himself into SCLC with such force that Dr. King assigned him to Operation Breadbasket, its economic arm, and put him to work in Chicago as a way of channeling his raw audacity. Instead of being chastened by this assignment, Jackson thrived. His oratorical abilities in the northern Baptist idiom plus his brilliant understanding and use of the media quickly made him a nationally significant civil rights personage. Jesse Jackson also resumed his formal education at the Chicago Theological Seminary, but the pull of full-time civil rights activism was too strong. In the particular context of Chicago, Operation Breadbasket was a safe instrument through which black clergy could demand economic progress in the private sector without incurring the political ire of a Catholic-dominated political machine under the dictatorial leadership of mayor Richard J. Daley. Operation Breadbasket called for greater inclusion of blacks at decision-making levels within the corporate structures of companies with a large black clientele. This meant, in Jackson's words, "kingdom control" or community approval of business policy in the black community. He was the uncontested midwestern "king" of this organization. Under his leadership, Chicago's Operation Breadbasket had some flashy and mixed successes in persuading a number of national food and beverage companies to hire and elevate more African-Americans than they had intended. Some companies also upgraded the quality of service rendered inner-city consumers.

In addition to pressuring some companies to make cash deposits in black-owned banks, Jackson targeted other banks for demands that they end racially discriminatory hiring and lending practices. The fact that some of the individuals upgraded to managerial positions were unsuited for their new role did not deter Jackson's determination to hold businesses to high standards of fairness in their operations. Jackson's use of news conference publicity and boycott threats often resulted in companies' bowing to his wishes. Operation Breadbasket, however, did not have the staff nor Jackson the interest in detailed monitoring of agreements with companies anxious to minimize negative publicity and eager to change as little as possible.

The concept behind Operation Breadbasket was not new. In Philadelphia, nearly two decades earlier, the Reverend Leon Sullivan pioneered the modern technique of community mobilization for economic pressure against corporations identified as treating African-Americans unfairly as customers and as potential employees. The idea of pledges of civic rectitude went back to the Fair Employment Commissions of the 1940s. Jesse Jackson, the individual, was *the* new ingredient appearing at a time of unprecedented black militancy. Operation Breadbasket gave Jackson the community legitimacy to become a voice in local politics. He entered the lists for economic justice for black Chicago's Southsiders, a once acquiescent part of the Democratic machine that ran Chicago. A nascent black business class needed more than the good word of an alderman or the goodwill of someone in City Hall to protect and enhance their interests. They needed some leverage to deal with large multistate corporations as well as the muscle to apply the boycott pressure of numbers when desired. Certainly no previous Chicago-based leader was able to generate as much national news from a local struggle as Jesse Jackson. The assassination of Dr. King in 1968 left Jackson the most audible, if not totally trusted, black voice in the nation.

By the seventies, Jackson had thoroughly eclipsed the Atlanta roots of Operation Breadbasket. This situation led to charges of insubordination and fiscal mismanagement of the Chicago Breadbasket's annual business showcase extravaganza, Black Expo. While not directly accused of wrongdoing, Jackson took the occasion of this conflict with Atlanta headquarters to resign from Operation Breadbasket. On December 18, 1971, he announced the formation of a new group, to be known as PUSH or People United to Save Humanity. This was a massive expansion of Jackson's vision of service. PUSH set up chapters in several other cities, although it was Chicago based and totally Jackson's creation. Its board of directors was a black roster of who's who in Chicago. Initially identified as a "civil economics program organized in a religious setting," PUSH had a variety of goals, among them the promoting of individual self-esteem, political involvement, prison reform, a "survival Bill of Rights," universal quality education, and greater involvement with issues related to Africa and the international scene. This agenda dwarfed the capabilities of the organization. It became the exhortatory platform of its leader, although its PUSH/Excel education program inspired some youths to take formal education more seriously. Jackson delighted in being the center of attention at Saturday morning PUSH pep rallies. These were usually attended by middle-aged working-class African-American men and women who felt important in his charismatic presence. It was Jackson's dream that these and additional millions would form a coalition so large that its power would be an automatic function of its size.

PUSH was an insufficient outlet for Jackson's ambitions, even though Jackson tried to make PUSH appear larger than its actual Southside Chicago base. He needed an agenda and a venue which would take him, with or without PUSH, quickly toward such a mainstream organization as the Democratic party. He bided his time, at first, and concentrated on Chicago politics. He used this role to gain the attention of the national Democratic party. In 1972, Jackson was the leader of an interracial reform group that challenged the validity of the Chicago delegation to the Democratic National Convention. The Chicago contingent had violated new rules on delegate selection. Its "official" delegates were disqualified because they had been secretly handpicked.

In the decade between 1972 and 1984, PUSH continued to tackle companies such as Burger King, Kentucky Fried Chicken, and Coca-Cola. It persuaded them to increase black management employees and franchisees. Jackson nonetheless felt frustrated. Nationally, conservative retrenchment of social programs plus the softening of the economy at the lower income levels contributed to a worsened quality of life in America's black communities. Chicago's Southside was no exception to these trends. Jackson realized that piecemeal wheedling of pledges of good behavior from businesses was a grossly inefficient way to solve the economic ills of black America. PUSH, despite its collective title, was an all-black economic uplift association with Baptist clerical leadership. It pursued its objectives by threatening black community economic retaliation against companies defined as guilty of racially unfair behavior, for the long term a dubious strategy for a relatively powerless group. Jackson decided to sever his ties with PUSH when the organization was accused of irregularities in financial management, including the alleged receipt of funds from suspect foreign sources. Jackson then turned his attention to the national political arena.

At the beginning of the 1980s, Jackson already had used PUSH for his Southern Crusade voter registration drive to increase the number and effectiveness of black voters. At Southern Crusade rallies, Jackson often heard the chant, "Run, Jesse, Run." During the Southern Crusade, some 650,000 black southerners were added to the voting rolls. When the national Democratic leadership failed to support Harold Washington in the Chicago mayor's race of 1983, Jackson declared his own independence from a party which took the black vote for granted. Few doubted that it was Jackson's voter registration-education drive which had led to the victory of Harold Washington. Jackson then announced that blacks should renegotiate their relationship to the Democratic party. He implied that he was willing to be the chief negotiator, with or without the approval of the black leadership establishment. He would "negotiate" by being a presidential candidate for the 1984 election.

Jackson's campaign drive went through a gauntlet because of off-handed negative references to Jews and the apprehensions of old-line black leaders that he was taking black voters on a winless, dead-end trip to the ballot box. Determined to remain in the campaign, he responded to criticism by declaring that "if you run, your friends can't take you for granted and your enemies can't write you off." In the nation's capital on August 28, 1983, when a quarter million people remembered Dr. King and the earlier March on Washington, Jackson spoke powerfully of the march from slavery to the courthouse to the White House. In the following months, he attempted to convert his "I Am Somebody" philosophy to a more populist "We Are Somebody." Perhaps millions of people of all races could be made to understand that acting collectively they were not powerless.

While the 1984 campaign reaffirmed Jackson's African-American base, it also proved that some non-African-American voters endorsed his politics. He denounced both Republican greed and Democratic timidity, urging the poor and powerless of all races to form a populist coalition that would give them respect and influence. In the 1984 primaries, Jackson won a total of 3.5 million votes, 750,000 of them from white Americans. Placing no higher than third in primary votes received, he was nonetheless the first African-American to be seen as a serious contender in this nation's presidential politics.

Jesse Jackson spent the next four years expanding his vision of a "rainbow coalition" America. By the campaign summer of 1988, Jackson's electoral program was now based on "interdependency." By appealing to the common interest of the excluded and underrepresented during the 1988 primary drive, he had doubled his primary votes to 7.5 million and tripled his convention delegates to 1,200. Never in the nation's history had an African-American received this level of electoral support for any office.

When Jackson spoke at the Democratic National Convention, he eloquently summarized the themes of his campaign. He called for a government "that's a tool for our democracy in service to the public, not an instrument of the aristocracy in search of private wealth." He hoped that such a democratic government could be created by forming a rainbow coalition. Individual groups were isolated and defeated. They needed to be brought together like a patchwork quilt held together by the common thread of interdependency: "Farmers, you seek fair prices and you are right but you cannot stand alone. Your patch is not big enough. Workers, you fight for fair wages. You are right. But your patch, labor, is not big enough. Women, you seek comparable worth and pay equity. You are right, but your patch is not big enough. African Americans and Hispanics, when we fight for civil rights, we are right, but our patch is not big enough. Gays and lesbians, when you fight against discrimination and for a cure for AIDS, you are right, but your patch is not big enough." The populist quilt, when completed, would give the group collective "power to bring about health care and housing and jobs and education and hope to our nation." This was the Reverend Jesse Jackson at his most expansive and ecumenical, blending insight and empathy with a call for a reformist coalition beyond race and gender.

Jackson's work in voter registration and speech-making notwithstanding, many white voters concluded that the Democratic party would face certain rather than probable defeat if it nominated Jackson as its standard-bearer. Thus it nominated the Massachusetts governor Michael Dukakis, a mainstream Democrat of Greek ancestry. Perhaps Jackson's major contribution was breaking the silence of the Democratic party on many of the crises facing the nation.

Jackson's populism was a fusion of his personal experience with the alienated and dispossessed of urban and rural America. We often forget how increasingly difficult and financially challenging it is for anyone from the "wrong side of the tracks" to ascend to the pinnacles of public visibility in the realm of governance. When seen in this context, perhaps Jackson's alleged opportunistic political style becomes more understandable. He did his share of self-propulsion with comparatively little money. He and the media used each other. The hard times of the 1980s, to which the Republican presidential party was fundamentally indifferent, aided his promotion of the concept of a neo-populist politics. In 1988, however, the nation was not ready for a Jesse Jackson–led coalition to go any farther than the convention which sent Dukakis and Lloyd Bentsen out to defeat. Times would have to become more difficult and the bankruptcy of trickle-down laissez-faire economics more apparent before the nation could elect as president William Jefferson Clinton in 1992.

By the early 1990s, there seemed to be an anti-climactic character to the career of Jesse Louis Jackson. Having become the largely symbolic "shadow senator" for the District of Columbia, and having moved beyond racial uplift associations, including leadership of the NAACP, Jackson again was an enigma. To the old query "What does Jesse want?" was added a new one: "What will Jesse do next?" If he was an opportunist, in this he was no different from anyone else contending for high office in the United States. Starting with nothing but himself in the late sixties and failing to develop a stable independent power base by the early nineties, Jesse Jackson, nonetheless, enriched the national dialogue about social justice.

Bibliography

Barker, Lucius J., and Ronald Walters, eds. *Jesse Jackson's 1984 Campaign: Challenge and Change in American Politics*. Urbana: University of Illinois Press, 1989.

Collins, Sheila. *The Rainbow Challenge: The Jackson Campaign and the Future of U.S. Politics*. New York: Monthly Review Press, 1986.

Colton, Elizabeth O. *The Jackson Phenomenon: The Man, the Power, the Message*. New York: Doubleday, 1989.

Fairclough, Adams. "What Makes Jesse Run?" (review article), *Journal American Studies* 22 (April 1988): 77–86.

Faw, Bob, and Nancy Skelton. *Thunder in America*. Austin: Texas Monthly Press, 1986.

House, Ernest R. *Jesse Jackson and the Politics of Charisma: The Rise and Fall of the PUSH/Excel Program*. Boulder, CO: Westview Press, 1988.

Jackson, Jesse. *Keep Hope Alive*. Boston: South End Press, 1988.

———. *Straight from the Heart*, rev. ed. Minneapolis: Fortress Press, 1987.

———. *A Time to Speak: The Autobiography of Jesse Jackson*. New York: Simon and Schuster, 1988.

Marable, Manning. "The Rainbow Coalition: Jackson and the Politics of Ethnicity," *Cross Currents* 34 (Spring 1984): 21–42.

Morris, Lorenzo, ed. *The Social and Political Implications of the 1984 Jesse Jackson Campaign*. New York: Praeger, 1990.

Reed, Adolph. *The Jesse Jackson Phenomenon: Crisis of Purpose in Afro-American Politics*. New Haven: Yale University Press, 1986.

Walters, Ronald. *Black Presidential Politics in America: A Strategic Approach*. Albany: SUNY Press, 1988.

White, John. *Black Leadership in America: From Booker T. Washington to Jesse Jackson*, 2d ed. New York: Longman, 1990.

Russell L. Adams

C.L.R. JAMES (1901–1989)

Democratic Marxist, Pan-Africanist

The gifted West Indian scholar and activist C.L.R. James spent some twenty-five years in the United States as a journalist, teacher, and spokesperson for Pan-African, African-American, and leftist causes. Indeed, many of his finest articles and books were inspired by, and aimed toward, a U.S. audience. While the impact of his ideas on the North American social movements of the 1960s and 1970s was uneven at best, his theoretical and practical work on black liberation, socialist organization, and the fundamental nature of Soviet bloc societies made a lasting impression on a select number of leftist political currents and journals.

Cyril Lionel Robert James was born in the town of Tunapuna, Trinidad, and was raised in a cultural environment characterized by easy access to Brit-

C.L.R. James. Photo courtesy of C.L.R. James Institute.

ish and Continental literature, embryonic black nationalism, and incessant cricket matches. As a young adult he contributed to indigenous literary journals and began to develop a distinctive writing style and political persona. Chafing at the social and economic limitations of West Indian colonial society, he moved to England in 1932 and became radicalized in the context of the global depression of the 1930s. Unimpressed by developments in the Soviet Union, he joined the ranks of the Trotskyist movement and simultaneously worked on behalf of the decolonization of Africa and Caribbean nations. At the urging of Leon Trotsky he moved to New York in 1938 in order to prod the Socialist Workers party to take up the struggle for black emancipation.

Not only New York City but America itself held a marked fascination for James. Having already produced a considerable oeuvre—*Minty Alley* (1936), a novel; *World Revolution 1917–1936: The Rise and Fall of the Communist International* (1937); and *The Black Jacobins: Toussaint L'Ouverture and the*

San Domingo Revolution (1938), among other works—he embarked on an ambitious research program designed to comprehend the dynamics of global capitalism in the age of the American century. From the late 1930s until his expulsion from the United States in 1953 he collaborated with a small circle of radicals (Raya Dunayevskaya, Grace Lee, Martin Glaberman, and others) in order to realize this program in a way that would relate Marxian precepts to the everyday struggles of black people, blue-collar workers, young people, and women. Breaking with the Trotskyist movement in the early 1950s, James and his associates formed an independent socialist organization, Correspondence. In 1955, a majority of the organization, led by Raya Dunayevskaya, split off to form the Detroit-based "Marxist-Humanist" organization, News and Letters. Some of the key Jamesian documents issued in this period include "The Invading Socialist Society" (1947, with Dunayevskaya and Lee); "The Revolutionary Answer to the Negro Problem in the U.S.A." (1948); *Notes on Dialectics: Hegel, Marx, Lenin* (1948); *State Capitalism and World Revolution* (1950); and *Notes on American Civilization* (1950, mimeo).

For several months in the early 1950s James was interned on New York's Ellis Island, awaiting the outcome of an unsuccessful appeal for U.S. citizenship. On Ellis Island he finished *Mariners, Renegades and Castaways: Herman Melville and the World We Live In* (1953), a bold reinterpretation of Melville's *Moby Dick* which signaled a return to literary and cultural themes. In 1958 he returned for the first time to Trinidad in order to join forces with his former pupil Eric Williams and contribute his talents to the Peoples' National Movement in the run-up to national independence. Relations between Williams and James soured shortly after James returned from independence celebrations in Ghana (formerly the Gold Coast) in 1960 and found Williams moving toward a tacit alliance with the U.S. authorities. Returning to England in 1962—only days before Trinidad secured full independence—James published the autobiographical *Beyond a Boundary* (1963), his most critically celebrated work.

From the early 1960s onwards the *éminence grise* of West Indian letters lectured extensively to a variety of audiences on several continents. In the late 1960s and 1970s he taught at several U.S. colleges and universities. Between 1981 and his death in 1989 at the age of eighty-eight James lived in Brixton, London. Many of his writings have been reissued, with *The C.L.R. James Reader* (ed. Anna Grimshaw) containing a number of seminal essays. Paul Buhle has published a helpful biographical study, *C.L.R. James: The Artist as Revolutionary* (1988), and further biographical projects are now underway.

James's unorthodox Marxism has enjoyed a discernible impact on small but intellectually vibrant sectors of the American Left from the late 1930s onwards. This impact can be measured in terms of three sets of concerns: the political meaning of race, the question of political organization, and the critique of the Soviet Union and Soviet-style systems. Profiting from his singular profile as a radical West Indian writer, James managed to make a sharp impression on many of those who passed through anti-Stalinist and Trotskyist organizations in the 1940s, 1950s, and 1960s. His influence has also been felt on such quintessential New Left publications as *Radical America* (1967–) and *Cultural Correspondence* (1975–). Dan Georgakas and Marvin Surkin report that James's writings on black politics influenced the leadership of the League of Revolutionary Black Workers and Detroit Revolutionary Union Movement (DRUM), which emerged out of the Black Power movement in the late 1960s. His writings on race, class, and politics have also contributed to the political thought of Vincent Harding, Robin Kelley, Manning Marable, Cedric Robinson, and other African-American intellectuals.

Black politics in America was the topic of a series of lengthy discussions held between James and Trotsky in Coyoacán, Mexico, in 1939. In a document prepared for their first meeting, James argued that the time was propitious for the creation of an all-black organization that would campaign for civil liberties and democratic rights. James believed that the Negro was the most revolutionary element in the U.S. population. The task for American socialists should be to encourage the autonomous development of independent organizations in a way that recognized the inherently oppositional and radicalizing potential of black self-activity. Instead of commandeering black organizations, leftists could assist in the spontaneous mobilization of the black masses.

While Trotsky was sympathetic to James's "pro-autonomy" position on the so-called Negro question, most socialists emphasized the importance of fostering black-white unity around basic economic demands. James, in a report presented at the Socialist Workers party's 1948 convention, argued against those who wanted to subordinate black struggles to class conflict or socialist doctrine. James's view that the black movement for equal rights represented "a constituent part of the struggle for socialism" made a profound impression on at least one listener, auto worker Charles Denby:

> He said the workers as a whole are the ones we must rely upon. But that didn't mean that the Negroes must not do anything until the labor movement actually came forward. The Negro struggle would help bring the workers forward. . . . I felt good. Now we had something, something to go by. (*Indignant Heart*, p. 173)

Those on the American Left who drew inspiration from James's overall approach had reason to be encouraged by several developments in the 1960s, including Malcolm X's break with the Black Muslims and the emergence of DRUM and similar workplace-based black groupings. The very fact that the Civil Rights movement of the 1950s had encouraged the emergence of a number of different progressive and anti-capitalist groupings seemed to confirm James's forward-looking prognosis. Cognizant of the powerful energies unleashed by independent black self-activity, he nevertheless rejected the notion that European history and philosophy had nothing to offer African-Americans. In a talk given at Federal City College in 1969, James emphasized that he was not merely asserting that "black is beautiful," but that black history was central to an understanding of human civilization.

As a revolutionary Marxist and subsequently as an independent radical, James saw socialism as the deepest expression of the democratic self-activity of blacks, industrial workers, and other subaltern groups. *Facing Reality* (1958, co-written with Grace Lee) defined socialism in almost libertarian terms:

> The whole world today lives in the shadow of the state power. . . . It robs everyone of initiative and clogs the free development of society. This state power, by whatever name it is called, One-Party State or Welfare State, destroys all pretence of government *by* the people, *of* the people. All that remains is government *for* the people. Against this monster, people all over the world, and particularly ordinary working people in factories, mines, fields, and offices, are rebelling every day in ways of their own invention. (p. 5)

The critic Paul Berman recalled that *Facing Reality*, which circulated widely among anarchists in the 1960s, was a useful antidote to then-popular Marxist-Leninist dogma. It was the central function of radicals to provide information to workers so that they could make their own decisions.

The group Correspondence attempted to apply James's radically democratic framework to concrete conditions in the postwar United States. Their eponymous newspaper was intended to provide an outlet for Americans to address political, social, and even cultural issues from a radical, anti-bureaucratic, and anti-Stalinist viewpoint. *Correspondence*'s first issue, published in late 1953, exemplified the group's unorthodox approach: the front page featured a "Worker's Journal" (by auto worker Charles Denby), an original cartoon, a statement by the editor ("You will find in the pages of *Correspondence* a total hostility to all forms of bureaucratic domination"), and a spirited account of Lucille Ball's appearance in front of the House Un-American Activities Committee ("In those days," she remembered, speaking about the 1930s, "it was almost as bad to be a Republican" as to be a Communist). Although James's deportation, and the 1955 split, seriously damaged the group's prospects—its successor organization, Facing Reality, was eventually disbanded in 1970—Correspondence's idiosyncratic form of Socialist organization exemplified the spirit of the pro-autonomy, "post-Leninist" politics James and his co-thinkers advanced from the 1950s onwards.

A key component of the Jamesian perspective was a thoroughgoing rejection of Soviet-style Communism, a system of organizing the economy that Dunayevskaya and James termed "state-capitalism." Their critical perspective was first developed in the context of Trotskyist debates over the class character of the Soviet Union. James and his associates strongly rejected Trotsky's "degenerated workers' state" analysis, repudiating the notion that the USSR retained any progressive features. They also firmly rejected the idea that the Soviet Union represented a new type of social system, a "bureaucratic collectivist" state. In *State Capitalism and World Revolution*, James described the Soviet Union and the newly created "people's democracies" in Eastern Europe as a special variant of capitalist development, as "the result of the world tendency to centralization" (p. 106):

> The Stalinists are not class-collaborationists, fools, cowards, idiots, men with "supple spines," but conscious clear-sighted aspirants for world-power. They are deadly enemies of private property capitalism. They aim to seize the power and take the place of the bourgeoisie. . . . Theirs is a last desperate attempt under the guise of "socialism" and "planned economy" to reorganize the means of production without releasing the proletariat from wage-slavery. Historical viability they have none; for state-ownership multiplies every contradiction of capitalism. (*State Capitalism and World Revolution*, p. 7)

Given his anti-Stalinism, it is perhaps not surprising that James welcomed the explosive growth of the Polish independent trade union movement Solidarnosc in the early 1980s, which he heralded as "part of the organic movement of the working class in capitalist society" (p. 271) at a New York support rally held in 1981. For James, Solidarnosc's emergence effectively symbolized the democratic yearnings of the Polish people. That its leadership came to favor "private property capitalism" was of secondary importance for James; the crucial issue was the fact that ordinary citizens in Poland had mobilized in defense of their autonomous interests. In the long run, according to James, industrial workers, rural dwellers, and other subordinate groups in the Soviet bloc would find ways of linking their concerns with those of similar sectors of advanced capitalist societies. Although he died just before the Communist edifice collapsed in Eastern Europe and the former Soviet Union, it seems likely that he would have welcomed the dramatic events of 1989–1990 and would have insisted upon the continued relevance of the socialist tradition for the ex-Communist nations.

In important respects, James's core teachings anticipated and even stimulated developments within anarchist, feminist, and radical democratic sectors of the post-1968 American Left. In terms of both its form and its program, the Jamesian-inspired Correspondence organization foreshadowed New Left efforts. In addition, James's writings on black politics, socialist organization, and state capitalism played a circumscribed but distinguished role in shaping post-sixties radical social thought in the United States and elsewhere. The positive reception given the republication of his most important works suggests that his ideas may find a new audience in the 1990s and beyond.

Bibliography

Buhle, Paul. *C.L.R. James: The Artist as Revolutionary.* London: Verso, 1988.

———. ed. *C.L.R. James: His Life and Work.* London: Allison and Busby, 1986.

C.L.R. James Journal. (Wellesley, MA: Calaloux Publications, ca. 1989–).

Denby, Charles. *Indignant Heart: A Black Worker's Journal*. Detroit: Wayne State University Press, 1989.

Georgakas, Dan, and Marvin Surkin. *Detroit: I Do Mind Dying*. New York: St. Martin's Press, 1975.

"James, C.L.R.," in *Contemporary Literary Criticism*, vol. 33. Detroit: Gale Research, 1985: 218–25.

James, C.L.R. *American Civilization*. Cambridge, MA: Basil Blackwell, 1993.

———. "Black Studies and the Contemporary Student" (1969), reprinted in *At the Rendezvous of Victory*. London: Allison and Busby, 1984.

———. *C.L.R. James and Revolutionary Marxism: Selected Writing of C.L.R. James, 1939–1949*, Scott McLemee and Paul LeBlanc, eds. Atlantic Highlands, NJ: Humanities Press, 1994.

———. *The C.L.R. James Reader*, Anna Grimshaw, ed. Oxford: Blackwell Publishers, 1992.

———. *C.L.R. James's Caribbean*. Durham, NC: Duke University Press, 1992.

———. Interview, in *Visions of History*, Henry Abelove, Betsy Blackmar, Peter Dimmock, and Jonathan Scheer, eds. New York: Pantheon Books, 1983: 265–77.

———. *State Capitalism and World Revolution*. Chicago: Charles H. Kerr Publishing Company, 1986 [1950].

James, C.L.R., and Grace Lee. *Facing Reality*. Detroit: Correspondence, 1958.

Levi, Darrell E. "C.L.R. James: A Radical West Indian Vision of American Studies," *American Quarterly* 43 (Sept. 1991): 486–501.

Wohlforth, Tim. "Trotskyism," in *The Encyclopedia of the American Left*, Mari Jo Buhle, Paul Buhle, and Dan Georgakas, eds. New York: Garland Publishing, 1990: 782–86.

Kent Worcester

MARGARET (MAGGIE) KUHN (1905–   )

Founder and convener of the Gray Panthers, social activist

Margaret E. Kuhn spent most of the 1960s in Philadelphia with the United Presbyterian Church, her employer since the end of World War II. Kuhn was at the forefront of the denomination's reform efforts. She was writer and editor of its magazine, *Social Progress*; an observer, representing Presbyterians, at peace rallies at the United Nations; and a third vice president of the church's health, education, and welfare association.

Kuhn's preretirement career resembles that of many well-educated women of her cohort. She was born in Buffalo to Samuel Frederick and Minnie Louise (Kooman) Kuhn, and graduated from Case Western Reserve University in 1926. Kuhn worked with the YWCA in Cleveland and Philadelphia, and later was affiliated with the General Alliance of Unitarian Women in Boston.

Maggie Kuhn's true radicalism did not become apparent until she reached age sixty-five. When the Presbyterian church forced her to retire, she rebelled. With four other people, Kuhn founded the Consultation of Older and Younger Adults for Social Change in 1970. A year later, the group officially adopted the name the Gray Panthers, an image created by the media in recognition of the dramatic and sometimes radical tactics advocated by Kuhn and her associates. In 1973, the group merged with Ralph Nader's Retired Professional Action Group; that same year the Gray Panther Project Fund was established to receive donations and allocate funds. Lest this sound unduly bureaucratic, Kuhn declared in 1977 that she financed herself and the Gray Panthers' many activities "by hustling." (Her modest lifestyle was supported by lecture fees, royalties, and a pension; she shared a home with several younger people.)

By 1985 there were more than 120 Gray Panther chapters (or "networks," as the group prefers) in forty states. Membership had grown to 60,000 by the mid-1980s. A national convention is held every two years; a central office helps to coordinate media watches, prepare congressional testimonies, publish and distribute educational materials, and file lawsuits in the public interest. Much of the real action takes place, however, at the grassroots level. Local chapters enjoy genuine autonomy in identifying issues. Members (25 percent of whom are under age thirty) expose abuses in nursing homes, demonstrate against housing and labor practices unfair to older and younger people, and rally around other neighborhood concerns. Calls for intergenerational justice matter greatly. Probably the Gray Panthers' most publicized moment featured guerrilla-theatre skits at an AMA convention in Chicago in 1974 to protest America's health-care industry.

Three factors propelled Maggie Kuhn into the limelight, making her one of this nation's most quotable and admired radicals. First, Kuhn was outraged about losing her job on account of age, when it was clear that she still was physically and mentally competent, not to mention enormously productive. She felt that too many Americans—including people her age—accepted negative images of what it means to grow older. As she told a reporter for the *Saturday Evening Post* in 1979:

> Old people are supposed to be all alike. In society's view, at age 65 we all become mindless, unable to learn anything. It's only a matter of time before senility sets in. This, of course, is ridiculous. . . . There's a similar myth that old people are useless. As soon as they retire, their skills are suddenly outdated, old-fashioned. In a society centered on the work ethic, mandatory retirement perpetuates this attitude. . . . We also seem to believe that old age is powerless. Much of our lack of power comes from our isolation from the rest of society. We must defeat that isolation through coalitions with other groups who are also victimized by discrimination—the young, the women, the handicapped.

Maggie Kuhn did not coin the term *ageism*. The word was first used in 1968 by Robert N. Butler, M.D., who became the first director of the National Institute on Aging. But Kuhn sprinkled her speeches (nearly 200 a year between 1970 and 1985) and interviews with Butler's term.

The second factor that transformed Kuhn into a Gray Panther was her recognition that older women are particularly well suited to fight ageism. Betty Friedan (3*), of course, had issued the clarion call in the 1950s with her *Feminine Mystique*. College-aged and middle-aged women would play a major role during the 1960s and early 1970s in advancing the Civil Rights movement and protesting the U.S. role in Vietnam. But it was Maggie Kuhn whose vigor, rapier wit, and utter commitment to fighting "good" causes showed why women should not retire to rocking chairs. As she suggested in a 1974 interview in *Prime Time*:

> I think of consciousness-raising as catalyzing the motivation to work for the larger public good. . . . In order to be liberated from the second childhood myth (of playpen and shuffleboard) we must have a consciousness of our own powers and the validity of accumulated wisdom and skills. . . . The fact that we are male and female is so influential in determining who we are and how we perform and how we relate to others! Indeed, it is the material of life itself and to deny it in old age is to deny life itself.

Liberating herself from sexism influenced Kuhn's assault on ageism.

This is hardly surprising. Many gerontologists believe that people become more androgynous in later years: men become more accepting of the need to cooperate with others; women become more confident in asserting their opinions. It is reasonable to hypothesize that Kuhn was taught to conform to sex-specific conventions in her youth, but learned how to break some rules in building a successful career as a church official. Denied a meaningful role in retirement, she created a model that affirmed her rights and responsibilities as an older woman.

The third factor that sparked Maggie Kuhn's radicalism was the social ferment of the 1960s. "This is a new age—an age of liberation, self-determination, advocacy," Kuhn declared in 1979. The number of people over sixty was growing far faster than the population as a whole. Public and private institutions were not dealing with the adverse effects of ageism, especially the isolation of the elderly from the young. Kuhn envisioned a truly integrated society in which people of all ages participated actively and interacted with one another.

> To be eliminated, racism, sexism, and ageism will require sweeping changes in society as well as in personal attitudes and life-styles, social theories and policies, our national priorities and political processes. I like to think that age may be the unifying force. We are all aging. Age is the one factor every living thing shares.

Kuhn considered herself "radical" in a classical sense: "A radical, by definition, is the person who looks to the roots of the problem." As she told a 1978 congressional committee, in opposition to an omnibus bill under consideration:

"Public welfare in this country does not need re-forming, it needs radicaliza-tion. . . . What is necessary is to uproot the system, to re-examine it, and design a new system to meet the needs of this society."

Whereas anger over ageism, advocacy of feminism, and social ferment im-pelled Kuhn to act, two other factors probably did not influence her much. For instance, given Kuhn's involvement in Presbyterian politics and social-action movements, it seems plausible that in convening the Gray Panthers she was motivated by some religious-liberal impulse. William R. Hutchinson has suggested that the 1960s should be interpreted as a religious revival. Yet it is important to recall that it was the church that dismissed her. And despite the fact that mainstream Protestant denominations are aging faster than any other institution in America (more than a quarter of their membership is over sixty-five, compared to 12 percent in the population as a whole), clergy and lay leaders alike have done remarkably little to alter their ministries to respond to the contributions that older congregants can make.

Thus when Kuhn speaks of older people as "elders of the tribe," as those who safeguard the survival of the larger community by attending to the larger public interest, she evokes a role ascribed to the old in the Bible. Here again Kuhn's radicalism reveals itself. Despite interest in recovering biblical canons, few churches heed what Scripture says about growing old. Kuhn also has expressed reservations about the mission of the National Interfaith Coalition on Aging: she feels NICA is too service oriented, more interested in palliatives than the pain and anxiety in later years.

Maggie Kuhn also chases sacred cows in the gerontological pasture. Golden Age Clubs, in her opinion, are "glorified playpens . . . run by well-meaning professionals who are not old and who seldom consult their clients as to what they need or want." Likewise, Sun City, Leisure World, and "section 202" senior-citizen housing projects are "ghettos." She remains angry at academics who formulated disengagement theories—which "prepared people to step down and out of involvement in community life, increased the dead weight of social apathy, and deprived millions of experienced survivors of the incen-tive and opportunity to contribute to the world around them"—because the concept justified deleterious social policies such as mandatory retirement.

When Maggie Kuhn was well into her eighties, she and the Gray Panthers faced some tough choices. The "wrinkled radical" embodied her movement. Replacing such a charismatic leader will be difficult, especially since Kuhn's notion of empowerment presupposes highly autonomous networks of people doing what they think best. The Gray Panthers have cultivated better rela-tionships with local media than they have with Washington lobbyists, the National Council of Senior Citizens, or the American Association of Retired Persons.

More important, Kuhn and her supporters must decide whether they are primarily advocates for older Americans or whether theirs is a more global agenda. The media and most of her constituency viewed the Gray Panthers as a vehicle for advocating senior-citizen rights. Kuhn long felt that her goals went beyond "senior power," however. As she noted in *Maggie Kuhn on Aging* (1977), the Gray Panthers has a stake in the struggles of nonwhites, women, the young and old, and Third World countries against oppression: "All these struggles are linked in the worldwide struggle for a new humanity. Together they have the potential of a new community-based social justice system of human compassion and selfhood. Old people have a large stake in this new community—in helping to create it and extend it."

To Maggie Kuhn, empowering the aged has been part of a more radical effort to rework human relations. While she and the Gray Panthers were quick to act on behalf of older people in demanding redress for past discrimination and insisting upon better access to health care, housing, employment, and income, Kuhn insisted that "responsible contributions of old people are essential to the survival and well-being of society." It remains to be seen whether a nation accustomed to viewing the aged as "others" will grasp Kuhn's theme of interdependency. More likely, either the Gray Panthers will be stereotyped as a group for the old, or its message will seem so fuzzy as to appear irrelevant.

Bibliography

"Gray Power," *The Nation* 250 (May 28, 1990): 127–28.

Huckle, Patricia. *Tish Sommers, Activist, and the Founding of the Older Women's League.* Knoxville: University of Tennessee Press, 1991.

Kuhn, Maggie. "Advocacy in This New Age," *Aging* no. 297–298 (July-August 1979): 2–4.

———. "Foreword" to *Ageism*, Jack Levin and William C. Levin, eds. Belmont, CA: Wadsworth Press, 1980.

———. *Get Out There and Do Something.* Philadelphia: Fortress Press, 1972.

———. "Gray Panthers," in *The Encyclopedia of Aging*, George L. Maddox, ed. New York: Springer Publishing, 1987, p. 297.

———. "Gray Power" (interviewed by Rebecca Blalock), *Saturday Evening Post* 251 (March 1979): 32+.

———. Interviewed by Francesca Lyman, *The Progressive* 52 (Jan. 1988): 29–31.

———. *Maggie Kuhn on Aging*, Dieter T. Hessel, ed. Philadelphia: Westminster Press, 1977.

———. Testimony in the *Congressional Digest* 57 (May 1978): 147–51.

Kuhn, Maggie, Christina Long, and Laura Quinn. *No Stone Unturned: The Life and Times of Maggie Kuhn.* New York: Ballantine Books, 1991.

Powell, Lawrence A., John B. Williamson, and Kenneth J. Branco. *The Senior Rights Movement: Framing the Policy Debate in America.* New York: Twayne Publishers, 1994.

Wallace, Steven P. and John B. Williamson. *The Senior Movement: References and Resources.* Boston: G. K. Hall, 1992.

W. Andrew Achenbaum

WILLIAM MOSES KUNSTLER (1919–   )

Civil liberties activist in the courts; founder of the Center for Constitutional Rights

William Kunstler, after hearing a partial list of people included in this book, remarked that it resembled a list of his present and former clients. From the early 1960s to the 1990s, Kunstler was a prominent, highly visible, and effective legal advocate for unpopular causes in the United States. He has been an activist by defending within the courts the legal rights of activists. He has described himself as a "civil-rights lawyer."

Born in Manhattan on July 7, 1919, to Jewish parents, William Kunstler grew up on the Upper West Side. Although neither of his parents was politically active, they reflected the liberalism of much of the Jewish professional community of the time. He describes their politics as "Roosevelt Democrats." His parents were not particularly religious people, although they did observe the high holy days. His mother, Frances, "sometimes attended church and temple both—just to make sure." Kunstler described himself as a rebellious child from the beginning, both at home and in school. His social consciousness even this early is evidenced in his inability to understand why his father, Monroe, who was a doctor, charged poor people for his medical services.

Kunstler graduated from DeWitt Clinton High School in New York City in 1937. He went on to earn a B.A. from Yale in 1941, displaying his literary ambitions by publishing the first of twelve books, a collection of poems entitled *Our Pleasant Vices*, in 1941. It was also in that year that he entered the army and served in the Southwest Pacific Theater. During this period he reached the rank of major and earned a Bronze Star. Returning to school, he got his law degree from Columbia University in 1948. (He continued his army connection by being a judge advocate for the army reserve until 1960.)

There is a certain irony that Kunstler's first activist sentiments were aroused by his experiences as a young man in the army, beginning in 1941. He was sent for training in such southern towns as Memphis and Nashville, in Tennessee, where he saw for the first time and at close hand a rigid segregationist culture. Even those whom he has described as "mild segregationists" insisted to him that "It's gotta be this way." He came away from these experiences with a reinforced aversion to racism and its patterns of segregation. Following this, he was sent to the Southwest Pacific Theater, where he was shocked by the racially segregated units there. Further, he was aware that there was only one African-American general in the entire United States Army at that time,

William Moses Kunstler. Copyright *Washington Post*; Reprinted by permission of D.C. Public Library.

General Benjamin O. Davis, Jr., who was in charge of African-American units. By the time he got to Columbia Law School, he understood racism, and it disturbed him deeply. The course had been set for much of his later civil rights advocacy.

Among the earliest heroes in William Kunstler's pantheon were Clarence Darrow and William Goodrich Thompson. Both attorneys were known as effective defenders of the underdog. Clarence Darrow became an American folk hero, having gained national attention, for example, by defending John Scopes for teaching evolution in the "Monkey Trial" of 1926. William Thompson was the defense attorney for the 1920s anarchists Sacco and Vanzetti. Both attorneys, like Kunstler himself, were ardent advocates of the rights of the citizen before the organized power of the state. They represented a tradition that valued the individual more than the state. Kunstler came to see the courts as a potentially powerful weapon for the weak, disenfranchised, and exploited.

Here was an arena in which they could fight back, thereby expanding the power of democracy. In addition, intellectual and legal influences on him came from two giants of jurisprudence, Justice Brandeis and Justice Cardozo. Both men were progressives and advocates of legal activism in the tradition of Roscoe Pound.

In one of his more pivotal works, *Deep in My Heart* (1966, with forewords by James Forman and Dr. Martin Luther King, Jr.), Kunstler tells how he was drawn into civil rights advocacy. The name of the first chapter is "It All Begins." It was 1961 and an urgent call from the legal director of the ACLU for help in defending the first Freedom Riders in Jackson, Mississippi, triggered his involvement. The book covers the critical years between 1961 and 1965 and the *Shuttlesworth v. Moore*, and the *State v. Lowry* cases. It is the history of Kunstler's first encounter and subsequent work with Dr. King and his supporters in cracking the wall of segregation in the Deep South. Twenty years after he had encountered southern segregation as a raw army recruit, he was unexpectedly given the opportunity to attack it in the courts. The struggle was long and bitter, with appeal after appeal and jail sentence after jail sentence until finally the movement began to achieve significant breakthroughs. Unforgettable place-names like Jackson, Mississippi; Birmingham, Alabama; Albany, Georgia; and Monroe, North Carolina, reverberate throughout the book. To read it is to relive those years and to learn the legal strategies and tactics adopted by the Freedom Riders and their advocates.

While pursuing these ideals of justice, Kunstler was never at a loss for employment. He always maintained a stable institutional base for his work. For thirty years, from 1949 through 1978, Kunstler was a partner in the New York law firm of Kunstler, Kunstler (his daughter), and Hyman. He worked as trial counsel for the Freedom Riders in 1961, was special trial counsel for the Reverend Martin Luther King, Jr. (1*), from 1962 through 1968, and legal advocate for such figures as Adam Clayton Powell (1966), Stokely Carmichael (1967), Daniel Berrigan and the Catholic anti-war activists (1968), and the Chicago Seven (1970). He subsequently defended Indian nationalist Sikhs, native American Indian Movement leaders, gay and lesbian rights groups, and prisoners rights groups, most notably at the uprising at the Attica Correctional Facility in New York State in 1971. (Litigation involving Attica was still in the courts in 1993.)

During the late 1960s and early 1970s the government's use of the courts to repress and harass dissident and unpopular social and political movements reached new depths. The seemingly endless string of Black Panther trials during this period is perhaps the best example of using the courts as a political weapon to maintain the status quo. The state was not particularly concerned if it failed to get a guilty verdict. None of the Black Panther cases resulted in conviction, but the government's legal campaign against the Panthers exhausted the organization's financial and psychic resources. This eventually contributed to the collapse of the Black Panther party. The same tactic was used against progressive student movements and anti-war groups. Kunstler was passionately opposed to this government ploy. He understood that the courts could be used for either repressive or progressive purposes.

Between his nationally publicized legal struggles, Kunstler was gainfully employed with his New York law firm. In 1966, he became the founder and staff attorney for the Center for Constitutional Rights. The Center operated as a private, nonprofit organization, guided by officers and a board of trustees, and funded by private, tax-deductible contributions. It has provided vigorous and innovative legal support to progressive movements across the country. Dedicated to using the law for social change, the Center has a speakers bureau and a student program, and publishes numerous pamphlets, newspapers, and books, such as Arthur Kinoy's *Rights on Trial: The Odyssey of a People's Lawyer* (1983) and Randolph Scott-McLaughlin, *Racially Motivated Violence Litigation Strategies* (1984). Just as his private law practice and his activities with the Center for Constitutional Rights gave Kunstler a stable economic base, the Center in particular created a solid network of constant contact with other progressive organizations and individuals. He never allowed himself to be isolated from other progressive groups. The Center gave him the opportunity to be in ongoing contact with the attorneys representing organizations such as the ACLU and many other groups defending unpopular and minority rights.

William Kunstler was also on the faculties of a variety of law schools over the years and was a lecturer in law at the New School for Social Research, Cooper Union, and other institutions of higher learning. His writings have been published widely in both professional journals and mass media publications, including the *Columbia Law Review*, the *Yale Law Review*, the *Nation*, the *New York Times*, the *National Law Journal*, *Saturday Review*, *Juris Doctor*, and *Rolling Stone*. He has appeared on many national television programs. Over the decades, he became a nationally known controversial figure, much loved and much hated. The 1990–1991 docket for Kunstler's Center for Constitutional Rights had cases in the following categories: government misconduct, racial justice, women's rights, lesbian and gay rights, AIDS, native American rights, Puerto Rico, right to housing, nuclear and environmental hazards, criminal justice, and international human rights. This list tells the story of William Kunstler.

It could be argued that William Kunstler was never the "radical" that much of the media claimed. For example, a *New York Newsday* magazine cover story featuring him was titled "Always Versus." Instead, he may have been simply an attorney who could not give up the conviction that the Constitution and the Bill of Rights can work—if pushed. His credo has been that the less perfect can be made better through legal struggle and challenge, and that the better can be made best through further court challenges. The Italian anarchists called this strategy "spingere," to push. He has always been a champion of individual freedom over state-supported oppression, bigotry, and racism.

Over the years, the staunchest institutional support for his civil rights work has come from religious groups, especially from African-American churches in the tradition of the Reverend Martin Luther King (1*) and the Reverend Jesse Jackson (*). The more mainstream, established institutions of church and temple tended to shy away from the social controversy that his legal activities aroused.

Throughout the course of his career, William Kunstler displayed superb skills in courtroom drama, mass publicity, and legal tactics. He seemed to be always at the right place at the right time. He maintained and nurtured his initial inspirations and ideals even through difficult times. Things were simpler in the early days of the fight for desegregation. By the 1990s, the enemy was not so easily identified and pinned down. The side of righteousness may have become less obvious. There was, for example, the painful case of Tawana Brawley in 1989. Although it turned out that Brawley was the fabricator of groundless accusations, her charges did raise larger issues of the victimization of black women, sexually, socially, and economically. The courtroom, as a theater of democracy, may have many unexpected conclusions, and sometimes even when you lose you win. As for Kunstler, he promised in the 1990s to continue to "dream up ingenious ways to confront the state."

Bibliography

Belknap, Michal R. *American Political Trials*. Westport, CT: Greenwood Press, 1981.

Christenson, Ron. *Political Trials: Gordian Knots in the Law*. New Brunswick, NJ: Transaction Books, 1986.

Ginger, Ann Fagin, and Eugene M. Tobin. *The National Lawyers Guild: From Roosevelt through Reagan*. Philadelphia: Temple University Press, 1988.

Hoffman, Abbie, Peter Babcox, Deborah Babcox, and Bob Abel. *The Conspiracy*. New York: Dell, 1969.

Kunstler, William Moses. "Back to Attica." *The Nation* 252 (March 25, 1991): 364.

———. *Beyond a Reasonable Doubt? The Original Trial of Caryl Chessman*. New York: Morrow, 1961.

———. *The Case for Courage*. New York: Morrow, 1962.

———. *Deep in My Heart*. New York: Morrow, 1966.

———. *The Hall-Mills Murder Case*. New Brunswick, NJ: Rutgers University Press, 1980 (1964).

———. *Trials and Tribulations*. New York: Grove, 1985.

Margolick, David. "Still Radical After All These Years," *New York Times*, July 6, 1993, B1: 2.

Shklar, Judith. *Legalism: Law, Morality and Political Trials*. Cambridge: Harvard University Press, 1986.

"William Kunstler and the Calls of the Wild," *Washington Post*, Feb. 3, 1992, C1, C6.

John Wildeman

SIDNEY LENS (1912–1986)

Labor radical and anti-war activist

Beginning in the late 1950s, Sidney Lens advocated the formation of a new American radicalism to revitalize both the labor movement and democratic politics. He was also a strong critic of cold war policy and of American intervention in the affairs of other countries, especially Vietnam. Among other organized efforts, he was a leading figure in Voters for Peace, the New Mobilization Committee to End the War in Vietnam, and the March on the Pentagon. Lens was the longtime editor, with A. J. Muste, of *Liberation* and the author of numerous books and articles on politics, labor, social change, and foreign policy.

He was born Sidney Okun. His Russian-Jewish parents in Newark, New Jersey, strongly influenced his early political sympathies. Although he went to work for a Wall Street brokerage firm after his graduation from New York's DeWitt Clinton High School in 1929, he lost that job in the Great Crash. In 1932, while working for a resort hotel, Lens persuaded the hotel's waiters and busboys to strike against management. The principal result of the strike was to get Sidney beaten up by the local sheriff. Soon after, he began to study Marxism and became embroiled in the factious world of left-wing politics. During the late 1930s, he dedicated himself to union work, hitchhiking over 40,000 miles to organize workers for radical action, including a sit-down strike in Detroit. He changed his name to Sidney Lens in the 1930s when he was blacklisted for union activities.

These were exciting years when Lens felt the exhilaration of riding what he thought was the wave of the future to the workers state. After World War II, however, hope gave way to rising anti-communism and retreating radicalism. Having become the head of a local Building Services Employees union in Chicago, Lens grew ever more disgusted with the failure of the national unions to organize workers into a movement for radical change. By the end of the 1950s, his disgust extended to a variety of former radicals who had publicly repudiated their past and transformed themselves into cold war partisans.

He was even more concerned with the degenerative effects of material prosperity, especially in corrupting workers into passive sports-oriented, television-watching consumers. He called on unions to find ways to integrate education into work so that the worker would be inspired to "enlarge his personality." He also criticized society for failing to provide idealistic youth with something worthy to do, warning that while Americans were much better off economically than they had been in the 1930s they were worse off spiri-

Sidney Lens at *Progressive* 75th Anniversary Benefit. Photo courtesy of Dennis Church.

tually: "Where can youth," he asked in 1961, "learn of the values of dedication, self-sacrifice, idealism? Not at home, not in the universities, not in the institutionalized unions, not in the complacent churches." He hungered for some new idealism that would restore what he called the "insurgent impulse" and reactivate workers and other people in the cause of social democracy.

He was convinced that much of the malaise that afflicted the labor movement was caused by the reactionary policies of George Meany as head of the AFL-CIO and by the domination of the unions by a conservative labor bureaucracy. He believed that this situation had alienated many workers, especially the younger ones, and tied organized labor to the status quo. Hoping to break the grip of leadership by "tired old men," Lens supported efforts to give union members a meaningful influence on decision making in their unions. His call for "participative rather than manipulative democracy" in the union movement won him an invitation in 1962 to address the Port Huron Conference convened to organize Students for Democratic Action, but he declined on what he later recognized was the mistaken belief that SDS would be too moderate. Similarly, he was slow to recognize the idealistic power of the Civil Rights movement, although he had long advocated racial justice, organizing in the late 1940s a branch of the NAACP in his Chicago neighborhood.

Lens was primarily concerned with the labor movement, but he also had a strong interest in global radicalism. An ardent traveler, he visited ninety-four countries between 1950 and 1970, searching amid the cold war for successful forms of social radicalism that had escaped what he considered to be the twin blights of Russian Stalinism and American imperialism. In the early 1960s, he praised Castro's Cuban Revolution for reinvigorating radicalism, and he publicly condemned the Bay of Pigs invasion. The Cuban missile crisis deepened his hostility to cold war policy, leading him in 1962 to run for Congress as a write-in candidate with the hope of creating a constituency favorable to peace; he polled less than 2,000 votes. Two years later, he published his *The Futile Crusade: Anti-Communism as American Credo*, where he condemned the anticommunism of the previous decade as threatening freedom at home and abroad.

Much of his concern focused on American interference with the efforts of other peoples to pursue social justice in ways suited to themselves. On this matter, Lens attacked not only the national government but also the AFL-CIO, which under the direction of Jay Lovestone, an ex-communist who headed its international affairs department, was using its influence to subvert radical movements throughout the world. For many years, he directed his harshest criticisms against Lovestone for his active support of intervention in such countries as Zaire and the Dominican Republic.

By the mid-1960s, he was concentrating his fire on the escalating war in Vietnam. In 1964, he visited Southeast Asia and concluded that the American government had placed itself in opposition to the real will of the Vietnamese people. He was one of the first critics of the war to urge immediate and unconditional withdrawal of all American military forces, principally to end what he called the mass murder of innocent civilians. The continuation of the war deepened his belief that the United States had long been dominated by militarism and imperialism. In *The Military-Industrial Complex* (1970), he estimated that since 1946 the United States had spent nine times more on its armed services than on all of its social programs. He warned that the influence of the military extended into virtually every area of American life, including organized labor. This had occurred, he believed, not for national security reasons but because the military establishment created to win World War II was determined to maintain itself by inciting the cold war. Instead of assuring peace, the military generated insecurity both at home and abroad, developing a dangerous "momentum for war."

Convinced that the Vietnam War was leading Americans to question this militarism, Lens redoubled his efforts. In *The Forging of the American Empire* (1971), he traced the history of national foreign policy to refute the myth that America was more moral than any other nation and to support his claim that since World War II the United States had forged "an imperialistic empire such as man has never known before," one intended to assure the global dominance of American business. He dedicated this book to "the Children of Vietnam, Who Are Being Murdered and Maimed by My Government and Yours."

Lens was radical in practice as well as thought. For years, he refused to pay income taxes in protest against militarism, leading the IRS to seize his checking account. In 1967, he headed an American delegation to the international conference in Stockholm against the Vietnam War. Soon after, he began to advocate a turn from "protest to resistance," arguing that the Johnson administration had initiated an illegal war without the consent of the people. On the premise that the government was "the most flagrant lawbreaker in the nation," he urged Americans to emulate the long line of dissenters who had resorted to civil disobedience against unjust policy. A firm believer in nonviolent protest, he placed himself near the head of the mass march of peace activists on the Pentagon, where he was tear-gased but not arrested.

The growing strength of the organized war movement revived his long-cherished dream for an independent radical political party. Throughout his life, he refused to support either of the two major political parties in the belief that both were tied into the same military-industrial system which, he said in 1968, "spawns alienation, dehumanization, racism and imperialism." He warned that even the victory of a "peace" Democrat like Eugene McCarthy would do little to eliminate the essential forces directing the nation toward war. Heartened by the rising tide of protest against both the war and racism, he dreamed of a grand coalition of radical labor with radical youth which, in combination with the black liberation movement, would form a new American politics dedicated to social justice. He thought that the idealism of youth would awaken workers from their infatuation with material things while the traditions of radical labor would provide direction for the young.

As an ideological base for the new politics, Lens urged radicals to break away from orthodox Marxism, which he believed had been rendered obsolete by the ability of a prospering capitalism to buy off the working class. He called for a New Left ideology that would be "multi-class," involving students, racial minorities, and the poor. It would also be strongly in tune with the varied forms of international radicalism which had risen in the Third World outside the spheres of both Russian communism and American capitalism. It would be a basically new Marxism adapted to new situations and dedicated to new principles like democratic participation and nonviolence.

As a member of the steering committee of the National Mobilization against the Vietnam War in 1969–1970, he advocated a broadening of the anti-war movement to include other issues, eventually helping to form the National Coalition against War, Racism, and Repression, which he hoped would become a new peace and freedom party dedicated especially to popular involvement in decision making at all levels of government and to public management of the economy.

In the early 1970s, the collapse of the student and Black Power movements forced Lens back to more limited goals, but he continued to agitate for radical change. Along with his continued war on the reactionary union leadership of men like George Meany, he attacked government for its neglect of the poor and its support of wealth, a "welfare state for the rich" rather than for the needy, a class government which, he warned, was creating a new aristocracy to ride on the backs of an apathetic and despairing people. To counter what he believed was a redistribution of wealth favorable to the rich, he again called on organized labor to take the lead in creating an independent popular party.

Completing his retirement from union work in 1976, Lens devoted even more of himself to attacking the cold war as a threat to social justice and human life both at home and abroad. Since World War II, he said, the United States had pursued a policy of aggression against the Soviet Union in the effort to establish its world domination, driven by the desire for victory to a constant escalation of the arms race, "a lunatic process" that unless stopped would lead to catastrophe. Convinced that the war-makers in Washington were preparing for the use of nuclear weapons, Lens formed Mobilization for Survival in the hope of organizing a popular movement against nuclear terror in any form. In "The Doomsday Strategy" (1976), he denounced not only the arms race but all forms of nuclear energy, warning that nuclear reactors could produce materials for bombs and might themselves explode, while more certainly they would leave wastes threatening to human health. When the first Strategic Arms Limitation Treaty was negotiated in 1979, he joined with a radical minority in condemning SALT as doing more to sustain than to control the arms race.

Lens carried his crusade against war into the 1980s, focusing his attack on what he continued to believe was a foolish and self-defeating effort by the United States to find security through nuclear terror and imperialistic intervention. Having lost faith in national government, he urged all peace-loving Americans to join with the like-minded everywhere in working for the creation of international agencies strong enough to abolish nuclear weapons and to deal with the problem of world poverty. Only then, with the establishment of an effective world state, would humanity be safe from the twin dangers of mass destruction and totalitarian rule.

Impelled by a radical's strong optimism, the Chicago-based Lens hoped for a new upsurge of radicalism. In 1984 he called on the "many thousands who consider themselves socialists" to abandon the two major political parties in order to revitalize socialism. Convinced that the American economy was headed toward another crisis like that of the 1930s, he succeeded in the fall of 1985 in convening nearly a thousand radicals for a conference in New York City on activism and socialism. Although suffering from ill health, he began to organize an even bigger conference, only to die suddenly in 1986 from cancer.

Sidney Lens remained true to his mission. Radicals, he said, must agitate in favor of the "injured and oppressed" against privileged wealth and dangerous power. A fellow activist Phil Berrigan, once complimented him by saying, "I don't think I've ever met a person more passionately committed to life, or so willing to struggle for it." And so it was until the very end.

Bibliography

Knoll, Erwin. "Under Surveillance," *The Progressive* 50 (Jan. 1986): 4.

Lens, Sidney. *The Bomb*. New York: Lodestar Books, 1982.

———. *The Day before Doomsday*. New York: Doubleday, 1977.

———. *The Forging of the American Empire*. New York: Crowell, 1971.

———. *Labor Wars: From the Molly Maguires to the Sitdowns*. New York: Doubleday, 1973.

———. *The Maginot Line Syndrome*. Cambridge, MA: Ballinger, 1982.

———. *The Military-Industrial Complex*. Philadelphia: Pilgrim Press, 1970.

———. "Our Real Strength Is in the Streets," *The Progressive* 47 (Nov. 1983): 18–19.

———. *Permanent War*. New York: Schocken Books, 1987.

———. *Poverty*. New York: Crowell, 1973.

———. *Radicalism in America*, updated. New York: Crowell, 1966.

———. *Strikemakers and Strikebearers*. New York: Dutton, 1985.

———. "U.S. Labor Needs Solidarity Too," *The Nation* 238 (Jan. 14, 1984): 7–8.

———. *Unrepentant Radical: An American Activist's Account of Five Turbulent Decades*. Boston: Beacon Press, 1980. Reviewed: *Labor History* 25 (Spring 1984): 279–81.

———. *A World in Revolution*. New York: Praeger, 1986.

New York Times Biographical Service 17 (June 1986): 802.

Obit, *The Progressive* 54 (Dec. 1990): 4.

Besides his books, Sidney Lens wrote hundreds of articles, especially for two periodicals of which he was an editor (*Liberation* and *The Progressive*), and also for *Christian Century*, *Commonweal*, and *The Nation*.

Edward K. Spann

HERBERT MARCUSE (1898–1979)

Marxist philosopher; influence on the New Left

Herbert Marcuse developed his own version of "critical Marxism" in an attempt to update the Marxian theory in response to changing historical conditions from the 1920s through the 1970s. Marcuse gained notoriety as "father of the New Left" in the 1960s when he was perceived as both an influence

Herbert Marcuse. Photo courtesy of Beacon Press.

on and defender of the so-called New Left in the United States and Europe. Marcuse was the teacher of Angela Davis (*) and other New Left radicals and lectured frequently to large and enthusiastic audiences during the 1960s and the 1970s. He influenced many leaders of SDS, as well as the more radical segments of the left and counterculture. Marcuse's book *Eros and Civilization* provided a celebration of art, play, love, and eros which influenced the 1960s counterculture and helped make the New Left less ascetic and prudish than the Old Left. His theory of "one- dimensional" society provided critical perspectives on contemporary capitalist and state communist societies and his notion of "the great refusal" won him renown as a theorist of revolutionary change and "liberation from the affluent society."

Marcuse was born in an upper-middle-class Jewish family in Berlin and experienced a typical bourgeois upbringing. Later when he served in the military in World War I, he read Marxist literature and was especially influenced by Rosa Luxemburg's concept of revolution as a totality of upheaval. Marcuse joined the SPD (Social Democratic party) as a protest against the war, but joined the more revolutionary workers' council movement in 1918 during the German revolution. He became drawn to Luxemburg's Spartacus movement, attending meetings, rallies, and demonstrations. With the outbreak of the German revolution in 1918, he joined a civilian security force which was formed to defend the revolution against counterrevolutionary attacks. In November 1918, Marcuse found himself standing in Berlin's Alexanderplatz un-der orders to fire at snipers who shot periodically at demonstrators and at those involved in the revolutionary movement.

After his discharge from the army in December 1918, Marcuse quit the Social Democratic party in protest against its actions and policies. The SPD was increasingly compromising and making conciliatory gestures toward the old Prussian-bourgeois establishment, while it supported and perhaps insti-gated repression of the Left. It was widely believed, for example, that the SPD was instrumental in the murder of Rosa Luxemburg and Karl Liebknecht. In 1967, Marcuse told students in Berlin,

> Let me say something personal. If you mean by revisionism the German Social Democratic Party, I can only say to you that from the time of my own political education, that is since 1919, I have opposed this party. In 1917 and 1918 I was a member of the Social Democratic Party. I resigned from it after the murder of Rosa Luxemburg and Karl Liebknecht, and from then on I have criticized this party's politics. Not because it believed that it could work within the frame-work of the established order—for we all do this, we all make use of even the most minute possibilities in order to transform the established order from inside it—that is not why I fought the SPD. The reason was rather that it worked in alliance with reactionary, destructive, and repressive forces.

Marcuse went to Freiburg after the war and got a degree in literature. After a short career as a book dealer in Berlin, he returned to Freiburg to study philosophy with Martin Heidegger. Marcuse's first published article in 1928 attempted a synthesis of phenomenology, existentialism, and Marxism which decades later would be carried out again by various "existential" and "phe-nomenological" Marxists. Marcuse argued that much Marxist thought had de-generated into a rigid orthodoxy and thus needed concrete phenomenological experience to revivify the theory. At the same time, Marcuse believed that Marxism neglected the problem of the individual and throughout his life he was concerned with individual liberation and well-being in addition to social transformation and the possibilities of a transition from capitalism to socialism.

Marcuse published the first major review in 1933 of Marx's just published *Economic and Philosophical Manuscripts of 1844*. The review anticipated the tendency to revise interpretations of Marxism from the standpoint of the works of the early Marx. His *Hegel's Ontology and Theory of Historicity* (1932) con-tributed to the Hegel renaissance that was taking place in Europe.

In 1933, Marcuse joined the *Institut fur Sozialforschung* (Institute for Social Research) in Frankfurt and soon became deeply involved in their interdisci-plinary projects which included working out a model for radical social theory, developing a theory of the new stage of state and monopology capitalism, and providing a systematic analysis and critique of German fascism. Marcuse deeply identified with the "Critical Theory" of the Institute and throughout his life was close to Max Horkheimer, T. W. Adorno, Leo Lowenthal, and others in the Institute's inner circle.

In 1934, Marcuse fled from Nazism and emigrated to the United States, where he lived for the rest of his life. His first major work in English, *Reason and Revolution* (1941), traced the genesis of the ideas of Hegel, Marx, and modern social theory. It demonstrated the similarities between Hegel and Marx, and introduced many English-speaking readers to the Hegelian-Marxian tradition of dialectical thinking.

After serving in the U.S. government from 1941 through the early 1950s, which Marcuse always claimed was motivated by a desire to struggle against fascism, he returned to intellectual work and in 1955 published *Eros and Civilization*, which attempted an audacious synthesis of Marx and Freud and sketched the outlines of a nonrepressive society. While Freud argued in *Civilization and Its Discontents* that civilization inevitably involved repression and suffering, Marcuse argued that other elements in Freud's theory suggested that the unconscious contained evidence of an instinctual drive toward happiness and freedom. This evidence is articulated, Marcuse suggests, in daydreams, works of art, philosophy, and other cultural products. Based on this reading of Freud and study of an emancipatory tradition of philosophy and culture, Marcuse sketched the outlines of a nonrepressive civilization which would involve libidinal and nonalienated labor, play, open sexuality, and production of a society and culture which would further freedom and happiness. His vision of liberation anticipated many of the values of the 1960s counterculture and helped Marcuse to become a major influence on the New Left in that decade.

Marcuse argued that the current organization of society produced "surplus repression" by imposing socially unnecessary labor, unnecessary restrictions on sexuality, and a social system organized around profit and exploitation. In light of the diminution of scarcity and prospects for increased abundance, Marcuse called for the end of repression and creation of a new society. His radical critique of existing society and its values and call for a nonrepressive civilization elicited a dispute with his former colleague Erich Fromm, who accused him of "nihilism" (toward existing values) and irresponsible hedonism. Marcuse had earlier attacked Fromm for excessive conformity and idealism and repeated these charges in the polemic around *Eros and Civilization* and Marcuse's use of Freud.

During his period of government work, Marcuse had been a specialist in fascism and communism, and he published a critical study of the Soviet Union in 1958 (*Soviet Marxism*) which broke the taboo in his circles against speaking critically of the USSR and Soviet communism. While attempting to develop a many-sided analysis of the USSR, Marcuse focused his critique on Soviet bureaucracy, culture, values, and the differences between the Marxian theory and the Soviet version of Marxism. Distancing himself from those who interpreted Soviet communism as a bureaucratic system incapable of reform and democratization, Marcuse pointed to potential "liberalizing trends" which countered the Stalinist bureaucracy which indeed eventually materialized in the 1980s under Gorbachev.

After part-time jobs at Columbia and Harvard's Russian Research Institute, Marcuse got a professorship at Brandeis University where he taught philosophy from 1954 until 1965, when his contract was not renewed. His students included Angela Davis, Ronald Aronson, Abbie Hoffman, William Leiss, Erica Sherover, and other activists and scholars associated with the New Left (although Davis was to join the Communist party).

During this period, Marcuse published a wide-ranging critique of both advanced capitalist and communist societies in *One-Dimensional Man* (1964). This book theorized the decline of revolutionary potential in capitalist societies and the development of new forms of social control. Marcuse argued that "advanced industrial society" created false needs which integrated individuals into the existing system of production and consumption. Mass media and culture, advertising, industrial management, and contemporary modes of thought all reproduced the existing system and attempted to eliminate negativity, critique, and opposition. The result was a one-dimensional universe of thought and behavior in which the very aptitude and ability for critical thinking and oppositional behavior was withering away.

Not only had capitalism integrated the working class, the source of potential revolutionary opposition, but capitalists had developed new techniques of stabilization through state policies and new forms of social control. Thus Marcuse questioned two of the fundamental postulates of orthodox Marxism: the revolutionary proletariat and inevitability of capitalist crisis. In contrast with the more extravagant demands of orthodox Marxism, Marcuse championed nonintegrated forces of minorities, outsiders, and radical intelligentsia and attempted to nourish oppositional thought and behavior through promoting radical thinking and opposition.

One-Dimensional Man was severely criticized by orthodox Marxists and theorists of various political and theoretical commitments. Despite its pessimism, it influenced many in the New Left as it articulated their growing dissatisfaction with both capitalist societies and Soviet communist societies. Moreover, Marcuse himself continued to defend demands for revolutionary change and defended the new, emerging forces of radical opposition, thus winning him the hatred of establishment forces and the respect of the new radicals.

One-Dimensional Man was followed by a series of books and articles which articulated New Left politics and critiques of capitalist societies in "Repressive Tolerance" (1965), *An Essay on Liberation* (1969), and *Counterrevolution and Revolt* (1972). During this era, Marcuse traveled throughout the world to promote his revolutionary message. He urged students and others to join Left organizations and struggle to create a new society. Marcuse did not, however, join any specific organizations himself, and often defended the workers' council movement of his youth, which advocated that individuals take control of the institutions in which they work, study, and live and practice a form of self-management, or people's power.

Marcuse's main writings of this period include "Repressive Tolerance," which attacked liberalism and those who refused to take a stand during the controversies of the 1960s. It won Marcuse the reputation of being an intransigent radical and ideologue for the Left. *An Essay on Liberation* celebrated all of the existing liberation movements from the Viet Cong to the hippies and exhilarated many radicals while further alienating establishment academics and those who opposed the movements of the 1960s. *Counterrevolution and Revolt*, by contrast, articulates the new realism that was setting in during the early 1960s when it was becoming clear that the most extravagant hopes of the 1960s were being dashed by a turn to the right and "counterrevolution" against the 1960s.

During this period—of his greatest influence—Marcuse also published many articles and gave lectures and advice to student radicals all over the world. Never surrendering his revolutionary vision and commitments, Marcuse continued to his death to defend the Marxian theory and libertarian socialism. Eschewing blueprints of the future or recipes for social change, Marcuse stressed the importance of the utopian vision of freedom and happiness which articulated the qualitative difference between existing societies and a future emancipated society.

Marcuse also dedicated much of his work to aesthetics and his final book, *The Aesthetic Dimension* (1978), briefly summarizes his defense of the emancipatory potential of aesthetic forms of so-called high culture. Marcuse thought that the best of the bourgeois tradition of art contained powerful indictments of bourgeois society and emancipatory visions of a better society. Thus he attempted to defend the importance of great art for the projection of emancipation and argued that cultural revolution was an indispensable part of revolutionary politics.

Marcuse's work in philosophy and social theory generated fierce controversy and polemics, and most studies of his work are highly tendentious and frequently sectarian. Although much of the controversy involved his critiques of contemporary capitalist societies and defense of radical social change, in retrospect, Marcuse left behind a complex and many-sided body of work comparable to the legacies of Ernst Bloch, Georg Lukacs, T. W. Adorno, and Walter Benjamin.

In retrospect, Marcuse's vision of liberation—of the full development of the individual in a nonrepressive society—distinguished his work, along with sharp critique of existing forms of domination and oppression. Since Marcuse was primarily a philosopher, his work lacked the sustained empirical analysis in some versions of Marxist theory and the detailed conceptual analysis found in many versions of political theory. Yet he constantly showed how science, technology, and theory itself had a political dimension and produced a solid body of ideological and political analysis of many of the dominant forms of society, culture, and thought during the turbulent era in which he lived and struggled for a better world.

Bibliography

Kellner, Douglas. *Herbert Marcuse and the Crisis of Marxism.* London and Berkeley: Macmillan and the University of California Press, 1984.

Marcuse, Herbert. *The Aesthetic Dimension.* Boston: Beacon Press, 1978.

———. *Counterrevolution and Revolt.* Boston: Beacon Press, 1972.

———. *A Critique of Pure Tolerance.* Boston: Beacon Press, 1965.

———. *Eros and Civilization.* Boston: Beacon Press, 1955.

———. *An Essay on Liberation.* Boston: Beacon Press, 1969.

———. *Five Lectures.* Boston: Beacon Press, 1970; reprinted London: Free Association Press, 1988.

———. *Negations.* Boston: Beacon Press, 1968; reprinted London: Free Association Press, 1989.

———. *One-Dimensional Man.* Boston: Beacon Press, 1964.

———. *Reason and Revolution.* New York: Oxford University Press, 1941; reprinted Boston: Beacon Press, 1960.

———. *Soviet Marxism.* New York: Columbia University Press, 1958; second edition, 1988.

———. *Studies in Critical Philosophy.* Boston: Beacon Press, 1973.

Pippin, Robert, Andrew Feenberg, and Charles P. Webel, eds. *Marcuse, Critical Theory and the Promise of Utopia.* South Hadley, MA: Bergin and Garvey, 1988.

Douglas Kellner

I. F. STONE (1907–1989)

Publisher and editor of I. F. Stone's Weekly, *anti-war spokesperson*

I. F. Stone's Weekly, a four-page newsletter operated out of its editor's residence in the northwest sector of Washington, D.C., served as a model for the underground publications which abounded during the 1960s and as an intellectual touchstone of sorts for many involved in the anti-war movement. Founded in early 1953, as the fires of McCarthyism still burned, the *Weekly* condemned those who fueled the cold war, whether at home or abroad. During the days of America's version of Camelot, I. F. Stone criticized the readiness of President Kennedy to reach for the gun, whether in Cuba or Vietnam, and his seeming ambivalence toward the Civil Rights movement. Consequently, the early New Left all but regarded Stone as one of its own, viewing

I. F. Stone. Copyright *Washington Post*; Reprinted by permission of D.C. Public Library.

him not as a discarded Old Left relic but rather as a fount of hard-to-find information. Indeed, of those who had passed through the sectarian wars of the Old Left, only A. J. Muste was viewed with such esteem by the latest version of young American political rebels. As U.S. involvement in Vietnam dramatically escalated starting in 1965, the *Weekly*'s analyses provided intellectual armor for the anti-war movement. The *Weekly* became a model for those determined to provide an "underground" perspective, while Stone served as an exemplar for many on the Left and, by the close of the decade, for some within the ranks of the Establishment itself.

I. F. Stone was born Isidor Feinstein in Philadelphia on December 24, 1907, the son of Russian Jewish immigrants. He was raised in the nearby town of Haddonfield, where he attended public schools and first became fascinated with the craft of journalism. In early 1922, he put out his own little newsletter, *The Progress*, which ran for all of three issues before his father demanded it come to a halt. No matter, his academic success in Haddonfield, as later at the University of Pennsylvania, remained mediocre at best, overshadowed by his dogged determination to become a reporter. He left Penn without a diploma and worked for a string of papers in the Philadelphia metropolitan area before publisher J. David Stern assigned him in 1931 to work on the editorial page at the *Philadelphia Record*. During the height of the Great Depression, he wrote for other publications as well, ranging from H. L. Mencken's iconoclastic magazine, the *American Mercury*, to V. F. Calverton's independent radical journal, the *Modern Monthly*. In December 1933, he moved to the *New York Post*, the top pro–New Deal paper of the era, where he served as chief editorial writer until 1939. During the same period, he contributed to the *New Republic* and *The Nation*, the leading progressive publications of the times, becoming an associate editor with *The Nation* in 1938. In 1940, he started a six-year stint as Washington editor of *The Nation* and began writing for *PM*, a new, experimental left-wing newspaper. *PM*'s financial woes, which caused it to fold in 1948, continued to plague its successors, the *New York Star* and the *New York Daily Compass*, both of which featured a column by I. F. Stone. When the *Compass* closed its doors in late 1952, Stone was unable to find work and considered himself a victim of the times. Driven by necessity, he put out his own newsletter, which opened in January 1953. There were 5,300 initial subscribers, including Albert Einstein, Eleanor Roosevelt, and Bertrand Russell. By late 1971, the circulation figures of the *Weekly* had surpassed 70,000. Stone went on to serve as contributing editor to the *New York Review of Books*. Even after he resigned from that post, he continued to write for this and other publications, particularly *The Nation*. During this period, Stone searched for a way to fuse socialism and freedom. He decided to examine the history of free thought and expression. That led him to the study of classical Rome and Greece, where he believed the notion of individual liberty had begun. This intellectual odyssey resulted in *The Trial of Socrates*, which in 1988 became Stone's first best-seller. The following summer, he died in a Boston hospital room.

Over the course of his lengthy career, I. F. Stone determinedly remained a man of the left. At various times he expressed left-of-center ideas of many kinds, ranging from progressivism to democratic socialism to communism. He was enmeshed in some of the ideological struggles of the Old Left, opting to support both the New Deal, the anti-fascist Popular Front, and Henry Wallace's 1948 presidential bid. He was likewise strongly supportive of the emergence of a New Left in America and became an intellectual figure of considerable influence within the ranks of the 1960s movement. Nevertheless, Stone was not an organization man, but a maverick who went his own way.

Stone was often a loner, but he was also a man whose political ideals had been shaped in depression-era America. Like the Old Left, he believed both in the desirability of social and economic reform and in the necessity of wholesale change when the need arose. But other than a brief flirtation with communism at the very height of the depression—a time when other American intellectuals moved far to the left—Stone supported peaceful change in Western democracies while accepting the need for revolutionary action in other lands. Consequently, while in the thirties he had viewed Soviet Russia as a great socialist experiment, he later believed Castro's Cuba could break the stranglehold of U.S.-sponsored Latin American oligarchies. All the while, he supported—albeit critically—calls for gradual, democratic reform in America and in Europe as well, from the New Deal to the Great Society and from the Marshall Plan to Czechoslovakia's Prague Spring, while continuing to envision the possibility of socialism with a human face.

While remaining consistent in his theoretical musings, Stone was blessed with the good fortune of having a supportive environment. He had long been afforded the privilege of working for publishers who largely allowed him to go his own way, including J. David Stern of the *Philadelphia Record* and the *New York Post*, Freda Kirchwey of *The Nation*, Ralph Ingersoll of *PM*, and Ted Thackery of the *New York Daily Compass*. Then, in 1953, he became his own boss, as he began publication of his own newsletter. Supported mainly by his wife, Esther, who ran the business end of operations, Stone was able to stake out the positions he truly believed in, regardless of whom he might offend in the process. Readers were sometimes offended. Some were put off by his damning 1956 reports on his visit to the Soviet Union, his condemnation of left-wing criticisms of the Warren Commission, and his sometimes scathing analyses of the sectarianism, overheated rhetoric, and propensity for violence exhibited by a certain portion of the Civil Rights and anti-war movements. But as Stone's reputation grew, the subscription figures of the *Weekly* and his bank account did likewise. In 1960, Stone was still well known for his earlier work with *The Nation* and *PM*, and the *Weekly* struggled to make a go of it. By the close of the decade, the number of readers of the newsletter had increased manyfold, and such publications as *Time*, *Newsweek*, and the *Wall Street Journal* were singing his praises.

Over and over again, Stone was extolled for his investigative techniques. Because of problems with his hearing, which first became pronounced in the 1930s, Stone had determined to go directly to the source, to official records, to dig out information not to be found in press releases or coming out of the mouths of spokespersons. Occasionally, his scoops were dramatic ones, as when he forced the Atomic Energy Commission to admit that it had not been telling the public everything it knew about the possibility of verifying underground nuclear tests.

While many within the ranks of the anti-war movement and outside of it too were increasingly drawn to Stone's analyses, some continued to view him as a highly controversial figure. As a portion of the movement, much to Stone's chagrin, veered hard-leftward, he was dismissed by would-be American revolutionaries as only a muddling liberal. Others on the opposite side of the political spectrum, by contrast, denounced him as little better than a Soviet dupe.

Nonetheless, Stone's star continued to shine long after he ceased to put out the *Weekly*. His essays for the *New York Review of Books* were likely to cause a stir whenever members of the American intelligentsia and/or Left gathered. So too did his commercially successful *The Trial of Socrates*, the product of his Greek studies, which admittedly received mixed reviews. Even years after his death, however, some conservatives were willing to assail his reputation by promoting the astonishing claim that Stone had been an agent of the Soviet secret police. The detailed discussion of this claim, in such publications as *The New York Review of Books* (Oct. 8, 1992, p. 21 and Dec. 3, 1992, p. 49) and *The Nation* (Sept. 28, 1992, pages 310, 312, and 313), established the motive of character assassination by right-wing ideologues. Stone had always been a gadfly, never anyone's kept pet.

Bibliography

Alterman, Eric. "The Ironies of Izzymania," *Mother Jones* 13 (June 1988): 34–37.

Birkhead, Douglas. "Muckraking Free Speech: I. F. Stone and the Trial of Socrates," *Communication Research* 16 (April 1989): 289–98.

Cochran, David. "I. F. Stone and the New Left: Protesting U.S. Policy in Vietnam," *The Historian* 53 (Spring 1991): 505–20.

Cottrell, Robert. *Izzy: A Biography of I. F. Stone*. New Brunswick, NJ: Rutgers University Press, 1992.

Greider, William. "The Crotchety Wisdom of I. F. Stone," *Rolling Stone*, April 21, 1988, pp. 37–38.

Obits. *Current Biography* 50 (Aug. 1989): 63; *Mother Jones* 14 (Sept. 1989): 17; *The Nation* 247 (July 10, 1989): 37+; *New Republic* 201 (July 10, 1989): 8+; *New York Times* (early city edition), June 19, 1989, D13; *New Yorker* 65 (July 24, 1989): 21–22; *The Progressive* 53 (Aug. 1989): 4; *Time*, July 3, 1989, p. 72; *Utne Reader*, Sept./Oct. 1989, p. 144.

Patner, Andrew. *I. F. Stone*. New York: Pantheon Books, 1987.

Stone, I. F. *The Haunted Fifties*. New York: Little, Brown, 1988 (1963).

———. *The Hidden History of the Korean War*. New York: Monthly Review Press, 1969 (1952).

———. *I. F. Stone's Weekly Reader*. New York: Random House, 1973.

———. *In a Time of Torment*. New York: Little, Brown, 1989 (1967).

———. *The Killings at Kent State: How Murder Went Unpunished*. New York: Vintage Books, 1971.

———. *Polemics and Prophecies, 1967–1970*. New York: Little, Brown, 1989 (1970).

———. *The Trial of Socrates*. Boston: Little, Brown, 1988.

———. *The Truman Era*. New York: Little, Brown, 1988 (1953).

Robert C. Cottrell

JAMES WEINSTEIN (1926–   )

Journalist for democratic socialism, activist, and historian

James Weinstein was a member of the editorial board of *Studies on the Left* from 1959 to 1967. This journal was a major ideological link between the Old Left and the New Left. Weinstein became known as a leading socialist intellectual who served as both a guide to and a critic of New Left activists. After the 1960s he continued to promote American socialism in his subsequent periodicals, such as *Socialist Revolution* (which was published under this name from 1970 to 1975) and *In These Times*, which he began publishing in 1976. He worked to create a vehicle for the effective political expression of his ideas. As an activist, he was a candidate for the U.S. House of Representatives as an independent Socialist in 1966 in New York's Nineteenth Congressional District, and he was one of the founders of the New American Movement in 1971.

Weinstein grew up in New York City where he was involved in left-wing political activities as a member of a Communist front group called American Youth for Democracy. After service in the U.S. Navy at the end of World War II, he earned a B.A. at Cornell University. Thereafter he worked full-time for the Young Progressives, joined the Communist party, and held factory jobs. He was an active unionist, becoming a steward in the International Brotherhood of Electrical Workers. He left the Communist party in 1956, the year of the Soviet repression of the Hungarian Revolution and of Khrushchev's admission of Stalin's crimes. The next year Weinstein earned an M.A. at Columbia University in American history. For his thesis he undertook an inquiry into indigenous American radicalism. This was later published as a book entitled *The Decline of Socialism in America, 1912–1925*. He joined the editorial board of *Studies on the Left*, which was based in Madison, Wisconsin, then a hub of leftist intellectual life. Through that seminal journal, he helped make known the traditions of grassroots activism in the American past. Weinstein was convinced that a sense of history and of clearly defined principles was necessary for leftist growth. In his writings he encouraged the Left to build on American traditions rather than on imported ideologies. He noted that earlier social democrats had done this successfully, and he cautioned against the rampant doctrinaire factionalism of the Communist and Marxist groups. Any New Left that emerged in the 1960s should benefit from the experiences of previous radical movements, develop a coherent and attractive program, and identify what groups it would attempt to organize. Weinstein criticized, for example, the claim that oppressed blacks and farmers were the key revolutionary agents of potential change. Instead, he asserted that the natural constituency of the New Left should be students.

Weinstein's major views were remarkably consistent for more than thirty years. While the essence of his thought changed little, some of the particulars evolved. As a graduate student he had discovered what he termed American socialism's "hidden heritage." In the early twentieth century, the Socialist party of America had created a dynamic movement that made notable inroads into segments of American public opinion. It achieved widespread cultural acceptance and some electoral success. That knowledge has informed his thinking ever since as a social democrat interested in building a socialist consensus in the United States. While his views of appropriate theoretical struc-

James Weinstein. Photo courtesy of James Weinstein.

tures changed, he maintained the fundamental goal of building a broad-based political movement to promote the transformation of American competitive capitalism into a more humane and democratic socialist system.

Weinstein's goal, even before his involvement in the New Left, was the socialization of the economy of the United States. He encouraged the democratic control of the economic and political system to insure that the people are in fact sovereign. He condemned piecemeal reforms for, like the earlier socialists, he argued that such reformism would serve to strengthen the extant system. He maintained that a socialist movement must speak to existing American economic and social conditions rather than imitate Soviet or Third World models of correct strategy and means of social transformation. He did not view workers, especially unionized workers, as a potential constituency for revolutionary change because the union bureaucracy had become tied into the existing system. The poor were also seen as unlikely converts because of their necessary focus on basic survival, at least until there was a viable movement that addressed their needs. What Weinstein termed a post-industrial socialist movement must appear. This would recognize that modern corporate capitalism had reduced even middle-level managers and professionals to mere technicians. This reflected Marx's expectation of increasing proletarianization. A socialist movement should give direction to any emerging social activism so that it could become more than a transient phenomenon. A socialist party, he held, was required that had both a vision of a new society and the expertise for taking over the economy. It should develop the theoretical and technical competence to plan and manage a new society. The party, thus, had to be the agent of change which ultimately would engage the workers, the poor, minorities, and even the bourgeoisie. Their interests, he believed, were counter to those of corporate liberalism that upheld the existing structure. A socialist party could clarify that truth for them.

By the late 1960s Weinstein was moving away from the old Leninist model of a vanguard party and from the Marxist notion of economic determinism. He believed in the primacy of political action through a multisector movement that could appeal to potential radicals whom it could lead to recognize their own oppression. A firm structure was vital whereby activists could be encouraged away from aimless and chaotic protests.

As the editor and publisher of *In These Times*, Weinstein oversaw a newspaper which was a microcosm of alternative, advocacy journalism. It, like the earlier journals to which he contributed, attacked corporate capitalism and promoted a social democratic society. Weinstein maintained that socialism was not the private property of self-proclaimed revolutionary elites but that it represented the struggles of the entire people. He endorsed an all- inclusive view of the Left, and favored diversity within the struggle for socialism involving a multiplicity of parties and movements. This is where his search for agents of change led him. While he once believed that a visionary party was crucial, he no longer required a socialist party or movement per se, or perhaps he simply abandoned hope for such a possibility. Weinstein ceased to look for theoretical models and had scaled back his definition of the Left. His immediate aim as a journalist was to stimulate discussion among potential forces of change. He encouraged social critics in various areas and promoted their unification. He urged that they declare capitalism itself an issue so that the status quo forces no longer set the terms of public debate. What he termed "a truly new American left" could emerge which encompassed everyone for whom the first principle of government is the meeting of human needs. Environmentalists, feminists, anti-nuclear power adherents, civil rights advocates, minorities, gays, and other dissenting voices together have the potential of representing the majority of Americans. He has recommended that they run political candidates at the local level. These single-issue movements must transcend their narrow foci and coalesce not around individual and immediate topics but around fundamental issues. They must work to reorganize the priorities of American government so that neocolonialism and cold war–era military spending would cease being the givens of public policy. Then a new value system would prevail. With this, Weinstein's vision of an alternative society seems to have come to closure.

Paralleling his intellectual odyssey, James Weinstein belonged to a group called the New American Movement, which was organized in 1971 to influence activists of various schools toward socialist thought. He endorsed the group's 1982 merger with the Democratic Socialist Organizing Committee under the leadership of Michael Harrington (*). The combined organization, which also absorbed the environmentalist Citizens party, became known as the Democratic Socialists of America.

By the 1990s, James Weinstein had, for thirty years, articulated Left programs that were grounded in the lessons of the past. He encouraged an active socialist presence in U.S. politics which would avoid factionalism and ideological hairsplitting. It would present to the American people reasoned arguments for moving public policy discussions beyond the framework of the economic interests of wealthy elites. Weinstein succeeded in developing an audience for his ideas through small journals in the 1960s and 1970s. and, in the late 1970s and during the 1980s, through *In These Times*. Although the latter's subscription list was modest (less than 35,000), no other socialist newspaper had achieved this during the last generation.

This publication, however, was frequently in perilous financial condition. A fund-raising letter (dated January 19, 1993) probably did not exaggerate when it said that the newspaper survived "by constantly juggling debts and enduring high levels of tension." In 1992, it was repackaged as a biweekly magazine, with a new subtitle: "the alternative newsmagazine." This illustrated both past weaknesses and the possibility, with a new format and the friendlier context of a Democratic administration, that it might attract a larger readership. Many similar journals had died in the previous years, such as *Democracy, New Times*, and *The Guardian*. Many that survived were demoralized by "the confusion and disillusionment that spread through the American left as the Soviet Union collapsed and free market ideology triumphed temporarily throughout the world" (Editorial, *In These Times*, Feb. 8, 1993, p. 2). It was a time of broad reassessments.

Weinstein was faulted by some remaining ideologues on the left. They believed that he had moved too far from Marxist ideas and, even worse, had blurred the line between socialism and liberalism. Although Weinstein had been considered too close to the Old Left by some New Left activists in the 1960s, by the 1990s he was likely to be criticized as a closet capitalist or a confused liberal. Weinstein steadily defended his socialism, however, as appropriate for American society. He repeated that socialists needed to develop a broad vision of a humane and democratic society. They should work out specific "practical legislative programs" that embodied that vision, and develop constituencies through "issue conferences," coalitions with other groups, and running candidates for local offices. The results might not be ideologically pure, but they would mean some progress toward radical ideals (*In These Times*, Jan. 10–16, 1990, p. 17).

Bibliography

Harrington, Michael. *Socialism: Past and Future*. New York: Arcade/Little, Brown, 1989.

Howe, Irving. *Socialism and America*. New York: Harcourt Brace Jovanovich, 1985.

"In Hard Times," *The Nation*, Sept. 20, 1993, pp. 268–69.

In These Times, 1976–present. (Weinstein is editor and publisher.)

Socialist Revolution, 1970–1975. (Weinstein was an editor.)

Studies on the Left, 1959–1967. (Weinstein was an editor.)

Weinstein, James. *Ambiguous Legacy: The Left in American Politics*. New York: New Viewpoints, 1975.

———. *The Corporate Ideal in the Liberal State, 1900–1918*. Boston: Beacon Press, 1968.

———. *The Decline of Socialism in America, 1912–1925*. New York: Monthly Review Press, 1967.

———. "Studies on the Left," in *History and the New Left: Madison, Wisconsin, 1950–1970*, Paul Buhle, ed. Philadelphia: Temple University Press, 1990: 113–17.

———. "A Vital Political Force Needs Both a Vision and a Constituency," *In These Times*, Jan. 10–16, 1990, p. 17.

Weinstein, James, and David W. Eakins, eds. *For a New America*. New York: Vintage, 1970.

Sally M. Miller

INDEX

CONTRIBUTORS

W. ANDREW ACHENBAUM, Professor of History at the University of Michigan and deputy director of its Institute of Gerontology, is the author of *Old Age in the New Land* (1978), *Shades of Gray* (1983), and *Social Security* (1986). He is currently writing a history of gerontology. He admires Maggie Kuhn but is not a Gray Panther.

RUSSELL L. ADAMS, Chairman of the Department of Afro-American Studies at Howard University, is a political sociologist who has written extensively in the fields of human relations and history, and served as a curriculum consultant to government agencies in the United States and abroad.

REGINA T. AKERS, an archivist at the Operational Archives of the Naval Historical Center (Department of the Navy, Washington, D.C.), is a graduate student in the History Department of Howard University.

SARA ALPERN, Associate Professor of History, Texas A & M University, has taught and published on U.S. women's history, including *Freda Kirchwey: A Woman of the Nation* (1987) and (as co-editor and contributor) *The Challenge of Feminist Biography* (1992). She is currently working on a book-length history of women in U.S. business.

ERIC BURNER, employed at Cadwalader, Wickersham, and Taft (New York City), is author of *And Gentley He Shall Lead Them: Robert Parris Moses and Civil Rights in Mississippi* (1994).

KATE BRANDT, employed in a law firm in San Francisco, is a member of the Gay and Lesbian Historical Society of Northern California and has compiled a book of interviews, *Happy Endings: Lesbian Writers Talk about Their Lives and Work* (1993).

JOHN CLARK, Professor of Philosophy at Loyola University of New Orleans, also teaches at the Institute for Social Ecology in Plainfield, Vermont. He founded and has been coordinator of the Delta Greens, and is a member of the Left Green Network and Surrealists for Social Responsibility. He has written widely on anarchism, including *The Philosophical Anarchism of William Godwin* (1977) and *The Anarchist Moment: Reflections on Culture, Nature and Power* (1984). He is working on several book-length projects on social ecology and social criticism.

RONALD D. COHEN, Professor of History at Indiana University, Northwest (Gary, Indiana), has published books and articles, including *Children of the Mill: Schooling and Society in Gary, Indiana, 1906–1960* (1990). He is presently concentrating on the social history of American popular music while he is writing a history of folk music and American society from the 1940s through the 1960s.

ROBERT C. COTTRELL, Associate Professor of History at California State University, Chico, has published articles on I. F. Stone and a book entitled *Izzy: A Biography of I. F. Stone* (1992).

THOMAS JOSEPH DAVIS, Professor of History and African American Studies, SUNY, Buffalo, is co-author of *Africans in the Americas* (1994).

MACEO DAILEY, JR., Associate Professor of History at Spelman College, has taught at Smith College, Boston College, Brown University, and Howard University. He has published essays and articles on African-American history, and is working on a biography of Emmett Jay Scott.

DAVID DeLEON, Associate Professor of History at Howard University, has written *The American as Anarchist: Reflections on Indigenous Radicalism* (1978) and *Everything Is Changing: Contemporary U.S. Movements in Historical Perspective* (1988), and co-edited *Reinventing Anarchy: What Are Anarchists Thinking These Days?* (1979).

ROLLAND DEWING, Professor of History, Chadron State College (Nebraska), has edited the FBI files on Wounded Knee for the University Publications of America, and has presented various papers on the American Indian Movement and on Vernon Bellecourt.

GARY DORRIEN, Assistant Professor of Religion and Dean of Stetson Chapel at Kalamazoo College, is author of three books, including *Reconstructing the Common Good* (1990) and *The Neoconservative Mind: Politics, Culture, and the War of Ideology* (1993).

SEAN M. ENRIGHT, Program Manager at the Great Lakes Council (Buffalo, New York).

LESLIE FISHBEIN, Associate Professor of American Studies at Rutgers University, has publications that include *Rebels in Bohemia: The Radicals of "The*

Masses," 1911–1917 (1982) and articles in *Labor History, The Historian, Women's Studies, American Studies,* and *American Quarterly.*

SUSAN DOUGLAS FRANZOSA, Associate Professor of Education and Humanities and Coordinator of Graduate Studies in Education at the University of New Hampshire, has published various studies. She is the co-author of *Integrating Women's Studies into the Curriculum* (1984) and editor of *Civic Education: Its Limits and Conditions* (1988). She has articles on the history of educational thought, educational equity, and feminist pedagogy in *Urban Education, Vitae Scholasticae, Contemporary Education, The Canadian Journal of Education, The Magazine of History,* and *Educational Theory.*

LARRY GARA teaches history and peace studies at Wilmington College in Ohio. He is the author of four historical monographs, has written scholarly articles, and edited publications of the War Resisters League. A longtime activist, he has been jailed three times as a war resister.

GEOFFREY GARDNER is a widely published poet and essayist. *The Horses of Time,* his translations from the poetry of Jules Supervielle, was published in 1986. In 1987, he received a grant from the National Endowment for the Arts' Literature Program. He is a lifelong community and peace activist. At present, he is a member of the steering committee of the Cambridge Tenants Union in Cambridge, Massachusetts.

WILLIAM GRAEBNER, Professor of History at the State University of New York, College at Fredonia, is the author of *Coming of Age in Buffalo: Youth and Authority in the Postwar Era* (1990) and *The Age of Doubt: American Thought and Culture in the 1940s* (1991).

CECIL CONTEEN GRAY is an ordained minister of the United Methodist Church and a Ph.D. candidate in the Department of African American Studies at Temple University in Philadelphia.

DEBRA NEWMAN HAM, Specialist in Afro-American History and Culture at the Library of Congress, is the author of *Black History: A Guide to Federal Records in the National Archives* (1984) and editor of *The African-American Mosaic: The Library of Congress Guide to the Study of Black History and Culture* (1993).

LINDA HAMALIAN, Professor of English at William Paterson College of New Jersey, is the author of *A Life of Kenneth Rexroth* (1991) and editor of the revised and expanded edition of Kenneth Rexroth's *An Autobiographical Novel* (1991). She interviewed Allen Ginsberg and reviewed his *Collected Poems* for *The Literary Review* (Spring 1986).

JOHN C. HAMMERBACK, Professor of Speech Communication at California State University, Hayward, is co-author of *A War of Words: Chicano Protest of the 1960s and 1970s* (1985) and contributor of twenty articles and essays in scholarly journals and books. He is a past president of the Western States Communication Association, past chair of WSCA's Freedom of Speech Interest Groups, and Associate Editor of the *Western Journal of Speech Communication*. His research has focused on the rhetorical discourse of dissenters, reformers, and other people in public affairs in the United States.

SUSAN M. HARTMANN, Professor of History and Director of the Center for Women's Studies at Ohio State University, is author of *The Home Front and Beyond: American Women in the 1940s* (1982) and *From Margin to Mainstream: American Women and Politics Since 1960* (1989).

KATHRYN W. HAUSBECK, a Ph.D. student in the Department of Sociology at The State University of New York at Buffalo, is Associate Editor of *Current Perspectives in Social Theory* and has been employed at the Research Program in Environment and Society.

SYLVIA BENNETT HILL, Professor of Criminal Justice at the University of the District of Columbia, was a principal organizer of the Sixth Pan African Congress, the Free South Africa Movement, and the 1990 USA visit of Nelson and Winnie Mandela. She is on the Boards of TransAfrica, TransAfrica Forum, and the New World Foundation.

MAURICE ISSERMAN, Associate Professor of History at Hamilton College, is author of *Which Side Were You On? The American Communist Party during the Second World War* (1982), *If I Had a Hammer...The Death of the Old Left and the Birth of the New Left* (1987), and (with Dorothy Healey) *Dorothy Healey Remembers: A Life in the American Communist Party* (1990).

RICHARD J. JENSEN, Professor of Communication at the Greenspun School of Communication, University of Nevada at Las Vegas, has authored numerous articles and book chapters which focus on movements among minorities, in religious organizations, and in labor unions. He was co-author of *A War of Words: Chicano Protest in the 1960s and 1970s* (1985).

DAVID K. JOHNSON, a Fellow in the History Department at Northwestern University, was formerly employed by History Associates of Rockville, Maryland. He presented an earlier version of this entry at the 1992 conference of the Historical Society of the District of Columbia and is now researching the history of the Mattachine Society of Washington, D.C.

MILTON S. KATZ, Professor and Chair of the Liberal Arts Department at the Kansas City Art Institute, is the author of *Ban the Bomb: A History of SANE, the Committee for a Sane Nuclear Policy, 1957–1985* (1986). He has written numerous book chapters and journal articles on peace and social justice activists in contemporary U.S. history.

DOUGLAS KELLNER, Professor of Philosophy at the University of Texas at Austin, is the author of *Karl Korsch: Revolutionary Theory, Herbert Marcuse and the Crisis of Marxism* (1977), *Critical Theory, Marxism, and Modernity* (1989), *Jean Baudrillard: From Marxism to Postmodernism and Beyond* (1989), *Television and the Crisis of Democracy* (1990), and (with Steven Best) *Postmodern Theory: Critical Interrogations* (1991).

ANNE KLEJMENT teaches U.S. history at the University of St. Thomas in St. Paul, Minnesota. Her research interests include the evolution of Catholic pacifism, and she has published *The Berrigans: A Bibliography* (1979).

FRANCES ARICK KOLB, a founder of the Pittsburgh chapter of the National Organization for Women and an early national board member of NOW, was associated with The Network, a nonprofit research and training organization, from 1980 until her death of cancer in 1991. (See *New York Times* obit., Jan. 14, 1991.)

JOHN KULTGEN, Professor of Philosophy at the University of Missouri–Columbia, is active in the Peace Studies Program at the University of Missouri and teaches a course in Philosophies of War and Peace. Among his research interests is the morality of nuclear deterrence.

PETER B. LEVY, Assistant Professor of History at York College, Pennsylvania, is the author of *The New Left and Labor* in the 1960s (1994) and the editor of *A Documentary History of the Modern Civil Rights Movement* (1992). He has had articles published in *Labor History, Peace and Change*, and *The Industrial and Labor Relations Review*. He is engaged in a study of the relationship between the cold war and the Civil Rights movement.

ROBBIE LIEBERMAN, Assistant Professor of History at Southern Illinois University at Carbondale, is the author of *My Song Is My Weapon: People's Songs, American Communism, and the Politics of Culture* (1989).

RALPH E. LUKER, Associate Professor of History at Antioch College and Associate Editor of the Papers of Martin Luther King, Jr., is the author of *The Social Gospel in Black and White: American Racial Reform, 1885–1912* (1991). His articles have appeared in *The American Quarterly, Church History, Fides et Historia, The Journal of American History, The Journal of Negro History, The Journal of Urban History, The New England Quarterly, Slavery and Abolition, The South Atlantic Quarterly, Southern Studies*, and *The Virginia Quarterly Review*.

CLIFFORD M. LYTLE, JR., Professor of Political Science and Director of the Honor's Center at the University of Arizona, has written several books on Indian affairs with Vine Deloria, Jr., including *American Indians, American Justice* (1983) and *The Nations Within* (1984).

GENNA RAE McNEIL, Professor of History at the University of North Carolina, Chapel Hill, concentrates on African-American history and twentieth-century U.S. history. She is the author of *Groundwork: Charles Hamilton*

Houston and the Struggle for Civil Rights (1983) and editor, with Michael R. Winston, of *Historical Judgments Reconsidered* (1990). She is currently editing, with John Hope Franklin, *African Americans and the Living Constitution*, which will appear in 1994.

THOMAS R. MADDUX, Professor of History at California State University, Northridge, has published articles and a book in the field of Soviet-American relations. His present research is on the experiences of Americans involved with Vietnam.

LAWRENCE H. MAMIYA, Professor of Religion and Africana Studies at Vassar College, is co-author, with C. Eric Lincoln, of *The Black Church in the African American Experience* (1990). Professor Mamiya has studied the Nation of Islam and the Muslim movement for twenty years. He and Dr. Lincoln are planning a major book.

WALDO E. MARTIN, JR., Professor of History at the University of California at Berkeley, is the author of *The Mind of Frederick Douglass* (1984) and articles on African-American cultural and intellectual history, such as "The Making of Black America," in *Making America*, edited by Luther S. Luedtke (1991). He is currently working on a book entitled *A Change Is Gonna Come: Black Cultural Politics and the 1960s.*

SALLY M. MILLER, Professor of History at the University of the Pacific, has published numerous books and articles on U.S. radical history, including *Flawed Liberation: Socialism and Feminism* (1981) and *From Prairie to Prison: The Life of Social Activist Kate Richards O'Hare* (1993).

KAY MILLS, a former writer and editor at the *Los Angeles Times*, is the author of *This Little Light of Mine: The Life of Fannie Lou Hamer* (Dutton/NAL, 1993). She held a Rockefeller Foundation Fellowship at the Carter G. Woodson Institute at the University of Virginia while conducting research on the biography. She is also author of *A Place in the News: From the Women's Pages to the Front Page*, published by Columbia University Press (1990).

L. G. MOSES teaches U.S. Indian history and the history of the U.S. West at Oklahoma State University, Stillwater. He is the author or editor of several books on U.S. Indian history and the history of American anthropology.

KENNETH O'REILLY teaches history at the University of Alaska, Anchorage, and is the author of *"Racial Matters": The FBI's Secret File on Black America, 1960–1972* (1989), *Hoover and the Un-Americans: The FBI, HUAC, and the Red Menace* (1983), and *Black Americans: The FBI Files*, David Gallen, ed. (1994).

CARLOS P. OTERO, Professor of Romance Linguistics at the University of California in Los Angeles, is the author of several books and many articles in linguistics and other fields, in particular on the work of Noam Chomsky. He has edited, with extensive introductions and notes, two books of Chomsky's writings: *Radical Priorities* (1981; 1984) and *Language and Politics* (1989).

GLENN PERUSEK teaches in the Department of Political Science at Albion College. He received his Ph.D. from the University of Chicago in 1988. His articles and reviews on political philosophy, political economy, and the labor movement have appeared in scholarly journals.

PAULA F. PFEFFER, Associate Professor of History at Loyola University of Chicago, is author of *A. Philip Randolph: Pioneer of the Civil Rights Movement* (1990). She is contributing the article on Randolph for the forthcoming Oxford University Press *American National Biography*, edited by John A. Garraty. Pfeffer's primary interest is U.S. reform movements, on which she has written several articles.

DAVID PICHASKE, Professor of English at Southwest State University (Minnesota), is editor-publisher of the Spoon River Poetry Press. His books include *Beowulf to Beatles* (1972), *A Generation in Motion: Popular Music and Culture in the Sixties* (1979), *The Jubilee Diary* (1982), *Beowulf to Beatles and Beyond* (1982), *Visiting the Father and Other Poems* (1986), and *Late Harvest: Recent Rural American Writing* (1992). He spent August of 1989 to September of 1991 as Senior Fulbright Lecturer in Lodz, Poland.

MEL PIEHL, Professor of History and Humanities at Valparaiso University, is the author of *Breaking Bread: The Catholic Worker and the Origin of Catholic Radicalism in America* (1982).

BEATRICE KAY REYNOLDS, formerly Professor of Humanities at the University of Houston–Victoria, is currently part-time lecturer at the University of Southern Maine. She has published before on Ti-Grace Atkinson.

PRISCILLA RAMSEY, Associate Professor of Literature in the Afro-American Studies Department at Howard University, teaches African-American, Caribbean, and African literature. She has published on such diverse topics as Marcus Garvey, Richard Wright, Nella Larsen, Stephen Henderson, E. Ethelbert Miller, and nineteenth-century "passing" fiction. Her publications have appeared in *The Dictionary of Literary Biography*, *The Journal of the College Language Association*, *The Journal of the Middle Atlantic Writers*, *Studies in Black Literature*, and *Negroes in New York Life and History*.

DONALD ROE, an Audiovisual Archivist and Reference Specialist in the Motion Picture, Sound, and Video Branch at the National Archives, is a Ph.D. candidate in the History Department at Howard University.

W. J. RORABAUGH, Professor of History at the University of Washington in Seattle, is the author of *Berkeley at War: The 1960s* (1989).

CHARLES T. RUBIN, an Associate Professor in the Political Science Department at Duquesne University, has published on environmental ethics.

JENNIFER SCARLOTT, has been a Fellow at the World Policy Institute in New York, and is now an editor at the Campaign for Peace and Democracy.

ROBERT C. SMITH, Professor of Political Science at San Francisco State University, has written extensively on African-American politics and leadership. He is General Editor of the State University of New York Press Afro-American Studies series and Associate Editor of the *National Political Science Review*.

PETER ANDRE SOLA, Professor of Education at Howard University, is editor or co-editor of the following books: *The New Servants of Power: A Critique of the 1980s School Reform Movement* (1989), *Building Bridges for Educational Reform: New Approaches to Teacher Education* (1989), and *Ethics, Education, and Administrative Decisions* (1984).

EDWARD K. SPANN, Professor of History and Urban Regional Studies at Indiana State University, is the author of four books, including *Brotherly Tomorrows: Movements for a Cooperative Society in America, 1820–1920* (1989). He has been working on a history of the baby-boom generation from 1943 to 1976.

ALAN SPEARS is a graduate of Clark University in Worcester, Massachusetts, where he majored in U.S. history. He has completed two years of graduate work in history at Howard University. In 1992, Mr. Spears edited *Fast Talk, Full Volume*, an anthology of African-American poetry, for the Gut Punch Press.

TAYLOR STOEHR, Professor of English at the University of Massachusetts, Boston, was Paul Goodman's friend and is his literary executor. In addition to his editions of Goodman's writings, he is working on a biography. He has also published books on Dickens, Hawthorne, the New England Transcendentalists, and the Free Love Movement in America.

STEPHEN L. TANNER, Professor of English at Brigham Young University, is the author of books on Ken Kesey, Paul Elmer More, and Lionel Trilling.

ALAN WALD, Professor of English Literature and American Culture at the University of Michigan, has written *The New York Intellectuals* (1987), *The Revolutionary Imagination* (1983), and *James T. Farrell: The Revolutionary Socialist Years* (1978).

THOMAS R. WEST, Associate Professor of History at the Catholic University of America, has published *Flesh of Steel: Literature and the Machine in American Literature* (1967), *Nature, Community and Will: A Study of Literary and Social Thought* (1976), and, with David Burner, *The Torch Is Passed: The*

Kennedy Brothers and American Liberalism (1984), and *Column Right: Conservative Journalists in the Service of Nationalism* (1988). He was assisted, in this entry, by Laura Mentz and Mark Buckley.

KINGSLEY WIDMER, Professor of English and Comparative Literature at San Diego State University, has been a peace and libertarian activist for more than forty years in the military, a prison, and ten universities. He is author of ten books of literary and cultural criticism on such topics as Melville, Miller, Lawrence, utopias, and rebels.

JOHN WILDEMAN (d. 1993) was Professor of Sociology at Hofstra University on Long Island and author of such publications as *The Problem of Crime: A Peace and Social Justice Perspective*, with Richard Quinney (1991). His area of specialization in sociology was crime and social control (*New York Times*, Dec. 7, 1993, B13).

LILLIAN SERECE WILLIAMS, Assistant Professor in the Women's Studies Department at the State University of New York at Albany, is a specialist in the history of African-American women.

RAYMOND WILSON, Professor of History at Fort Hays State University (Kansas), is author of *Ohiyesa: Charles Eastman, Santee Sioux* (1983) and is the co-author, with James S. Olson, of *Native Americans in the Twentieth Century* (1984) and, with L. G. Moses, of *Indian Lives: Essays on Nineteenth and Twentieth Century Native American Leaders* (1985).

ANN WITHORN, Professor of Social Policy at the University of Massachusetts, Boston, has been an activist for welfare rights and women's rights since the 1960s. She has been an editor for *Radical America* magazine since 1975 and is currently book review editor of *The Journal of Progressive Human Services*. She has written *Serving the People: Social Services and Social Change* (1984) and co-edited, with Rochelle Lefkowitz, *For Crying Out Loud: Women and Poverty in the United States* (1986).

KENT WORCESTER is revising for publication his manuscript "C.L.R. James: A Political Biography." His research interests, which include modern social theory, are reflected in publications in the *World Policy Journal*, *Critical Sociology*, *Research in Political Economy*, *Research and Society*, and *New Politics*.